Computers and Applications

Daniel L. Slotnick
University of Illinois

Evan M. Butterfield
The American University

Ernest S. Colantonio
University of Illinois

Daniel J. Kopetzky
Compion Corporation

Joan K. Slotnick

Computers and Applications

AN INTRODUCTION TO DATA PROCESSING

D. C. Heath and Company
Lexington, Massachusetts   Toronto

To the memory of Dan Slotnick.

Cover: Steve Niedorf / Image Bank

International Standard Book Number: 0-669-08675-4 (hardcover)
International Standard Book Number: 0-669-11223-2 (paperback)

Library of Congress Catalog Card Number: 85-80262

Preface

Hardly a day goes by that we aren't affected by or don't interact directly with computers in some way. The tremendous recent growth in the introduction to data processing course and all its relatives, such as courses in computer literacy and microcomputer applications, is only one indicator of a society-wide computer revolution. The reader of this text may be fulfilling a requirement, satisfying curiosity about computers, looking for ways to use a newly purchased personal computer, or trying to keep up with a trend. Whatever his or her goal, *our* goals in writing this book were to present enough details about the actual workings of hardware and software to dispel the mystery without overwhelming the reader with more technical detail than is needed for competency. Add to that a touch of humor, imaginative use of graphics, and substantial emphasis on real-world examples and applications, and you have a practical yet entertaining introduction to computers and their applications.

Our approach to this text and package has been one of learning and application. In order to succeed with that approach, we have brought a unique variety of perspectives to this project. In much the same way that the introduction to data processing course is aimed at an increasingly diverse audience, this book was conceived by authors from diverse, yet related, academic and professional backgrounds. Two of us have been active teachers of the introductory course, one of us brings a writer's skills to his work, three of us have worked at different levels in the computer industry, and our senior author (see About the Authors) brings considerable technical and management expertise to the project. Our publisher, D. C. Heath and Company, brought in additional insight from the experts—those on staff who know how to publish successful textbooks, those who teach the introductory course, and those who currently work in the computer industry. D. C. Heath surveyed over 2000 course instructors, personally interviewed over a dozen others, and had the text manuscript reviewed by twenty-five teachers. The result, we feel, is a perfect fit of teaching package with classroom reality.

The *Computers and Applications* package is a four-part instructional system featuring the following components:

1. *Text content.* Exceptionally well-explained and accurate coverage of all key computer and data processing concepts.
2. *Text learning aids.* Extensive pedagogical features integrated throughout the text.
3. *Student supplements.* A variety of study aids designed for flexibility within any course structure.
4. *Instructor's supplements.* A complete teaching package fully coordinated with the text, for both full- and part-time instructors.

 ## TEXT CONTENT

This text has been carefully designed for use in any first course in computer data processing or for any individual who is learning more about computers. It meets or exceeds the requirements for CIS-1, Introduction to Computer-Based Systems, the first course proposed by the Data Processing Management Association (DPMA); serves as an introduction to management information systems as recommended by the American Assembly of Collegiate Schools of Business (AACSB); conforms with the curriculum units recommended by the Association for Computing Machinery (ACM) for data entry operations, computer operations, entry-level programming, and Courses 2 and 3 in the ACM's program for small colleges; meets the requirements of ISI, the ACM's first recommended course in information systems; and can be used for Modules 2.1 and 2.2 proposed recently by UNESCO-IFIP. It is intended to prepare students in two-year colleges who plan to transfer to curricula in four-year institutions, as well as for those taking courses offered at four-year schools.

As you can see, the table of contents lends itself to a wide range of course types— from those that deal only lightly with programming to the programming-intensive, from hands-on applications courses to more traditional surveys, from the business-oriented to the technical.

Above all, the content of this book has been organized for maximum flexibility. Its 23 chapters are divided into 7 modules which can, with some exceptions, be taught in any order. We recommend covering Part 1 (Chapters 1 and 2) first. After that, Part 2, Hardware (Chapters 3 through 7); Part 3, Software (Chapters 8 through 11); Part 4, Systems (Chapters 12 through 14); Part 5, The Miraculous Micro (Chapters 15 and 16); Part 6, Applications (Chapters 17 through 21); and Part 7, Implications (Chapters 22 and 23) can be read in any order.

We also recommend, however, that the software module's introductory material on programming style and languages (Chapters 8 and 9 in Part 3) be covered before the BASIC Appendix. Note, too, that the programming materials in the text require neither a computer nor mathematical skills beyond high school algebra. However, the BASIC Appendix becomes progressively more complex, giving the instructor a variety of choices—from teaching only the programming material in Part 3 to devoting nearly half the course to programming. Similarly, a computer may not be used at all, used only occasionally, or used frequently, depending on the availability of computer facilities and on course objectives.

Not only is the text coverage comprehensive, but it also emphasizes topics of growing interest to those teaching and taking the introductory course. Part 5 includes substantial material on the personal computer—from hardware and software basics to a special section after Chapter 15 on selecting a personal computer plus a full chapter on embedded micro-processors. Microcomputers are also discussed as applicable throughout the text. Because applications have become such a significant part of the introductory course, we devote the five chapters in Part 6 to them, as well as a full chapter (10) to application packages. Further, detailed walkthroughs of such popular microcomputer applications software as Lotus 1-2-3 and word processing are provided in Chapters 10 and 17. Look, too, for state-of-the-art coverage of topics like artificial intelligence and the fifth generation, voice input, flat-panel screens, micro-mainframe links, the electronic office, decision support systems, ergonomics and stress, robotics, "Star Wars" defense computers, and the ethical concerns that go with all these developments.

TEXT LEARNING AIDS

Computers and Applications includes an outstanding array of pedagogical features designed to make familiarization with what amounts to a "foreign language" as painless as possible. Combined with a relaxed writing style, they facilitate understanding and encourage reader enthusiasm.

Chapter Preview and Review Materials

Since we believe that repetition of preview and review materials helps a student to skim a chapter and later to study for exams more effectively, we have structured each chapter around such materials. Each chapter opens with *In This Chapter*, a preview outline of the chapter's headings annotated with easily remembered study phrases. These study phrases are then repeated for guided study in the text margins. Finally, the chapter summary is structured for review around the same outline of chapter headings.

Chapter Opening Situations

Each chapter opens with a Focus on a real-world situation closely related to the chapter content. These selections have been chosen from popular computer magazines and from such nonfiction views of the computer world as *Soul of a New Machine* and *Hackers* to give readers a taste of the real, somewhat eccentric, world of the computer literate. More than just frilly adjuncts to each chapter, each Focus also has followup questions (A Sharper Focus) at the end of the chapter, which challenge readers to apply what they have just read to the Focus.

Boxed Features

Every chapter includes an Issues in Technology question boxed within the running text to encourage students to pause, reflect, and take a stand on an ethical question related to the chapter content. Technology Closeups provide a more in-depth look at such topics as super-computers and systems design.

Careers Guidance

Because many readers will be looking for job opportunities in the computer industry, most chapters include Careers in Technology, a thumbnail sketch of a career area related to the chapter topic, which provides a job description, qualifications, job outlook, and suggested career paths.

Application Perspectives

At the end of each of the first six text modules, an Application Perspective provides concrete, colorful examples of everyday computer use which combine schematics, text, and photographs.

Readability

To ensure accessibility for students, the reading level has been carefully monitored by the editors and course instructors.

Design and Illustrations

Introduction to data processing students of the 1980s are part of a visually oriented society and need a textbook that will hold their interest. To that end, we have a colorful, yet accurate, design that reflects the excitement and dynamism of the computer field.

Chapter-End Materials

A carefully graded set of chapter review materials is provided at the end of each chapter. First, the Computer Concepts exercise reviews vocabulary, providing page references to the chapter's boldfaced glossary terms. From fifteen to twenty Review Questions follow, providing a rote review of the chapter's major topics and paralleling the chapter outline. Two or three Sharper Focus questions challenge students to apply what they have learned to the chapter opening Focus. Finally, three to ten special Projects encourage students to stretch their learning beyond the chapter content.

 ## SUPPLEMENTS

Throughout the development of the text and its supplements, we have aimed to create a total package that would be interesting, easy to use, and well integrated. Each supplement has been prepared by an experienced teacher of the introduction to data processing course.

Student Supplements

Available for students are a study guide and software.

Study Guide. Prepared by Fred L. Head of Cypress College, the Study Guide has been designed as a thorough review and self-test of text mastery. Included for each chapter are

- Learning objectives written especially for the guide.
- Making the Chapter Work, learning and study tips for making the most of the chapter.
- Chapter Review, a summary of the chapter organized by text headings and written in entirely new terms.
- A true-false pretest to assess mastery.

- Applying Your Knowledge, an assortment of different exercises, both objective and subjective.
- A multiple-choice posttest to assess learning.

All answers are supplied at the end of the Study Guide.

Software. Prepared by Technology Training Associates, *Introduction to Microcomputer Applications* is a software package for Apple® and IBM-PC® microcomputers, designed to familiarize students with word processing, spreadsheet, and data base applications software. Hands-on computer experience and cases are provided as part of the software.*

Instructor's Supplements

The supplements designed for instructors include an instructor's guide, a test item file, and transparencies.

Instructor's Guide. Prepared by Marilyn Meyers of Fresno City College, the Instructor's Guide includes a wealth of materials for busy instructors. For each chapter we provide learning objectives, chapter overviews, annotated lecture outlines, answers to text questions, and additional classroom and lecture materials.

Test Item File. Prepared by Carole Colaneri of Mid-Florida Technical Institute, the Test Item File includes close to 2000 possible test questions: 40% true-false, 50% multiple choice, and 10% fill-in. *Archive,* a computerized test generator for Apple IIe and IBM-PC microcomputers, is also available.

Transparencies. The transparency pack includes 50 color transparency acetates.

ACKNOWLEDGMENTS

The number of individuals contributing to a textbook like this is, of course, countless. We do want to give special thanks to C. Brian Honess of the University of South Carolina for his significant contributions to the end-of-chapter projects and to Gayle M. Ross of Copiah-Lincoln Junior College for her ideas for BASIC exercises. Brian Prorok of Bell Laboratories and Dan Mitchell of the University of Illinois, Urbana-Champaign, also provided valuable insights as the book developed.

Our special gratitude and appreciation to Sue Gleason and Pam Kirshen at D. C. Heath. And, last but not least, the following people at D. C. Heath helped make this book possible: Marret McCorkle, Mark Fowler, Martha Shethar, and Ruth Thompson.

D. L. S.   D. J. K.
E. M. B.   J. K. S.
E. S. C.

*Apple is a registered trademark of Apple Computer, Inc. IBM is a registered trademark of International Business Machines Corp.

ACKNOWLEDGMENTS

Special thanks are due the following instructors for their reviews of manuscript materials.

Gerald H. Anderson, COWLEY COUNTY COMMUNITY COLLEGE

Joseph J. Cebula, COMMUNITY COLLEGE OF PHILADELPHIA

Carole Colaneri, MID-FLORIDA TECHNICAL INSTITUTE

William Cornette, SOUTHWEST MISSOURI STATE UNIVERSITY

Robert Dependahl, Jr., SANTA BARBARA CITY COLLEGE

Don Distler, BELLEVILLE AREA COLLEGE

Diane Ebling, INDIAN RIVER COMMUNITY COLLEGE

Henry A. Etlinger, ROCHESTER INSTITUTE OF TECHNOLOGY

Stuart S. Fink, NEW YORK UNIVERSITY

William E. French, ALBUQUERQUE TECHNICAL-VOCATIONAL INSTITUTE

Fred L. Head, CYPRESS COLLEGE

Elizabeth Williford Hodges, NORTH CAROLINA STATE UNIVERSITY

C. Brian Honess, UNIVERSITY OF SOUTH CAROLINA

Enid Irwin, SANTA MONICA COLLEGE

Robert Marshburn, WEST VIRGINIA INSTITUTE OF TECHNOLOGY

William O'Hare, PRINCE GEORGE'S COMMUNITY COLLEGE

Jerry T. Peters, LAMBUTH COLLEGE

Charles C. Philipp, MONTGOMERY COUNTY PUBLIC SCHOOLS

Herbert F. Rebhun, UNIVERSITY OF HOUSTON—DOWNTOWN

Gayle M. Ross, COPIAH-LINCOLN JUNIOR COLLEGE

Alfred St. Onge, SPRINGFIELD TECHNICAL COMMUNITY COLLEGE

Frank T. Vanecek, NORWICH UNIVERSITY

Kenneth W. Veatch, SAN ANTONIO COLLEGE

R. Kenneth Walter, WEBER STATE COLLEGE

Charles M. Williams, GEORGIA STATE UNIVERSITY

ABOUT THE AUTHORS

Daniel L. Slotnick

Dr. Slotnick has had a business background that includes a decade of active technical management for such firms as IBM and Westinghouse. For the past twenty years—while a Professor of Computer Science at the University of Illinois—he has also been a consultant to domestic and foreign computer corporations and United States government agencies, including NASA, the Department of Defense, Standard Oil of Indiana, Atlantic Refining Company, Intel, and Burroughs.

Most recently Professor of Computer Science at the University of Illinois at Urbana-Champaign, Dr. Slotnick earned his M.S. at Columbia University and his Ph.D. at New York University's Institute of Mathematical Sciences. Dr. Slotnick's early academic experience includes participation in the development of the IAS machine, the earliest general-purpose computer, from 1952 to 1954. From 1965 to 1974 Dr. Slotnick was Director of the ILLIAC IV Computer Project, which produced what was the world's fastest computer from its completion in 1972 until it was removed from service in 1982. He has also served as a corporate director of seven companies.

Dr. Slotnick is the author of more than forty reviewed publications. Among his awards are the McDowell Award, the major award of the nation's principal computer professional organization; the AFIPS Prize of the American Federation of Information Processing Societies; the annual Mellon Award of Carnegie-Mellon University; and selection by graduate and undergraduate students every semester as an outstanding teacher.

Evan M. Butterfield

A professional writer and editor, Evan Butterfield brings to *Computers and Applications* a strong background in both writing and teaching. He received his undergraduate and master's degrees at the University of Illinois and studied at the University of Sussex, Brighton, England. Currently teaching writing at The American University, Mr. Butterfield has also taught courses in writing at the University of Illinois, including classes specifically designed for engineering students.

Ernest S. Colantonio

Ernest Colantonio brings combined teaching, technical, and writing skills to this textbook. Currently a research associate and programmer at the University of Illinois' Human Attention Research Laboratory, he received his undergraduate degree in psychology and completed graduate work in computer science at the University of Illinois. Mr. Colantonio has also taught introduction to computer science courses for nontechnical majors at the University of Illinois.

Daniel J. Kopetzky

Author of the BASIC Appendix to *Computers and Applications*, Daniel Kopetzky has an especially strong computer science background. Principal computer scientist for Compion Corporation, a systems design firm in Urbana, Illinois, he received his undergraduate and M.S. degrees in electrical engineering from the University of Notre Dame and his doctorate from the University of Illinois.

Joan K. Slotnick

Joan Slotnick, an experienced textbook author and project coordinator of this text, received her undergraduate degree in mathematics from Columbia University and her master's degree in agricultural economics from the University of Illinois.

Brief Contents

Contents

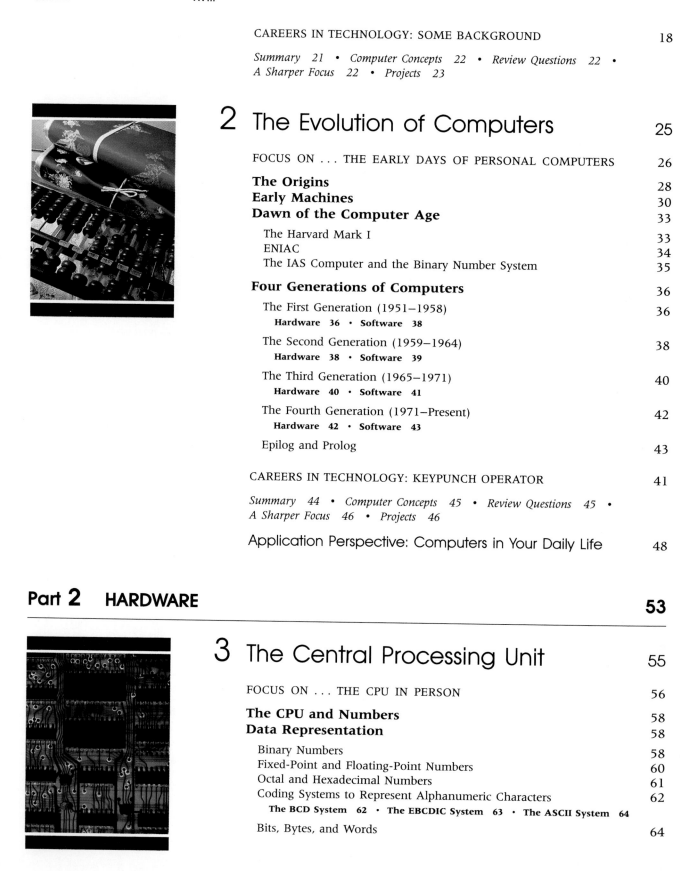

Part 2   HARDWARE   **53**

4 Input   87

5 Storage Devices and File Organization   119

Part 3   SOFTWARE   211

8 Program Development   213

9 Programming Languages   245

10 Application Packages 277

11 Operating Systems   313

Part 4   SYSTEMS   **343**

12 Systems Analysis and Design   345

Part 5   THE MIRACULOUS MICRO 429

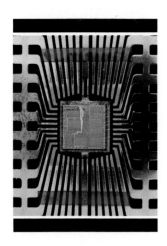

Part 6   APPLICATIONS   489

18 Design and Manufacturing   521

Part 7   IMPLICATIONS   **623**

23 The Next Twenty Years 653

Appendix: An Introduction to BASIC Programming A1

Part 1

COMPUTERS AND COMPUTING: AN OVERVIEW

You may have heard the story of the four wise men sent out one night by the king to examine a strange new beast that had just wandered into the kingdom. On returning to the castle, the first wise man reported that the creature was a long tube, like a snake. The second said it was like the trunk of a tree; the third, like a wall; and the fourth claimed that in fact it was like an enormous leaf. At daybreak, the controversial beast was revealed to be an elephant. Each wise man had accurately described one part of the whole: the trunk, a leg, the side, or an ear.

Computers are analogous to that elephant in one basic way. Our understanding of them can be as incomplete as that of any of the wise men if we fail to see the whole picture before we pounce on the details. Chapters 1 and 2 provide this essential overview, describing in general terms the applications, functions, and history of computers.

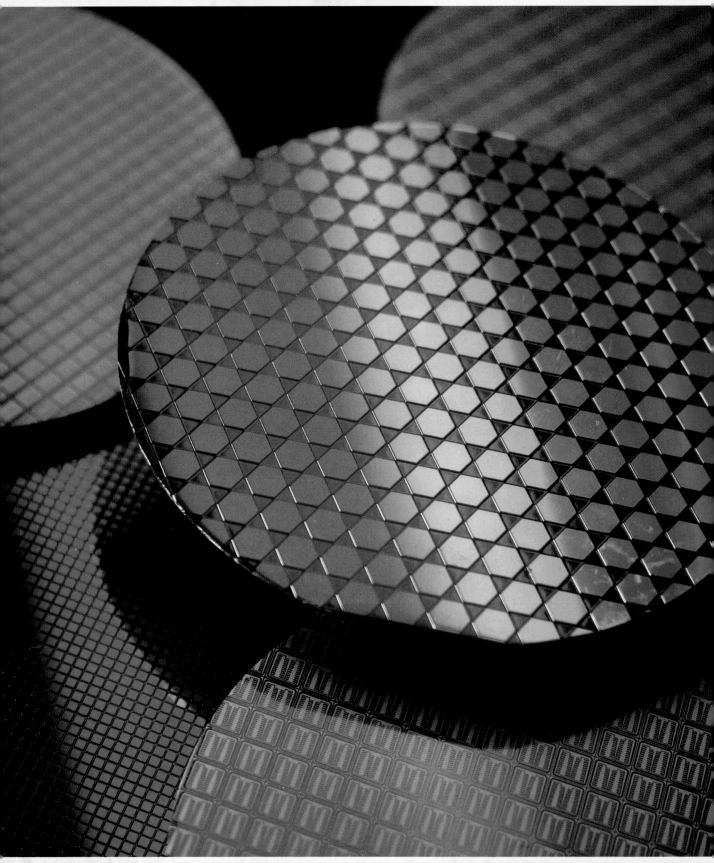

1

Computers: What They Do, What They Are, What They Aren't

▶

FOCUS ON . . . THE COMPUTERIZED
CAMPUS: USES AT CARNEGIE-MELLON

Peter Corless, an art illustration major at Carnegie-Mellon University, picks up his artist's tools in the classroom and begins the assignment: draw a self-portrait.

He starts with his sloping nose, moves swiftly to the bushy eyebrows, then makes a sweeping semicircle for the facial outline. Slowly he fills in the features, using a brilliant color for each: green for the forehead, purple for hair, red for the mouth, gold for the face.

Finally he stares intently at the canvas—a computer screen. Satisfied, he jerks a disk out of the computer and lays down the electromagnetic stylus that is his paintbrush. Later he will insert the disk into another computer to show his professor his work.

Whether in the classroom or dormitory, the cafeteria or library, the computer has become very much a part of Mr. Corless's everyday life on campus. By plugging into special "accounts," he uses computer terminals to write papers for his creative writing class and turn them in, to send and receive electronic mail, and even to find out whether a certain soft drink machine is empty.

Mr. Corless generally accomplishes these miracles at the art building or the University Computation Center, but other terminal rooms and personal computer clusters are scattered about the campus. Not counting individual students' own computers, more than 3500 terminals are on campus now, compared with fewer than 50 two decades ago.

. . . Corless's daily life shows how a computer these days practically becomes an appendage. On Thursday mornings, for example, he goes to his art-and-the-computer class, where a software program enables him to choose from up to 16 million color mixtures to design pictures like his self-portrait. After class, he dashes to lunch, where a computerized cash register credits his hamburger, fries, and soft drink to his room-and-board bill. The only time he needs cash is when the computer tells him he has exceeded his meal limit for the week. If there is time before his illustration class in the afternoon, Mr. Corless seeks out a nearby terminal to check his electronic mail or catch up on classwork.

One recent night, Mr. Corless spent nearly 13 hours pecking away at a terminal keyboard, first creating two self-portraits, then struggling to convert Celsius temperatures to Fahrenheit for his introduction to programming course. By the time he forwarded the work directly into his professor's computer file, it was 7:30 A.M. He stayed awake to play computer games, tapping into Rogue, a computerized version of the popular Dungeons and Dragons game, until a 9 A.M. class.

On Thursday nights, Mr. Corless works at the library and shows other students how to use the computerized card catalog system, with its 550,000 book and 500 journal entries. This system is a good example of what computers can do.

The turn of the century approaches. The last time it arrived, the automobile, the telephone, the phonograph, the radio, photography, and motion pictures were radically altering a horse-and-buggy society. Then, during this century, new scientific developments—relativity and atomic structure, the airplane, television, the exploration of space, and the electronic computer—seemed at times to change our lives overnight.

The end of such an eventful century is a good time to think about what we're heading toward. Although we're near the end of a calendar era, our society is currently in the midst, or maybe even just at the beginning, of a technological revolution unparalleled in history. That's why you're reading this book: you need to be prepared to function in a vastly altered world.

Forty years ago, computers were the mysterious "thinking machines" of scientists and the top-secret weapons of generals. Today, they are toys, typewriters, and microwave ovens. They do your taxes, transact your banking, and make your movies. You play with them, work with them, and talk to them on the telephone. Their technology is even changing the language, adding new nouns like *technocrat* and *hacker* and new verbs like *input* and *access*. The computer's impact is greater than the telephone's and more pervasive than the automobile's. And, like any important new invention, the computer provokes a variety of reactions.

Few machines other than computers are assigned such a variety of roles to play. Magicians, accountants, servants, thieves, dictators, expediters, secretaries, miracle-workers—computers are called all of these and more. People have so many opinions about them that it's very easy to get a distorted idea of what computers *really* are and can do. The truth is often hidden under such thick layers of half-truths, prejudice, wishful thinking, and advertising slogans that it's hard to see.

This chapter is a time for getting it all straight—for sorting out the accumulated misinformation about a subject that seems to generate nonsense nonstop, for organizing in your mind those things about computers that you already know to be true, and for learning some new things. We don't have to tell anyone that computers are important, that Silicon Valley isn't Detroit, and that more and more of our lives are recorded in electronic bits and bytes. These things are common knowledge. The changes, the technological developments we're experiencing today, are rapidly being integrated into our lives and even becoming commonplace: a six-second wait for a computer to do something that would have once taken hours to do "by hand" now seems an intolerable annoyance. Nonetheless, none of us should simply accept these technological changes. We must take the time to understand the tools with which our society is being rebuilt, so that we can use them properly.

6

Figure 1.1 The Impact of Computer Technology
Computers are at the center of a technological revolution that extends from the depths of the ocean into outer space. (a) The U.S. Navy's exploratory minisubmarine is computer powered. (b) Although a kitchen isn't its best natural habitat, this microcomputer stores a restaurant chef's recipes. And (c) shuttle astronauts rescue a satellite.

COMPUTERS: WHAT THEY DO

It is difficult to think of an activity that hasn't been profoundly affected by computers since their appearance about thirty years ago. It would take more pages than this book could hold to list all the current applications of computers, or to count the ways they interact with us in our daily lives. Business, medicine, science, government, finance, industry, energy, entertainment—in virtually every imaginable field and enterprise, computers have had an enormous impact (see Figure 1.1).

The Computer's Role

In all the activities we might list, no matter how many there were, the computer would be employed for the same fundamental reasons: *to increase speed, to reduce costs,* and *to improve quality.* Although individuals and enterprises have always aspired to these goals, the opportunity to achieve them has never been so great. The computer stands alone as a means of reinvigorating old industries and creating entirely new ones. And whoever fails to take advantage of its unique capabilities can be sure that others will not (as the Swiss discovered in 1980, when their 90% share of the international watch market was cut to 30%, largely due to the wide-spread emergence of less-expensive electronic quartz watches). Competition at both the international and intercorporate levels is fierce, with companies pouring money into research and development in order to come up with a faster chip, a larger memory, or a more effective application. This intense rivalry produces rapid change and a lot of computers—all the more reason to take a closer look at the basic three-part role of the computer in our lives.

Increase Speed

In what ways do computers speed up our daily routines?

- In Detroit, Chrysler's automation efforts have increased productivity by 20%.   *Saving time and resources*
- It is estimated that the average secretary spends more than a quarter of each workday "holding" on the telephone; electronic mail eliminates that wasted time.
- Sixty billion checks are processed annually by the nation's banks. Trying to manage this enormous volume of paperwork without computers would bring the whole financial world to a standstill. With them, more than $100 million per second moves through the Federal Reserve's electronic Fedwire system.
- In seconds, a computer can figure the payroll for a medium-sized company, score 3000 SAT tests, or evaluate 100 electrocardiograms.
- At the supermarket, the electronic check-out system can read and interpret the bar code (see Figure 1.2) on an item, transfer the necessary information from

Figure 1.2 The Universal Product Code and the Automated Grocery Store
(a) The Universal Product Code (UPC) identifies each item for the computer. (b) The computer "looks up" the price of the item identified by the code and then transmits the information back to the point of sale. (c) The bar code also provides assistance in inventory management. Using a hand-held scanner, a clerk enters the UPC code from the shelf and counts the number of items. The computer, with this information, can determine when items should be reordered to restock the shelves. It can also verify that what is there matches what inventory and sales records say ought to be there.

(a)

(b)

(c)

scanner to computer to check-out terminal, do the calculation, and print both the item's description and price on the tape in less time than it would take a clerk to locate a printed price on an item and punch it into a cash register.

Reduce Costs

We all know computers are expensive. How, then, do they *reduce* costs?

Reducing development and operating costs

- Crash testing a prototype car can take more than two weeks and cost an automobile manufacturer more than $30,000. Through the use of computer simulation (see Figure 1.3), an unlimited number of tests can be run, under very different conditions, at a fraction of the cost, and with no mess to clean up later. Modifications in the design can also be made on the computer, drastically reducing the number of expensive and time-consuming rebuildings of the traditional clay model.

- In 1965, a typical communications satellite held about 240 telephone circuits at a cost of $22,000 each; such satellites now carry 100,000 circuits for only $30 each. This plummet in costs opened the door to numerous telecommunications activities, from international phone conferencing to pay-TV movies.

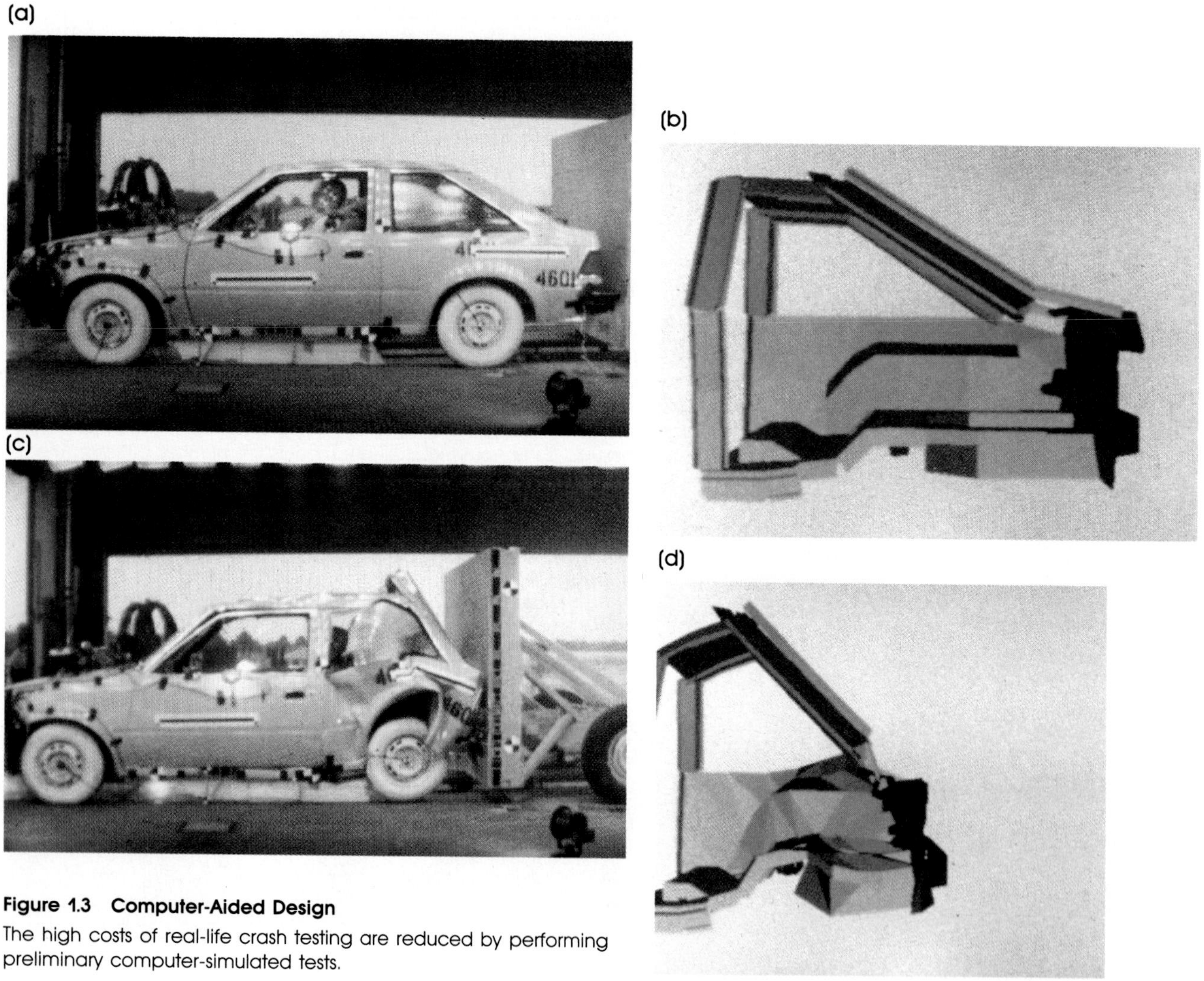

(a)

(b)

(c)

(d)

Figure 1.3   Computer-Aided Design
The high costs of real-life crash testing are reduced by performing preliminary computer-simulated tests.

- The cost of keeping an exploratory drilling crew on an oil rig in the North Atlantic can be tens of thousands of dollars per day, and many holes are "dry." The indispensable help of the computer in exploratory decision making increases the likelihood of payoff and minimizes the risk.

- The wages of supermarket checkers and stock clerks have increased by a factor of approximately 10 during the thirty-odd years in which the computer's cost has decreased by a factor of roughly 100,000. The clerk's wages are still increasing; the computer's cost is still decreasing.

- Because an automated assembly line can operate 24 hours a day without breaks, a major investment in automation can pay for itself within one or two years.

Improve Quality

Because computers, in some manufacturing situations, operate more reliably and precisely than the most skilled human workers, their use can improve the quality of goods and services.

- A robot at General Dynamics makes 30 parts for the F-16 fighter plane every shift, with no rejects; human workers averaged 6 parts per shift, with a 10% rejection rate.

Improving the quality of goods and services

- Computer-based management information systems provide fast, reliable, and accurate statistics on sales, marketing, financial, and personnel activities, thus helping executives make better decisions. Information networks help professionals in financial, legal, scientific, and other fields keep up with current issues, trends, and discoveries, which makes them better qualified to solve complex problems in a constructive and profitable way.

- Contrary to all the jokes and horror stories about computer errors, the fact is that computers perform complicated arithmetic 24 hours a day, day after day, and—for the most part—make no errors.

Why Study Computers?

Even though its effects are so far-reaching, the computer isn't a very visible element of our society. You don't often see the actual machine that toils behind the scenes at the supermarket or the bank. Its role is often less apparent, but no less important, in other areas as well. In industry and government, we are confronted with the need to plan and manage in an environment of increasing complexity: from manufacturing and marketing in a multinational or store-front enterprise to fighting crime, collecting taxes, and planning national defense policy in a nuclear age. The computer is the best means for organizing the increasing quantities of data with which decision makers must contend.

The increased complexity of our activities

Each of us has a profound personal interest in understanding computers. If you don't learn something about computers, at least enough to be able to communicate with computer professionals, your career prospects are likely to be limited. Computers are the single largest source of higher paying jobs in our current economy. (We will describe many of these jobs in the Careers in Technology section of each chapter.) Furthermore, the low-cost personal computer embodies unique opportunities for intellectual and business achievement by linking the incomparable reasoning ability of the human mind with the speed and accuracy of the computer. The intense international competition, both commercial and military, to

New businesses and jobs

gain the greatest advantage from this powerful technology is another reason why a balanced understanding of computers is worth achieving. Finally, we live in a world in which we literally leave a trail of computer records behind us. Computerized records are kept of our earnings, our savings and spending habits, our travel, and our organizational affiliations. These records may influence how we are treated by companies seeking our business or by credit-granting agencies; thus we should study computers because they are used to study us.

COMPUTERS: WHAT THEY ARE

Now that we've summarized some of the parts computers play in our daily lives, let's take a first look at what computers really are. What we want to provide here is a quick introduction to the different types of computers and an initial exposure to the principal parts of the computer system and their interfunctionings. Words that are printed in **boldface** in this chapter are key to the general understanding you should be trying to achieve here. The important word is "general"—don't worry about mastering the specifics yet. *All of the concepts introduced in this chapter will be treated more extensively in subsequent chapters.* (Throughout the rest of the book, all terms that are essential to this study of computers appear in **boldface** at the first place where they are fully defined. These terms are collected at the end of each chapter for review and are also listed alphabetically in the glossary. Terms that are important in the context of a given section are printed in *italics* where they are first used.)

Types of Computers

Price range

As we'll show in Part 2, computer **hardware** (the physical parts of a computer system) varies widely in performance and price as well as in size and appearance. For example, to give you some idea of just how wide the price range is, the systems of computer hardware discussed in this book range in price from about $200 to $10 million. The upper limit is 50,000 times the lower one. In contrast, car prices run from roughly $5000 to $100,000; the upper limit is only 20 times the lower one.

Let's look at the three basic types of computers: microcomputers, minicomputers, and mainframes.

Microcomputers

Microcomputers and the silicon chip

Microcomputers are the smallest and cheapest computer systems. The part of a microcomputer that does the actual computing is the tiny **silicon chip**, the symbol of "high tech." A portable, battery-powered microcomputer is about the size of a notebook. The economy and small size of the microcomputer have made possible the spread of individually owned and operated **personal computers**. Figure 1.4 indicates the wide range of available microcomputer systems.

Minicomputers

The midsize minicomputer

Minicomputers make up the middle class of computer size and power. The largest, called *superminis,* are the size of a few file cabinets, and the smallest can fit on a desk top. Since minicomputers generally have no special environmental or

(a)

(b)

(c)

Figure 1.4   Microcomputer Systems
(a) The heart of the microcomputer is the tiny silicon chip. Chips are incorporated into a wide variety of personal computers, from (b) inexpensive portable systems that are battery-powered to (c) systems with substantial storage and a printing capability.

personnel requirements, such as for air conditioning or a data-processing staff, they are particularly popular with small and medium-sized businesses. They are also sturdy enough to withstand the rigors of the industrial and military environments in which they are frequently employed. Figure 1.5 shows typical minicomputer systems.

Figure 1.5   Minicomputer Systems

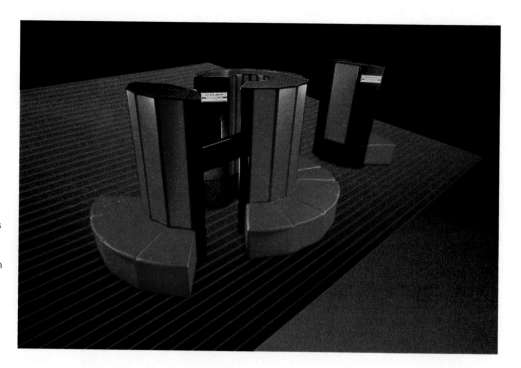

**Figure 1.6 The Cray X-MP
Supercomputer**
This is the most powerful of
the current group. Despite its
power, its size is moderate—
those are standard-size
bench seats surrounding it. In
order to be fast, it can't be
too big, since electrical signals, though they travel at
nearly the speed of light,
would take too long to get
from one end to the other.

Mainframes

*Mainframes and
supercomputers*

The large-scale **mainframe computer** is used principally by large organizations. Although the minicomputer is generally specialized to serve the needs of a relatively small number of users, the mainframe typically serves an entire organization and runs hundreds of different jobs each day. The largest and most powerful of the mainframes, used primarily by government and by industrial engineers and scientists, are called **supercomputers** (see Figure 1.6).

These are the basic distinctions. We'll look next at what all these computers, from the smallest microcomputer to the biggest mainframe, have in common.

The Physical Machine: A Hardware Overview

Components and systems

Computers aren't very exciting machines to watch. No wheels turn, no gears grind. All you see is the flickering of a few lights or the display of some values on a screen. If the computer is connected to a nearby printer or tape or disk drive, the mechanical parts of those units will produce some whirring and clattering, but most of the noise generated by a computer comes from a legion of small cooling fans that keep air currents swirling around the electronic circuits.

The minicomputers shown in Figure 1.5 are bolted into a standard rack of a type used to house many different kinds of electronic units. The units comprising a computer system are bought separately, as you buy stereo components, and then connected together. The computer itself comes packaged on a metal chassis, again, much like a stereo amplifier or a TV receiver, with a cover or front plate.

A **terminal**, which looks like a small TV screen with an attached keyboard, is connected to the computer. An operator uses the terminal to turn the computer on and off, to enter (**input**) data and computer programs, or to print or otherwise display (**output**) information stored by the computer. The terminal is also used when the computer is out of order (''down'') to help the operator locate and fix the problem. While the computer is routinely running a job, the terminal plays no role. Since input and output of a job usually take longer than running it, however, the terminal is usually in use.

We've made a quick survey of the external aspects of computer hardware. Now let's take up how computers do their jobs, how the principal hardware units work together.

The Principal Hardware Units

Memory

The most important thing to keep in mind about a computer is that everything it deals with must be represented numerically—all it can do is manipulate numbers. The data, or raw information, that describe a problem and the step-by-step list of instructions that tells the computer how to solve that problem (the **program**) must be reduced to numerical form.

Memory storage of both data and programs

The **memory** is where all of these numbers—the data and the program—are stored, at the center of the computer system. In fact, this storage of data and program together is the defining characteristic of the modern computer, which was originally called the *stored-program computer*.

We have mentioned the remarkable silicon chips that are the building blocks of computers, as well as of most other electronic devices. Some of these chips consist of more than a million microscopic transistors (see Figure 1.7). The transistors store numbers either as tiny electrical charges or as patterns of electronic pulses.

(a)

Figure 1.7 A Memory Chip

Each silicon chip (a) can store more than a million individual items of information. Each item is stored as an electrical signal or pattern of pulses by the chip's transistors. The chips are packaged in plastic components from which metal leads project. These leads are used to assemble the components onto *boards* where printed circuits interconnect them. (b) plastic package; (c) memory board.

(c)

(b)

(There is no brief way to explain how an individual transistor stores values, but, fortunately, neither is there any real need to do so here. In Chapter 3, we'll have more to say on the subject—just enough to remove the aura of mystery it might have.)

The transistors store numeric values, and a silicon chip may contain more than a million of these transistors. A computer's memory consists of many chips and can thus store millions of numbers. The transistors in the memory are connected into small groups, called memory locations. Each **memory location** is an electronic circuit in which one number may be stored, although how many digits this number may have varies among different kinds of memories and computers.

Addresses, locations, and contents

Each memory location has an **address**, a unique number that identifies it. The address of a memory location serves the same purpose as the number given to a section of a shelf that holds one hat in a check room (see Figure 1.8). In order to retrieve your hat, all you need to do is give the attendant the ''address'' of the location, the number printed on your hat check. Similarly, when a value is stored in a computer's memory, it is assigned a specific location. The value stored, or the **contents**, can only be retrieved from the memory location by giving the address to the memory circuits.

Just like the pieces of data, the instructions the computer is to follow to do a job are also reduced to numerical form and stored in memory. Remember that computers deal only with numbers. In Chapter 2, you'll see that representing instructions as numbers was crucial to the evolution of computers.

Arithmetic and Logic Unit (ALU)

Processing in the ALU

When numbers held in memory chips are to be manipulated in any way, they are transmitted as electronic signals to other chips designed to do this work. These chips make up the computer's **arithmetic and logic unit (ALU)**. The ALU can perform arithmetic operations, compare two numbers to determine if they are equal, and manipulate values in other ways, which we'll discuss in detail in Chapter 3.

Control Units

Managing the whole system

Other collections of silicon chips constitute the computer's control units. The **main control unit**, as its name reveals, controls all computer activities. For example, it transmits numbers to be added to the ALU and then transmits the sum

Figure 1.8 Addresses and Contents in Memory

The memory address identifies a location in memory where a number is stored. The number is the contents of that location. Similarly, a hat check number (an address) identifies the location on a shelf where a hat (the contents of that location) is sitting. This analogy of the hat, the shelf location, and the hat check number should make it easier to keep the memory contents, location, and address straight.

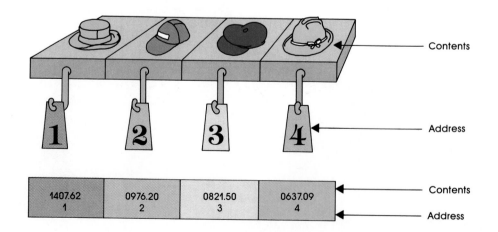

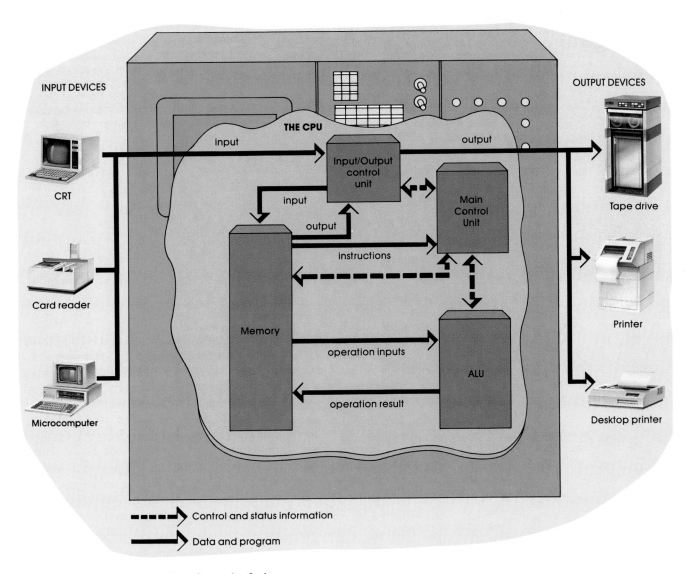

Figure 1.9   Information Flow in a Computer System
The main control unit supervises the entire computer system. The dashed lines represent commands from the main control unit to the other units. The solid lines trace the movement of data and program through the system.

back to the memory. The memory, the ALU, and the main control unit are collectively referred to as the **central processing unit**, or **CPU** (see Figure 1.9).

The main control unit generally has a subordinate **input/output (I/O) control unit**, which has the special job of overseeing the **peripheral equipment**, such as keyboards, screens, and printers. The peripherals get the data and programs into the computer and get the results back out. We'll discuss them next, and then turn to software.

Peripheral Equipment

The peripheral equipment connected to the computer is the means by which data and program are put into the memory and results are communicated to the user.

Getting data in and results out

Figure 1.10 Communicating with the Computer

A computer terminal is the easiest means for entering data or program. The screen displays what the user keys in, allowing a visual check of the correctness of the input. Results can be communicated to the user by being displayed on the same screen or printed.

Figure 1.10 shows a computer terminal with the type of keyboard that is commonly used for input. The TV-like screen displays what the user types in (or, more accurately, what the user "keys" in, since no actual type is involved). The screen display allows the user to check the input visually and correct any typographical errors before the information is transferred to the computer's memory.

Output can be communicated to the user on the same screen used to display the keyed input. A **printer** can be added as a peripheral to even the smallest computer system to provide **hard copy** (something you can walk away with). Large computer systems employ a wide variety of peripheral equipment to handle specialized data input sources, such as light tables or joysticks, and to provide output to other machines as well as humans. In fact, in medium and large systems, the I/O control units that operate the peripheral equipment may themselves be full-scale computers.

Solving Problems with Software

The Process

Data and information

Let's first clarify a useful distinction between data and information. **Data** are the raw materials of a problem, which the computer processes. **Information** is the finished, human-usable product—the answer to the problem. Data are *input*; information is *output*. The process that transforms data into information is described by the computer program, and the ALU is the place where the steps in this process are carried out. Figure 1.11 demonstrates this distinction. There is, however, no magic moment when data become information, and the distinction between the two cannot be drawn with great precision. A general rule that may be worth keeping in mind is "data in, information out."

Remember that it is always a program, in fact, more often a whole group of interdependent programs, that drives the hardware comprising a computer system. These controlling programs are called **software** to distinguish them from the

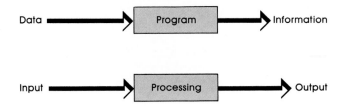

Figure 1.11 Data and Information

A sometimes useful, though imprecise, distinction can be made between data (what is input) and information (the results produced by executing a program).

hardware. A computer does nothing meaningful without a program, and a program is created by a **programmer** to do a specific computing job. A group of people called **systems analysts** have the responsibility of understanding what a program is supposed to do and how it fits into its operating environment. They must painstakingly formulate the job to be done and specify the overall plan for doing it. After systems analysts develop the refined plan of attack, programmers devise the precise sequence of operations that the computer must perform to produce the desired result.

The problem-solving process

An Example

To fit some of the facts we've been relating into a meaningful context, let's consider a simple computing job. Our example shows basically how a computer goes about adding two numbers together and outputting the result. The two numbers in this case are wages received for the year and interest income for the year. These are to be added together as part of a four-step program for income tax preparation. This calculation is simple enough that no great programming effort is involved. However, some programs have hundreds of thousands of steps. Writing such a program may be a combined effort of dozens of programmers, all of whose individual contributions must mesh together perfectly for the whole thing to run correctly. But that's a story for a later chapter—let's get back to our example.

First, the memory must be loaded with both the data (the numbers to be added) and the step-by-step program that will actually get the job done. Part of the memory will contain the data, and another part will store the program, as shown in Figure 1.12.

The steps in the example program are easy to follow. The main control unit causes the execution of the first step in the program: the wage figure is moved from the memory to the ALU (where, remember, all actual processing is done). The

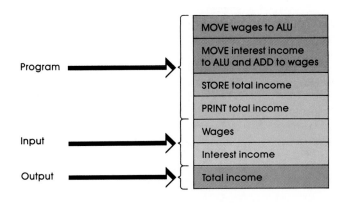

Figure 1.12 The Contents of Memory: A Taxing Example

The four-step program is loaded into consecutive locations in memory, followed by the input data. At the completion of the program, the result has been stored in memory and printed.

CAREERS IN TECHNOLOGY
Some Background

You now have a basic idea of what computers are and what they can do. In sections like these throughout the rest of the book, we'll describe many career opportunities centering around these remarkable machines, particularly jobs in the growing data-processing and computer-related fields. Here, however, is an overview of the computer-related job market itself: its history, its current outlook, and its future.

Data Processing: An Overview In 1980, nearly a million and a half people were employed in computer-related occupations, according to figures compiled by the U.S. Bureau of Labor Statistics. This bureau, the Department of Labor, and a number of private studies all project that by 1990 well over two million people will hold jobs directly associated with computer operation, computer maintenance, and systems analysis. That number doesn't include the millions more whose jobs in retailing, manufacturing, and service industries will involve the daily use of computers or those who will make, market, and sell computer hardware and software. The growth rate for jobs whose existence depends on computers (data processing and related occupations) is three times faster than the expected growth rate for all other jobs in the nation!

Furthermore, computer-related jobs will be available nearly everywhere. In the late 1970s and early 1980s, more than two-thirds of such jobs were concentrated in major metropolitan areas, where the money and facilities to support computer systems were more likely to be found. But the increasing use of minicomputers and distributed data processing is rapidly decentralizing computer systems and creating more opportunities for high-technology employment in all geographic regions.

More than 80% of all data-processing personnel are employed in only five fields. In descending order, these are data-processing service organizations (over half of all computer professionals are employed by such companies, which provide computing services to business and industry); manufacturing firms; insurance, finance, and real estate companies; banking; and wholesale or retail trade. Transportation, communications, chemical and pharmaceutical companies, public utilities, petro-leum and gas companies, government, mining, construction, and agriculture together account for only about 20% of computer-related employment. The highest salaries are paid by manufacturing firms, with public utilities a close second.

Data processing is clearly an attractive field. The number of associate's and bachelor's degrees awarded in computer science (including general computer and information sciences, data processing, computer programming, and systems analysis) has increased by more than 100% in the last ten years, as has the number of people who completed computer training courses in public and private vocational education programs. However, since more and more workers will be needed to bring the increasing number of computer applications "on-line," shortages of qualified computer personnel are anticipated.

Beyond Data Processing The growing use of computer systems makes a background in data processing (such as you have chosen to receive) a valuable asset even in job markets not directly related to computer operations. Secretaries, typists, and file clerks, for example, will find that experience in word processing is increasingly important, that many employers do in fact already require it. According to the U.S. Department of Labor, as new applications are developed for computers, more and more workers in noncomputer jobs will have to adapt to using computers. This, of course, means that some background in computers will prove valuable to almost every job seeker.

Among the occupations expected to be most affected by computers in the next decade are journalist, editor, real estate broker and agent, actuary, and stock broker; banker, loan officer, accountant, accounting clerk, auditor, and bank teller; doctor, lawyer, scientist, teacher, librarian, pilot, and engineer. Also, in an otherwise depressed market for teachers, those trained in computer science, mathematics, and natural sciences have very favorable employment prospects. High schools and colleges are adding new computer courses to their curricula and utilizing computers in traditional classes. Over a third of current college undergraduates use computers in their course work, and this number is

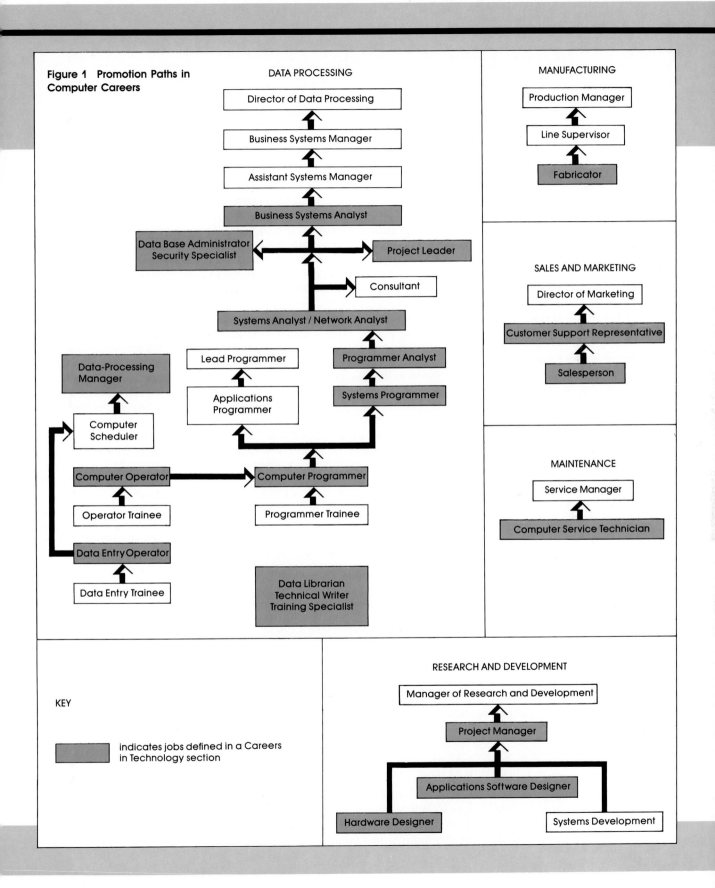

Figure 1 Promotion Paths in Computer Careers

19

increasing. Private industry's demand for graduates with computer skills is far outstripping schools' ability to produce them.

Today's Uncertain Market   Long-term, even short-term, employment projections can only be educated guesses based on an analysis of past economic, employment, and business forces; they are, like the Ghost of Christmas Yet to Come, a shadow of things that might be, not of things that will be. In fact, what looks like an exciting prospect one day may look really dismal the next. In the middle of 1985, for example, the experts who had assured everyone of the computer industry's unlimited profitability and employment prospects got a big surprise. In the space of only a few weeks, IBM stopped producing the PCjr and both Apple and Wang announced temporary factory shut-downs. A number of once-booming small computer and software manufacturers folded. There started to be new talk of "limited markets" for computers, suggestions that perhaps a computer in every home and office was an unrealistic goal. It was suddenly discovered that people could be just as unemployed in Silicon Valley as they could be in Detroit.

Today, we are in the midst of a realignment of the computer industry, and its impact on employment prospects is still unclear. It has been suggested that the day of the computer entrepreneur has passed and that in the near future there may be only two or three big computer companies that really control the marketplace. That would limit the kinds of hardware available to users, which would in turn dictate the applications, the personnel required, the necessary training, and a host of other areas vital those considering computer careers. So take our projections as the general trends and conditions that they are, and look into the current reality for yourself. In the end, it's up to you to check out the up-to-the-minute situation in any career area.

A Look Ahead   In upcoming Careers in Technology sections, we'll look in depth at such jobs as computer operator, computer programmer, systems analyst, and service technician. We'll also examine the job description, qualifications, and outlook for a wide range of computer-related careers, from applications software designers and network analysts to data base administrators, technical writers, and customer support representatives. In the last chapter, Careers in Technology will discuss the practical strategies of the job search, resumé, and interview. All of this should give you a clear picture of the doors your computer skills can open into the professional world beyond this book.

So that you may better understand the relationships among the jobs we'll be discussing, and perhaps begin to plan your own career path, Figure 1 shows likely routes up the corporate ladder from entry-level jobs to top-level positions.

---

control unit then instructs the ALU to execute the next instruction, which moves the interest income to the ALU and adds it to wages. The ALU then contains the result, the total income. The next program instruction causes this total to be stored back in the memory, freeing the ALU for other work. The last instruction outputs the total income figure so that someone can use the information.

Beyond the CPU   Our example focused on the activities of the CPU, the computer's "brain," which in many cases is augmented only by a keyboard from which a human can directly feed in small amounts of input and by a screen or printer via which results can be output to a human who may or may not take some action. Some computers are far more independent of direct human control. They are equipped with sensors and scanners that let them observe and assess what's going on, and they can output to *actuators* that take action on the basis of their assessments. Although it's difficult to comprehend, even in such complex systems a program—written by a human—is ultimately directing the whole show, relating the outputs to the inputs.

COMPUTERS: WHAT THEY AREN'T

Even this brief discussion of computers begins to clarify just what they are and what they can do. Computers produce such impressive results that we need to remind ourselves from time to time that all they're really able to do is store numbers and do arithmetic. Computers don't decide how they will be used. That decision is our responsibility alone. Computers can't perform the research and analysis that capture the essence of problems, and they don't write the programs that attempt to solve them. They don't enter the input data, and they don't make policy decisions based on the results. These are our jobs, our responsibilities. Computers can't anticipate the economic or social side effects of an application. This, too, is our responsibility. Only through an enlightened understanding of what computers are and how they work can we possibly expect to use their capabilities as effectively and as wisely as we should.

Limits to what computers can and ought to do

ISSUES IN TECHNOLOGY
Shortly after the new computer-controlled subway system opened in Washington, D.C., a runaway train was stopped by a passenger who unlocked the control booth with her hair barrette. What other things can people do that computers can't? Is that list likely to change? What changes are likely, and in what ways might they affect how we work, think, and feel?

SUMMARY

Computers: What They Do
In little more than thirty years, the computer has been applied to nearly every activity conducted within our increasingly technology-dependent society.

The Computer's Role The computer's basic three-part role is to increase the speed with which we deliver goods and services while reducing costs and improving quality.

Why Study Computers? The computer is essential to our ability to cope with issues and problems of increasing complexity. Computers continue to create new jobs and are a principal basis for establishing new enterprises. The computerized information accumulated about every one of us increasingly affects how we are treated.

Computers: What They Are
Types of Computers Computer types range from the simplest microcomputer systems owned and operated by individuals and priced at a few hundred dollars, to medium-sized and medium-priced minicomputers, to supercomputers that cost around $10 million.

The Physical Machine: A Hardware Overview All systems consist of equipment to input programs and data, to process the data by executing the program, and to output the results. Computer systems are often assembled from components, much like stereo systems are.

The Principal Hardware Units The memory contains a problem's data as well as the program to be executed, both stored in numerical form. Memory is divided into areas called locations; each location stores a number, its contents, and is referred to by its address.

Processing is done in the arithmetic and logic unit (ALU). The main control unit interprets the program's sequence of instructions and causes the transmission of data and results between the memory and the ALU. The memory, the ALU, and the main control unit constitute the heart of the computer—the central processing unit (CPU). A wide variety of peripheral equipment is employed to put data in and get results out.

Solving Problems with Software Data are the raw materials that go into the computer, and information is the results that come out. The program converts the former into the latter. A programmer prepares the program only after the problem has been formulated and specified, in detail, by a systems analyst.

Computers: What They Aren't

All computers do is store and manipulate numbers. Although this permits them to do impressive jobs, every one of these jobs is directed by a program, written by one or more people on the basis of requirements supplied by other people.

COMPUTER CONCEPTS

As an extra review of the chapter, try defining the following terms. If you have trouble with any of them, refer to the page number listed.

hardware 10	program 13	input/output (I/O) control
microcomputers 10	memory 13	unit 15
silicon chip 10	memory location 14	peripheral equipment 15
personal computers 10	address 14	printer 16
minicomputers 10	contents 14	hard copy 16
mainframe computer 12	arithmetic and logic unit	data 16
supercomputers 12	(ALU) 14	information 16
terminal 12	main control unit 14	software 16
input 12	central processing unit	programmer 17
output 12	(CPU) 15	systems analysts 17

REVIEW QUESTIONS

1. What are the three principal advantages underlying the trend toward computer-based automation?
2. What new kind of service enterprise has been created by the use of computers?
3. How can computers influence how we are treated by certain agencies?
4. What are the three types of computers?
5. What are the main characteristics of each type of computer?
6. Describe how memory works.
7. Distinguish between memory location and address, between location and contents.
8. What is the job of the ALU? of the main control unit?
9. Name the units that make up the CPU. Describe how each relates to the others.
10. Describe some typical peripheral equipment and its functions.
11. Distinguish between data and information, between software and hardware.
12. Of what use are computers without programs? Why?
13. Distinguish between the job of the systems analyst and that of the programmer.
14. List some of the things computers can't do, things that must remain the responsibility of their human users.

A SHARPER FOCUS ▬▬▬▬▬

Now that you've completed this chapter, you should be able to answer the following questions about the chapter opening.

1. To what extent did the availability of computer facilities influence where you applied to college?
2. Some students at Carnegie-Mellon are concerned that all the computers on campus bring about depersonalization. Others feel that computers promote closer personal relationships. Which side do you agree with? Support your argument.
3. How do the computers on campus increase speed, reduce costs, and improve quality in everyday school life?
4. What types of computers are in evidence at Carnegie-Mellon?

PROJECTS ▬▬▬▬▬

1. Make a list of specific situations in which you come into contact, somehow, with a computer. What benefits do you derive from these encounters? Are there any drawbacks? Try to find out how the functions you've listed were carried out *before* computers existed. How have things improved since then?
2. Computers are portrayed in many different ways by the print and broadcast media. For example, many magazine articles, movies, and TV shows depict computers as magical "superbrains," while others depict them as nothing more than extremely complex electronic devices. Discuss some examples of these and other views (identify your sources).
3. Other than jobs in the data-processing industry itself (computer engineer, data entry operator, programmer, and so on), what *new* jobs and careers have resulted from the entry of the computer into the business world?
4. The computerized supermarket check-out system mentioned in the chapter hasn't met with universal praise. Ralph Nader, for example, finds fault with these systems. Research the complaints about such a system, and discuss what merit you find in the complaints.
5. We've stated that "all that the computer can do is manipulate numbers," yet we constantly read about a computer being used to predict the winner of the Superbowl or to find the ideal mate. How can tasks like these be accomplished if all a computer does is store and operate on numbers?

2

The Evolution of Computers

▶

FOCUS ON . . . THE EARLY DAYS OF PERSONAL COMPUTERS

Despite the illusion that personal computers have been around a long time, there was a fairly recent era when you had to build your own or do without. Stephen Gray, contributing editor to *Creative Computing* magazine, reminisces:

> Twenty years ago, while I was the computers editor of *Electronics* magazine at McGraw-Hill, I realized there was much I could learn from building a computer. It didn't take long to find out how difficult it was just to get started. There were no kits, no "cookbooks." Computer textbooks usually contained partial schematics, but none told how to connect the various sections.
>
> After several years of trying to build a digital computer in my spare time, I began to realize how difficult it must be for other hobbyists. . . .

Back in the mid-sixties, to build a simple computer accumulator, which could do no more than add successive inputs, using toggle switches for input and lamps for output, cost several dollars per bit. To build an extremely simple "computer" with four-bit words and without memory, and which divided the easy way (by repeated subtraction without shifting), could cost two or three hundred dollars. . . .

Building one's own computer was such a complicated undertaking that very few were ever completed, and nearly all of those were built by electronics engineers working in the data processing industry.

The main problem in building a computer was (and still is) the many technologies involved. Computer companies had specialists in logic, input/output, core memory, mass memory, peripherals, and other areas. To build one's own computer required learning a great deal about each one.

If the computer hobbyist was an electronics engineer working for a computer manufacturer, he could drop in on a friend down the hall or in the next building and ask what kind of drivers might be needed for a core memory with such-and-such specs. Most hobbyists had no such resources.

In addition to having to learn a great deal about computer electronics, the hobbyist also had to get into mechanical areas such as packaging, back-plane wiring, metal working, plastics, and many others.

Eventually, the young personal computer industry began to market kits, then kits *or* completed computers, and finally finished products.

Four Generations of Computers

People have always needed to add things up: how many mammoths killed in a season, how much grain to store for the winter, or how much fuel to get a rocket to the moon. In fact, a cave wall in Lascaux, France, may have been the first "adding machine." About 16,000 years ago, anonymous hunters wanted to keep track of how many bison, deer, horses, and wild cattle were available in the region but lacked an abstract concept of number, so they drew a portrait of each animal. Later, because it was much easier to draw a little abstract shape than to paint a realistic picture of the individual animal, the Phoenicians used the symbol *aleph* (a triangle with horns) to represent a cow. Inverted, aleph later became the Greek alpha and subsequently the Roman letter A. The use of symbols for objects was a step in the right direction, but can you imagine a rancher drawing thousands of alephs every time someone asked him for a record of how many head of cattle he owned?

Computers are the logical end product of centuries of humanity's pencil-breaking frustration with having to add things, subtract things, and perform other feats of arithmetic derring-do. "Make it easier; make it more accurate; make it faster!" has been the universal cry, and an ever-progressing technology has been the response. From portable notched bones (themselves a large technological leap forward from the bulky, hard-to-carry cave wall) to the abacus, from unwieldy mechanical adding machines to the silicon chip, from no numbers at all to magnetic spots on plastic disks, technological developments have answered the demand that computations be made faster, better, and easier. It's a long way from the cave wall to the silicon chip, but this chapter will trace the major steps that led from then to now.

The main thread of the story concerns the sequence of ever-improving calculating and computing machines created by a succession of inventive geniuses. Each of these inventors used the technology, that is, the parts and tools, available in his or her era. Frequently, the existing technology was the determining factor in whether or not an idea for a machine would actually work or could be built for a price anyone was willing to pay.

THE ORIGINS

The concept of number

What would life be like without numbers? What if there were no words for numbers, no symbols for numbers, in fact, no concept of number at all? How could we engage in agriculture or plan the hunt to meet the needs of a tough winter if we couldn't count our population or reckon the passage of time? How could we even define or describe "a tough winter" without using some kind of numerical measurement? Without numbers, how could we manufacture or build? How could we buy or sell or trade?

It's obvious that the concept of number must have coincided with the earliest advances of civilization. At first, the concept covered no more than the distinction between one and many. Later, one, two, and many were distinguished—a vital step forward. Then came the realization that there is a concept of "twoness" that is the same whether it refers to two rabbits or two trees. Further generalization and application of this idea, over the millenia, gave rise to the words and symbols that enable us to record and communicate numbers.

Symbols for numbers

The idea and the symbol came together with the first calculation—counting. The earliest surviving records unearthed by archeologists are notched bones about 30,000 years old. Two notches in a bone or stick stood for two head of cattle; a third notch was added when a calf was born. This type of counting tool persisted for thousands of years, marked by a transition to counting in groups of five (the

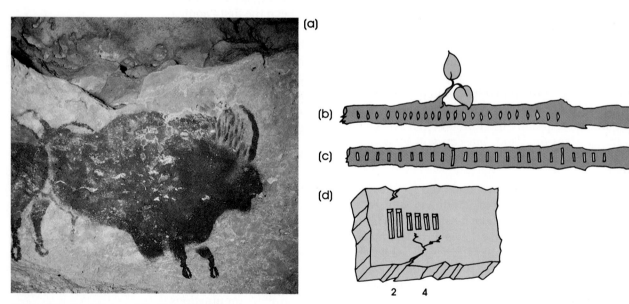

Figure 2.1 Counting and Positional Notation

(a) Before anyone had thought of numbers, in order to represent, for example, a herd of cattle, someone had to draw the actual number of cows in the herd on a cave wall. (b) Sticks (the first great counting innovation) are portable, unlike cave walls, and it was easier to make notches than to draw portraits. But the notches often became too numerous, making it difficult to grasp the number at a glance or to compare the number of notches to the number of cattle. (c) A great leap forward occurred when every tenth notch was made longer, greatly facilitating record keeping. (d) It was then just a small step to positional notation, in which each big notch represents 10 and each little notch stands for 1. The notches shown here correspond to 24 in our number system.

Figure 2.2 The Counting Board

The counting board, a great advance over a heap of stones, depends on positional notation; each column of the board represents a digit position. More than ten stones in a position result in a carry: one stone to the next higher position, and the removal of ten stones from the position that caused the carry. Unlike the notched stick, the counting board was "erasable." It was undoubtedly a precursor of the abacus.

Figure 2.3 The Abacus

The Japanese abacus (*soroban*) appeared late in the sixteenth century and is completely harmonious with decimal notation. The beads on each wire can represent all nine digits. When pushed to the bar, the bead at the right stands for a value of 5. When pushed to the bar, the beads to the left of the bar each count for a value of 1.

Romans) and ten (in eastern India and Arabia) and the development of *positional notation,* which is illustrated in Figure 2.1.

The first counting "machine," shown in Figure 2.2, was the *counting board,* dating back about 3000 years. More than a thousand years went by before the stones in a column of the counting board evolved into the "high-tech" beads on the wires of the *abacus.* The origin of this first calculator is obscured in Chinese, Arabic, European, and Egyptian antiquity. The abacus shown in Figure 2.3 is clearly lighter and more portable than the counting board, and it enables addition to be done more rapidly and accurately.

The earliest aids to counting

As the centuries passed, an influential merchant class arose in Europe, the sign of a growing international and even intercontinental commerce. The more complex social and economic system called for elaborate account keeping, with calculations of interest and currency exchange. Science awakened to computation; mathematical theories concerning the motions of the earth, moon, planets, and sun used equations to compute planetary positions and daily variations in daylight and tides. Seasonal effects were estimated more accurately, increasing agricultural productivity and creating the food surpluses necessary to feed a burgeoning urban population. Government clerks calculated tariffs and other taxes. In 1642, Galileo died, Newton was born, and the French mathematician Pascal built the first gear-driven mechanical calculator.

Figure 2.4 The Pascaline
Pascal's mechanical calculator performed addition and subtraction. Each digit was entered manually by turning the appropriate gear. This turning also carried out the operation and produced the display of the result in the window.

  EARLY MACHINES

The first mechanical calculating machine

Blaise Pascal (1623–1662), the son of a mathematically gifted tax official, spent long hours with his father adding columns of figures. He later became an entrepreneur who built and sold 50 of the far-from-perfect mechanical calculators he invented. Figure 2.4 shows his *Pascaline,* a gear-driven machine that performed addition and subtraction. Pascal's calculator was **digital**; that is, like the abacus, it dealt with whole numbers and produced precise results. Another class of instruments and calculators, such as certain surveying and astronomical instruments, was **analog**; these machines, like the conventional mechanical wrist watch, gave only a visual depiction of the result, in contrast to the precise read-out of a digital watch (see Figure 2.5).

Figure 2.5
Analog and Digital

(a) The traditional clock presents an analog indication of the time and is capable of representing every possible value. However, it provides only an approximation of the true value, perhaps to two or three reliable digits. (b) The digital clock gives precise readings to as many digits as are required. (c) The analog slide rule was the universal calculator of engineering students before the invention of (d) the digital electronic calculator. After centuries of use, slide rules are no longer manufactured.

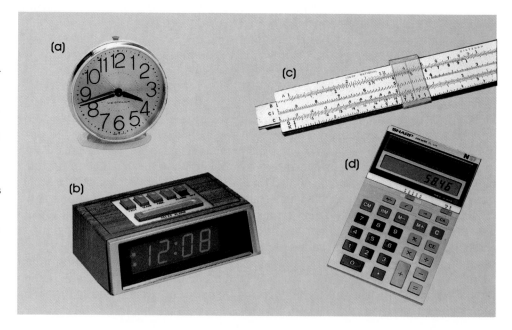

Figure 2.6
Leibniz's Calculator

Leibniz's calculator not only added and subtracted but also multiplied and divided. The complicated and unreliable mechanism formed products by adding the multiplicand first to itself and then to the preceding subtotal, as many times as indicated by the value of the multiplier. To multiply 23 by 8, for example, it added 23 to itself and then added 23 to 46, and so on. This is essentially the method used in modern computers, although countless refinements have been made.

Later in the seventeenth century, the German mathematician *Gottfried Wilhelm von Leibniz* (1646–1716) built the first calculator designed to do multiplication and division as well as addition and subtraction. The complexity of this machine was, however, somewhat beyond what could be effectively built out of the contemporary mechanical gears and levers, and the machine, shown in Figure 2.6, was not very reliable.

In the nineteenth century, the British inventor and mathematician *Charles Babbage* (1792–1872), who had very little practical success, achieved the intellectual triumph of clearly anticipating most of the logical principles on which the modern computer is based. Babbage designed his *analytical engine* (Figure 2.7) as a result of his boredom with long calculations and his distress at the inherent errors they involved. He incorporated a mechanical memory in his design to store intermediate calculated results so they wouldn't have to be copied onto paper and subsequently reentered—a process that was one of the principal sources of error. He

A precursor to the modern computer

(a)

(b)

Figure 2.7 Babbage's Analytical Engine and the Jacquard Loom
(a) A model of Babbage's analytical engine, built from his plans. The machine read data and programs from cards adapted from (b) the Jacquard loom, which used holes in a sequence of cards to control which threads were picked up by hooks and inserted into a woven pattern.

also provided for the entry of both numbers and calculation steps on punched cards. He adapted this idea from *Joseph Jacquard* (1752–1834), who, late in the eighteenth century in France, had built a weaving machine that used punched cards to select the threads to be incorporated into a pattern. However, Babbage's steam-powered analytical engine proved too complex for him to build: his idea was ahead of the currently available technology.

It is largely due to the efforts of *Ada Augusta,* Countess of Lovelace (1816–1852), daughter of the romantic poet Lord Byron and now generally regarded as the first computer programmer, that we remember the work of Babbage today. A mathematical prodigy, the Countess of Lovelace became interested in Babbage's ideas, and in 1842, at the age of 27, she translated a description of Babbage's machine from French into English. She added some of her ideas about programming to the translation and corrected Babbage's errors. Ada Lovelace is credited with developing the programming loop (see Chapter 8), in which a sequence of operations is repeated within a program.

Not until 1886 did *William Seward Burroughs* (1855–1898) introduce the first commercially successful mechanical adding machine. A million Burroughs Adding and Listing Machines (Figure 2.8) were sold by 1926, and Henry Ford even produced a car, the Burroughs Special, with a rack designed to carry the popular device.

At about the time that Burroughs was building his mechanical adder, another important development occurred in the United States. There had been a census in 1880, and manual tabulation of the data had taken seven years. Since the population was growing rapidly and more information was to be included on the census forms, it was clear that the data from the 1890 census wouldn't be compiled before it was time to start on the 1900 census. *Dr. Herman Hollerith* (1860–1929) was an employee of the Census Office when he recognized this problem. He struck out on his own and developed the first electromechanical punched-card tabulator, shown in Figure 2.9. Data were represented by the positions of punches on cards that

Figure 2.8 The Burroughs Adding and Listing Machine

Each column of keys corresponds to a decimal digit position. Numbers were entered and then accumulated into the total by pulling down on the handle.

Figure 2.9 Hollerith's Tabulating Machine

This is the historic machine that was the basis for what today is the IBM Corporation.

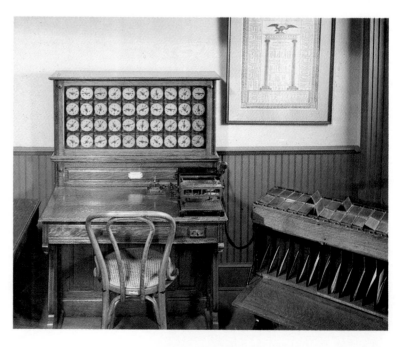

were fed into the tabulator. (In Chapter 4, we'll describe the Hollerith code, which is still in use today to represent data on punched cards.) The tabulator then automatically totaled the data from selected parts of the card.

*Punched cards and the
beginning of IBM*

Hollerith took another major step. He recognized that the punched data could be "sorted" to determine how many people had more than two children, or non–English-speaking family members, or any other attribute on which data had been collected. He built a sorting machine, powered by electricity rather than muscle or steam, to do this automatically. As a result of Hollerith's work, the tabulation of the 1890 census was completed in three years, and vastly improved analysis and use of the data had been made possible.

The Tabulating Machine Company, founded by Hollerith on the basis of his machines, proved to be a profitable venture. *Thomas J. Watson, Sr.* (1874–1956) joined this company in 1914. After an initial period of less-than-perfect harmony, the technical genius of the founder was subordinated to the business mastery of his successor. In 1924, with Watson as its president, it was renamed the International Business Machines Corporation (IBM), and the Hollerith card became the IBM card. In 1914, the company had 1300 employees; today, more than 600,000 people work for the $40-billion-a-year firm. Watson's commercial vision led to his sponsorship of another technical pioneer, Howard H. Aiken, whose work was instrumental in the development of the modern computer.

DAWN OF THE COMPUTER AGE

The Harvard Mark I

By the end of the 1930s, the production of punched card tabulating equipment based on Hollerith's initial inventions had turned IBM into a large and profitable company. These machines served many routine business needs, with unmatched accuracy and speed. In 1939, Professor *Howard H. Aiken* (1900–1973) of Harvard University sought backing from Watson, who had established IBM's policy of enlightened corporate self-interest and demonstrated it by generous gifts to universities. Aiken wanted to design and construct a computer that, like Babbage's, could be programmed to execute an entire sequence of instructions automatically. Watson responded with financial support of nearly a million dollars and the assistance of some of IBM's best technical people.

IBM and Aiken

The *Harvard Mark I,* as the computer came to be known, became operational in 1944 (see Figure 2.10, p. 34). It employed new electromechanical devices called **relays**, which consisted of an electromagnet and a switch. Hollerith had already used electricity rather than muscle power to move the mechanical parts in his machines. The relay was the next big step in the advance of early twentieth century computing technology; it soon entirely replaced the gear.

Relays

Harvard Mark I's relays were much quicker than mechanical gears; each switch took only a few thousandths of a second to open or close. This seemed like a very short time indeed, but three seconds had elapsed by the time all of the thousands of relays required to multiply two numbers had operated. The process was held up by the fact that some of the relays couldn't start operating until others had finished (for example, those responsible for making "carries" from one digit position to the next). Some of the calculations performed by the Harvard Mark I involved many thousands of multiplications. There are 3600 seconds in an hour—enough time for the Harvard Mark I to do only 1200 multiplications—so the total time per calculation sometimes ran to many hours.

Figure 2.10 The Mark I and ENIAC

(a) The Mark I executed a sequence of instructions automatically. It was built out of electromechanical relays.
(b) ENIAC, though not yet a general-purpose computer, used fully electronic components to achieve its then unparalleled speed.

ENIAC

With its 51-foot length and 500 miles of wire, the Harvard Mark I was a significant accomplishment, but it was to be eclipsed in 1946 by the first of the totally electronic machines, *ENIAC* (Electronic Numerical Integrator And Computer), shown in Figure 2.10. Development of ENIAC began during World War II under Army sponsorship. It was designed to compute the numerical tables used to target artillery, that is, to calculate the ballistic trajectories of artillery shells and of the first generation of U.S. military rockets.

The machine

The principal designers of ENIAC were *John Presper Eckert, Jr.* (b. 1919) and *John W. Mauchly* (1908–1980) of the Moore School of Electrical Engineering at the University of Pennsylvania. ENIAC wasn't a general-purpose computer by our current standard; substantial manual set-up (plugging units together and setting switches) was required to vary even its rather narrow repertoire of calculations. But ENIAC started a revolution in arithmetic speed by doing away with the electromechanical relay altogether. Instead, ENIAC employed an electronic switch—the

Vacuum tubes

vacuum tube, which was used at that time in radio and radar equipment. The relay, in which an appreciable mass must move a finite distance, completes its task in *milliseconds* (thousandths of a second); the vacuum tube, in which only electrons move, operates in *microseconds* (millionths of a second).

ENIAC was an enormous machine: it was 100 feet long, 10 feet high, and 3 feet deep, and weighed 30 tons. It contained 18,000 vacuum tubes, 70,000 resistors, and 6000 switches, and required 140 kilowatts of power to operate. But it carried out a multiplication operation in 3 milliseconds—a thousand times faster than the Mark I!

Eckert, Mauchly, and Atanasoff

Assigning credit for initiating the electronic computer age to the designers of ENIAC is open to question. In 1941, two years before the start of the ENIAC project, Mauchly visited the laboratory of *John V. Atanasoff* (b. 1903) at Iowa State University. Atanasoff had already built a specialized computer to solve systems of linear equations. Although Atanasoff's computer employed vacuum tubes and was not as flexible or as powerful as ENIAC, nonetheless it was fundamentally a kind of electronic computer. Atanasoff sued Mauchly and his associates when they tried to patent what he claimed were his ideas. A federal court finally decided in 1974 that his claim was valid. This controversy, however, had little impact on ENIAC's development or its significance in the evolution of computer technology.

It must also be pointed out that in two important ways ENIAC itself did not qualify as a modern electronic computer: it worked with decimal rather than binary numbers, and its calculations could be varied only by tedious manual altering of its set-up rather than by simply changing a numerically coded program. But, all disclaimers aside, ENIAC was certainly of great historic importance. For one thing, the principals of the ENIAC project stayed in the forefront of the developing computer field. Eckert and Mauchly went on to found the company that built *UNIVAC,* the first commercial electronic computer. John von Neumann, one of the world's leading scientists, was a consultant to the project, and he would later bring the computer age into full flower.

The IAS Computer and the Binary Number System

John von Neumann (1903–1957), of Princeton's celebrated Institute for Advanced Study (IAS), the academic home of Albert Einstein and many other great scientists, was a true scientific genius. He had a virtually photographic memory, was a prodigious mental calculator, and made broad and fundamental contributions to science. He was a consultant to the U.S. government and was actively involved in the World War II atomic weapons research at Los Alamos. Consulting on the ENIAC project was only the start of his work on computers. Before ENIAC was complete, von Neumann formulated plans with Eckert and Mauchly for a new computer, *EDVAC* (Electronic Discrete Variable Automatic Computer), which was to store program as well as data as numbers in memory, just as is done by computers today.

John von Neumann

Also, von Neumann abandoned the decimal system, once and for all. He reasoned (as had Atanasoff) that the switches out of which computers were built had two states: on and off (or conducting and nonconducting for the vacuum tubes he employed). Using such switches to represent decimal digits (the numbers from 0 through 9) is somewhat inefficient (as we will see in the next chapter) and complicates the arithmetic circuitry as well. Rather naturally, von Neumann concluded that the **binary system** of notation, in which the digits indicate what powers of 2 (1, 2, 4, 8, 16, etc.) a number contains, would be better suited to computers. In the binary system, since the base is 2, each digit can have a value of either 0 or 1. One binary digit (either a zero or a one) is called a **bit**. The two possible values of a bit are represented by the two possible states of a switch.

The binary system

In 1945, long before EDVAC's completion in 1950, von Neumann went on to direct his own computer project. The machine this project produced at Princeton, the *IAS computer* (Figure 2.11), rather than the solely military EDVAC, was the immediate precipitant of the explosion of computers onto the commercial scene. At Princeton, von Neumann created not only a computer but an intellectual environment in which the application of computers was the focus of broad and deep investigation.

The IAS computer

Unlike its predecessors, the IAS computer possessed the hallmark of the truly general-purpose computer—the ability to turn instantly from one program to another, to solve equations of atmospheric motion one second and those describing nuclear detonations the next. The versatility of the IAS machine meant that it had more than one use. Although its major role was in the design of U.S. nuclear weapons, it ran hundreds of other pioneering programs written at Princeton, from the simulation of genetical processes to the first electronic checker player.

Figure 2.11 The IAS Computer
The first truly general-purpose electronic computer was built at the Institute for Advanced Study in Princeton, New Jersey, by a group headed by John von Neumann. Compare its size to that of the Mark I or ENIAC; it was vastly more powerful than either.

After the IAS computer and EDVAC, things began to move quickly. In 1951, Eckert and Mauchly delivered UNIVAC I to the U.S. Bureau of the Census, and a year later IBM unveiled its first computer. The computer age had begun.

FOUR GENERATIONS OF COMPUTERS

The years from the delivery of the first UNIVAC in 1951 to the present can be separated into four periods. Each is identified primarily by the hardware components used during that particular *generation*. The generations are generally defined like this:

Generation	Dates	Hardware
First	1951–1958	Vacuum tubes
Second	1959–1964	Transistors
Third	1965–1971	Integrated circuits
Fourth	1971–Present	Large-scale integration

With each generation, costs decreased, performance improved, utilization became easier, and the computer industry continued its rapid growth.

The First Generation (1951–1958)

The first commercial electronic computers

The first generation began with Eckert and Mauchly's UNIVAC I (Figure 2.12) and IBM's 701. These machines were the first computers to be used by businesses, mostly for accounting functions such as payroll and billing. Previous computers had been used mainly for military and scientific computation.

Hardware

Many thousands of vacuum tubes were required to build a single first-generation CPU. Vacuum tubes were notoriously unreliable because of, among other factors, the heat generated in using them and the imperfection of the vacuum (enough air

Figure 2.12   UNIVAC I
The UNIVAC I being used by CBS and Walter Cronkite to predict the outcome of the 1952 presidential election.

remained inside the glass to slowly burn up the metallic parts). The aging of the seal between the glass body of the tube and its metal and plastic base accelerated this process. A dedicated maintenance effort, checking and replacing aging tubes, was necessary to keep a first-generation computer operating.

Relatively few numbers could be stored using a vacuum tube to represent each binary digit. Although several other electronic storage techniques were used during the first generation, most of these have since become extinct. The abiding contribution of the first generation to computer technology was the use of magnetic storage media.

Magnetic storage

Magnetic drums (cylinders with a magnetizable outer surface) were used as internal memory for many of the first-generation computers. Programs and data were usually first punched on IBM cards. Since reading and punching IBM cards is a slow process, the data were, upon input, transferred to a magnetic drum. The drum was the internal memory, or **primary memory** (sometimes also called the **primary storage unit**); that is, it was directly connected to the ALU and control unit and held the active data and program. Intermediate results were written on and retrieved from the drum. No slow card punching and reading was necessary. Although magnetic drums were very slow by today's standards, they were still much faster to access than punched cards, which were the first generation's secondary storage. **Secondary storage** refers to memory with higher capacity but slower accessibility; data to be processed are transferred from secondary storage to the primary storage unit.

Even though they represented an improvement in speed, drums did have a limited capacity; only a few thousands or tens of thousands of numbers could be held on a drum. To augment this capacity, secondary storage on magnetic tape was developed toward the end of the first generation. The amount of data that can be stored on tapes is virtually limitless, but the price for this high capacity is paid in terms of the longer time it takes to access the data. If the data you want to use were recorded in the middle of a tape, you might have to wait several minutes until that spot unreels under the *read head*, where an electromagnet converts the magnetic spots on the tape into the electronic impulses handled by the processor. (Of course, if the reel of tape is on a shelf in another room, the time it will take to access the data will be even longer.) Like data on cards, specific data on magnetic tape secondary storage were transferred to a magnetic drum primary storage unit to be processed.

Software

Keeping first-generation hardware running was tedious and exacting, but programming for it was even worse. The first programs were expressed in the long strings of binary digits, zeros and ones, that the machine dealt with. That is, the program instruction we encountered in Chapter 1:

ADD wage income and interest income

might have looked like this:

110001101001101011001110100100010011001

where the first 12 digits instructed the machine to add and the remaining digits described the locations in memory of the numbers to be added. Arranging the digits in groups of three or four, in ways we'll explain in Chapter 3, made the programming task somewhat easier, but not much. Writing programs in **machine language** consisting of long sequences of such instructions was error-prone, and checking page after page of ones and zeros tested many a programmer's endurance.

Assemblers

The first big software breakthrough was the development of **assembly language**. An assembly language allowed programmers to use *mnemonics* (easily remembered names) for operations and symbols for variables. An assembly language instruction looked like this:

ADD A and B

where A and B are symbols representing variables. Programs were written in assembly language and punched on cards; then each instruction was converted by the computer itself (that is, under the direction of a program called the **assembler**) into the string of zeros and ones that the machine could manipulate. Assembly language was a definite improvement over machine language, but it was still hard to work with. Had programming remained at that level of difficulty, there's no question that we'd still be in the dark ages of computers.

The Second Generation (1959–1964)

The second generation was defined by two advances that produced fundamental changes in the manufacture and use of computers: the invention of the transistor and the development of programming languages that were more like English.

Hardware

The transistor

At Bell Telephone Laboratories in 1948, three men changed the young world of computing. *John Bardeen* (b. 1908), *Walter H. Brattain* (b. 1902), and *William B. Shockley* (b. 1910) invented a new electronic device, the **transistor**. In 1956 they were jointly awarded the Nobel Prize for this achievement. Transistors could be made of solid material and were consequently more mechanically rugged than the delicate assemblies of vacuum tubes. They were also small and lightweight, and employed no heater. Because of their cool operation, they had a long life. By 1959, when they were being produced in volume and thus at a relatively low price, transistors were the dominant component of the typical CPU.

Magnetic cores and disks

Primary memory was also radically transformed during the second generation. Powdered magnetic material was pressed into tiny doughnut-shaped (*toroidal*) **magnetic cores**, which were strung together on wires. Each tiny core can store one bit. Memories built out of magnetic cores have a striking advantage over drums and tapes: the data are instantly available. There is no waiting for a part of a drum or tape to arrive under a read head. No physical motion at all is involved in the accessing of a magnetic core memory.

The magnetic tape of the first generation was joined in the second generation by the **magnetic disk**, a large, flat, stereo-record-like magnetic storage surface. With magnetic disk secondary storage (which we will discuss in greater detail in Chapter 5), less time is required to move data into primary memory for processing. Disks rotate rapidly; each item on a disk passes under the read and write heads every 30 or 40 milliseconds—a great improvement over the many seconds, or even minutes, it could take for data on a tape to reach the heads.

During the second generation, computer hardware in general became smaller, more reliable, and more easily maintainable. Components were "packaged" onto **printed circuit boards**, each of which could easily be removed and replaced with a nondefective spare. While the faulty part on the removed board was located and replaced, the system went right on working. **Diagnostic programs**, which test the machine and locate faulty parts quickly (the computer is patient and doctor simultaneously), were developed and improved during the second generation.

Software

The second generation ushered in **high-level languages**, programming languages that resemble written English in vocabulary and syntax. They were essential to the proliferation of computers in every walk of life. We will have much more to say about high-level languages in Chapter 9; here we say that, with their help, programming changed from writing the long strings of digits that are meaningful to computers to writing statements that can be understood by other humans, such as

High-level languages

$$LET\ C = A + B$$

The job of translating such a statement into the zeros and ones on which the computer depends was performed by a complex computer program called a **compiler**, or **translator**. A compiler had to be written only once. It then served to compile, or translate for the computer, any program written in the language it was designed to handle.

The two earliest high-level languages, which are both still flourishing today, were *FORTRAN* (FORmula TRANslator), designed for scientific problems, and *COBOL* (COmmon Business-Oriented Language), created for business use. (These languages will be described in Chapter 9.) In addition to making programming efforts far less strenuous, high-level languages had another important impact on computer technology: they made possible the **portability** of programs among computers of different manufacturers. In other words, a single high-level language program (or **source program** as it is called) can be translated by different compilers into various **object programs**, or **machine codes** ("code" is a frequently used synonym for "program"). Each compiler is designed to translate from a particular high-level language into a specific machine language.

At the beginning of the era of high-level languages, however, things weren't that straightforward. Different manufacturers used their own **dialects**, or versions of a language, which meant there were difficulties in conversion. Different machines, then and now, work with numbers of different lengths (numbers of digits). This, and the details of each machine's handling of input/output, added to the difficulties. It wasn't until later, with the establishment of industry-wide standards, that the promise of portability became a reality.

The Third Generation (1965–1971)

The economy and reliability of transistors made computers available to entirely new classes of users. High-level languages made it easier to write programs for business users, enabling them to apply computers to their jobs. A period of explosive growth in the computer industry was taking place within a generally buoyant economy. It was becoming common for a business to buy a computer and then quickly outgrow its capacity. Buying a more powerful computer usually meant that many of the company's existing programs had to be scrapped, all of the ones written in assembly language, for example, and perhaps even the high-level language source programs. The necessity for program conversion was definitely a negative factor to any organization looking to change computers.

IBM and compatibility

IBM made a $5 billion bet on an answer to this problem—a compatible *family* of computers. IBM's 360 product line started at its low end with a relatively small and economical computer and progressed through half a dozen others to a large, ultra-high-speed machine. The family possessed **upward compatibility**: any program written for one of these machines could be run, without change, on any larger machine in the series. IBM was offering users a means to cope with growth without having to convert most of their programs. The business of manufacturing computers was permanently changed. From this time on, companies built product lines rather than just a single model.

Hardware

During the third generation, the manual assembling of transistors and other components on printed circuit boards gave way to the mechanized manufacturing of small solid pieces of silicon that contained all these components, as well as all their necessary interconnections.

Integrated circuits

These new **integrated circuits** were much smaller, more efficient (in terms of power consumption), more reliable, and ultimately far cheaper than their slower second-generation counterparts. The resulting increases in computing speed were also dramatic. It became necessary to think in terms of a new time unit, the *nanosecond* (a billionth of a second). Soon after, an even less comprehensible unit of time, the *picosecond* (a trillionth of a second), had to be added to the general computer vocabulary.

Memory technology was transformed by integrated circuits. By 1969, approximately 1000 transistors could be built on a single piece of silicon (a *silicon chip*), making the transistor primary memory, in which a transistor circuit is used to store each bit, more competitive in price with magnetic core memory. Magnetic core memory does have one advantage over transistor memory: it is *nonvolatile;* that is, the information remains stored even if the power is shut off. Even the most reliable electric power systems have momentary outages that, in the absence of special safeguards, will destroy the information in a transistor memory. In situations where it is vital that the contents not be lost, magnetic core primary memories remain in use today.

Integrated circuits and miniaturized core memories made low-cost minicomputers possible. These small, rugged machines are generally used for a single application, or at most a small set of applications, as opposed to the mainframes, or large computing center machines, which run hundreds or even thousands of different jobs every day.

The human user was linked more directly to the computer with the development of the *terminal*. Instead of punching cards on some off-line device, then

Job Description A keypunch operator operates a key-punch machine, keying data from a variety of sources onto computer-readable cards. It is important to note that some employers have converted from keypunching to direct data entry, but still use their old vocabulary. You may see advertisements for "keypunchers" that actually refer to job openings in word processing or direct data entry.

Qualifications A high school diploma, plus some vocational keypunch training, is required by most employers. All demand excellent typing skills. A keypunch operator must be able to concentrate in a noisy environment, to perform highly repetitive operations with speed and accuracy, and to work under the stress of tight deadlines and strict production requirements. There is little opportunity for individual initiative, but plenty of work to do in firms where keypunching is performed.

Outlook According to the Bureau of Labor Statistics, there were about 272,570 keypunch operators at work in the United States in 1970, representing 40% of all people employed in computer-related industries. By 1980, while all other computer-related jobs were undergoing a dramatic boom, that number had been cut in half. The bureau estimates there will be a further 15% decline by 1995, and it seems that the virtual extinction of the position in the first quarter of the twenty-first century is inevitable.

The collapse of keypunching is directly related to technological advancements in the field it helped create. Today, such direct input methods as key-to-disk (see Chapter 4) are eliminating the need for keypunched cards and thus for keypunch operators. Some openings will occur as a result of retirements or deaths, and those companies with a large capital investment in keypunch machines will continue to hire. Virtually every employment projection, however, shows that the number of job opportunities will inevitably dry up, and IBM's recent closing of its last card-making plant means that the disappearance of the position has only been accelerated.

---

giving them to an operator who would, some time later, place them in a card reader for processing, programmers could now type their programs directly into computer memory, and check them on the printed output. Terminals were also perfect for data entry and the operation of minicomputers; they continue to play a large role in communications between humans and computers.

Magnetic disks represented an increased percentage of the volume memory market in the third generation. **Disk packs** became prevalent. These are like other rotating disks but with removable disk storage surfaces. This gives a disk unit the same ability as a tape unit to make rooms full of data accessible to the computer, while maintaining the speed advantages of the disk.

Software

Software became more sophisticated during the third generation. The number of high-level languages continued to grow. Languages adapted to more specific applications began to make their appearance: *RPG* (Report Program Generator) for generating business reports; *APT* (Automatically Programmed Tools) for fabricating parts on automatically controlled machine tools; and *BASIC* (Beginner's All-purpose Symbolic Instruction Code) for easy programming.

The expanded power of the CPU and the increased quantity and variety of input/output equipment with which it was surrounded created a need for more efficient management of these complex and costly resources, some worth several million dollars. A new class of computer program, the operating system, answered this need. In the first and second generations, jobs were run successively under the supervision of a human operator. Great improvements in efficiency were made by placing the computer system's resources under the control of an **operating system**, a program that could match the jobs that needed to be done with the equipment that was available. With an operating system, much more work can be accomplished by the same equipment.

Time-sharing operating systems

A natural extension was **time sharing** of an operating system. The CPU is so fast that it can keep up with many users communicating with the system from a number of terminal keyboards. In fact, in time sharing, the operating system parcels out successive connection times of a few milliseconds' duration to several users. Unless traffic is particularly heavy, each user has the illusion of having sole and immediate access to the computer.

The Fourth Generation (1971–Present)

During the third generation, computers penetrated deeply and permanently into the fabric of industry, commerce, government, and higher education. In the fourth generation, computers have reached the common thread of all these institutions: the individual at work, school, and home. Two innovations that enabled this extension of the technology are the microprocessor (the hardware means by which the power of the computer was delivered to virtually everyone) and user-friendly software (the means by which the complexities of using the machine were made easily comprehensible).

Hardware

We've followed a progression from the abacus to gears, vacuum tubes, transistors, and the integrated circuits of the third generation. But progress didn't stop there; that was just another starting point.

VLSI and the microcomputer

In the early 1970s, integrated circuit technology, by which a dozen or so transistors were included on a single chip, was supplanted by the techniques of *large-scale integration (LSI)*, which manufactured chips with a few thousand transistors. By the mid 1970s, *very large-scale integration (VLSI)* was used to produce a chip containing an entire **microprocessor**, or microcomputer CPU (even including small amounts of primary memory). (We'll have a great deal more to say about microcomputers in Part 5.)

One consequence of VLSI was the virtual replacement of magnetic core memory with transistor memory. Single memory chips now contain up to a million bits, and an upper limit is still not in sight. The number of transistors on today's VLSI chip is enough to build 20 ENIACs. The process used to make these ever-smaller patterns of transistors and their interconnections on a chip was originally based on photographic techniques. These techniques, which can produce features as small as a micron (a millionth of a meter or 39 millionths of an inch), have become too crude, and electron beams are currently used to create the patterns on the chip.

As long as we're on the subject of fourth-generation hardware, we should at least mention two larger-scale developments. First, as we'll see in Chapters 5 and 13, secondary storage has grown to a large enough capacity to contain all the data needed to operate a big corporation or a major government agency. This has led to the development of special programming techniques and programs to manage such vast quantities of data. Second, each generation of computers has featured its largest, fastest, and generally scientifically oriented computers—the *super-computers*. They have played a special role in a variety of fields, which we'll discuss in Chapter 20.

Software

The special software created to handle the huge quantities of data that fourth-generation systems are able to store is also capable of handling the communication function such **data bases** serve. For example, in an airline reservation system, many geographically dispersed users are constantly referencing and modifying the data. The system must be updated instantly when the status of a piece of the data changes. Selling the same seat on the same flight to three different people isn't the way to keep the customers happy. Solving software problems of this magnitude is a labor-intensive job whose costs continue to rise. Since the cost of hardware has decreased regularly, software and operating costs now generally exceed hardware costs.

At the other end of the software spectrum are the numerous programs now available for the personal computer that have been built around the microprocessor chip. This software, designed for inexperienced users, makes every attempt to guide the user by containing built-in instruction and answers to questions; in other words, it is designed to be **user-friendly**.

Personal computers and user-friendly systems

The growing scope and complexity of programming efforts have meant that greater and greater intellectual discipline and organization have had to be imposed on frequently large programming teams, whose efforts must mesh together perfectly. A set of techniques called **structured programming** has made an important contribution to the standardization of such efforts. It is a vital underpinning of the complex fourth-generation software (and is discussed in detail in Chapter 8).

ISSUES IN TECHNOLOGY

In little more than 30 years, computer technology has moved through four generations. Computers commonly available today were almost inconceivable 30 years ago. Is this technology moving too fast for society to assimilate the changes it brings?

Epilog and Prolog

The fourth generation is not the end of the story. Following a Japanese initiative, a worldwide effort is currently underway to develop a radically different fifth generation of computers. This effort centers on work in a field called *artificial intelligence,* the goal of which is to produce the first "thinking" machine by 1990. The fifth generation is described more fully in Chapter 23.

The fifth generation

SUMMARY ≡

The Origins

The computer story begins with the concept of number. With the use of symbols for numbers came the earliest aids to counting, which culminated in the first calculator, the abacus.

Early Machines

The mathematician Pascal developed the first mechanical calculator. Pascal's machine was digital, which distinguished it from earlier analog instruments. Leibniz built a more ambitious calculator that performed multiplication and division. Charles Babbage's analytical engine anticipated the main principles underlying the modern computer. William Seward Burroughs developed the first commercially successful calculator. Herman Hollerith invented punched card tabulating machines for the 1890 census. Thomas J. Watson joined the company Hollerith founded and later renamed it the International Business Machines Corporation.

Dawn of the Computer Age

The Mark I   With financial and technical support from IBM, Howard Aiken of Harvard built the Mark I using relays, electromechanical devices that replaced the purely mechanical gears of earlier machines.

ENIAC   John Presper Eckert and John W. Mauchly built ENIAC at the University of Pennsylvania. The U.S. Army sponsored the project in order to achieve faster and more accurate calculation of artillery and rocket trajectories. ENIAC was built with vacuum tubes, purely electronic switches that replaced relays. Eckert and Mauchly later went on to produce UNIVAC I, the first commercial electronic computer.

The IAS Computer and the Binary Number System   John von Neumann took the vital step of representing program steps numerically and storing them, together with data, in the computer's memory. He was also responsible for making the binary system, whose two digits perfectly match the on or off state of a switch, the basis of computer arithmetic and logic.

Four Generations of Computers

The year 1951 marked the start of commercial production of computers. Since then, machines have been grouped into four generations, defined mainly by the hardware components used to build them.

The First Generation (1951–1958)   The first UNIVAC and the early IBM machines had vacuum tube CPUs and magnetic drum memories. Programs were written in numerical machine language until the development of assembly language, which brought the first significant reduction in programming labor.

The Second Generation (1959–1964)   As a result of the replacement of vacuum tubes with transistors, computers became smaller and cheaper, more powerful and more reliable. Magnetic cores were used increasingly to build primary memory, and magnetic disks were the common form of secondary storage. The first high-level languages, FORTRAN and COBOL, were developed. As a result, portability became possible, and program conversion was less of a nightmare.

The Third Generation (1965–1971)   IBM developed the first upward-compatible family of computers, the 360 series. Integrated circuits produced further performance increases and cost reductions for mainframe computers and made minicomputers possible. High-level languages continued to proliferate, and operating systems and time sharing appeared.

The Fourth Generation (1971–Present)   The computer's decreasing cost and improving performance extended its range of application into the home. Techniques of LSI and VLSI ultimately produced the microprocessor, the single-chip CPU of the personal computer. The needs of a rapidly growing community of users are served by user-friendly software.

The greater size and complexity of programming undertakings are managed more efficiently with structured programming.

Epilog and Prolog The fifth generation of computers, machines possessing artificial intelligence, is currently being developed.

COMPUTER CONCEPTS

As an extra review of the chapter, try defining the following terms. If you have trouble with any of them, refer to the page number listed.

digital 30
analog 30
relays 30
vacuum tube 34
binary system 35
bit 35
magnetic drums 37
primary memory (primary storage unit) 37
secondary storage 37
machine language 38
assembly language 38
assembler 38

transistor 38
magnetic cores 38
magnetic disk 39
printed circuit boards 39
diagnostic programs 39
high-level languages 39
compiler 39
translator 39
portability 39
source program 39
object programs (machine codes) 39

dialects 39
upward compatibility 40
integrated circuits 40
disk packs 41
operating system 42
time sharing 42
microprocessor 42
data bases 43
user-friendly 43
structured programming 43

REVIEW QUESTIONS

1. What were some of the first counting devices?
2. What contribution did Blaise Pascal make to the evolution of computers?
3. Name some digital and analog machines you use every day.
4. Who built the first calculator that could do multiplication and division as well as addition and subtraction?
5. What was the significance of Charles Babbage's analytical engine?
6. In what type of machine was the punched card first used?
7. Who is generally credited with writing the first computer program?
8. In the context of the computer story, what was noteworthy about the 1890 U.S. census?
9. What electromechanical device was used by the Mark I?
10. What was the first totally electronic computer, and what was it created to do?
11. Who is credited with the idea of using the binary number system for computer representation of numbers and storing both data and program in memory?
12. What were some of the problems whose solutions the IAS computer made possible?
13. What hardware component is usually associated with the first generation of computers?
14. What was the first commercial electronic computer? Who founded the company that produced it?
15. Why was the invention of the transistor so important to the development of computers?
16. What very important software development is associated with the second generation of computers?
17. Which computer generation is marked by the introduction of the integrated circuit and the operating system?
18. The computer has been the heart and soul of automation. Whose job does the operating system automate? What is the result?
19. In which generation did the microcomputer make its debut?
20. What new advance does the fifth generation promise?

A SHARPER FOCUS

Now that you've completed this chapter, you should be able to answer the following questions about the chapter opening.

1. During which computer generation did people begin building their own personal computers? What connections can you draw between this event and the other events of that generation?
2. What sort of software do you think was available for early personal computers? Where would users obtain it?

PROJECTS

1. Research some of the capabilities of UNIVAC I, the first commercial electronic computer. Compare features such as its memory capacity, speed, size, and cost with those of a popular personal computer sold by a local computer retail store.
2. One of the ways in which computers have drastically changed through the four generations is in "cost per million calculations." Of course, there's a range of costs within each generation, too. Prepare a short report on the results of your research into these costs, utilizing charts and graphs wherever possible.
3. In 1950 the average qualifying speed at Indianapolis was 131 miles per hour. In 1960 it was 144, in 1970 it was 167, and in 1980 it was 197. Contrast this, as well as changes in other speed-related statistics, with computer speeds within corresponding time frames.
4. Early computers suffered from relatively low reliability, beset with problems like burned out tubes. Businesspeople were naturally skeptical about such performance, and many decided to wait until computers became more reliable. With the VLSI circuitry in today's computers, these early concerns about reliability don't seem applicable today. The tremendous drop in prices, accompanied by increases in speed and in the variety of available software products, would seem to put a computer within the reach of every business. Yet many people still resist. Why? Write a short report giving three or more reasons. Your data gathering might include some short interviews.

Application Perspectives

An Introduction

At the end of Parts 1 through 6 of this book, we will present an Application Perspective, a feature whose purpose is to give you a visual appreciation of computers' penetration into a variety of applications. The first Application Perspective is fairly general; the remaining ones will be somewhat more detailed. We hope the Application Perspectives will stimulate reflection. Use them to assimilate the material in each part, to ask yourself questions about how the concepts in each part fit together in a specific computing job.

You'll notice that each Application Perspective includes both photographs and simplified flowcharts. We have combined visuals in this way to demonstrate how real situations (the photos) can be described in data-processing terms (by means of flowcharts). For a thorough explanation of how flowcharts work, see Chapter 8. For now, though, the only flowchart convention you need to know about is the *connector:* the small circle labeled A on the next page. This connector simply means "to be continued"; it is a symbol that connects the first flowchart with the second.

Application Perspective: Computers in Your Daily Life

1. Filling Your Gas Tank

① Deciding where to drill for oil is the all-important first step in the production of gasoline. This decision depends heavily on computers. They process the information obtained from setting off patterns of small explosions in holes drilled into the earth and recording the vibrations produced at the surface. From this seismic data, geophysicists locate the geological formations most likely to contain oil. The number of exceedingly costly "dry holes" is greatly reduced as a result of these computations. This reduces your cost at the gas pump.

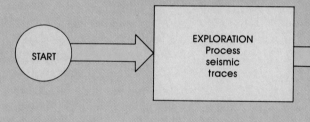

START ⟶ EXPLORATION Process seismic traces

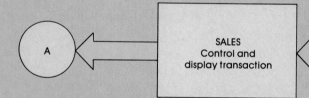

A ⟵ SALES Control and display transaction

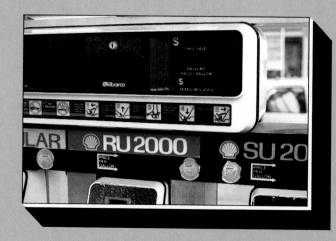

④ A special computer measures the gas pumped into your tank and computes the price, displaying both. It can also keep track of the total quantity of gas pumped during any time period selected by the station owner.

(2) The crude oil is shipped from the well to the refinery. Here, a decision is made about what products to produce. Computers analyze prices and help to determine the most profitable product "mix" (of aviation fuel, automobile gasoline, heating fuel, lubricants, and asphalt). Other computers then monitor and control the production cycle.

```
                    ┌──────────────────┐
                    │                  │
═════════════════>  │   PRODUCTION     │
═══════════════╗    │   Monitor and    │
               ║    │  control refinery│
               ║    │                  │
               ║    └────────┬─────────┘
               ║             │
               ║             ▼
               ║    ┌──────────────────┐
               ║    │                  │
               ╚══> │   DISTRIBUTION   │
                    │    Generate      │
                    │  dispatch plans  │
                    │                  │
                    └──────────────────┘
```

(3) Trucks are dispatched to deliver the refined products requested by each retailer. A computer is used to determine the route assignments for 20 to 100 trucks. The object is to make all the deliveries at the lowest total cost, or the lowest total mileage traveled by all the trucks. This process also generates the information needed for billing.

Application Perspective: Computers in Your Daily Life

2. Paying by Check

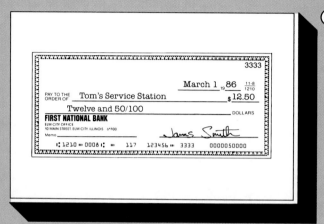

5 The information that identifies your bank and your checking account is preprinted on your personal checks, using special numerals and symbols that can be read automatically by bank equipment.

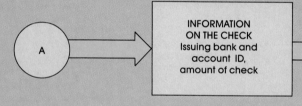

A

INFORMATION ON THE CHECK
Issuing bank and account ID, amount of check

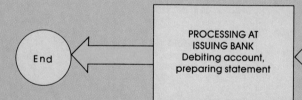

End

PROCESSING AT ISSUING BANK
Debiting account, preparing statement

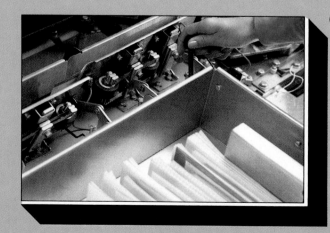

8 The check is finally "home." The information identifying your account and the amount of the check is read into your bank's computer, and your account is debited. This information is used to generate your account statement. Note that every step in your check's odyssey could be reconstructed if there should ever be a need to do so.

(6) An operator types the amount you paid to the gas station onto the check, using the special machine-readable numerals. The information identifying the station owner's bank and the date of deposit are entered automatically. The information on the check is read into the computer at the station owner's bank. His account is credited, and your check is batched with all the others that go to the same regional Federal Reserve Bank for clearance, the process that ultimately (sometimes all too soon) results in your account being debited.

PROCESSING AT
PAYEE'S BANK
Crediting account,
preparing for clearance

PROCESSING AT THE
FEDERAL RESERVE BANK
Batch information
and checks for
transmission to
issuing banks

(7) All the checks cashed at banks in your region are sent to the regional Federal Reserve Bank. There, check-sorting machines separate them according to the issuing bank. The checks are then returned to the issuing bank; your check is returned to your bank: First National Bank, Elm City. The Federal Reserve Bank's computer can send out information concerning checks written for large amounts immediately over telephone lines.

Part 2

HARDWARE

Computer hardware—the physical parts of a computer system—varies widely in performance, price, size, and appearance. The structure and function of the central processing unit, the numerous peripheral devices, and the various media for the input, storage, and output of data are of primary importance to your understanding of data processing. Part 2 covers these physical aspects of computers and computing.

Chapter 3 focuses on the heart of the computer, the CPU. Chapter 4 moves outside that central core, to cover the devices and media used to present data to the computer. Chapter 5 tells how the data are organized and stored. Chapter 6 describes the devices and media used to present the results of processing to the user. Finally, Chapter 7 discusses data communications, that is, sending data from one computer to another computer.

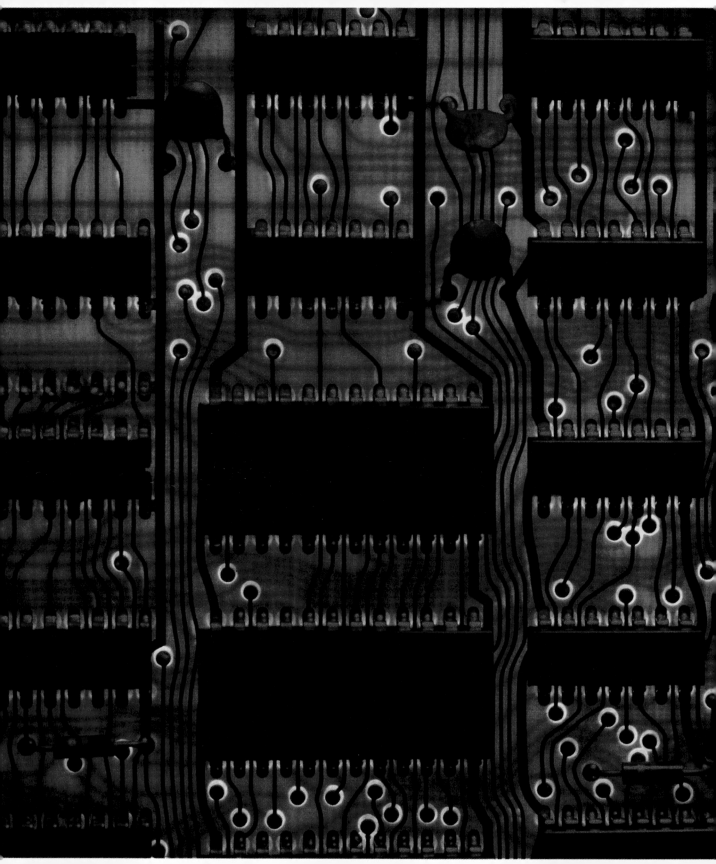

3

The Central Processing Unit

IN THIS CHAPTER

▶

FOCUS ON . . . THE CPU IN PERSON

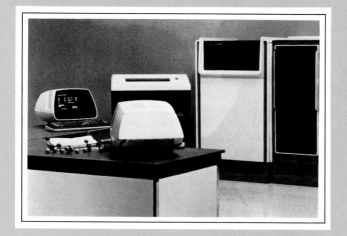

In researching his Pulitzer Prize—winning *The Soul of a New Machine,* journalist Tracy Kidder had the fascinating experience of witnessing the entire developmental process for a new minicomputer (the Eagle). During his observations, Kidder "descended . . . into Eagle's engine room" for an introduction to how its CPU works:

> . . . The task was to make an engine that would obey—without fail and at great speed—each of the roughly four hundred chores named in Eagle's instruction set. One night after work, Microkid Jon Blau described for me the progress of just one of these basic chores, or assembly-language instructions, through the engine. . . .

With Blau, I descended, as it were, into Eagle's engine room. He pointed out the main parts of Eagle and spoke of them as if they were sensate things that asked questions, looked up answers, sent and received messages. It's a way of talking about computers that makes some people nervous, but it was one of the ways he thought about the machine when he was working on it.

In order to execute an instruction in a user program, the engine has to do a lot of work first, Blau explained. We should assume that a special program—a program of programs, let's call it—is already running. This program communicates with people using the computer and it does jobs for them. . . .

Okay, said Blau, someone out there at a terminal, a user, wants to run a program; call it "program FOOBAR." Through a terminal, this user tells the program of programs: "Run program FOOBAR." The program of programs tells the IOC (Input/Output Control Board) to move *part* of that program from a storage disk outside of the CPU into the CPU's "Main Memory," and to do so at high speed. This accomplished, the program of programs turns over control to program FOOBAR. The machine then starts executing the instructions of program FOOBAR, one after the other.

Before the engine can execute an instruction, it has to find it, of course. Then it has to fetch it and decode it. Thus we came to the printed-circuit board known as the Instruction Processor—the IP, it was called, and it was quite a tricky thing. The IP has a relatively small memory of its own. In a sense, the IP makes assumptions about what the next instructions in the user program will be, and it keeps those instructions handy in its storage. Acting on its assumptions, it finds, fetches, and decodes instructions ahead of time. It "gets them in the pipeline." . . .

Thirty years or so ago, it was common for people unfamiliar with computers to refer to them as "electronic brains." Today, people are more sophisticated about computers, and no longer astonished by their computational abilities. Most of us know that they have to be programmed in order to do anything and that there are limitations on what they can and can't do. So where did that "electronic brain" label come from, and why does the attitude it represents persist today?

The labeling of computers as "brains" is based on a certain limited similarity between the two complex entities, one organic and the other electronic. The comparison is faulty at best—like comparing apples with oranges because both are round and both are fruit. So the analogy is rather a weak one, drawn from certain superficial similarities between brains and computers: a computer's central processing unit resembles a brain insofar as both are places where input is transformed into output and where the control of the peripheral equipment (arms and legs, or terminals and printers) is centered. Also, without a brain or a CPU, a body or a computer is useless.

The first two chapters in this book introduced the modern computer—its operation and role and its origins and development. This is sufficient conceptual background for a more detailed study of the machine itself. In this chapter, we begin to see how a computer really works, how it goes about making the trillions of calculations we demand of it every day.

THE CPU AND NUMBERS

In Chapter 1 we studied the principles of operation of the CPU's main subsystems: memory, ALU, and control unit. Now we will study these subsystems in greater detail. We will see how they differ and how computers of different types are made up of these differing subsystems. We've also mentioned, several times, that numbers are the currency of computers. So, before we get into our discussion of the CPU, we will need to describe the different ways in which numbers are arranged so that CPUs can operate on them.

DATA REPRESENTATION

The CPU in any contemporary computer system deals only with the zeros and ones of the binary system, which correspond to the on and off states of an electronic switch. People, however, find data more readable when they're presented as **alphanumeric characters** (letters, numbers, and punctuation marks). This difference raises the problem of how to get from the alphanumeric representations that are convenient for people to the binary ones and zeros that are necessary for computers.

Encoding data for computer processing

Various number systems and coding schemes have been employed to address this problem. We'll first examine the most common ones in use today. Then we'll discuss the fundamental data units of computers: bits, bytes, and words.

Binary Numbers

The number system we are most familiar with, the decimal system, uses 10 symbols (the digits 0 through 9) to represent numerical quantities; single digits represent quantities smaller than 10, and groups of two or more digits represent quantities larger than 9. A digit's position in a group and its value contribute to the overall value of the group. Since each position stands for a certain power of 10, the decimal system is said to have a *base* of 10.

Binary integers

The binary system, with a base of 2, uses the symbols 0 and 1 to represent values less than 2, in the same way that the decimal system uses 0 through 9 for values less than 10. Quantities larger than 1 are represented by groups of zeros and ones. The digit positions in these groups represent successive powers of 2, rather than powers of 10. For example, in the decimal system, the number 57 is a shorthand expression meaning

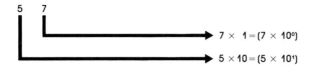

In the binary system, the decimal number 57 is expressed as 111001:

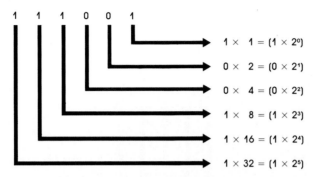

Figure 3.1 lists the decimal values of the powers of 2. If you work around computers for any length of time, you'll become as familiar with these as you are with the powers of 10. Note that a 10-digit decimal number can represent any of 10 billion values (from 0,000,000,000, or just 0, through 9,999,999,999), while a 10-digit binary number can only represent 1024 different values (0000000000 through 1111111111). It may clarify this to note that 9,999,999,999 is 1 less than 10,000,000,000 and, similarly, 1111111111 is 1 less than 10000000000 (which is

2^0	=	1
2^1	=	2
2^2	=	4
2^3	=	8
2^4	=	16
2^5	=	32
2^6	=	64
2^7	=	128
2^8	=	256
2^9	=	512
2^{10}	=	1024
2^{11}	=	2048
2^{12}	=	4096
2^{13}	=	8192
2^{14}	=	16,384
2^{15}	=	32,768
2^{16}	=	65,536

Figure 3.1   Powers of 2

Just as the decimal number system uses successive powers of 10 (that is, 1, 10, 100, 1000, . . .), the binary number system uses successive powers of 2. These powers and their decimal equivalents are listed here.

Binary fractions and mixed numbers

2^{10}, or 1024). It is customary, by the way, to use no commas or spaces when writing binary numbers. Binary numbers can be used to represent fractions and mixed numbers as well as whole numbers (integers). For example, let's examine the decimal number 43.75. Its whole number or integer part is 43; the period is called the decimal point; its fractional part is 75. Figure 3.2(a) shows how this number breaks down in the decimal system, and Figure 3.2(b) shows how it breaks down in the binary system. In the second case, the period is called the **binary point** (instead of the decimal point). The binary digits to the left of it represent positive powers of 2, and the binary digits to the right of it represent negative powers of 2.

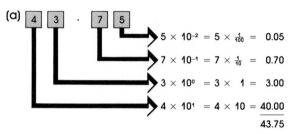

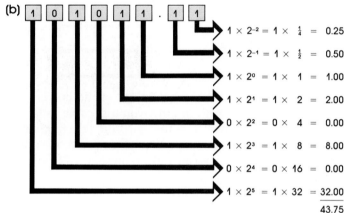

Figure 3.2 Decimal and Binary Mixed Numbers
(a) Breaking down the decimal number 43.75 into its powers of 10 demonstrates what the digits and positions really mean. (b) Similarly, the binary number equal to 43.75 can be broken down into powers of 2.

Fixed-Point and Floating-Point Numbers

As we'll see later in this chapter, in the section titled Types of ALUs, one of the principal attributes that distinguishes a computer's speed and cost is what kind of numbers its hardware can handle. The two main types of numbers are fixed-point numbers and floating-point numbers.

A **fixed-point number** is one whose point (decimal or binary) is in a fixed place in relation to the digits. For example, both integers and fractions can be represented as fixed-point numbers. For integers, the point is fixed at the extreme right; for fractions, the point is fixed at the extreme left. Since the point position is fixed and predefined, it does not have to be stored in memory with the value. A **floating-point number** (also called a **real number**, one in which the position of the point can vary from number to number), in contrast, can be used to represent a mixed number (integer part plus fractional part). You may already be familiar with this concept in its application known as *scientific notation*, since it's used with most pocket calculators. One number is used for the fractional part, called the *mantissa*, and another number is used for the power of the base, or the *exponent*. For example, the mixed number 43.75, which can't be stored as a fixed-point number because it has both an integer part and a fractional part, can be stored as a floating-point number like this:

$$\begin{array}{cc} 4375 & 2 \\ \text{mantissa} & \text{exponent} \end{array}$$

Positioning the decimal (or binary) point

The decimal point in the mantissa is assumed to be at the extreme left, and thus is not explicitly stored. The exponent indicates that the decimal point is really lo-

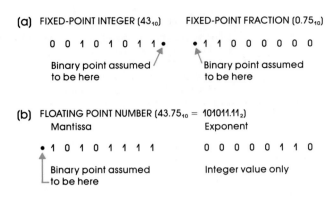

(a) FIXED-POINT INTEGER (43_{10})

0 0 1 0 1 0 1 1 •

Binary point assumed
to be here

FIXED-POINT FRACTION (0.75_{10})

• 1 1 0 0 0 0 0 0

Binary point assumed
to be here

(b) FLOATING POINT NUMBER ($43.75_{10} = 101011.11_2$)

Mantissa

• 1 0 1 0 1 1 1 1

Binary point assumed
to be here

Exponent

0 0 0 0 0 1 1 0

Integer value only

Figure 3.3 Fixed-Point and Floating-Point Binary Numbers

(a) Fixed-point binary numbers can express either integers or fractions. The binary point is assumed to be at the extreme right in the case of an integer and at the extreme left in the case of a fraction. (Subscripts show the base of the number system used, as in $10_2 + 10_2 = 4_{10}$.) (b) Floating-point binary numbers can represent mixed numbers. The mantissa holds the digits of the number as a fraction, with the binary point assumed to be at the extreme left. The exponent holds the power of 2 by which the mantissa must be multiplied. In this case, the mantissa, which is normalized, meaning there are no leading zeros, must be multiplied by 2^6 ($110_2 = 6_{10}$) to get the actual value, or 101011.11. Another way to look at this is to see that the binary point, assumed to be at the extreme left of the mantissa, must be shifted six places to the right to get the correct value.

cated two positions from the left of the mantissa. In other words, the exponent indicates that the mantissa (.4375) is to be multiplied by 10^2 to get the real value. Most of the time, it is desirable to have the mantissa shifted all the way to the left, that is, to have a mantissa with no leading zeros. A floating-point number stored in this way is said to be *normalized*. Figure 3.3 illustrates these concepts for binary numbers. We'll have more to say about floating-point numbers when we discuss the arithmetic and logic unit (ALU) later in this chapter.

Octal and Hexadecimal Numbers

You've probably realized from the few examples given here how unsuited people are to the routine handling of binary numbers. Their length (six digits to represent the decimal value 43) and their monotony (nothing but zeros and ones) make dealing with them tedious and error-prone for humans. Two compromises between binary and decimal—the **octal system** (base 8) and the **hexadecimal system** (base 16)—are often used for communication between people and computers (see Figure 3.4).

Base 8 or base 16 as a compromise between binary and decimal

The octal system uses eight symbols: 0, 1, 2, 3, 4, 5, 6, and 7. Since 2^3 is equal to 8, the octal system is a convenient shorthand for binary; each octal digit is equivalent to three binary digits. This is illustrated more graphically in Figure 3.5, which shows how each digit of an octal number can stand for three binary digits.

Figure 3.4 Powers of 8 and 16

(a) Octal numbers are based on successive powers of 8.
(b) Hexadecimal numbers are based on successive powers of 16.

$8^0 =$	1
$8^1 =$	8
$8^2 =$	64
$8^3 =$	512
$8^4 =$	4096
$8^5 =$	32,768

(a)

$16^0 =$	1
$16^1 =$	16
$16^2 =$	256
$16^3 =$	4096
$16^4 =$	65,536
$16^5 =$	1048,576

(b)

Figure 3.5 Octal Numbers

Octal numbers, consisting of successive powers of 8, are a convenient shorthand for binary numbers.

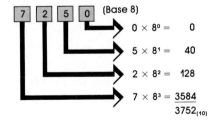

| 7 | 2 | 5 | 0 | (Base 8) |

$0 \times 8^0 = \quad 0$
$5 \times 8^1 = \quad 40$
$2 \times 8^2 = \quad 128$
$7 \times 8^3 = \underline{3584}$
$\qquad\qquad 3752_{(10)}$

1 1 1   0 1 0   1 0 1   0 0 0 ← Base 2

7   2   5   0 ← Base 8

(a)

Base 16	Base 10
0	0
1	1
2	2
3	3
4	4
5	5
6	6
7	7
8	8
9	9
A	10
B	11
C	12
D	13
E	14
F	15

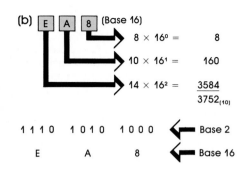

Figure 3.6 Hexadecimal Numbers

(a) Because it must represent values from 10 through 15 with single digits, the hexadecimal system employs six letters as symbols.
(b) Hexadecimal numbers are built up of successive powers of 16 and are a convenient shorthand for binary numbers.

The hexadecimal number system uses 16 symbols, which are listed in Figure 3.6(a) with their decimal system equivalents. Although using letters as numbers might seem strange, it is necessary in order to have a single character to represent each value from 10 through 15. Since each hexadecimal digit is equivalent to four binary digits (2^4 is equal to 16), the hexadecimal system is also a shorthand way to express binary numbers, as illustrated in Figure 3.6(b).

Coding Systems to Represent Alphanumeric Characters

In order to store and represent text in a computer, some scheme must be employed to convert letters, punctuation marks, and special characters to binary numbers. In fact, one way to think of octal numbers is as a set of 3-bit codes that represent the characters 0 through 7. Similarly, the hexadecimal system can be thought of as a 4-bit system for representing the characters 0 through 9 and A through F. These codes can only represent decimal and binary values, however. To represent more than 16 characters, some scheme is required that uses codes of more than 4 bits. Various coding systems have been developed over the years using 6-bit, 7-bit, and 8-bit codes. Of these, three are common today: BCD, EBCDIC, and ASCII.

The BCD System

In its original form, the **BCD (Binary Coded Decimal) system** was a 4-bit code used to represent the decimal digits. Each digit in a decimal number is converted to a 4-bit binary number. For example, the decimal number 3752 can be represented in 4-bit BCD like this:

3	7	5	2	←—— base 10
0011	0111	0101	0010	←—— 4-bit BCD

You should note an important difference between BCD and a hexadecimal or octal number. The hexadecimal and octal systems encode the entire number and then group the bits, but BCD encodes each digit separately and then combines these "subcodes" into a single string of zeros and ones. This may seem pretty straightforward, but it's actually somewhat inefficient. Using 4 bits to represent just 10 different values in a sense "wastes" 6 values since 4 bits can represent 2^4, or 16, distinct quantities. This is one reason why ENIAC, which used switches arranged to work with 4-bit BCD, was rather inefficient.

The inefficiency of BCD

**Figure 3.7
Character Representation
with 6-bit BCD**

A unique 6-bit BCD code
represents each of the decimal digits, capital letters, and
28 punctuation marks and
other characters.

CODE	Character
110001	A
110010	B
110011	C
110100	D
110101	E
110110	F
110111	G
111000	H
111001	I
100001	J
100010	K
100011	L
100100	M
100101	N
100110	O
100111	P
101000	Q
101001	R
010010	S
010011	T
010100	U
010101	V
010110	W
010111	X
011000	Y
011001	Z
010000	0
000001	1
000010	2
000011	3
000100	4
000101	5
000110	6
000111	7
001000	8
001001	9
011011	,
111011	.
100000	—
001100	@
001011	/
101100	*
101011	$
etc.	etc.

Figure 3.8   EBCDIC and ASCII Codes
The two coding systems for alphanumeric
characters used in most computers are
EBCDIC and ASCII.

CHARACTER	EBCDIC	ASCII
A	1100 0001	100 0001
B	1100 0010	100 0010
C	1100 0011	100 0011
D	1100 0100	100 0100
E	1100 0101	100 0101
F	1100 0110	100 0110
G	1100 0111	100 0111
H	1100 1000	100 1000
I	1100 1001	100 1001
J	1101 0001	100 1010
K	1101 0010	100 1011
L	1101 0011	100 1100
M	1101 0100	100 1101
N	1101 0101	100 1110
O	1101 0110	100 1111
P	1101 0111	101 0000
Q	1101 1000	101 0001
R	1101 1001	101 0010
S	1101 0010	101 0011
T	1110 0011	101 0100
U	1110 0100	101 0101
V	1110 0101	101 0110
W	1110 0110	101 0111
X	1110 0111	101 1000
Y	1110 1000	101 1001
Z	1110 1001	101 1010
0	1111 0000	011 0000
1	1111 0001	011 0001
2	1111 0010	011 0010
3	1111 0011	011 0011
4	1111 0100	011 0100
5	1111 0101	011 0101
6	1111 0110	011 0111
7	1111 0111	011 1000
8	1111 1000	011 1001
9	1111 1001	011 1010

With the addition of two more bits on the left (called *zone bits),* the original 4-bit BCD was expanded to 6-bit BCD. The various combinations that can be obtained using 6 bits allow the representation of 64 different characters, enough to code the 10 decimal digits, the 26 upper-case letters, and 28 other special characters and punctuation marks (see Figure 3.7). Because it is limited by a lack of codes for lower-case letters, 6-bit BCD is no longer widely used as a general alphanumeric coding system; however, it is used on 96-column punched cards, which we'll encounter in Chapter 4.

The EBCDIC System

The **EBCDIC (Extended Binary Coded Decimal Interchange Code) system** is an 8-bit BCD code that allows 256 (2^8) possible bit combinations. This code can be used to represent upper-case and lower-case letters, decimal digits, punctuation marks, and special characters. The 4 leftmost bits are the zone bits, and the 4 rightmost bits are the numeric bits. As shown in Figure 3.8 a unique combination *The code used by IBM* of the zone and numeric bits represents each character. This code was established by IBM and is used primarily in IBM mainframe computers and peripheral devices.

The ASCII System

The standard code for microcomputers

The **ASCII (American Standard Code for Information Interchange) system** is a 7-bit code cooperatively developed by several computer manufacturers whose objective was to produce a standard code for all computers. Their objective has been fulfilled, at least for microcomputers—virtually every such machine marketed today uses the ASCII code. Although ASCII is officially a 7-bit code (see Figure 3.8), in practice it is an 8-bit code because an extra bit is almost invariably added for error detection (we'll see how this works in Chapter 4).

Bits, Bytes, and Words

How binary digits are grouped

You know by now that the most fundamental unit of data processing is the bit: 0 or 1, off or on. All data handled by computers are ultimately reduced to bits. The **byte** is simply a group of 8 bits. A single character coded in EBCDIC or ASCII constitutes a byte. A **nibble** is half of a byte (or 4 bits), and also a good example of computer scientists' whimsical sense of humor. Bits, bytes, and nibbles are constant from machine to machine; a bit is always a 0 or a 1; a byte is always 8 bits; a nibble is always 4 bits.

A computer **word** is a group of adjacent bits that are manipulated and stored as a unit. The number of bits in a word depends on the computer. A computer's word length is a key element of its design. As we'll see later in this chapter, the smallest computers handle 4-bit words, and the largest can deal with words of 128 bits. Computers that use *fixed-length words* store a fixed number of characters at each address. For example, a fixed-length word of 16 bits contains 2 bytes (characters) that are stored at a single address. On the other hand, computers that use *variable-length words* have a separate address for each byte of storage. In this type of machine, the word length can be tailored to the individual job, and each byte of a word is accessed by its own address.

Finally, words can be defined by the types of numbers they hold. *Fixed-point words* hold fixed-point numbers, and the binary point is assumed to be at one end or the other. *Floating-point words* hold floating-point numbers and are comprised of two parts: one part for the mantissa, the other for the exponent.

PRIMARY STORAGE

You may recall from Chapter 1 that the CPU is made up of primary memory, the ALU, and the main control unit. Now that we've taken a look at the ways in which data are represented in the CPU in general, let's examine how they are handled in primary memory, otherwise known as primary storage.

The Two Basic Functions of Primary Storage

One basic function of primary storage is to hold the program that is being executed. In Chapter 2 we emphasized the importance of the idea that computer **instructions**, which describe actions to be carried out by the computer, could be

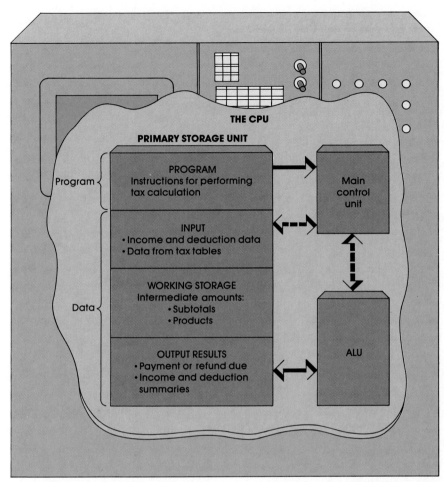

Figure 3.9 The Contents of Primary Storage
In order to be executed, a program and its related data must first be loaded into the primary storage unit. For a program that does a simple income tax calculation, the input data are from two sources: the individual's income and deduction data, and the tax tables. Working storage holds quantities that are the results of intermediate calculations, such as income and deduction subtotals. The principal result to be output is the payment or refund due; other results to be output are appropriate income and deduction summaries.

represented numerically. What this means is that a program, which is nothing more than a sequence of instructions, is just a list of numbers that can be stored in the primary storage unit as if it were a list of prices or any other data. The instructions, of course, are used by the computer in a totally different way than data are used: the instructions determine what the computer *does* with data to produce the desired results. We will look at instructions in more detail later.

Primary storage: holding both program instructions and data

The other basic function of primary storage is to hold the input data that are required by the program being executed. In an extensive calculation, the results of carrying out the instructions using the input data are usually twofold: there are some intermediate results, which are used in subsequent calculations; and there are final results, which are to be output. Primary storage thus includes *working storage* (space to hold the intermediate results) as well as space for input data and the final results (see Figure 3.9). Now let's look at the logical structure of primary storage and then at its physical structure and components.

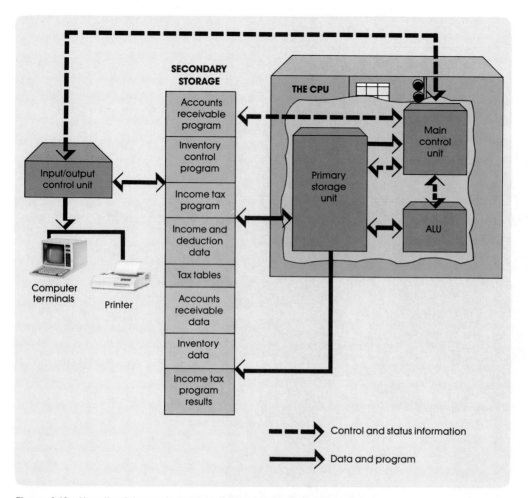

Figure 3.10 How the Primary Storage Unit Fits into the Computer System
Much of the hardware in the computer system and a great deal of software is devoted to maintaining efficient transfer of data between the primary and secondary storage units. Programs and input data are maintained in the secondary storage unit, which communicates with the peripheral equipment through the input/output control unit. To be executed, the programs must be loaded into the primary storage unit. Two sets of data—the income and deduction data and the tax tables—are needed as input by the income tax program. The results of program execution are to be output.

The Logical Structure of Primary Storage

Figure 3.10 illustrates the relationship of the primary storage unit to the rest of the components in the computer system.

Capacity of Primary Storage

In a mainframe computer system at a given time, many programs may be in secondary storage, together with their data, awaiting the availability of the CPU and space in the primary storage unit. One feature of primary storage that distinguishes it from secondary storage is that its contents can be transmitted very rapidly to the ALU for processing. Also, its physical size is small compared to that of secondary

Unit Prefix	Traditional Meaning	Computerese
kilo	1,000	$1,024 = 2^{10}$
mega	1,000,000	$1,048,576 = 2^{20}$
giga	1,000,000,000	$1,073,741,824 = 2^{30}$
tera	1,000,000,000,000	$1,099,511,627,776 = 2^{40}$

Figure 3.11   Prefixes for Units Used with Computers

storage since it must be both close to the main control unit and ALU and built out of the fastest (and therefore most expensive) memory chips in the system. For these reasons, the overall capacity of the primary storage unit remains limited compared to the slower, cheaper, physically larger secondary storage.

As we've implied, the capacity of primary storage is always a major concern. In fact, we'll see in Chapter 9 that part of the art of programming is making the most efficient use of limited primary storage space.

Measuring the size of primary storage

For a variety of historical reasons, the number 1024, or 2^{10} (as shown in Figure 3.1), has become the basic measure of memory size. It was the total size of some early computer memories and was later the number of bits on a single LSI memory chip. The memory size 1024 bits is somewhat imprecisely called 1K (K stands for *kilo*, meaning thousand). When we refer to a 4K word memory, we don't mean it holds 4000 computer words, we mean 4 times 1024, or 4096. This is the number of different words that can be specified in an **address space** of 12 bits ($2^{12} = 4096$). In other words, 12 bits are required to specify 4096 different addresses.

If the word length of the computer is 8 bits—that is, each word *is* a byte—the **kilobyte**, or 1024 bytes, is equal to the **kiloword**, which is 1024 computer words. With the transition from LSI to VLSI has come the need for the unit **megabyte** (the prefix *mega-* stands for million). A **megaword** is the number of different computer words that can be specified with an address space of 20 bits (see Figure 3.11). **Gigabyte** and **gigaword** (the prefix *giga-* means billion) correspond to a 30-bit address space, and **terabyte** and **teraword** (the prefix *tera-* means trillion) mean a 40-bit address space.

Random Versus Sequential Access

An important characteristic of primary storage is that it takes the same amount of time to retrieve a word from any of its locations. Since any randomly selected location in a primary storage unit can be accessed in the same amount of time, the unit is called a **random access memory (RAM)**. In contrast, sequential access is characteristic of magnetic tape storage, which we will study in Chapter 4. The time required to get information from a tape clearly depends on the location of that information, since it takes time for it to come under the read/write head. Figure 3.12 (page 68) illustrates the distinction between random and sequential access.

Accessing data in primary storage

Communicating with Primary Storage

Before leaving the subject of primary storage, let's examine the central role that it plays, functionally, both in the CPU and in the computer system as a whole.

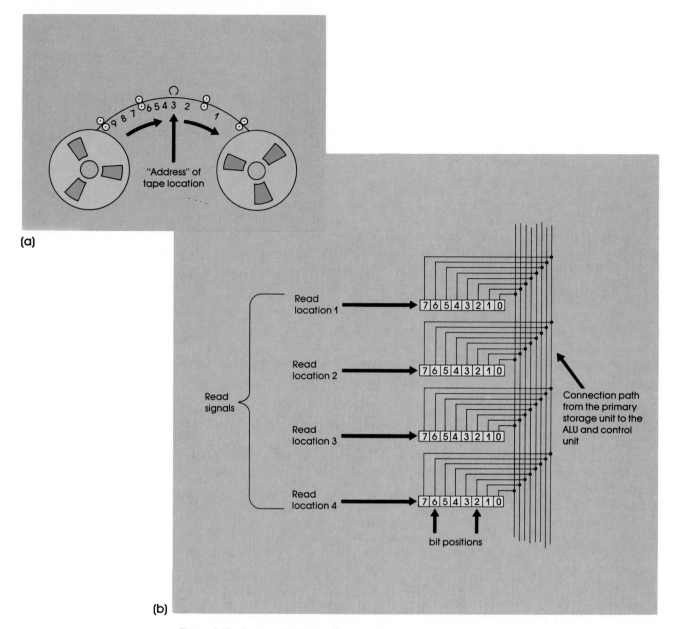

(a)

(b)

Figure 3.12 Sequential Versus Random Access

(a) The information at location 3 on the tape is available immediately, since it is directly beneath the read/write head. The information at location 9 will have to be brought beneath the read/write head before it can be accessed. Information on a typical magnetic tape can take many seconds (even minutes, depending on where on the tape it is) to reach the read/write head—virtually an eternity of computer-measured time. (b) Each of the locations in the primary storage unit (four 8-bit locations are shown here) has its own, independent connection to the path that connects the primary storage unit to the ALU and the main control unit. The information in any randomly selected location is available in the same amount of time.

Communication Between Primary and Secondary Storage

For the entire computer system to operate efficiently, all of its parts must work at or near their maximum speeds. But, as we've seen, different subsystems work at different speeds. Recall that, although it has a smaller capacity, the primary storage unit operates more rapidly than tape or disk secondary storage does. The problem is how to avoid periods of idle waiting by the primary storage unit when it's necessary for it to receive data from the slower secondary storage. (If the primary storage unit is idle, the ALU and main control unit will also be mostly idle, since they depend on primary storage for data and programs.)

Part of the solution is to minimize the frequency and maximize the efficiency of communication between primary and secondary storage. Complex computer programs monitor the operation of the computer system. They ensure that data and programs are loaded into the primary storage unit as they are needed and in a sequence that permits efficient operation. For example, if a program loaded from secondary into primary storage is to perform operations on certain data, then those data are also loaded.

Another part of the solution is that special hardware is sometimes used to reduce the delays when primary storage must communicate with secondary storage. For example, a type of memory with a size and an access speed that are intermediate between those of primary and secondary storage, called **bulk memory**, is sometimes used (see Figure 3.13 page 70). The overall computer system is controlled by software in such a way that when required data or program steps are not already in the primary storage unit, they are usually held in bulk memory. This eliminates idle periods for the primary storage unit, which would have to wait while information was transferred from slower secondary storage. The software, in fact, transfers information from bulk memory to the primary storage unit during periods when the ALU and main control unit are performing operations and are not calling on the primary storage unit. Bulk memory is described more fully in Chapter 5. *Bulk memory*

Finally, in systems designed to permit many user programs to share the resources of the CPU simultaneously, specialized software and hardware mediate between primary and secondary storage. Such simultaneous use of computer facilities is called *time sharing,* and we'll discuss it in detail in Chapter 11.

Communication in the CPU

Just as bulk memory mediates between primary and secondary storage, **cache memory** bridges the gap between primary storage and certain faster circuits in the CPU. The CPU contains a relatively small quantity of memory even faster than primary memory. Each word of this special memory is called a **register**. Registers are special storage locations directly connected to the main control unit and to the ALU, where the actual manipulation of the data is done. With the help of the cache memory and its elaborate controls, the primary storage unit is made to appear faster to the ALU and main control unit, which in fact communicate only with the cache memory (via the registers), rather than with the primary storage unit. The cache memory communicates with the primary storage unit when the main control unit and the ALU are busy and have no immediate need for new information. As a result of this communication, the cache memory acquires the data or program steps that will be needed for processing next. The relationship of the cache memory to the other parts of the CPU is illustrated in Figure 3.14 (page 70). The size and speed of cache memory and the number of registers and their operating speed are limiting factors in the overall performance achievable by a CPU. *Cache memory*

Cache memory and bulk memory are both examples of **buffer storage**: units inserted between two different forms of storage in order to synchronize their activities more efficiently.

Figure 3.13   An Intermediary Between Primary and Secondary Storage
Bulk memory has an operating speed and a capacity between those of primary and secondary storage. It facilitates communication between the two storage units.

Figure 3.14   An Intermediary Between Primary Storage and Other Parts of the CPU
Cache memory has an operating speed and capacity between those of the primary storage unit and the set of registers also in the CPU. It facilitates communication within the CPU.

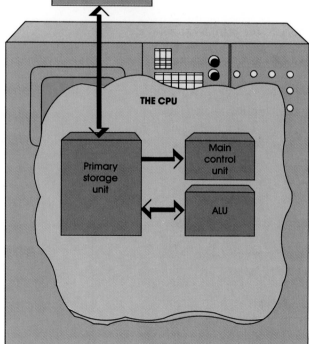

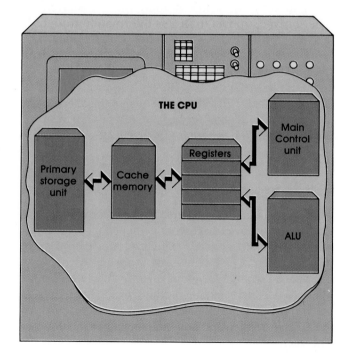

THE ARITHMETIC AND LOGIC UNIT (ALU)

Babbage called the place in his analytical engine where the input was transformed into results "the mill." Similarly, today's computers are sometimes irreverently referred to as "number crunchers." The **arithmetic and logic unit (ALU)** is the part of the CPU where mathematical and logical operations are carried out. The data values to be used in the arithmetic and logical operations are transferred to the ALU, where the operations are performed. We've already seen how data and instructions, represented as binary numbers, are stored in the primary storage unit. We'll look at how the main control unit causes the data to be transmitted to registers and operations to be performed. For now, we'll assume that the data are in registers and that the CPU is ready to execute an instruction.

Where operations are performed

Registers and Accumulators

The data are transmitted from registers to the ALU, and the result of an operation is transmitted from the ALU to a special register called an **accumulator**. As its name suggests, an accumulator is a location in the CPU used to hold, or accumulate, the results of ALU operations.

Special storage connected to the ALU

Once an operand is in a register, its journey from an input device has nearly ended. This journey included brief stopovers in at least some of the following: secondary storage, bulk memory, primary storage, and cache memory. Now, finally, the ALU circuits perform an arithmetic or logical operation on the operands and transmit the result to an accumulator in the CPU. The accumulator, in turn, communicates with other registers (the details of the connections vary from system to system), and the results start on the journey to an output device.

All CPUs contain an internal accumulator and some registers, and large systems may be augmented with additional registers and accumulators. Figure 3.15 is a diagram of the usual arrangement.

Figure 3.15   Information Flow to and from the ALU
Operands are transmitted to the ALU from registers, and results of an operation are transmitted from the ALU to an accumulator.

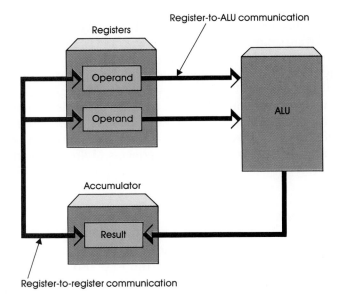

Types of ALUs

*Processing operands at
different speeds*

Different types of ALUs are designed to do arithmetic operations at different speeds (and the faster they work, the more they cost, in general). The simplest type of ALU does operations involving a single pair of bits at a time, one from each operand. It adds two multidigit numbers, for example, much as we do manually, beginning with the two digits in the least significant position of the numbers and proceeding to the most significant position (right to left), adding in the carried values along the way. Such an ALU is called a *serial-by-bit ALU.* Doing arithmetic in a serial-by-bit fashion is, by computer standards, a very slow process. As a result, serial-by-bit ALUs are found only in a relatively few, specialized systems.

Calculations can be performed faster if more transistors are included in the ALU's arithmetic circuits, to process all of the digits in the operands (all of the bits in the computer words) simultaneously. An ALU that has the transistors necessary to do this simultaneous processing is called a *parallel ALU.* The continuing decrease in the cost of transistors means that virtually all ALUs currently marketed are parallel ones. Parallel ALUs require that the programmer completely specify the handling of the binary point in the operands. That is, if 101.1 (the decimal value 5.5) is to be added to 1.01 (the decimal value 1.25), it is the programmer's responsibility to ensure that both numbers are entered in registers in the proper alignment:

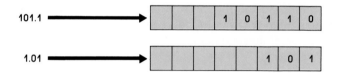

The programmer must also keep track of the location of the binary point in the result.

While keeping track of the binary point is not difficult in such operations as our simple example, this task can be a more complex one. In fact, it represented a major programming challenge before the advent of elaborate *floating-point software,* written for early machines, which lifted this burden from the programmer. The price of this software solution to the problem was, and is, slower speeds: the time to execute a significant program is the time required for a single ALU operation. Many current models of personal computers, whose users can generally live with slower operating speeds, still use floating-point software. Larger minicomputers and mainframes, however, must be as fast as possible in order to satisfy their users' needs, and they contain larger, more costly *hardware floating-point ALUs.* These ALUs are equipped with several additional hardware units that perform the required operations on the mantissas and exponents of floating-point numbers.

Logical Operations

The examples we've referred to in our discussion of the ALU have involved arithmetic operations, but we did mention that the ALU also performs logical operations. We've been using the term *logical operations* rather loosely, without going into how they differ from arithmetic operations. In this section, we'll describe the structure and purpose of these operations, which are fundamental to the design and use of computers.

Logical Expressions

To exercise their full power in applications, computers must be able not only to calculate the values of algebraic expressions, but also to deal somehow with the occurrence (or nonoccurrence) of conditions and events. For example, if a computer is used to control an office building's heating and cooling system, it might be programmed to turn on the air conditioning when the temperature *(T)* exceeds 80°F (26.67°C) *and* the humidity *(H)* exceeds 70%. The computer in that case would have to be programmed to recognize when the event "*T* greater than 80°F *and H* greater than 70%" had occurred. The computer might also be programmed to turn the system off if either it was *not* a weekday *or* the temperature was between 60°F (15.56°C) and 80°F. Both of these situations represent conditions that can be described by **logical expressions**: statements constructed by connecting simpler statements with the *logical connectives and, not,* and *or.* The truth or falsity of the overall statement can be determined from the truth or falsity of its component statements.

The need for logical expressions

How can the computer work with logical expressions when we've seen that it can only deal with numbers? Obviously, logical expressions must be expressed somehow as numbers. For example, we can define a variable A to be equal to 1 when the statement "*T* greater than 80°F" is true and to be equal to 0 when it is false. Similarly, we can define a variable B to be equal to 1 when the statement "*H* greater than 70%" is true and to be 0 when it is false. In this sense, the *logical variables A* and *B* represent the statements "*T* greater than 80°F" and "*H* greater than 70%," respectively. Then the product $A \cdot B$ represents the statement "*T* greater than 80°F *and H* greater than 70%." If A is true and B is true, then both A and B have the value 1. Thus the product $A \cdot B$ also has the value 1, and the statement it represents is true. If either of the statements is false, then the product $A \cdot B$ will have the value 0 (because one of the factors is 0), and the statement it represents will be false.

Logical variables and binary values

Using the direct association of the values 0 and 1 of a variable with the truth and falsity of a statement it represents permits logical relationships to be manipulated arithmetically and logical inferences to be drawn by computer programs. This is illustrated in Figure 3.16 (page 75), which shows the logical flow of the program to control a heating and cooling system.

Logical Comparisons

The example of the computer control of a heating and cooling system illustrates the importance of comparisons (comparing the value of T to 80 and the value of H to 70) for steering a program through alternative paths. The ALU can perform a basic set of logical comparisons, including the determination of at least the following conditions:

$$A > B \quad (A \text{ greater than } B)$$
$$A = B \quad (A \text{ equals } B)$$
$$A < B \quad (A \text{ less than } B)$$

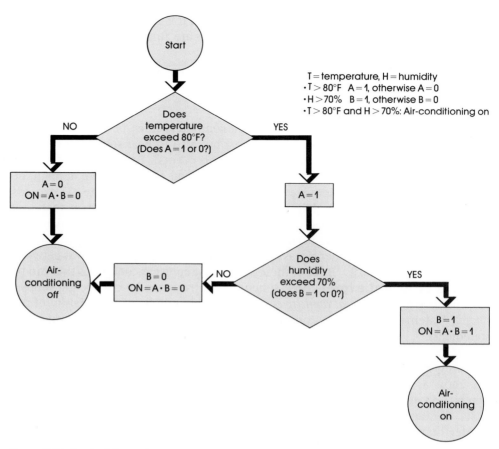

Figure 3.16 Logical Flow of a Program to Control a Heating and Cooling System
The logical flow of a program to control a heating and cooling system is presented above in the form of a flowchart. (See Chapter 8 for a complete discussion of flowcharts.) For now we just need to point out the key role of decision elements, the parts of the program represented by the diamonds. Measuring devices communicate the values of the physical variables T (temperature) and H (humidity) to the computer, which then calculates the corresponding values of A and B, the logical variables. Then the program simply computes the value of the product $A \cdot B$, which equals the variable ON, to determine the appropriate action to take.

Some ALUs can also perform these useful compound comparisons:

$A \geq B$ (*A* greater than or equal to *B*)
$A \leq B$ (*A* less than or equal to *B*)
$A \neq B$ (*A* unequal to *B*, or, *A* greater than or less than *B*)

How logical comparisons are used

Comparisons are the basic means for controlling a program's flow. In a payroll program, the condition that the hours worked *(H)* exceed 40 will steer the program to a path that takes into account the payment of an overtime premium and multiplies the difference between *H* and 40 by $1\frac{1}{2}$ times the regular hourly pay rate. Since the income tax rate differs depending on the payer's tax bracket, an income tax program must perform comparisons to determine in what numerical range of values the net income lies.

Comparisons are also central to *sorting,* the single most basic function of data processing. Sorting is used to facilitate the retrieval of a desired data item from among a large number of stored items. Can you imagine, for example, trying to find a specific name in an unalphabetized (unsorted) telephone directory for a major city? Comparisons are utilized in programs that sort data items to determine where in an alphabetic or numeric sequence a given item belongs. (Sorting is discussed in more detail in Chapter 5.)

THE MAIN CONTROL UNIT AND PROGRAM EXECUTION

The **main control unit** is a collection of circuits that orchestrates the functioning of all of the computer system's components. Based on program instructions it takes from the primary storage unit, the main control unit causes required data to be transmitted back and forth between ALU, primary storage, secondary storage, and input/output devices and tells the ALU what operations are to be performed. The main control unit is the part of a computer system that makes it a system—like the captain of a drill team, it gets a collection of individual units to perform their various roles in a precise and constructive way.

Coordinating the entire system

We know that data and program must be held in the primary storage unit in order to be executed. We also know that the sequence of operations listed in the program is carried out on the specified data in the ALU. Let's trace the steps in the execution of a simple program, a somewhat streamlined version of an ADD operation. The program is already in primary storage, and the computer is ready to execute the instruction stored in the memory location identified by address 17. How the instruction got to memory location 17 will be described later; for now we'll just assume that's where it is.

Executing an Instruction

To be executed, the instruction at a given address is transferred to a special register in the main control unit called the *instruction register.*

An instruction consists of two parts: an operation and an address. The **address** specifies the memory location of a data value; the **operation** specifies what's to be done with that value. In Chapter 1, we said that an address is the number that labels a particular storage location, and a location is an actual physical place in the memory.

Parts of the instruction: operation and address

Let's say that the instruction stored in binary form at memory location 17 is ADD 35, which means "Add the value at memory location 35 to the number currently in an accumulator in the ALU." When it's time for this instruction to be executed, it's transmitted from where the programmer stored it (memory location 17) to the instruction register in the main control unit, as shown in Figure 3.17.

The main control unit then executes the instruction. Each portion of the instruction—the operation and the address—is processed by different hardware in the main control unit. When the address of 35 is transmitted to the primary storage unit, it is accompanied by a signal from the main control unit. The signal informs the primary storage unit to send the value held at address 35 to the ALU for processing. At the same time, the main control unit sends another signal to the ALU informing it to do an ADD operation on the value it will receive next from the

Figure 3.17 The Instruction Register

When a program instruction is to be executed, it is transmitted from the memory location where it is stored to the instruction register in the main control unit.

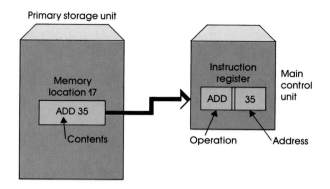

primary storage unit. That is, the ALU is instructed to add the value to the current contents of the accumulator. The ALU simultaneously receives both the word stored at address 35 and the current contents of the accumulator. It adds them together and transmits the result back to the accumulator (see Figure 3.18).

This is a brief overview of instruction execution; let's look more closely at how the main control unit gets the ALU to execute the desired instruction.

Decoding Operations: Microcode and Read-Only Memory

The operation portion of the instruction is a pattern of binary digits. Each pattern (or *operation code,* as it's called) corresponds to a different operation; a unique set of signals must be sent to the ALU to cause that operation to be executed. All these sets of signals are stored in a special memory called the **operation decoder**. An address for this memory is the bit pattern representing an operation. The memory contents for each such bit pattern are the proper sequence of signals (called the **microcode**) that cause the ALU to execute that operation. The bit pattern or

Figure 3.18 Overview of Instruction Execution

The instruction to be executed is in the instruction register in the main control unit. Two things happen first (indicated by the circled ones): the address portion, 35, is transmitted to the primary storage unit with signals to send the word at that location to the ALU; and the ALU is sent a signal telling it to do an ADD operation on the word it will receive next from the primary storage unit. Then (see the circled twos), the word is transmitted to the ALU which simultaneously receives the current contents of the accumulator. Finally (see circled three), the ALU adds the two operands and transmits the result back to the accumulator. All of these steps in the sequence of events that is the execution of an instruction are controlled by electronic signals from the main control unit.

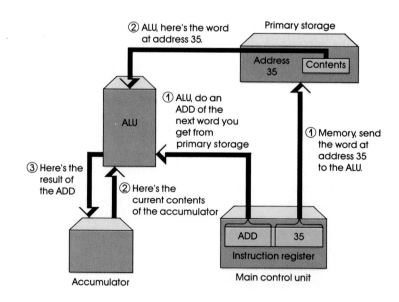

sequence of signals is unvarying: an ADD is an ADD is an ADD. If everything is working right, a given operation will always be executed by the same sequence of signals. Thus, the operation decoder is an example of a type of memory that is only written into once; after being written into, it is only read. For this reason, it is called a **read-only memory (ROM)**.

Even though they can't be written into and are thus unalterable, there are several advantages to the use of ROMs. First, the information they hold is stored in a form that persists even in the absence of power; that is, ROMs are nonvolatile. Clearly, it would be more than just inconvenient to have to redefine the computer's instructions every time it was turned on. Also, because ROMs are structurally somewhat simpler than the memories we've previously discussed that a user can write into as well as read (called read/write memories) they generally cost less and work faster.

There are a number of ROM variants. The contents of basic ROMs are loaded by the manufacturer and, as we said, are thereafter essentially unalterable. The contents of a *programmable read-only memory (PROM)* may be loaded by the user. This feature is important mainly to hardware designers and to research scientists who use PROMs to circumvent the long delays usually associated with ordering preloaded ROMs from manufacturers. Since the information stored in ROMs is usually quite complex, programming in an error of some kind is possible (in fact, it's quite likely). For this reason, *erasable read-only memory (EROM)* and *erasable programmable read-only memory (EPROM)* were developed. Their contents can be changed to correct errors. Such alterations can't be done while they're inside the computer, though—in operation they remain securely nonvolatile. Changing their contents requires that they be removed from the system and inserted into special equipment. Even though this reprogramming process is somewhat time-consuming, it's certainly more efficient than starting from scratch with a new ROM or PROM. (Three sections in Chapter 5—ROM Cartridges, Optical Disks, and Optical Cards—deal with applications that utilize ROMs.)

ROMs, PROMs, EROMs, and EPROMs

We can now add another level of detail to the overview of instruction execution illustrated in Figure 3.18. Figure 3.19 shows the processing that takes place inside the main control unit to generate the signals that must be transmitted to the ALU and to the primary storage unit.

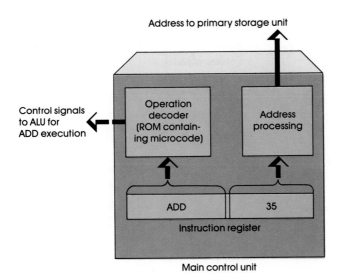

Figure 3.19   Instruction Processing in the Main Control Unit

The bit pattern stored in the operation portion of the instruction is an address in the operation decoder, a ROM containing microcode. The contents at that address are the actual source of the control signals that cause execution of the operation in the ALU. The address portion of the instruction is processed by special hardware in the main control unit; this hardware, as we'll see later when we study loops, allows the same program to be applied to data at successively updated memory locations.

The Instruction Counter and Branching

In our description of the execution of an instruction, we began by assuming that the instruction was stored at the memory location identified by address 17 and was transmitted to the main control unit when it was time for it to be executed. In fact, in addition to controlling the execution of each instruction, the main control unit also determines the sequence in which the instructions are executed.

Role of the instruction counter

A special register in the main control unit called the **instruction counter** contains the address of the instruction that is just about to be executed. To return to our earlier example, let's assume the instruction counter contains 17. This causes the instruction stored in the primary storage unit at the memory location with address 17 to be transmitted to the instruction register for execution. The diagram in Figure 3.20 clarifies the function of the instruction counter.

When writing a program, a programmer assigns consecutive addresses to its instructions. The instructions are executed sequentially, in the order of their assigned addresses (unless some alternative order is specified). That is, execution of a program starts with the address of its first instruction in the instruction counter. After that instruction has been executed, the instruction at the next consecutive address (obtained by adding 1 to the contents of the instruction counter) is executed, and so on, until all of the program's instructions have been executed.

If computers were limited to executing instructions in a single, fixed sequence, their applications would be few and uninteresting. However, as our earlier example of the program that controls the heating and cooling system of an office building reveals, computers can be programmed to use computed or input values to determine which of several alternative paths to take. For example, if the temperature is greater than 80°F, an instruction to turn on the air conditioning would probably be the next to be executed; if less, a different instruction would follow. With a tax program, if more tax was withheld than is owed, a refund is calculated; otherwise, the amount of tax due is calculated. Few really useful programs could be written

Figure 3.20   The Instruction Counter
The instruction counter contains the address of the instruction about to be executed. The instruction stored at that memory location is transferred to the instruction register for execution. Then, the address in the instruction counter is increased by 1 to obtain the address of the next instruction to be executed.

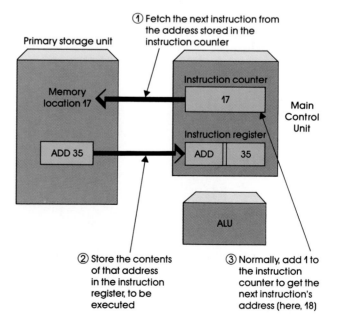

TECHNOLOGY CLOSEUP
A Closer Look at Supercomputers

The first supercomputers go back to the early 1960s: the IBM STRETCH (which "stretched" the technological state of the art) and the UNIVAC LARC (Livermore Automatic Research Calculator; the Department of Energy laboratory at Livermore, California, was and remains a principal nuclear research site) executed roughly one million floating-point operations per second (megaflops). Their immediate successor, Control Data Corporation's CDC 6600, was approximately three times faster. Today's supercomputers achieve peak rates of above 600 megaflops.

Two U.S. companies supply almost all of the domestically manufactured supercomputers: ETA Systems, created and partially owned by CDC, and CRI (Cray Research Incorporated). CRI founder Seymour Cray has been at the forefront of supercomputer designers since, while at CDC, he designed the CDC 6600. Recently, three Japanese companies, Fujitsu, Hitachi, and NEC, have entered the supercomputer competition.

What is the importance of this relatively small supercomputer market, which is no more than about 1% of the total computer market? Mainly, supercomputers have been the technological trailblazers. Hardware and design technology developed for the top of the line soon finds its way down into the entire product line, making all of a manufacturer's machines more powerful and thus more competitive.

And how have supercomputers achieved their great speed? The first decade of supercomputers accomplished their speedups more or less as a direct result of component speed increase: faster switches. As the generations of transistors got faster and faster, however, it got correspondingly more difficult to squeeze out additional speed. The limitations of the speed of light loomed closer and closer in view. We are still not at the end of the line in raw component speed; further size reductions and the use of new semiconductor materials, gallium arsenide in particular, leave perhaps another factor of 20 or so to be gleaned from this approach.

Looking at the past, however, a factor of 20 offers little comfort. We have in less than 30 years consumed more than a factor of 100 in supercomputer speed increase and still are surrounded by important computer applications thirsting for additional speed. Today's supercomputers provide their power not only as a result of their component speed but also because of the way in which the components are organized into the functional units that do the processing work; in other words, their architecture.

There have been two principal architectural innovations: *parallelism,* the simultaneous use of several functional units that operate cooperatively to execute a program; and *pipelining,* a design technique that breaks a calculation down into consecutive parts, connected in a pipeline fashion, and permits a stream of operands to simultaneously be in the pipeline, at various stages of completion. The latest and most powerful supercomputer, the Cray X-MP, combines both parallelism and pipelining to achieve its extraordinary peak speed of over 600 megaflops.

without this ability to go through different sequences of instructions *(branches)* based on the values of data. This programming technique of constructing alternative paths is called **branching**. When branching is utilized in a program, the instruction counter, instead of simply being *incremented* (increased regularly by a fixed number, such as 1), at critical points receives a new value from the program itself. This value determines which branch of the program will be executed next. The branching of program instructions is based on the outcomes of the logical comparisons we've already described.

Taking alternative paths

The details of how branching is accomplished, an important part of the study of programming, are discussed in Chapters 8 and 9. For the modern programmer, high-level programming languages eliminate the need to be concerned with the numerical contents of the instruction counter. However, branching remains the very essence of program structure.

With this description of branching instructions we have completed our discussion of all of the basic types of instructions (arithmetic, logical, and branching) that, together, constitute a computer's complete *instruction set* or *repertoire*.

 COMPUTER TYPES REVISITED

CPU characteristics and computer types

In Chapter 1, we classified computer systems in general according to size, price range, and function. Now we can elaborate on those classifications in a much more meaningful way—based on the speed and capacity of the computer and the types of functional units that make it up (the **architecture**). Here, it is primarily CPU architecture that establishes a system's place in the classification. Note that these classifications are not static. The size and cost of electronic components continue to decrease, so that today's mini becomes tomorrow's micro, and so on.

Microcomputers

The original microcomputers handled 4-bit words, but this word length soon grew to 8 bits and 16 bits. A recent model, the Motorola MC68020, even handles 32-bit words. Most microcomputers have fixed-point parallel ALUs, but relatively slow floating-point operation may be programmed using fixed-point operations. Special floating-point hardware attachments are becoming available as options on some microcomputers.

Word lengths of 8, 16, or 32 bits

Memory capacities of microcomputers range in size from a few kilobytes up to 16 megabytes, and their memory access times are about 100 nanoseconds.

The types of peripheral equipment available for microcomputer systems are multiplying rapidly, but their sophistication is somewhat limited by the relatively simple architecture of microprocessors. Chapters 15 and 16 are concerned exclusively with microcomputer systems and microprocessors.

Minicomputers

The first minicomputers were machines that processed 8-bit words. Currently, the most advanced minicomputers, the so-called **superminis**, such as the Vax 11/785 and the Gould PN9000, have hardware that works with 32-bit words and can even do some operations on 64-bit words. Hardware floating-point ALUs are available on most minicomputers and are standard for superminis.

The most advanced minicomputers

Minicomputers have memory capacities of up to 32 megabytes, and ones that use sizable cache memories can maintain access times of 75 nanoseconds.

A wide range of conventional peripheral equipment is available for minicomputers. Also available is a large assortment of special peripheral devices that facilitate the incorporation of minicomputers into automatic monitoring and control systems.

Mainframes

The word length used by mainframes is usually 64 bits (in machines built by IBM and most other companies), but it is 60 bits in some mainframes (notably those manufactured by Control Data Corporation, or CDC). Fast hardware floating-point ALUs are standard equipment in mainframes. Execution rates of arithmetic operations exceed 10 million floating-point operations per second *(megaflops)*. The IBM 4331 and the CDC Cyber 175 are examples of recent mainframes.

The largest, most powerful computers

Incorporating bulk memory (see Chapter 5) and large cache memories, mainframes achieve memory access times of 15 nanoseconds and have memory capacities in excess of 100 megabytes.

Mainframes' architectural features include the ability to attach from two to four ALUs and main control units to the same primary memory, with hardware and software features that keep them all working productively.

The peripheral equipment available for mainframes is virtually endless, as we will learn in Chapters 4, 5, and 6.

Supercomputers

A word length of 64 bits is the standard for supercomputers, the fastest of the floating-point mainframe computers. They can also handle 128-bit words, but at reduced speed.

The fastest supercomputer, the Cray X-MP, executes floating-point operations at peak rates exceeding 600 megaflops. Using bulk and cache memories, supercomputers achieve memory access times of less than 10 nanoseconds.

The fastest of the mainframes

Supercomputers often have multiple ALUs and separate specialized units that work simultaneously to perform each of the different arithmetic operations. Additional aspects of current supercomputer architecture are discussed in Chapter 20.

SUMMARY

The CPU and Numbers
Data Representation

Data must be translated from the alphanumeric characters that are conveniently presented to people to the binary numbers that computers must handle.

Binary Numbers   The binary system, with its base of 2, is well suited to computers because of the two-state nature of electronic switches.

Fixed-Point and Floating-Point Numbers   One of the distinguishing characteristics of any computer is the kind of numbers its hardware can process. Fixed-point numbers have the decimal or binary point in the same location, invariably. In floating-point numbers the position of the decimal or binary point can vary from number to number.

Octal and Hexadecimal Numbers   The octal (base 8) and hexadecimal (base 16) systems are convenient as shorthand ways to express binary numbers since each of their digits can stand for three or four binary digits, respectively.

Coding Systems to Represent Alphanumeric Characters   Alphanumeric characters must be translated into binary numbers for computer processing. Three principal coding systems are used to accomplish this: BCD, which can represent only 64 characters and whose use is therefore limited; EBCDIC, which represents 256 characters and is the standard IBM code; and ASCII, which is the standard code for almost all microcomputers.

Bits, Bytes, and Words   The byte is a group of 8 bits. Computer word lengths vary from 4 bits (a nibble) to 128 bits for the largest machines. Words are fixed-length or variable-length and fixed-point or floating-point.

Primary Storage

A vital part of the CPU is primary storage, or primary memory.

The Two Basic Functions of Primary Storage   In addition to holding the program being executed, primary storage provides storage space for the input data, intermediate results (working storage), and end results.

The Logical Structure of Primary Storage   Logical structure, as opposed to physical structure, is concerned exclusively with function. The distinguishing feature of primary storage is that its contents can be transmitted rapidly to the ALU. Primary storage size is often expressed in units of 1024 bytes (kilobytes) or words (kilowords), but larger sizes may be measured in megabytes, gigabytes, or terabytes. Words are retrieved from primary storage using the random access method (all words are retrievable in the same amount of time), as opposed to the sequential access method that is used for magnetic tape storage.

Communicating with Primary Storage Primary storage operates much faster than secondary storage, but a bulk memory can be placed between the two to make their intercommunication more efficient. For even better system performance, a cache memory can be similarly employed between primary storage and the CPU registers.

The Arithmetic and Logic Unit (ALU)

All mathematical and logical operations are performed in the ALU.

Accumulators Operands are transmitted from registers to the ALU. Results are held in accumulators.

Types of ALUs The simplest type of ALU is the serial-by-bit ALU, which processes binary numbers one bit at a time. Parallel ALUs process all digits of fixed-point numbers simultaneously. Hardware floating-point ALUs are equipped to process the exponents and mantissas of floating-point numbers.

Logical Operations Computers must be able to deal with logical expressions in order to evaluate conditions that determine the path a program should take. A logical variable can take on the binary value of 1 or 0 to represent the occurrence or nonoccurrence of a condition. Logical comparisons are performed by the ALU and are the basic means to control a program's flow.

The Main Control Unit and Program Execution

The main control unit coordinates the entire computer system, supervising the operation and intercommunication of all its components and sees that they communicate with one another in the proper sequence.

Executing an Instruction The instruction register holds both parts of a computer instruction: the operation and the address.

Decoding Operations: Microcode and Read-Only Memory The instruction register sends the operation portion of the instruction to an operation decoder. These decoders are one type of read-only memory (ROM). The address portion of the instruction identifies the operand.

The Instruction Counter and Branching The instruction counter determines the sequence in which instructions are executed, that is, the sequence of memory addresses from which instructions are transmitted to the instruction register. It contains the address of the instruction that is going to be executed next. Branching is used to alter the value in the instruction counter based on the outcome of comparisons.

Computer Types Revisited

The main classifications for computer systems also apply when we consider the architecture of their CPUs.

Microcomputers Originally limited to 4-bit words, some sophisticated microcomputers now work with 32-bit words. Memory access times are about 100 nanoseconds, and memory sizes range up to 16 megabytes.

Minicomputers While most minicomputers deal only with fixed-point words, the newest superminis process 32-bit words with hardware floating-point ALUs and can perform some operations on 64-bit words. Special peripheral equipment is available to facilitate the incorporation of minicomputers in automatic monitoring and control systems.

Mainframes Word lengths for mainframes are 64 or 60 bits. Execution rates are in excess of 10 million floating-point operations per second.

Supercomputers Fastest of the mainframes, supercomputers achieve memory access times of less than 10 nanoseconds.

COMPUTER CONCEPTS ≡

As an extra review of the chapter, try defining the following terms. If you have trouble with any of them, refer to the page number listed.

alphanumeric characters 58

binary point 60

fixed-point number 60

floating-point (real) number 60

octal system 61

hexadecimal system 61

BCD (Binary Coded Decimal) system 62

EBCDIC (Extended Binary Coded Decimal Interchange Code) system 63

ASCII (American Standard Code for Information Interchange) system 64

byte 64

nibble 64

word 64

instructions 64

address space 67

kilobyte 67

kiloword 67

megabyte 67

megaword 67

gigabyte 67

gigaword 67

terabyte 67

teraword 67

random access memory (RAM) 67

bulk memory 69

cache memory 69

register 69

buffer storage 69

arithmetic and logic unit (ALU) 70

accumulator 71

logical expressions 73

main control unit 75

address 75

operation 75

operation decoder 76

microcode 76

read-only memory (ROM) 77

instruction counter 78

branching 79

architecture 80

superminis 81

REVIEW QUESTIONS ≡

1. Explain why the binary system was chosen for computers.
2. What do the digits to the right of the binary point represent in base 2 mixed numbers?
3. How does a floating-point number represent a mixed number?
4. Why is the octal system a convenient shorthand for binary numbers?
5. Why are coding systems necessary?
6. Why is 4-bit BCD somewhat inefficient?
7. How many characters can be represented using 6-bit BCD?
8. What are the two most popular coding systems used by computers today?
9. How many bits are in a computer word?
10. What are the two basic functions of primary storage?
11. What factors limit the capacity of primary storage?
12. What are the distinctions among storage location, address, and contents?
13. What units are used to express the capacities of primary storage units?
14. What is the major difficulty in communication between primary and secondary storage? What is done to overcome it?
15. What differentiates the three principal types of ALUs?
16. In the statement "If you have a bone and a carrot and some water, then you can make soup," what are the logical connectives?
17. Why are logical comparisons essential to computer programs?
18. What are the two parts of a computer instruction?
19. What makes ROMs attractive to use?
20. What is the "normal" sequence in which program instructions are executed? How does branching alter this sequence?
21. Differentiate the general computer types according to some characteristics of their CPUs.

A SHARPER FOCUS

Now that you've completed this chapter, you should be able to answer the following questions about the chapter opening.

1. The Eagle is a 32-bit supermini. Explain what that means.
2. Although Tracy Kidder uses terms slightly different from those used in this chapter, it's apparent that he's talking about the CPU. What, in this chapter's terms, is the "Instruction Processor"? (*Hint:* What does it do?)
3. Does the Eagle have accumulators?
4. In what part of the Eagle's CPU does the "program of programs" reside?

PROJECTS

1. Convert your Social Security number from base 10 to base 2, base 8, and base 16. How many digits does it take to represent a 9-digit decimal number in each of the other number systems? Can you write a formula that expresses the general relationship between number of digits and base of system? (Show all your work.)
2. Consider the diagram of the logical flow of a program to control a heating and cooling system (Figure 3.16). Using the six logical comparisons listed in this chapter, draw a similar diagram for a method of determining which of any three numbers (represented by the variable names *A*, *B*, and *C*) is the largest.

57,881   60,775   63,814

430   750

57,451   60,025   63,114

28,951   30,387   31,912

28,500   29,638   31,202

11,528   11,150   12,496
896   932   941

| File Manager | Load Data | Store Data | Visuals Main |

4

Input

▶

FOCUS ON . . . TYPEWRITERS THAT TAKE DICTATION

On a cloudy November afternoon, a visitor sat before a blank computer screen in an IBM laboratory preparing to dictate a message that the computer would try to transcribe. The IBM scientists demonstrating the system handed him a list of suggested sentences to read aloud. Instead he made up his own, pausing between words as they had instructed him: "I . . . am . . . really . . . surprised . . . that . . . this . . . computer . . . can . . . understand . . . what . . . I . . . say . . . period." As he spoke, each word popped up instantly in blue letters on an adjacent screen that monitored the inner workings of the computer as it tried to decide what it was hearing. As the sentence grew longer, words began to change from blue to a rich green—in IBM's system, the color is certainty. A fraction of a second after the visitor shut his mouth, the complete sentence was delivered to the screen in front of him.

IBM's experimental device is one of the first talkwriters—machines that transform speech into text. It can understand 5,000 words, a small fraction of the more than 100,000 the average adult knows, but enough for composing routine business correspondence. Talkwriters promise to make computers accessible to millions of people who can't type, and to speed the journey of ideas to paper, now slowed by stenographers, pens, and keyboards. It is too early to reliably forecast the potential, but industry participants think the market for talkwriters could grow as quickly as for word processors, now over $2 billion a year. Such machines also represent an important step toward computers that can converse with humans, long the stuff of science fiction. . . .

Mere child's play for people, speech represents one of the thorniest problems in all computerdom. Many words sound alike; each word can be pronounced in many ways. Machines often have difficulty identifying the same word spoken by two speakers. The devices have to filter out ums, ahs, sneezes, coughs, and the sound of crumpling paper, all of which can be mistaken for words. Words spoken in sentences spell even more trouble: they bob around in pitch, volume, duration, and inflection, and blend together at their edges, so that "meet her" becomes "meter," "this guy" becomes "the sky." . . .

Word recognizers on the market today rely mainly on a pattern-recognition technique called template matching. A microphone translates sound waves of a spoken word into an electrical signal from which the recognizer derives a pattern, or template, similar to the voice spectrograms used by researchers to study pronunciation. Like the fairy tale prince with the glass slipper, the recognizer then tries to match the pattern against templates stored in its memory.

Magnetic Tape	*Reels, cartridges, and cassettes. Data from keyboard to tape. How data are input on tape. Why tape is used.*
Magnetic Disks	*Direct versus sequential access. Input via floppy disks. Input via hard disks.*
Source Data Input Methods	*Media and devices used to enter data directly into the computer from the source.*
Magnetic Ink Character Recognition	*Machine-readable characters printed in special ink.*
Magnetic Strips	*Machine-readable strips on cards.*
Optical Input	*Machine-readable marks, characters, and bar codes.*
On-Line Input Methods	*Media and devices used when data are entered directly into the computer and processed immediately.*
Terminal Input	*Direct input from terminal to computer.*
Point-of-Sale Input	*Computerized check-out.*
Graphic Input	*Digitizers, light pens, and the mouse.*
Touch-Panel Input	*Sensitive computer screens.*
Touch-Tone Input	*Input via telephone.*
Voice Input	*Talking to the computer.*

This chapter deals with input—probably one of the most important concepts you'll come across in your study of computers. Bits and bytes are certainly significant, and computer-aided manufacturing, management information systems, data storage, and the production of movie special effects are all compelling aspects of computer technology. But input is the very foundation of the Information Age, of high tech, of Silicon Valley—of practically everything related to computers. Whether it's the Cray X-MP, capable of carrying out 600 million operations per second, or a desktop microcomputer that processes words, a computer is just an expensive place to set your coffee cup unless someone has it do something. And if the necessary data aren't entered correctly, all of the computer's programmed wizardry may as well not exist.

Simple as the idea is, then, input is vitally important. In this chapter, we'll look at the ways data are entered, or input, and weigh the advantages and disadvantages of many of the most widely used methods. We'll also consider some of the techniques used to ensure that input's most important quality—accuracy—is maintained.

DATA ENTRY

Computers can only process numbers; in fact, as we discussed in the last chapter, they can only process numbers represented by patterns of electrical signals. Somehow raw data, the collected facts and figures that are to be processed, must be converted into this machine-readable form before the computer can accept and manipulate them. *Data entry* is the process of gathering a specific type of factual material, converting it to machine-readable form (if necessary), and either storing it temporarily or presenting it directly to the CPU.

Where the data come from

Given the wide range of tasks performed by computers, it isn't surprising that input data come from an equally wide variety of sources. In the business world, data are collected from sales, inventory, and payroll records, customer orders, or market research reports. Data used by scientific research organizations often consist of instrument measurements collected during experiments. Educational institutions gather data about their students in the form of attendance records, grade reports, and personal histories. Data collected by government agencies such as the IRS are taken from forms filled out by individuals and corporations.

Regardless of the source, the facts and figures must be correctly transcribed and transmitted or the results of processing them will be useless. Before we look at the methods, media, and devices used to enter data into computers, let's consider this clearly essential characteristic of input—accuracy.

Hardware Checks on the Accuracy of Data

Data errors due to hardware malfunctions

Unfortunately, even computers aren't perfect; computer errors do occur. For example, a bit of data can be lost or altered during transmission within or between computers. Such losses, although rare in relation to the enormous numbers of computations and data transfers that take place, happen often enough to be of concern. Dust, moisture, magnetic fields, and equipment failures are the most frequent causes of machine errors. Given the number of data-processing operations and of possible disturbances, such errors simply cannot be eliminated completely. It is necessary, therefore, to have some way of detecting machine errors, of pinpointing when and where they have occurred. Furthermore, since these errors originate in some problem with the equipment, it makes sense that the means to check for and if possible correct them should be built right into the computer hardware. Two of the most common built-in means of maintaining the accuracy of data are parity checks and redundancy checks.

Parity Checks

The **parity bit** is an extra bit that is added to a machine code for error-detecting purposes. For example, with the ASCII 7-bit code for the letter A (1000001), the parity bit is added to the leftmost position, resulting in an 8-bit code. If a computer uses *even parity,* the added bit is whichever bit produces an even number of ones in the 8-bit code. Similarly, *odd parity,* used by some computers, adds the binary digit that makes the total number of ones odd. With odd parity, the 8-bit code for A is 11000001. With even parity, the correct 8-bit code for A is 01000001. The zero added in the leftmost position results in an even number of ones; if a one had been added, the code would have had three.

The parity bit is generated by the computer circuitry before data transmission. Upon reception, the computer circuitry checks each byte to see whether or not it has an even (or odd) number of ones. If it does, it is accepted as correct. If it doesn't, at least one of its bits must have been changed during transmission; the data transfer is tried again. If the error persists, something serious is wrong, and the computer user is informed.

Notice that, although the parity bit is used successfully to detect one erroneous bit in a byte, two erroneous bits in the same byte will cancel each other out and thus will not be caught. This might sound like a serious setback for computer designers, but in fact it isn't—the probability of machine errors occurring twice in the same byte is very small. The parity check also cannot detect when data have been entered incorrectly. We'll discuss how to catch those kinds of errors in the section on software checks.

Redundancy Codes

The parity check employs one redundant bit per word, the parity bit. Redundancy codes use additional redundant digits. To give a simple example, storing a given 3-bit code for a one and another 3-bit code for a zero provides some powerful error-detection capabilities. It might seem wasteful to store 3 bits for every single bit of input data, but in fact it pays off handsomely.

Let's say that 111 is stored for every bit that is a 1, and 000 is stored for every bit that is a 0. So, for example, the 7-bit ASCII code for the letter A is stored as 21 bits:

111	000	000	000	000	000	111	Redundancy code for A
1	0	0	0	0	0	1	ASCII code for A

What is gained by using redundancy codes? First, a single-bit error in any of the triplets is immediately detectable since all of the triplets should consist of three identical bits. If, after transmission, the leftmost bit is 011, 101, or 110, it is obvious that some error has occurred in that bit. Furthermore, and here is the bonus, it is also immediately apparent in which bit the error has occurred, and the error can be *automatically* corrected. Thus, unlike the parity bit, the redundancy code can be used to eliminate all single-bit errors automatically. Not only is it an error-detecting scheme but, in the case of single-bit errors, it is an error-correcting scheme. Also, unlike the parity bit, the redundancy codes can be used to determine if two bits in a byte are erroneous.

Hamming codes, the most frequently used redundancy codes, actually use much less redundancy than we used in our example. They are a very powerful method for detecting and correcting random errors.

Software Checks on the Accuracy of Data

Even perfectly functioning computer hardware is limited by the reliability of what is input. Given correct data and programming, computer processing is predictable and reliable. But computers cannot evaluate the quality of the data they're given. For all their technological sophistication, if you provide them with inaccurate data, they will produce erroneous results. The programmer's phrase *garbage in, garbage out (GIGO)* says it all: the computer's output is only as good as the input data it is given. The vast majority of the "computer errors" people are so fond of citing are not hardware malfunctions at all, but rather the result of mistakes made in programming or data entry—two essentially human functions. Blaming such mistakes on the computer is a little like putting apples in a food processor and then complaining to the manufacturer that a "food processor error" produced applesauce instead of tomato puree.

There are two main types of input errors: (1) those due to the incorrect collection or recording of data; and (2) those due to mistakes in entering or keying in the

Detecting human input errors

data. Quite a few techniques for detecting input errors have been developed. Although often performed manually, these checks are most successful if they are programmed into the software that controls data input. Because the computer is well suited to the repetitive task of checking details, it can play a major role in the process of ensuring the accuracy of its own input data.

These are some of the accuracy-checking techniques that are included in computer software:

- *Checking for correct data types.* If a letter or punctuation mark turns up within a particular data item that is supposed to consist only of numbers, an input error has occurred. Many programs that are used for inputting mailing addresses can check for such errors. For example, such a program would identify the zip code 606A2 as invalid (because it includes a letter of the alphabet) and would alert the operator accordingly.

- *Checking for reasonable data values.* It is often possible to predetermine what range of input values will be acceptable. Checks to see if particular data items are reasonable can be included in input software to avert certain inaccuracies. For example, programs that input data concerning people's ages can be designed to recognize that three-digit numbers above 125 are unreasonable values for a person's age in years. Similarly, some types of data have very specific ranges of acceptable values, and software can reflect this. For example, there are only 12 months in a year, so 14 should be rejected as out of range for a month value.

- *Checking for data consistency.* Two separate data items may be related in some way that can be used to check their accuracy. An item that seems correct when viewed on its own may really be invalid when viewed in relation to some other item. For example, software that inputs data on educational histories might check high school graduation dates against college graduation dates. A high school graduation date of 1983 and a college graduation date of 1979 for the same person would mean that at least one date was probably incorrect.

- *Checking control totals.* Input data often consist of columns of numbers. One way to help ensure the correct entry of such numbers is to use **control totals**, or sums that are computed twice: by hand before input and by computer afterwards. If the two totals match, the numbers were probably entered correctly. For example, software that inputs the daily number of hours an employee works may use control totals to see if the number of hours entered matches the total number of hours reported.

- *Using a check digit.* The digits themselves can be used to help ensure the accuracy of numerical input data. Through the use of some predefined mathematical formula, an additional **check digit** is calculated for a number to be input and appended on that number. After input, the same calculation is performed again to see if the same check digit is obtained. If it isn't, then some error has occurred during input. This method, which is usually built into the input software, is similar to the parity check we discussed previously.

INPUT METHODS

Many different approaches have been developed to deal with the problem of getting data into a computer. **Batch input methods** involve collecting, or batching, data before entry into the computer. This usually means waiting until enough data have been collected to form a batch, and it requires the use of some medium for storing the data during collection, either cards, tapes, or disks. **Source data input methods** represent an attempt to reduce human errors by taking data right from the source and inputting them directly into the computer via some type of scanning device. Finally, **on-line input methods** are used to enter and process individual pieces of data as they become available. This type of input method relies on a terminal, scanner, graphic device, touch panel, or even the user's voice. Let's look more closely at these three approaches to data entry.

BATCH INPUT METHODS

Batch input methods typically capture data from source documents, such as inventory lists, employee payroll forms, income tax returns, sales receipts, or customer invoices. Data can be gathered directly from the source if they are in machine-readable form. In any case, the distinguishing characteristic of batch methods is that input data are temporarily stored until large quantities, or batches, are collected. At scheduled intervals, these accumulated batches are sorted into some convenient processing order, input into the computer, and processed. Batch input media, such as punched cards, paper tape, magnetic tape, or magnetic disks, are used to hold the input data during processing intervals. Devices that enable raw data to be recorded on these media include keypunches and key-to-tape or key-to-disk devices.

Media and devices used when data are batched

It is important to note that batch input is collected and stored temporarily before it is entered into the computer. Batch input media, therefore, are also storage media. (Since magnetic tapes and disks are commonly used to hold data, we will also discuss them as storage media in Chapter 5.)

Punched Cards

Everyone in our society has at some time been warned not to fold, spindle, or mutilate those perforated rectangles of stiff paper. **Punched cards** were, as we saw in Chapter 2, one of the very first ways of presenting data to calculating machines, and they are still being made and used by the billions each year. As we also discussed in Chapter 2, Dr. Herman Hollerith first developed the punched card for use in the 1890 census. Hollerith's coding scheme, the **Hollerith code**, and cards with formats similar to his 12-row, 80-column card are still used today. The most popular cards in current use are the 80-column card introduced in 1928 and the 96-column card introduced in 1969, both from IBM. Figure 4.1 shows the far more common 80-column card with all possible characters punched. The overall process of using punched cards for computer input involves a keypunch machine, a card verifier, a card sorter, a card reader, and the computer itself (see Figure 4.2).

Advantages of using punched cards as an input medium include:

- *Cards are standardized.* Since there are essentially only two kinds of punched cards in use today and the 80-column variety is by far the more common, cards punched at one installation can usually be read into other computer systems with card-reading capabilities.

- *Cards are reliable and familiar.* Punched cards have been in use for so long that most of the bugs have been worked out of the machines that punch and handle them. The technology is familiar, and many computer installations have the machines to handle punched cards.

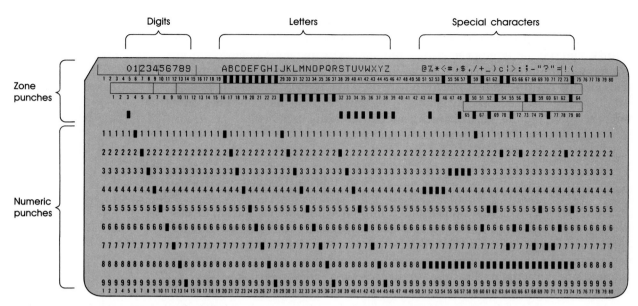

Figure 4.1 The 80-Column Punched Card

(*above*) The Hollerith code is used to represent data on the 80-column card. Each column holds one character. This card shows the punching patterns for all of the possible characters. Each number is encoded by a single hole in its row. Each letter requires two punches: one in one of the three zone punch rows, and one in a numeric row. Special characters are represented by unique patterns of one, two, or three punches.

Figure 4.2 Punched Card Input Process

(*below*) Inputting data using punched cards is accomplished with a keypunch, a card verifier, a card sorter, a card reader, and a computer. A keypunch operator types data from source documents onto cards. The accuracy of the data on the cards is verified, and the cards are sorted if necessary. The card reader translates the punches on the cards into the electrical pulses that are processed by the computer's CPU.

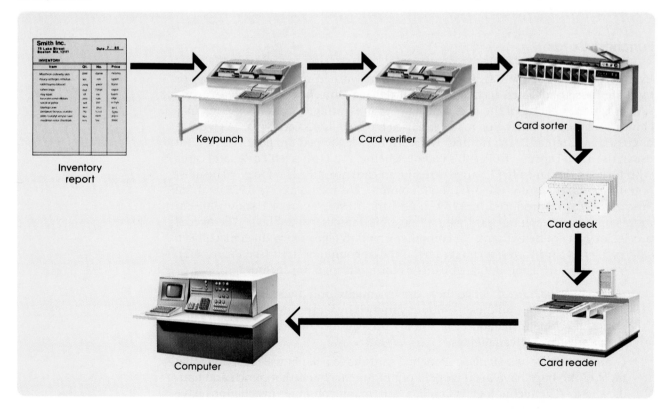

- *Cards are human-readable.* The characters punched on each card are also printed across the top. This makes cards easy for people to check visually.

- *Cards are cheap and easy to handle and mail.* These factors make them handy to use for customer billing. A punched card with the customer's name, account number, and balance is sent along with the bill and returned with the payment. The amount paid is then punched on the card, and the record is ready to be input with an accounts receivable program.

- *Cards can be updated relatively easily.* If the data on a card must be changed, that card is simply replaced by a new card with the new data punched on it.

There are also some disadvantages to using punched cards:

- *Card reading is relatively slow.* Card readers operate at speeds ranging from 100 to 2000 cards per minute (133–2667 characters per second); they are not as fast as other input devices. Card reading is slow primarily because so many mechanical operations must be performed to move the cards and access the punched data.

- *Cards in large quantities are bulky.* Although a single card is fairly light and thin, a stack of cards containing the names of all the people in New York City would be nearly a mile high.

- *Cards have a limited capacity for data.* The amount of data that can be put on each card is limited to 80 or 96 characters. Because of the standardized formats used, there is no way to squeeze more data on a card.

- *Cards can be easily folded or mutilated.* If a punched card is damaged, its data are no longer machine-readable.

- *Cards can be easily lost, misplaced, or disordered.* Anyone who has dropped a big deck of carefully ordered punched cards knows that putting all the scattered cards back in their original order can be quite a feat.

- *Card punches cannot be erased.* On most keypunches, typing errors can be corrected only by punching another card. Furthermore, once a card has been punched, the only way to change the data on it is to punch a new card.

Why the use of cards is declining

Magnetic Tape

Magnetic tape is a recording medium used extensively for computer batch input and data storage. It consists of a long strip of thin, tough plastic called *Mylar,* which is coated on one side with a film of an easily magnetizable substance such as iron oxide. Data are recorded on tape in the form of tiny magnetized spots induced in the iron oxide coating by electrical pulses (as we described in Chapter 2). Magnetic tape can be reused many times since recording new data automatically erases the data previously recorded in that location.

Magnetic tape is perhaps most familiar as a data storage medium. Therefore, we will postpone until Chapter 5 a detailed description of how data are represented and organized on tape. In this section, we will concentrate on how magnetic tape is used in the context of data input.

The magnetic tape used for data input and storage is very similar to that used for audio recording. The major differences are that data tapes are usually of much higher quality and are often packaged differently than sound tapes. Data tapes have three basic physical formats (shown in Figure 4.3).

(a)

(b)

(c)

Figure 4.3 Magnetic Tape
The magnetic tape commonly used for data input and storage is packaged in three formats: reels, cartridges, and cassettes. Reels are generally used with mainframes and some minicomputers, cartridges with minicomputers, and cassettes with microcomputers. (a) Reels are 10½ inches in diameter and hold up to 2400 feet of ½-inch-wide tape. (b) Cartridges hold 140–450 feet of ¼-inch-wide tape. (c) Cassettes hold 150–300 feet of ⅛-inch-wide tape.

Reels, cartridges, and cassettes

- **Tape reels**, commonly used with mainframes and minicomputers, are 10½ inches in diameter and typically hold 2400 feet of ½-inch-wide tape (300-foot, 600-foot, and 1200-foot lengths are also used). The usual **data density** (number of bytes per given area) for such tape is 1600 bytes per inch, giving a full reel a capacity equivalent to 576,000 punched cards.
- **Tape cartridges**, commonly used with minicomputers, are plastic cases enclosing small reels that typically hold 140 or 150 feet of ¼-inch-wide tape. Data densities of 400 bytes per inch are common.
- **Tape cassettes**, commonly used with microcomputers, are just like those used in audio cassette recorders. These tapes are typically ⅛ inch wide and 150 or 300 feet long. The data density is usually about 200 bytes per inch.

Key-to-Tape Input

Key-to-tape devices allow magnetic tape to be used as an efficient batch input medium. Such devices record data typed in at keyboards directly onto magnetic tape. Mohawk Data Sciences Corporation brought the first key-to-tape data re-

Figure 4.4 The First Key-to-Tape Device
The first key-to-tape data recorder was sold in 1965 by Mohawk Data Sciences Corporation. Such devices allow direct data entry onto magnetic tape.

corder to the market in 1965 (see Figure 4.4). Although there are many different kinds of key-to-tape devices, using various kinds of tapes, they can all be categorized as either single-station units or multistation units.

The **single-station unit** has a keyboard, a view screen, a limited amount of memory, and a tape-recording mechanism. The operator sits at the keyboard and types in the data, which appear on the view screen and are placed in the unit's memory. A single piece of data is entered at a time, allowing the operator to check the accuracy of the data displayed on the view screen before it is actually recorded on the tape. Once all the data have been recorded, the operator can rewind the tape and recheck the data, piece by piece, on the view screen. If an error is found, that data item must be retyped correctly into memory and written back onto the tape at the same location.

Data from keyboard to tape

Multistation units, or **clustered devices**, as their names suggest, have several keyboards and view screens connected to a central controller. This controller, which is in fact a small computer dedicated to this specific task, consolidates the data coming in from the different keyboards and sends them to one or more magnetic tape units to be recorded. From an operator's point of view, a multistation unit works just like a single-station unit, with the same entry, storage, and correction procedures. The multistation unit is, however, more economical for high-volume data entry because the expensive controller and magnetic tape units are shared by several keyboard-and-screen combinations.

Processing Tapes

Once the data have been checked for accuracy and placed on a tape, that tape can be loaded onto an on-line magnetic tape unit. This unit, which we will describe in more detail shortly, reads the data on the tape and sends them to the CPU, as illustrated in Figure 4.5.

How data are input on tape

The devices that write and read the data on magnetic tape are known as **tape drives**, **tape transports**, or **magnetic tape units**. The technology used in this equipment is essentially the same as that used in audio tape recorders. In fact, microcomputers may use the same tape recorders as are used to record music on

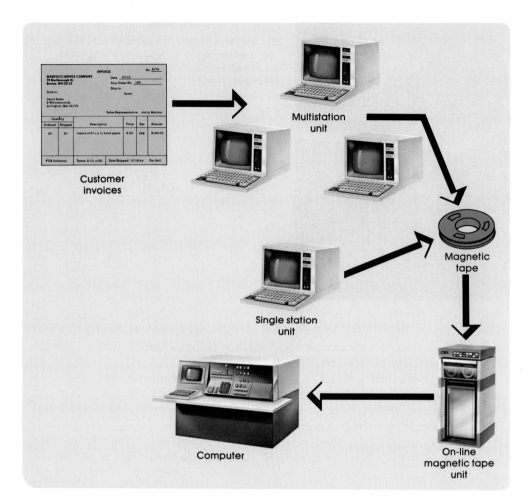

Figure 4.5 Magnetic Tape Input Process

Using magnetic tape for batch input requires a single-station or multistation key-to-tape unit, an on-line tape drive, and a computer. Data from source documents are keyed in by an operator at a key-to-tape device, checked for accuracy, and edited if necessary. The magnetic tape is then loaded onto an on-line tape drive that sends the data to the computer's CPU.

cassette tapes. Tape drives commonly used with mainframes and minicomputers, on the other hand, resemble large reel-to-reel decks (see Figure 4.6).

The first 10 or 15 feet of a reel of tape are always blank. This blank section of a tape, called the **leader**, may be safely handled when loading the tape unit. The tape is first threaded from the **supply reel** (the removable reel on which the tape is stored) into an airtight vacuum chamber, where it hangs in a long slack loop to prevent breakage from sudden starts and stops. From the vacuum chamber, the tape is threaded over rollers and past the **read/write heads**. These are tiny, sensitive electromagnets, one for each track on the tape. The heads read data by detecting the magnetic spots on the tape and generating electrical impulses, which are sent to the computer. When the heads are writing data, the process is reversed: an electric current is sent through the heads, magnetizing spots on the tape as it moves beneath them. After passing by the heads, the tape is fed through another vacuum chamber and onto the tape unit's permanent **take-up reel**.

Advantages and Disadvantages of Magnetic Tape Input

Magnetic tape is superior to punched cards in several significant ways. Input to the computer is much faster with magnetic tape, and tape has a higher data density. Verification of data and error correction are faster and easier with tape. Magnetic

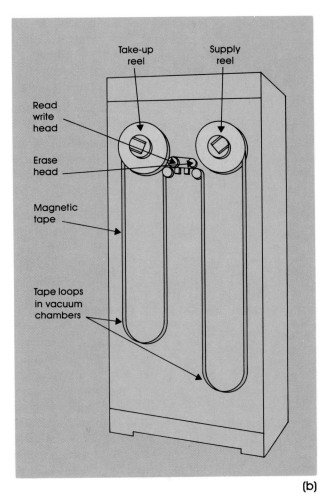

Figure 4.6   The Tape Drive
The magnetic tape unit, or tape drive, is the device that reads and writes data on magnetic tape. (a) A unit that holds tape on large reels is commonly used with mainframes and minicomputers. (b) The principal parts of such a tape drive, showing how the tape is threaded through the device.

tape is also cheaper per character recorded than punched cards. We can summarize the advantages of magnetic tape:

- *Greater data item lengths are possible with magnetic tape.* Individual units of data aren't limited to 80 or 96 characters as on cards.

- *Tapes have high data densities.* Up to 6250 characters per inch can be recorded on magnetic tape. A 10½-inch reel containing 2400 feet of tape can hold as many characters as 2.25 million cards, which would make a stack 1320 feet high.

- *Tapes are inexpensive, reusable, and easily handled.* At a cost of about $20 for a 10½-inch, 3-pound reel, tape is an even cheaper medium than punched cards. Since magnetic tape can be written over and reused, correction is faster and easier.

- *Tapes speed up the input process.* Between 15,000 and 1,250,000 characters per second can be transmitted from tape drive to computer, compared to 3000 characters per second with the fastest card readers.

Why tape is used

Magnetic tape also has some disadvantages, however:

- *Tapes are sequential in nature.* A particular piece of data can only be accessed by first going through all the data that come before it on the tape. The songs on a tape for a cassette player are also recorded sequentially. If you want to hear a song from the middle of a tape, you have to run the tape on "fast forward" until you find it. However, when it's a matter of accessing vital data such as a patient's medical record, there may not be time to rely on a sequential medium.

- *Tapes aren't human-readable.* Users can't even see, much less read, the magnetic spots.

- *Tapes are sensitive to dust and extremes of temperature and humidity.* If a tape is exposed to such adverse conditions, its data may be lost. To prevent this, tapes that are not in use are usually kept in tight canisters on racks in rooms where temperature and humidity are controlled.

Although magnetic tape is still a valuable and economical medium for storage and input, key-to-tape devices have lost much of the popularity they enjoyed between 1965 and 1975, when more than 10,000 were installed. The primary reason for their decline in popularity was the development of key-to-disk devices.

Magnetic Disks

Direct versus sequential access

Magnetic disks are flat, circular platters similar to phonograph records in appearance. They are coated on one or both sides with an easily magnetized film of a metallic oxide. As with magnetic tape, data are recorded on disks in the form of tiny magnetic spots induced by electromagnetic pulses. Consequently, magnetic disks can be used over and over again—new data are simply recorded over the old data. However, unlike magnetic tape, which is a **sequential access medium**, the magnetic disk is a **direct access medium**. This means that any particular piece of data on a disk can be read at any time, without having to go through all the preceding data.

Magnetic disk storage is an essential part of almost every major computer system currently in use. Disks, like tapes, are used extensively for both batch input and data storage. In Chapter 5, therefore, we will examine disk storage devices and show how data are organized on disks. In this section, we will focus on how magnetic disks are used for batch input.

Key-to-Diskette Input

Input via floppy disks

The **floppy disk**, or **diskette**, is a thin, circular sheet of flexible plastic coated on one or both sides with iron oxide. Each disk is enclosed in a square vinyl or cardboard envelope, within which it can spin freely. A "slice" of the disk is exposed through a slot in the envelope, allowing the data to be read and written. The most popular diskette sizes are $5\frac{1}{4}$ inches (commonly used with microcomputers) and 8 inches (often used with word processors and minicomputers). Several types of **microfloppies** are also marketed; the most popular is $3\frac{1}{2}$ inches in diameter and completely enclosed in a hard plastic shell.

The **key-to-diskette unit** (see Figure 4.7) is an independent system consisting of a keyboard, a view screen, and a floppy disk drive (the device that reads and writes data on floppy disks, which we will describe more fully in Chapter 5). The operator types in data at the keyboard, and they are stored as magnetic spots on the diskette. The view screen allows easy verification and correction of any data item before or after it is recorded on the diskette. Figure 4.8 illustrates this input proc-

Figure 4.7   Key-to-Diskette Unit
The key-to-diskette unit allows direct data entry
onto floppy disks.

Figure 4.8   Floppy Disk Input Process
Data from source documents are keyed in by
an operator at a key-to-diskette unit, checked
for accuracy, and edited if necessary. The data
are recorded on a floppy disk, which is then
loaded into an on-line floppy disk drive. The disk
drive transmits the data to the computer's CPU.

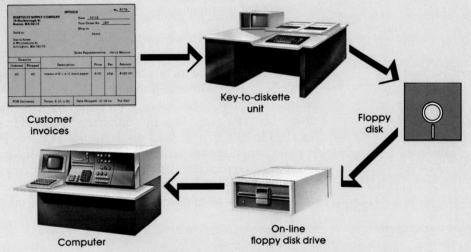

ess. Key-to-diskette units have become very popular, replacing keypunch and
key-to-tape devices in many organizations.

Advantages and Disadvantages of Floppy Disk Input

Evaluating diskettes as an input medium, we find they have several advantages:

Diskettes allow greater data item lengths. The length of a particular piece of data is
theoretically limited only by the capacity of the diskette. A typical 8-inch,
single-sided diskette can hold about 256,000 characters, making it equivalent
to 3200 punched cards. In practice, it is rare for a diskette to be filled by a
single lengthy string of data.

Diskettes have high data densities. Up to 1.4 million bytes of data can be put on
some $5\frac{1}{4}$-inch diskettes.

Diskettes are inexpensive, portable, and easily handled. A $5\frac{1}{4}$-inch diskette costs
less than $3.00, weighs only an ounce, and is convenient to carry or mail.

Diskettes are reusable. Writing new data onto a diskette automatically erases
any previous data from that area.

- *Diskettes allow fast input speeds.* Entry of 30,000 characters per second is possible with many floppy disk systems.

- *Diskettes are a direct access medium.* They allow fast access to any stored record and are easy to verify and correct.

Disadvantages of diskettes as an input medium include:

- *Diskettes are not human-readable.*

- *Diskettes are sensitive to dust and extremes of temperature and humidity.* If subjected to extreme conditions, the data on diskettes can be lost or become unreadable. Moderate care must be taken not to damage diskettes by exposing them to such conditions.

- *Diskettes can be erased by magnetic fields.* If placed near magnets or electrical equipment that produces strong magnetic fields, diskettes may lose the data recorded on them.

Key-to-Disk Input

Input via hard disks

A **hard disk** is a rigid metal platter, usually made of aluminum, which is coated on one or both sides with a thin magnetizable film. Their rigidity allows hard disks to be spun very fast. This, along with their high data densities, results in rapid data storage and retrieval. Usually completely enclosed in plastic cases or permanently installed in disk drives, hard disks are not as portable as floppy disks. The most popular hard disks are $3\frac{9}{10}$, $5\frac{1}{4}$, 8, or 14 inches in diameter. Two or more hard disks together in a removable unit constitute a *disk pack* (see Figure 4.9). Storage capacities of hard disk systems range from about a million bytes on the smallest, least expensive units to hundreds of millions of bytes on the largest.

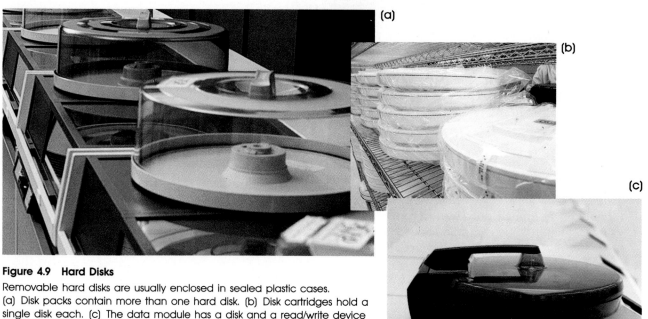

(a)

(b)

(c)

Figure 4.9   Hard Disks
Removable hard disks are usually enclosed in sealed plastic cases.
(a) Disk packs contain more than one hard disk. (b) Disk cartridges hold a single disk each. (c) The data module has a disk and a read/write device inside one case.

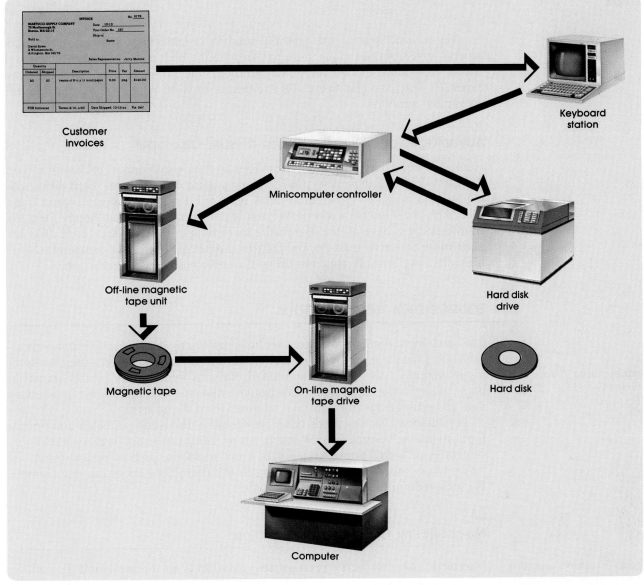

Customer invoices

Keyboard station

Minicomputer controller

Off-line magnetic tape unit

Hard disk drive

Magnetic tape

On-line magnetic tape drive

Hard disk

Computer

Figure 4.10   Hard Disk Input Process

Data from source documents are keyed in by operators at keyboard stations, checked for accuracy, edited if necessary, and stored on a hard disk. The contents of the disk may then be transferred to magnetic tape for later batch input to the computer. The transfer to tape is necessary if the key-to-disk unit is not connected to the computer or if its hard disk is not removable.

The **key-to-disk unit**, which allows direct data entry onto hard disks, represents the most advanced device for batch input. Various types of key-to-disk systems are currently in use, but most have from 2 to 64 input stations (each with a keyboard and a visual display screen) connected to a single hard disk controller (usually a minicomputer) that coordinates the input from the multiple keyboards and stores it on one or more hard disks. Data can be verified and corrected while they are still in the controller's memory. After the correct data have been stored on hard disks, they may be transferred to magnetic tapes for later batch input to a computer. The reason for this transfer is that many key-to-disk systems are not connected to the computers that eventually receive the entered data. In addition, the hard disks used in such systems may not be removable. Thus, the fastest, most economical way to get the data from the key-to-disk system to the desired computer may be via magnetic tape. Figure 4.10 summarizes the hard disk input process.

Key-to-disk systems are typically used in organizations that must regularly process large volumes of batch input. Despite the high cost of these sophisticated hard disk systems, many companies find them efficient enough to justify the extra expense. This cost-effectiveness is the primary reason why these systems are increasingly common.

Advantages and Disadvantages of Hard Disk Input

Hard disk input has the same advantages as floppy disk input, except that hard disks are neither inexpensive nor (generally) portable. However, hard disks have higher data densities (10 million bytes per hard disk is typical) and faster input speeds (1,250,000 characters per second is not uncommon) than floppy disks do. Hard disks also have all the disadvantages of floppy disks. In fact, hard disks are even more sensitive than floppy disks to dust and extremes of temperature and humidity. As a result, they require and receive costly extra protection.

SOURCE DATA INPUT METHODS

Inputting data directly from the source

The batch input media and devices we have just discussed all require human operators to key data from source documents into a machine that records them on some input medium. As we have mentioned, humans make errors as they transcribe data. Source data input methods eliminate this type of human error by allowing data to be input directly into the computer from the source.

We discuss these methods here, between the discussions of batch and on-line input methods, because source data input methods can really be classified as subcategories of both. Some source data input methods, such as optical input, are basically on-line methods, while magnetic ink character recognition, for example, is used predominantly with batched data.

Magnetic Ink Character Recognition

Machine-readable characters printed in special ink

Magnetic ink character recognition (MICR) is an input method that utilizes characters printed with magnetizable ink to make them machine-readable. If you have a checking account, you've probably noticed the chunky black numbers printed along the bottom of your checks (see Figure 4.11). Those symbols, consisting of the ten decimal digits and four special characters, allow an MICR reader-sorter unit to process up to 2600 checks per minute. The MICR input method is widely used by banks to process the large numbers of checks written every day.

When you pay for something with a check, an operator at the first bank to receive your check after it's cashed will print the amount, in magnetizable ink, in the lower right-hand corner of the check and batch it with other checks received that day. These batches are placed in the *input hopper* (a tray or shallow bin that neatly holds the checks) of an **MICR reader-sorter unit**. One at a time, the checks are passed through a magnetic field that magnetizes the iron oxide particles in the special ink. The MICR characters on your check can then be detected by read heads that can "interpret" these magnetic symbols in a way similar to how data are read from tapes or disks. The data can be input directly into a computer or placed on magnetic tape for later processing. The reader-sorter unit also sorts all the checks according to their identification codes, and eventually your check ends up back at your bank.

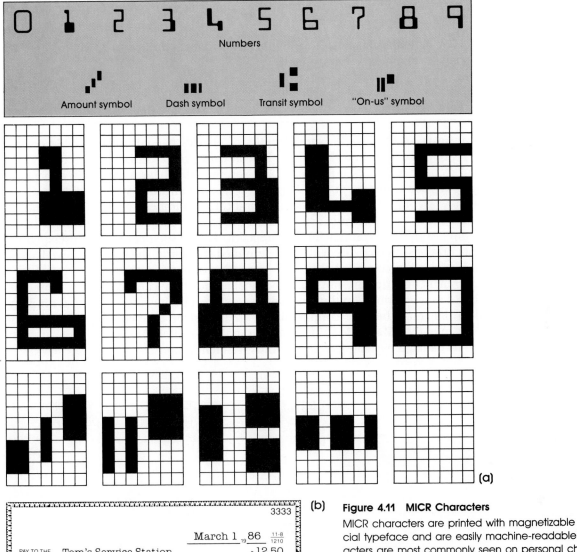

(a)

(b)

Figure 4.11 MICR Characters

MICR characters are printed with magnetizable ink in a special typeface and are easily machine-readable. These characters are most commonly seen on personal checks. (a) The magnetic ink character set, with its underlying grid pattern. (b) A check with MICR characters.

The advantages of using MICR include:

- *MICR characters are not easily damaged.* Checks can be folded, wrinkled, written on, and stamped. Character recognition is magnetic, so minor mutilation will usually not affect the accurate reading of data.

- *MICR allows faster input and processing.* Since the data are directly entered from source documents, input speeds are not limited by an operator's typing abilities.

- *MICR reduces errors.* Inaccurate input due to human keying mistakes is largely eliminated.

•*MICR characters are human-readable.* Only the four special characters require any getting used to.

The chief disadvantage to using MICR is that it's limited to 14 characters. No alphabetic characters are available.

Magnetic Strips

Machine-readable strips on cards

Magnetic strips are the short lengths of plastic-covered, magnetizable coating that are often found on the backs of credit cards, bank cards, identification cards, and security badges (see Figure 4.12). You probably have a card with a magnetic strip in your wallet or purse. Magnetic strips are encoded with confidential data such as account numbers, personal identification numbers, privacy codes, and access codes. The data encoded on a magnetic strip can be read and input into a computer by a special machine equipped to accept such cards from users. If the data on the strip coincide with predetermined standards, the user is allowed access to his or her account or is granted some type of entry authorization.

Magnetic strips are not human-readable, but they can hold much more data than could be printed in the same space. As a result, they are excellent for holding data that must be kept confidential or that must be entered often, quickly, and conveniently. Magnetic strips, however, have the disadvantage of being susceptible to damage by magnets, fingerprints, scratches, and bending.

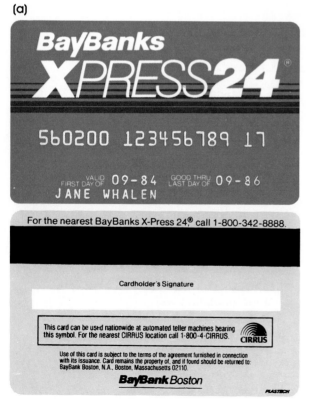

Figure 4.12 Magnetic Strips

Magnetic strips are used to encode confidential data. Special devices are required to read this data. (a) A bank card with a magnetic strip (the dark band across the back). (b) Automated teller machines are programmed to read the data encoded on the magnetic strips of bank cards.

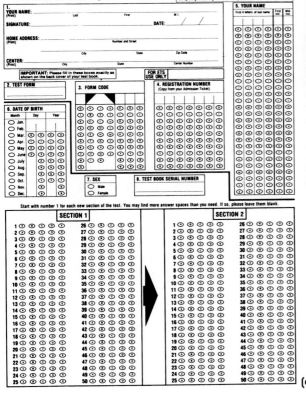

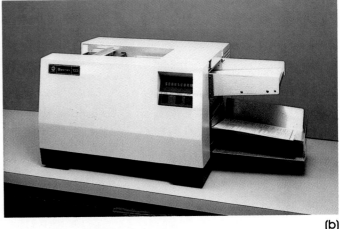

(b)

Figure 4.13   Optical Mark Recognition

(a) Optical mark recognition (OMR) is often used for scoring answer sheets for multiple-choice tests such as the Scholastic Aptitude Test (SAT). A pencil mark must fill the oval designating each desired answer. (b) An optical mark sensing device is used to read the pencil marks and to input the data to a computer.

(a)

Optical Input

Optical input, the reading and direct entry of visible symbols not printed in special ink, is accomplished using any one of three techniques: optical mark recognition, optical character recognition, and bar code recognition.

Machine-readable marks, characters, and bar codes

Optical mark recognition (OMR), or **mark sensing**, is widely used in the scoring of test forms, such as the SAT answer sheet shown in Figure 4.13. A pencil is used to mark a box or other space representing the selected answer. Test forms are scored by an optical mark sensing device that uses light beams to convert the presence of pencil marks into electrical signals that can be input to a computer.

Optical character recognition (OCR) is a widely used input technique that employs light beams to read alphanumeric characters. Machine-printed characters are produced in a standard typeface, called **OCR-A**, which can be easily read by optical character recognition techniques. However, machines are available that can read well-defined, carefully formed handwritten characters. Figure 4.14 illustrates machine-readable characters.

Optical character readers scan the input, and their photoelectric devices convert the reflected light patterns into electrical pulses. These are then compared with standard character patterns that have been programmed into the readers. A common OCR input device is the **hand-held wand** used in many large department stores.

Figure 4.14 Machine Readable Characters

Optical character recognition (OCR) devices can read characters printed with regular ink. The characters, however, must conform to certain standards. The most commonly used typeface for optical character recognition is OCR-A. Some OCR devices can read carefully formed handwritten characters.

Legible handwriting
INPUT

Poor handwriting

Bar code recognition is a technique that depends on the familiar black and white stripes of the **Universal Product Code (UPC)** that appears on most supermarket items and even books and magazines (see Figure 4.15). **Bar codes**, which were first used by railroads in the 1960s to track freight cars, represent data as a series of light and dark marks. The UPC bar codes identify the manufacturer and product and are read either by wands or by **fixed bar code readers**. As items are scanned, the identification data are transmitted to a store's computer, which finds the current price, updates inventory and receipts, and sends the price back to the check-out counter. The use of bar codes in supermarkets has resulted in more

Figure 4.15 Bar Code Recognition

The most common bar code is the Universal Product Code (UPC) printed on virtually every item in today's supermarkets. The device most often employed to read these codes is a fixed bar code reader that scans the surfaces of products with laser beams.

(a)

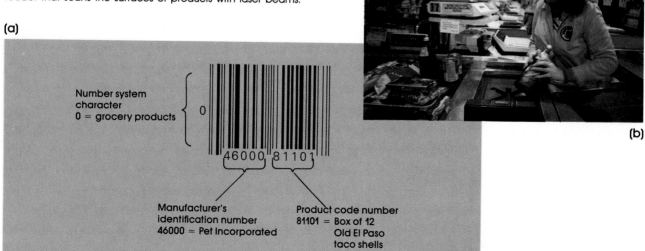

Number system character
0 = grocery products

0

46000 81101

Manufacturer's identification number
46000 = Pet Incorporated

Product code number
81101 = Box of 12 Old El Paso taco shells

(b)

accurate prices, faster check-out, decreased training and labor costs, and easier inventory control (see Chapter 19). Because of this success, bar codes are being adapted for such applications as library books and student identification cards.

The only disadvantage of optical input results from the sensitivity of the readers and their strict requirements for characters or symbols. The accuracy of optical input devices can, as a result, be diminished by poor penmanship, stray marks, bits of dust, or invisible scratches.

ON-LINE INPUT METHODS

On-line input, in contrast to batch input, is processed by the computer immediately, without being temporarily held on some intermediate storage medium. The entering or updating of any piece of data, often called a **transaction**, is handled when it occurs, without waiting for other similar occurrences. On-line input methods and devices are used wherever the data to be input require some immediate response or other action, for example, bank account updating, and hotel, car rental, and airline reservation handling.

Media and devices for on-line input of data

The on-line input methods we will look at here are terminal input, point-of-sale input, graphic input, touch-panel input, touch-tone input, and voice input.

Terminal Input

The computer **terminal** is by far the most popular on-line input device in use today. Its output portion, the display screen or printer, will be discussed along with other devices for computer output in Chapter 6. Terminal input originates from typewriterlike keyboards that send alphanumeric data directly to a computer. Although the alphabetic keys of these keyboards are almost always in the same positions, each manufacturer seems to have unique ideas about how many other special-function, special-character, and numeric keys should be on a keyboard and how they should be arranged (see Figure 4.16). **Local terminals** are at the same

Direct input from terminal to computer

Figure 4.16 Terminal Keyboards

This montage of photographs of keyboards reveals the nonstandardization of their layouts.

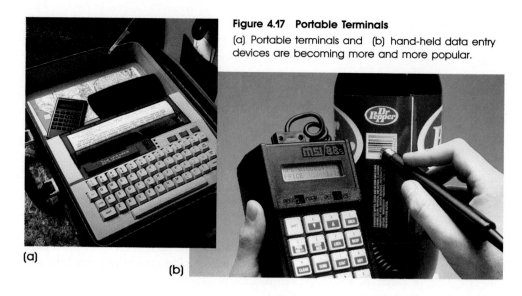

Figure 4.17 Portable Terminals

(a) Portable terminals and (b) hand-held data entry devices are becoming more and more popular.

(a)

(b)

site as the computer; **remote terminals** are located at some distance from but are connected to the computer by long cables or phone lines. Terminals are also classified as dumb, smart, or intelligent. A **dumb terminal** can only be used to send data to and receive them from a computer. A **smart terminal** has its own microprocessor and some internal storage, enabling it to do some data editing prior to transmission. An **intelligent terminal** is a smart terminal that can be programmed by the user to perform certain simple processing tasks independently of the computer to which it is connected.

A relatively new type of terminal for computer input is the **portable terminal**, shown in Figure 4.17. Some of these handy little devices are small enough to fit in your hand. Some portable terminals are used for specialized purposes, such as retail inventory taking, and have either limited ability to display information to the user or none. Others function like full-sized computer terminals, with small but complete keyboards and miniature display screens. Portable terminals may be small, but the market for them is large and is expected to continue its growth.

Point-of-Sale Input

Computerized check-out

Point-of-sale (POS) input is data that are fed to a computer by specialized terminals located at check-out counters in retail stores. A hand-held wand or fixed bar code reader is an integral part of such a terminal, in addition to its sophisticated type of cash register keyboard. These terminals pass along item identification codes to a store computer, which updates sales and inventory figures and sends back price information. Some POS terminals can also process credit card transactions by checking customers' credit status and updating their credit accounts (see Chapter 19).

Graphic Input

Digitizers, light pens, and the mouse

Graphic input to a computer consists of data that describe a drawing or a particular place on a screen; it is transmitted to the computer from a number of different devices, shown in Figure 4.18.

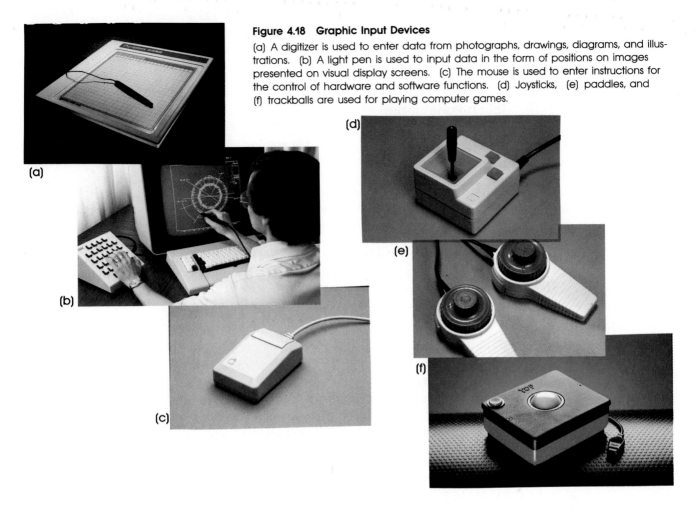

Figure 4.18 Graphic Input Devices
(a) A digitizer is used to enter data from photographs, drawings, diagrams, and illustrations. (b) A light pen is used to input data in the form of positions on images presented on visual display screens. (c) The mouse is used to enter instructions for the control of hardware and software functions. (d) Joysticks, (e) paddles, and (f) trackballs are used for playing computer games.

A **digitizer**, also called a **graphics tablet**, is a flat surface on which the user draws with a special stylus. The tablet senses each location where the stylus touches it, produces signals communicating the x-y coordinates of the contact points, and inputs these to the computer. A digitizer can be used to trace over a picture, converting it into a series of x-y coordinates that represent, to the computer, a digital map of the points comprising the picture.

A **light pen** is a light-sensitive rod used with special graphics terminals. The touching of the light pen to the display screen of such a terminal closes a photoelectric circuit, and the terminal identifies the contact point as an x-y coordinate. With such a system, the user can draw any image on the display screen, and it is converted to digits and stored.

The **mouse** is an input device that has become increasingly popular since its adoption by many user-friendly microcomputer systems, such as the Apple Macintosh. It consists of a small plastic box, with two wheels or a ball roller, that produces electrical pulses when rolled around on a flat surface. The wheel or ball rotations are converted to x-y coordinates that are stored as numbers. The mouse is used to direct the movement of a *cursor,* a small blinking light spot indicating a particular position on the screen. With the mouse, a user can point the cursor at symbols (also called *objects* or *icons*) representing the available activities to be performed. Systems employing a mouse have a traditional keyboard as well for entering text; the mouse is a convenient accessory for accomplishing certain tasks.

The *trackball, joystick,* and *paddle* (familiar to video game enthusiasts) operate on the same principle as the mouse. Ball, stick, or knob positions are translated into x-y coordinates to be input.

Touch-Panel Input

Sensitive computer screens

Touch-panel screens (Figure 4.19) employ either a pressure-sensitive surface or crisscrossing beams of infrared light to enable the user to enter data. The computer is programmed to display instructions or items to be manipulated on the touch-panel screen. The user instructs the computer to perform a specified action simply by touching the appropriate place on the screen. Since the touch panel can detect where it is touched, these data can be relayed to the computer, which completes the desired action. Even though touch panels are a relatively recent innovation, they have already been applied fairly extensively in education and with user-friendly microcomputer systems. By allowing users to simply point to what they want the computer to do, touch panels reduce the use of the keyboard and thus the time required to learn how to operate the computer.

Touch-Tone Input

Input via telephone

Touch-tone devices send input data, in the form of sounds of varying pitch, over telephone lines from remote locations to a central computer. Touch-tone devices are by no means full-fledged alphanumeric terminals; they have limited capabilities and are generally used only for specialized tasks, such as verifying credit card transactions or updating warehouse inventories. These devices use the pushbuttons of a touch-tone telephone as a keyboard. Some have the ability to store up small quantities of data on magnetic belts or punched plastic cards before transmitting them.

Voice Input

Wouldn't it be convenient if users could simply tell the computer what to do and forget about learning how to use keyboards, tablets, mice, or touch panels? To some extent, voice input is already a reality. Although it will probably be decades

Figure 4.19 Touch-Panel Screen
The touch-panel screen allows the user to input data by simply touching an area of the display. These data are usually an instruction concerning some hardware or software function. The Hewlett-Packard HP 150 microcomputer utilizes a touch-panel screen.

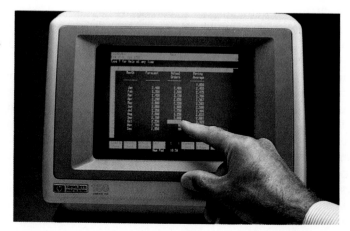

CAREERS IN TECHNOLOGY
Data Entry Operator

Job Description Data entry operators are clerical personnel who work in an organization's data-processing center, keying data into the computer system. Documents are sent from all departments to such a center, where they are logged in by a supervisor and assigned to an operator. Once in the system, documents can be called up quickly on an operator's terminal screen for necessary revisions or for printing. When keypunch devices were the state of the art, keypunch operators were the data entry personnel. Today, key-to-tape, key-to-disk, OCR, and word-processing technologies have all but eliminated keypunching (as noted in Chapter 2's Careers in Technology). Data entry operators work at quiet terminals in a clean, air-conditioned environment (see Chapter 22 for a discussion of potential health hazards faced by data entry operators).

Qualifications A high school diploma and the ability to type at least 30 words per minute accurately are basic requirements (and many organizations have a 60-wpm minimum). Since data entry systems differ, on-the-job training is generally provided. Familiarity with data entry techniques and data processing in general will certainly influence potential employers.

Outlook The Bureau of Labor Statistics predicts a decline in the number of job openings for data entry operators through the end of this century, due to the growing number of on-site systems that reduce dependence on centralized computer service organizations. Data entry comprised about 7% of computer service employment in 1980, but this figure may drop to as low as 3.5% by 1995. Optical input technology will also contribute to the decline, since it eliminates most keying functions. On the other hand, it must be noted that the bureau's statistics are limited to the computer service industry. As employment falls in that area, firms that are installing their own systems will be adding data entry personnel, thus creating new jobs—although the distinction between secretaries, data entry operators, and computer operators (see Careers in Technology in Chapter 6) may blur. In such a rapidly changing field, success requires diversity in training and flexibility in career goals.

before effective vocal dialogues with computers are possible, some **voice recognition modules (VRMs)** have been developed that can recognize from 40 to 200 isolated sounds, words, and phrases. In order to be understood, however, speech to these devices must be distinctly and slowly pronounced, for example: "print" (pause) "trans" (pause) "ac" (pause) "tion" (pause) "file." Such devices, which convert voice input into the digital codes acceptable to computers, are being employed in a limited number of applications involving small vocabularies.

Talking to the computer

Speaker-dependent systems are the most prevalent type of voice recognition module. The individual user repeats required words such as "run" or "print" to the system several times to create **templates**, the speech patterns against which the computer compares all subsequent voice commands. The computer can recognize these commands when spoken by other users if their pronunciations closely resemble those of the template maker. Most manufacturers of speaker-dependent systems claim an accuracy rate of better than 90% for their machines. In other words, the user's commands will be recognized at least nine times out of ten (unless his or her voice is distorted by a cold or sore throat).

The less common **speaker-independent systems** can theoretically recognize the words in their vocabularies no matter who says them. Such systems have an accuracy rate of 95%, due to the many built-in templates for each word. Their drawback, however, is their very small vocabularies—some are limited to "yes," "no," and the digits "zero" through "nine."

Currently, VRMs are used in voice-activated executive computer systems (for the executive who has everything), nonflight controls in sophisticated aircraft, automated inventory systems and assembly lines that require input from workers who are using their hands to move stock or build components, certain phone-answering machines that handle requests for information or service, and robots that carry out simple tasks for the physically disabled.

ISSUES IN TECHNOLOGY

It's debatable whether rolling a little plastic box around on a desktop is really more efficient than tapping two keys. Nevertheless, the mouse is currently highly acclaimed, particularly by its manufacturers. And VRMs will probably be the next candidate for unqualified praise as the ultimate input device. But computers function under the direction of clear and precise instructions, and spoken English is full of ambiguity and even illogic. How, for example, could a word processor that takes dictation deal with the problem of words that sound the same but are spelled differently, such as "blue" and "blew" or "to," "too," and "two"? Also, would it really be easier to say "move the cursor right to column 63 and down to line 17" than to press four keys? Consider the implications and the drawbacks of voice recognition technology. Where is it truly useful? Are some of its applications just cases of using the latest technology so as to seem "on the cutting edge"?

SUMMARY

Data Entry

All computer input consists of numbers, but it originates from various sources.

Hardware Checks on the Accuracy of Data Parity bits or redundancy codes are used to detect and correct data errors caused by hardware malfunctions.

Software Checks on the Accuracy of Data The accuracy of computer input is critical—garbage in, garbage out. Error detection is accomplished by checking for correct data types, reasonable data values, or consistency of data or by using control totals or check digits.

Input Methods

The three major approaches to data entry are batch input methods, source data input methods, and on-line input methods.

Batch Input Methods

With batch input methods, the data are collected in groups before being entered into the computer.

Punched Cards These perforated rectangles of stiff paper have either an 80-column or a 96-column format. Data entry using cards requires a keypunch machine, a card verifier, a card sorter, a card reader, and a computer.

Magnetic Tape   Used extensively for batch input and storage of data, magnetic tape is a long strip of plastic coated on one side with iron oxide. Data are recorded on the coating in the form of magnetic spots. Tapes come in three formats: reels, cartridges, and cassettes.

Key-to-tape devices record data entered at keyboards directly onto magnetic tape; they may be either single-station or multistation units (clustered devices). Batch input via magnetic tape involves a key-to-tape unit, an on-line magnetic tape drive, and a computer.

Magnetic Disks   Also used extensively for batch input and storage of data, magnetic disks are flat, circular platters coated on one or both sides with a magnetizable film. Data are recorded as magnetic spots. Disks are categorized as either hard or floppy (diskettes).

The floppy disk, or diskette, is a thin, circular sheet of flexible plastic coated with iron oxide and enclosed in a vinyl or cardboard envelope. The key-to-diskette unit is an independent system consisting of a keyboard, a view screen, and a floppy disk drive.

The hard disk is a rigid aluminum platter coated with a thin magnetizable film. It is either completely enclosed in a plastic case or permanently installed in a disk drive. The key-to-disk unit allows direct data entry onto hard disks.

Source Data Input Methods

Source data input methods attempt to reduce input errors by eliminating the human operator—data are input directly into the computer from the source. Source data input methods are applicable to both batch and on-line input of data.

Magnetic Ink Character Recognition   Magnetic ink characters consist of the ten decimal digits and four special characters printed with magnetizable ink. These can be read by MICR reader-sorter units, which are used extensively by banks to process checks.

Magnetic Strips   Magnetic strips are found on credit cards, bank cards, identification cards, and security badges. They hold confidential data for direct computer entry.

Optical Input   Optical input is the reading and direct entry of visible symbols not printed in special ink. Optical mark recognition is often used in scoring test forms. Optical character recognition techniques allow the machine reading of printed and carefully handwritten characters. The Universal Product Code, a bar code, encodes identification and price information on products found in supermarkets.

On-Line Input Methods

On-line input is processed by the computer immediately, without being held on some intermediate storage medium. On-line input methods are necessary for applications in which the input requires an immediate response or other action.

Terminal Input   The computer terminal is the most popular on-line input device. Full-sized terminals are categorized as local or remote, and as dumb, smart, or intelligent. Portable terminals are small, sometimes specialized, input devices.

Point-of-Sale Input   Specialized terminals, often incorporating optical input devices, are used in retail stores to input sales data to computers from check-out counters.

Graphic Input   Graphic input consists of data describing a picture or a place on a screen. It originates from a number of different devices, including digitizers, light pens, mice, trackballs, joysticks, and paddles.

Touch-Panel Input   Touch-panel screens allow users to enter data simply by touching the display.

Touch-Tone Input   Touch-tone devices employ telephone pushbuttons and lines to send data, in the form of sounds, to a central computer.

Voice Input   Voice recognition modules enable computers to accept a limited number of vocal commands from users. Voice input systems are either speaker-dependent or speaker-independent.

COMPUTER CONCEPTS

As an extra review of the chapter, try defining the following terms. If you have any trouble with any of them, refer to the page number listed.

parity bit 90
Hamming codes 91
control totals 92
check digit 92
batch input methods 92
source data input methods 93
on-line input methods 93
punched cards 93
Hollerith code 93
magnetic tape 95
tape reels 96
data density 96
tape cartridges 96
tape cassettes 96
key-to-tape devices 96
single-station unit 97
multistation units (clustered devices) 97
tape drives (tape transports, magnetic tape units) 97
leader 98
supply reel 98
read/write heads 98

take-up reel 98
sequential access medium 100
direct access medium 100
floppy disk (diskette) 100
microfloppies 100
key-to-diskette unit 100
hard disk 102
key-to-disk unit 103
magnetic ink character recognition (MICR) 104
MICR reader-sorter unit 104
magnetic strips 106
optical input 107
optical mark recognition (OMR) (mark sensing) 107
optical character recognition (OCR) 107
OCR-A 107
hand-held wand 107
Universal Product Code (UPC) 108
bar codes 108

fixed bar code readers 108
transaction 108
terminal 109
local terminals 109
remote terminals 110
dumb terminal 110
smart terminal 110
intelligent terminal 110
portable terminal 110
point-of-sale (POS) input 110
graphic input 110
digitizer (graphics tablet) 111
light pen 111
mouse 111
touch-panel screens 112
touch-tone devices 112
voice recognition modules (VRMs) 113
speaker-dependent systems 113
templates 113
speaker-independent systems 113

REVIEW QUESTIONS

1. List some of the sources of computer input.
2. How are parity bits used to detect data errors?
3. What are the two main types of input errors?
4. Name and describe five error-detecting techniques that can be used to minimize input errors.
5. What are the three categories of input methods?
6. What are the two most popular types of punched cards, and what coding scheme is used to record data on the more common type?
7. Describe the general process of using punched cards for computer input.
8. How are data stored on magnetic tape?
9. What are the three physical formats of magnetic tapes?
10. Outline the overall process of using magnetic tape for batch input.
11. What factors make magnetic tape superior to punched cards as an input medium?
12. How is the way in which data are accessed on magnetic disk different from the way they are accessed on magnetic tape?
13. Outline the overall process of using floppy disks for batch input.
14. What are some of the advantages of using floppy disks as an input medium?
15. List some general characteristics of key-to-disk systems.
16. Outline the overall process of using hard disks for batch input.
17. In what ways are hard disks better than floppy disks for batch input? In what ways are they worse?

18. What makes source data input methods attractive?
19. What is the major disadvantage of using magnetic ink character recognition as an input technique?
20. What are the three techniques for optical input?
21. How has the use of bar code input affected supermarkets?
22. What kinds of applications require the use of on-line input methods?
23. What is the most popular on-line input device?
24. Where are point-of-sale input methods put to use?
25. What function does the mouse serve in some microcomputer systems?
26. How does a touch panel simplify the input process for the user?
27. What is the major limitation of touch-tone input?
28. What are some current applications of voice recognition modules?

A SHARPER FOCUS

Now that you've completed this chapter, you should be able to answer the following questions about the chapter opening.

1. Besides the word-recognition problems mentioned in the chapter opening, what other input difficulties can you envision for talkwriters?
2. What memory capacity do you think would be adequate for an efficient talkwriter?
3. Based on what you've read in this chapter, what might be some advantages and disadvantages of this use of voice input?

PROJECTS

1. Throughout this chapter, we listed the advantages and disadvantages of the various input methods, highlighting their individual strengths and weaknesses and comparing each with other methods. Based on what you've read here and on your own experience and research, prepare a report on the advantages and disadvantages of on-line input devices, covering terminals, point-of-sale devices, graphic input devices, touch panels, touch-tone devices, and voice recognition modules (the Issues in Technology feature on page 114 should help you get started). What are the best—and worst—attributes of each device? Where is each best suited? How do they compare with one another?

2. Find out whether or not punched cards are used at your school or company. If they are, explore the reasons behind their continued use. If they're not used, see if you can identify any situations in which they might be as good as or better than the media currently being used.

5

Storage Devices and File Organization

▶

FOCUS ON ... CATALOGING A LIBRARY—
IT'S NO LONGER IN THE CARDS

The main card catalog at the Library of Congress—the rows and rows of massive wooden cabinets that hold 23 million well-thumbed index cards—is gradually becoming obsolete as the library moves toward automation.

Traditionalists worry that they are losing a cherished national institution, a place where scholars can make serendipitous discoveries among the cards and where more than a few romances have started from chance encounters.

Library officials, on the other hand, assert that the evolving computerized catalog is a physical necessity at the world's largest library, which has to add two million index cards each year. The general collection's card catalog, which dates back to 1800, occupies several rooms—about the size of half a city block—and has 22 trays of cards on Shakespeare alone.

Even with increasing automation, the old card catalog will not be abandoned for at least four more years, according to library spokesman Craig D'Ooge, mostly because the cards are being microfilmed. "And it's for certain that as long as there's a need for it, it will be accessible [to] scholars," he said. But it is obvious that the card catalog's days are numbered. In 1981, the catalog was "frozen" so that books obtained after January 2, 1981, were recorded only in the computerized files. And by the end of 1984, virtually all of the library's English-language books were cataloged in the automated system and available to researchers through 40 terminals in the library's reading rooms, according to John W. Kimball, head of the automation and reference collections section in the general reading rooms.

The automation has proceeded on two fronts. Since 1968, the library has cataloged new acquisitions in its machine-readable cataloging (Marc) computer system, and recently the library converted its 1979 list of 5.5 million books into computer format to cover pre-1968 items, in what is called the pre-Marc system.

Consequently, a researcher looking for English-language books on Shakespeare, for example, now could use a computer terminal to find at least 90% of the library's books on the subject, Kimball said. . . .

The library has about 71 million items now that could be cataloged. "We're talking now about having only cataloged about 7.5 million books in machine-readable form, so we've got a long way to go," Kimball said.

To handle the huge data base, he added, the library will replace its two IBM 3033 mainframes in the next few months "with whatever is equivalent to IBM's best computer now," because the data files simply require faster and more powerful processors. . . .

The automation projects will continue as the library undergoes a major renovation, to be completed by 1992. By January 1987, Kimball explained, the number of computer terminals will increase to between 75 and 100. The wood cabinets, with their elaborate and historic carvings, will survive as part of the high-tech catalog, Kimball said, by way of some artful carpentry work.

Computers perform more than 25 trillion calculations a day just in the United States. The federal government holds dozens of computer files on every individual, and the 1980 census gathered more than 5 billion facts about Americans. In business, medicine, education, finance—in practically any field—people constantly create new data for computers to analyze. But just as you can't remember everything you've read in books, magazines, and newspapers, no computer can hold in its primary memory all the data it will need to process in carrying out the variety of jobs it is asked to do. That's why computers need secondary storage.

There are a variety of media on which to store data. Once the data are stored, there are a number of methods for organizing them into useful, quickly accessible pieces of information. The choice of organizing method depends in large part on the storage medium being used. And the choice of a storage medium is based on a careful analysis of how quickly and how often the data need to be accessed, how frequently they will be changed, whether or not copies are necessary—in other words, how the data should be filed.

In this chapter, we'll take a look at the various media and devices used to store data—at the strengths and weaknesses of each and at the methods for organizing the data they hold.

THE NEED FOR SECONDARY STORAGE

In Chapter 3, we saw that in order to do any processing a computer must have both a program and the data called for by that program in its primary memory. **Secondary storage**, also called **auxiliary storage**, supplements primary memory by providing a place to keep programs and data when the computer isn't processing them. Secondary storage may be either **on-line** (physically connected to and controlled by the CPU) or **off-line** (must be manually connected to the computer to be accessed). Since accessing secondary storage usually involves some mechanical operation, such as threading tape, mounting disk packs, or waiting for tape to wind or for read/write heads to move, it is much slower than accessing primary memory, which involves no moving parts. Despite its access advantage, primary memory has several shortcomings that make secondary storage a necessity:

Why primary memory isn't enough

- *Primary memory has a limited capacity.* Even though technological advances produce a steady increase in the amount of primary memory that can be installed in computers, the upper limit is still far less than most users need for all of their programs and data. There's virtually no limit to the amount of secondary storage a system can have.

- *Primary memory is expensive.* Technological advances are also steadily reducing the cost of primary memory, but the cost of secondary storage remains lower.

- *Most primary memories are volatile.* When the power is shut off, the contents of most types of primary memory are lost. Because secondary storage is usually magnetic rather than electronic, its contents are not affected by power losses.

- *Primary memory is nonportable.* The contents of a computer's primary memory cannot be transferred to another computer or device unless a communications link exists. Many forms of secondary storage can be transported between machines.

 ## MAGNETIC TAPE STORAGE

In Chapter 4, we introduced magnetic tape as an input medium and described some of the devices used to write and read data on it. As a secondary storage medium, tape has been a vital element of mainframe computer systems for years. Today, magnetic tape storage remains an efficient, economical, and reliable method for keeping backup copies of large quantities of data. Whether the system is a word processor or a supercomputer, some type of magnetic tape unit can be incorporated in it as a valuable component. To see exactly how magnetic tape storage is utilized in computer systems, let's examine how data are represented and organized on tape.

Data Organization on Tape

How data are represented on tape

Data are represented on magnetic tape by tiny, invisible, magnetized spots. Once recorded, these magnetic spots persist until they're either erased or written over by new data. A spot magnetized in one direction represents a binary one, and a spot magnetized in the opposite direction, a zero. The tape has a gridlike organization of its surface, with short vertical columns called *frames* and long horizontal rows called *channels,* or *tracks.* The most common tapes have nine tracks, and data are encoded on them in EBCDIC (the 8-bit data representation code that we introduced in Chapter 3). One character is stored in a frame; there is one track for each of the eight EBCDIC bits and an extra track for the parity bit, which is used by the computer to see if an error has occurred in the storage, transmission, or copying of a character. As we mentioned in Chapter 4, tape is a sequential access medium, in which characters are stored one after another along the length of the tape. A decision to use magnetic tape for data storage must take into account the limitations imposed by its sequential nature. Figure 5.1 shows how data are represented on magnetic tape.

A sequential access medium

Unfortunately, it usually isn't possible to store characters one after another for the entire length of a tape. If it were, the tape's data density—expressed in **bytes per inch (bpi)** or **characters per inch (cpi)**—could be used to calculate its maximum capacity. Data density varies with the quality of the tape and the equipment used to read from and write on it. The usual data density is 1600 bpi, but some $\frac{1}{2}$-inch wide magnetic tape has a density of 6250 bpi. The maximum capacity of a $10\frac{1}{2}$-inch reel holding 2400 feet of such tape is 180 million characters, which would fill 2.25 million punched cards. That's 694 Social Security numbers per inch, or almost 20 million Social Security numbers per reel.

How data are grouped into records

Adjacent characters are usually arranged in consecutive groups called **fields**, each of which holds some particular data category. A social security number, for instance, could be stored in a field nine characters long. Fields are further grouped into **records**, each of which is a collection of adjacent fields treated as a unit. For example, a mailing list record could consist of three fields: a name, a Social Security number, and an address. Since they reflect the fact that there is some intrinsic relationship among their fields, these records are often called **logical records**.

Sometimes it's necessary for the logical records stored on a tape to be individually accessible, and because the starting and stopping of the tape motion by the tape drive require some leeway, a blank space, or **interrecord gap (IRG)**, must be left to separate adjacent records. If the records are short, these gaps (usually about $\frac{1}{2}$ inch long) can easily take up more space on the tape than the data do.

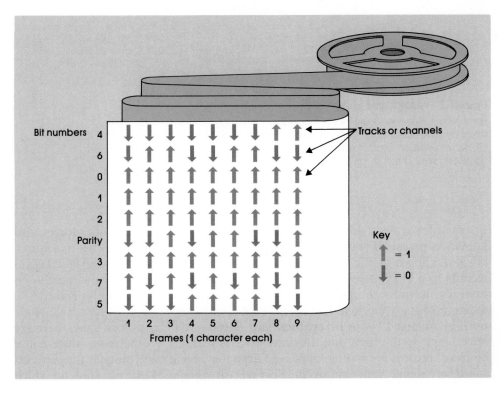

Figure 5.1 Data Representation on Tape

Data are stored on tape in the form of spots magnetized in one direction or the other. Here, arrows pointing up represent binary ones, and arrows pointing down represent zeros. Each vertical column, or frame, is made up of 9 bits and contains one 8-bit EBCDIC character and a parity bit. The 9 horizontal rows are called tracks, or channels.

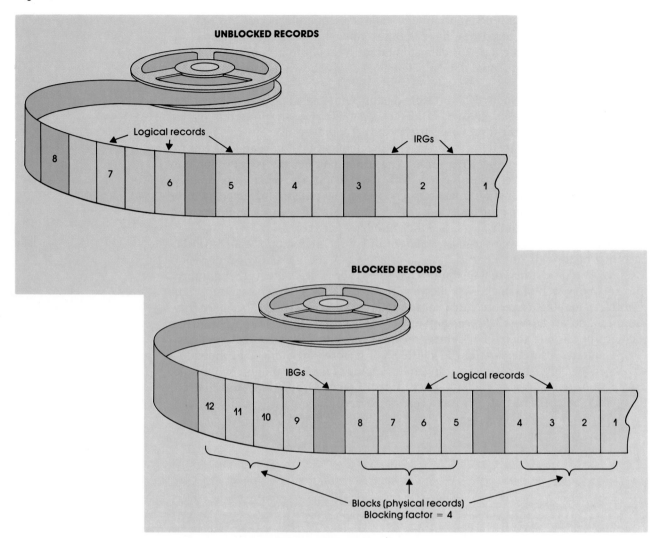

Figure 5.2   Records and Blocks
For logical records on tape to be individually accessible, they must be separated by interrecord gaps (IRGs). However, if records can be grouped into
blocks (physical records), then processing is faster and less tape is wasted
because fewer gaps, in this case called interblock gaps (IBGs), are needed.

In order to avoid this waste of tape, records are often grouped into **blocks**, also
known as **physical records**. The fixed number of logical records that make up a
block is known as the **blocking factor**. For example, if there are four logical
records to a block, the blocking factor is 4. The blocking factor must be chosen
carefully, in order to optimize overall processing. As you can see in Figure 5.2,
when records are blocked, interrecord gaps aren't necessary. However, each block
must be followed by an **interblock gap (IBG)**. With interblock gaps, there are
fewer gaps on the tape, and thus less space is wasted. Furthermore, since entire
blocks of records are written to or read from the tape at once, storage and retrieval
speeds are significantly improved. However, the programs that use tapes on which

records have been blocked are fairly complex since they must reserve enough primary memory to hold entire blocks and must perform the blocking and deblocking of records.

Advantages and Disadvantages of Magnetic Tape Storage

The use of magnetic tape as a storage medium has both advantages and disadvantages, all of which determine how it is best used. Its strengths include:

- *Magnetic tape is inexpensive, reusable, and easily handled.*
- *Magnetic tape has a high data density, can be read from and written on very quickly, and can hold records of different lengths.*
- *Magnetic tape is nonvolatile.* Magnetic tape is widely utilized for making off-line backup copies of important data just in case some unforeseeable erasure of on-line data occurs.

Best features of magnetic tape

The weaknesses of magnetic tape as a storage medium include the following:

- *Magnetic tape can only be accessed sequentially.* Tape isn't the best storage medium for data that must be accessed in an unpredictable sequence; thus it is not useful for such applications as the storage of airline or hotel reservation information that must be constantly accessible to any number of users. It is useful, however, for holding large quantities of data that will be accessed in order and only periodically, such as payroll, billing, and personnel files.
- *Magnetic tape is not human-readable.*
- *Magnetic tape is vulnerable to dust and extremes of temperature and humidity.*

MAGNETIC DISK STORAGE

The magnetic disk is the most popular on-line secondary storage medium for microcomputers, minicomputers, and mainframes. Superficially, disks look like phonograph records: they have the same shape and they rotate on a spindle in the disk drive. However, a phonograph record has a spiraling groove that starts at the outside edge and ends near the center, and a magnetic disk stores data in separate concentric rings, or *tracks,* of magnetic spots. Both types of magnetic disks we covered in Chapter 4 are used for storage of data.

Hard Disks

Hard disks are the major secondary storage medium for most mainframes and many minicomputers. Recent technological developments have made hard disks available for most microcomputers as well. These hard disks for microcomputers have already been widely adopted in science and business and are expected to become even more popular.

Storage for any computer system

Several different kinds and arrangements of hard disks are in common use today. Hard disks are either *fixed* (that is, permanently installed) or removable. A single side of one disk, both sides of one disk, or a group of as many as 12 disks may be used as a unit. A group of disks that can be mounted and removed as one unit is called a *disk pack*. One double-sided 5¼-inch hard disk can store 20 megabytes of data (that's 20 million bytes). Some large disk packs have capacities of hundreds of millions of bytes.

Floppy Disks

Floppy disks, also called diskettes, are presently the most prevalent secondary storage medium used with microcomputers. **Single-density diskettes** hold 3200 bits of data per inch, and **double-density diskettes** can accommodate 6400 bits per inch. In addition, floppy disks are either *single-sided* (data can be recorded on one side only), or *double-sided* (both sides can be used). As an example of floppy disk capacity, a 5¼-inch, double-sided, double-density floppy disk used with a typical personal computer can hold 362,496 bytes of data.

Disk Drives

The machines that record and retrieve data on magnetic disks are known as *disk drives*. Disk drives, like disks, are of different sizes and capacities. The operating principles, however, are generally similar for all disk drives, both hard and floppy. The differences are primarily ones of precision, speed, and capacity.

General Operating Principles

Inside the disk drive, each disk is spun on a spindle at speeds that may exceed 3600 rpm (about 150 mph). Read/write heads mounted on **access arms** move in and out across the surface of the disk (see Figure 5.3), creating and detecting magnetic fields on it. Read/write heads in floppy disk drives actually touch the disk surface, but those in hard disk drives do not. The combination of disk rotation and access arm movement allows a read/write head to be positioned over any spot on any track of a disk. The disk drive must have an access arm for each disk surface: if a disk pack containing four double-sided disks is to be used in a disk drive, the drive must have eight access arms.

The classic challenge for designers of disk drives is how to achieve higher data densities and faster storage and retrieval speeds. Two factors that directly affect the data density that can be achieved are the closeness of the read/write head to the disk surface and the precision of the access arm movements. Higher data densities are possible with closer heads and more precise arm movements because smaller magnetic spots can be used and tracks can be placed closer together (and thus more of them can be fit on a disk). Another factor influencing data density is the quality of the disk's magnetizable coating. Achieving faster storage and retrieval is mainly a matter of improving the speed of disk rotation.

Hard disk drives outperform floppy disk drives on all but one of these measures. Hard disk drives have more precise access arm movements, and their read/write heads are very close to the disk surface. Also, hard disks' coatings are of higher quality than are those of floppy disks. As a result, a disk pack containing 11 hard disks (a popular format) can hold 300 million characters, 2.5 million more than will fit on 11 floppy disks. Because hard disks are rigid, they can be spun faster than their flexible counterparts (centrifugal force would eventually bend and damage a floppy disk that was spun too rapidly).

Figure 5.3   The Disk Drive
The disk drive spins (a) a disk or (b) a group of disks (a disk pack) on a spindle at a very high speed. Access arms, one for each disk surface, position the read/write heads that create and detect the magnetic spots.

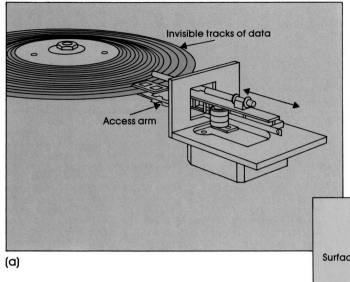

Invisible tracks of data

Access arm

(a)

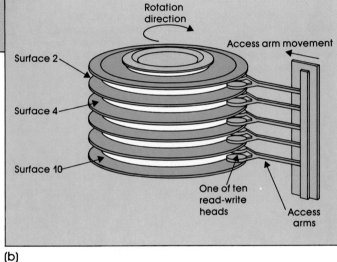

Rotation direction

Access arm movement

Surface 2

Surface 4

Surface 10

One of ten read-write heads

Access arms

(b)

Hard disk drives, however, are rather expensive. They must be carefully sealed because of the disks' sensitivity to contamination by dust, smoke, and fingerprints. If a hard disk drive's read/write head collides with one of these minute obstructions as it glides 20 millionths of an inch above a disk spinning at more than 100 mph, the resulting **head crash** can destroy the data, disk, and read/write head all at once (see Figure 5.4). Floppy disk drives are less susceptible to such mishaps, even

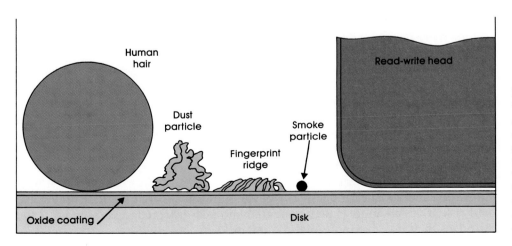

Human hair

Dust particle

Smoke particle

Fingerprint ridge

Read-write head

Oxide coating

Disk

Figure 5.4   Head Crash
This illustration depicts the extreme sensitivity of hard disks to contamination. That smoke particle, only 250 millionths of an inch in diameter, is about to collide with the read/write head, which is only 20 millionths of an inch above the surface of the disk.

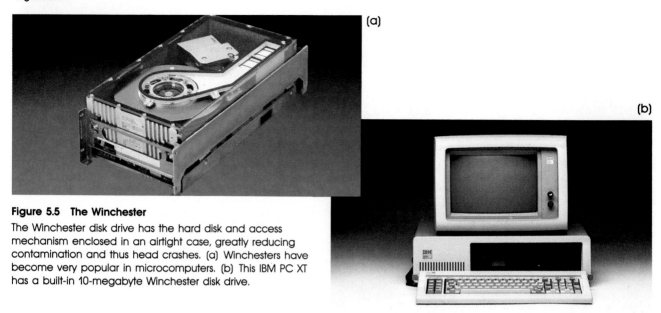

(a)

(b)

Figure 5.5   The Winchester
The Winchester disk drive has the hard disk and access
mechanism enclosed in an airtight case, greatly reducing
contamination and thus head crashes. (a) Winchesters have
become very popular in microcomputers. (b) This IBM PC XT
has a built-in 10-megabyte Winchester disk drive.

though the heads actually come into contact with the floppy disks. Floppy disks
can be damaged by contaminants, but their flexibility and slower rotation speeds
minimize the consequences of collisions. In general, floppy disk drives are much
cheaper and more rugged than hard disk drives.

The Winchester

The Winchester disk

In the early 1970s, in an effort to increase the storage capacity, access speed, relia- ◄
bility, and economy of hard disks, IBM developed the **Winchester disk drive.**
This device has the access arms and read/write heads as well as the hard disk or
disks completely enclosed in a sealed, airtight housing (see Figure 5.5). This virtually eliminated contamination from airborne particles and dramatically increased
both access speed and storage capacity (to 70 million bytes on four 8-inch disks).
The result was hard disk storage that was much more reliable and much less expensive than previously. Prior to 1980, the most common medium for high-speed disk
storage was large, removable disk packs. Since then, Winchester disk drives have
become more popular and have increased the power of affordable small computer
systems.

Recent technological advances have produced Winchester disk drives that
employ removable hard disk cartridges (Figure 5.6). This innovation has the hard
disk (and sometimes the read/write head) housed in a removable, airtight plastic
cartridge, which makes the hard disk safer to transport than a floppy disk. With
this type of disk drive, backup copies can be conveniently made: the data are
written to one disk, then another disk cartridge is inserted into the drive, and the
same data are written again to a second disk. Furthermore, the total amount of
storage capacity, already quite large with just one disk, can be expanded by simply
purchasing additional cartridges. The obvious drawbacks are that these removable
hard disk drives are more expensive than their fixed-disk predecessors and that the
cartridges they use cost more than floppy disks.

Figure 5.6 The Removable Hard Disk Cartridge
Recently, disk drives featuring removable hard disk cartridges have become fairly commonplace. The hard disk and the access mechanism are enclosed in an airtight housing.

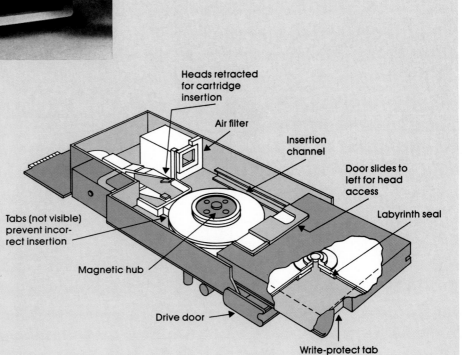

Heads retracted for cartridge insertion

Air filter

Insertion channel

Door slides to left for head access

Labyrinth seal

Tabs (not visible) prevent incorrect insertion

Magnetic hub

Drive door

Write-protect tab

Data Organization on Disk

Data are stored on disks as they are on tape, in the form of tiny magnetic spots that represent binary zeros and ones. An 8-bit representation code such as EBCDIC or ASCII is used to encode data on disks. Characters stored on disks are usually grouped into records—again, as they are on tape. But there the similarities end.

How data are arranged on disks

As we said earlier, data on a disk are arranged in concentric rings called tracks, which are numbered from 0 starting at the outer edge (see Figure 5.7). On one side of a disk, there may be as few as 35 tracks (on some floppies) or more than 800 (on some hard disks). Regardless of its circumference, every track on a particular disk holds the same number of characters. By moving the access arm in or out over the proper track and rotating the disk to the proper position, any record on a disk can be read or written. This is why the magnetic disk is a direct access medium. Any record on a disk can be accessed directly, as long as its position is known. The records on a disk can also be accessed sequentially, another way in which magnetic disks are similar to phonograph records. You can start a record album at the beginning and play all the songs on that side sequentially, or you can cue the tone arm and set the needle on the record in a specific place to play a particular song.

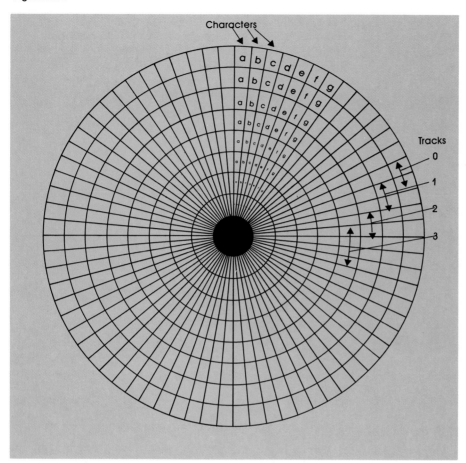

Figure 5.7 Disk Tracks
Data are recorded on disks in concentric rings called tracks, which are numbered starting with 0 at the outer edge. Each track, regardless of its circumference, holds the same number of characters.

The Sector Method

Sectors shaped like slices of pie

The **sector method** is the approach to data organization that is used on virtually all floppy disks. The disk surface is divided into shapes like slices of a pie, called *sectors*. A record on a disk organized by the sector method is located by its *address*. Such a record's address has three components: the *surface number* (if there is more than one surface), the *track number* on the surface, and the *sector number* within the track. Figure 5.8 shows how these three parts of an address identify the exact location of a record.

The Cylinder Method

Disks and cylinders

Another approach to the organization of data on disks, the **cylinder method**, is used only for disk packs. All of the disks in a pack are fixed to the same spindle, and for each surface there is a read/write head on an access arm. All of the access arms move in concert. Since the disks are stacked, each track on a surface lines up with the same track on all the other surfaces. Thus, all the tracks with the same number make up a *cylinder*; that is, each set of vertically aligned tracks forms one of a series of nested cylinders, as shown in Figure 5.9. A stack of disks has as many cylinders as the number of tracks on each individual disk; all the access arms are positioned at the same cylinder at any given time. The location of a record stored on a disk pack is specified by an address made up of the *cylinder number*, the *surface number*, and the *record number* within the cylinder.

Clearly, there is an advantage to using the cylinder method of data organization with disk packs. When the access arms are in position at the appropriate cylinder, they don't have to be moved again until all the data on that cylinder have been accessed. If the data to be accessed are on one cylinder, this shortens the **access time**, or how long it takes for data to be written on or read from the storage medium. In order to speed up the storage and retrieval of data, this time must be kept as short as possible. (Keep in mind that access time is measured in milliseconds and usually adds up to only 10–60 milliseconds for hard disks and 100 milliseconds or more for floppy disks.)

Disk access time

Access time for disks can be broken down into three segments that represent three separate events in the data storage and retrieval process. **Seek time**, the longest segment, is how long it takes for the access arm to position its read/write head over the proper track or, on disk packs organized by the cylinder method, to position the read/write heads at the proper cylinder. **Rotational delay** is the time it takes for the turning motion of the disk to bring the desired record under the read/write head once the access arm is in position. **Data transfer time**, generally the shortest of the three segments, is how long it takes for the data to be transmitted to or from the CPU.

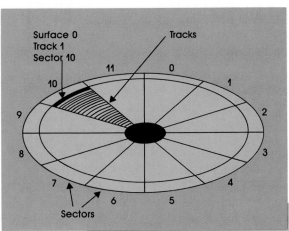

Figure 5.8   The Sector Method
The sector method subdivides the disk surface into areas shaped like wedges of a pie, which are called sectors. Accessing a given record requires the surface number, the track number, and the sector number.

Figure 5.9   The Cylinder Method
The cylinder method, used only with multiple disks, is based on the grouping of all tracks having the same number to form a cylinder. A stack of disks has as many cylinders as each disk has tracks. Accessing a record requires the cylinder number, the surface number, and the record number.

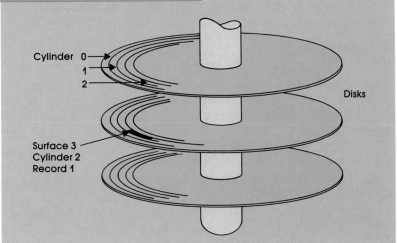

Advantages and Disadvantages of Magnetic Disk Storage

Magnetic disks also have advantages and disadvantages as a storage medium, which affect the ways in which they can be effectively used. The advantages of magnetic disk storage include:

Best features of magnetic disks

- *Magnetic disks can be accessed directly or sequentially.* This makes disks more flexible than magnetic tape.
- *Magnetic disks can be read from and written to very quickly.* The fastest hard disk drives can transfer more than 2 million characters per second to or from the CPU.
- *Magnetic disks have high data densities.* Magnetic disk storage, especially hard disk storage, is very compact. Hard disks can hold 750 characters per inch of track and may have 400 tracks per inch of diameter.
- *Magnetic disks are portable.* Removable hard disks and floppy disks can be taken off-line and are easily transported.

Disadvantages of magnetic disk storage include:

- *Magnetic disks are relatively expensive.* Although magnetic disks are becoming more and more economical, they still cost more than magnetic tape. The higher cost makes disks less suitable than tape for storing large quantities of periodically accessed off-line data.
- *Magnetic disks are easily damaged.* Fixed-disk units are fragile, and removable disks and floppy disks can be damaged by heat, dust, and magnetic fields.

These characteristics indicate that magnetic disks are applicable for general, on-line secondary storage. Magnetic disk storage is best suited to situations where data must be accessed directly and in no particular order.

OTHER TYPES OF SECONDARY STORAGE

Although magnetic tapes and disks are the most common, there are some other types of secondary storage you should know about. These are either being used currently or promise to become important in the near future.

Bulk Memory

An intermediary between primary memory and disks

The access time for magnetic disk storage is somewhere between that for primary memory and that for sequentially accessed magnetic tapes. On high-performance computers, the difference between the access time for primary memory and that for high-speed disks constitutes an opening for another type of storage called *bulk memory* (see Chapter 3), which can be accessed faster than disks but as much as ten times slower than primary memory. Bulk memory is often accessible only in blocks, rather than as individual bytes. The data transfer time between bulk memory and primary memory is about the same as that for accessing the fastest disks. The difference is that accessing bulk memory involves no seek time or rotational delay. Also, data transfers from most disk drives must start at a sector boundary, and there is no way to transfer only part of a sector to the CPU. When data are in bulk memory, any byte or group of bytes can be transferred into primary memory.

Bulk memory is sometimes configured as *cache memory*. In other words, when access to a particular disk sector is called for, the entire track or cylinder on which the sector resides is transferred into bulk memory as a cache (pronounced "kash" and meaning literally a container for safekeeping). If a program requires data from another sector that is among those just transferred, the request may be satisfied without having to go back to the disk. This eliminates most of the seek time and rotational delay associated with disk access.

Mass Storage

Mass storage is one of those computer terms that has had many meanings, but it currently refers to a particular class of secondary storage devices. Such devices hold enormous quantities of data, as much as hundreds of billions of bytes, but their access times may be measured in tens of seconds. Although this is very slow compared to magnetic disks, the large storage capacity makes up for the lack of speed. No disk system currently available has anywhere near that capacity of on-line storage, and the time required to find and insert the proper off-line disk could easily be several minutes. Thus mass storage devices are a welcome system component in organizations that must maintain on-line access to extremely large volumes of data.

Storing enormous archives

The classic example of a mass storage device is the IBM 3850 Mass Storage System (see Figure 5.10), which consists of a honeycomblike rack with 9440 cells. Each cell holds a cylindrical data cartridge that is 2 inches in diameter and 4 inches long. Each data cartridge houses a spool of tape; the tape is 770 inches long and can hold 50 million bytes of data. The total capacity of the system is thus 472 billion bytes of data, which makes it equivalent to about 50,000 reels of magnetic tape or about 218,000 books the size of this one. When data are requested, a mechanical arm moves to the proper cell and extracts the cartridge. The data on the tape within that cartridge are then transferred to a magnetic disk. This entire access process can take as long as 15 seconds. Mass storage devices are most useful for applications dealing with large quantities of data, where access time is not critical.

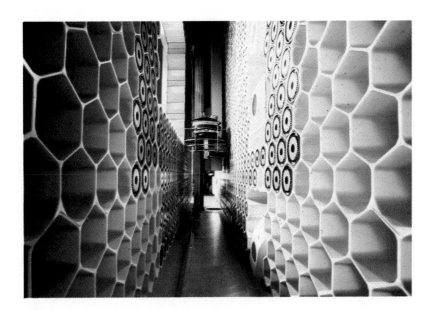

Figure 5.10 Mass Storage
The IBM 3850 Mass Storage System has a capacity of 472 billion characters.

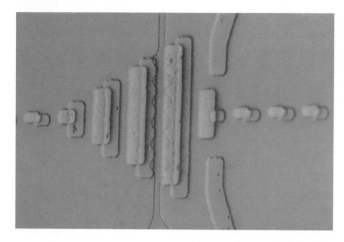

Figure 5.11   Magnetic Bubble Storage
In magnetic bubble storage, solid-state chips store thousands of tiny magnetic fields. This nonvolatile type of memory is used in some portable computers.

Magnetic Bubble Storage

Secondary storage without moving parts

Magnetic bubble storage utilizes thousands of tiny floating magnetized areas (the ''bubbles'') induced on chips of synthetic garnet (a hard, glasslike mineral), as shown in Figure 5.11. The presence of a bubble indicates a binary one, and its absence, a zero. The magnetic bubbles can be moved across the chip to be read, written, or erased. An important feature of this type of storage is that, like tapes and disks, it keeps its magnetic configuration even after the power is turned off. However, its biggest advantage, and the characteristic that differentiates it from magnetic tape and disk storage, is its solid-state nature. Magnetic bubble chips operate completely by electromagnetic forces, and thus magnetic bubble storage has no mechanical or moving parts. Because of this, magnetic bubble storage systems are potentially much more reliable than magnetic tape or disk storage systems, which typically have many moving parts. Magnetic bubble storage is used in a variety of portable computers, intelligent terminals, robots, and communications equipment.

Introduced and widely utilized in the late 1970s, magnetic bubble storage was heralded as the future replacement for magnetic disks. However, the relatively slow access speeds and the high cost of the chips, in conjunction with recent phenomenal advances in hard and floppy disk technology, makes this changeover seem much less likely today.

ROM Cartridges

Storage for permanent programs

In Chapter 3, we saw that a ROM (read-only memory) chip is a semiconductor component of primary memory whose contents are permanently fixed, usually during its manufacture. A **ROM cartridge** consists of one or more ROM chips mounted on a small printed circuit board inside a plastic case, with an edge connector at one end so the case can be plugged into a slot in a computer. Many inexpensive personal computers have one or more slots that can accept a ROM cartridge.

ROM cartridges aren't a very flexible storage medium, because the user can't add to their contents. They most often hold programs to be run. These programs are usually computer games, but more practical applications, such as word-processing programs, are also available as ROM cartridges. ROM cartridges have several advantages: access is very fast, and they are rugged, almost impossible to erase accidentally, and inexpensive. Also, the unauthorized copying of a ROM cartridge is very difficult—a clear advantage for software authors and manufacturers.

Optical Disks

Optical storage is promising as a means for storing massive amounts of data inexpensively. The **optical disk**, also known as the **laser disk**, is a circular platter covered with a thin metallic film beneath a layer of glass or plastic, as shown in Figure 5.12. Optical disks are very durable and reliable because the metallic film is protected by the glass or plastic and isn't as easily damaged by extremes of temperature or humidity, scratches, or dust. Compared to magnetic media, optical media are almost indestructible; they can easily last ten years or more.

Storing data using light

Optical disks are similar in principle to the laser-driven videodisks that have been commercially available for home use since 1979. To store data on an optical disk, a laser is used to either burn holes or raise blisters in the metallic film. The presence of a hole or blister represents a binary one, and the absence, a zero. Another, less powerful, laser is used to read the recorded disk by detecting the differing amounts of reflected light caused by the presence or absence of holes or blisters. The biggest advantage of optical disks is their high data densities: the holes can be made so tiny that 100 of them could fit into a space the diameter of an eyelash. Optical disks currently being marketed have capacities of from 1 to 4 gigabytes (recall from Chapter 3 that a gigabyte is 1 million kilobytes). Some research labs have reported achieving a data density of 1 gigabit per square centimeter. At this density, the contents of all the 18 million volumes in the Library of Congress could be recorded on just 100 optical disks!

Most currently available optical storage systems can only be used to read stored data and write new data; previously written data cannot be erased. However, much research is being directed toward the development of erasable optical disks, and at least one company has marketed a model. Such disks are made of plastic coated with special materials (known as *amorphous glasses*) that change state when hit by laser light. As a result, lasers can be used to write, read, and erase spots in

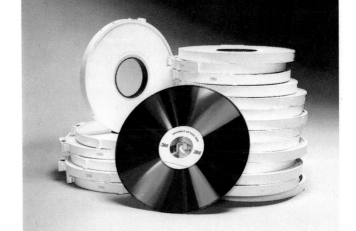

Figure 5.12 Optical Disk Storage
Optical disks are a possible answer to the need for inexpensive storage of huge quantities of data. An optical disk is a platter coated with metallic film that is covered with glass or plastic.

these materials. This general concept was hit upon by self-trained physicist Stanford Ovshinsky more than 15 years ago and has since been successfully incorporated into the Optical Document File System of the Japanese company Matsushita. The end-product of a $600-million-a-year research program at Matsushita, this system stores 10,000 documents on 8-inch optical disks that hold 700 megabytes each.

Despite the development of erasable optical disks, current applications of optical storage systems are mainly limited to the holding of large quantities of data that must be read but are not expected to change. For example, libraries and other archives can use optical disks to store more compactly much information that is now in paper form. NASA, the Air Force, and the Library of Congress have all instituted pilot programs to test the use of optical storage systems.

Optical Cards

Supercards

The **optical card** or **laser card**, as it is sometimes called, consists of a laser-encoded metallic strip on an inexpensive rectangle of plastic. This strip, which is written to and read from in much the same way as an optical disk is, holds as much as 2 megabytes of data and can store fairly complex programs. Optical cards are easy to handle and transport, and the data they hold can be loaded into a computer by means of a reading device that is simpler and less expensive than a floppy disk drive. Invented by Jerry Drexler, president of Drexler Technology Corporation, optical cards have the potential to be widely used as credit and bank cards, as portable medical histories, and as a low-cost, copy-protected medium for software distribution. Although not yet widely available, these cards are already being marketed by several companies for microcomputer applications. At least 13 companies, including Canon, Fujitsu, Honeywell, NCR, Toshiba, and Wang, have paid licensing fees to adapt and market Drexler's optical card technology.

 FILE ORGANIZATION

Fields, records, and files

All secondary storage media hold collections of data that need to be maintained outside a computer's primary memory. These collections, generically known as **files**, are characterized by their relative permanence and large size. They exist independently of the programs that create, modify, and use them. Files are necessary to hold data that will not fit into primary memory or that are to remain intact after the computer is shut off.

A file is a collection of records, and a record is subdivided into fields, which are meaningful groupings of characters. The characters in a field are adjacent, related, and treated as a single entity. In the following sections, we will look at three file organization methods: sequential, direct access, and indexed sequential.

Sequential Files

One record after another

A **sequential file** is organized so that one record follows another in some fixed succession, as shown in the example in Figure 5.13. To access a particular record, it is necessary to search through the file from the beginning until the desired item is

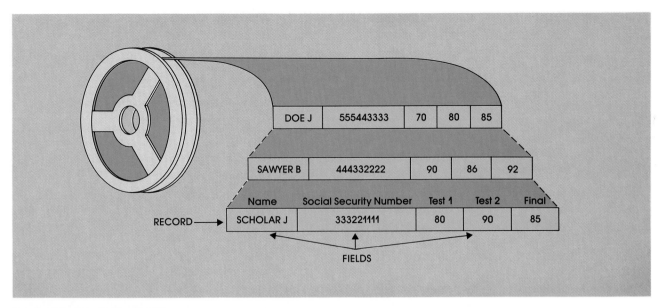

Figure 5.13 The Sequential File
This file of student grades is a sequential file. Note that the characters are grouped into fields and the fields into records, and that the records follow one another in a specific order in the file.

reached. Also, new records can be added only at the end. Keeping large sequential files *sorted*, that is, keeping them in a predictable ascending or descending order (like the names in a phone book, for example), is crucial to their efficient use and maintenance. To achieve this end, a particular field in each record is chosen as the **key**, or item on which the sorting will be based. If, for example, the name field is chosen as the key in the student grades file in Figure 5.13, the records can then be sorted in alphabetical order by name.

This sorting of files, while seemingly an obvious thing to do, is an extremely important aspect of data processing. Most computer resources are devoted to data processing, and most data processing consists of sorting, searching among, and combining files. Many business and organizational applications of computer hardware and software, such as inventory control, customer billing, and payroll accounting, are dependent on these processing operations. As a result, computer science professionals put a lot of time and effort into the development of efficient methods of sorting files, searching them for particular records, and *merging* them (combining them in order) with other already sorted files.

The importance of sorting

The maintenance of sequential files involves keeping them sorted in the proper order and keeping the records up to date. Additions, deletions, and changes to be made are known as *transactions* and are temporarily batched into **transaction files**. Transaction files are sorted, then merged at regularly scheduled intervals with the files to be updated, known as **master files**. Sequential files are often used for payroll, billing, and statement preparation, and for check processing by banks.

Some of the advantages of sequential files include the following:

- *Sequential files have a simple organizational principle.*
- *Sequential files have a range of applications.*

- *Sequential files are an efficient storage method if a large number of records are to be processed.*
- *Sequential files are inexpensive to use.* Magnetic tape is not a costly medium.

Some of their disadvantages are:

- *Sequential master files must be completely processed and new ones created every time records are updated.*
- *Sequential files must usually be kept sorted.*
- *Sequential files are hard to keep current.* The master file is up to date only immediately after the transaction file is merged in.
- *Sequential files cannot be accessed directly.* Individual records of a sequential file can only be accessed by checking the key in all preceding records of the file.

Direct Access Files

Records and their addresses

A **direct access file** (also called a **random access file**) consists of records stored on a direct access medium, such as a disk, according to some addressing scheme (see Figure 5.14). If the address of a record is known, that record can be accessed directly, without going through the records preceding it. The address, or *location*, is determined in some way from the record itself. Either the address is one field in the record or the address is obtained through some transformation of the record key—a method known as **hashing**, or **randomizing**. For example, using the Social Security numbers of bank customers as addresses at which to store their savings account records on a disk wouldn't work because Social Security numbers have nine digits, and the disk would have to have 1,000,000,000 locations to correspond to all the possible different Social Security numbers. There are no single disks with such a large capacity, and besides using such a long address would be a great waste of disk space. However, since every possible Social Security number isn't actually used, the nine-digit Social Security number could be reduced to four or five digits. Figure 5.15 describes one way this hashing might be done.

Direct access files should be used if a few records must be updated frequently. They are also useful for situations in which additions, deletions, and changes must be made immediately on the master file (such as an airline flight's seat availability

Figure 5.14 The Direct Access File

This savings account file is a direct access file. Each record is stored on the disk according to its address, obtained through some manipulation of the customer's Social Security number and stored as part of the record, the customer number. The records need not be sorted, and any one can be accessed without going through the preceding ones. If the disk locations are numbered sequentially from 0000 starting at side 0, track 0, sector 0, then the customer number can be used directly to access the disk.

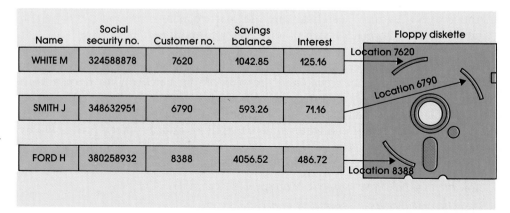

Name	Social security no.	Customer no.	Savings balance	Interest	Floppy diskette
WHITE M	324588878	7620	1042.85	125.16	Location 7620
SMITH J	348632951	6790	593.26	71.16	Location 6790
FORD H	380258932	8388	4056.52	486.72	Location 8388

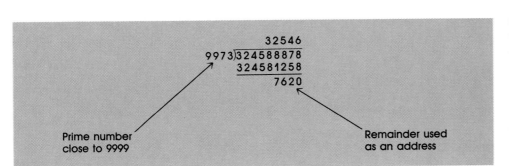

Figure 5.15 Hashing

Hashing is the transformation of a record key into a number that can be used as a storage address. For example, a nine-digit Social Security number is divided by a prime number (a number that is evenly divisible only by itself and 1) that is close in value to the largest desired result, and the remainder is used as the address.

list) or for situations in which transactions cannot be batched. Besides being used for bank account files (as shown in Figure 5.14), direct access files are used for factory production records and for processing travel, hotel, and car rental reservations.

Direct access files have several advantages:

- *Direct access files eliminate the need for separate transaction files.* Transactions are processed as soon as they occur.
- *Direct access files do not have to be kept sorted.*
- *More efficient processing is possible with direct access files.* Only the portion of the file that needs to be changed is processed.
- *Retrieval of data stored in direct access files is fast.* It takes essentially the same time to access any record in a file, no matter where it is.
- *Several direct access files can be updated at the same time.* Because transactions are processed as soon as they occur, without using separate transaction files, more than one file can be immediately updated from a single transaction.

Some of their disadvantages are:

- *Backup files may need to be kept.* Records are modified by being written over; thus the old data will disappear forever unless they have been copied.
- *Direct access files show greater potential for accidental data destruction and security breaches.*
- *Available storage space may be used less efficiently with direct access files than with sequential files.*
- *Complex hardware and software are needed to implement direct access files.*

Indexed Sequential Files

The **indexed sequential file** (Figure 5.16) combines the best features of the sequential file and the direct access file. Records are kept sorted so that transactions can be processed in batches, but an index is also used to speed up access when records are updated one at a time. An **index** is a table of selected record keys with their corresponding addresses that is stored on the same disk as the file. To locate a specific record, the index is first searched to get an idea of its approximate location. The sequential search for the desired record starts at an indexed record that precedes it slightly, rather than at the beginning of the whole file. Figure 5.16 illustrates the concept of the index.

The best of both methods

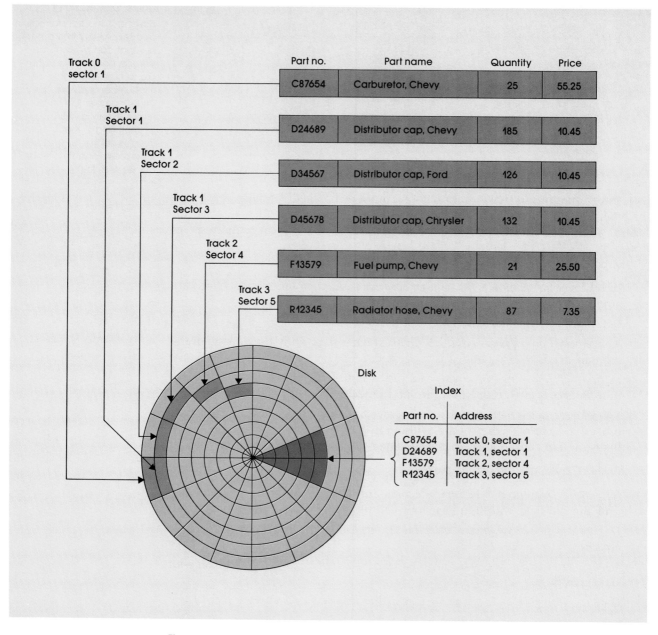

Figure 5.16 The Indexed Sequential File

This parts inventory file is an indexed sequential file. The index, stored on the same disk as the file, is a table of selected record keys and their addresses. The index is searched first, speeding up the retrieval of records. Indexed sequential files, however, must be kept sorted.

For example, to find the record for part number D34567, the index would be searched first to find the address of the closest preceding record. In this case, this record is that for part number D24689, found at track 1, sector 1. The disk is searched sequentially from there, one sector at a time, until the desired record for part number D34567 is found at track 1, sector 2. With indexed sequential files, a

CAREERS IN TECHNOLOGY
Data Librarian

Job Description The data librarian, generally employed in large hardware or software firms, supervises an organization's collection of tapes, disks, microfilm, microfiche, cards, printouts, documentation, reports, forms, and journals. He or she is responsible for maintaining backup copies of all software and for keeping magnetic media in good condition—that is, making sure the storage environment is clean and periodically checking for physical damage. Data librarians also perform conventional library tasks, such as checking out items to users, ensuring prompt returns, and establishing logical and efficient filing, storage, and cataloging routines. A program librarian deals only with programs and their supporting documentation. He or she keeps track of programming work in progress, incorporates revisions into existing documentation, and monitors who is working on a program and what is being done. This position is a bit more specialized than that of the data librarian.

Qualifications Some firms require that data librarians have only a high school diploma and some familiarity with data processing. Increasingly, however, companies want college graduates, although not necessarily ones with degrees in library or computer science, but simply with some exposure to data-processing concepts. Most firms are willing to train data librarians in the necessary technology; they look more for organizational skills and a general aptitude than for a strong computer-oriented background. The position of program librarian, however, usually calls for specific training in data processing and some knowledge of programming concepts and techniques.

Outlook The growth in job opportunities for data librarians is limited and will not be as dramatic in coming years as, for example, the growth in the number of programming jobs. This is simply because even the largest firms need only one or two data librarians. Even so, jobs will steadily become available as more firms find that accumulated material must be organized in order to be useful.

given record can be accessed more quickly than with purely sequential files because there is no need to examine every record on the disk preceding the desired one.

Indexed sequential files are useful if both batch and on-line updating of records will be necessary. Their applications therefore include inventory files that must be used by different departments (such as the one shown in Figure 5.16) and customer billing files that are also used for credit checks.

Indexed sequential files have certain advantages, for example:

- *Indexed sequential files are well suited to both batched and individual transactions.*
- *With indexed sequential files, access to any particular record is faster than with sequential files.*

Disadvantages of indexed sequential files include the following:

- *Access is not as rapid as with direct access files.*
- *Some extra storage space is required to hold the index.*
- *Complex hardware and software are required to implement indexed sequential files.*

However, if an organization has sufficient need for indexed sequential files, obtaining the means to employ them would be cost-effective.

SUMMARY ≡≡≡≡≡≡≡≡≡≡≡≡≡≡

The Need for Secondary Storage

Primary memory is limited in capacity, expensive, volatile, and nonportable. Therefore, secondary storage is necessary.

Magnetic Tape Storage

Magnetic tapes have proven to be an efficient, economical, and reliable storage medium for all computer systems.

Data Organization on Tape   Data on tape are represented as tiny magnetized spots. The tape's surface has a gridlike pattern of channels and tracks. Characters on tape are grouped in a sequential fashion into records, and records are usually grouped into blocks.

Advantages and Disadvantages of Magnetic Tape Storage   Magnetic tapes have high data densities and are reusable and transportable; and variable record lengths are possible. However, they are accessible only sequentially and are physically vulnerable.

Magnetic Disk Storage

The magnetic disk is the most important on-line secondary storage medium for all types of computer systems.

Hard Disks   Hard disks have very high data densities. Because they are rigid, they can be spun, and thus accessed, very quickly. They may be fixed, removable, or Winchester, or packaged in disk packs.

Floppy Disks   Floppy disks (diskettes) are the most prevalent secondary storage medium used with microcomputers.

Disk Drives   A disk drive is a device that reads and writes data on magnetic disks. Read/ write heads mounted on access arms can access any location on a disk surface. Hard disk drives surpass floppy disk drives in both access speed and precision.

The Winchester disk drive has the access mechanism and the hard disk completely enclosed in an airtight housing.

Data Organization on Disk   Data are recorded on disks in the form of tiny magnetic spots arranged in concentric tracks. Because of this arrangement, disks are a direct access storage medium.

With the sector method, each disk surface is divided into sectors resembling pie slices. The cylinder method, used with disk packs, has all tracks on the various disks arranged into cylinders.

Access time is how long it takes to store or retrieve a piece of data. It includes seek time, rotational delay, and data transfer time.

Advantages and Disadvantages of Magnetic Disk Storage   Magnetic disks can be used as a direct or sequential access medium, are very fast, have very high data densities, and can be transported. However, they are more expensive than tape and are physically vulnerable.

Other Types of Secondary Storage

Besides tapes and disks, other forms of secondary storage are becoming more common.

Bulk Memory   Bulk memory is a type of electronic storage used to speed up the transfer of data to primary memory.

Mass Storage   Mass storage devices hold enormous quantities of data but have relatively slow access speeds.

Magnetic Bubble Storage   Magnetic bubble storage employs solid-state chips to hold data in the form of tiny magnetized bubbles. It is used in a variety of specialized systems.

ROM Cartridges   ROM cartridges are plastic cases that house one or more ROM chips. They permanently store ready-made programs for microcomputers.

Optical Disks   Optical storage systems utilize lasers to create and detect tiny holes or blisters in metallic film. They have great potential, as they can store large volumes of data that can be accessed very quickly. However, most systems available today use nonerasable disks.

Optical Cards   Optical cards consist of a laser-encoded metallic strip on a plastic rectangle. They are likely to be used more and more for credit cards, medical histories, and software distribution.

File Organization

Files are collections of records stored on secondary storage media.

Sequential Files   Sequential files have their records organized in a fixed order. They must be kept sorted and cannot be accessed out of order. With sequential files, a master file is usually updated from transaction files.

Direct Access Files   The records in direct access files are stored according to their addresses, which are often determined by hashing. These records can be accessed in any order.

Indexed Sequential Files   Indexed sequential files share certain characteristics with both sequential files and direct access files. They employ an index to store the locations of selected records.

COMPUTER CONCEPTS

As an extra review of the chapter, try defining the following terms. If you have trouble with any of them, refer to the page number listed.

secondary storage
   (auxiliary storage) 121
on-line 122
off-line 122
bytes per inch (bpi) 123
characters per inch (cpi)
   123
fields 123
records 123
logical records 123
interrecord gap (IRG) 123
blocks (physical records)
   124
blocking factor 124
interblock gap (IBG) 124
single-density diskettes
   126

double-density diskettes
   126
access arms 126
head crash 127
Winchester disk drive 128
sector method 130
cylinder method 130
access time 131
seek time 131
rotational delay 131
data transfer time 131
mass storage 133
magnetic bubble storage
   134
ROM cartridge 134

optical disk (laser disk)
   135
optical card (laser card)
   136
files 136
sequential file 136
key 137
transaction files 137
master files 137
direct access file (random
   access file) 138
hashing (randomizing)
   138
indexed sequential file
   139
index 139

REVIEW QUESTIONS

1. Why is secondary storage necessary?
2. What are currently the two most important media for secondary storage?
3. How are data represented on magnetic tape?
4. How are data organized on magnetic tape?
5. What important characteristic of magnetic tape results from the way data are stored on tape and the way tape drives work?

6. Why is blank space left on magnetic tape to separate records?
7. Why are logical records grouped into blocks on magnetic tape?
8. What determines the choice of a blocking factor?
9. What types of applications are best suited to magnetic tape? Why?
10. What is the most popular on-line secondary storage medium?
11. How are magnetic disks similar to phonograph records? How are they different?
12. Describe how any spot on the surface of a magnetic disk can be accessed, in any order.
13. What are the two overriding concerns in the development of better disk drives?
14. Explain why hard disk drives surpass floppy disk drives in both access speed and precision.
15. Why are floppy disks less susceptible to head crashes than hard disks?
16. What prompted the development of the Winchester disk drive?
17. How are data represented on magnetic disks?
18. Explain, in terms of access time, why the cylinder method of data organization is used with disk packs.
19. Compare magnetic disk storage with magnetic tape storage. What are its advantages and disadvantages?
20. Why is bulk memory faster to access than magnetic disks?
21. What types of applications can best employ mass storage devices?
22. Why hasn't magnetic bubble storage been as widely used as was originally expected?
23. What is the major limitation of ROM cartridges?
24. What is the biggest advantage of optical storage systems?
25. Why must sequential files be kept sorted?
26. In what two ways are addresses determined for records in a direct access file?
27. How is a record accessed in an indexed sequential file?

A SHARPER FOCUS

Now that you've completed this chapter, you should be able to answer the following questions about the chapter opening.

1. How does the Library of Congress application exemplify both secondary storage and file organization?
2. Keeping users' needs in mind, which of the three file organization methods is best suited for the Library of Congress catalog files?
3. How does the computerized catalog system save time, expense, and effort?
4. Do you think that most library users will be content with being able to access a computer's storage, or will they resist this innovation and insist on their right to browse the bookshelves?

PROJECTS

1. To get a concrete example of how much information can be stored on magnetic media, figure out approximately how many bytes of information any well-known encyclopedia contains (remember that one character equals a byte). Then determine how many 5¼-inch floppy disks it would take to hold the contents of the entire set, assuming that each disk has a capacity of 360,000 bytes. What would be the best storage medium and method of file organization for this byte-sized version of the encyclopedia?
2. Suppose data are written on magnetic tape at a density of 1600 characters per inch, and records are 80 characters long. Between each pair of records is a blank space (the interrecord gap) that is ½ inch long. A tape reel holds 2400 feet of usable tape. What percentage of such a tape is blank? How many records can be written on it?

3. Find out what files are stored on magnetic tape at your school or company. What criteria are used to determine what files are put onto magnetic tape and when? Are tape files eventually disposed of, or do they just keep accumulating? What procedures would you suggest for managing the addition of tapes to the tape library and their eventual disposition?

4. Claims in magazine ads concerning the longevity of floppy disks are somewhat exaggerated. Research the actual life span of a typical floppy disk (perhaps in "number of read/write operations" or some other appropriate measure), and write a short report on your findings. You might want to interview several users or salespeople.

5. Find out which file organization method is used at your school for student records. Why was this method originally chosen? About how many times is a typical record accessed during a school year? Would one of the other organizational schemes offer any advantages?

6

Output

▶

FOCUS ON . . . HIGH-POWERED GRAPHICS

At Martin-Marietta Aerospace in Denver, Colorado, the software engineering team uses several Apple Computer [Macintosh] systems for a variety of graphics tasks. According to departmental staff engineer Jerry Simonson, the graphics systems have paid off in a number of ways. Staff drawing time is reduced, illustrations are finding their way into more documents and presentations for improved communications, and there's a substantial cost savings. While software engineers aren't involved in the drafting work of mechanical or electrical engineers, they do use block diagrams and flowcharts to visualize the programs they're working on.

"Before we got the [Macintosh] systems," Simonson says, "we used to send out diagrams to the art department or do them on a big CAD/CAM [computer-assisted design/computer-assisted manufacture] system. We allocate our costs for expensive equipment to individual departments," he says, "and with our $500,000 CAD/CAM system, we figured flow diagrams were costing about $200 a page to produce."

With several software engineers doing flow diagrams constantly, the costs added up quickly. The introduction of [the new systems] into the department quickly converted the engineers from the CAD/CAM system. With the [systems] and an Apple printer, flow diagrams can be produced at a fraction of the cost. Now that the . . . systems are available, some of the engineers haven't used the CAD/CAM system in months. Ease of use is an important feature that allows users of all levels to get up on the system quickly. "We had a new person," Simonson says, "and we showed him the . . . system on a Friday night. He came in and played with it on Saturday, and did 10 to 12 viewgraphs for a meeting on Tuesday."

In addition to block and flow diagrams that are photocopied for distribution or made into transparencies for overhead projection at meetings, the department also creates organizational charts and timelines. These documents are stored . . . and when changes are made, it's easy to recall the file and edit the chart. With the organizational charts, for example, individual boxes can simply be moved to new locations during a reorganization.

The power of graphics to make a point has been shown again and again in the department. "For example," Simonson says, "I was doing facilities planning for some of our software engineers. We wanted to partition everybody in their own space to give them more privacy. We were going back and forth with the facilities people about how big each space should be, and I finally sat down and drew the desk, table, and computer terminal in each module to scale so they could see how a 6' × 8' cubicle wasn't big enough. It was amazing how easily they could see the problem once I showed the graphic. Otherwise, I could have spent quite a few days or months arguing, and they probably would have gone ahead and committed to a smaller space."

What goes up eventually comes down, and what is input somehow becomes output. Output (computerese for "that which is put out") is whatever is produced when the computer does what it is instructed to do with the data it is given. Output isn't always words or numbers on paper. It can also be an image on a screen or a series of sounds. Output can be formed of light or ink or dancing bits of phosphorus. A government check, a business report, or a Space Invader—it's all output.

The information that computers produce augments the three basic management functions we all perform every day: planning, organizing, and controlling. Whether one is preparing a household food budget or the annual financial report for a multinational corporation, information is vital. If information is well ordered, we are organized; if it is detailed, we can make intelligent, thoughtful decisions; if it is easily interpreted, we can plan for the future. Computer output can be all of these things if the data and programs used to produce it are sound (don't forget GIGO).

In this chapter, we'll look at the physical aspects of computer output, of how the results of processing are presented to users. We'll examine and compare the various media, machines, and methods associated with this final product of data processing.

INFORMATION OUTPUT: AN OVERVIEW

As we said in Chapter 1, the major role of the computer is transforming raw input data into useful output information. In Chapters 3 through 5, we examined how data are input, processed, and stored. Now we turn our attention to the ways the data in the computer get back out to the users—in the form of information that is both understandable and usable.

A large number of specialized machines have been developed to convey the results of data processing to users. Before we examine them, however, let's consider some criteria for judging the usefulness or applicability of any output device.

Evaluating Output Devices

The factors that determine which particular output device is best for a given situation depend, of course, on the demands that will be made of it, the type of computer it will be connected to, and the type or format of output desired. These considerations can vary widely from user to user, but there are six basic qualities that must be considered when evaluating any output device:

Choosing the best device

1. *Speed.*   How fast can the device produce information? Speed is not an especially critical attribute of output devices for single-user microcomputers. It is, however, a major criterion for the high-volume output devices necessary for heavily used mainframe computer systems.

2. *Quality.*   Is the information presented clearly? How readable are the characters; how compelling are the graphics; how distinct is the voice? If the information that is output cannot be deciphered because of poor quality of presentation, it will be useless.

3. *Efficiency.*   How well does the device utilize the energy and materials it requires? Does it waste power, paper, ink, or film?

4. *Lifetime.*   How long will the device and its parts last? Will the mechanism wear out quickly and have to be replaced?

5. *Reliability.*   How often does the device require routine, scheduled maintenance? How often does it break down? Are customer support and service readily available from the manufacturer or retailer?

6. *Cost.*   How much does the device cost? The price of a piece of equipment depends to some extent on the other five factors.

Types of Output

Paper, microfilm and microfiche, display, and voice output

The storage media we discussed in Chapter 5 are *triple-purpose media;* that is, they can be used for output as well as for input and storage. In this sense, "output" means that the information stored on disks and tape is computer-generated and transferred from the computer onto exterior media. It is not human-readable, but it *is* output. For the purposes of this chapter, however, we'll focus our attention on output that is directly conveyed to the human user. Using that distinction, we'll discuss four major types of output media: paper output, microfilm and microfiche output, display output, and voice output.

 PAPER OUTPUT

The most popular permanent output medium

Paper is by far the most popular permanent medium for computer output. Also called *hard copy,* paper output is produced using many different kinds of paper and is presented in many ways. Text, tables, reports, graphs, charts, and drawings are some of the typical formats of paper output, as Figure 6.1 illustrates. Three major types of devices are used to produce paper output: printers, printing terminals, and plotters.

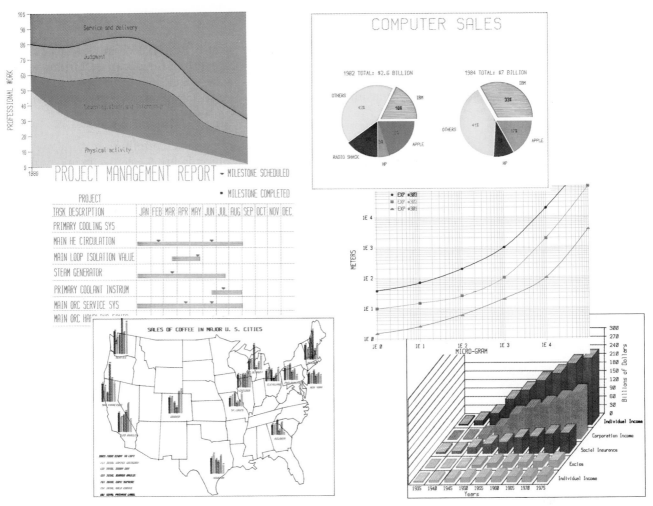

Figure 6.1   Paper Output
Paper output, or hard copy, may be presented as text, tables, reports, graphs, charts, or drawings.

Printers

A **printer** is a machine that outputs human-readable alphanumeric characters on paper. There is wide variation in the size, speed, cost, and operation of the devices classified as printers. For example, speeds range from 3 cps (characters per second) for character printers to more than 60,000 cps for the most advanced laser printers. Also, cost varies from less than $100 for the cheapest electrostatic printers to as much as $300,000 for laser printers with built-in minicomputers. Printers are usually categorized according to how much they print at one time and how they produce characters.

Devices that output characters on paper

Character Printers

Character printers (also called **serial printers**) print a single character at a time, one after another, across the paper from margin to margin. As you might guess, this is the slowest class of printer, with printing speeds ranging from 3 to 900 cps.

A character at a time

Character printers are used either where *letter-quality text* (like that produced on a good electric typewriter) is required or where slowness is acceptable (because the price is right). Consequently, character printers are often used in word-processing systems and in microcomputer systems. Character printers can be further subdivided according to printing method: daisy wheel and dot matrix printers use impact methods; and inkjet, thermal, and electrostatic printers employ nonimpact methods.

■ IMPACT METHODS **Impact methods** of character printing are similar to the working of typewriters, in the sense that an object is struck against an inked ribbon and the paper in order to produce an image of a character. Since they use physical pressure to produce output, impact printers can make simultaneous multiple copies with carbon or pressure-sensitive paper (nonimpact methods, discussed below, cannot). For this reason, impact printers are often chosen for applications that require extra or file copies.

Daisy wheel printers (Figure 6.2) have a printing mechanism with solid, raised characters embossed on the ends of arms that are arranged like the spokes of a wheel or the petals of a daisy. As the wheel spins, a tiny hammer strikes the back of the proper character as it passes. The impact of the hammer bends the spoke and forces the embossed character against the ribbon and paper. Daisy wheel printing

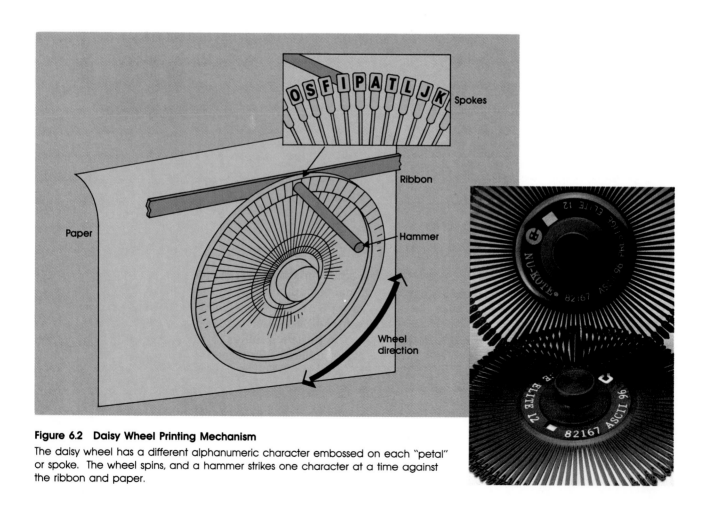

Figure 6.2 Daisy Wheel Printing Mechanism
The daisy wheel has a different alphanumeric character embossed on each "petal" or spoke. The wheel spins, and a hammer strikes one character at a time against the ribbon and paper.

is rather slow, not that much faster than typewriting, but the print is of a high quality.

Dot matrix printers are cheaper and faster than daisy wheel printers. The print quality, however, isn't nearly as good. The dot matrix *printhead* constructs the character images by means of a vertical column of from seven to nine pins that is struck repeatedly against the ribbon and paper. Electrical signals cause the appropriate pins to be pushed out to form the successive columns of dots that make up a character's image. Each column of the character is struck in its turn against the ribbon and the paper until the complete image has been formed (see Figure 6.3). Dot matrix printers are used primarily where speed is the most important consideration and where the aesthetic appeal of the output is less important.

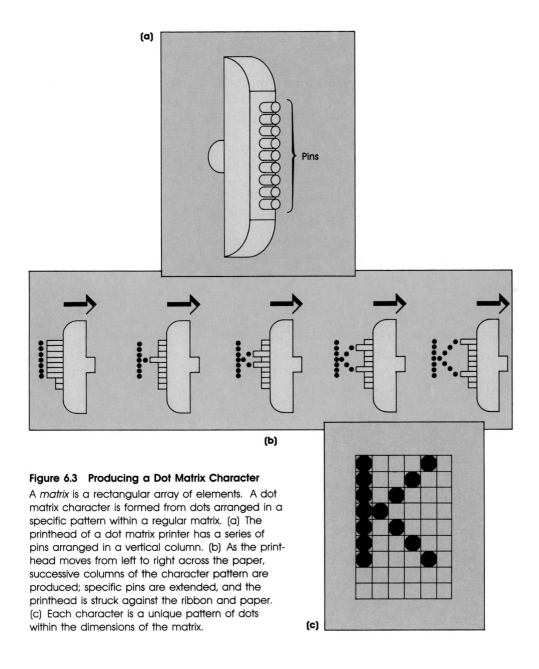

Figure 6.3 Producing a Dot Matrix Character

A *matrix* is a rectangular array of elements. A dot matrix character is formed from dots arranged in a specific pattern within a regular matrix. (a) The printhead of a dot matrix printer has a series of pins arranged in a vertical column. (b) As the printhead moves from left to right across the paper, successive columns of the character pattern are produced; specific pins are extended, and the printhead is struck against the ribbon and paper. (c) Each character is a unique pattern of dots within the dimensions of the matrix.

Figure 6.4 Inkjet Printing
This nonimpact method of printing produces characters using a stream of tiny ink droplets shot out of a nozzle and guided to their proper positions by electrically charged deflection plates.

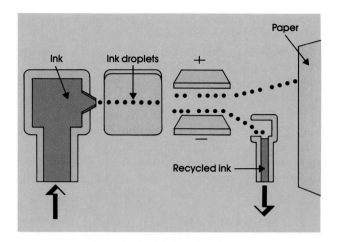

■ NONIMPACT METHODS **Nonimpact methods** of character printing employ inkjet, thermal, or electrostatic processes to form alphanumeric images on paper.

Inkjet printers have a mechanism that shoots tiny, electrically charged droplets of ink out of a nozzle; the droplets are guided to their proper positions by electrically charged deflection plates (see Figure 6.4). Ink that isn't used for a particular character is recirculated. Although inkjet printers are fast and quiet and produce high-quality print, they are more expensive than dot matrix and daisy wheel printers. Inkjet printing is well suited for offices where the noise of impact methods would be distracting and where speed and high-quality print are important.

Two types of printers produce output that is literally "hot off the presses." **Thermal printers** use heat to produce characters that resemble dot matrix ones on special heat-sensitive paper. The printing mechanism resembles that of a dot matrix printer, except that the pins produce the columns of dots by heating up *near* the paper instead of actually striking it. **Electrostatic printers**, on the other hand, use static electrical sparks to burn away aluminum from special aluminum-coated, black-backed paper. Thermal printers are the least expensive of the character printers, but they produce poor-quality output. Furthermore, the special papers they use are expensive, and the distinctive appearance of the output limits its applicability.

Figure 6.5 includes an example of some of the types of character printers we've described.

Line Printers

An entire line at a time

Line printers, which print an entire line at a time, are often part of larger mini-computer or mainframe systems. Since the print quality is usually not as good as that of typewriters, line printers are often used for producing output whose appearance is not important, such as internal reports, rough drafts, and hard copies of computer programs. Line printers print from 300 to 3000 lines per minute (generally by impact methods) and can be subdivided into wheel, drum, band, and chain printers.

■ WHEEL PRINTERS **Wheel printers** can print up to 150 lines a minute. The mechanism features a series of *print wheels*, one for each position in a line. Each

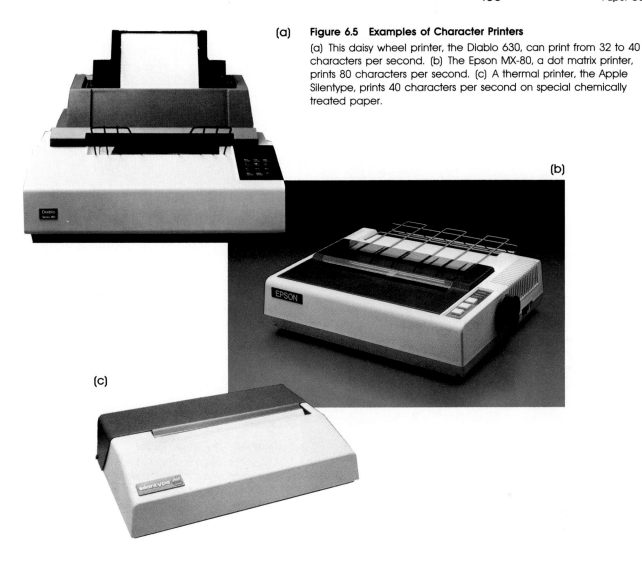

(a)   **Figure 6.5 Examples of Character Printers**
(a) This daisy wheel printer, the Diablo 630, can print from 32 to 40 characters per second. (b) The Epson MX-80, a dot matrix printer, prints 80 characters per second. (c) A thermal printer, the Apple Silentype, prints 40 characters per second on special chemically treated paper.

print wheel has 48 characters, including alphanumeric and special characters, embossed around its outside circumference. Each wheel rotates to align the appropriate character and position on the paper, and then a long hammer strikes from behind the paper, pressing the paper against the ribbon and the ribbon against the aligned wheels to produce a line of text [see Figure 6.6 (page 156)].

■ DRUM PRINTERS **Drum printers** are similar to wheel printers, except that instead of a series of print wheels, a drum printer has a solid metal cylinder embossed across its outside surface with rows of characters—as many as there are character positions in a line. It's as if the whole series of print wheels had been soldered together [see Figure 6.7 (page 156)]. Behind the paper, at each print position, is a small hammer. As the drum rotates at high speed, each hammer strikes the paper against the ribbon and drum as the appropriate character moves into position. For example, all the A's in the line are printed, then all the B's, and so on until all of the characters included on the drum have been rotated past the array of hammers. Thus a complete rotation of the drum is required to print each line. Although this might sound like a time-consuming process, drum printers work at rates as fast as 3000 lines per minute.

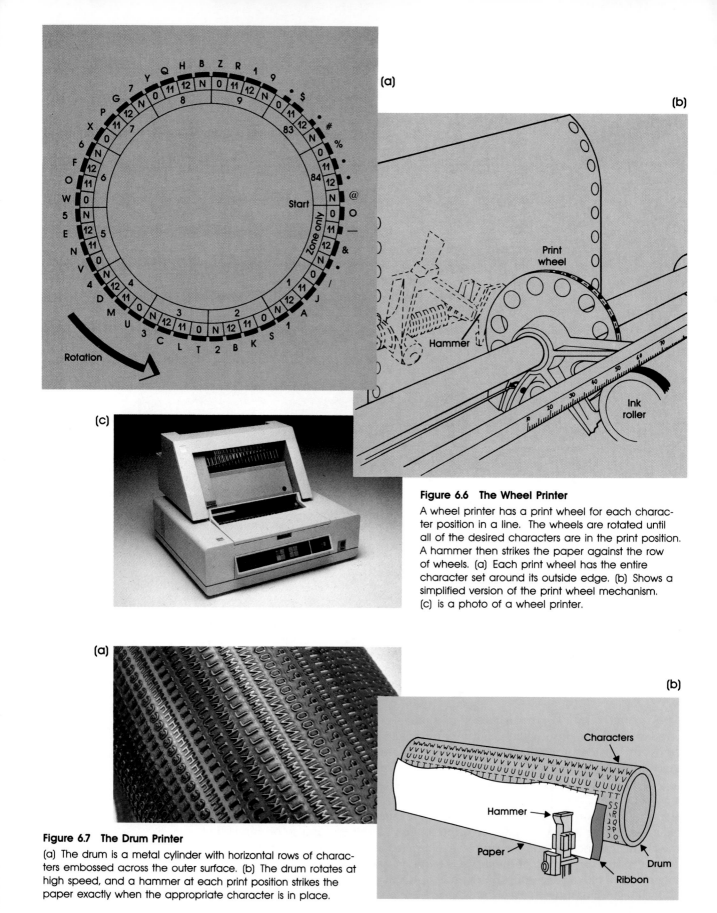

Figure 6.6 The Wheel Printer

A wheel printer has a print wheel for each character position in a line. The wheels are rotated until all of the desired characters are in the print position. A hammer then strikes the paper against the row of wheels. (a) Each print wheel has the entire character set around its outside edge. (b) Shows a simplified version of the print wheel mechanism. (c) is a photo of a wheel printer.

Figure 6.7 The Drum Printer

(a) The drum is a metal cylinder with horizontal rows of characters embossed across the outer surface. (b) The drum rotates at high speed, and a hammer at each print position strikes the paper exactly when the appropriate character is in place.

(a)

Figure 6.8   The Band Printer

(a) A band printer. (b) The printing mechanism of a band printer is a moving steel band on which characters are embossed. A hammer at each character position of the line strikes against the paper, ribbon, and band just as the proper character arrives at that position.

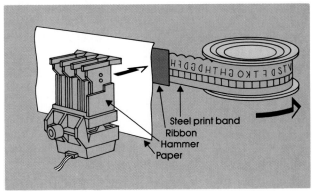

Steel print band
Ribbon
Hammer
Paper

(b)

■ BAND AND CHAIN PRINTERS   **Band printers** have a printing mechanism consisting of a scalloped steel band with five sections of 48 characters each and an array of hammers, one hammer for each position in the line. As the band moves at high speed, the hammers are timed to hit the paper and ribbon against the proper characters as they pass by (see Figure 6.8). Band printers can print as many as 3000 lines per minute.

Chain printers (see Figure 6.9) are similar to band printers, except that the characters are embossed on small pieces of metal joined as links in a looped chain. A chain printer operates just like a band printer and at the same speed.

Figure 6.9   The Chain Printer

Similar in operation to a band printer, a chain printer has a print chain, however, instead of an embossed band.

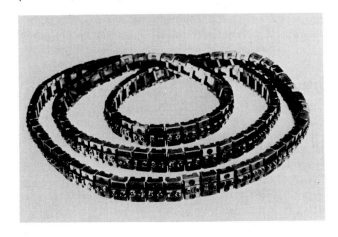

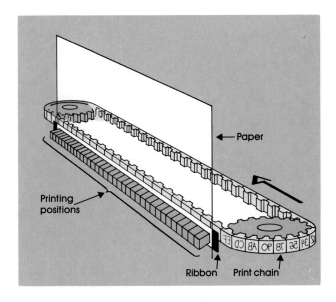

Paper

Printing positions

Ribbon   Print chain

Page Printers

An entire page at a time

Page printers, which print entire pages at a time, are the most sophisticated and expensive of the paper output devices. Their very high-speed, nonimpact printing methods are based on either xerographic (like a Xerox copy machine) or laser technology. Such printers are necessary equipment at installations where large volumes of paper output must be produced every day. The quality of the print produced by page printers is quite good, but their very high cost (as much as $300,000, or more) limits their use to organizations such as large law firms, central government agencies, and major publishers, which produce so much paper output that speed is a vital factor.

Xerographic printers utilize photocopier techniques enhanced by microprocessor technology to print up to 4000 lines per minute. Electrically charged paper is passed over photoconductive surfaces (*photoconductive* refers to material that becomes electrically charged when exposed to light) covered with a powdery ink. The charged images on the paper attract the dry ink to form an entire printed page at one time.

Laser printers represent the most advanced printing technology; they are generally faster than xerographic printers and have built-in microprocessors to control the printing process. Laser beams are reflected from spinning disks onto electrically charged paper. The reflected beams form electrostatic images on the paper, which is then passed through an ink solution containing oppositely charged particles. The ink adheres to the charged images on the paper, resulting in high-quality print. The most advanced laser printers are capable of producing more than 60,000 lines per minute. Recently, a new class of relatively inexpensive ($3500 to $10,000) laser printers has been developed for use with microcomputers. Compared to their more expensive counterparts, these smaller laser printers have slow output rates (about 530 lines per minute). However, even this comparatively lazy pace is much faster than that of the fastest character printers.

Printing Terminals

Terminals without screens

Printing terminals are specialized computer terminals that produce output on paper instead of displaying it on a screen. A printing terminal consists of a keyboard, a print mechanism, a paper-feed mechanism, and the necessary circuitry to link it with a computer. This output device is essentially a character printer with an attached keyboard. The print mechanism may be a daisy wheel, a dot matrix printhead, or a traditional typewriter mechanism (see Figure 6.10). In fact, some electric typewriters have optional interfaces that allow them to be used as printing terminals. Printing terminals are employed where output must be immediately produced as hard copy, and speed isn't an important consideration.

Plotters

Devices that produce graphics

Plotters are computer-controlled drawing machines used to produce paper output in the form of maps, graphs, charts, or illustrations.

Graphic output from plotters can be used to clarify complicated statistics or to make dry material more interesting. A recent study by the Wharton Business School found a 10% increase in persuasiveness for presentations that used graphics. Graphics can be very effective communicators; computer-generated graphics

Figure 6.10   The Printing Terminal
A printing terminal is a computer terminal that produces paper output, such as this DECWriter V, which has a dot matrix printing mechanism.

are particularly neat, clear, and professional-looking. Architects, artists, and sales departments also use computer-generated color graphics to clarify ideas. Outside the business world, computer-generated graphic output is relied on by seismologists studying earth tremors, by engineers performing stress tests on various materials, and even by obstetricians monitoring fetal heartbeat and the strength of contractions during delivery.

Inkjet plotters (such as that shown in Figure 6.11) produce images by spraying droplets of different-colored inks on paper rolled over a rotating drum. The computer to which the inkjet plotter is connected controls the movement of both the drum and the ink jets, which are mounted on a carriage above it. Inkjet plotters can produce complicated multicolored drawings quickly, quietly, and accurately. Consequently, they are often used for drawing large, detailed, and colorful maps.

Pen plotters produce images in a way similar to manual drawing—a pen or pens move across the paper's surface. Useful for graphing, charting, and diagramming, pen plotters are often used to present statistical data in graphic form. They are most often found in engineering and manufacturing applications (as will be discussed in Chapter 18), but many medical and research organizations employ them as well. There are two basic types of pen plotters: flatbed and drum.

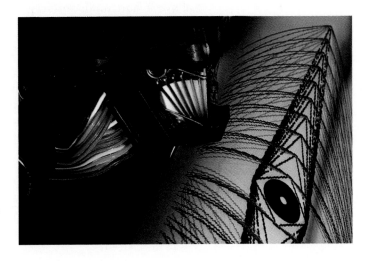

Figure 6.11   The Inkjet Plotter
An inkjet plotter produces pictures by spraying droplets of different-colored inks on paper wrapped tightly around a drum.

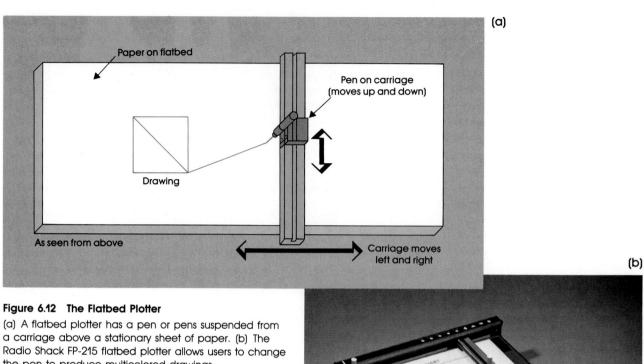

Figure 6.12 The Flatbed Plotter
(a) A flatbed plotter has a pen or pens suspended from a carriage above a stationary sheet of paper. (b) The Radio Shack FP-215 flatbed plotter allows users to change the pen to produce multicolored drawings.

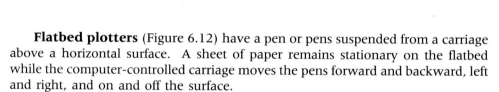

Flatbed plotters (Figure 6.12) have a pen or pens suspended from a carriage above a horizontal surface. A sheet of paper remains stationary on the flatbed while the computer-controlled carriage moves the pens forward and backward, left and right, and on and off the surface.

In **drum plotters**, a continuous sheet of paper rolls over a cylinder (the drum) beneath one or more pens (see Figure 6.13). The drum can move the paper forward and backward by rotating in either direction, while the pen or pens can move back and forth perpendicular to the paper's motion, and can also be retracted from the paper's surface. Both drum and pen movements are controlled by the computer; various combinations of movements yield a full range of lines, curves, and shapes.

One final note: pen plotters aren't limited to drawing on paper. Some flatbed plotters have light-emitting ''pens'' suspended over light-sensitive Mylar sheets. Such plotters produce images on the Mylar sheets, which are used as transparencies for overhead projectors. The high-precision technology used for two-dimensional control in pen plotters has also been applied in certain industrial processes (which

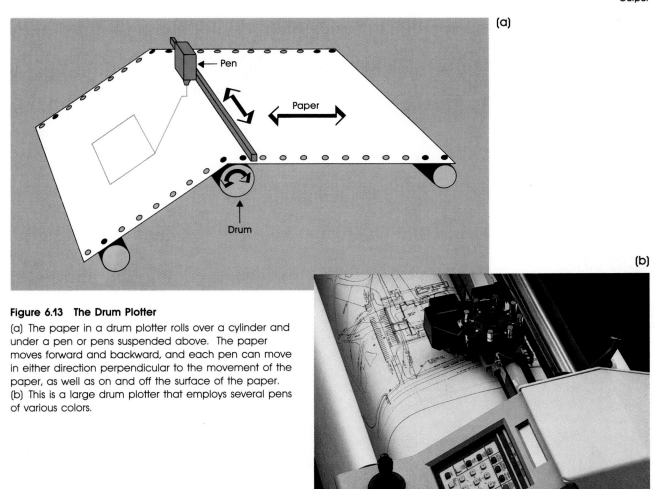

(a)

(b)

Figure 6.13 The Drum Plotter
(a) The paper in a drum plotter rolls over a cylinder and under a pen or pens suspended above. The paper moves forward and backward, and each pen can move in either direction perpendicular to the movement of the paper, as well as on and off the surface of the paper.
(b) This is a large drum plotter that employs several pens of various colors.

we'll discuss in Chapter 18) that employ devices very much like pen plotters as cutting tools. For example, a laser can be used to cut patterns from fabric in much the same way as a pen can be used to draw them.

MICROFILM AND MICROFICHE OUTPUT

Sometimes paper isn't the most desirable medium for output. In large quantities, it is heavy and bulky, taking up a lot of file cabinet or shelf space. It is rather expensive, and individual sheets are often defaced, lost, or destroyed. Fortunately, there is an alternative medium for situations in which these disadvantages are significant.

Computer-produced film output

Computer output microfilm (COM) is either rolls or sheets (called **microfiche**) of thin plastic film on which output text is reproduced photographically at greatly reduced size. Computer output **microfilm** is a much more sensible form than paper output for organizations that handle very large quantities of information. Banks, insurance companies, and public utilities can store their massive accounting, billing, and personnel records in a few small file drawers rather than warehouses. A single 4-by-6-inch sheet of microfiche weighs 1 ounce and holds as

Figure 6.14 Producing and Using Computer Output Microfilm

In the computer output microfilm process, data from either an on-line or off-line device are read into a microfilm recorder. The output text is displayed on a CRT, photographed a screenful at a time, and reduced. After the film is developed, it can be viewed at a viewing station and can also be printed from to produce a paper document.

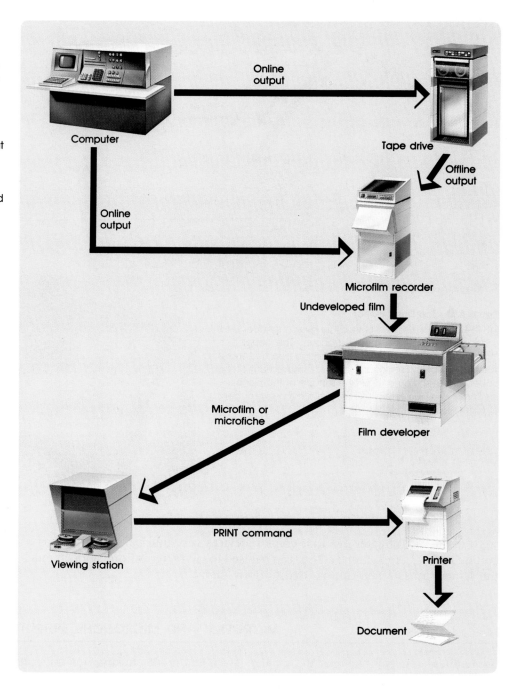

much information as about 10 pounds of computer paper. The information is more quickly accessible and relatively inexpensive to produce (at least for high-volume users): it costs about eight times as much to print a 1000-page report on paper as to output it on microfilm. Also, microfilm is more durable than paper.

Let's look at how computer output microfilm is produced (see Figure 6.14). The information to be output is transmitted from an on-line or off-line device and read into a *microfilm recorder,* where it is displayed sequentially on the screen of a cathode ray tube (CRT), which we'll describe more completely in the next section. A high-speed camera (loaded with 16-mm, 35-mm, or 105-mm photographic film) in the recorder snaps a picture of each full screen of displayed material, at recording speeds of up to 32,000 lines per minute. The photographic film is then developed, in either the microfilm recorder or a separate machine.

After being developed, the microfilm or microfiche can be viewed at a *viewing station,* which is basically a magnifying slide projector. Some COM systems require that the user search manually for the particular frame (screenful or page). Other, more sophisticated systems utilize *computer-assisted retrieval (CAR) techniques* to speed up the accessing of information. Each document is cataloged in an index along with its exact location on a roll or sheet. A small computer stores the index, presents it on request, and automatically retrieves the selected document so that it can be viewed. Whether the search is manual or automatic, it is important to note that users must have a special machine to read the output on microfilm or microfiche. However, most COM systems are connected to a printer so that selected pages can be output on paper.

DISPLAY OUTPUT

Computer display screens, which output text and other images, are by far the most widely used computer output devices. As with most equipment in the ever-changing world of computer hardware, there are many variations in the types and uses of display screens. As you know, a terminal is a unit that has a keyboard and a display screen. A unit consisting solely of a display screen is called a **monitor**. Display screens are either cathode ray tubes or flat panels. The display may be **monochrome** (of one color) or multicolored, alphanumeric or graphic. Sizes range from the 1-line, 12-character display screen of the smallest portable pocket computer to the full-page, 80-character-per-line, 66-line display screen of a word processor.

On-line screen output

The Cathode Ray Tube

The majority of computer display devices currently in use are built around the **cathode ray tube (CRT)**, in which a raster-scan technique produces images on a screen. A beam of electrons moves rapidly and steadily back and forth, from top to bottom, across the phosphor-coated backing of the display screen. The phosphor coating glows wherever it is hit by the beam. The computer controls precisely when the electron beam is on or off, thus causing images to be formed on the screen. This is essentially the same process used to produce television images; picture tubes in television sets are cathode ray tubes.

The traditional display screen

Monochrome CRT displays are produced when only one electron beam hits phosphor that glows in only one color. Multicolored displays contain triplets of phosphor dots that glow red, blue, or green when hit by one of three electron beams. Computer-controlled coordination of the three beams yields colored images.

CAREERS IN TECHNOLOGY
Computer Operator

Job Description Computer operators are responsible for the actual processing of data. They prepare the computer for operation by testing the equipment and loading the input and output units (for example, putting a disk pack in the disk drive and paper in the printer) and then run the programs. Also, while programs are running, operators don't just babysit the hardware; they must monitor the system for malfunctions and be able to diagnose, locate, and attempt to correct problems as they arise—whether due to mechanical failures or faulty programs. Computer operators are responsible for the stability of the computer's environment, which means seeing that proper conditions of temperature, ventilation, and humidity are maintained in the computer room (see Chapter 22). Finally, computer operators must be able to write clear and well-documented reports describing operations activities.

Qualifications Most organizations want job applicants to have a degree or certificate in data processing or computer operations, and many also require a familiarity with one or two programming languages (such as RPG, JCL, or COBOL), since operators should be able to read the programs they run. Some employers, however (the Federal Civil Service among them), require only a high school diploma and some specialized training or on-the-job experience in data processing. Prospective employees are almost invariably given logical reasoning and aptitude tests. Also, newly hired candidates must often undergo a probationary training period of several months before taking on the full responsibilities of the position.

Outlook In 1970, there were 117,222 computer and peripheral equipment operators, accounting for less than one-fifth of total computer industry employment. By 1984, that number rose to well over 500,000; it is projected to exceed 850,000 by 1990. More than 1 million people will be employed as computer operators by the end of this century. Out of every 10 openings, however, only 4 are filled by people who have had no hands-on experience with the equipment used by a particular company. But, college courses are the primary sources of experience in computer operations (along with vocational, military, and in-house training).

One word of caution, however, for would-be computer operators. The replacement of large, centralized systems by decentralized business-oriented personal computers may result in a relative decline in employment of operators by the data-processing service firms that are currently the largest source of such jobs. More and more of the new job openings will be in firms in other fields, such as marketing or manufacturing. Thus a broader job search and more field-related academic training will be necessary.

The Flat-Panel Screen

A portable display screen

The other type of computer display screen currently in use is the **flat-panel screen**. Although CRTs are still the dominant type of display screen, flat-panel screens are the focus of a great deal of current research and have already found a place in several specialized applications. Far less bulky than CRTs, flat panels are ideal for the popular pocket-, notebook-, and briefcase-sized portable computers (their major area of application), and have also been incorporated in a few types of terminals. Current flat-panel screens may be one of four general types: liquid crystal, electroluminescent, electrophoretic, and plasma.

Table 1. Outlook Summary: Employment in Computer Operations.

Job Title	Employment			% Change	Average Number of Annual Openings	Average Entry-Level Salary
	1970	1980	1990			
Computer Operator	117,222	522,000	850,000	+63	69,000	$16,000

Source: U.S. Bureau of Labor Statistics.

Figure 1 Outlook Summary: Employment in Computer Operations

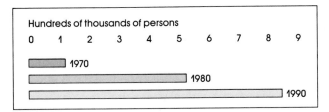

Table 2. Where the Jobs Are.

Industry	1978	1990	% Change
Agriculture, forestry, and fisheries	337	625	85.5
Mining	5,397	11,650	115.9
Construction	3,641	7,725	112.2
Manufacturing	103,093	215,000	108.5
Transportation, public utilities, and communications	26,057	52,300	100.7
Wholesale/retail trade	44,455	90,000	102.5
Finance, insurance, and real estate	69,026	147,500	113.7
Services	103,647	236,000	127.7
Government	37,340	89,200	138.9
Total, all industries	392,993	850,000	116.3

Source: U.S. Bureau of Labor Statistics.

The technology of the **liquid crystal display (LCD)** has been used in watches, calculators, and other small electronic devices for years. More recently, LCDs have been used in tiny television sets and many portable computers. These displays are made of a thin layer of a liquid crystalline material between two polarized sheets of glass, in which are embedded thin wires. The wires in one sheet run horizontally, and in the other vertically. When current passes through a wire in each sheet, the crystals at the intersection align themselves in a certain way, producing a dark dot. Unfortunately, since LCDs emit no light of their own, they must either be illuminated somehow or be viewed from a certain angle to be seen clearly. An LCD screen with a capacity of 24 lines of 80 characters each costs about

Figure 6.15 A Liquid Crystal Display
The Apple IIc portable computer uses a liquid crystal display (LCD) screen that can present 24 lines of 80 characters each.

four times as much as a comparable CRT. The advantage is, of course, that the LCD screen weighs less and is comparatively flat, being only 1 to 2 inches thick (see Figure 6.15).

An **electroluminescent display (ELD)** has an image composed of orange and yellow dots. A thin layer of zinc sulfide and manganese is sandwiched between glass panels; parallel wires running through one panel are perpendicular to those in the other. When current is passed through a wire in each panel, a glowing dot is produced in the sandwiched layer at the point where the wires cross. Although they are used in some portable computers, ELDs aren't as popular as LCDs, probably because of their considerably higher cost.

An **electrophoretic display (EPD)** is produced with electrically charged particles of pigment suspended in a fluid of a different color that is sandwiched between two glass panels containing an embedded network of wires. The particles of pigment are attracted to the glass surface when current passes through the wires, creating dots. Once these dots are formed, no further power is needed to maintain them. The screen "remembers" the image being displayed. The image is erased by reversing the electric field, which puts the pigment particles back in suspension. EPDs are still mostly experimental and are thus the least commercially available of the four types of flat-panel screens.

The **plasma display panel (PDP),** on the other hand, is a relatively new type of flat-panel screen that is already commercially viable. As in the other flat panels we've discussed, glass sheets criss-crossed with wires are used to sandwich some material, in this case, neon gas that glows orange at the points where current is flowing through intersecting wires. PDPs are currently used in mainframe computer terminal screens and some touch-sensitive screens.

Alphanumeric Displays

Displaying text

The most common format for computer display output is the **alphanumeric display**. It is usually produced on a monochrome CRT, but color CRTs and flat-panel screens are becoming more and more popular. The purpose of alphanumeric displays is to present various types of text, and most do so using both upper-case and lower-case letters and an assortment of punctuation marks and special characters.

Monochrome screen colors include green, blue, white, and amber. The brightness and contrast of the characters being displayed contribute more to the overall ease of reading than the screen color does: a dim amber display and a glaring blue one are equally likely to produce eyestrain (see Chapter 22). The most popular alphanumeric displays have 24 lines of 80 characters, but other sizes are available. For example, 66 lines of 80 characters (the equivalent of a full typewritten page) is the most appropriate display size for word-processing systems.

Most output devices that present alphanumeric displays have built-in features such as scrolling, paging, and highlighting. **Scrolling** is the ability to move lines of text up or down on the screen, as if they were on a large scroll that was being rolled and unrolled. **Paging** is the ability to call up entire screenfuls (pages) to be displayed. **Highlighting** consists of emphasizing particular sections of text via underlining, increased intensity, blinking, or *reverse video* (dark characters against a light background).

Graphic Displays

A **graphic display** is one that includes pictorial images as well as alphanumeric characters. Color CRTs are often used to produce vivid and intricate effects. Drawings, maps, charts, graphs, and even motion pictures (as we'll see in Chapter 20) can be output on display screens with graphic capabilities. Some graphic display devices can simulate the "rotation" of the image in space or movement past it, giving the user the option of viewing the image from any angle. With some systems, the user can give the computer a basic shape, pattern, or set of coordinates and then watch while a complex geometric design is traced out on the screen. Previously applied mainly in engineering and computer-aided design (discussed further in Chapter 18), graphic displays have become much more common in recent years, and are now an accepted tool in many businesses, homes, and educational institutions. For example, graphic displays are used in many computer-assisted instruction systems (discussed in Chapter 20). When used in combination with graphic input devices, graphic displays enable users to view the images they produce.

Displaying pictures

Many graphic displays are enhanced by screen control features such as windowing and viewporting. **Windowing** allows the user to select any section of the screen image and have it presented by itself, usually on a larger scale. **Viewporting** allows the user to have several different images displayed on the screen simultaneously. Windowing and viewporting, when used together, enable the user to examine different features of an image simultaneously. For example, an automobile designer can look at both the overall design of a prototype car and at close-ups of specific details on the same screen and can thus examine the effects of small design modifications on the car's overall aspects.

VOICE OUTPUT

Computer-generated voice output, like graphic displays, has been growing in popularity in recent years. Voice output capabilities are now incorporated into many general-purpose computer systems and are available as an option for most home computers (although additional interface hardware must be purchased).

Computer-generated speech

Voice output devices convert data into spoken words using either prerecorded speech samples or computer-synthesized sounds. The technology behind such devices is not that complicated, and so they are relatively inexpensive and widely applied. For example, voice output emanates from children's toys, automobile dashboards, cash registers, video games, telephones, vending machines, and greeting cards. A less trivial application of voice output is a reading machine for the blind that can scan printed text and pronounce the words aloud.

ISSUES IN TECHNOLOGY

Sophisticated graphic display technology can be used to create highly realistic images. During a recent manslaughter trial, a computer simulation of an automobile accident was presented to the jury on a graphic display screen. The prosecution, which produced the simulation, claimed that this method of presenting the circumstances of the accident gave the jury a better view of what actually happened than did verbal testimonies and reports. The defense, on the other hand, felt that the jury might forget that the stunning graphic images only simulated what might have actually happened. What are the pros and cons of using computer output in this way?

Text-to-speech converters break down words into their smallest distinct sounds, called phonemes. Stored inside these converters are the instructions that specify how all of the phonemes are pronounced. Because of this, text-to-speech converters have the ability to output a virtually unlimited vocabulary: if it can be spelled, it can be spoken. However, exceptions to pronunciation guidelines are not allowed for, and these devices do tend to speak in a rather stilted and choppy fashion. Despite these imperfections, computer-synthesized speech is easily understood by humans.

SUMMARY

Information Output: An Overview

The major role of the computer is transforming input data into output information. Output devices are the specialized machines that convey this information to users.

Evaluating Output Devices Factors that must be considered in the evaluation of an output device include speed, presentation quality, efficiency, lifetime, reliability, and cost.

Types of Output Storage media can be considered output media. Paper, microfilm and microfiche, display, and voice output are the major types of user-directed output.

Paper Output

Paper is by far the most popular permanent medium for computer output.

Printers A printer is a machine that outputs alphanumeric characters on paper. Character printers print one character at a time, by impact or nonimpact methods. Impact methods are used in daisy wheel and dot matrix printers. Nonimpact methods are used in inkjet, thermal, and electrostatic printers. Line printers print an entire line at a time and can be subdivided into wheel, drum, band, and chain printers. Page printers print an entire page at a time, by means of xerographic or laser technology.

Printing Terminals Printing terminals are specialized computer terminals that produce output on paper instead of displaying it on a screen.

Plotters   Plotters are computer-controlled drawing machines used to produce paper output such as maps, graphs, charts, and illustrations. Inkjet plotters produce images by spraying droplets of ink on paper rolled over a rotating drum. Pen plotters produce images by moving one or more pens across paper and can be classified as either flatbed or drum plotters.

Microfilm and Microfiche Output

Computer output microfilm (COM) is either rolls or sheets (microfiche) of thin plastic film on which text is reproduced at reduced size. Microfilm recorders are used to produce COM, which must be read at a viewing station. Sophisticated COM systems utilize computer-assisted retrieval (CAR) techniques to improve the speed of microfilm access.

Display Output

Computer display screens are by far the most widely used computer output devices.

The Cathode Ray Tube   The majority of computer display devices are built around cathode ray tubes (CRTs), which use a rapid scanning technique to produce images.

The Flat-Panel Screen   Many of the newest portable computers employ flat-panel screens. Four types have been developed: liquid crystal displays (LCDs), electroluminescent displays (ELDs), electrophoretic displays (EPDs), and plasma display panels (PDPs).

Alphanumeric Displays   The alphanumeric display, which presents various types of text, is the most common format for computer display output. Screen control features for alphanumeric displays include scrolling, paging, and highlighting.

Graphic Displays   Graphic displays present pictorial images as well as alphanumeric characters. Windowing and viewporting are screen control features that enhance some graphic displays.

Voice Output

Voice output devices convert data into spoken words using either prerecorded speech samples or computer-synthesized sounds.

COMPUTER CONCEPTS ▬▬▬▬▬▬

As an extra review of the chapter, try defining the following terms. If you have trouble with any of them, refer to the page number listed.

REVIEW QUESTIONS ≡≡≡≡≡≡

1. How can computer output help people in their daily activities?
2. What characteristics distinguish quality computer output?
3. What factors are used to evaluate the usefulness of a computer output device?
4. In what sense are storage media also output media?
5. What is the most popular medium for permanent computer output?
6. Describe the different types of character printers.
7. What types of applications are most suitable for character printers?
8. Describe the different types of line printers.
9. What types of applications are most suitable for line printers?
10. What types of applications are most suitable for page printers?
11. In what situations are printing terminals useful?
12. Describe two devices that adapt pen plotter techniques to other uses.
13. What advantages does computer output microfilm have over paper output?
14. What are the most widely used computer output devices?
15. In what types of devices are flat-panel screens used?
16. What is the purpose of alphanumeric displays?
17. Name several applications utilizing graphic displays.
18. Name several devices that use computer-generated voice output.

A SHARPER FOCUS ≡≡≡≡≡≡

Now that you've completed this chapter, you should be able to answer the following questions about the chapter opening.

1. How did Martin-Marietta's software engineering team use computer output?
2. How did the new Macintosh systems compare with Martin-Marietta's CAD/CAM system in terms of the six evaluation factors for output devices? Was there any question that the smaller systems represented an improvement?
3. Do you suppose the quality of the output produced by the Apple dot matrix printer was as good as that from the CAD/CAM system? Do you think it was good enough for its intended use?

PROJECTS ≡≡≡≡≡≡

1. Go to a computer store, and find out more about the output devices available for personal computers. Prepare a report on these devices, including information on models, manufacturers, features, and prices. If you were buying a personal computer today, what output devices would you select? Why?

2. In this chapter, we mentioned some of the particular applications most suited to the various types of output currently available. Pick out some specific types of computer users with which you're familiar, such as students, small and large retailers, research organizations, manufacturers, hospitals, libraries, police departments, and schools. Which types of output are most appropriate for each user's needs? Why would other types not be suitable?

3. One sign that a computer has been used to produce a piece of mail is when your name and address is inserted into the body of a printed letter or advertising message. Collect some computer-generated junk mail, your own and your friends . Try to identify the types of printers used, special features such as double-width letters and varied type fonts, and so on. Prepare a short report of your findings.

4. Page printers can print both the general elements of a form itself and the individual information it contains, thereby eliminating the necessity of preprinting blank forms. For example, when customers' statements or bills are printed, blank paper can be used, on which the itemized particulars are inserted automatically as the printer also reproduces a standard format, including a letterhead, the company's logo, and maybe even a drawing of the home office. Find out what typical preprinted forms and blank paper cost. Also, investigate the cost of the average page printer and of a comparable chain printer. Summarize your conclusions about the two ways of handling the output of forms.

5. Early dot matrix printers produced output that was quite obviously composed of dots. This is no longer the case; the output from many small dot matrix printers is almost indistinguishable from that produced by daisy wheel printers, even though the dot matrix printers still print dots in a matrix. Find out what accounts for this improvement.

7

Data Communications

▶

FOCUS ON . . . REAL ESTATE TO GO

The woman and her real estate agent were being chauffeured up Manhattan's swank Park Avenue in a repainted London taxi cab in search of a two-bedroom condominium with doorman, priced at around $700,000. But wait. Did she mention that she required a concierge? And that she really preferred a penthouse?

No problem. The broker reached for his cellular mobile phone and computer keyboard and listened for the high-pitched tone indicating that the mobile modem had connected to the central office computer. A few seconds later, several listings appeared on the 5-inch screen. The broker downloaded the details. The woman seemed particularly interested in one apartment in the East Sixties, so he flipped the switch from data to voice transmission and arranged a visit.

Breaking into the tightly knit world of Manhattan real estate brokerage isn't easy, but Clark Halstead has technology on his side. The managing partner in the Halstead Property Management Co. opened for business this fall with an IBM System 36 minicomputer and 14 terminals in his townhouse office. But his real edge may be parked out front. The cab is not only a rolling billboard—it is a way of shuttling clients around with the office computer virtually in tow. The cab is outfitted with an IBM Portable Computer, cellular telephone and 2400-baud modem.

From the backseat a broker can type in the apartment hunter's requirements. Calls are transmitted from a small antenna above the rear window. If an apartment description appeals to the client's fancy, the show, as they say, is already on the road.

To keep the backseat more spacious, the computer and modem are kept on foam padding in the trunk. Both are plugged into a 120-volt generator, which feeds off the car's electrical system. Only the keyboard, phone and monitor are inside with the passengers. . . .

Halstead had a little experience with computers. . . . He turned, however, to Barry Fagan, an outside programmer, to install the computer system—inside and out.

"Anything we can do in the office we can do in the car," asserts Fagan. Data is not lost in transmission even when the cab hits a pothole or when the data crosses from one cell into another, because each block of bytes is echoed back to the sender to check for a match.

Components of Data Communications Systems

Communications Hardware	*The equipment used to construct systems.*
Terminals	*Input/output devices at the ends of communications lines.*
Modems	*Devices that enable computers to send and receive data over telephone lines.*
Interface Units	*Devices that coordinate data transmission and reception: multiplexers, concentrators, message switchers, and front-end processors.*
Computers	*Machines that process the data.*
Communications Software	*The programs used to control data flow through systems.*
Communications Channels	*Pathways for data.*
Physical Structure	*What channels are made of: wire cables, microwave systems, and fiber optic cables.*
Transmission Speed	*How much data can be sent at a time: narrowband, voiceband, and broadband channels.*
Transmission Direction	*Allowed direction of data transmission: simplex, half-duplex, and full-duplex channels.*
Transmission Mode	*How data are sent over channels: asynchronous and synchronous transmission.*
Line Configuration	*How channels connect terminals to computers: point-to-point and multidrop lines.*
Leased Versus Switched Lines	*Weighing factors of access and cost.*
Protocols	*Rules and procedures governing data communications.*
Common Carriers	*Companies licensed to transmit data.*
Distributed Data-Processing Networks	*Decentralized processing of data.*
Network Configurations	*Basic designs of DDP networks: star, ring, and hierarchical networks.*
Advantages and Disadvantages of Distributed Data-Processing Networks	*Benefits and drawbacks of DDP networks.*
Local Area Networks	*Connecting nearby computers.*

Computers were first linked across distances in 1940, when Dr. George Stibbitz sent data over telegraph lines from Dartmouth College in New Hampshire to a Bell Laboratories calculating machine in New York City. That event marked the birth of **data communications**, the sending of data between geographically separated computers.

Since 1940 advances in computer and communications technology have resulted in vast communications networks and a worldwide explosion of data communications. Data are sent over telephone lines, bounced off satellites, and carried through the air by microwaves. Any business or home with a computer (and there are more than 20 million computers in the United States) and a telephone has easy access to a multitude of data communications services ranging from electronic mail and stock reports to retail catalogs and games. You name it, and you can probably subscribe to a network that offers it. Data communications is an $80-billion-a-year industry and clearly here to stay.

In this chapter, we'll look at the physical aspects of data communications—how (and why) networks are set up and what hardware and software resources are involved—and at some of its most significant applications.

 ## APPLICATIONS OF DATA COMMUNICATIONS

Applications of the principles and technology of data communications are rapidly transforming society. Let's look at some of the many ways data communications is being used today.

Information Services and Videotex

Networking of home computers

Information services offer interactive networking to users who have an inexpensive terminal or a personal computer. These services are easy to use and can be accessed with most types of microcomputers. Customers can choose from a multitude of services including:

> information retrieval (news, weather, home education, financial data, sports, etc.);
>
> electronic mail (which we'll discuss in the next section);
>
> computing (computer languages, application packages, computer games);
>
> telemonitoring (home security systems);
>
> home shopping and banking; and
>
> travel, theater, restaurant, and sports reservations.

The two largest information services in the United States are The Source and CompuServe (see Figure 7.1). The Source, now owned by Reader's Digest, was the first information service in the United States. News, financial data, games, electronic mail, and other options are available nationwide to home computer users who subscribe to The Source. CompuServe, owned by H&R Block, offers news, games, want ads, travel reservations, and financial data, among other services.

Videotex (or **viewdata**) is a general term describing interactive information services that rely heavily on color displays and graphics. Regular information services like The Source and CompuServe can only transmit and receive plain, monochrome text. Although they offer similar services, videotex systems employ color graphics to make the format in which the information is presented more flexible and interesting. Consequently, many videotex services require their customers to purchase or lease special terminals capable of displaying color graphics. This extra cost is justified for many users, who appreciate such enhancements as multicolored bar graphs presenting the Wall Street picture at a glance or color-coded seating plans for choosing tickets to theater performances or sports events.

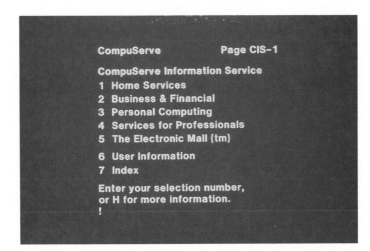

Figure 7.1 Information Services
A wide variety of options is available to home computer users who subscribe to one of the large information services such as CompuServe or The Source.

In the United States, general-interest videotex services are currently available only in selected regions. For example, Viewtron, run by Viewdata Corporation, serves southern Florida; Gateway, owned by Times-Mirror, operates in Orange County, California; and Keyfax, a joint venture of Honeywell, Centel Corporation, and Field Enterprises, is available only in the Chicago area. However, IBM, CBS, and Sears Roebuck have announced a joint, long-term project to set up a national videotex system, as have RCA, J. C. Penney, and Citicorp.

Electronic Mail and Bulletin Boards

Electronic mail is a data communications service that employs computers and telecommunications lines to store and send messages that would otherwise take the form of a memo, telephone call, or letter. Such services are offered independently as well as being an option of some videotex systems. In fact, electronic mail is one of the "hot" new business services. Nearly a third of all U.S. businesses use some form of electronic mail, paying nearly $2 billion annually for the services. Electronic transmission of business messages accounts for more than 20% of all business mail in the United States. (In Chapter 17, we'll look more closely at electronic mail in the context of interoffice communications.)

Messages sent via computer

Similar communications services, known as **electronic bulletin boards**, have become quite popular among home computer users and hobbyists. These systems provide a means for their users to exchange messages, programming tips, advice, comments, and software. To access an electronic bulletin board, all one needs is a microcomputer (almost any kind), a modestly priced communications device known as a modem (which we'll discuss later in this chapter), and a telephone. Such systems generally consist of a central personal computer that is equipped to answer the telephone automatically and to allow callers to link up their own computers. Once communication has been established between two computers, callers can "post" messages or read messages left for them by other users. Costing as little as $500 for a complete system (personal computer, modem, software, and phone), electronic bulletin boards have proven to be an entertaining and educational way for computer enthusiasts to "get together" and trade notes. There are hundreds of them across North America, operated by all kinds of groups.

ISSUES IN TECHNOLOGY

The use of electronic mail is expected to continue to grow in both office and home environments. What consequences might this have for traditional postal and telephone services? What possible problems might arise from an increased dependence on electronic message systems?

Electronic Funds Transfer

Money moved via computer

Electronic funds transfer (EFT) is the electronic movement of money into, out of, and between bank accounts. EFT systems are a very important application of data communications. In 1985, nearly a quarter of all financial transactions in the United States were handled electronically. (Chapter 19 examines EFT as a major use of computer systems in business.) One of the most obvious signs of the growth of EFT has been the proliferation of the **automated teller machine (ATM)**. Operating 24 hours a day, ATMs are programmed to perform many of the functions of human tellers—to dispense cash, receive deposits, and report account balances. To use an ATM, a bank customer must have a specially coded plastic card and a personal identification number that maintains security and privacy.

Computer Conferencing

Conferring via computer

Data communications can be applied in ways that eliminate the need for a certain amount of travel. The result can be significant savings in travel costs and time. **Computer conferencing** involves the use of a link joining distant computers and terminals so that users can exchange information or messages directly and immediately, in effect, to have a meeting. As we will see in Chapter 17, computer conferencing is a convenient, economical alternative to business travel.

Telecommuting

Working at home using a computer

Enormous amounts of energy and time are spent every day by people commuting to work. Almost two-thirds of the employees and the vast majority of the commuters in the United States are white collar workers. The combination of microcomputers, data communications networks, and computer conferencing techniques makes **telecommuting**, or working at home using a computer, a feasible alternative to traditional work patterns. Companies such as Control Data Corporation, Walgreen, McDonald's, and Mountain States Telephone & Telegraph have limited telecommuting projects allowing professional, managerial, and clerical employees to work at home.

COMPONENTS OF DATA COMMUNICATIONS SYSTEMS

We've seen that various data communications systems have become an essential facet of modern life. Of what elements are such systems composed? Although their complexity and configuration vary widely, systems such as the one illustrated in Figure 7.2 basically involve some arrangement of the following components:

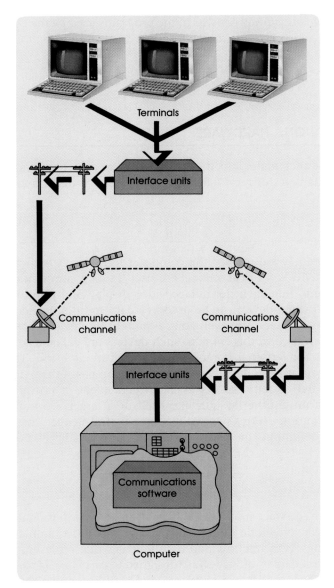

Figure 7.2   Components of a Typical Data Communications System

The principal components of a typical data communications system are terminals, interface units, some communications channels, at least one computer, and communications software.

- *Video display terminals* and *printing terminals* are both widely utilized in data communications systems, as are other input/output devices.

- *Interface units* are the hardware components that enable data to be transmitted over communications lines. They include such devices as modems and data communications interface units.

- *Communications channels* (also called data links or communications lines) are the means by which data are sent to and from a computer. They include telegraph and telephone lines, various types of cables, and microwave and satellite systems.

- *Computers,* ranging from microcomputers to supercomputers, are an essential element of data communications systems. A system may have one large central computer, a number of small scattered computers, or both.

• *Communications software* consists of the programs used by the computers in data communications systems to control, coordinate, and monitor the data transmissions.

Now let's look more closely at each of these components.

COMMUNICATIONS HARDWARE

The equipment that makes up the hardware of a data communications system includes various types of terminals, modems, interface units, and computers.

Terminals

Input/output devices at the ends of communication lines.

In earlier chapters, we discussed the computer terminal as both an input and an output device. All types of terminals are used in data communications systems: dumb, smart, and intelligent terminals; video display and printing terminals. In fact, any input/output device can be used in a data communications system. Card readers, printers, plotters, and even voice input/output devices may be part of such a system. When used in this context, such devices are called terminals since they are at the ends (or terminal points) of communications lines. This usage of the label *terminal* can be extended even further to encompass other computer systems. A small computer system can act as a terminal when it transmits data to and receives data from another system like itself or a larger, centrally located computer. Data communications systems that employ full-fledged computers as terminals have, by definition, the ability to do local processing at the terminal sites.

Modems

Devices for sending and receiving data over telephone lines

A **modem** is an interface unit that enables a computer or terminal to transmit and receive data over telephone lines. Both computers and terminals employ *digital signals* consisting of discrete low and high voltages that represent zeros and ones. Ordinary telephone lines, however, are designed to carry *analog signals* with continuous voltage ranges which represent the sounds of human voices. Digital signals must be converted to analog signals before they can be sent over phone lines. Such conversion is called **modulation**. At the other end, where the data transmission is received, the analog signals must be converted back into digital signals. This is called **demodulation**. A modem, then, is a *mo*dulator/*dem*odulator (see Figure 7.3). Note that modems are necessary only when analog communications channels (normal telephone lines) are used. Recently, phone companies have been installing lines especially designed to carry digital signals, for example, those of AT&T's Advanced Communication Service. As such digital channels become more widely available, the need for modems will decrease.

Various types of modems are available. **Intelligent modems** can simultaneously transmit both voice and data, automatically dial telephone numbers, automatically answer incoming calls, and test and select transmission lines. **Direct-connect modems** plug right into phone jacks. In contrast, an **acoustic coupler** converts digital signals into sounds that are emitted into a telephone receiver cradled in rubber cups (see Figure 7.4). Acoustic couplers are often used to connect portable terminals or computers to telephone lines. Modems also vary in their

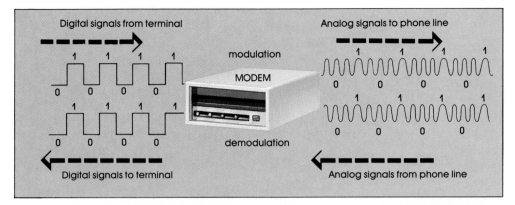

Figure 7.3   The Modem
The modem's name reflects its dual role: it modulates, or converts digital signals from a terminal into analog signals to be sent over telephone lines; and it also demodulates, or converts analog signals from telephone lines into digital signals to be sent to a terminal.

Figure 7.4   The Acoustic Coupler
An acoustic coupler converts digital signals into sounds that are emitted into a telephone receiver cradled in rubber cups.

transmission speeds, which typically range from 300 **baud** (pronounced "bawd," and equivalent to bits per second) for low-speed modems to 9600 baud for high-speed modems.

Interface Units

Many data communications systems employ interface units that coordinate various aspects of data transmission and reception. These units greatly increase the overall efficiency of the systems in which they are used. Such devices include multiplexers, concentrators, message switchers, and front-end processors.

Devices that coordinate data transmission and reception

Multiplexers

A **multiplexer** is a device that combines the signals from several terminals into a single transmission that can be carried by one communications channel. Since communications lines almost always have a greater capacity than can be filled by transmission from a single terminal, the use of a multiplexer ensures that this carrying capacity isn't wasted. In essence, a multiplexer treats a high-speed communications line as if it were multiple lower-speed lines, resulting in a much more economical use of these expensive channels. Note in Figure 7.5 how the multiplexer *interleaves* the data streams from different terminals one character at a time so that one combined stream can be sent over a single line.

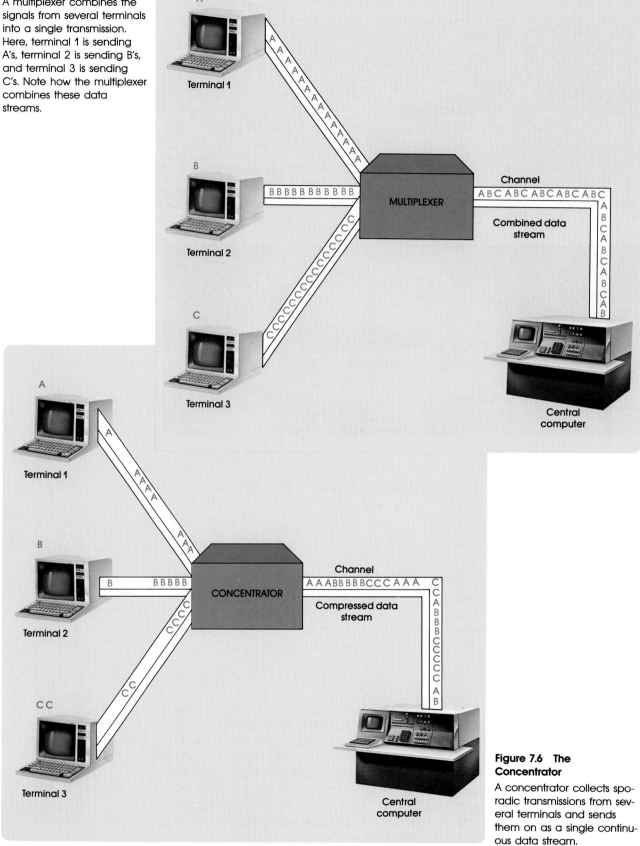

Figure 7.5 The Multiplexer

A multiplexer combines the signals from several terminals into a single transmission. Here, terminal 1 is sending A's, terminal 2 is sending B's, and terminal 3 is sending C's. Note how the multiplexer combines these data streams.

Figure 7.6 The Concentrator

A concentrator collects sporadic transmissions from several terminals and sends them on as a single continuous data stream.

183   Communications Hardware

Concentrators

A **concentrator** is a minicomputer or microcomputer that combines the data from a number of terminals onto a single high-speed line to a central computer. Its role is similar to that of a multiplexer, but a concentrator is a more sophisticated piece of equipment, often having an internal memory. This gives the concentrator the ability to store data temporarily until enough is collected to forward significant chunks to the computer at high speed. A concentrator also differs from a multiplexer in that it waits until a group of characters is collected from each terminal, instead of interleaving the data streams character by character (see Figure 7.6). Transmissions from several terminals are collected and compressed, one after another, into a continuous, high-speed stream. Again, more efficient use of expensive communications channels is the main reason for employing concentrators.

Message Switchers

A **message switcher** is a device that receives all transmissions from all terminals in a data communications system, analyzes them to determine their destinations and proper routing, and then forwards them to the appropriate locations (see Figure 7.7). Many message switchers are capable of storing transmissions if the

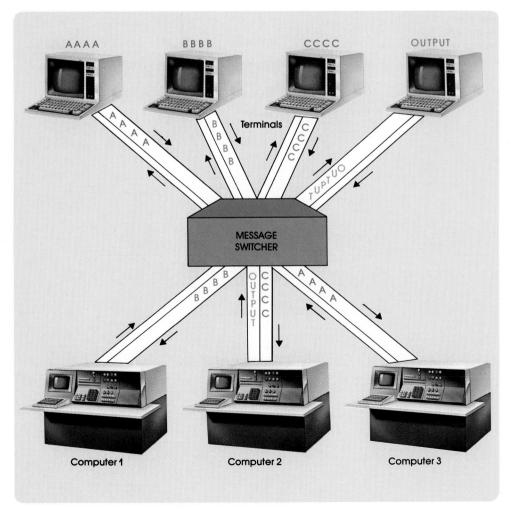

Figure 7.7 The Message Switcher

A message switcher handles the routing of data transmissions between terminals and computers.

appropriate communications lines aren't immediately available. Message switchers increase the efficiency of a data communications system by relieving the main computer of routing responsibilities.

Front-End Processors

A **front-end processor** is a computer that is usually located at the same site as the central computer in a data communications system. Its function is to relieve the central computer of routine transmission-oriented tasks. This leaves the central computer free for processing applications programs, thus increasing the amount of processing that can be accomplished in a given amount of time by more than 30%. Front-end processors can be programmed to do message switching, error checking, data translation, and transmission coordination and control. They can keep logs, compile statistics concerning data communications activities, and maintain security by limiting access to authorized users (see Figure 7.8).

Figure 7.8 The Front-End Processor

A front-end processor is a computer that contains communications software that enables it to relieve the central computer of many routine data communications tasks.

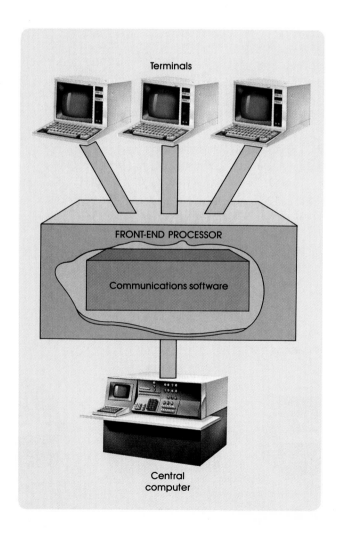

Computers

As we mentioned earlier, the computer or computers in data communications systems vary widely in size and capabilities. The ultimate purpose of any such system is to transmit and process data. Data are usually sent from terminals to some computer for processing and then sent from that computer back to the terminals. Where there is a single computer designated as the central processing component of a data communications system, it is called the **host computer**. In very large data communications systems, this host might be a supercomputer, but in a very small system, the host can be a microcomputer.

Machines that process the data

COMMUNICATIONS SOFTWARE

Communications software consists of the programs that enable the host computer and/or front-end processor to establish, coordinate, monitor, and control the flow of data through data communications systems. Here are some of the tasks accomplished by such programs:

The programs used to control data flow

- *Opening and closing communications lines.* Certain programs direct the computer to establish the correct connection to make a transmission and to break the connection when the transmission has been sent. These programs may also maintain banks of phone numbers for establishing such connections.

- *Finding and correcting transmission errors.* Data may be garbled or bits may be lost during transmission. It is essential to have programs that can determine if errors have occurred and cause the data to be retransmitted if necessary.

- *Coordinating multiple use of communications lines.* When several terminals must share communications channels to a computer, programs that coordinate data transmissions are needed. **Polling** is one technique for maintaining smooth flow of data in which each connected terminal, in turn, is "asked" if it has data to send. With another similar technique, called **contention**, each terminal is instructed to "listen" to see if any other terminal is transmitting and, if so, to wait.

- *Routing data transmissions.* Data must be sent to the appropriate destination. Programs that handle routing may also perform *queuing*, or ordering transmissions into some sequence, or priority, if more than one are to be sent to the same place.

- *Keeping statistics.* Some programs compile useful facts about system performance, such as the number of errors that have occurred and how many transmissions have been sent.

COMMUNICATIONS CHANNELS

Communications channels are the pathways over which data are sent. Also called communications lines or data links, they connect the various hardware components of a communications system. Communications channels are classified in various ways, each based on a particular characteristic. Thus channels can be

Pathways for data

described in terms of physical structure; speed, direction and mode of transmission; line configuration; and whether lines are leased or switched.

Physical Structure

What channels are made of   Communications channels can consist of wire cables, microwave systems, or fiber optic cables.

Wire Cables

Ordinary telegraph and telephone lines are cables consisting of bundles of twisted copper wires that carry information in the form of analog electrical signals and are widely used for data communications. Since a worldwide network of these lines already exists, they have the advantages of economy and accessibility. The telephone system, however, was intended to handle voice transmission and isn't the ideal medium for transmission of digital signals. Its analog nature and its susceptibility to electromagnetic interference limit the transmission speeds that can be achieved. During phone calls, you can often hear faint conversations in the background caused by *crosstalk,* a phenomenon in which high-speed transmissions in one pair of twisted wires interfere with those in nearby pairs. Although crosstalk is merely a nuisance with voice communications, it seriously impairs the high-speed transmissions necessary for some sophisticated types of data communications.

Invented in 1929, **coaxial cables** are efficient transmission lines developed primarily to combat crosstalk. They consist of a central cable completely surrounded by, but insulated from, a "tube" of outer wires (see Figure 7.9). This outer layer of wires shields the inner cable and thus helps to reduce electromagnetic interference. Coaxial cables are widely used in data communications systems because they allow signals to be sent faster and with less interference than do ordinary twisted wire cables. Coaxial cables can be laid underground and underwater. They are often used in local area networks, which will be described later in this chapter.

Figure 7.9 Coaxial Cable
This cross section of a coaxial cable shows the special shielding used to reduce transmission distortion.

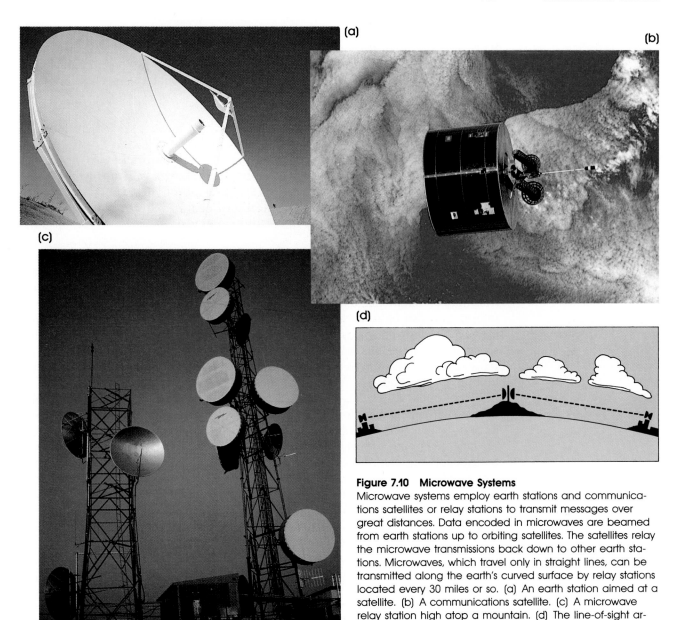

Figure 7.10 Microwave Systems
Microwave systems employ earth stations and communications satellites or relay stations to transmit messages over great distances. Data encoded in microwaves are beamed from earth stations up to orbiting satellites. The satellites relay the microwave transmissions back down to other earth stations. Microwaves, which travel only in straight lines, can be transmitted along the earth's curved surface by relay stations located every 30 miles or so. (a) An earth station aimed at a satellite. (b) A communications satellite. (c) A microwave relay station high atop a mountain. (d) The line-of-sight arrangement necessary for microwave relay stations.

Microwave Systems

Microwaves are radio signals with high frequencies that can be used to transmit any kind of data. Microwave systems transmit data over the earth's surface by transferring them to and from relay stations on tall buildings, towers, and mountains. Such stations must be located every 30 miles or so because microwave transmissions are line-of-sight signals—they won't bend to follow the earth's curvature. Microwave systems may also utilize *communications satellites,* which relay microwave transmissions they receive from one earth station back to another earth station at some distance from the first (see Figure 7.10). Many such satellites are presently in orbit, circling the earth 22,300 miles above the equator at the same speed at which the earth rotates. Due to this matching of the earth's rotational speed, such satellites appear stationary with respect to earth stations. Initially used for voice and video transmissions, communications satellites can relay very large quantities of data rapidly.

Fiber Optic Cables

Fiber optic cables are used throughout the world to transmit voice, television, and data signals. A fiber optic cable consists of very thin glass filaments that transmit light (see Figure 7.11). Lasers generate the off-and-on pulses of light that carry binary data over fiber optic cables. Instead of electrons moving through metallic wires to carry signals, light waves travel through tiny glass fibers to accomplish the same purpose.

The greatest advantage of fiber optics lies in the extremely wide bandwidth of light transmission. **Bandwidth**, which we will discuss further when we talk about transmission speed, refers to the range of frequencies that can be accurately transmitted. Light has a wide range of frequencies, so an immense volume of information can be sent over a single circuit at very high speed. Light does not travel much faster through fiber optic cables than electrons do through wires; the speed advantage results primarily from the fact that light can be turned on and off more rapidly than can electricity. Some single optical fibers can transmit 576 million bits per second—the equivalent of 7680 simultaneous telephone calls.

Fiber optics also offers other significant advantages. Lightweight cables with very small diameters are formed from the hairlike optical fibers. For example, 900 pairs of copper wires in a bundle 3 inches thick can be replaced by a 0.005-inch-diameter fiber optic cable in a $\frac{1}{4}$-inch jacket. Also, crosstalk is negligible even when many fibers are cabled together. Since optical fibers are immune to electrically generated interference (such as that caused by lightning and nearby electric motors), error rates are as much as a million times lower than they are with metallic wires. (Optical fibers do not produce undesirable electromagnetic interference either.) Since it is almost impossible to wiretap optical fibers, data transmission over fiber optic cables is much less liable to security breaches. Finally, fiber optic cables are safer (no electrical sparks to cause fires or explosions), last longer (no corrosion), and can operate under conditions of high temperatures (at which copper wire cables would melt).

Figure 7.11 Fiber Optic Cable
Fiber optic cables consist of very thin glass filaments that transmit light pulses generated by lasers. This photograph shows a thin fiber cable in contrast with a thick wire cable cross section.

There are, of course, disadvantages to fiber optic cables. They are somewhat difficult to handle and install, and they require complex, expensive interface units. The drawbacks of fiber optics are mostly due to its relative newness. Although the technology has proven to be cost-effective for long-distance voice and video communications, it is still somewhat expensive for data communications applications. Nonetheless, fiber optics has the potential to play a major role in the data communications systems of the near future.

Transmission Speed

The transmission speed of a channel refers to how much data can be sent over that channel in a given time. This rate is dependent on the bandwidth (also called *grade*) of the channel, the range of frequencies that can be transmitted. The greater the bandwidth, the greater the number of frequencies at which information can be transmitted. For example, your ears differentiate the frequencies of sound wave vibrations as tones of distinct pitches. All the tones a person can normally hear make up the bandwidth of audible sound, which is the range from about 20 to 20,000 *hertz* (or cycles per second). Since each tone can express a single bit per unit of time (if the tone is on at that time, the digit 1 is transmitted; if off, the digit 0), the number of bits per unit of time that can be transmitted with audible sound is limited by the number of frequencies that can be distinguished. Thus, the greater the bandwidth, the greater the amount of information that can be simultaneously sent in a given time period and the greater the transmission speed. Channels are classified by bandwidth into narrowband, voiceband, and broadband.

Classifying channels by how much data can be sent at a time

Narrowband channels have a bandwidth of less than 3000 hertz and a transmission rate between 5 and 30 characters per second. Telegraph lines are examples of narrowband channels. Such channels are too slow to be used for modern data communications. They have been widely used for low-speed data transmission to devices such as news service teletype machines.

Voiceband channels have a bandwidth of about 3000 hertz and transmission rates of up to about 960 characters per second. These channels are named for the fact that they are commonly used for voice communications—telephone lines are voiceband channels. The lines used to connect such devices as video display terminals, card readers, and slow printers to computers are also voiceband channels.

Broadband channels have a bandwidth greater than 3000 hertz and transmission rates of up to several million characters per second. Coaxial cables, microwave systems, and fiber optic cables are all broadband channels. In terms of transmission speed, these three types rank as follows: the fastest by far are fiber optic cables, followed by microwave systems, and then by coaxial cables. Broadband channels are primarily used for high-speed, high-volume data transmissions between computer systems.

Transmission Direction

Channels can be classified according to the direction in which they allow transmission. There are three directional classifications: simplex, half-duplex, and full-duplex (see Figure 7.12).

Classifying channels by allowed direction

Simplex channels allow transmission in one direction only. Devices connected by simplex channels can either send or receive, but not both. Even though

Figure 7.12 Simplex, Half-Duplex, and Full-Duplex Channels

The classifications of simplex, half-duplex, and full-duplex refer to the direction of transmission allowed for a channel.

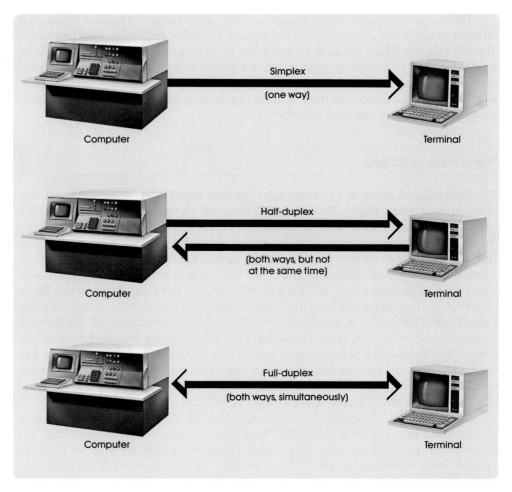

they are inexpensive, simplex channels are rarely used for data communications. They are found only in a few one-way applications such as weather and news wire service teletype lines.

Half-duplex channels allow transmission in either direction, but not simultaneously. Devices connected by half-duplex channels can send or receive, but not at the same time. A pair of walkie-talkies is a good analogy to a half-duplex channel; although both users can talk and listen, only one can talk at a time. Half-duplex channels are commonly used to connect terminals, modems, printers, and other peripheral devices to computers. Because the receiving unit must wait until the transmitting unit has finished sending and then switch over to its transmitting status to send a reply, these channels are characterized by a certain amount of delay between the transmission of a message and the reception of a reply.

Full-duplex channels allow transmissions in both directions, simultaneously. A telephone line, for example, is a full-duplex channel because the two parties can both talk and listen at once (although such a conversation would be confusing). A full-duplex channel is very efficient since signals can flow in two directions at the same time. This ability to carry a constant two-way "traffic" means that full-duplex channels are ideal for high-speed, high-volume computer-to-computer communications.

Transmission Mode

Channels can be classified according to the way in which data are transmitted over them. Inside computers and terminals, data are handled in parallel fashion, that is, a byte at a time. Over communications channels, however, data must be transmitted in a serial fashion, or one bit after another. Two common modes of serializing data for transmission are called asynchronous and synchronous.

How data are sent over channels

Asynchronous transmission involves the sending of one character at a time. In order to separate the characters, *start bits* and *stop bits* are added to each end of the individual 8-bit character codes. This means that for each character 12 bits are actually sent. The start bits are a signal to the interface unit that a character is coming next; the stop bits signal the end of a character. For example, Figure 7.13(a) shows how the letter x would be sent asynchronously. The ASCII code for x (101100) is preceded by two start bits (00) and followed by two stop bits (11). Asynchronous transmission is appropriate for devices that communicate at rates from 30 to 240 characters per second. Consequently, it is quite adequate for and is commonly employed in channels that connect terminals and modems to computers.

Synchronous transmission involves the rapid sending of blocks of characters, sometimes called *frames*, or *packets*. These groups of characters are sent without start and stop bits, as shown in Figure 7.13(b). Instead, the transmissions are carefully timed (or synchronized) so that interface units "know" where the first character begins (then each 8 bits is another character). If 100 8-bit ASCII characters are sent synchronously, the message will be 800 bits long (it would be 1200 bits with asynchronous transmission). Because fewer bits are sent, synchronous transmission is more commonly used than asynchronous transmission for sending high volumes of data at rates exceeding 480 characters per second. Therefore, synchronous transmission is most often used in the channels that connect mainframe computers.

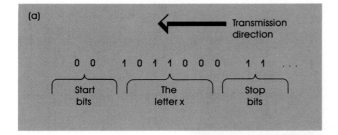

Figure 7.13 Asynchronous and Synchronous Transmission
Channels can be classified according to how data are sent over them. (a) With asynchronous transmission, one character is sent at a time, preceded by start bits and followed by stop bits. (b) With synchronous transmission, groups of characters are sent without start and stop bits. The transmissions are carefully timed so that the interface unit can "recognize" the individual characters.

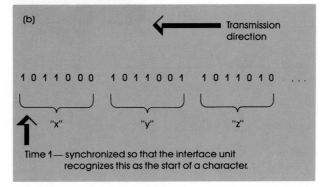

Line Configuration

Channels that connect terminals to a computer have two principal line configurations: point-to-point and multidrop (see Figure 7.14).

Point-to-point lines connect each terminal directly to the computer by a separate line. Because point-to-point line configurations are expensive (each terminal must have its own channel and interface unit), their use is generally limited to situations in which each terminal must have uninterrupted access to a computer or a small computer system is acting as a terminal.

Multidrop lines, on the other hand, connect several terminals to the computer via a single channel. Such a configuration is more economical because communications channels and interface units are shared by more than one terminal. Although multidrop lines allow several terminals to receive data simultaneously, only one terminal at a time can send data. Earlier, we described how the techniques of polling and contention enable communications software to coordinate data transmissions over multidrop lines.

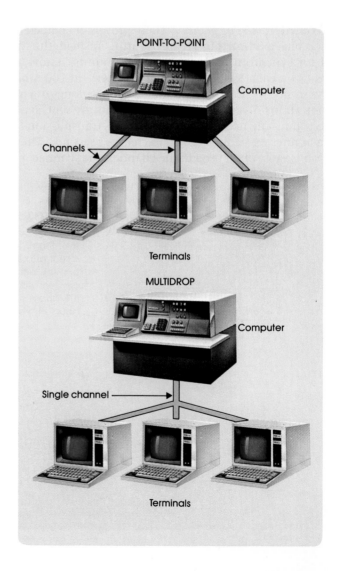

Figure 7.14 Point-to-Point and Multidrop Lines

Point-to-point lines connect each terminal directly to the computer. Multidrop lines connect several terminals to the computer via a single channel.

Leased Versus Switched Lines

Finally, some channels can be classified according to whether they are leased or switched. **Leased lines** (also called *private lines* or *direct lines*) connect a computer to fixed destinations. If you had a private telephone line that ran directly to your best friend's house, it would be similar to a leased line in that you could call no one but your friend on that line and your friend could call no one but you. A **switched line**, in contrast, is one that can connect a computer through switching centers to any of a number of destinations. This type is like an ordinary telephone line—you can call up anyone who has a phone connected to the telephone system. Because their use is limited to transmissions between two fixed end points, leased lines are more expensive than switched lines. However, leased lines are always available to their users and in some cases can be enhanced, or *conditioned*, to increase the transmission rate.

Weighing factors of access and cost

PROTOCOLS

As you've probably concluded by now, data communications systems are complex entities. Setting up a working system requires the careful consideration of many hardware and software options. Contributing to this complexity is the fact that manufacturers and data communications professionals employ a variety of transmission techniques. In a move toward standardization, various national, international, and industrial groups have attempted to set up guidelines to which data communications hardware and software should conform. One result has been the establishment of several **protocols**, or sets of rules and procedures spelling out how to initiate and maintain data communications. These protocols are intended to enable the components of data communications systems to work together harmoniously.

Standards for data communications

A necessary function of protocols is to define the rules by which receivers can properly interpret transmitted messages. Without protocols to guide the orderly exchange of data between components of communications systems, messages would be impossible to decode. Protocols determine who transmits when, how transmissions are made, how errors are detected and handled, and how received messages are interpreted and decoded. Protocols establish operating standards for data communications systems and have greatly increased the efficiency with which messages can be sent and received. Examples of protocols include teletypewriter (TTY), binary synchronous communication (BSC), synchronous data link control (SDLC), and high-level data link control (HDLC).

COMMON CARRIERS

Although some private data communications systems have been established by large government agencies and business firms, most data communications are handled by common carriers. A **common carrier** is a company licensed and regulated by the state or federal government to carry the property of others at approved rates. In the context of data communications, common carriers are organizations licensed to transport data belonging to others. The two largest such carriers in the United States are American Telephone and Telegraph (AT&T) and Western Union, but there are more than 3000 others.

Companies licensed to transmit data

In the United States, communications are regulated by the Federal Communications Commission (FCC) and various state agencies. Since 1968, the FCC has allowed companies to compete with AT&T (which previously had a virtual monopoly over data communications) by producing equipment (such as modems) that could be interfaced with AT&T's telephone network. In 1982, the U.S. government agreed to drop an antitrust suit against AT&T if the company divested itself of the 22 local telephone companies making up the Bell System. At the same time, AT&T became free to enter areas from which it had formerly been barred, such as data processing and computer equipment manufacturing.

An important result of the increased competition in the communications industry has been the rise of specialized common carriers and value-added carriers. **Specialized common carriers** are companies, such as MCI Communications Corporation and ITT World Communications, that offer a limited number of data communications services in and between selected metropolitan areas. These carriers often employ microwave systems or communications satellites.

Value-added carriers are companies that lease channels from common carriers and add extra services beyond the basic ones provided, such as error detection or faster transmission. Such a carrier thus creates a **value-added network (VAN)**. Some value-added networks, such as Tymnet, Inc. and GTE's Telenet, are **packet-switching networks**; that is, messages from several customers are combined into a packet and transmitted as a unit at high speed. The packets are disassembled into the various messages at the carrier's office closest to their final destinations. Customers use local leased or switched lines to get their messages from this office.

More and more businesses are finding value-added networks to be a fast and economical means for data transfer. The two largest of these networks, Tymnet, Inc. and GTE's Telenet, share more than 80% of the total market. Telenet serves 325 U.S. cities, interconnects with similar networks in 53 foreign countries, and handles data transmitted among 1400 customer computers, which serve a total of 200,000 terminals. Tymnet is somewhat smaller, providing a broad range of services throughout a network of hundreds of computers and tens of thousands of terminals.

DISTRIBUTED DATA-PROCESSING NETWORKS

As we mentioned earlier, many data communications systems consist of remote terminals connected via channels to a central host computer. Such systems, with one computer and many distant terminals, are often called **teleprocessing systems** (a combination of telecommunications and data processing). Teleprocessing systems operate under either a time-sharing or a batching scheme. *Time sharing,* which we briefly described in Chapter 2 and will discuss in more detail in Chapter 11, involves dividing the host computer's capacity among many users. In **remote job entry systems**, the host computer receives tasks to be processed from distant terminals and batches them. Both of these types of systems have problems, however, which have led to the development and rapid growth of distributed data-processing networks.

Decentralized processing of data

Instead of a single computer and many remote terminals, **distributed data-processing (DDP) networks** have several widely dispersed computers that are interconnected to form a data communications system. Thus, there is not one host computer, but several computers with independent processing capabilities. Although DDP networks may have a computer that is designated as the central computer to do generalized processing, each of the outlying computers can do much of its own processing.

There are many examples of private and public organizations that use DDP networks. Hewlett-Packard has a worldwide network consisting of 10 mainframes, 195 minicomputers, and at least 2500 terminals, linking over 100 manufacturing sites and sales offices to corporate centers in California and Switzerland. Texas Instruments has an equally complex network of hundreds of different-sized computers and over 7000 terminals scattered in Europe, South America, Asia, and the United States. At least 50 computers, ranging from minicomputers to supercomputers, at about 40 universities and research institutions in the United States and Europe are part of the U.S. Defense Department's ARPANET (Advanced Research Projects Agency Network). Finally, airline reservation networks such as the Apollo system of United Airlines and the Sabre system of American Airlines give thousands of travel agencies up-to-the-minute access to flight schedules and rates and allow them to make car rental and hotel reservations as well as to print out tickets and itineraries.

Network Configurations

Three basic designs are used for distributed data-processing networks, each with its own advantages. These configurations are commonly known as the star network, the ring network, and the hierarchical network.

Basic designs of DDP networks

The **star network** consists of several computers connected to a central computer, as shown in Figure 7.15(a). This central computer, usually located at an organization's headquarters, controls the communications to and from the outlying computers. The star network is well suited to organizations that must centrally control and coordinate the operations of distributed branch outlets (such as banks).

In a **ring network**, several computers are connected directly to each other; there is no central, dominant computer, as is shown in the diagram in Figure 7.15(b). This type of network is often used in organizations in which there is no need for central control of the distributed processing sites. Ring networks are somewhat more reliable than star networks because their functioning doesn't depend on a central coordinating computer. Although more expensive to implement, ring networks are less vulnerable than star networks because the failure of a single link still leaves an alternate communication path; that is, the malfunction of any one computer doesn't disable the entire network. In a star network, on the other hand, the failure of the central computer effectively crashes the whole network. A ring network is the best design for situations in which the maintaining of communication is the critical factor, such as in military and national security agencies.

The **hierarchical network** reflects the chain-of-command type of management structure found in many organizations. Computers are connected together in a pyramidlike arrangement, reflecting their relative levels of importance, as shown in Figure 7.15(c). The *root computer* at the top of the hierarchy exercises control over all of its immediate subordinates. This highest-level computer communicates with computers on the level beneath it, which in turn communicate with computers on the level beneath them. The Texas Instruments network mentioned above is arranged in a hierarchical fashion. At the top are five large mainframes that serve as corporate information and control centers. Next in the hierarchy are a

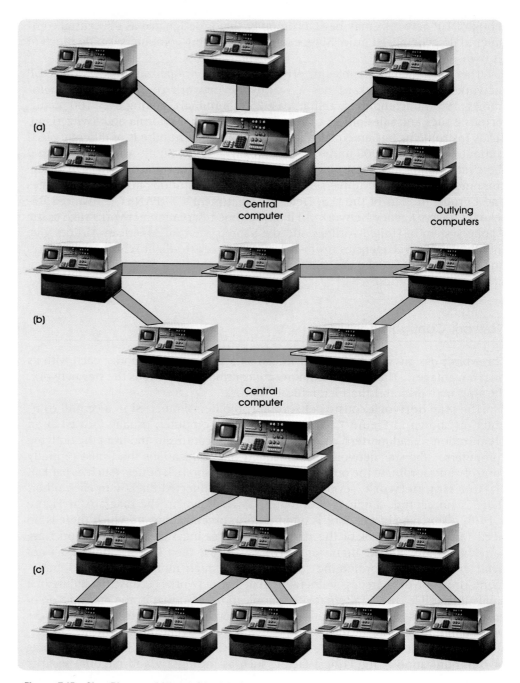

Figure 7.15   Star, Ring, and Hierarchical Networks
The three basic designs of distributed data processing networks are (a) the
star, (b) the ring, and (c) the hierarchical network.

number of medium-sized mainframes responsible for data processing at major
manufacturing plants and administrative offices throughout the world.   Below
these are many minicomputers that serve the computing needs of individual departments.   At the lowest level are the intelligent terminals used by employees for
routine tasks.

CAREERS IN TECHNOLOGY
Network Analyst

Job Description A network analyst determines ways to link computer systems together into information networks, which provide users with practically unlimited access to a wide variety of information and expertise. The network analyst's responsibilities include organizing the individual elements of the network; choosing, purchasing, distributing, and setting up the necessary equipment; and testing and supervising the completed network. This job requires scientific, business, and social expertise, since any network should be technically efficient, economical, and easily accessible to all potential users.

Qualifications A B.S. degree in computer science, with an emphasis on communications and network theory is the basic academic requirement. In addition, an applicant should have four to five years of hands-on experience in communications programming. A network analyst must have good logical and analytical skills, be detail-oriented, and be able to communicate well both on paper and face to face. Research skills are also essential, as the job requires keeping up with new developments in technology.

Outlook As computer networks play an increasingly important role in both business and domestic life and as the number and types of available services invariably multiply, there will be a corresponding demand for people who can analyze and apply their various qualities. This job requires a large investment of time to achieve the necessary training and experience, but the evergrowing need for analysts in all fields should make such a choice pay off in future job opportunities.

Advantages and Disadvantages of Distributed Data-Processing Networks

Distributed data-processing networks are very popular, largely because they alleviate some of the problems inherent in single-computer teleprocessing systems. DDP networks are favored because they:

Benefits and drawbacks of DDP networks

- *Decentralize the system work load.* The central computer is relieved of the burden of being the only processing unit available to all of the users in the network.
- *Speed up response times.* Because there are more computers to do the work, it gets done faster.
- *Provide access to more users.* Vital computer resources are readily available to more users since more than one computer is employed.
- *Allow flexibility.* Since hardware configurations can be customized, individual user needs can be met.
- *Reduce communications costs.* Many jobs can be performed locally and do not have to be sent to the central computer for processing.
- *Increase system reliability.* If one computer or some communications lines go down, processing can still be done by the computers at intact local sites.

DDP networks also have their drawbacks, however, including the following:

- *Limitations of the local computers.* Each site is to some extent dependent on its computer's processing capabilities, memory, and software. A centralized host computer facility is generally better staffed and equipped.

- *Incompatibility between local computers.* Equipment and software used at one local site may not work smoothly with the equipment and software at other local sites. This is usually the result of employing different protocols.

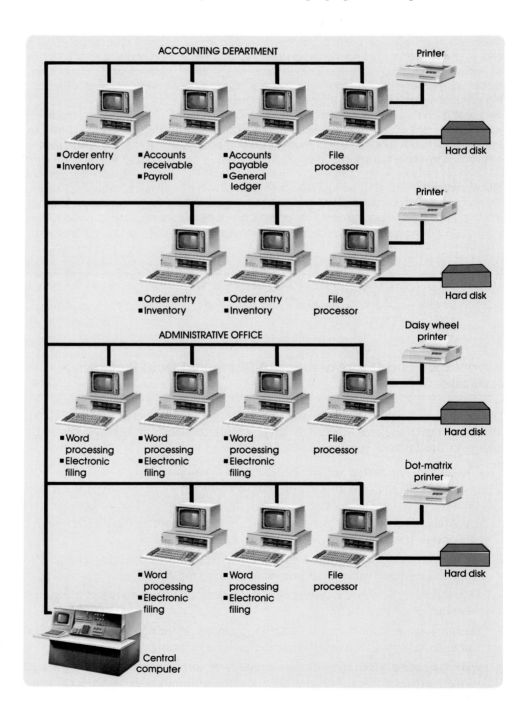

Figure 7.16 A Local Area Network

An organization can increase its efficiency by linking small computers and peripheral devices into a local area network.

- *Increased complexity of the system.* The bigger the network, the more complications inevitably arise.
- *Difficulties in ensuring the confidentiality and integrity of user programs and data.* These important issues of privacy and security are dealt with in Chapter 22.

Local Area Networks

Recently, the increasing technological sophistication and decreasing costs of microcomputers and minicomputers have brought about significant growth in the application of data communications systems in the office environment. A lot of what we've described in this chapter has to do with data communications systems as a means of exchanging information over relatively long distances. Businesses and other organizations have discovered, however, that as much as 80% of their communications occur across relatively short distances, such as within a large office, between offices in a building, or among a group of neighboring buildings. The result has been the rapid rise of a new branch of data communications known as local area networking.

Connecting nearby computers

A **local area network (LAN)** basically consists of two or more microcomputers physically connected together with some type of wire or cable that forms a data path over which data are transmitted (see Figure 7.16). Typically, coaxial or fiber optic cables and specialized interface units provide very fast data transmission. Once established, a local area network enables all of its users to exchange programs, data, and essential information at high speeds. In addition, local area networks allow expensive equipment such as large-capacity hard disk drives and letter-quality printers to be shared more efficiently by users within the same organization. This can promote greater productivity, as well as encourage individuals to use available computer resources more effectively.

Most local area networks connect a number of microcomputers together, but there has been a great deal of recent interest in *micro-to-mainframe links,* which are LANs that enable microcomputer users to take advantage of local mainframe resources. Local area networks such as Xerox's Ethernet and Datapoint's Arcnet system are currently causing quite a bit of excitement in the computer industry, and they are sure to continue to do so for quite some time.

SUMMARY

Applications of Data Communications
Data communications has changed many aspects of modern life.

Information Service and Videotex Information services offer interactive networking to users who own inexpensive terminals or personal computers. Videotex services add color graphics.

Electronic Mail and Bulletin Boards Electronic mail employs computers and communications lines to enable users to send and receive messages. Electronic bulletin boards serve as a means of electronic message exchange between home computer users.

Electronic Funds Transfer EFT systems use data communications to move money among bank accounts.

Computer Conferencing   Computer conferencing enables users to interact directly and immediately.

Telecommuting   Telecommuting utilizes microcomputers and communications channels to allow people to work at home.

Components of Data Communications Systems

The components of most data communications systems are communications hardware, communications software, and communications channels.

Communications Hardware

The devices that a data communications system includes are terminals, modems, interface units, and computers.

Terminals   All types of input/output devices can be used as terminals in data communications systems. Small computers can act as terminals when they send data to and receive data from other computers.

Modems   A modem (modulator/demodulator) is an interface unit that enables a computer to send and receive data over telephone lines. Intelligent modems, direct-connect modems, and acoustic couplers all convert digital signals to analog signals for transmission and convert received analog signals back to digital signals.

Interface Units   These are devices that coordinate data transmission and reception. Multiplexers combine signals from several terminals into a single transmission that can be carried by one channel. Concentrators collect data transmissions from several terminals and compress them, one after another, into a continuous, high-speed stream. Message switchers route transmissions from several terminals to their proper destinations. Front-end processors are computers that relieve the host computer of many routine data communications tasks.

Computers   Several computers or a single host computer of any size may be used in a data communications system.

Communications Software

Communications software consists of programs that coordinate, monitor, and control data transmission, routing, and reception.

Communications Channels

Channels are the communications lines or pathways over which data are sent.

Physical Structure   Channels can consist of wire cables (ordinary or coaxial), microwave systems (possibly involving satellites), or fiber optic cables.

Transmission Speed   How much data can be sent over a channel in a given time is determined by the bandwidth of the channel and classifies channels into narrowband, voiceband, and broadband.

Transmission Direction   Simplex, half-duplex, and full-duplex are the channel classifications that describe the direction of allowed transmissions.

Transmission Mode   Data are transmitted over channels one character at a time (asynchronous transmission) or in groups of characters (synchronous transmission).

Line Configuration   Two principal ways of connecting terminals to a computer are with point-to-point lines (a direct connection exists between each terminal and the computer) and with multidrop lines (several terminals share a single channel).

Leased Versus Switched Lines   Leased lines connect the computer to a limited number of fixed destinations, and switched lines connect the computer via switching centers to a large number of destinations.

Protocols

Protocols are sets of rules and procedures that govern the initiation and maintenance of data communications.

Common Carriers

Most data communications are handled by companies licensed and regulated by the state and federal governments. Specialized common carriers offer data communications services in and between certain metropolitan areas. Value-added carriers lease channels from common carriers and provide special services via value-added networks or packet-switching networks.

Distributed Data-Processing Networks

Instead of one host computer, several computers, each with processing capabilities, can be interconnected in a distributed data-processing network.

Network Configurations The three basic designs for DDP networks are the star network, the ring network, and the hierarchical network.

Advantages and Disadvantages of Distributed Data-Processing Networks DDP networks decentralize the computer work load, speed up response times, provide more users with ready access, allow flexibility, decrease communication costs, and increase system reliability. However, local computer capabilities may be limited, resources at different sites may be incompatible, system complexity is usually increased, and data confidentiality and integrity may be compromised.

Local Area Networks Local area networks link the small individual computers in an organization.

COMPUTER CONCEPTS ▬▬▬

As an extra review of the chapter, try defining the following terms. If you have trouble with any of them, refer to the page number listed.

REVIEW QUESTIONS

1. List three applications of data communications.
2. List the components of a typical data communications system.
3. What advantage is there to using a full-fledged computer as a terminal in a data communications system?
4. What does a modem do and why is it a necessary component of many data communications systems?
5. What do interface units do in data communications systems?
6. What is the difference between a multiplexer and a concentrator?
7. How can a message switcher increase the efficiency of a data communications system?
8. How can a front-end processor increase the efficiency of a data communications system?
9. What kinds of computers are used in data communications systems?
10. What kinds of tasks does communications software perform?
11. How do coaxial cables differ from ordinary telephone cables?
12. Why are microwave relay stations placed on top of tall buildings, towers, and mountains about 30 miles apart?
13. What role do communications satellites play in microwave systems?
14. What carries data over fiber optic cables and how is it produced?
15. Why are broadband channels faster than narrowband channels?
16. What are half-duplex channels commonly used for?
17. What are full-duplex channels commonly used for?
18. Which is usually faster, synchronous or asynchronous transmission?
19. Why are point-to-point lines usually more expensive than multidrop lines?
20. What are the two largest common carriers of data in the United States?
21. What has been one of the most significant results of increased competition in the communications industry?
22. Why are ring networks generally more reliable than the star networks?
23. In what ways are distributed data-processing networks better than teleprocessing systems?

A SHARPER FOCUS

Now that you've completed this chapter, you should be able to answer the following questions about the chapter opening.

1. What data communications hardware does real estate broker Clark Halstead use?
2. Which type of line configuration does this system have?
3. Which transmission mode is employed?
4. Approximately what transmission speed is involved?

PROJECTS

1. Find out more about one of the available videotex services (such as The Source or CompuServe), and make as complete a list as possible of what the service offers. What equipment must a subscriber have, and how much does the service cost?
2. Prepare a report on one of the large value-added networks (such as Telenet or Tymnet). What do they offer their users, and what kinds of organizations do they serve?

3. Most large libraries have access to data retrieval networks. Investigate the typical costs and features of these systems and prepare a report of your findings.

4. Modems, even those used with small home computers, differ significantly in features and price. Prepare a report delineating available features and corresponding costs.

5. Find out the exact roles data communications plays at your school or company. To supplement your written report, draw diagrams showing all the communications channels used and indicating the type of channel, transmission mode, and transmission speed. Also, explain why data communications is used for each application, what other possibilities are available, and why they aren't being used.

Application Perspective: The Airline Industry

1. You Make a Plane Reservation

(1) Seats on a flight are an expensive and perishable form of inventory; they're worthless once the airplane leaves the ground. As a result, they are intensively managed. Your shopping for a flight may involve compromises, for example, between the most convenient departure and arrival times and the lowest fare. Current flight information, kept updated in airline computers' memories, is presented on the travel agent's terminal screen for review.

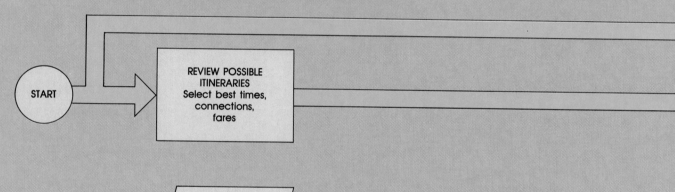

START

REVIEW POSSIBLE ITINERARIES
Select best times, connections, fares

END

ISSUE TICKET
Entry to accounting system for direct billing or credit card charge

(4) Your ticket is ready; all that's left to do is to pay for it. The agent makes the appropriate entry debiting your credit card account. If you're a regular customer, your account number is on file in a computer record along with your seating preferences. In that case, you don't even have to go to the travel agency—a phone call will take care of the whole thing.

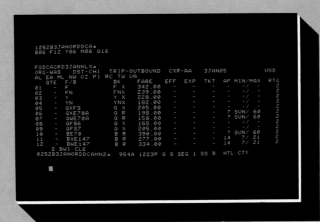

(2) The seats on the flight you select can be sold by travel agencies and airline offices all over the world. Their terminals must be linked with the computers of the various airlines to keep the seating availability information current. When you buy a ticket, one seat is no longer available, and this must be reflected on all those terminal screens as quickly as possible. Although the inventory can't be managed perfectly, the frequency with which there are more confirmed passengers at the gate than there are seats is remarkably low.

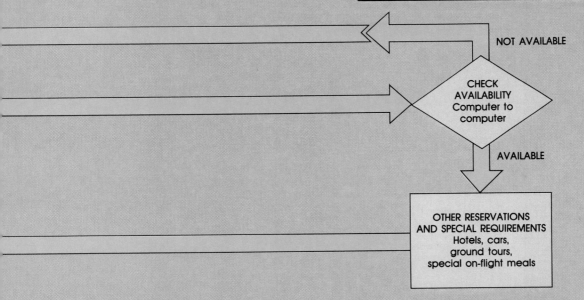

NOT AVAILABLE

CHECK
AVAILABILITY
Computer to
computer

AVAILABLE

OTHER RESERVATIONS
AND SPECIAL REQUIREMENTS
Hotels, cars,
ground tours,
special on-flight meals

(3) Having entered your seat selection and noted any special in-flight services you request, the travel agent can use the reservation system to arrange other services: a car at the best available rate, a conveniently located hotel, and perhaps a ground tour package.

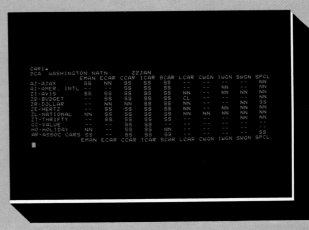

Application Perspective: The Airline Industry

2. Your Flight Takes Off

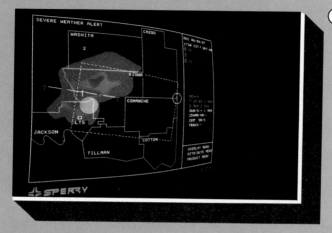

(5) The most important factor in planning the route for any flight is the weather. A computer logs observations made by pilots in the air about the actual weather conditions at flight altitudes. The Weather Bureau uses large mainframes to produce forecasts for use by pilots. The captain uses this information to choose a route that minimizes the likelihood of severe turbulence.

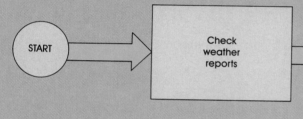

START → Check weather reports

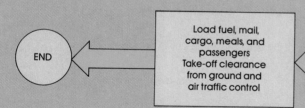

END ← Load fuel, mail, cargo, meals, and passengers Take-off clearance from ground and air traffic control

(8) The airplane takes on sufficient fuel for the filed flight plan plus a required reserve. Passenger baggage and other cargo, as well as the required number of meals, are loaded. In the tower, FAA personnel use computerized systems to monitor air and ground traffic. Your flight is assigned a position on an approaching runway and in its turn is cleared for takeoff.

6 Each airplane's position is continuously monitored en route for adherence to its filed flight plan. The pilot is kept advised via radio communications of all nearby aircraft, and Federal Aviation Administration (FAA) controllers quickly respond to any unexplained flight deviations. The flight plan information is also transmitted to the destination airport, where it is used in the assignment of ground personnel, equipment, and gates.

File flight plan
Personnel, equipment, and gate assignment

Ticketed and standby passenger check-in

7 The airline's computer holds the names of all confirmed passengers for your flight. As passengers check in at the gate, the agent records each one. Shortly before departure time, a count is made of the "no-shows." Those people who are standing by because the computer showed the flight as full are ticketed until all seats are filled. The final passenger manifest is then stored in the computer's memory.

Application Perspective: The Airline Industry

3. A Reflection: The Data-Processing Viewpoint

This Application Perspective presents two views of a complex system: a view of its actual functioning, as shown in photographs, and a view of the data processing that supports this functioning. In the latter case, we no longer look at airline passengers as individual people. They are represented by information to be processed through the creating and maintaining of computer records of physical movements.

A passenger reserves a seat on an airline flight; at that moment the seat is removed from the available "inventory" and a passenger record is created. When the passenger arrives at the gate for check-in, the record is brought up on a terminal screen by an agent and the fact that the passenger has shown up is appended to the passenger record. The passenger information is then incorporated in a new record, the passenger manifest.

What has happened here? Has anyone been stripped of his or her identity by the computer? Of course not. The maintenance of accurate records is essential to the efficient operation of an airline's flights—it must be known how many seats are available, who is booked, who has actually shown up, and whether passengers have any special requirements such as special meals or wheelchairs. This is the only way airlines can safely and efficiently manage an activity as complex as getting a 747 filled with passengers, baggage, and freight from Boston to Los Angeles.

Whether the data are managed by computers or by people isn't the issue. Any complex activity can be carried out only if the information goes in correctly, gets processed correctly, and comes out correctly. However, what is an issue is the management of costs and time. The use of a computer is mandatory when a job is just too big to be otherwise handled efficiently in the required time. Imagine an agent at a departure gate pawing through 500 scraps of paper to find out whether Mrs. Smith has made a reservation on the flight for which she has appeared and then typing up a final passenger manifest with the "no-shows" deleted and the stand-bys added.

The computer is a necessary tool whenever a job is too complicated to be done reliably by people under the stress of deadlines. If a job must be done, it is in everyone's interest that it be done as quickly, correctly, and economically as possible.

Part 3

SOFTWARE

To imagine a world without computers isn't hard; but to imagine a world *with* computers and without software, without the programs that tell the hardware what to do, is impossible. Just as a computer needs electricity, it needs software in order to do anything. In Part 2, we looked at all the computer's various component devices. In Part 3, we'll discover what makes them work.

Chapters 8 and 9 are about the tools and concepts relied on by programmers to write software. Chapters 10 and 11 are about two of the most significant types of software: application packages (''canned'' programs) and the operating systems that oversee program execution.

8

Program Development

▶

FOCUS ON . . . VIDEO GAME PROGRAMMING

When Michael Wise sits down at a keyboard, he never knows when he will get up. The plump, bearded computer programmer often works twelve, 24, even 36 hours without a break, filling a green screen at the San Rafael, Calif., offices of Broderbund Software with words and numbers that only he and his computer completely understand. Since December, Wise has written 40,000 lines of instructions for a video game he calls Captain Goodnight, after the old *Captain Midnight* radio series. By the time the program is ready for release this summer, it will have grown to 50,000 lines and swallowed up some 900 hours of programming time, or nearly 40 days and 40 nights.

Wise's first task in writing his program was to create the objects displayed on the screen. These are actually just patterns of colored dots, with each dot controlled by an individual on-off switch. Wise sketched the images on an electronic drawing tablet that translated his lines into patterns of ones and zeros, where one represents a dot of color and zero a blank space. The image of Captain Goodnight's airplane is stored in the computer as a list of 798 zeros and ones that look like this: 11111100 00000001 10000000 . . .

After the objects were drawn, Wise began creating a series of small, self-contained miniprograms called subroutines. One subroutine, for example, moves the captain's jet. Another controls the enemy planes. A third fires a missile. In all, the finished program will have 400 different subroutines. Wise writes it one subroutine at a time, making sure that each new one works before continuing. A typical section of coding reads:

```
EMIS-HIT? LDA JETY
          SBC EMISY
          CMP #10
          BGE EMISEXIT
PLAYR-HIT?LDA #01
          STA JETCOND
```

Those commands tell the computer to determine the jet's altitude (JETY) and subtract the altitude of the enemy missile (EMISY). If the result is ten or more, the two objects have missed each other. If it is less than ten, the program puts a one in a special switch called JETCOND that sends the jet into a flaming crash.

As the pieces of the program fall together, their interrelationship becomes maddeningly complex. Even one letter misplaced in 10,000 lines of code is enough to throw the whole program out of kilter. At one stage in the game's development, the computer had the captain walking in mid-air because one subroutine was inadvertently modifying another subroutine's instructions. "I almost went blind trying to find that bug," Wise recalls.

Wise does his best work at night. Every evening after dinner he picks up where he left off at work. "My wife is a computer widow," he confesses. During the past month, he has been working until dawn with increasing regularity. "When I'm done, we're taking a vacation," says the 29-year-old programmer. "I'm almost getting too old for this."

We've covered the essential facts about all kinds of hardware, and now we can shift our emphasis to what makes that hardware work—software. In this chapter, we'll discuss how software is created, that is, the program development process, and what the role of the computer programmer is in that process. Since computers deal only with numbers and logical comparisons, the process of developing a program basically involves treating a concrete, real-life problem (such as organizing a company's payroll records or tracking the paths of satellites) by formulating a systematic, detailed sequence of instructions very carefully stated and ordered so that a computer can do what needs to be done. Thus, a **computer program** is a precise, ordered group of statements that tells a computer how to execute a well-defined task.

The words *precise* and *ordered* are crucial. A computer won't tolerate ambiguity, nor can it generalize or infer. It does *exactly* what it is told to do. Because of this, computer programming can be difficult and even frustrating. The more complex the program, the more likely it is to contain an inadvertently erroneous statement, telling the computer to do something that was not intended. Since many programs are quite complex (consisting of hundreds of thousands of lines in some cases), the process of developing a computer program must be disciplined and systematic if the result is to be useful and correct.

THE PROGRAM DEVELOPMENT PROCESS

Recognizing that a computer can be used for some job is a far cry from having a useful program. The **program development process** is the series of activities necessary for the creation of a successful computer program. Before examining these activities, let's list the characteristics of a successful computer program.

How successful programs are created

correct　it does what it's supposed to do

usable　it's easy to use

reliable　it works without failing

understandable　it can be easily comprehended

modifiable　it can be enhanced and updated

maintainable　it can be corrected when errors are found

flexible　it can be modified to supply other information as required

general　it isn't overly specialized

efficient　it doesn't waste computer resources

The program development process can be divided into seven stages: (1) defining the problem; (2) developing the software requirements; (3) designing the program; (4) coding the program; (5) testing the program; (6) installing and maintaining the program; and (7) documenting the program.

Following these steps won't guarantee that a program will be successful. However, unless the program is very simple, not following these steps is likely to detract from the program's quality.

Defining the Problem

Pinpointing what needs to be done

The programmer's first task is to determine just what the problem is and how to solve it. This can often be accomplished simply by talking with the people who work in an organization, learning about the facilities and the perceived shortcomings of the current way of operating. The programmer sometimes receives only vague or generalized verbal descriptions of what's needed; in that case, he or she will have to help determine what the program should do. Even then, it's not uncommon for both beginning and experienced programmers to end up with a program that bears no resemblance to what was originally intended. It's vitally important to take a complete view of the whole project at the outset, so that the problem is clearly defined and understood. Because they can have a bearing on how the problem is defined, the other stages of the program development process must also be considered at the beginning. We've presented the program development process as a sequence of distinct steps, but they are all interrelated and must all be kept in mind throughout the entire process.

Developing the Software Requirements

Software requirements specify exactly what a program should do without giving any details concerning how it should be done. This second stage produces the program *specifications*. From specifications, the program can be designed. If the solution to the problem is very complex, the specifications may be expressed in a *software requirements document (SRD)*, a set of precisely stated constraints that the finished program must satisfy. If the program satisfies these constraints, it's an acceptable solution to the problem.

Specifying the output, input, and processing

Developing software requirements also involves specifying the type and exact form of the output to be produced by the program, the type and form of the necessary input, and the types of processing that must be done to convert the input data to output information.

Desired Output

Since the output is the whole reason for developing a program in the first place, specifying the output is as important as defining the problem. The following characteristics of the output must be determined:

- *Content* What information must the output convey? How detailed should this information be? The answers to these questions depend on the definition of the problem being solved.

- *Format* How is the information to be presented? What output device or devices are to be used, and how is the information to be arranged? For example, if the output is to appear on a display screen, how it will look, where it will be placed, and what color it will be are some of the factors to be considered.

- *Timing* When is the information to be presented? Is the information to be output immediately or batched and output periodically?

Required Input

Since the output of a program represents the results obtained from the processing of the input, a careful analysis must be made of the input data. The programmer must know what data are needed, whether they are available and accessible, and how they are formatted:

- *Necessary data* What data are needed in order to get the desired output? A thorough list of all data that must be input is a very important part of developing software requirements.

- *Availability and accessibility of data* Where will the necessary data come from? Are the input data already stored somewhere, or must they be gathered? Will the data be obtained directly from on-line input devices or from secondary storage media such as disks or tapes?

- *Format of data* What is the physical arrangement of the input data? If a program receives data in a format it was not designed to handle, it may fail or yield unpredictable results.

Necessary Processing

The computer operations indicated in the program perform the processing of input into output. The software requirements must list the processing tasks to be executed, define the way users will communicate with the program, and designate the necessary equipment:

- *Processing tasks* What operations must be performed in order to process the data? For example, input data may have to be sorted or mathematical calculations may have to be carried out. The software requirements should specify exactly what is to be done with the input data.

- *User interface* How will the users interact with the program? The **user interface** is the means by which the people using the program communicate with it. How this interface should work largely depends on the sophistication of the intended users. If the users are computer professionals, familiar with the equipment and programming, the interface may be relatively sophisticated, allowing much to be done quickly with only a few commands. If, on the other hand, the users are relative beginners, the interface should be *user-friendly;* that is, it should be easy to learn to use the program.

● *Necessary equipment*   Exactly what computers, peripheral equipment, and other programs will be needed to run the program? The software requirements should list the hardware resources that must be available if the program is to run successfully. For example, a program may be designed to run only on one computer model with a specific kind of display unit and disk drive. On the other hand, some programs are designed to run on a number of machines with a variety of peripheral equipment.

Designing the Program

How to solve the problem

Once the programmer has determined *what* the program must do, the next step is spelling out *how* it will be done, designing the problem solution. Before instructing the computer in detail as to how to perform a task, the programmer must develop a step-by-step method for getting from input to output. This set of steps is called an **algorithm**. Drawing up the algorithm, which specifies a particular method for solving a problem or performing a task, is the first step of program design.

As any programmer will tell you, good algorithms don't grow on trees. Finding a suitable algorithm for the task at hand can be something of a challenge, and is sometimes made even trickier by the fact that there may be more than one algorithm that will do the job. For example, let's say we want to sort a list of names into alphabetical order. There are a number of different algorithms that will let us accomplish the same result. We might pick out all the names beginning with A, then those beginning with B, and so on. Alternatively, we could start with one name and then place other names one by one into their proper relative positions.

The search for the right algorithm may be made less difficult by the fact that for tasks like sorting, which have been done many times before, workable algorithms have been collected and printed in reference books. On the other hand, for tasks that are new or somehow different from what has been done before, original algorithms must be developed. This part of the job tests a programmer's problem-solving and puzzle-working abilities. Sometimes mathematical skills are needed to develop a working algorithm, and sometimes solutions come from outside sources—coworkers, friends, or other projects may supply new approaches to a problem.

How to express the solution

Once the general algorithm that best solves the problem has been chosen or developed, the programmer must express it clearly in words, diagrams, charts, or tables. The means for doing this is a **program design aid**, a tool for building a computer program. A design aid either outlines the program's overall organization or gives some of the specific steps of the program. Programmers use such aids to help them plan programs, and we will introduce a few of the more established ones: flowcharts, pseudocode, decision tables, structure charts, and HIPO charts.

Flowcharts

Diagramming the algorithm

A **flowchart** is a graphic form of an algorithm in which standard symbols represent the necessary operations and show the order in which they will be performed. In other words, it's a diagram of the sequence of steps that a program must perform to produce the desired output. (See Figure 8.1.) Flowcharts are one of the oldest and best methods of planning a program. They allow an algorithm to be expressed graphically, giving a good view of the sequencing of the program. One way to think of a flowchart is as a talking map that says something like this: "Start here. Then go here and do this. Then go there and do that. Now make a decision and go here or there. Go back to the beginning and start over until this happens. Finish here."

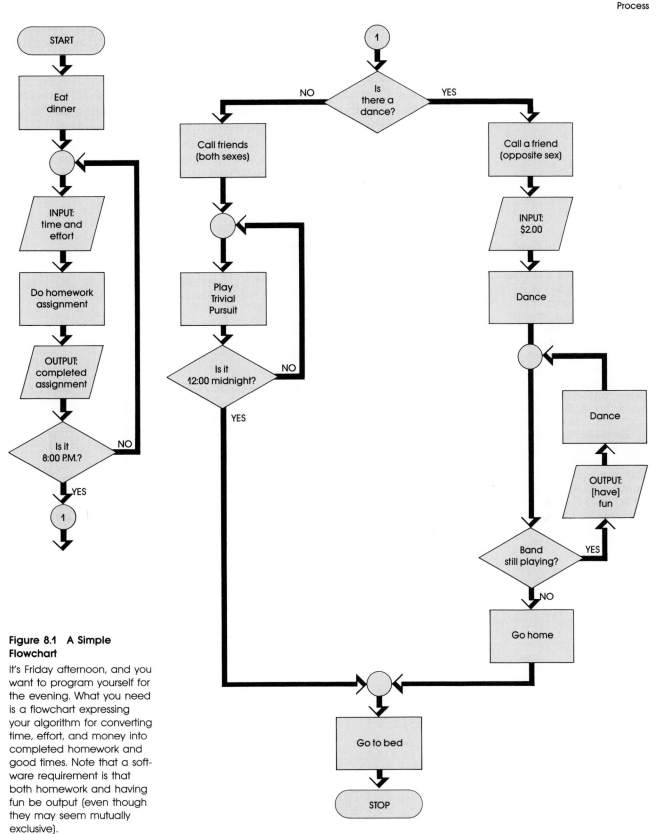

**Figure 8.1   A Simple
Flowchart**

It's Friday afternoon, and you
want to program yourself for
the evening. What you need
is a flowchart expressing
your algorithm for converting
time, effort, and money into
completed homework and
good times. Note that a software requirement is that
both homework and having
fun be output (even though
they may seem mutually
exclusive).

Flowcharts have become a traditional tool of programmers because they work as well for designing highly complex programs as for simple ones. In fact, they are often the first design aid taught to beginning programmers. The simple flowchart in Figure 8.1 illustrates the appearance and basic function of this useful design aid. The Technology Closeup section on flowcharting on pages 224 and 225 contains a more complete introduction to the various symbols and formatting guidelines.

One of the interesting features of the flowchart is its flexibility with respect to the amount of detail that can be represented. Programmers can use flowcharts to diagram both the general structure of a large program system and specific sections of a single program module. The programmer is free to include the amount of detail he or she feels is most appropriate for the particular design level being worked on.

Figure 8.2 Levels of Detail in Flowcharts

A company called Keyboard Koncepts, Inc., is an innovator in the production of superbly engineered computer terminal keyboards. To illustrate how different flowcharts can depict various degrees of detail, we've partially designed a simple accounting system to serve the firm's needs. This accounting system will provide Keyboard Koncepts with computer software to handle their inventory control, accounts receivable, accounts payable, payroll, and general ledger. (a) At the most global level, the system flowchart presents the overall picture of what the entire system will do.

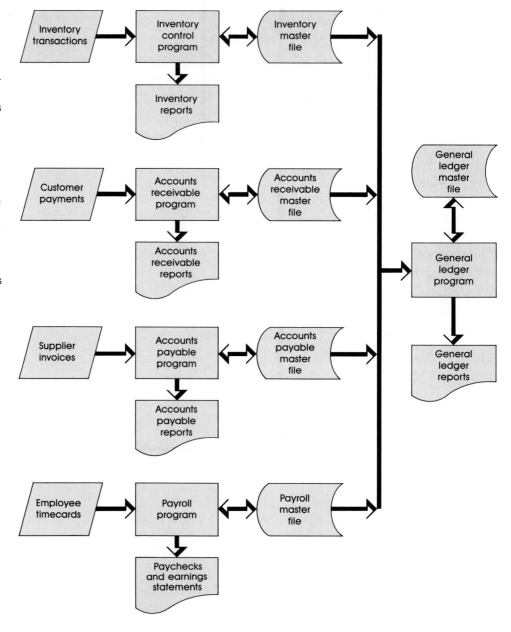

The designer might begin with a **system flowchart**, such as the one shown in Figure 8.2(a), a flowchart that provides a broad overview of the entire operation without itemizing all of the specific input, processing, and output steps that will actually be performed. The idea is to present the total picture without worrying about taking care of every little detail. A system flowchart may include components from several separate computer programs.

After the outline of the whole system is complete, the designer might construct **macroflowcharts**, or *program flowcharts*, like the one in Figure 8.2(b). A macroflowchart depicts the main segments of a complete computer program. If a program, in turn, is composed of smaller program modules, the designer may then

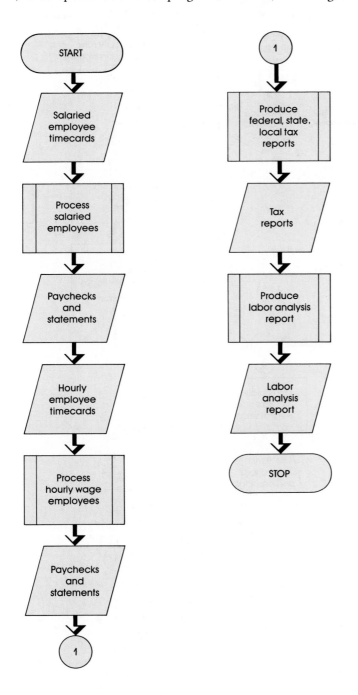

Figure 8.2

(b) Focusing on the payroll subsystem (which is a complete computer program itself), a macroflowchart specifies the individual modules that will handle the company's payroll.

Figure 8.2

(c) At the most detailed level, a microflowchart describes the module that handles the payroll of hourly employees. These employees, the assembly line workers who put together the keyboards from components, are paid an hourly wage (base pay) plus an incentive bonus for every keyboard in excess of the minimum 40 required each week. Employee records are input from time cards one at a time. The base pay is computed. Then, if more than 40 keyboards were assembled by the employee, bonus pay is computed and added to the base pay. Tax withholding is computed, and a paycheck and an earnings statement are printed. The whole procedure is repeated as long as there are more employee records to be processed.

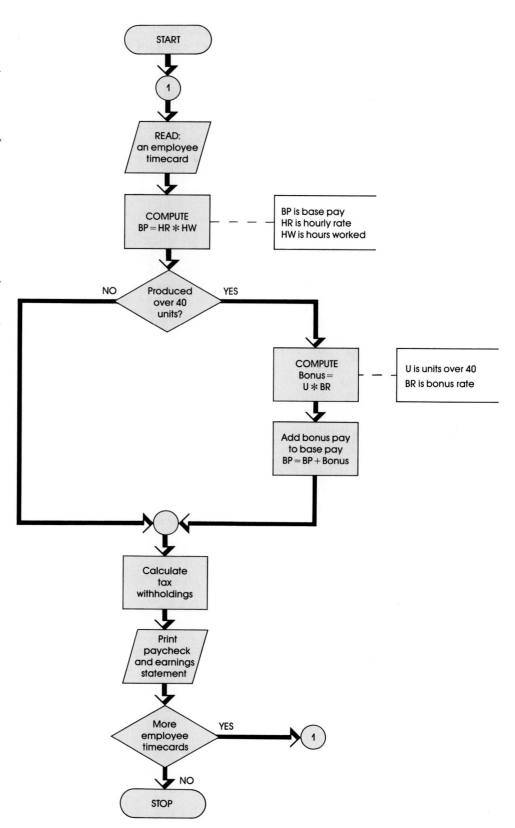

prepare **microflowcharts** similar to the one shown in Figure 8.2(c). These are very detailed flowcharts that illustrate the processing steps within a program module. Quite often, program coding can be done directly from well-prepared microflowcharts.

Pseudocode

Pseudocode is an informal expression of a program algorithm, using words and mathematical symbols to present the elements and flow. This program design aid allows the programmer to specify the problem solution with enough precision that it can later be almost directly translated to a formal programming language. Pseudocode is a "pidgin" computer language—it includes statements and grammar from various computer languages along with English phrases. The informality of pseudocode and its lack of standard rules free the programmer to concentrate on the general structure and flow of the program without getting bogged down in the requirements of a particular programming language.

Pseudocode has become a very popular alternative to flowcharts for the design of simple to moderately complex programs. Pseudocode is easier to revise, more compact, and often easier to convert into an actual program than a flowchart is. Pseudocode is also quicker to write since no time is spent drawing symbols and connecting lines. On the other hand, flowcharts are sometimes better than pseudocode because they graphically portray programs with complex logic.

Although there is a lot of individual variation in pseudocode and no "official" standards, a lot of pseudocode appears generally the same because there are a few widely accepted formatting rules. Figure 8.3 presents some general pseudocode rules and an example of how a simple algorithm is expressed in pseudocode.

A step toward a programming language

Figure 8.3 Pseudocode
(a) Since there is no standard form of pseudocode, there are no hard-and-fast rules telling exactly how to write it. Programmers can make up their own rules for the most part. However, there are certain overall formatting rules that are worth following because they help to make the pseudocode readable and unambiguous. (b) The algorithm for Friday evening from Figure 8.1 as it might be written in pseudocode.

SOME PSEUDOCODE RULES

(a)

1. Certain key words and phrases, such as DO UNTIL, are written in capital letters.
2. Levels of indentation are used to show the logical structure.
3. A set of operations to be performed in sequence is bracketed by the words BEGIN and END.
4. A decision between two alternatives is presented as follows:

```
IF (some condition is true) THEN
      one or more operations
ELSE
      one or more operations
END IF
```

5. Repetition of a sequence of operations is indicated in one of the following two ways:

```
DO WHILE (some condition is true)
      one or more operations
END DO
```

(This tests the condition each time *before* the operations.)

```
DO UNTIL (some condition is true)
      one or more operations
END DO
```

(This tests the condition each time *after* the operations.)

(b)

```
BEGIN (Friday evening)
      eat dinner
      DO UNTIL 8:00 pm
            input time and effort
            do homework assignment
            output completed assignment
      END DO
      IF there is a dance THEN
            call a friend (opposite sex)
            input $2.00
            dance
            DO WHILE band still playing
                  dance
                  output (have) fun
            END DO
            go home
      ELSE
            call friends (both sexes)
            DO UNTIL 12:00 M
                  play Trivial Pursuit
            END DO
      END IF
      go to bed
END (Friday evening)
```

TECHNOLOGY CLOSEUP
Flowcharting

Flowcharts are such a common and useful program design aid that they merit a closer look. Let's examine the symbols and construction of flowcharts and the advantages and disadvantages of using them.

Flowchart Symbols The symbols used in flowcharts include geometric shapes, lines and arrows, and mathematical operators. Of course, words are also used. The widespread use of flowcharts by computer programmers has led to the adoption by the American National Standards Institute (ANSI) of a set of Standard Flowchart Symbols for Information Processing. This standard set contains two overlapping subsets: system flowchart symbols and program flowchart symbols. Tables 1 and 2 summarize the most common of these symbols. Although many more symbols are included in the standard set, those shown in the tables here are encountered most frequently.

Flowcharting Guidelines Even though the programmer is free to decide on the amount of detail to incorporate in a flowchart, he or she should follow certain suggested guidelines for overall format. These general guidelines apply to all flowcharts, regardless of the complexity of the program or the level of detail included:

1. Always use ANSI standard symbols. (Flowchart symbols are not the proper outlet for expressing your artistic or imaginative drives.)
2. Construct your flowcharts to read from top to bottom and from left to right, as much as possible.
3. Don't crisscross flowlines (use labeled connectors, if necessary), and use arrowheads to indicate direction of flow.
4. Make the messages and labels in the flowchart symbols direct and descriptive.
5. Strive for neatness, clarity, and simplicity. If necessary, break a large flowchart down into microflowcharts and use labeled connectors. Use a *flowcharting template* and print clearly to ensure legibility.

Advantages and Disadvantages of Using Flowcharts
The use of flowcharts as program design aids has advantages and disadvantages. Some of the benefits of using flowcharts include:

- *Flowcharts supply graphic representations.* A flowchart depicts the structure of a program, and this picture can quickly communicate the relationships between the various components.
- *Flowcharts provide standardization.* Flowchart symbols, their meanings, and their usage are described by the official ANSI standards. A flowchart that conforms to the standards is meaningful to anyone who knows them.
- *Flowcharts have application to both large systems and small program segments.* Flowcharts can be used to get the overall picture of a large, complex system of programs and also to describe small sections of programs in great detail.
- *Flowcharts provide documentation.* Flowcharts serve as excellent means of documenting how a program works. A set of comprehensive and correct flowcharts can greatly facilitate the understanding, debugging, and maintenance of a computer program.
- *Flowcharts make coding easier.* Flowcharts can often be converted directly into computer-language programs, if they have been carefully constructed.

There are also some disadvantages to flowcharts, however:

- *Flowcharts can be time-consuming and difficult to construct.* Drawing correct flowcharts for programs of any complexity can be quite a chore. Planning the physical arrangement of the symbols on paper alone can use up a lot of time.
- *Flowcharts can be unwieldy.* Flowcharts tend to take up a lot of space, filling multiple sheets of paper to capacity. This can make them difficult to read and understand.
- *Flowcharts are hard to modify.* Once a flowchart has been committed to paper, changing even a small part of it can be difficult. Small changes often have repercussions throughout the entire chart, making extensive redrawing necessary.
- *Flowcharts can be challenging to design.* Although the lack of specific standards determining the amount of detail that should be included in flowcharts makes them very flexible, it can also leave programmers without a basis for deciding how much detail is enough.

Table 1 ANSI Standard Symbols for System Flowcharts.

Process symbol. Represents a major processing step in the system. Can be a program segment or an entire program that is detailed by a separate flowchart.

Input/output symbol. Stands for any type of input data or output information. Represents generic input/output functions of all kinds.

On-line storage symbol. Can depict any type of on-line storage device; often used for files residing on magnetic media that are referenced and updated.

Document symbol. Represents paper documents and reports of all kinds, source data documents or hard copy output.

Flowlines. Indicate the flow of data through the system, the processing sequence. Show the pathways by which data travel and which processes control which functions.

Punched card symbol. Represents punched cards both as input and as output.

Magnetic tape symbol. Stands for magnetic tape storage, input, or output.

Off-line storage symbol. Indicates any storage not directly connected to the computer, including paper, cards, and magnetic and optical media.

Manual input symbol. Represents data supplied to the computer by an on-line input device such as a terminal keyboard.

Display symbol. Stands for information being output to a display device such as a terminal screen or plotter.

Table 2 ANSI Standard Symbols for Program Flowcharts.

Input/output symbol. Represents any input/output function, just like the system flowchart input/output symbol.

Flowlines. Indicate direction of flow of data and processing, just like system flowchart flowlines.

Process symbol. Stands for one or more program instructions. Typically contains one algorithm step, or minor processing function.

Predefined process symbol. Represents a group of operations not detailed at that particular point but usually defined in a separate microflowchart. May be either procedures and functions that are used repeatedly or steps that would overly complicate the flowchart.

Terminal symbol. Indicates the beginning, end, or a point of interruption in a program.

Decision symbol. Marks a branching point in the algorithm, where the flow is directed to one set of instructions or another based on the answer (yes or no) to a question. Usually has one flowline entering and two flowlines exiting to alternate paths.

Connector symbol. Marks a junction of several flowlines or an entry from or exit to another part of a flowchart. Used to simplify flowcharts with many or very long flowlines, as in Figure 8.2(b).

Annotation symbol. Holds additional descriptive comments, explanatory notes, or clarifications; connected by dashed line to the symbol being commented on. Used as needed to aid understanding.

Figure 8.4 The Decision Table

Decision tables help the programmer allow for every possible case in a problem with a number of conditions and corresponding actions to be taken. This example shows a procedure that might be followed in the processing of credit card applications.

HEADING

Issuing Credit Cards	RULES						
	1	2	3	4	5	6	7
Stable employment?	Y	Y	Y	Y	N	N	N
Previous loans?	Y	Y	N	N	—	Y	N
Other charge accounts?	Y	N	Y	N	Y	N	N
Issue card, full credit	X	X	X				
Issue card, half credit				X			
Run full credit check		X	X	X	X	X	
Reject, but keep file (encourage to reapply)						X	X
Reject, dispose file							X

CONDITION STUB · CONDITION ENTRIES · ACTION STUB · ACTION ENTRIES

Decision Tables

Clarifying complex logic

The **decision table** is a program design aid used for specifying complex logical conditions and actions. Most often employed in conjunction with other aids, decision tables help a programmer verify that every possible outcome has been considered and provided for. A programmer is often faced with problems that have multiple combinations of conditions and possible actions. By constructing a decision table for each portion of a program that will handle this complex decision-making process, the programmer can be sure that no likely combination has been left unaccounted for. Decision tables give the programmer a clear, concise way of enumerating every possible case, and therefore reduce errors in finished programs.

Figure 8.4 is a simple decision table that might be used in a computer program for processing credit card applications. The *condition entries* are based on the applicants' answers to the questions on the application. A condition entry of Y means the answer to the question in the same row was yes, N means it was no, and — means the question doesn't apply or the answer doesn't matter. The *action entries* indicate what should be done about applications for each combination of conditions. An X indicates that the action in the same row is to be taken in response to the combination of conditions entered above in the same column. Each rule ties a specific action or actions to a given set of conditions. Rule 5 on the decision table in Figure 8.4, for example, indicates that any applicant that does not have stable employment and does have other charge accounts (regardless of previous loans) is to be checked out and rejected but encouraged to reapply.

A series of criteria that is fairly complicated to put in words is relatively easy to express in a decision table. The example in Figure 8.4 is a very simple decision table. More complex ones with greater numbers of condition and action rows and rule columns are usually necessary.

Structure Charts

The big picture

The **structure chart** is a program design aid that helps the programmer organize large, multipart programs. It shows the overall structure of a complex program and illustrates the relationships among its various parts, called modules. A **module** is

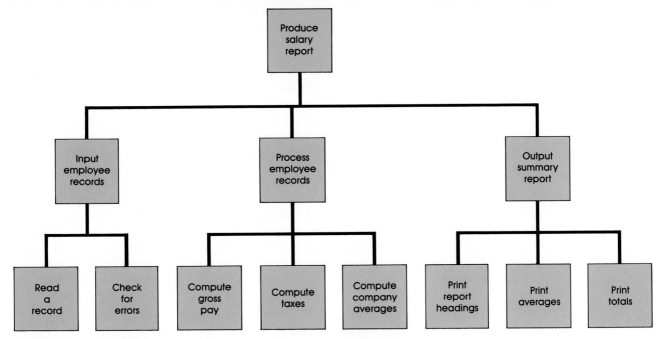

Figure 8.5 The Structure Chart

This simple structure chart shows the overall organization of a program that produces a summary report of employee salaries. The boxes, which represent modules, are connected by lines that indicate the flow of control. Higher modules control the modules directly beneath them. Note the lack of detail, even in the modules on the lowest level. The idea is to give a broad picture of the structure of the whole program.

a relatively independent, identifiable group of related program statements that can be treated as a unit. The structure chart shows how the modules of a program are interrelated but does not reveal any details about how they work. A structure chart presents the broad picture—the overview of a program's organization. Like decision tables, structure charts are usually used in conjunction with other design aids.

The typical structure chart is arranged in a hierarchical (ranked by level) fashion and looks like an upside-down family tree or a corporate organizational chart (see Figure 8.5). Labeled boxes represent the program modules and the connecting lines indicate which modules control or are controlled by others. There is usually a single topmost module, which controls the entire program much as a president runs a corporation. It directly controls the modules just beneath it, which in turn control the ones beneath them. The modules at the very bottom of the chart are the ones that do the "real" work, the specific tasks required to get the job done.

As we'll discuss later when we talk about structured programming and top-down design, very large or complex problems are best solved by such a "divide-and-conquer" approach. Thus, a structure chart is useful for showing the overall layout of very large programs, but it must be supplemented by other design aids that detail the lower-level modules.

HIPO Charts

The **HIPO chart** (Hierarchy plus Input-Process-Output chart) was originally developed at IBM as a tool for documenting programs. A HIPO chart clearly displays what a program does, what data it uses, and what output it creates. For many programs, HIPO charts are easier to read than flowcharts. They are highly detailed and yet flexible and easy to modify and maintain.

Producing a HIPO chart requires constructing three types of diagrams: the visual table of contents (VTOC), overview diagrams, and detail diagrams.

Three levels of detail

The *visual table of contents* is very similar to the structure chart, as you can see by comparing Figure 8.6(a) with Figure 8.5. The only difference is that each module is given a reference number that reflects its place in the hierarchy. A *legend* listing these numbers along with a short description of each module's purpose accompanies the VTOC. The VTOC shows the overall structure of the program and gives a general impression of what it does. The use of the sequence numbers and the legend allows lower-level design details to be referenced and located.

The second type of diagram in the HIPO chart, the *overview diagrams* present a general summary of the input, processing, and output done in each module identified in the VTOC. If there are 12 modules, there are 12 overview diagrams. The overview diagram for one module of the VTOC in Figure 8.6(a) is shown in Figure 8.6(b). Again, no attempt is made at this point to go into great detail. The major logical divisions are shown, and the flow of data through the module is indicated by arrows.

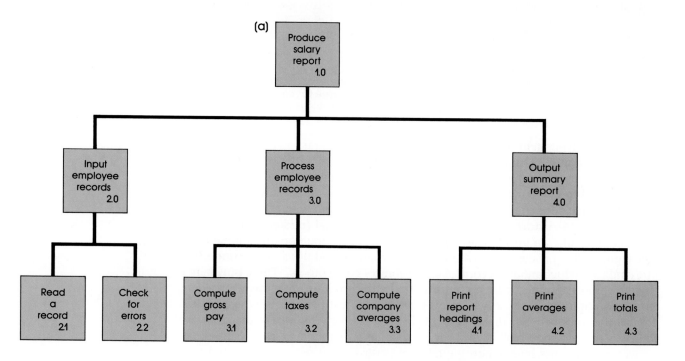

Figure 8.6   The HIPO Chart

A HIPO chart consists of three types of digrams: (a) a visual table of contents (VTOC) (the number in the lower-right corner of each VTOC box reflects the hierarchical position of that module and enables it to be specifically referenced in overview and detail diagrams); (b) an overview diagram for each module; and (c) one or more detail diagrams for each module.

VTOC LEGEND

Ref. No	Description
1.0	Produces a summary salary report
2.0	Inputs salary records of all employees
3.0	Computes necessary totals and averages
4.0	Formats and outputs summary report
2.1	Reads in employee salary records
2.2	Checks for invalid record or terminated employee
3.1	Computes each employee's gross pay
3.2	Computes each employee's taxes
3.3	Totals and computes company salary and tax averages
4.1	Prints summary report headings
4.2	Prints company averages
4.3	Prints company totals

The third type of diagram in the HIPO chart and the most specific are the *detail diagrams,* which further describe the logical flow of data through the modules and contain complete details about the processing to be done. Each module has a single overview diagram but may have more than one detail diagram if it is complex. Figure 8.6(c) is a detail diagram for one of the modules in Figure 8.6(a). Detail diagrams are translated by the programmer almost directly into program instructions in some programming language.

Coding the Program

Once an algorithm has been developed and its design has been completed, the next step is to code the program. **Coding** is the process of expressing the fully detailed algorithm in a standard programming language. This stage of the program development process requires strict adherence to the specific rules of format and **syntax**

Expressing the design in a programming language

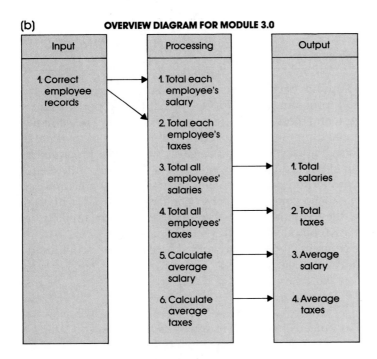

(b)   **OVERVIEW DIAGRAM FOR MODULE 3.0**

Input	Processing	Output
1. Correct employee records	1. Total each employee's salary	
	2. Total each employee's taxes	
	3. Total all employees' salaries	1. Total salaries
	4. Total all employees' taxes	2. Total taxes
	5. Calculate average salary	3. Average salary
	6. Calculate average taxes	4. Average taxes

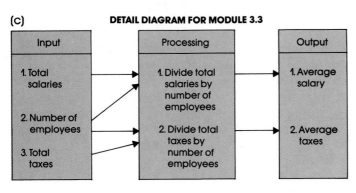

(c)   **DETAIL DIAGRAM FOR MODULE 3.3**

Input	Processing	Output
1. Total salaries	1. Divide total salaries by number of employees	1. Average salary
2. Number of employees	2. Divide total taxes by number of employees	2. Average taxes
3. Total taxes		

(vocabulary, grammar, and punctuation) of the language being used. A programmer who has done a good job of working out all the details of the design and who is familiar with the chosen language will have little trouble getting through the coding stage. In fact, coding is usually the easiest and least time-consuming of the seven stages of program development.

Since there are a number of programming languages, as we'll see in Chapter 9, the first task of program coding is to decide which one to use. (Actually, the choice of language is often made before the program development process begins and in that case will effect the program design.) The different languages have been developed to answer the different needs of specific applications, so the particular job at hand may dictate the choice of a language. On the other hand, a particular language may be chosen because of its availability, standardization, or manufacturer support.

The program expressed in a programming language, the **source code** as it is also known, must be entered (input) into the computer. This means that someone has to type it in on a keyboard. Programmers may do this themselves, working directly from the design documents, or they may fill out *coding forms* that list the program exactly as it is to be entered and give them to a keyboard operator.

Testing the Program

Making sure the program works

After the program has been coded and entered comes the moment of truth: does it work? Testing a program to see if it does what it's supposed to do is usually the hardest, longest, and most frustrating stage in the program development process. It has been estimated that testing takes from 50% to 90% of total program development time. Program testing is the stage in which the programmer is tested as well—the task of perfecting source code so it is accepted by the computer can take on immense proportions. Emotionally, programmers want (and secretly expect) their programs to be completely correct and run without a hitch the first time. Intellectually, they should realize that this is extremely unlikely, especially if a program has any complexity at all.

Testing a program completely requires three separate activities: desk checking, translation, and debugging.

Desk Checking

Proofreading the program for errors

Desk checking means just what it says—it's the process of sitting at a desk and checking the source code, proofreading for obvious syntax errors as well as looking for not-so-obvious logic errors. *Syntax errors* are violations of the rules of the specific programming language being used; they can be the result of an error in entering the source code or a misinterpretation or unawareness of a syntax rule. An example of a syntax error is using a comma where a period is required. Syntax errors can be easily uncovered by careful proofreading and can be reduced if the programmer looks up new or unfamiliar language features in a reference manual. *Logic errors* are mistakes in the algorithm, or program design, and are much more difficult to spot during desk checking. An example of a logic error is forgetting to divide the total value of all salaries by the total number of employees to get the average salary.

Desk checking is a monotonous chore that many programmers would like to avoid. As boring as it can be, not doing it usually just postpones the frustration of discovering errors that must be corrected for the program to work.

Translation

Translation is the conversion of the source code to the internal instructions that the computer requires. This process is carried out by the computer. During translation, another computer program (the *translator*) checks for and finds all syntax errors. If the programming language has been used improperly or entered incorrectly, the translation may be ambiguous or impossible to complete. The computer then issues *diagnostic messages*. Having a comma where a period should be, for example, might yield the message "PERIOD MISSING" or "INCOMPLETE STATEMENT." (We'll have more to say about translation in Chapter 9.)

Submitting the program to the computer for checking

Translation is not a check of the logic of a program; that is, it will not reveal whether the program will work the way it was intended to. Therefore, logic errors will remain undetected by the translation process. The translator only checks that all of the syntax rules of the programming language are followed; it has no way of checking a program for illogical structures, or ensuring that it won't produce garbage as results.

Debugging

Debugging is the process of detecting, locating, and correcting logic errors (or *bugs*) by submitting a translated program to the computer for execution and seeing what happens. In order to debug a program completely, the programmer must create suitable *test data* that simulate as many as possible of the real-life conditions under which the program will be run. This means that test data should include both normal items and incorrect or unusual ones to reveal their effect on the program. For very complex programs, it may be next to impossible to test all of the possible variations in data and conditions. The result is that a great many programs in daily use have hidden bugs just waiting to appear at some inopportune moment, such as the one that nearly kept Apollo 14's lunar module from descending or the one that made Voyager II's computer refuse to carry out a number of orders from Mission Control.

Finding and fixing mistakes

ISSUES IN TECHNOLOGY

One of the latest controversies in the world of software development concerns *program proving*, a concept that has been enthusiastically promoted by some of the leading academics in the computer science field. Program proving is a means of gaining confidence that an algorithm is correct without resorting to testing cases with a computer; program proving instead uses a special formal notation to prove mathematically that a program will do what it is supposed to do. Its proponents claim that the traditional approach of entering a program into a computer, translating it, and testing a few cases can never lead to absolute confidence in a program's correctness because the number of potential test cases can be infinite. On the other hand, many data-processing professionals assert that program proving is applicable to only a few, small, mathematical functions, that most practical applications programs tend to be long and intricate. Proving such programs, they claim, would be prohibitively time-consuming or, in effect, impossible. Proponents of program proving maintain not only that their techniques can be applied to complex systems but that for such systems exact mathematical reasoning is even more urgently necessary. Is the resistance to this new idea justified? Or are its opponents just trying to avoid doing math?

Installing and Maintaining the Program

Setting up the program and keeping it useful

Once the program has been as thoroughly tested as possible, it must be *installed,* or put into everyday operation at the site where it will be used. This involves making sure that it will work properly with the particular equipment at the designated site. If a program has many unique features or complicated operation procedures, installation may also involve training the personnel who will use it. If it is a replacement for an old program currently in use, both programs may be kept around until users adapt to the change.

Program maintenance is an ongoing process of correcting bugs discovered during operation, upgrading the program to accommodate new hardware or software, and introducing minor improvements. Essentially, it is the correction, expansion, updating, and improvement of a program after its installation. The environment in which most programs are used constantly changes because of such factors as new company policies, revision of laws or government regulations, and new equipment. Therefore, regular maintenance is essential to the continued usefulness of a program. And proper maintenance depends on the existence of complete documentation.

Documenting the Program

Describing the program to others

Documentation is a detailed description of a program's algorithm, design, coding method, testing, and proper usage. Documentation is a necessity for the users who will rely on the program on a day-to-day basis, as well as for the programmers who may be called on to modify or update it.

Creating and collecting documentation should be an ongoing activity throughout all stages of program development. No programmer's memory is good enough to hold all the important facts about a program's development or proper use. Also, someone who was originally involved in creating a program may no longer be available. Therefore, written records should be kept during all stages of the program development process.

There are no universally accepted standards concerning what should be included in a program's documentation. Although its contents will vary somewhat depending on the complexity of the program, in general, comprehensive documentation consists of the following:

A description of what the program is supposed to do (the software requirements document).

A description of the problem solution (the algorithm) in general terms.

A description of the program's design, including any aids used (flowcharts, pseudocode, decision tables, structure charts, and/or HIPO charts).

A description of the program testing process, including the test data used and the results obtained.

A description of all corrections, modifications, and updates made to the program since it was put into operation.

A *user manual,* or set of instructions telling the average user how to work with the program.

STRUCTURED PROGRAMMING

Structured programming refers to a set of software development techniques that includes many important concepts. Although it has had a major impact on data processing, structured programming is difficult to define succinctly. Originating in the latter half of the 1960s, structured programming was basically a response to two problems: the productivity of programmers was unacceptably low, and nearly all programs of any complexity were filled with bugs and almost impossible to maintain. This "software crisis" was at least partly due to the widespread perception of computer programming as a mysterious, esoteric art rather than a systematic, definable task. Programmers strove to be clever, tricky, and very concise, and thus produced cryptic code that was often unintelligible to other programmers. Programming projects were difficult to keep on schedule because low productivity made estimations of completion dates notoriously unreliable. In short, the state of the art of computer programming was near chaos.

Disciplining the job of software development

The objective of structured programming, then, was to bring order to this unsettled scene. Specifically, structured programming techniques have produced the following results:

- *Greater productivity.* More code can be written by fewer programmers in less time.

- *Increased economy.* The costs (in time and dollars) of producing software are reduced.

- *Better programs.* Programmers develop software with fewer bugs.

- *Decreased debugging time.* Errors that do occur are easier to locate and correct.

- *Clearer source code.* Structured programs can be readily understood, modified, and maintained by people other than the original programmer.

- *Longer software lifetimes.* Programs that can be easily modified, updated, and maintained are more flexible and can remain in service for longer periods of time.

Control Structures

The central principle of structured programming is that all programs can be constructed from just three basic control structures (see Figure 8.7). A **control structure** is a pattern for the flow of logic in a computer program; in other words, it is a framework that indicates the order in which operations are performed. The three control structures of structured programming—the sequence, selection, and iteration control structures—have one important property in common. Each of them has one entry point and one exit point, which is what makes structured programs so much easier to understand and correct.

Three basic formats for logical structures

The **sequence control structure** simply orders one step after another in a linear fashion. This structure is essentially the same as the BEGIN-END sequence of pseudocode operations as described in the general rules in Figure 8.3(a). The **selection control structure** is a two-path structure reflecting the IF-THEN or IF-THEN-ELSE logical structure of pseudocode, which is also included in Figure 8.3(a). The **iteration control structure** is a *loop*, or a structure that allows for the repeated processing of a set of operations. The flow exits the loop when a

(a)

SEQUENCE CONTROL STRUCTURE

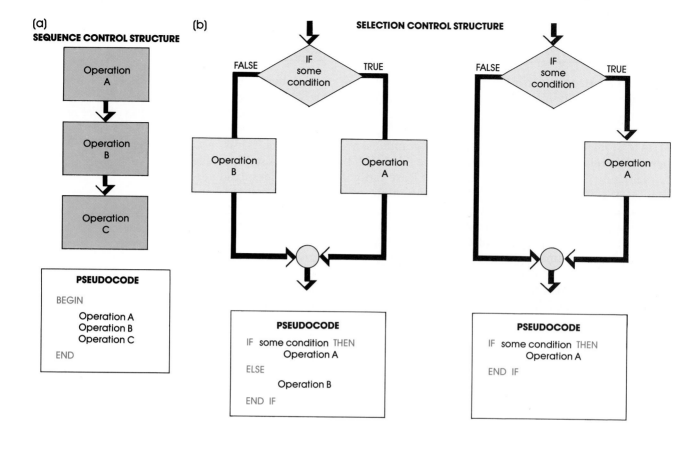

SELECTION CONTROL STRUCTURE

(b)

ITERATION CONTROL STRUCTURE

(c)

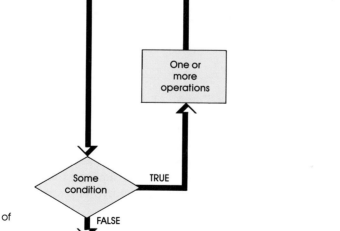

Figure 8.7   The Three Control Structures

Structured programming employs only three types of control structures, all of which have a single entry point and a single exit point. The three control structures are (a) the sequence control structure, (b) the selection control structure, and (c) the iteration control structure.

condition tested at the start is false. This corresponds to the DO WHILE structure in the pseudocode rules in Figure 8.3(a). The DO UNTIL structure is a variant of the DO WHILE that is also acceptable in structured programming but not strictly necessary. It has been mathematically proven that any computer program can be constructed using just sequence, selection, and DO WHILE iteration structures. The DO UNTIL iteration structure is used because it is often more convenient.

In the DO WHILE structure, the condition is tested *before* the operations are performed, and in the DO UNTIL structure, the condition is tested *after* the operations are performed. In other words, the test for exiting is at the top of a DO WHILE loop, but at the bottom of a DO UNTIL loop. This means that the operations in a DO WHILE will not be performed at all if the test condition is initially false. However, the operations in a DO UNTIL will always be executed *at least once,* because the test condition follows them.

Regardless of where a condition is tested in an iteration control structure, it must be carefully considered. If for some reason the condition never changes, the program will become stuck in an *infinite loop,* repeating certain operations over and over again like a broken record. In order to avoid this undesirable event, a programmer must make sure that an operation within a loop somehow changes the value or values being tested.

Originally, structured programming simply meant the use of these three basic control structures. These one-entry, one-exit structures made even complex programs easier to design, code, debug, understand, and maintain. Structured programming, however, has gradually come to include a number of related concepts and techniques. As the advantageousness of these innovations has become apparent, structured programming has not only been widely accepted but has become synonymous with proper programming. A few of these techniques are especially relevant to our discussion of structured programming: the avoidance of GOTO statements, top-down design, modularity, egoless programming, structured walkthroughs, and the chief programmer team.

Avoiding GOTO Statements

Many programming languages include a **GOTO statement** that causes an unconditional branch from one part of a program to another. In other words, a GOTO statement enables a programmer to make the flow jump from one point in a program to any other and continue from that point on. Before the advent of structured programming techniques, most programs were characterized by many GOTO statements that broke up the sequential flow.

Limiting unconditional branches

One of the motivations for the development of structured programming techniques was the realization in the late 1960s that the excessive, undisciplined use of GOTO statements often resulted in programs that were difficult to understand and to modify, overly complicated, and likely to contain errors. In short, GOTO statements can alter the logical flow of processing in a very unstructured way. However, this conclusion was not universally accepted: a great controversy arose among computer professionals. Those accustomed to using GOTOs as much as they pleased resisted the notion of limiting this use in any way. In the end, though, the foes of the GOTO won out. It's now generally accepted that the indiscriminate use of unconditional branches is poor programming practice. Most experts agree that sticking to the three basic control structures results in the best programs. Some programming languages lack built-in expressions for selection and iteration control structures, so it is acceptable to use GOTOs to construct them.

Top-Down Design

The technique of **top-down design** is a divide-and-conquer approach that involves breaking down a large task into successively smaller subtasks, organized hierarchically. The design process starts with the highest level and proceeds through the middle levels to the lowest level. Higher levels control the lower levels. Structure charts and HIPO charts are direct reflections of this design strategy.

Top-down design entails three steps:

1. Define the output to be produced, the input required, and the major processing tasks that must be performed to convert input to output.
2. Break down each major processing task into a hierarchy of independent modules.
3. Create the algorithm for each module, starting with the top one (or *main module*) and proceeding downward.

This approach is a major component of structured programming. It requires that the problem be clearly defined and that software requirements be explicitly stated before the design process can begin. This systematic manner of handling the design process makes program development more efficient. Coding is much easier, and testing takes less time because there are fewer errors. Finally, programs designed from the top down are much easier to maintain than those designed in a less organized fashion.

Modularity

A module, as we said earlier, is a set of related program statements that can be treated as a unit. The desirability of breaking down a large program into modules, or small *subprograms,* has been acknowledged for years. The concept of program modularity, however, takes this recommendation one step farther by being concerned with how modules are constructed and the relationships between them. To be useful, a module should be not merely a collection of related statements but a well-defined program segment. It should have a name and carry out a specific program function. Furthermore, like a control structure, a module should have only one entry and one exit. Although there is no limit to the number of statements a module can contain, it is generally accepted that a module should not be too large. About 50 lines (or one page) of source code is considered to be an appropriate size.

Coupling

One of the terms describing the relationship between modules is **coupling**, a measure of the strength of interconnection between two modules. *Highly coupled modules* are strongly interconnected; they are interdependent, so to understand one, we must also understand the other. *Loosely coupled modules,* on the other hand, have little dependence on each other. Modules are said to be *decoupled* if they are completely independent, with no interconnections. Basically, two modules of which one in some way controls the other or that pass data back and forth are coupled. The greater the extent of this control or data sharing, the higher the degree of coupling. Programs having loosely coupled modules are the easiest to understand, debug, and maintain because one module can be studied or changed without having to know very much about any of the other modules in the system. If modules are highly coupled, changes in one will very likely lead to changes in another.

Cohesion

Cohesion is a structured programming term used to describe the closeness of the relationships among the elements within a module. Ideally, the components of a module should be very closely related and directed toward achieving a single function. A highly cohesive module contains only those statements necessary for performing a single, well-defined task. Cohesion can be thought of as the glue that holds a module together. The clearest examples of program modules with high levels of cohesion are those that perform mathematical functions. For example, a module to compute a square root is certain to be highly cohesive. Nothing will be included that is not directly related to the single function of computing a number's square root.

As you may have guessed, coupling and cohesion are related. In general, the greater the cohesion of individual modules, the looser the coupling between them. Programmers who strive to make modules functionally cohesive will find that the resulting program demonstrates minimal coupling, which generally means easier maintenance.

Egoless Programming

We've been looking at some structured programming techniques that programmers can use to achieve the desirable end of well-designed, understandable, error-free programs. But what about the programmers themselves? Are there personality traits that facilitate good programming practice? In 1971, Gerald Weinberg published *The Psychology of Computer Programming*. In this book, Weinberg explored the relationship between programmers' attitudes and the quality of the programs they produced. He found that programmers and their employers often think of programming as a rather asocial job. This fosters the image of programmers as mysterious loners, working privately to find hidden solutions to esoteric problems. As a result, many programmers, though proud of their skills, are secretive or defensive about their work. Some are reluctant to share their techniques with others, afraid that their weaknesses may be uncovered and their images as software wizards destroyed. In short, Weinberg proposed that many programmers are egotistical about their work.

It's fairly obvious that such an attitude leads to the production of many programs that contain costly, hidden errors or that are difficult for others to understand. As the software industry grew and the scope of projects became greater, secretive, lone-wolf programmers became more and more of a liability. Weinberg suggested the practice of **egoless programming** as an alternative. According to this model, programming is a social activity, open to and benefiting from the inspection of colleagues, who check each other's work for errors in a constructive rather than a negative, fault-finding way. Complex programming is virtually impossible to do without making mistakes, but review by other programmers at all stages of program development can catch most of them and thus results in programs that are very nearly error-free. Since the emphasis is on the program rather than on who produces it, the software product is seen as a team achievement.

Cooperation rather than confrontation

CAREERS IN TECHNOLOGY
Computer Programmer

Job Description A computer programmer creates solutions to problems in business, science, and engineering in the form of logically constructed computer programs. On the basis of a systems analyst's recommendations (see Careers in Technology in Chapter 12), the programmer determines what data and instructions the computer requires in order to solve the problem. Next, the program is tested and debugged, and then a set of instructions is written for the computer operator (see Careers in Technology in Chapter 6) to follow in order to run it. A simple program may take a few hours to create, but a more complex program, using complicated mathematical formulas or numerous data files, may occupy a whole team of programmers for more than a year.

In many organizations, a programmer is responsible for both the analysis of problems and the creation of appropriate programs. Such a person is called a programmer analyst, and he or she fulfills the roles of both programmer and systems analyst, working on developing new programs or extending and maintaining existing ones—thus analyzing *and* solving problems.

Programmers usually work about 40 hours a week, but those hours often occur early in the morning, late at night, and on weekends, depending on when the computer is available for use. They are also expected to be on call to help the computer operator when a new program is run. This job is pretty demanding, but whether it puts the demands on the workers or the workers created the pressures to suit their inclinations is a good question. Programmers are often characterized as workaholics— ultradedicated and intensely professional individuals (often at the expense of their families and friends), who perform best under pressure, whether self-generated or job-related.

Qualifications Most employers require a bachelor's degree or certificate in data processing or in business administration with a data-processing background. Scientific or technological research organizations, however, generally require a graduate-level degree in some scientific field, along with a basic background in advanced mathematics and computer programming. Some businesses also want an MBA. A general knowledge of some specific programming language, such as BASIC, COBOL, RPG, or C (see Chapter 9), and familiarity with data base management systems (see Chapter 13) are often required, as is some experience with the particular hardware and systems used by the employer. Well-developed communication and administrative skills, as well as the ability to function efficiently both independently and as part of a team, are considered valuable assets.

Outlook The number of people employed as computer programmers rose from 170,000 in 1970 to over 300,000 by 1984. By 1990, the number of programmers is expected to climb to 500,000, mostly employed in large manufacturing firms, data-processing services, government agencies, and insurance companies. As a rule, more programmers are hired by large firms, which can afford their own expensive systems, than by smaller firms, which either use a data-processing service or have a simpler system running packaged programs.

In the last few years there has been a shortage of qualified programmers, and more than half of all job openings are still filled at the entry level by people lacking previous professional experience, although computer operators are prime candidates for promotion to a programming position. However, as for any good job, competition is increasingly intense and the shortages do not seem to be destined to last long. Chase Manhattan Bank in New York City recently received over 200 applications for a single entry-level programming job. The growing number of people seeking jobs in programming has resulted in a stiffening of the qualifications: many large companies now report that most certificates or two-year associate degrees are no longer enough— hands-on experience (at school or on the job) is necessary.

Another discouraging development is that programming is very prone to accelerated obsolescence, which means that the COBOL and FORTRAN you learned

Table 1. Outlook Summary: Employment in Computer Programming

Job Title	Employment			% Change	Average Number of Annual Openings	Average Entry Salary
	1970	1980	1990			
Computer programmer	161,337	341,000	500,000	+ 47%	38,000	$22,000[a]

Source: U.S. Bureau of Labor Statistics.
[a]The Center for Survey Research reported in 1984 that female programmers earn roughly 91 cents for every dollar earned by male programmers.

Figure 1 Outlook Summary: Employment in Computer Programming

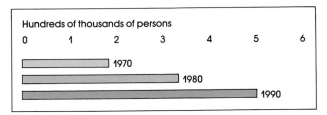

Table 2. Where the Jobs Are.

Industry	1978	1990	% Change
Agriculture, forestry, and fisheries	269	600	102.4
Mining	3,176	6,300	123.0
Construction	2,481	4,500	98.4
Manufacturing	73,830	129,000	74.7
Transportation, public utilities, and communications	12,445	23,000	84.8
Wholesale/retail trade	19,409	35,000	80.3
Finance, insurance, and real estate	26,300	51,000	93.9
Services	84,366	204,000	141.8
Government	24,722	46,600	88.5
Total, all industries	246,998	500,000	102.4

Source: U.S. Bureau of Labor Statistics.

in school may be replaced by some new programming language. Many programmers complain that they're constantly struggling to catch up with the technology they thought they'd mastered. A second common complaint is that programming jobs have become too routine and repetitive, with as much as 75% of the work involving the maintenance of old programs on outdated equipment—not a very glamorous occupation. The upshot of all this negative news is that you should be prepared for anything and surprised by nothing.

Figure 8.8 Egoless Programming
The concept of egoless programming rejects the notion of the programmer as a lone-wolf artist. Instead, it promotes programming as a social activity in which collegues constructively work together to develop more error-free software.

Programmers are not criticized for making errors (errors are seen as unavoidable), but they are praised for discovering them. In addition to minimizing the occurrence of errors in programs, the practice of egoless programming produces a more pleasant and effective working environment. (See Figure 8.8.)

Structured Walkthroughs

Step-by-step peer reviews

One specific way of implementing the practice of egoless programming is to schedule **structured walkthroughs**, or peer reviews of the design or coding of a computer program. It has been found that structured walkthroughs are one of the most effective ways to improve the quality of computer programs. Typically, a walkthrough is a meeting of the members of a programming team, each taking a specific role. For example, one member presents the design or code, another coordinates the activities, another takes notes, and others point out implications for future maintenance, standardization, and user needs. Usually, no managers or bosses attend, since their presence might inhibit honest evaluation of the program.

The basic purpose of a structured walkthrough is to detect errors, not to correct them; suggestions for better algorithms or justifications for the existing design or code have no place in a walkthrough. It's also necessary that all participants keep in mind that the program, not the programmer, is being reviewed. Ideally, if the proceedings follow formal guidelines no one's feelings will be hurt. Some data-processing managers aren't convinced that structured walkthroughs are worthwhile. Perhaps they aren't applicable to every programming situation, but they are another tool in the useful kit of structured programming.

The Chief Programmer Team

The coordination of a large programming project may require more than the general principles of egoless programming or the use of structured walkthroughs. The greater the number of people working on a program, the more likely it becomes that the design will suffer from too many contributions. What such a group undertaking needs is *conceptual integrity;* that is, the design appears and is developed as a unit instead of as a collection of disjointed ideas. The best way to achieve conceptual integrity is to have one person in charge of the design, thus ensuring consistency of purpose. This realization led to the implementation of chief programmer teams.

A **chief programmer team** is a collection of specialized personnel directed by a chief programmer, who prepares the software requirements, designs the overall structure of the program, and oversees all of the lower-level activities of the entire program development process. The team consists of several specialists whose roles are defined so the work will progress in an efficient manner. For example, the team may include an assistant administrator, a documentation editor, a code tester, a programming language specialist, and a secretary. Although each member of the team has responsibility for certain lower-level decisions, the chief programmer makes all major decisions. This organizational division helps to ensure communication among the personnel.

An organizational means for achieving design unity

The chief programmer team seems to work well for large programming projects. However, in some ways this model violates the principles of egoless programming. The chief programmer is sometimes perceived (and often self-perceived) as a superprogrammer. Since one person at the top is making all the important decisions, the potential is there for egotism to detract from the quality of the product. The situation is by definition not democratic, and if the chief programmer decides to review all the code personally rather than delegating some of the responsibility or making it a group activity, the result may well be confrontation instead of cooperation.

SUMMARY

The Program Development Process

The program development process is the series of activities that is necessary to create a successful computer program.

Defining the Problem This crucial first step involves determining exactly what needs to be done.

Developing the Software Requirements This involves drawing up exact specifications of the desired output, the required input, and the processing for converting input to output.

Designing the Program This very important step is the determination of how the requirements are to be fulfilled. An algorithm is developed, and one or more program design aids are employed to express the logic of the computer program. Flowcharts, pseudocode, decision tables, structure charts, and HIPO charts are some of the most commonly used of these aids.

Coding the Program Once the design is complete, it must be expressed in a programming language before it can be entered into the computer.

Testing the Program The finished computer program must be thoroughly tested to make sure that it does exactly what it was intended to do. Testing includes desk checking, translation, and debugging.

Installing and Maintaining the Program The tested program must be put into everyday operation, and any overlooked bugs must be fixed. Modifications, updates, and improvements may also occasionally need to be made.

Documenting the Program Compiled throughout the entire program development process, documentation is a detailed description of the program's algorithm, design, coding method, testing, and proper usage.

Structured Programming

Structured programming is a set of techniques for program development; it is a discipline that has produced greater productivity, increased economy, fewer errors, decreased debugging time, clearer source code, and longer software lifetimes.

Control Structures   Structured programming minimizes complexity by using only three basic control structures: sequence, selection (IF-THEN or IF-THEN-ELSE), and iteration (DO WHILE or DO UNTIL).

Avoiding GOTO Statements   The overuse of GOTO statements (unconditional branching statements) in computer programs results in complex, error-prone code. Programmers should stick to the three basic control structures.

Top-Down Design   This design approach involves breaking down large tasks into hierarchically organized, smaller subtasks. Then the subtasks, or modules, are designed from the top, or the highest level, down to the lowest.

Modularity   Modules should be well-defined program segments with one entry and one exit. Coupling, or the degree to which modules are interdependent, should be minimized. Cohesion, or the degree to which the statements within a module reflect a single function, should be maximized.

Egoless Programming   This practice recommends that programming be viewed as a social activity, open to and benefiting from the involvement of colleagues.

Structured Walkthroughs   Structured walkthroughs are formally organized sessions for peer group review of program design or coding. Their purpose is the discovery of errors.

The Chief Programmer Team   A large programming project may best be carried out by a collection of specialized personnel directed by a chief programmer, who prepares the software requirements, designs the overall structure, and oversees all aspects of development. Having a single person in charge helps ensure that a large program will have conceptual integrity.

COMPUTER CONCEPTS

As an extra review of the chapter, try defining the following terms. If you have any trouble with any of them, refer to the page number listed.

computer program 215
program development process 215
software requirements 216
user interface 217
algorithm 218
program design aid 218
flowchart 218
system flowchart 221
macroflowcharts 221
microflowcharts 223
pseudocode 223
decision table 226
structure chart 226

module 226
HIPO chart 227
coding 229
syntax 229
source code 230
desk checking 230
translation 231
debugging 231
program maintenance 232
documentation 232
structured programming 233
control structure 231
sequence control structure 231

selection control structure 231
iteration control structure 231
GOTO statement 235
top-down design 236
coupling 236
cohesion 237
egoless programming 237
structured walkthroughs 240
chief programmer team 241

REVIEW QUESTIONS

1. Describe what is meant by a successful computer program.
2. List the seven stages of the program development process.
3. What do the three main parts of the software requirements specify?
4. What factors must be considered in specifying a program's output?
5. What factors must be considered in specifying a program's input?
6. What must the software requirements say about a program's processing tasks?

7. What is the first task of program design?
8. How is a flowchart like a map?
9. Why has pseudocode become a very popular alternative to flowcharts?
10. How do decision tables help in the design of logically complex programs?
11. How is a structure chart like a corporate organizational chart?
12. What are the three types of diagrams in a HIPO chart?
13. What factors may influence which computer language is chosen for coding a program?
14. What is usually the most difficult, and time-consuming stage of program development?
15. What are the three phases of thorough program testing?
16. Why do programs have to be maintained?
17. When should program documentation be compiled?
18. What problems instigated the development of structured programming?
19. Why should GOTO statements be avoided?
20. What are the three steps of top-down design?
21. To what degree should modules be coupled, and why?
22. How cohesive should a module be, and why?
23. How does egoless programming reduce errors?
24. What is the basic purpose of a structured walkthrough?
25. Why create a chief programmer team for a programming project?

A SHARPER FOCUS

Now that you've completed this chapter, you should be able to answer the following questions about the chapter opening.

1. Does Michael Wise follow the principles of egoless programming? of structured programming?
2. How do the stages of the program development process apply to the creation of the video game "Captain Goodnight"?
3. What does the chapter opening tell you about coding, debugging, and modules?

PROJECTS

1. Use a flowchart to design a program that will compute your grade-point average. Assume the input consists of a record containing 10 letter grades, one for each course you've taken so far. A letter grade of A is worth 5 points, a B is worth 4, a C is worth 3, a D is worth 2, and an F is worth 1. Add up the total number of grade points, and divide by the number of courses to get the grade-point average. The program should output a printed grade-point average.

2. Modify the program you designed in the first project so it drops the lowest grade and averages the remaining 9 grades. Draw a flowchart of the new design.

3. Prepare a report that explores the extent to which the various structured programming techniques described in this chapter are actually used in the "real world" of data processing. Recent books, magazines, and newspapers such as *Computerworld* will be helpful. If possible, talk to programmers at a local business and ask them if they are familiar with such things as HIPO charts, structured walkthroughs, and chief programmer teams.

4. Most of us encounter algorithms daily; they weren't invented just for the computer. For example, there may be an algorithm on the back of your bank statement, showing how to balance your checking account using the checks and deposit slips that were returned. List and briefly describe five more algorithms that you frequently use.

5. Draw up and make a flowchart of an algorithm that will help you select the courses you'll take next term. Your algorithm should take into account various conditions that will affect your selection, such as closed sections, prerequisites, conflicting class times, etc. Confine your algorithm to your personal situation.

9

Programming Languages

FOCUS ON . . . THE GRASS ROOTS OF A PROGRAMMING LANGUAGE

It was there that someone showed [Bob Albrecht] BASIC, the computer language developed by John Kemeny of Dartmouth to accommodate, Kemeny wrote, "the possibility of millions of people writing their own computer programs. . . . Profiting from years of experience with FORTRAN, we designed a new language that was particularly easy for the layman to learn [and] that facilitated communication between man and machine." Albrecht immediately decided that BASIC was *it*, and FORTRAN was dead. BASIC was interactive, so that people hungry for computer use would get instant response from the machine (FORTRAN was geared for batch-processing). It used English-like words like INPUT and THEN and GOTO, so it was easier to learn. And it had a built-in random number generator, so kids could use it to write games quickly. Albrecht knew even then that games would provide the seductive scent that would lure kids to programming—and hackerism. Albrecht became a prophet of BASIC and eventually cofounded a group called SHAFT—Society to Help Abolish FORTRAN Teaching. . . .

Albrecht thought that some sort of publication should chronicle this movement, be a lightning rod for new developments. So the group started a tabloid publication called *People's Computer Company.* . . .

There was little response from the ivory towers of academia or the blue-sky institutions of research. Hackers like those at MIT would not even blink at PCC—which, after all, printed program listings in BASIC, for God's sake, not their beloved assembly language. But the new breed of hardware hackers . . . who were trying to figure out ways for more computer access for themselves and perhaps others, discovered the tabloid and would write in, offering program listings, suggestions on buying computer parts, or just plain encouragement. . . .

The success of the newspaper led Dymax to spin off the operation into a nonprofit company called PCC, which would include not only the publication, but the operation of the burgeoning computer center itself, which ran classes and offered off-the-street computing for fifty cents an hour to anyone who cared to use it. . . .

As always, planners like Bob Albrecht would talk about the *issues* of computing, while the hackers concentrated on swapping technical data, or complained about Albrecht's predilection for BASIC, which hackers considered a "fascist" language because its limited structure did not encourage maximum access to the machine and decreased a programmer's power. It would not take many hours before the hackers slipped away to the clattering terminals, leaving the activists engaged in heated conversation about this development or that.

In Chapter 8, we looked at the general process of program development. In this chapter, we examine some of the most popular and important languages that programmers employ to do their job.

During the past 30 years, the development of a new programming language has been a fairly common event. Today, more than 100 languages are being used for programming computers, and new ones are still being introduced every year. This abundance contrasts sharply with the fact that most programmers don't even attempt to use more than a few languages. In the face of so many widely different choices, how do programmers know which ones to learn in the first place? Just how does one decide which language is best suited for a given purpose? To answer these questions, in this chapter we present an overview of the characteristics and applications of programming languages in general and more closely examine several of the most important high-level ones in detail.

PROGRAMMING LANGUAGES IN GENERAL

A language, as you know, is a means of communicating, usually via human speech or written symbols. A computer **programming language** is a set of symbols and usage rules employed to direct the operations of a computer. Just like any human language, a programming language consists of a set of symbols; rules of *syntax* or *grammar* governing how those symbols are combined; and *semantics,* or meanings associated with certain symbol combinations. However, unlike human languages,

What a programming language is

programming languages have very limited vocabularies and very specific functions. Human languages are used to express the vast, rich world of human experience and thus are full of colorful, context-dependent words and ambiguous rules. The single purpose of programming languages is the construction of computer programs.

Characteristics of Programming Languages

Instructions found in every language

Although there are many different programming languages, each one designed to solve certain types of problems, all of them have the basic function of directing the operations of a computer. Therefore, certain general classes of instructions are present in every programming language, which can be categorized as follows:

- *Instructions for input and output.* These instructions tell the computer to get data and present information. They usually provide details indicating which input or output device to use, where the data or information is stored, and what formatting rules to use.

- *Instructions for calculations.* These instructions direct the computer to perform common mathematical operations such as addition, subtraction, multiplication, and division.

- *Instructions for transfer of control.* These instructions allow deviations from the normal sequential processing of operations. A deviation may be based, for example, on the value of a computed result or the existence of some specified condition. These instructions are used to transfer program control (to *branch*) to an instruction other than the one immediately following. (The selection and iteration structures we introduced in Chapter 8 are examples of how control is transferred based on the outcome of some logical or arithmetical comparison. The GOTO statement, also introduced in Chapter 8, is an example of an unconditional transfer of control.)

- *Instructions for data movement, storage, and retrieval.* These instructions cause the movement, storage, and retrieval of data in primary memory. For example, a data item may be copied from one location to another, the result of a computation may be stored at a specified location, or an intermediate result may be retrieved from a given location.

All programming languages must be able, in one way or another, to perform the above types of operations. As we'll see, however, there are marked differences in how the various languages accomplish these things.

In addition to the above kinds of statements, almost every computer language includes some provision for programmers to insert explanatory notes within their programs. These descriptive sections of text are known as **comments** and are ignored by the computer during program translation and execution. Their purpose is to help clarify the program's operation for users. Different languages have different ways of denoting and delimiting comments.

Levels of Language

Four general categories of languages

Although there are many different computer languages, most of them fall under one of only four broad categories. These groupings are also known as *levels* of language because they can be arranged hierarchically. The lowest level in this hierarchy is occupied by those languages that are closest to what computers use, which is binary zeros and ones. The highest level is occupied by languages that appear similar in many ways to English (or some other language that people speak). Going from the lowest to the highest level, the classifications are

Machine languages
Assembly languages
High-level languages
Nonprocedural languages

MACHINE LANGUAGES

The only language that can be directly used by a particular computer is its own machine language. A machine language program consists of binary numbers that represent the instructions, memory locations, and data necessary to solve a specific problem. Thus any machine language consists entirely of zeros and ones, but their arrangement differs for each model of computer. A machine language instruction is generally made up of two parts. The first part is a binary code representing the operation to be performed. Each computer has such an **operation code**, or **opcode**, for every operation it can perform. The second part of the instruction specifies the **operand**, that is, the number on which the operation is to be performed. This can be a piece of data itself or the memory location of the desired piece of data. For example, the machine language instruction to add 8 to the value in the accumulator looks like this for the IBM Personal Computer (it might be helpful to review Chapter 3, particularly the discussion of what the accumulator is):

The languages of zeros and ones

$$\underbrace{00000101}_{\text{ADD}} \quad \underbrace{00001000}_{\text{8 (in binary)}}$$

In the early days of computing, all programming was done in machine languages. However, since every instruction, memory location, and piece of data have to be specified in strings of zeros and ones, machine language programming is extremely difficult, time-consuming, and error-prone. People aren't very happy, accurate, or efficient when they have to write zeros and ones all day. As a result, languages that are easier for people to use have been developed. Programs written in any of these other languages are automatically translated, after they are entered into the computer, by other computer programs into machine language. Machine languages are now rarely used for programming. However, it's important to realize that programs written in any other language must always be translated into machine language before they can be executed by a computer.

ASSEMBLY LANGUAGES

At a higher level than that of machine languages, but still on a fairly low level, are assembly languages. An assembly language consists of easy-to-remember abbreviations, or **mnemonic symbols**, that represent the zeros and ones of machine language. For example, an assembly language might use ADD, MUL, and STO instead of the binary codes for the computer's addition, multiplication, and storage operations. **Symbolic addressing**, or the practice of using representative names

Machine-specific symbolic languages

instead of numeric memory addresses, is usually allowed when using assembly language. That means a programmer can call a memory location TOTAL rather than 00001001. In doing this, the programmer creates a *variable*, a meaningful abstraction for a given location. In addition to symbolic addressing, most assembly languages allow programmers to use octal, hexadecimal, or decimal numbers for data values. All of these factors make assembly languages much easier to use than machine languages.

Figure 9.1 presents a simple example of an assembly language program for the IBM Personal Computer. Assembly languages, like machine languages, are specific to particular machines; that is, the assembly language shown here for the IBM Personal Computer isn't the same as the assembly language for the Apple Macintosh. Another similarity between assembly languages and machine languages is that individual assembly language instructions aren't very powerful. In other words, many instructions may be needed to get the computer to perform even the simplest tasks.

Figure 9.1 An Assembly Language Program

A very simple example of an assembly language program for a popular microcomputer, the IBM Personal Computer. Assembly language is often used for programs or parts of programs that must execute very efficiently or must deal intimately with some machine-dependent task. Each computer model has its own unique assembly language. This program isn't of any practical use; it is intended to be extremely elementary, so you can get a feel for what assembly language programming is like. All it does is to calculate the sum of two numbers that have been placed in primary memory, subtract a third number, and place the result in another memory location. Note the use of *comments* (any text to the right of a semicolon) to annotate the program.

```
; Assembly Language Program Example
;
; This program calculates the sum of two numbers, subtracts a third number
; and stores the result in memory.
;
;
DATA      SEGMENT                  ; Define the data to be used.
;
NUMBER1   DW      20               ; Store the 1st number (20) in memory.
NUMBER2   DW      35               ; Store the 2nd number (35) in memory.
NUMBER3   DW      12               ; Store the 3rd number (12) in memory.
RESULT    DW      ?                ; Reserve a place in memory for the result.
;
DATA      ENDS
;
;
CODE      SEGMENT                  ; Describe the processing steps.
          ASSUME  CS:CODE,DS:DATA  ; Tell computer where to find code and data.
;
          MOV     AX,NUMBER1       ; Move the 1st number into the accumulator.
          MOV     BX,NUMBER2       ; Move the 2nd number into the BX register.
          ADD     AX,BX            ; Add the two and place result in accumulator.
          MOV     BX,NUMBER3       ; Move the 3rd number into the BX register.
          SUB     AX,BX            ; Subtract 3rd number from previous sum.
          MOV     RESULT,AX        ; Move the result from accumulator into memory.
;
CODE      ENDS
          END
```

Unlike a machine language program, an assembly language program must be translated before it can be executed. A special program called an **assembler** translates the assembly language for a particular computer into that computer's machine language. A program in the form in which it's written by a programmer in assembly language (or in any other language that must be translated) is known as *source code*. After the source code has been converted by the assembler (or other translator program) to machine language, it's referred to as **object code**.

Although much more efficient than machine language programming, assembly language programming is still rather tedious and error-prone because of the tremendous amount of detail that must be attended to. The use of assembly language is, however, worth the extra effort when the unique characteristics of a particular computer must be allowed for or when the most efficient use of computer resources is a crucial factor. Because assembly language gives programmers control of the internal functioning of the computer at a very basic level, it is often used when peripheral devices are to be interfaced, or connected to the computer. Also, because of this control, assembly language can be used by skillful programmers to produce programs that run faster and take up less space in memory. Thus assembly languages have a significant role in the programming of certain types of machine-dependent tasks.

HIGH-LEVEL LANGUAGES

By far the most utilized category of programming languages is the high-level languages, whose statements are closer to human language or mathematical notation than are machine or assembly languages. High-level languages were developed to help programmers focus their attention on the task to be performed and pay less attention to machine-specific details. These languages are more abstract than low-level languages; they make it easier for programmers to express more complex processing operations using fewer statements.

Abstract languages

The high-level languages are often subdivided into procedure-oriented languages and problem-oriented languages. A **procedure-oriented language** is a general-purpose language designed to let programmers express the logic of problem solutions without having to pay attention to the details of how the computer processes a program. Some examples of procedure-oriented languages are FORTRAN, COBOL, BASIC, Pascal, C, and Ada. A **problem-oriented language** is a more specialized language, designed so programmers can easily handle a certain rather narrow range of predefined problems. When using a problem-oriented language, a programmer may only have to specify the input and output requirements and the problem parameters. The problem-oriented language provides self-contained handling of the logic necessary to produce the desired results. Two examples of problem-oriented languages are RPG, used to produce reports and update files, and APT, used to program automated machine tools.

We'll describe each of the important high-level languages a bit later. First, let's deal with some important general aspects that affect their application.

Compilers and Interpreters

Like assembly language programs, high-level language programs must be translated into machine language before they can be run by a computer. Unlike

Translator programs

assembly languages, however, most high-level languages have the advantage of **machine-independence**; that is, they can be run on any computer as long as it has the applicable translator program. Most high-level languages are translated, or *compiled*, into machine language by special programs known as **compilers**. Compilers are to high-level languages what assemblers are to assembly languages: they translate the language into computer-usable form. As an indication of the machine-independence of high-level languages, a FORTRAN program written and compiled (with the IBM FORTRAN compiler) on an IBM Personal Computer can often be run on an Apple II microcomputer with few changes if it is simply recompiled with the Apple FORTRAN compiler.

Some high-level languages can also be translated into machine language by programs called **interpreters**. A compiler translates an entire high-level language program all at once, producing a complete, executable machine language program; an interpreter translates and executes one statement at a time as it's entered into the computer. This ongoing translation allows a programmer to try out ideas or make changes to programs and see the results almost immediately. Consequently, an interpreter provides a more interactive programming environment, which can make it easier to write programs. The catch is that although they can speed up program development, interpreters often produce translated programs that run slower or take up more memory space than they would if they had been compiled. Once a program has been compiled, the compiler is no longer needed to run it because it has been fully translated into machine language. An interpreter, on the other hand, must be used each time the high-level language program is run because the translation isn't stored. A compiler is like a human translator who is given a book written in English and returns the Russian version of the whole text. Once the book has been translated into Russian, the translator's job is done. An interpreter is like someone who works at the United Nations converting English into Russian as it is being spoken—he or she must be present for every English speech.

For some high-level languages, both compilers and interpreters are available for program translation. BASIC, for example, is usually translated by an interpreter, but BASIC compilers are also fairly common.

The Advantages of High-Level Languages

What high-level languages have to offer

High-level languages offer many advantages over assembly and machine languages: they are easier to learn, write, correct, and revise. Furthermore, because of their greater degree of abstraction, they allow programmers to pay more attention to the problem at hand and to be less concerned with machine-dependent details of processing. As a result, very large, complex programs can be written in high-level languages (it would still be a demanding job but a much less difficult one than with lower-level languages). Programming errors are easier to avoid when high-level languages are used and easier to find when they do occur. It's also easier to follow the principles of structured programming with high-level languages, which offer all the advantages we discussed in Chapter 8. Finally, the machine-independence of high-level languages means that programs can be transported from computer to computer, which frees programmers from having to learn a different language for each computer they work with.

MAJOR HIGH-LEVEL LANGUAGES

Now that we've placed high-level languages in the general hierarchy of computer languages, let's look closely at several of the most important ones in use today: FORTRAN, COBOL, BASIC, Pascal, C, Ada, and RPG. Each of these languages is noteworthy because of its widespread use or profound influence. If you use computers, it's very likely that you'll hear about or even learn at least one of these high-level languages.

The most widely used and influential languages

We'll briefly examine some important aspects of each of these languages, including features, program format, data types, and control statements. By *features*, we mean those characteristics that make a language useful as well as those that limit its use. The program format specifies what elements a program written in a particular language must contain and how they must be arranged. The **data types** of a computer language are the kinds of data that can be processed using that language; they indicate what applications the language is best used for. **Control statements** show how the flow of program logic is determined and reveal how structured a language is. Finally, we include a brief example of a program written in each of these languages (except RPG) so you can see what they look like. For continuity, we've shown how parts of the accounting software for Keyboard Koncepts (the company we invented in Chapter 8) could be programmed in the different languages.

FORTRAN

FORTRAN, or FORmula TRANslator, was developed by IBM and introduced in 1957. Designed with scientists, engineers, and mathematicians in mind, it was the first commercially available high-level language. To this day, FORTRAN is the programming language that is the most widely used in the scientific community.

A number-crunching language

Features

FORTRAN's most outstanding feature is the ease with which it enables programmers to express complex computations. Because of its mathematical orientation, efficient execution, and numerical precision, it is the top "number-crunching" language. Noted for its simplicity and conciseness, FORTRAN is probably the most highly standardized computer language. These things, along with its familiarity, have made it a favorite of many mathematically inclined users. In addition, it's commonly and effectively used on all types of computers, from microcomputers to supercomputers.

However, FORTRAN isn't very good at handling alphabetic data or performing file processing tasks. It doesn't have a wide variety of data types or control statements. Furthermore, the logic of FORTRAN programs is often difficult for users to follow. Programming errors occur frequently and can be difficult to find and correct. In general, FORTRAN isn't particularly well suited to business applications, which typically require extensive manipulation of files containing nonnumeric data.

Figure 9.2 shows an example of a simple FORTRAN program.

(a)

```
2850 25 08350
3850 93 10265
4850 41 11500
5858 10 12025
6850 15 13500
7850 20 15000
```

(b)

MODEL	DOLLAR VALUE
2850	$ 2087.50
3850	$ 9546.45
4850	$ 4715.00
5858	$ 1202.50
6850	$ 2025.00
7850	$ 3000.00

Figure 9.2   A FORTRAN Program

This simple FORTRAN program, compiled and run using the IBM Personal Computer FORTRAN compiler, implements a part of the software for Keyboard Koncepts. It calculates the dollar values of various keyboard models in stock.   (a) The input file contains each keyboard model number, how many units are in stock, and the unit price. The decimal points are assumed to be two places from the right in the unit prices. The decimal points do not have to be entered with the input because FORTRAN allows the programmer to specify where they should be when the numbers are entered. (b) The output of the program, presented on the microcomputer's display screen, lists the model number and the total dollar value of all units of that model in stock.   (c) In the FORTRAN program, all lines beginning with C are comments that are ignored by the computer.

(c)

```
      C          FORTRAN Program Example
      C
      C          This program calculates the dollar values of various keyboard models
      C          in stock.
      C
      C
      C          Declare the variables:
      C
                 INTEGER MODEL, UNITS
                 REAL    PRICE, VALUE
      C
      C
      C          Tell the computer the input file this program will use.
      C
                 OPEN(3, FILE='INFILE', STATUS='OLD')
      C
      C          Print a heading for the output.
      C
                 WRITE(*,50)
      50         FORMAT(1X,'MODEL   DOLLAR VALUE')
      C
      100        CONTINUE
      C
      C          Get the data from the input file. If there's no more, then stop.
      C
                 READ(3, 200,END=400) MODEL, UNITS, PRICE
      200        FORMAT(I4, 1X, I2, 1X, F6.2)
      C
      C          Calculate the dollar value.
      C
                 VALUE = UNITS * PRICE
      C
      C          Write the information to the display.
      C
                 WRITE(*, 300) MODEL, VALUE
      300        FORMAT(1X, I4, 3X, '$', F8.2)
      C
      C          Loop again to process more data.
      C
                 GOTO 100
      C
      400        STOP
                 END
```

Program Format

FORTRAN was originally developed when keypunch machines were the dominant input device. Consequently, FORTRAN programs have an 80-character-per-line fixed format. A FORTRAN program consists of a series of statements, which begin in predefined line positions, concluded with an END statement. Statements that are to be branched to must be preceded by line numbers so that they can be referenced. Variables are introduced as they are needed and often lack an explicit declaration as to what type of data they are to hold. Large programs are often subdivided into subprograms, of which FORTRAN has two types: subroutines and functions. A **subroutine** is a sequence of statements, or module, that performs a particular processing task and can be called on from various locations in the main program. A **function** is like a subroutine except that it returns a single value (for example, the square root of a number) to the main program.

Data Types

The data types that can be processed by FORTRAN programs reveal its mathematical orientation. Integer (fixed-point), real (floating-point), and complex (containing the square root of -1) numbers can be processed, as well as logical values (also called *Boolean values,* and consisting of true and false). FORTRAN offers a *double-precision capability,* which means results can be calculated to twice as many significant digits as are in regular real numbers (in other words, results are very accurate). Some newer versions of FORTRAN include a character data type that facilitates the processing of alphanumeric characters. FORTRAN also allows the use of **arrays**, ordered sets or lists of data items identified by a single name.

Control Statements

FORTRAN has three major control statements: the GOTO statement (an unconditional transfer of control), the IF statement (a conditional transfer), and the DO statement (a loop structure). This rather limited collection of simple control structures makes it somewhat difficult to apply the principles of structured programming with FORTRAN (and is due to the fact that FORTRAN was invented before the blossoming of structured programming). Newer and more commonly used versions of FORTRAN, however, such as FORTRAN-77 and WATFIV-S, do have enhanced control structures.

COBOL

The name COBOL stands for COmmon Business Oriented Language. COBOL was introduced in 1960, after having been developed by the Conference on Data Systems Languages (CODASYL), a committee of government and industry representatives called together by the Department of Defense. COBOL was the first high-level language suitable for business data processing, and its use was greatly encouraged by the U.S. government. Consequently, it has been applied extensively throughout business and industry and may well be the most widely known and used computer language in the world.

The business-as-usual language

Figure 9.3   A COBOL Program
This program represents the same algorithm as in Figure 9.2, but here it is expressed
in COBOL. The input file and the output are not repeated because they would look
the same. This program was run on a Control Data Corporation mainframe computer, the CYBER 175. Comments in COBOL are preceded by an asterisk.

```
        IDENTIFICATION DIVISION.

*   THIS DIVISION CONTAINS GENERAL DOCUMENTATION DETAILS.

        PROGRAM-ID.     COBOL-PROGRAM-EXAMPLE.
        AUTHOR.         ERNIE COLANTONIO.
        DATE-WRITTEN.   FEBRUARY 24, 1986.
        REMARKS.        THIS PROGRAM CALCULATES THE DOLLAR VALUES OF VARIOUS
                        KEYBOARD MODELS IN STOCK.

        ENVIRONMENT DIVISION.

*   THIS DIVISION CONTAINS MACHINE-SPECIFIC DETAILS.

        CONFIGURATION SECTION.
        SOURCE-COMPUTER.        CYBER-175.
        OBJECT-COMPUTER.        CYBER-175.

        INPUT-OUTPUT SECTION.
        FILE-CONTROL.
                SELECT INPUT-FILE ASSIGN TO INFILE-FZ.

        DATA DIVISION.

*   THIS DIVISION DESCRIBES THE FORMAT OF THE FILES AND DATA.

        FILE SECTION.

        FD      INPUT-FILE
                LABEL RECORDS ARE OMITTED
                DATA RECORD IS MODEL-RECORD.
        01      MODEL-RECORD.
                02      MODEL-NUMBER-IN         PIC 9(4).
                02      FILLER                  PIC X.
                02      NUMBER-OF-UNITS         PIC 99.
                02      FILLER                  PIC X.
                02      UNIT-PRICE              PIC 999V99.

        WORKING-STORAGE SECTION.

        01      DOLLAR-SUM                      PIC 9(5)V99.
        01      MODEL-VALUE-RECORD.
                02      MODEL-NUMBER-OUT        PIC 9(4).
                02      FILLER                  PIC X(3).
                02      DOLLAR-VALUE            PIC $ZZZZZ.99.
        01      END-OF-FILE-INDICATOR           PIC X VALUE "N".
                88 END-OF-FILE VALUE IS "Y".
                88 NOT-END-OF-FILE  VALUE IS "N".
```

```
PROCEDURE DIVISION.

*   THIS DIVISION CONTAINS THE ACTUAL PROCESSING INSTRUCTIONS.

    MAIN-PROGRAM.
            OPEN INPUT INPUT-FILE.
            DISPLAY "MODEL   DOLLAR VALUE".
            READ INPUT-FILE RECORD
                AT END MOVE "Y" TO END-OF-FILE-INDICATOR.
            PERFORM PROCESS-RECORDS UNTIL END-OF-FILE.
            CLOSE INPUT-FILE.
            STOP RUN.

    PROCESS-RECORDS.
            MOVE UNIT-PRICE TO DOLLAR-SUM.
            COMPUTE DOLLAR-VALUE = NUMBER-OF-UNITS * DOLLAR-SUM.
            MOVE MODEL-NUMBER-IN TO MODEL-NUMBER-OUT.
            DISPLAY MODEL-VALUE-RECORD.
            READ INPUT-FILE RECORD
                AT END MOVE "Y" TO END-OF-FILE-INDICATOR.
```

Features

COBOL's outstanding features include its ready handling of the input and output of large volumes of alphanumeric data, its machine-independence, and its Englishlike vocabulary and syntax. Business data processing usually involves a great deal of input, output, and file manipulation, with few and relatively simple mathematical computations. COBOL functions well in such an environment. Another strength of COBOL lies in its specifically designed machine-independence. What this means is that COBOL programs can be run on different computer systems with few modifications, meaning that the programs have both portability and longevity. Finally, COBOL is noted for its Englishlike statements that often make programs understandable even to casual readers. For this reason, COBOL is sometimes referred to as a *self-documenting language*.

This self-documenting capability, however, is also the source of much of the criticism directed at COBOL. COBOL programs are quite wordy—it's next to impossible to write a "short" one. COBOL has a long list of **reserved words**, words with set meanings that aren't available for programmers to use as data or variable names. This frequently frustrates programmers. In addition, COBOL requires a relatively large and sophisticated compiler, which can make it difficult to implement on some small computers. Although there are COBOL compilers for microcomputers, they tend to be expensive and slow and to use a lot of space in memory. Despite these drawbacks and its unsuitability for complex computations, COBOL is likely to remain a very important language in the business world for the foreseeable future because so much business software has already been written in it.

Figure 9.3 is an example of a COBOL program.

Program Format

All COBOL programs have a specified, uniform format. The basic unit of a program is the *sentence*, which ends with a period. Sentences make up *paragraphs;*

paragraphs make up *sections;* and sections make up *divisions.* Every COBOL program must have four divisions. The *IDENTIFICATION DIVISION* contains the name of the program and its author, the date it was written, and other documentation details. The *ENVIRONMENT DIVISION* specifies the computer on which the program is to be run and lists the names of the input and output files to be used by the program. The *DATA DIVISION* lists and describes the exact formats of all variables, records, and files that the program will use. Finally, the *PROCEDURE DIVISION* contains the instructions that perform the data processing.

Data Types

A central rule of COBOL is that all data are in character form unless explicitly declared to be numeric. Only numeric quantities can be used in computations. This reflects COBOL's data-processing orientation and simplifies the handling of common items like names, addresses, model identifications or code numbers, inventories, and dollar amounts. COBOL allows the use of simple single variables, as well as more complex hierarchical record structures and tables. All data must be defined and their exact formats specified in the DATA DIVISION.

Control Statements

COBOL has three major control statements: the GOTO statement, the IF-ELSE statement, and the PERFORM statement. As in FORTRAN, the GOTO is an unconditional transfer of control, and the IF-ELSE is a conditional transfer of control. The PERFORM statement serves both as a looping structure and as a call to execute a named set of instructions (that is, a module). COBOL, like FORTRAN, was developed before the principles of structured programming became accepted. However, the combination of COBOL's control statements and its sentence-paragraph-section-division format produces fairly structured, modular programs.

BASIC

A beginner's language

BASIC, or Beginners' All-purpose Symbolic Instruction Code, was developed by Dr. John Kemeny and Dr. Thomas Kurtz at Dartmouth College in 1965. Originally designed as a simple, instructive, interactive language for use with time-sharing computer systems, BASIC has become the most widely used high-level language for microcomputers.

Features

BASIC's most striking feature is its simplicity. It is very easy to learn and to use. Users can often begin to write and run functional programs after only a few hours of instruction and practice. Derived from both FORTRAN and ALGOL, BASIC in many ways resembles a somewhat simplified version of FORTRAN. As an interactive language by design, BASIC is most often translated by small, compact interpreters. However, BASIC compilers are also quite common. Applicable to both computational and alphanumeric data-processing tasks, BASIC has been extensively employed by users of all types of small computers. BASIC is very suitable for microcomputers, and pared-down versions are even available for notebook and pocket-sized computers. Figure 9.4 is an illustration of a BASIC program.

(a)

```
2500.00
5286.50
1525.25
1870.50
3205.75
2150.00
4100.25
1000.00
895.25
3651.75
2225.25
3525.75
2100.25
4050.00
3150.50
```

Figure 9.4   A BASIC Program

This simple BASIC program computes the total of a month's customer payments to Keyboard Koncepts. This program was written and run with the IBM Personal Computer BASIC interpreter. (a) The input file to this program consists of a list of customer payments, one to a line. (b) The output, presented on the display screen, consists of a single line reporting the sum of all the payments in the input file.
(c) In the BASIC program, the lines on which REM (REMark) appears are comments.

(b)

```
Sum of payments is $41237
```

(c)

```
10   REM    BASIC Program Example
20   REM
30   REM    This program calculates the sum total of a month's customer
40   REM    payments for Keyboard Koncepts.
50   REM
65   REM    "C" is the variable holding the payment counter.
70   REM    "S" is the variable holding the sum of payments accumulator.
75   REM
80       LET C = 0
90       LET S = 0
100  REM
110  REM    Tell the computer what the input file is.
120  REM
130      OPEN "INDATA" FOR INPUT AS #1
140  REM
150  REM    Get a payment (P), if there are no more, go to line 280
160  REM
170      IF EOF(1) THEN 280
180      INPUT #1, P
190  REM
200  REM    Increment the counter and accumulator.
210  REM
220      LET S = S + P
230      LET C = C + 1
240  REM
250  REM    Loop again.
260  REM
270      GOTO 170
280      PRINT "Sum of payments is $"; S
290  REM
300      END
```

Leading the list of BASIC's negative features is its lack of standardization; it sometimes seems that each computer uses a different version, or dialect, of BASIC. Fortunately, a core of certain BASIC features is common to almost every version, but program transportability is still a frequent problem. Also, BASIC's very simplicity can be a drawback when it lacks some needed capability. Furthermore, this simplicity does make it rather difficult to write very long or very complex programs. Finally, the ease of programming in BASIC is often offset by slower running times and less efficient programs.

Program Format

The format of BASIC programs is quite simple and unrestrictive. A program consists of a series of statements terminated by an END statement. Statements are entered in a free format, one or more to the line. The lines must be consecutively numbered. BASIC programs can be subdivided into subprograms, but this capability isn't as sophisticated as in most other high-level languages.

Data Types

Although the data types that are acceptable vary somewhat depending on the version of BASIC, all BASIC dialects handle real numbers and *strings,* or groups, of characters. And almost all BASIC dialects support arrays of real numbers and arrays of character strings. The small set of data types was intentional; it was part of BASIC's overall simplicity. Most manufacturers have augmented the original set with such additions as integers and double-precision numbers.

Control Statements

BASIC's control statements are much like those found in FORTRAN: a GOTO statement, an IF-THEN statement, and a FOR-NEXT loop. As with FORTRAN, these limited control statements make structured programming in BASIC somewhat difficult. Some BASIC dialects, however, have additional statements that lend themselves more readily to structured programming techniques. An example is True BASIC, a version created by the original coauthors (Kemeny and Kurtz) with several other colleagues. Introduced late in 1984, True BASIC retains all the strengths of the original language but is faster, more powerful, and more portable and contains many new features that allow structured programming as well as sophisticated graphics, mathematics, and text processing.

Pascal

A structured programmer's dream

Pascal, named in honor of the seventeenth-century French philosopher and mathematician Blaise Pascal, was invented by the Swiss computer scientist Niklaus Wirth. Introduced in 1971, it was originally intended as a general-purpose, high-level language for teaching the concepts of structured programming and top-down design. Pascal's simplicity, elegance, and embodiment of structured programming principles have made it quite popular with computer scientists and students, scientific programmers, and microcomputer users.

Features

Among all the computer languages currently in widespread use, Pascal is probably the best for demonstrating what structured programming is all about. It is simple, straightforward, and easy to learn, and it imposes rules that encourage good programming habits. In addition, Pascal is a versatile and powerful language that helps users avoid programming errors. Consequently, large, complex, relatively error-free programs are easier to write in Pascal than in many other languages. Furthermore, Pascal can be translated by small compilers. As a result, Pascal has become a popular alternative to BASIC on microcomputers as well as being commonly used on minicomputers and mainframes.

Pascal's main shortcoming is its limited input/output and file manipulation capabilities. This makes Pascal somewhat unattractive to business users, and it has not been utilized much in traditional data-processing applications. Designed to be a teaching language, Pascal wasn't originally intended to be employed outside of educational institutions. Its limitations, however, have been addressed to some extent by vendors selling extended versions of Pascal that incorporate additional features. These extensions themselves constitute another negative feature for Pascal—there are many different versions being sold. Even though there are standards, such as Wirth's original specifications and an ISO (International Standards Organization) set, vendors haven't consistently followed them. Despite these problems, Pascal has become a very influential language, especially in educational environments, and is a strong competitor of FORTRAN and BASIC.

An example of a Pascal program is shown in Figure 9.5 (page 262).

Program Format

Pascal has a very well-defined program format. The program name is first, followed by the data descriptions, then any subprograms used, and finally the body of code representing the main program. The internal organization of each subprogram, of which Pascal has two types (procedures and functions), mirrors this program format. The basic units of Pascal programs are statements, which can be entered in free format but must be separated by semicolons.

Data Types

Pascal provides users with a full range of simple and structured data types, in addition to supporting programmer-defined ones. Pascal's built-in simple data types include integers and real numbers, Boolean values (true and false), and characters. Its structured types include arrays, sets, records, and files. Programmer-defined data types are user-constructed, custom-made types that significantly contribute to Pascal's power and versatility.

Control Statements

Pascal is richly endowed with the control structures dear to the hearts of structured programming advocates. To handle conditional transfers of control, it has the old standby, the IF-THEN-ELSE statement, as well as a multiple-choice CASE statement. Pascal has three kinds of looping structures: the WHILE statement, the REPEAT-UNTIL statement, and the FOR statement (which sets up a *counted loop*

(a)

8200	595.00
8250	1587.25
8500	8462.75
8700	15000.00
9100	432.25
9200	20000.00

Figure 9.5 A Pascal Program

In this simple Pascal program, selection control structures (IF-THEN-ELSE statements) are used to route payment approval requests for the accounts payable subsystem of the software for Keyboard Koncepts. This program was compiled and run using the IBM Personal Computer Pascal compiler. (a) The input file of invoice records includes invoice numbers and the amounts to be paid. (b) The output consists of three files, one for each executive. (c) In the Pascal program, comments are enclosed in curly brackets.

(b)   FOR EXECUTIVE A

```
Approval request for invoice 8200, payment = $595.00
Approval request for invoice 9100, payment = $432.25
```

FOR EXECUTIVE B

```
Approval request for invoice 8250, payment = $1587.25
Approval request for invoice 8500, payment = $8462.75
```

FOR THE PRESIDENT

```
Approval request for invoice 8700, payment = $15000.00
Approval request for invoice 9200, payment = $20000.00
```

(c)

```pascal
{ Pascal Program Example

This program routes payment approval requests to three executives for the
   accounts payable subsystem of Keyboard Koncepts. }

program PAYMENT_APPROVAL (input, output);

const                                 { This is the section that defines    }
    executive_A_limit =   1000.00;    { constants - data values that don't  }
    executive_B_limit = 10000.00;     { change throughout the program.      }

type                                  { This is the programmer-defined data }
    invoice_number_type = integer;    { type definition section.            }
    payment_type        = real;

var                                              { This is the section that declares }
    invoice_number : invoice_number_type;        { the variables used.               }
    payment        : payment_type;
    input_file     : text;                       { Declare the files used. }
    executive_A    : text;
    executive_B    : text;
    president      : text;

begin
{ Tell the computer about the files to be used. }

    ASSIGN (input_file, 'INFILE');      RESET (input_file);
    ASSIGN (executive_A, 'EXEC_A');     REWRITE (executive_A);
    ASSIGN (executive_B, 'EXEC_B' );    REWRITE (executive_B);
    ASSIGN (president, 'PRES');         REWRITE (president);
```

```
{ Route the payment requests. }

    while NOT EOF (input_file) do     { while there is input }
      begin
          READLN (input_file, invoice_number, payment);
          if payment < executive_A_limit then
              WRITELN (executive_A,
                      'Approval request for invoice ', invoice_number:0,
                      ', payment = $', payment:0:2)
          else if payment < executive_B_limit then
              WRITELN (executive_B,
                      'Approval request for invoice ', invoice_number:0,
                      ', payment = $', payment:0:2)
          else
              WRITELN (president,
                      'Approval request for invoice ', invoice_number:0,
                      ', payment = $', payment:0:2);
      end;

  CLOSE (input_file);    CLOSE (executive_A);
  CLOSE (executive_B);   CLOSE (president);
end.
```

that executes a specified number of times). Finally, Pascal's GOTO statement accomplishes an unconditional transfer; however, it seldom appears in well-designed programs.

C

C is a simple, general-purpose programming language originally developed at Bell Laboratories as part of the UNIX operating system (about which we will have more to say in Chapter 11). Dennis Ritchie designed and implemented C in 1972 on a DEC PDP-11 minicomputer. He intended C to supplant assembly languages as the tool for the development of operating systems. The versatile and portable C is a high-level language that allows users to do some things that are normally only achievable with assembly languages. Similar to Pascal in its compatibility with structured programming techniques, C has become quite popular with microcomputer users. It's also commonly used on both minicomputer and mainframe systems.

A simple yet versatile language

Features

C differs from most high-level languages in that it doesn't divorce the programmer from the internal workings of the computer's hardware and software. In fact, C encourages programmers to use their knowledge of the computer's functioning. Because of this, C gives programmers great power, and is therefore often described as being "robust." C has a diversity of operations and commands that makes it a highly general-purpose language. At the same time, it is also clear, pragmatic, and concise. One of its most desirable attributes is the portability it conveys on programs—it's easy to take software written in C and run it on other systems with very

Figure 9.6　A C Program

This short C program implements the same algorithm as does the BASIC program in Figure 9.4. The input file and output would look the same. Note the use of the WHILE statement here in C, instead of the GOTOs in the BASIC program. This program was compiled and run on a DEC VAX-11 minicomputer. Comments are text situated between a forward slash and asterisk matched pair.

```
/*
 * C Program Example
 *
 * Sum the total of a month's customer payments for Keyboard Koncepts.
 *
 * Usage:  payments [filename]
 */
#include <stdio.h>

main(argc, argv)  char **argv;
{
    double      sum = 0.0;
    double      payment;

    if (argc > 1 && freopen(argv[1], "r", stdin) == NULL) {
        /*
         * report problems opening the input file
         */
        exit(perror(argv[1]));
    }

    while (scanf("%f\n", &payment) == 1) {
        sum += payment;
    }

    printf("Sum of payments is $%.2f\n", sum);
}
```

little modification. Although C is perhaps best suited to developing system software (such as operating systems, language compilers, word processors, and data base management systems), it has also become quite popular for writing applications software.

Even C's best features, however, have a negative side to them. The great power C provides to programmers at the same time makes it easy for them to make hard-to-find logic errors when writing programs. The conciseness that is characteristic of C programs means they can be difficult to understand for users who aren't skilled programmers. In addition, documentation, error messages, and even expository books written about C tend to be short and cryptic. C isn't a user-friendly language and can be difficult for novice programmers to learn. Despite these difficulties, C produces compact programs that run fast, and it's one of the most versatile programming languages available for microcomputers.

Figure 9.6 shows an example of a C program.

Program Format

A C program consists of a main module that must be named "main" and a number of subprograms called functions. The main module and each function must begin with a description of all the data items that are used within. After these data descriptions is the list of statements that actually direct the processing. Each statement must end with a semicolon. Functions can be placed after the main module in any order.

Data Types

C's fundamental data types are characters, integers, real numbers, double-precision real numbers, and pointers. A *pointer* is a value that indicates the storage address of a data item. C also supports arrays and special constructs called *structures*, which allow data items of different types to be grouped together.

Control Statements

The control statements of C are similar to those of Pascal. C has an if-else statement and a multiple-choice switch statement (parallel to Pascal's CASE statement) for conditional transfers of control. Also present but not recommended is the goto statement for unconditional transfer of control. Loop structures consist of the while, do-while (identical to Pascal's REPEAT-UNTIL), and for statements (the latter is again a counted loop). All the reserved words in C, as you may have concluded, must be entered in lower-case letters.

Ada

Named for Countess Augusta Ada Lovelace, "the first programmer" (of Babbage's analytical engine), Ada was introduced in 1980. Commissioned by the U.S. Department of Defense (the world's largest software consumer), Ada is a powerful, comprehensive language applicable to a wide range of problems. Although still too new to be available for many computers, Ada promises to become a major high-level language in the very near future.

The new kid on the block

Features

Ada was designed with the specific intent that it be a universal computer tongue. It is a structured language, encompassing the principles of modular, top-down program design. In fact, many of the concepts in Ada were derived from Pascal. Like Pascal, it requires all data items to be explicitly declared, so it allows the programmer more easily to achieve error-free programs. However, Ada goes well beyond Pascal in its applicability to almost any kind of programming task. For example, Ada was specifically designed to be effective for the programming of **embedded computers**. These are computers that are part of larger, electromechanical systems such as sophisticated weapons, aircraft, ships, space vehicles, rapid transit networks, and message switching systems. (You'll learn about embedded microcomputers in Chapter 16.) Ada was also designed to be used as a data-processing language, like COBOL. The vast amount of time and effort spent on its design has resulted in Ada's two most outstanding features: its power to accomplish almost any task and its wealth of programming structures.

Some experts, however, characterize Ada as a very "big" language, that is, one that has many features and can be difficult to learn. Presently, the number of machines that can compile Ada programs is limited, and this is the language's

Figure 9.7 An Ada Program

This Ada program is equivalent to the Pascal program in Figure 9.5. The input and output would look the same. Comparing this program with the Pascal version should make the similarities between the two languages evident.

```
-- Ada Program Example

-- This program routes payment approval requests to three executives for the
-- accounts payable subsystem of Keyboard Koncepts.

with TEXT_IO;
procedure PAYMENT_APPROVAL is
   use TEXT_IO, CHARACTER_IO;

-- Declare the data types, constants, variables, and files.

type INVOICE_NUMBER_TYPE is INTEGER;
type PAYMENT_TYPE is FLOAT;

EXECUTIVE_A_LIMIT : constant := 1000.0;
EXECUTIVE_B_LIMIT : constant := 10000.0;

INVOICE_NUMBER : INVOICE_NUMBER_TYPE;
PAYMENT        : PAYMENT_TYPE;
INPUT_FILE     : IN_FILE;
EXECUTIVE_A    : OUT_FILE;
EXECUTIVE_B    : OUT_FILE;
PRESIDENT      : OUT_FILE;

begin
-- Tell the computer to open the files to be used.

   OPEN ( INPUT_FILE, "INFILE" );       CREATE ( EXECUTIVE_B, "EXEC_B" );
   CREATE ( EXECUTIVE_A, "EXEC_A" );    CREATE ( PRESIDENT, "PRES" );

-- Route the payment requests.

   while not END_OF_FILE ( INPUT_FILE ) loop
      FIXED_IO.GET ( INPUT_FILE, INVOICE_NUMBER );
      FLOAT_IO.GET ( INPUT_FILE, PAYMENT );
      if PAYMENT < EXECUTIVE_A_LIMIT then
         PUT ( EXECUTIVE_A, 'Approval request for invoice ' );
         FIXED_IO.PUT ( EXECUTIVE_A, INVOICE_NUMBER );
         PUT ( EXECUTIVE_A, ', payment = $' );
         FLOAT_IO.PUT ( EXECUTIVE_A, PAYMENT );
      elseif PAYMENT < EXECUTIVE_B_LIMIT then
         PUT ( EXECUTIVE_B, 'Approval request for invoice ' );
         FIXED_IO.PUT ( EXECUTIVE_B, INVOICE_NUMBER );
         PUT ( EXECUTIVE_B, ', payment = $' );
         FLOAT_IO.PUT ( EXECUTIVE_B, PAYMENT );
      else
         PUT ( PRESIDENT, 'Approval request for invoice ' );
         FIXED_IO.PUT ( PRESIDENT, INVOICE_NUMBER );
         PUT ( PRESIDENT, ', payment = $' );
         FLOAT_IO.PUT ( PRESIDENT, PAYMENT );
      end if;

   CLOSE ( INPUT_FILE );       CLOSE ( EXECUTIVE_B );
   CLOSE ( EXECUTIVE_A );      CLOSE ( PRESIDENT );
end PAYMENT_APPROVAL;
```

major weakness. This situation is expected to improve steadily since the Department of Defense has made a massive commitment to Ada. Eventually, it will refuse to accept new software that isn't written in Ada. The DOD is such a major consumer of software that computer manufacturers are hustling to produce Ada compilers so as not to miss out on lucrative defense contracts. The Department of Defense has even registered Ada as a trademark so that it can have the final say as to what constitutes an acceptable Ada compiler. A few compilers that translate subsets of the full language are available for microcomputers, but Ada isn't expected to achieve the popularity of BASIC and Pascal among users of small machines.

Figure 9.7 is an example of an Ada program.

ISSUES IN TECHNOLOGY

Some people have proposed that the computer industry should choose one high-level language as the standard for all computers. Others say that this is not only impossible but undesirable as well. Take a position on this and defend it.

Program Format

In its simplest form, an Ada program has two parts: a *declarative part* that describes the data, and a *statement part* that describes the computations and processing. The declarative part lists the names and types of the variables that will be used in the program. The statement part, which is bracketed by the reserved words "begin" and "end," lists the operations that are to be done on the data. Ada, like Pascal, has two types of subprograms: *procedures* and *functions*. Ada also has two other program units known as packages and tasks. *Packages* are either separately compilable modules that contain collections of common data or groups of related subprograms that collectively carry out some activity. *Tasks* are similar to packages, except that they can be executed concurrently with other program units. They are useful for the programming of operations that must be carried out at the same time as some other operation, such as the simultaneous functioning of multiple input/output devices in a large computer system.

Data Types

Ada has all the built-in simple types that are found in other languages: integers, Boolean values, characters, real numbers, and double-precision real numbers. In addition, Ada also supports arrays, character strings, records, files, and programmer-defined data types. As you can see, Ada is fairly similar to Pascal in the types of data it accommodates, but it adds a couple of important ones. And, as with Pascal, this variety in data typing gives programmers the flexibility and versatility to solve many different kinds of problems.

Control Statements

Like Pascal, Ada has the basic control statements necessary for structured programming. It has the following statements: IF-THEN-ELSE (for conditional transfer), CASE (for selection among multiple choices), WHILE (for loops), and FOR (for counted loops). It does not have an exact parallel of Pascal's explicit REPEAT-UNTIL statement; however, Ada does have an EXIT statement that can be used to get out of a loop based on a condition tested at the end. These control statements are straightforward and provide the programmer with the basic tools of structured programming.

RPG

A convenient language for certain business tasks

RPG was introduced by IBM in 1964; the name stands for Report Program Generator. Unlike the other high-level languages we've described, RPG is a problem-oriented language, aimed at producing business reports. Originally designed for use with punched cards on small, batch-oriented computer systems, RPG has evolved into a modern, interactive, information-processing tool. Today, RPG is used widely for report generation, file maintenance, and other business applications of data processing. Users employ it with mainframes and minicomputers; it isn't generally used on microcomputers.

Features

RPG's main attraction is the ease with which it enables users to handle straightforward business tasks like accounts receivable, accounts payable, and file updating. The user "programs" in RPG by simply filling out special coding forms either interactively (at a terminal) or in batch mode (on paper to be entered on punched cards). The detailed *specification forms* require the user to describe the files to be used, the format of any input, any calculations to be performed, and the desired format of the output report. The user does not have to worry about the logical procedures actually involved in producing reports. Thus users need not be programmers. Since RPG is so easy to learn and use, it is quite popular with businesses that operate minicomputer systems.

RPG is a problem-oriented language, which limits the types of tasks to which it can be applied. It works well for those simple data-processing tasks for which it was designed, but it has neither the power nor the versatility of a general-purpose, procedure-oriented language such as COBOL. RPG has rather restricted mathematical capabilities and is not applicable to scientific problems. Finally, RPG is not a standardized language, although the versions produced by IBM tend to dominate the market.

Program Format

An RPG program consists of three or four specification forms. These forms give the RPG translator the information it needs to produce the desired report:

File description specification, which identifies the input and output files to be used.

Input specification, which describes the exact format of the data contained in the input file.

Output specification, which describes the exact format of the output report.

Calculation specification, which describes any mathematical computations to be performed.

Each user-provided line is entered into the computer either on a punched card or at a terminal. The user must stick to a fixed format because the RPG translator requires that entries be placed in predefined columns. If this is done, however, the translator takes care of everything else.

Other Important High-Level Languages

There are several other high-level languages that are not as prevalent as the ones we've just discussed, but are significant enough in some respect to be worthy of brief mention.

Other significant languages

ALGOL

ALGOrithmic Language, or ALGOL, was developed in the early 1960s after long study by an international committee. No other computer language has had such a far-reaching influence on the design of subsequent languages. Designed with the scientific community in mind, ALGOL is noted for its clarity, elegance, and excellent control structures.

APL

APL, or A Programming Language, was introduced by IBM in 1968 but was conceived by Kenneth Iverson in 1962. Expressly designed to be an interactive language, APL is especially well suited to handling data arrays and to performing mathematical computations quickly. It is characterized by the use of many special symbols, which requires a special APL keyboard.

APT

APT is short for Automatically Programmed Tools, and this language is a very specialized, problem-oriented one used for describing the operations involved in machine-cutting metal parts. Developed at the Massachusetts Institute of Technology (MIT) in the late 1950s, APT is a good example of a special-purpose language. It is important in industries employing automated manufacturing methods and is discussed further in the section on computer-assisted manufacture in Chapter 18.

Forth

Invented by Charles Moore in the late 1960s, Forth is a powerful, flexible combination of programming language and operating system. Although somewhat difficult for beginners to understand and use, Forth has the unique feature that users can define their own new commands. This capability gives Forth programmers much creative freedom and is mainly responsible for the growing number of Forth fans.

LISP

Developed by a group headed by John McCarthy at MIT and introduced in 1960, LISP (for LISt Processing) was designed to manipulate lists of abstract symbols. Often used interactively, LISP is noted for being almost tailor-made for applications such as game playing, robot control, pattern recognition, and mathematical proofs.

LOGO

LOGO, derived from LISP and also developed at MIT, but by Seymour Papert, is an interactive programming language with graphics output. LOGO was designed for children, who can draw pictures on the terminal screen by learning how to move a little triangular pointer, informally referred to as the "turtle." Intended to help build programming skills, LOGO lets users form statements by grouping commands together; the results of their instructions are immediately visible on the video display.

PL/I

PL/I, or Programming Language I, was sponsored by IBM and introduced in 1965. Intended as a general-purpose computer language applicable to both science and business, PL/I combines the best features of three earlier languages: FORTRAN, COBOL, and ALGOL. Even though it's an excellent language, PL/I for some reason never achieved the popularity reached by FORTRAN and COBOL.

Smalltalk

Sometimes classified as an *object-oriented language*, Smalltalk was invented at Xerox's Palo Alto Research Center by Alan Kay. It makes extensive use of the mouse, which, you'll recall from Chapter 4, is a graphic input device in the form of a little box the user moves about on top of a desk or table. Many of the concepts used in Smalltalk became the basis for the revolutionary, user-friendly operating system of the Apple Macintosh personal computer.

SNOBOL

Developed at Bell Laboratories during the 1960s, SNOBOL is a powerful and widely used language for processing character strings. Its major application is to problems in which substantial amounts of data in character-string form must be processed in complex ways. SNOBOL is often used in the development of text editors, word processors, and high-level language translators.

 NONPROCEDURAL LANGUAGES: LANGUAGES OF THE FUTURE?

Nonprocedural languages are the newest generation of programming languages—a special group of programming systems that has evolved since 1970. Also known as *very high-level languages, fourth-generation languages,* and *natural languages,* nonprocedural languages attempt to make it as easy as possible for users to tell the computer what to do. Using these types of languages, the user must typically supply very few instructions on *how* to achieve a particular result. Instead, the user gives instructions on *what* data are to be used and *what* the format of the output is to be. These languages therefore resemble problem-oriented languages in that they relieve the user of the procedural steps involved in producing output from input. However, unlike problem-oriented languages, nonprocedural languages look very much like human language. For example, nonprocedural languages make it possible to give a set of instructions very similar to a request to a human assistant:

Getting closer to human languages

CAREERS IN TECHNOLOGY
Training Specialist

Job Description Training specialists (also known as in-structors) are essentially educators: they teach computer users programming languages and methods, or about operating systems, communications technologies, systems analysis, or how to use the hardware. They are employed either by a computer organization to train its employees or by computer services to train customers. The people who take the courses do so to become familiar with new technology, for career advancement, to reinforce rusty skills, or simply for personal interest. Some companies require their new employees to take a course or two as a part of their on-the-job training. In addition, computer retailers often offer training courses to the public, as inducements to purchase personal computers or as premiums included in the price of a system.

Training specialists must plan and teach classes in any of a number of subject areas in a way specifically tailored to the interests and skills of a particular group of trainees. They give lectures, lead discussions, supervise lab sessions, assign and evaluate homework or projects, and locate and distribute applicable reading materials (textbooks specialized enough are rarely available). They must have a comprehensive understanding of the course material and must keep up to date on current technological developments.

Qualifications A B.S. in computer science or a related technological field, with a strong emphasis on business systems and concepts, is the basic requirement, and some companies look for an M.B.A. The majority of employers follow one of two approaches: they look for experienced teachers from any field and then expose them to the appropriate technology (assuming that teaching skills are the most important qualification), or they firmly demand a strong background in computer education so that instruction in the technological subject matter isn't necessary. In any case, training specialists must have good organizational and communications skills and must enjoy speaking to groups of people, conducting small seminars, and tutoring individual trainees. Some previous experience in teaching, programming, technical writing, or data processing is likely to be helpful.

Outlook The number of job openings depends very heavily on the computer market. Profitable companies will naturally be more willing to develop and staff training programs than will firms operating in the red. Furthermore, although opportunities for training specialists are expected to increase during the upcoming decade, due to the booming computer market and the general need for businesses to train and "retool" their personnel, employee education is always one of the first areas to be cut back when fiscal times get rough.

Get sales and personnel files and print names and salaries by department and by highest salary.

Because of the complexities and ambiguities of human languages, the development of nonprocedural languages is a tremendous challenge, and this new generation of languages is still in its infancy. Very complex translator programs are necessary to convert English sentences, for example, into executable object code. As a result, there are presently no nonprocedural languages available that enable computers to accept and respond to the entire range of word combinations and meanings in any human language. That is, nonprocedural languages currently still have limits on vocabulary and syntax. However, much research and development is underway to produce more unrestricted ones. If successful, such attempts will allow people with no formal training to program computers quickly, easily, and effectively. This will have the result of dramatically increasing productivity, creativity, and user satisfaction.

Some nonprocedural languages allow people to request certain specific kinds of tasks. **Query languages** enable users to interrogate and access computer data bases by means of Englishlike statements. A user request in a query language would be very similar to the example above. People can learn to use a query language with very little instruction; very quickly, users are efficiently retrieving the information they want. (We'll have more to say about query languages in Chapter 13 when we talk about data base systems.)

Examples of nonprocedural languages currently in use include RAMIS, FOCUS, NOMAD, INQUIRE, and NPL.

WHAT MAKES A LANGUAGE GOOD?

This section could also be entitled "How to Choose a Language." Since we've described or mentioned more than 20 popular computer programming languages and there are others as well, the task of choosing any particular one for a problem at hand might seem bewildering. In fact, in many cases, programmers have no choice—the decision as to what language is to be used has already been made by management. Whether the decision is made by management or programmer, the following characteristics should be taken as the criteria for judging the programming language:

Criteria for choosing a programming language

- *Suitability to the problem.* For example, because of its limited computational capabilities, COBOL is much less appropriate than FORTRAN for a program to compute a rocket's trajectory.

- *Clarity and simplicity.* A language with straightforward concepts and a simple program structure can help the user think about the solution before the program is even written and can help reduce errors discovered during and after development.

- *Efficiency.* Ideally, a language should allow (1) efficient program execution (it runs fast), (2) efficient program translation (it compiles fast), (3) efficient memory use (it takes up little room), and (4) efficient program development (programs can be written quickly).

- *Availability and support.* Is there a translator program available for the language for your computer, and can you get help using the language if you need to? Sometimes this factor winds up being the deciding one. Many organizations have only one or a few language translators and can't afford to purchase a new one for a specific application.

- *Consistency.* Many organizations have a policy that all their software is written in a single language or one of a small number of languages. Besides being easier for programmers, who only have to know one or a few languages, this policy means that new programs will work with already existing ones. A language is often chosen because it has been successfully and extensively used in the past.

SUMMARY ═══════

Programming Languages in General

A programming language is a set of symbols and usage rules employed to direct the operations of a computer.

Characteristics of Programming Languages Every programming language has instructions for input and output, for calculations, for transfer of control, and for data movement, storage, and retrieval. In addition, most languages allow comments.

Levels of Language The four general categories of computer languages can be arranged hierarchically. From the lowest to the highest level, the classifications are machine languages, assembly languages, high-level languages, and nonprocedural languages.

Machine Languages

A machine language consists of binary numbers that represent instructions, memory locations, and data so they can be processed by a specific computer model. Its own machine language is the only language that can be directly used by a computer.

Assembly Languages

An assembly language consists of mnemonic symbols that stand for the zeros and ones of machine language. An assembly language program is also machine-specific and must be translated into machine language by an assembler.

High-Level Languages

A high-level language consists of statements that are closer to human language or mathematical notation than are machine or assembly languages. High-level languages are machine-independent and can be classified as either procedure-oriented or problem-oriented.

Compilers and Interpreters High-level languages must be translated into machine language by either compilers or interpreters. A compiler translates an entire program all at once; an interpreter translates and executes one statement at a time.

The Advantages of High-Level Languages High-level languages are easier to learn, write, correct, and revise than are assembly or machine languages. The programmer using a high-level language can pay more attention to the problem at hand and less attention to machine-specific details.

Major High-Level Languages

The most important high-level languages are those that are widely applicable and/or influential in the development of other languages.

FORTRAN FORTRAN is a popular language among scientists, engineers, and mathematicians because of its simplicity, conciseness, standardization, efficiency, and numerical precision.

COBOL COBOL has widespread application in businesses and is noted for its ability to handle the input and output of large volumes of alphanumeric data, its machine-independence, and its Englishlike statements.

BASIC BASIC is a notably simple language that is easy to learn and to use. It is the most widely used high-level language for microcomputers.

Pascal Pascal is a general-purpose, high-level language. Its simplicity, elegance, and embodiment of the concepts of structured programming and top-down design have made it extremely popular.

C C is a simple but versatile and portable general-purpose language. It allows users to do some things normally done with assembly languages.

Ada   Ada, commissioned by the Department of Defense, is a new and powerful language applicable to a wide range of problems.

RPG   RPG is a problem-oriented language, designed to make it easy for users to handle common business tasks like report generation and file updating.

Other Important High-Level Languages   ALGOL is a highly influential language noted for its clarity, elegance, and excellent control structures. APL is especially well suited to handling data arrays and performing mathematical computations quickly. APT is a problem-oriented language used for programming automated machine tools. Forth is a powerful, flexible combination of programming language and operating system. LISP is designed to manipulate lists of abstract symbols. LOGO is designed to teach children elementary concepts of computer programming. PL/I combines the best features of FORTRAN, COBOL, and ALGOL and is suited to both science and business applications. Smalltalk is an object-oriented language that makes extensive use of the mouse. SNOBOL is widely used for processing character strings.

Nonprocedural Languages: Languages of the Future?

Nonprocedural languages attempt to make it as easy as possible for users to tell the computer what they want instead of having to specify exactly how to do it. The statements read very much like human language. Query languages, which enable users to interrogate and access data bases, are good examples of nonprocedural languages.

What Makes a Language Good?

Suitability to the problem at hand, clarity and simplicity, efficiency, availability and support, and consistency are the criteria to be used when choosing a programming language.

COMPUTER CONCEPTS

As an extra review of the chapter, try defining the following terms. If you have trouble with any of them, refer to the page number listed.

programming language 247

comments 248

operation code (opcode) 249

operand 249

mnemonic symbols 249

symbolic addressing 249

assembler 251

object code 251

procedure-oriented language 251

problem-oriented language 251

machine-independence 252

compilers 252

interpreters 252

data types 253

control statements 253

subroutine 255

function 255

arrays 255

reserved words 257

embedded computers 265

nonprocedural languages 270

query languages 272

REVIEW QUESTIONS

1. What is the difference between human languages and computer languages?
2. Describe the four general classes of instructions found in all computer languages.
3. What are the four levels of programming languages?
4. What are the two parts of a machine language instruction?
5. Why is programming in machine language so difficult?
6. How do assembly languages differ from machine languages?
7. Why would a programmer want to use assembly language?
8. Describe and give examples from the two functional classes of high-level languages.
9. What is the difference between a compiler and an interpreter? Why is each used?

10. What advantages do high-level languages have compared to low-level languages?
11. Give a short description of each of the major high-level languages covered in this chapter.
12. List and briefly characterize the other important high-level languages mentioned in this chapter.
13. How do nonprocedural languages differ from high-level languages?
14. What are the criteria that should be applied when choosing a programming language?

A SHARPER FOCUS

Now that you've completed this chapter, you should be able to answer the following questions about the chapter opening.

1. What differences set BASIC off from FORTRAN and made it seem, in the early 1970s, like the "people's computer language"?
2. Why did the programmers at MIT *prefer* to work with assembly language?
3. How might BASIC decrease "a programmer's power"?
4. How do you think early programmers would have felt about nonprocedural languages?

PROJECTS

1. Many computer games are programmed in assembly language. Find out why this is so, and write up your findings in a report.
2. Programs written in a high-level language for a particular computer won't always run on another computer, even though the other computer has a compiler for the same language. In other words, high-level language programs sometimes do not have 100% portability. Write a report that explains why this happens. Include some specific examples of this type of incompatibility.
3. What programming languages are being used in the computer center at your school or office? Why were those languages chosen for their particular applications?
4. Some of the high-level languages discussed in this chapter can't be used on personal computers. Find out which ones are available for use with the top four brands of microcomputers (IBM, Apple, Commodore, and Tandy–Radio Shack).
5. *Program-writing aids* let a user write specifications in an Englishlike format and use these to produce a program outline in one of the popular languages, such as BASIC. Do some research and prepare a report on these software systems, paying special attention to their advantages and disadvantages.
6. Many programming languages have a feature called a *trace,* which can be turned on or off while a program is being executed on a computer. What is a trace, and what are the advantages and disadvantages associated with its use? Write a report, and include a short example.
7. It has been reported that large bookstore chains sell more computer-related books than novels. From the titles of available books, it seems that a large percentage of the computer books sold are about programming languages. Survey local bookstores (and libraries) and report on the overall number of computer books available compared to the number on languages.

Application Packages

FOCUS ON . . . APPLYING APPLICATION PACKAGES

As personal computers become more commonplace in more and more corporations, the need for a fast and efficient way of teaching professionals how to use them is becoming acute. The desire of companies and individuals to tap the productive powers of computing has been short circuited by the difficulty in learning the ins and outs of applications software. Busy executives are the ones who can perhaps most benefit from personal computer applications. Yet, by definition, they are the ones with the least time to find out how.

The problem is not a shortage of software. There is plenty of it, almost an embarrassment of riches. It is more a matter of matching an appropriate software package to each professional's needs or, in many cases, simply selecting relevant parts of a given software package and then finding an efficient teaching approach.

To fill this need, a number of software companies have begun to provide packages which are not ends in themselves, but means to teach professionals how to use other programs. The hallmark of this new "teaching software" is that it is very easy to use. If it were not, the problem would not be solved.

Yale Dolginow, a retailing entrepreneur in Edina, Minn., turned to computer-aided instruction (CAI) to solve a specific problem. Two years ago, he bought an Apple II Plus and VisiCalc. Until very recently, however, his copy of this highly touted software remained unused. Why? "As an owner of 17 stores, I just didn't have time to work through the manual," says Dolginow. "But then I found out about the Cdex VisiCalc tutorial software. I can now program and use VisiCalc. I am really excited!" . . .

Savvy managers want to be part of the expanding possibilities of the information age and computer-aided instruction is helping pave the way. According to Rosalinde Torres, CAI trainer for Connecticut Mutual Life, there is no lack of motivation for decision-makers to become accomplished personal computer users. "Everybody wants to learn. The only problem is finding the time," says Torres. "Managers are impatient with flipping through pages of a manual and the tutorial programs have the added advantage of simulating the operation of the programs that managers will actually use in their work." . . .

Clearly, success with management training software will have effects beyond encouraging more effective management practices. Managers, seeing their own performance improve because of their work with these packages, have begun to insist that CAI software be developed for all echelons of their companies. The bottom line is increased productivity.

In the early days of computer use, companies and individuals had to produce their own software. Just as the pioneers in this country had to grow their own food, build their own homes, and make their own clothes, the first computer users had to be completely self-sufficient as far as programming was concerned; there were no ready-made programs. As time passed and the number of computers grew, many users realized that they had common needs. Companies and individuals began to see that many of the problems they were using computers to solve were quite widespread. Entrepreneurial programmers also noted this fact and started independent software firms. The dazzling array of products offered by such vendors is now referred to by the all-encompassing label of application packages. An **application package** is a collection of related programs or subprograms designed to accomplish some specified set of tasks. As we'll see in this chapter, these off-the-shelf packages of prewritten software opened up the world of computer use to virtually everyone.

ADVANTAGES OF USING PREWRITTEN SOFTWARE

Although in-house programming will always be a necessity for those users who require customized, specialized, or completely new software, many common computing needs can be fully satisfied by mass-produced application packages. The use of such software offers several significant advantages: quick installation, well-defined function, reduced cost, easy updating and revising, and familiarity.

Quick Installation

Use it right after purchase

Prewritten software can be installed and used as soon as it's purchased. This is a great advantage over software that is produced within an organization. Such software may take months to design, code, debug, and install. Vendors usually sell versions of their packages specifically designed for popular computer systems so that users generally find that installation and use is trouble-free. However, at times, modifications are necessary.

Well-Defined Function

You know what you're getting

Careful consumers know exactly what they're getting when they buy established application packages. If the product has been on the market for a while, it has probably been closely scrutinized by experts—other users and professional reviewers—who have published their findings in trade journals, magazines, and newspapers. Also, many users are often happy to relate their experiences and problems more informally. And popular application packages frequently attract loyal fans, who form users' groups and publish newsletters relating the advantages and capabilities of their "pet program." The strengths and weaknesses of a popular software package are readily uncovered by doing some prepurchase research.

In-house software may not be as thoroughly or objectively evaluated. Since fewer people use it, its unique capabilities and shortcomings may remain unknown. Also, the final program may not be exactly what was originally described, and users may not even be aware that discrepancies from the original design exist. Home-grown software may never receive unbiased review, so in many cases users simply don't know what they're getting.

Lower Cost

Less expensive

Purchased software is generally much less expensive than in-house software. Furthermore, purchasers of an application package know exactly how much they're paying: the listed retail price. Software vendors expect to sell many copies; their costs are spread over the total units sold. Therefore, they can sell each unit at a price far less than it cost them to develop the software and still realize a healthy profit.

The total cost of in-house software, on the other hand, must be fully absorbed by the developer. And that total is typically hard to pinpoint ahead of time since development may take longer or require more resources than originally projected. Furthermore, the program can't be used until it's finished, and any delay of implementation usually costs money.

Easy Updating and Revising

Established application packages are frequently revised, updated, or upgraded (improved) by their manufacturers, either in response to users' suggestions or in an effort to take advantage of new technology. As new features are introduced into the market and become popular among users, software vendors are eager to incorporate them into their products in order to remain competitive. New versions are frequently offered to owners of older versions at nominal or reduced costs, and users are usually happy to enhance their software capabilities this way since familiar features are still retained.

New versions

Upward compatibility is usually characteristic of new versions of application packages. This means that applications utilizing old features still work, but users have the option of incorporating new features. This important property ensures that users' established procedures need not be changed to accommodate revisions or innovations.

Software developed by users can, of course, be updated or revised, but the process can be expensive, time-consuming, and difficult. In fact, desirable new features often aren't added simply because it would be too much trouble to do so.

Familiarity

If an application package is in widespread use, some employees may already know how to use it. For a business, this built-in familiarity can greatly reduce the time and cost involved in training personnel. Furthermore, employees are often highly motivated to learn how to use popular packages because such know-how increases their own marketability; the more application packages they can use, the greater their attractiveness to potential employers. Becoming familiar with a popular software package may be made easier because there are others around who already know how to use it or there are "how to" books available about it.

Help from others

In-house software, on the other hand, is typically well understood by only a few people. Familiarity with it is likely to be of little value to other firms and employers, which may inhibit employee motivation to learn. Furthermore, such software may be more difficult to learn how to use, as a result of lack of documentation or supplementary reference materials.

DISADVANTAGES OF USING PREWRITTEN SOFTWARE

The main disadvantage of using prewritten application packages is that they may not do exactly what needs to be done. In order to cover the costs of software development, packages must be general enough to sell to a large number of diverse

Is it exactly what you need?

customers. The dentist, locksmith, and baker may all need the same basic accounting services, but there will be significant differences among their more detailed requirements. Thus, users must frequently adapt to their software instead of the other way around. A current general trend toward making software that can be somewhat customized by individual users to suit their own preferences does not go far enough to answer all user needs. Many businesses require specialized or completely new software that simply does not correspond to existing application packages.

The many other problems associated with using prewritten programs are the same as the difficulties that also exist for developed software. That is, there are application packages that are poorly documented, difficult to use, or full of bugs or that don't do what they're advertised to do. But there's probably just as much in-house software that exhibits the same deficiencies.

On the other hand, unless you happen to be a highly skilled programmer with lots of time, there's no way that you can develop all your own software. Most people have neither the means nor the desire to create their own programs; purchasing application packages is their only alternative. Even organizations that employ large programming staffs find that for certain applications purchasing software packages is much more feasible than developing the necessary programs from scratch. Because of the convenience and low cost, most software consumers are willing to live with the fact that the packages they purchase are not a perfect match with their needs.

WHAT MAKES A GOOD PACKAGE?

Factors to consider in choosing a package

How can a buyer even begin to choose among the overwhelming number of application packages on the market? Reading critical and comparative reviews of various packages in computer magazines as well as consumer guides to software is a good place to start. If possible, a buyer should see the product demonstrated on a system exactly like the one on which it will be installed. Some of the specific aspects that should be considered in an evaluation of a software package are its features, documentation, support, ease of use, flexibility, and upgradability.

Features

Fulfilling user requirements

Your primary concern should be whether or not a package satisfies your requirements. If you only need a word processor, you can rule out software packages that provide additional functions. You should not rely on written descriptions of a package's features in magazine ads or brochures; you should determine through in-store trials whether or not the software provides what the vendor says it provides. This recommendation isn't meant to imply that software vendors are unscrupulous but rather that products for sale are always presented in their best light—subtle deficiencies are not pointed out in advertising or promotional literature.

As suggested above, you should also make sure that any package you're considering will run on the computer system you have. The package should be compatible with (that is, should work smoothly with) the hardware and software you already own, unless you plan on purchasing additional system components. It's essential to know how much memory a program requires; if you have only 128K of memory in your machine, you can't run a package that needs 256K.

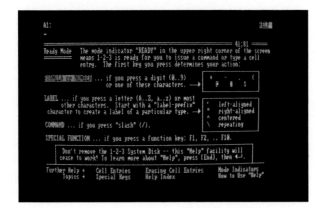

Figure 10.1   Help Facilities
Many application packages now incorporate on-line help facilities, which present usage instructions on the computer's display screen. This is an example of a screenful of instructions for using the Lotus 1-2-3 package.

Documentation

The best software package ever written in the history of computer programming would be practically useless if it didn't have adequate user documentation. There's nothing more frustrating than spending hours and hours trying to learn how to use an application package that has poorly written, confusing, or insufficient documentation. Unfortunately, inadequate documentation is all too often the reality with prewritten software, although the situation has been improving. Many current packages even include convenient on-line **help facilities**, which present usage instructions right on the user's display screen (see Figure 10.1). Whether it is on-line or in the form of a user manual, good documentation should have clear instructions for setting up, installing, and using the package as well as easy reference sections and information for advanced users.

Clear instructions

Support

Assuming that something will eventually go wrong as an application package is being used or that a significant question its documentation doesn't answer will arise (and these are safe assumptions), it's important to be assured that advice or assistance is available from the dealer or manufacturer. Some manufacturers have toll-free customer service numbers, while others charge some flat rate per customer call. For complex or heavily used packages, support can be essential, worth paying extra for.

More help

User-Friendliness

How user-friendly is the package? In other words, how easy is it for a novice to learn to work with the program? The commands for choosing various features and options should be straightforward, clear, simple, and easy to remember. The displayed output should be attractive, clear, and easy to read. The packages should operate quickly; there should be no long waiting times. Although these may seem to be obviously desirable software attributes, ones that would make any package more marketable, they can be difficult for designers to implement. Also, sometimes user-friendliness is deliberately sacrificed in order to use less memory or

Ease of use

provide more power. A compact or powerful package may have short, cryptic commands that allow users to perform complex tasks quickly. Such a package may also be difficult for beginners to learn how to use.

Cost

The price is right

Cost is a major concern of most consumers, but the same general rule applies for software as for other products: you get what you pay for. Usually (although by no means always), better products command higher prices. If a not-too-flashy, bare-bones program will do the trick, fine, but in most cases the more expensive package will offer more features, better documentation, and greater flexibility.

Flexibility

Adapting to users

Ideally, a package should be able to handle any combination of user demands and circumstances within the limits of its defined function. Adaptability to a wide variety of situations is definitely an attractive quality for an application package. For example, a word-processing program that works with only one or two printers isn't very flexible since users may have any one of a number of existing printer models.

Upgradability

Keeping up

Is the package going to be periodically revised and updated to keep it current with the latest technology and advances in programming techniques? If so, are these new versions going to be offered to owners of previous versions at a reduced price? Manufacturers aren't obligated to do these things, but upgradability is obviously a positive aspect of any package being considered.

TYPES OF APPLICATION PACKAGES

Many new packages and completely new concepts in application software are continually being developed. The software industry is an extremely fast-moving, competitive, and innovative environment, producing software for as many applications as you can imagine. Of course, we couldn't possibly describe (or even list) every type of useful application package on the market. What we'll do instead is to examine some of the most important general classes of packages. We'll cover all of the really "hot" software products, the ones you will be likely to encounter and use, for example, word-processing packages, electronic spreadsheets, file managers, data base management systems, communications software, and integrated software packages, to name a few. Many of the general classes of packages introduced here will be discussed again in more detail in later chapters.

The importance of the varied array of application packages is substantial. Software availability and applicability have been major factors in making computers—especially microcomputers— useful and attractive to many people. Most owners of microcomputers are not professional programmers. Consequently, prewritten software is essential for these users to employ their computers effectively, and the market for such software packages is huge. Although packages are available for computer systems of all sizes, those used on personal computers attract perhaps the most attention. The availability of desirable application packages for a particular microcomputer may be the single most important factor in its marketability. If a computer can't run the most popular software packages, people simply won't buy it. Some consumer experts have even suggested that people in the market for a personal computer should first choose the software they want to run, then select a model that can execute that software.

Word-Processing Packages

Almost everyone who uses a computer—especially if it's a microcomputer—uses a word-processing package of some kind. Over 90% of the microcomputer owners surveyed in the summer of 1984 by Venture Development Corporation, a market research group, said they owned a word-processing package. In fact, about 80% of them said they owned from one to five word-processing programs from various vendors. With total sales in excess of $300 million in 1984, word-processing packages are clearly one of the most popular of all software applications.

Capturing keystrokes and manipulating text

Just what is a word-processing package and what can it do for you? We'll be examining exactly how word-processing packages work in Chapter 17, so we will simply say here that a **word-processing package** is a piece of software that enables a computer and a printer to do everything a typewriter does and much more. Word processors apply the power of the computer to enable people to express themselves efficiently with written words.

Simply stated, word-processing packages make it very easy to enter, store, modify, format, copy, and print text. Many of the tedious, time-consuming manual tasks associated with using a typewriter, such as centering text, setting margins or tabs, performing carriage returns, and even checking spelling, are done automatically by many word processors. What makes the word processor such a valuable tool is that it enables the computer to ''capture'' and store keystrokes, in contrast to the typewriter, which merely converts keystrokes to mechanical movements of its hammers. Through this capturing of keystrokes as data to be stored, manipulated, and output (in other words, to be processed), word-processing packages put a tremendous power at a user's fingertips. Word processors have been demonstrated to boost office workers' productivity dramatically—by as much as 300%.

A wide variety of word-processing packages is available, and this diversity is reflected in the prices, which range from a few dollars to hundreds. The simplest, least expensive word-processing programs are basically computerized typewriters; the most complex and expensive can directly drive a typesetting machine. Keeping this great diversity in mind, examine Figure 10.2, which shows a typical display on a terminal screen when a popular word-processing program for microcomputers is being used.

Electronic Spreadsheets

The electronic spreadsheet is a type of application package that was first designed for and implemented on microcomputers, but became so popular and useful that it was later adapted to minicomputers and mainframes. In 1978, Dan Bricklin, an MIT graduate enrolled in Harvard Business School, decided that he was spending too much time laboring over the financial worksheets (spreadsheets) required for

Figure 10.2   A Word-Processing Package

This display is typical of what appears on a terminal screen when WordStar, a popular word-processing package for microcomputers, is in use. More than 40% of microcomputer owners have WordStar, making it the standard against which other word-processing programs are compared.

A new computer application

his accounting classes. He had only two alternatives at the time: do the many computations by hand with paper, pencil, and pocket calculator; or make use of the school's time-shared mainframe computer system. Neither of these alternatives suited him; the first was too time-consuming and error-prone, and the second was inconvenient. Small corrections or changes in a few places meant redoing the entire spreadsheet, and it was often difficult to visualize what was happening when using the mainframe computer. So Bricklin invented the electronic, microcomputer-based spreadsheet. In 1979, along with fellow MIT alumni Bob Frankston and Daniel Flystra, Bricklin formed a company named Software Arts. They sold a program for Apple microcomputers called VisiCalc (short for Visible Calculator), which opened up previously unheard of possibilities, fulfilling needs that businesspeople didn't even know they had. In addition, it paved the way for a whole new class of indispensable, user-friendly programs adaptable to many kinds of problems, not only business ones. Since it went on the market, more than 500,000 copies of VisiCalc have been sold.

An **electronic spreadsheet** is just like a conventional paper one in that it's a table of columns and rows of numbers and text labels. For financial applications, a spreadsheet might have places for entering all the income sources and costs (taxes, interest rates, and so on) that must be considered when making a business decision. The most important part of a spreadsheet is the *bottom line,* because that represents the final outcome of the series of calculations, the result that will indicate what decision to make. Figuring out your income taxes is a process much like constructing a spreadsheet. However, while you only have to do this once a year, many organizations must perform spreadsheet-type calculations every day.

The last section of this chapter includes a detailed description of a particular electronic spreadsheet that is part of a package called Lotus 1-2-3, but an immediate understanding of why these packages are so popular can come from considering a not unlikely situation. Let's say you've just spent five hours filling out your federal income tax forms. Then you suddenly realize you forgot to deduct the $600 you paid as interest on your car loan—that little oversight will mean refiguring almost everything. With a spreadsheet package, making that one change (the $600 deduction) will automatically cause all other dependent figures to be recalculated and the new results stored.

Rows and columns of figures

As you can see from Figure 10.3, the typical spreadsheet program displays labeled rows and columns on the terminal screen. Each particular position, or **cell,** is identified by its row and column. Quantities can be entered in the cells, columns and rows totaled, formulas applied, and headings specified. Most spreadsheets

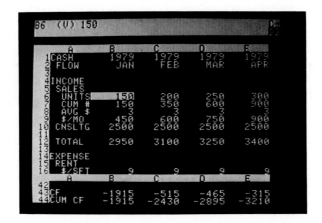

Figure 10.3 An Electronic Spreadsheet
VisiCalc was the first spreadsheet program to be marketed. In this particular example, Visi-Calc is being used to handle a firm's employee payroll records.

have a capacity of many more rows and columns than will fit on the screen at one time (overall dimensions of at least 254 rows and 64 columns are quite common). The user can shift *(scroll)* the screen view sideways or up and down to frame any portion of the spreadsheet. In addition, entire spreadsheets can be saved on secondary storage to be retrieved and added to at later times. *Templates,* or predefined formats with certain headings, columns, and formulas, can be used to reduce the initial work in setting up a new spreadsheet.

Electronic spreadsheet packages are useful, flexible tools that can be applied to a wide range of common problems. They can be used to monitor investments and to perform most typical business accounting chores (such as cash flow and depreciation calculations, balance sheets, and income statements), as well as to balance personal checkbooks and to work out home budgets. One of their most attractive features is that they allow the user to ask "what if" questions: once a worksheet has been set up, it's easy to change various figures and the results are immediately apparent. The possibilities are almost endless—imaginative users have started with spreadsheet programs and come up with games, questionnaires, conversion tables, statistical analyses, and financial models.

File Managers and Data Base Packages

In contrast to spreadsheet programs, file managers and data base packages were developed for and used on mainframe computers before they became available for microcomputers. This category really represents three major types of application packages: free-form indexing and filing programs, file managers, and full-fledged data base management systems. Here we will concentrate on the indexing and file management systems, and only briefly introduce data base management systems. Since data base management is such an important topic in the computer world, Chapter 13 is entirely devoted to it.

One of the major jobs of computers in our society is that of managing the data kept in huge secondary storage facilities. We often don't want computers to actually compute anything—we just want them to store, sort, locate, print out, or otherwise manipulate information. A file, as you learned in Chapter 5, is a collection of data held in secondary storage and organized as a set of records. A **data base** consists of one or more files of interrelated or interdependent data items stored together efficiently. A data base may serve one purpose or a number of

Managing and manipulating information

different ones. For example, a data base containing information about a magazine's subscribers may be used solely by the magazine for billing or copies of it may also be sold to other magazines and organizations for promotional or advertising uses. File managers and data base packages enable users to manage easily data they have stored and are handy whenever a sizable number of items must be kept track of. In business, such software can be used for inventory, accounts receivable, mailing lists and personnel files, among other applications. In the home, it can be used for indexing and retrieving letters, recipes, personal property inventories, financial or tax information, exercise logs, or any reasonably voluminous collection of information. Students, researchers, authors, and other professionals can use these packages to organize and retrieve instantly their notes about any subject. In short, file managers and data base packages are invaluable tools for dealing with the everpresent information explosion.

Free-Form Indexing and Filing Programs

Computerized index cards

Free-form indexing and filing programs don't have a great deal of power or flexibility, but they are generally quite inexpensive and easy to use. Primarily used on microcomputers, these types of packages basically allow you to attach a list of key words to a file that consists of text. This text might be a letter, memo, term paper, or report. After giving the program an indication of which words are to be the key words, you can then have the program search through your files for items containing those words. For example, let's say you created a file or set of files containing recipes, and you used your indexing program to identify the recipes by the key words SALAD, ENTREE, BEVERAGE, and DESSERT. Taking it another step further, let's say you've also indicated by key words the recipes that your relatives especially like. Then, any weekend when Grandma comes to visit, you can call up her favorite dessert recipes by having your program retrieve records identified by the key words DESSERT and GRANDMOTHER.

Free-form indexing and filing packages can be very useful with small computer systems and are quite reasonably priced. A popular example of such a program is illustrated in Figure 10.4.

Figure 10.4 A Free-Form Indexing and Filing Package

SUPERFILE, produced by FYI Inc., is an example of a popular free-form indexing and filing program for microcomputers.

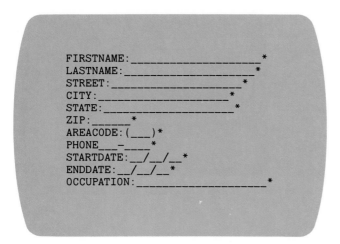

```
FIRSTNAME:_____*
LASTNAME:_____*
STREET:_____*
CITY:_____*
STATE:_____*
ZIP:_____*
AREACODE:(___)*
PHONE___-____*
STARTDATE:__/__/__*
ENDDATE:__/__/__*
OCCUPATION:_____*
```

Figure 10.5 A Sample Data Entry Form
An illustration of what a typical data entry form for a file manager or data base package looks like. *Keyboard World* is a popular (but imaginary) magazine catering to microcomputer owners. The publication's subscriber files are handled by a file manager that uses this data entry form. The underscores show where characters are to be entered, and an asterisk indicates the maximum length specified for each field. Whenever a new record is to be added to the data base, this empty form is presented on the display screen, and an operator keys in the new information.

File Managers

Stripped-down data base management systems

Different from and somewhat more complex than the free-form programs we've just discussed, **file managers** allow you to set up, store, retrieve, and manipulate collections of data items. In many ways, these packages are similar to the data base management systems we'll look at next: both require you to create a blank *data entry form,* which defines the information that is to be included. Figure 10.5 provides an example of what such a form might look like on a computer display screen. The whole form and its contents represent a record, and each labeled item represents a field. Each field must have both its length and the type of characters that it will hold (alphanumeric or strictly numeric) specified. Once this has been done, the form becomes a template for entering new records into the file. The blank form appears on the screen, and the new data are keyed "into" the proper lines. The difference between these records and the free-form ones used with the simpler category of filing and indexing programs is the structure. Each field here is explicitly defined as to its name, length, and contents. The records used by free-form indexing and filing programs aren't divided into subfields; they simply consist of blocks of text.

Entering all the data is a time-consuming chore, but the real payoff comes when it's time to locate some item of information. File managers and data base management systems offer efficient search and retrieval features. Any field can be the basis for a search, and multiple fields can often be used simultaneously. Furthermore, very specific retrieval instructions can be given to access particular data subsets. For example, by using the sample data entry form illustrated in Figure 10.5 with a file manager, the subscription renewal department of *Keyboard World* could retrieve all records of subscribers whose last name begins with B, who live in Florida, and who have only three weeks before their subscription expires. In addition, most file managers can output the retrieved information in a sorted order according to any key or keys. That is, to continue the example, subscribers' records could be printed out in alphabetical order by last name first, followed by first name, and also grouped by city.

File managers are used on all types of computers, but they are especially popular for microcomputers. There are many packages to choose from, with prices ranging from tens to hundreds of dollars.

Figure 10.6   Data Base Management Systems

Probably the most popular data base management systems used with microcomputers are Ashton-Tate's dBASE II and its updated version, dBASE III. This screen image is part of a dBASE III display.

Data Base Management Systems

Most file managers can handle only one file at a time, but data base management systems, large, powerful, flexible packages, can work with several files at once. These systems are also used as "engines" to drive a wide variety of other software, such as inventory, accounting, payroll, check-writing, and mailing list programs. Full-fledged data base management systems typically run on mainframe computers because of their great power, storage capacity, and speed. However, many smaller data base packages are also used on microcomputers; probably the most popular of these are Ashton-Tate's dBASE II and its new, improved version, dBASE III (see Figure 10.6). We'll look more closely into data base management systems in Chapter 13.

Graphics Packages

Presenting visual images

The most eye-catching of all application packages are undoubtedly the ones that enable users to create pictures—that is, *graphics packages*. Computer-generated graphics can transform mundane data into attractive and informative visual images. If a picture is worth a thousand words, then a good graphics package is worth at least ten programs that output characters only. Graphics packages are being marketed in ever increasing numbers, even though this software is greatly dependent on the memory and display hardware of the computer system it is run on. There are hundreds of graphics packages available just for microcomputers, and more come out every week. What's more, the demand among users is just as great as the seemingly endless supply.

There are several categories of popular graphics packages. One of these consists of programs for producing business graphics, that is, all types of bar and line graphs and pie charts. According to the magazine *Software Merchandising*, more than 25% of the firms that buy microcomputers eventually purchase a business graphics package (we'll have more to say about business graphics in Chapter 17).

Another category encompasses the interactive drawing or painting programs, which enable users to explore their artistic talents by employing display screens and graphic input devices instead of canvas and paintbrushes. Yet another category of graphics software is made up of packages that resemble graphics programming languages. These provide programmers with prewritten subprograms that draw *graphics primitives* such as dots, lines, circles, boxes, and other predefined shapes.

Other graphics packages are programs that present a kind of "slide show" display—a sequence of images that were previously created using other programs. (In Chapter 20, the creative role of graphics in movie making and art will be discussed at some length.) Some graphics packages allow users to "dump" the pictures they create on graphics display screens to printers or plotters in order to end up with permanent hard copy.

Some highly sophisticated graphics software combines several of the features we've discussed into a single package for designing and displaying all kinds of objects, from tiny machine parts to entire cars or whole buildings. These packages for CAD, or *computer-aided design,* are the cream of the graphics software crop and will be discussed in depth in Chapter 18.

At the most fundamental level, graphics packages manipulate tiny dots, or **pixels** (the name was coined from the words *picture elements).* Everything you see on most computer display screens, including characters, is composed of these minuscule dots of light, just as newspaper pictures are made up of thousands of tiny black ink dots. Strings of them form lines, and every type of curve and shape imaginable can be constructed. The clarity of the picture on a display screen depends on how many pixels its area contains (the density of the pixels on the screen surface). The measure of this density is known as the screen's **resolution**, and the higher the resolution, the clearer the picture is (because there are more pixels to delineate each area of the image).

As you can imagine, a remarkable amount of detail must be attended to within the computer so that these hundreds of thousands, or even millions, of dots are all turned off or on correctly to form a coherent image, especially if more than one color is involved. This is where the graphics package comes in. Instead of having to worry about controlling each little pixel, users can concentrate on what their graphs look like or what messages they want to convey with visual imagery; the graphics package handles all the details.

Figure 10.7 shows two examples of popular graphics packages.

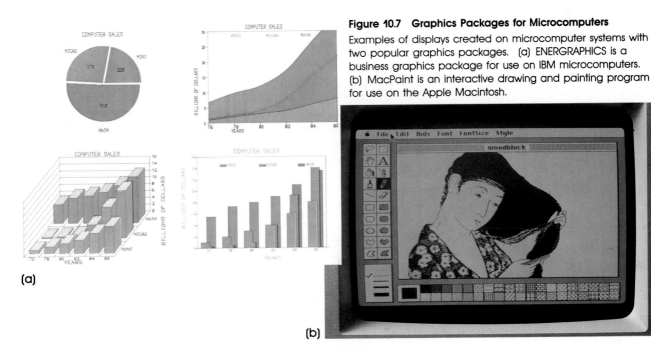

(a)

(b)

Figure 10.7 Graphics Packages for Microcomputers
Examples of displays created on microcomputer systems with two popular graphics packages. (a) ENERGRAPHICS is a business graphics package for use on IBM microcomputers. (b) MacPaint is an interactive drawing and painting program for use on the Apple Macintosh.

Mathematical and Statistical Packages

Perhaps the first thing that comes to mind when thinking of computers is mathematical computation, or, as it's known in computing circles, "number crunching." Since calculations with binary numbers are the very basis of any computer's operation, it's only natural that computers—especially big computers—have always been used to solve mathematical problems. Statistics, of course, is just a branch of mathematics, one that involves a lot of complex calculations and that is therefore handled readily by computers. As with other types of problems, many mathematical and statistical problems come up again and again within particular professional groups or organizations. Predictably, various mathematical and statistical packages have been developed to address these common problems. Originally intended for use with mainframes and supercomputers, such packages were relatively slow to filter down to the level of microcomputers. Given the great power and speed of the big machines, this is understandable. However, as microcomputers have become more advanced, useful mathematical and statistical packages have been adapted for them. Today, users with all kinds of computers have a choice among several of these packages.

Handling complex calculations

Mathematical software is used to carry out various types of complex calculations, many of which would be extremely difficult, if not impossible, to do by hand. Some packages consist of collections of prewritten subprograms that can be called upon by user programs written in high-level languages like FORTRAN and Pascal. Others are complete, self-contained programs with which the user interacts. Mathematical packages are available that perform complicated tasks like solving large systems of algebraic and differential equations (equations that involve quantities defined in the calculus). And simpler programs are available that make microcomputers function like programmable calculators.

Analyzing data

Although mathematical packages tend to be used mainly by mathematicians and physical scientists, *statistical packages* also attract users from business, the social sciences, and the biological sciences. Statistical packages enable users to analyze numerical data for certain patterns and may be used to support theories being researched or to predict possible future trends. Three of the biggest of the statistical packages for mainframe computers are the Statistical Analysis System (SAS), the Statistical Package for the Social Sciences (SPSS), and the Biomedical Computer Programs (BMDP). These packages are widely used at computer centers around the country, especially in colleges and universities. Recently, statistical packages have been adapted or developed for use on microcomputers, dispersing some of their power that was formerly available only to mainframe users. SPSS and BMDP, for example, have been adapted for use on some microcomputers. Even though these compact versions cannot do everything that the large original versions can and also tend to be comparatively slow, they do offer microcomputer users capabilities they never had before.

Modeling and Simulation Packages

Simulating reality

Modeling and simulation packages—some of the most interesting and educational software on the market—allow computer users to play "let's pretend." A **mathematical model** is a simplified representation, expressed in mathematical terms, of a real process, device, or concept. For example, economies and ecologies (processes), airplanes and automobiles (devices), and the theories of maximizing profits and optimizing the use of resources (concepts) can all be represented as mathematical models, and the use of a computer makes such representations much easier to achieve. Although such models are necessarily simplifications of what they represent, they can be very useful in that they isolate those features that are most important. A **simulation** is the representation of selected characteristics of a physical or abstract system by means of another system. For example, certain aspects of an airplane in flight (a physical system) can be represented (simulated) by a computer system consisting of a graphics input device, a computer, software, and a graphics display screen.

In short, modeling and simulation packages allow the computer to assume the role of the "universal machine" by enabling it to behave like almost any system imaginable. Computer capabilities for simulation and mathematical modeling originated primarily in connection with the physical sciences, and some of their more important aspects are discussed in Chapter 20.

Modeling packages tend to be quite mathematically oriented. As we'll see in Chapter 20, computer software has been written to model everything from gravity to the weather, but the prewritten application packages available from software vendors are usually more general in their scope. A common example of modeling packages are those that perform linear programming. **Linear programming** is a technique for finding the best or most favorable solutions to certain types of mathematical problems. Its processes usually involve maximizing some variables (like profit) while keeping others (like expenses) within specified bounds. For example, a manufacturer, such as our hypothetical Keyboard Koncepts, might use a linear programming package to determine its optimum production level, that is, how many keyboards it should make in order to maximize the profits that can result from some given level of expenditures (the *constraints* of the operation).

Modeling packages, including those for linear programming, tend to be used on large computers, although a few simple packages are available for microcomputers.

Simulation software is quickly becoming a powerful force in both entertainment and education. The recent crop of simulation packages for microcomputers is so good that the effects the programs produce often come startlingly close to real-world experiences. Simulations can be used to mimic situations that would be too expensive, inconvenient, dangerous, or nearly impossible to carry out in real life. A prime example is flight simulation. Microsoft's Flight Simulator program, which runs on the IBM Personal Computer and sells for about $50, reproduces the experience of flying a small, single-engine Cessna 182 airplane (see Figure 10.8). This

Figure 10.8 Flight Simulation
Microsoft's Flight Simulator program is one of the most popular application packages ever sold for the IBM Personal Computer. It so realistically simulates the experience of flying a small aircraft that it has been suggested for use in some flight schools.

Figure 10.9 Educational Simulation
Scholastic Inc.'s Operation: Frog is an excellent example of an educational simulation package. With this program, a microcomputer user can perform a realistic dissection of a frog.

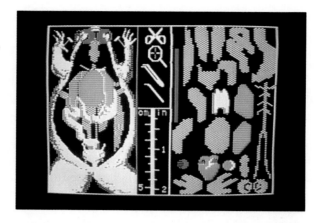

program approximates what it's like to be in the cockpit controlling the actions of a plane. On the display screen, users can see the effects of their actions reflected in the passing landscape and on the control panel gauges. The software so realistically simulates navigation and the natural elements of flight that it has been seriously considered for inclusion in curricula for training people to fly small aircraft. Much more powerful and realistic flight simulation systems have been used for years in commercial and military aviation training. However, it hasn't been until recently that the average owner of a modestly priced personal computer system could reap the benefits of similar software.

Other examples of inexpensive, yet highly realistic simulations available to personal computer users include Blue Chip Software's Millionaire and Tycoon programs, which simulate various financial markets; Human Engineered Software's Cell Defense, which teaches concepts of human immunology using a video game approach; and Scholastic Inc.'s Operation: Frog, which offers an odor-free, mess-free replication of a frog dissection (see Figure 10.9). These packages are an entertaining method of learning complex concepts. They *are* dependent on the graphics capabilities of the machine they run on, but simulation packages are still the state of the art in application programming.

ISSUES IN TECHNOLOGY

The latest of the inexpensive simulation software for microcomputers hasn't been accepted without reservation by all educators. Some of them are worried that the convenience, realism, and low cost of such computer simulation could lead to its replacing much of the real, hands-on instruction given in school labs. They wonder what influence this will have on those taught with simulation software. Does a budding biologist need to cut up an actual frog, or will a computer-simulated one do? How much should education depend on computer-simulated experience?

Business and Financial Packages

We've barely scratched the surface as far as the topic of application packages is concerned—we have yet to look into the massive volume of software devoted to helping commercial organizations and individuals manage their financial dealings.

In Chapter 19, we'll define and illustrate the use of business application packages in some detail, using the activities of a hypothetical business. Here we'll introduce two major types of packages: accounting packages and personal finance packages.

Accounting Packages

Accounting packages are concerned with managing financial information. They deal with the collection, storage, analysis, and presentation of data that represent all of a business's financial transactions. They usually include subprograms to handle the "big four" (general ledger, accounts payable, accounts receivable, and payroll). The computer is, of course, the ideal system to handle this multitude of numbers accurately. Available for all sizes of computers and ranging in price from about $90 to $600, accounting packages give large and small businesses the means by which they can utilize the full potential of their computers.

Business accounting

In Chapter 8, we outlined some of the design of a simple custom-made accounting package for a company we called Keyboard Koncepts. In reality, most companies don't write their own software to handle accounting needs. For years, software vendors have offered accounting packages for every type of business and every kind of computer. It's true that each business is unique, but accounting procedures tend to be quite consistent in many ways. Every firm must employ adequate accounting practices in order to survive and compete, and this fact translates into a large and profitable market for accounting software. An idea of the size of this market can be gained from considering just the microcomputer portion of it. Accounting packages represent one of the fastest growing software products for microcomputer application. The number of such packages has been increasing at an annual rate of more than 30%. Over 300 vendors currently produce more than 1500 accounting packages for microcomputers, an overwhelming assortment for businesspeople to choose among.

Personal Finance Packages

Personal finance packages, to the disappointment of their developers and vendors, haven't fared as well as accounting packages in the marketplace. By definition, this type of software is almost exclusively reserved for use on microcomputers, but this isn't the real crux of the problem. Personal finance packages were the first serious application packages to appear for microcomputers, and they have been cited in many advertisements as a major reason to buy a personal computer. Comprised primarily of budgeting, investment, and tax programs, personal finance packages are accounting packages pared down for individuals and families. They can do all they are advertised to—if individuals spend the time and effort to learn how to use them and enter all their transactions into the computer. A checkbook balancing program, for example, can't balance your checkbook if you don't provide the date, amount, and recipient's name for each check you write. This record-keeping discipline isn't a problem in the business world, where it has been accepted as an unavoidable necessity. However, when this requirement of personal finance packages is made clear to private individuals, many of them rightly conclude that the benefits simply aren't worth that much time and effort. When a checkbook can be balanced faster and easier using a pen and pocket calculator than using a computer, the checkbook balancing programs aren't likely to sell well. This has been the fate of most home budgeting programs. Only users who are especially conscientious or who are running big estates can make effective use of home budgeting

Personal finances

software. Most users find that spreadsheet programs suffice for their occasional home budgeting needs.

The problem of an unacceptably low payoff for the amount of work required doesn't occur for most investment and tax programs. For those personal computer owners who play the stock market, investment software can be worth its weight in gold—helping to sort out and evaluate the best ways to make money work and eliminating the need to consult expensive investment advisors. Where to invest—in stocks, bonds, real estate, futures, precious metals, foreign currency, or Treasury notes? With the right software, you can project the effect on your portfolio of any combination of actions. Shrewd investors use such software constantly to play "what if" games that require many calculations. Good investment programs analyze raw stock market data to uncover such worthwhile nuggets of information as what are "hot" industries, what stocks are outperforming the market, and what stocks are undervalued. These programs often employ sophisticated mathematical techniques and present their results in the form of clear and informative graphs rather than endless lists of numbers. Although no computer program can replace good judgment, investment packages can reinforce it considerably by reducing the number of choices to a more manageable level.

Software for tax planning and tax preparation is another useful type of personal finance package. Computers can dramatically reduce the time it takes to prepare tax returns and can eliminate arithmetic errors. Tax programs enable users to calculate quickly and easily a variety of filing alternatives from which they can choose the option that will maximize their refund or minimize their payment. By playing "what if" games like investors do, taxpayers can see, at any time during the year, the effects that salary raises, bonuses, stock options, pension plan participation, and other financial decisions may have on their year-end tax situation. Tax preparation software encourages users to be meticulously accurate, and some programs will even print out filled-in facsimiles of federal tax forms, which can be mailed as is. A disadvantage of, or at least a potential problem with, tax software is that tax laws change practically every year. If the manufacturer of a tax package fails to offer reasonably priced revised versions, the useful life of the program is likely to be short.

Figure 10.10 illustrates an example of a popular tax package.

Communications Software

Software for teleprocessing

As you learned from our discussion in Chapter 7 of data communications, it's software that establishes, coordinates, monitors, and controls the flow of data through teleprocessing systems. Telecommunications in a real sense owes its existence to packaged software. Although modems link computers to telephone lines, it's communications software that makes computer-to-computer interchanges possible. This type of software is so difficult to write and so tricky to make operate efficiently that most users leave all that to the experts by purchasing prewritten programs. Communications packages are available for every type of computer that can be part of a data communications network. As is true for much of the software we've introduced in this chapter, communications packages being marketed for microcomputers are selling like hotcakes. Because they effectively shrink the world and bring it under personal computer owners' fingertips, communications packages are high on the list of desirable and useful software.

What are the tasks that a communications package must perform for a user? Many programs let users do at least the following:

Figure 10.10   Tax Packages

Tax planning and tax preparation programs can help users considerably, provided the manufacturer makes yearly updates to reflect changes in the tax laws. One popular package for microcomputers is The Tax Preparer from Howard Software Services.

- *Set communications parameters.*   These are the protocols for coordinated computer communication, for example, the baud rate, the duplex setting (full or half), the type of parity (odd, even, or none), and how many start and stop bits are to be used (see Chapters 3 and 7).   A communications package should make it easy for users to set up and modify these parameters.

- *Dial the phone.*   Although this is not an absolutely essential feature, many packages enable users to dial the phone from the computer keyboard or automatically from phone directories stored on disk.   Assuming a user has a modem compatible with such a feature, it can make establishing communications fast and convenient.   (Modem manufacturers often supply free communications software with the purchase of a modem.)

- *Enter log-on information.*   Most time-sharing systems allow access only to users who have an account or permission to use the facilities.   The process by which users identify themselves as having a valid account is called **logging on**, or sometimes **signing on**.   It usually involves supplying some combination of name, address, identification number, account number, and password. Many communications packages can do this automatically once the user has programmed in his or her individual log-on sequence.

- *Capture incoming data.*   The communications package must allow a user's computer to receive and store data coming in from a remote computer.

- *Transmit data.*   Finally, the communications package must enable a user's computer to send messages, commands, and files to a remote computer.

Communications packages for microcomputers allow them to emulate, or behave as if they were, terminals of a remote (usually mainframe) computer. Since telecommunications is one of the few reasonably standardized areas of the computer industry (computers couldn't communicate at all if it weren't), most communications packages are functionally quite similar. Almost all will provide the basic features we've outlined; their differences lie in their ease of use, speed, and number of extra features.

Software Integration

Bundling several applications together

A recent development in application packages is a trend toward what has become known as software integration. Besides being one of the current buzzwords of the computer industry, **software integration** refers to the bundling of several applications into a single, powerful, easy-to-use package. The roots of software integration go back as far as projects undertaken at Xerox Corporation's celebrated Palo Alto Research Center in the 1970s, but it came into the marketplace quite suddenly in 1982 with the introduction of Lotus Development Corporation's 1-2-3 package and Context Management Systems' Context MBA package. The combination of 16-bit microcomputers (like the IBM Personal Computer), larger and less expensive primary storage, high-capacity hard disk secondary storage, and graphics input and display devices paved the way for this new generation of powerful software offering several functions "under one roof." Primarily a phenomenon associated with microcomputers, software integration is currently experiencing an explosive growth in popularity. According to a report prepared by Creative Strategies, Inc., a research firm in San Jose, California, the market for such software is expected to exceed $3.8 billion by 1987.

Software integration assumes one of two basic forms: the integrated software package and the software integrator package. Even though these two sound almost alike and ultimately provide users with similar capabilities, they take different approaches.

Integrated Software Packages

All-in-one packages

The **integrated software package** is the Swiss Army knife of application packages: it aims to provide just about every commonly used tool that will be needed in a business environment. Such packages typically include spreadsheet, data base management, word-processing, communications, and graphics capabilities, all within the same program. The primary goal achieved by this approach to software integration is ease of training and use—it's simpler to train someone to use a single set of commands for a large multifunction program than it is to teach a different set of commands for each separate application. Furthermore, switching between the various functions of an integrated software package is quick, straightforward, and problem-free. For many organizations, a single integrated software package may be the only application package needed. Such companies can turn on their computer in the morning and load the integrated package, and they're set for a whole day of business operations.

Integrated software is typically quite user-friendly and allows the computer display screen to be divided up into several *windows*. Each window can contain a different function, almost as if each one were a separate display screen (see Figure 10.11).

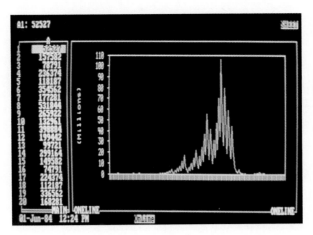

Figure 10.11 An Integrated Software Package
Symphony, produced by Lotus Development Corporation, is a popular integrated software package currently on the market. It offers spreadsheet, word-processing, data base management, graphics, and communications functions, as well as its own programming language for customizing advanced applications. On-screen windows are used to display and coordinate the different features. Symphony costs about $700, runs on IBM microcomputers, and requires a relatively large amount of primary memory.

Let's say, for example, that you need to prepare a report. Starting off using the word processor portion of your integrated software package, you discover that you need some figures from the regional sales office. At the touch of a button, the communications function is loaded and appears on the screen in its own window, either above or beside the word-processing window. The computer at the regional office is automatically called and logged onto, and you can get the information you need from its large data base. Feeding these figures into the spreadsheet function creates a new window, and the communications window is discarded since its role is ended. After computing some results, you use the graphics function to plot a pie chart, and you insert this into the text of your report with the word processor. All this and more can be accomplished with the same program.

Software Integrator Packages

Making your own custom package

Software integrator packages aren't quite as numerous or heavily advertised as integrated software packages; they're also not as popular, largely because they're somewhat less convenient. A **software integrator package** (or **integrated operating environment**) is best described as a shell that ties different application packages together. By itself, a software integrator is almost useless. Although it may include simple scratchpad, calendar, and calculator functions, a software integrator doesn't have word-processing, data base, spreadsheet, graphics, or communications functions. The user must supply these. Software integrators make independent application packages appear to be a set of interrelated modules by handling the transfer and sharing of data among them. Like integrated software packages, software integrator packages feature on-screen windows to display multiple functions simultaneously. Figure 10.12 shows how one software integrator presents more than one application package on the screen at once.

The unique advantages that users derive from these integrators are the ability to choose which application packages to include as components, and a high degree of flexibility. A user can upgrade or add to the existing environment as new or better programs become available. Some people prefer software integrators to integrated software for this reason. A particular integrated software package may have a great spreadsheet, for example, but what if you hate its word processor? You're stuck with it. With a software integrator, however, you can make a customized assortment of all your favorite application packages.

Figure 10.12 A Software Integrator Package

Software integrators allow users to bundle several application packages together so they act as a cohesive unit. Here DesQ displays WordStar, dBASE II, and other information all on the screen at the same time in overlapping windows.

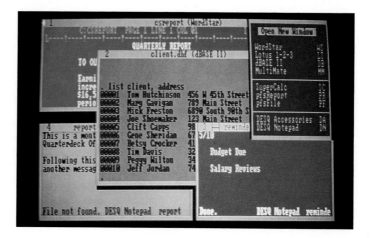

 AN IN-DEPTH EXAMPLE: LOTUS 1-2-3

An all-time best-seller

In addition to being one of the best-selling products in the microcomputer industry, Lotus 1-2-3 is an excellent example of an integrated software package. Shortly after its introduction in late 1982, 1-2-3 hit the top of the software best-sellers list, and it remains an extremely popular program to this day. It's a powerful, sophisticated package that combines (1) a state-of-the-art electronic spreadsheet, (2) exceptional business graphics, and (3) useful data management functions. Specifically designed to utilize the memory capacity and speed of 16-bit microcomputers such as the IBM Personal Computer, the 1-2-3 package includes one of the largest and fastest spreadsheets on the market.

Let's take a look at how the three basic elements of this package might be used by a small business. Kwik Key & Lock is a family-owned locksmith shop providing installation and repairs for home, business, and automobile locks. In addition to giving 24-hour emergency lock-out service, owners Karen and Karl Keating also duplicate keys and sell new locks over the counter of their neighborhood store. Since they run a relatively small operation (grossing about $100,000 a year), the Keatings decided that Lotus 1-2-3 should be able to handle their needs for financial analysis and record keeping. In particular, they plan to use it for producing yearly income statements, drawing a few graphs, and maintaining a customer mailing list. As we go over 1-2-3's spreadsheet, graphics, and data management functions, we'll see how they apply to these specific tasks for Kwik Key & Lock.

The Spreadsheet

Processing tables of numbers

As we've mentioned, 1-2-3 is first and foremost an electronic spreadsheet program. Like all spreadsheet programs, 1-2-3 is a computerized replacement for the traditional tools of financial analysis: the accountant's columnar pad, pencil, and calculator. A spreadsheet program facilitates the repetitive processing of tables of numbers and can in fact manipulate any kind of numerical data. Consequently, spreadsheet programs are applicable to a wide range of problems, not just those associated with financial analysis.

As we've mentioned before, the typical electronic spreadsheet configures the computer's memory so the display screen resembles a columnar pad of rows and columns. Because this configuration dynamically exists in the computer's memory, it can be much larger than an ordinary paper spreadsheet pad. Many electronic spreadsheets have 254 rows and 64 columns, but 1-2-3 has 2048 rows and 254 columns. In 1-2-3, the rows are numbered from 1 to 2048, and the columns are lettered starting with A to Z, then AA to AZ, BA to BZ, and so on, all the way to IV. Thus, 1-2-3 has 520,192 cells, or places to put data items, each one of which is identified by a unique column-row combination. For example, the cell at the intersection of column C and row 11 is identified as C11.

Cell Contents

The cells of an electronic spreadsheet can be filled with three basic types of information: (1) numbers; (2) text (or labels); and (3) mathematical formulas and functions. Numbers, of course, are the primary type of data inserted in electronic spreadsheets, and text is frequently used for headings and labels for columns and rows. Formulas and functions, however, give electronic spreadsheets much of their power.

A *formula* is a mathematical relationship that can be stored in a cell. For example, if the formula A1 + B1 is stored in cell C1, then cell C1 will automatically display the sum of the contents of cells A1 and B1. The cell names are like variables in an equation; no matter what values are in A1 and B1, C1 will always show their sum. Spreadsheet formulas can be much more complex than this simple example, of course. The contents of one cell can be added to, subtracted from, multiplied by, or divided by those of any other cell. In addition, formulas may contain functions.

A *function* is a sort of mathematical shortcut that lets a user perform common computations with a minimum of typing. Spreadsheet functions can help to abbreviate what would otherwise be long and cumbersome formulas. For example, the SUM function of 1-2-3 lets the user add up the contents of a range of contiguous cells without having to type in each cell name. The formula for the total contents of cells B1 through B25 can be concisely expressed as follows:

$$@SUM(B1..B25)$$

The symbol @ tells 1-2-3 that the word that follows it is the name of a function. The 1-2-3 spreadsheet offers users a wide range of mathematical, trigonometric, statistical, financial, and other special functions.

The Cursor

The *cursor* of 1-2-3 allows you to enter information into the cells, much as a pencil lets you write on paper. The cursor is displayed on the screen as a bright rectangle one row high and one column wide. It can be moved anywhere on the array of rows and columns (or the *worksheet*, as Lotus calls it) by pressing the arrow keys on the computer keyboard. If the cursor is at cell A1 and you want to move it to cell D5, you hit the right-arrow key three times and the down-arrow key four times.

Once the cursor is positioned at the desired cell, information is entered by typing it in at the keyboard and hitting the carriage return. As the characters are typed in, they appear in the upper left-hand corner of the display screen, along with the cursor's current location. The characters aren't actually put in the cell where the cursor is located until the user hits the carriage return. This allows the user to backspace over and fix typing errors before pressing the carriage return. After the

Figure 10.13 An Empty 1-2-3 Worksheet
In this empty 1-2-3 worksheet, the cursor is in cell C5. Note that the main menu is presented across the top of the array.

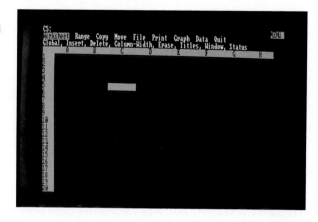

carriage return has been pressed, errors can still be fixed using the edit key. Pressing this key displays the contents from the current cursor location in the upper left-hand corner so that it can be modified.

Figure 10.13 shows how an empty 1-2-3 worksheet appears on the screen (the cursor is in cell C5).

Scrolling the Worksheet

Because the 1-2-3 worksheet is so large, it won't all fit on the computer display screen at one time. The screen serves as a window onto the worksheet, showing only a portion of it at a time. Typically, 20 rows and 8 columns can be viewed at once; however, how many columns will fit depends on their widths, which can be set by the user. To view other parts of the worksheet, the cursor is simply moved off the edge of the screen, and the worksheet automatically shifts, or scrolls, behind the display screen window until the desired portion is shown. As an analogy, imagine that you've got a large map spread out on a table. You can only look at the part of the map visible through a nine-inch-square hole cut in a piece of cardboard that completely covers the map. Although you can see only part of the map through the square window, the rest of it's still there. To see other portions, you must scroll the map by pulling it left, right, up, or down beneath the cardboard. The 1-2-3 worksheet is like the map, the display screen is like the hole in the cardboard, and the arrow keys do the pulling.

Commands

The user tells 1-2-3 how to manipulate worksheet contents through the use of *commands*. The *menu,* or list of available commands, appears at the top of the display screen when the user types in a slash (/). The user can make a selection from the menu, which will cause the display of another sublist of selections or the performance of some operation. For example, to mention just a few, 1-2-3 has commands to insert, delete, move, and copy rows and columns. Help is available to the user through the use of an on-line facility that presents additional information about menu selections. All the user has to do is press the appropriate key and 1-2-3 will display detailed information about itself on the screen. The combination of menus and on-line help makes 1-2-3 fairly easy for novices to use, without having to spend hours leafing through manuals.

Now that we've given a brief introduction to some of the features of Lotus 1-2-3, let's see how the Keatings used it to set up their yearly income statement.

The Income Statement

In order to summarize how their business does each year, the Keatings construct a yearly income statement. This report lists all the major income sources and expenses for each quarter of the year and gives their totals. The bottom line, or total income minus total deductions, indicates the profit for the year. Figure 10.14 shows the report that is the final product of this Lotus 1-2-3 worksheet example.

Backing up a bit, however, the first step in constructing the income statement is to set up the worksheet format. This means setting the width of each column and telling 1-2-3 how numbers are to be displayed. The Worksheet Column-Width command is used to set columns A, B, C, and D through G to widths of 16, 2, 10, and 11 characters, respectively. Since this worksheet is to contain dollar amounts, the number formats are set with the Worksheet Format command to have two places to the right of the decimal point and commas to indicate thousands.

Next, titles, headings, and some dividing lines are typed into appropriate cells to give the income statement a neat, easy-to-read appearance. To enter titles or headings, the cursor is simply moved to the cell the text is to start in, and the text is entered. Text can overflow cell boundaries, so that long headings like "YEARLY INCOME STATEMENT 1986" can be typed in all at once. Column and row labels can be automatically repeated, centered, or left- or right-justified by preceding them with one of the following *label-prefix characters:*

'   left-justifies

/\   centers

"   right-justifies

\   repeats

```
*******************************************************************
                        Kwik Key & Lock
                     1404   Silver Street
                    Urbana, Illinois  61801
*******************************************************************

                 YEARLY INCOME STATEMENT 1986


==================================================================
       Item      |            Quarters
                 |    First    Second     Third     Fourth      Total
==================================================================
        INCOME
 Sales Income    $ 10,523.50  13,459.25  17,752.00  11,543.50  53,278.25
 Labor Income    $  7,987.25  11,208.00  15,489.50  10,653.00  45,337.75
    Total Income $ 18,510.75  24,667.25  33,241.50  22,196.50  98,616.00
 -----------------------------------------------------------------

        EXPENSES
 Store Rental    $  1,500.00   1,500.00   1,500.00   1,500.00   6,000.00
 Telephone       $    750.00     750.00     750.00     750.00   3,000.00
 Utilities       $    450.00     450.00     450.00     450.00   1,800.00
 Advertising     $    600.00     600.00     600.00     600.00   2,400.00
 Insurance       $    250.00     250.00     250.00     250.00   1,000.00
 Vehicles        $    750.00   1,200.50   1,087.25   1,345.20   4,382.95
 Tax & Licenses  $    125.50     125.50     125.50     125.50     502.00
 Tools           $    327.80     892.50     479.00     589.50   2,288.80
 Office Supplies $    213.50     186.75     300.89     288.00     989.14
 Equipment       $    799.50     456.25     925.25     654.40   2,835.40
 Accountant      $                          350.00                 350.00
 Materials       $  2,500.50   2,785.75   3,111.25   2,354.20  10,751.70
 Payroll         $  7,200.00   7,200.00   7,200.00   7,200.00  28,800.00
 Misc. Services  $    258.00     129.50     321.70     150.50     859.70
    Total Expenses $ 15,724.80  16,526.75  17,450.84  16,257.30  65,959.69
 -----------------------------------------------------------------
 Depreciation    $    500.00     500.00     500.00     500.00   2,000.00
 Bad Debts       $                159.20     213.13      25.60     397.93
 -----------------------------------------------------------------
 Tot. Deductions $ 16,224.80  17,185.95  18,163.97  16,782.90  68,357.62
 -----------------------------------------------------------------
     Net Profit  $  2,285.95   7,481.30  15,077.53   5,413.60  30,258.38
==================================================================
```

Figure 10.14 An Income Statement

The income statement for Kwik Key & Lock after it's been printed out on a dot matrix printer.

The repeat label-prefix character (\) is useful for entering lines, such as those made up of dashes, asterisks, and equals signs that you see in the finished income statement.

After the format of the table has been completely set up, the next step is to enter all those numbers that are known beforehand. In this case, Karl Keating types in the figures from the first through the fourth quarter for sales income, labor income, expenses, depreciation, and bad debts. After this, all that's left are the empty cells that are to hold the column and row totals. This is where 1-2-3 gets a chance to shine. Formulas are entered for the remaining cells, and the totals are automatically calculated.

For example, Karl types this into cell C16: +C14+C15. This tells 1-2-3 to add the contents of the two cells directly above cell C16. The Copy command lets Karl replicate this formula in cells D16 through G16 so that 1-2-3 will properly compute all the total income amounts (see Figure 10.15). Note that the Copy command saved Karl a significant amount of typing; he only had to enter the formula once, and 1-2-3 changed the columns being summed as the formula was copied to each new cell. By entering just three more formulas (using the @SUM function for the expenses columns) and using the Copy command, Karl filled in all the remaining blank cells in practically no time at all.

At this point, the income statement worksheet can be stored on disk with the File Save command, printed out with the Print command, or experimented with further. The great advantage to an electronic spreadsheet program like 1-2-3 is that it easily handles "what if" speculations. What would the Keatings' profit be if their rent were $200 more a month? They could easily find out by using the edit key to change the figures in the Store Rental row for the four quarters. Any other cells in the entire worksheet that are based on the values of these cells would change automatically, and the new results would immediately appear on the screen.

As we've seen from this example, the 1-2-3 spreadsheet helps users perform three fundamental types of tasks:

1. Given an array of numbers, perform some calculations.
2. Present these numbers so that their meaning and organization are immediately clear.
3. Store these numbers accurately and reliably so that they can be quickly retrieved.

Figure 10.15 Computing Totals in the Worksheet

This display shows the screen filled with the top portion of the income statement worksheet just after the Total Income row has been computed.

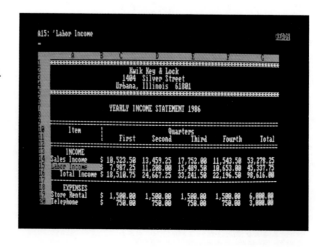

We've taken only a glimpse at what the 1-2-3 spreadsheet can do; it has many more commands and techniques that make it an extremely powerful and flexible tool. However, let's go on to examine how 1-2-3 can present information from worksheets in graphic form.

Graphics

Although Kwik Key & Lock doesn't have a board of directors to impress, the Keatings can still appreciate being able to see worksheet results displayed in a more striking form than as a table of figures. Lotus 1-2-3 allows users quickly and easily to set up various types of charts and graphs for immediate screen display (provided the computer being employed has graphics capabilities). Bar graphs, line graphs, and pie charts are the types of graphics most commonly used, and the Keatings have decided to set up one of each.

The 1-2-3 Graph command and its associated menus make it a snap to set up and display graphs. For example, it took Karen Keating only 5 minutes or so to

Displaying and printing charts

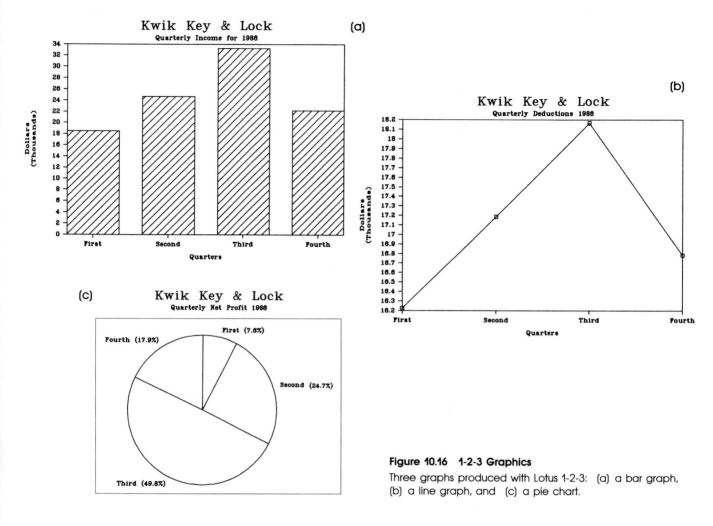

Figure 10.16   1-2-3 Graphics

Three graphs produced with Lotus 1-2-3:   (a) a bar graph, (b) a line graph, and   (c) a pie chart.

produce the bar graph shown in Figure 10.16(a). First, she invoked the Graph command, then selected bar graph as the type of graph she wanted. The total income value for the four quarters was chosen as the data range of the graph. Finally, titles and axis labels were typed in and the View option was selected. The display screen cleared, and the completed graph jumped into view in a split second.

The Keatings did two more graphs. Figure 10.16(b) shows the line graph they made of quarterly deductions, and Figure 10.16(c) shows the pie chart of quarterly net profit. The graphs were saved on disk with the Graph Save command and later printed on an IBM Personal Computer Graphics Printer using the Lotus 1-2-3 PrintGraph program.

Data Management

Storing and manipulating data records

The third element of the 1-2-3 package is the data management function. Although Lotus calls this feature "data base management," it's really too simple and too limited to be referred to by that term. What 1-2-3 allows the user to do is to set up a worksheet in which rows correspond to data records and columns correspond to fields within those records. Once this is done, 1-2-3's commands basically allow the user to sort and query this worksheet. Although it's not a full-fledged data base management system, 1-2-3 is adequate for simple applications, such as the mailing list file for which the Keatings decided to use it.

Inputting the data records is no different than entering data for any other worksheet. To set up the mailing list shown in Figure 10.17, the Keatings adjusted column widths to accommodate last names, first names, street addresses, cities, states, and zip codes. Then the data are simply typed in, one record after another. Once finished, the data base can be stored on disk, retrieved from disk, printed out, or manipulated just like the contents of any other 1-2-3 worksheet. The difference is that this worksheet will usually only be sorted and queried.

The customer mailing list for Kwik Key & Lock will be kept sorted according to the last name of each person. Records can be added in any order and sorted later with the Data Sort command. This command allows the user to sort on two keys: the primary key and an optional secondary key. For example, the Keatings could sort their mailing list by zip code (as the primary key) and then by last name (the

Last Name	First Name	Street Address	City	State	Zip
Abel	Larry	906 Busey #5	Urbana	IL	61801
Alexander	Barbara	604 Armory	Champaign	IL	61820
Banks	David	1104 Grant Pl.	Champaign	IL	61820
Becker	Molly	310 W Paddock	Savoy	IL	61821
Calhoon	Carrie	1007 Barclay	Tolono	IL	61880
Carver	George	402 Main	Watseka	IL	60970
Crawford	John	2012 Anderson	Urbana	IL	61801
Daily	Irene	2209 Philo	Urbana	IL	61801
Davis	Becky	2504 S Lynn	Urbana	IL	61801
Diamond	Jim	502 E Chalmers	Champaign	IL	61820
Eaton	Candy	701 Dover Pl.	Champaign	IL	61820
Edwards	Barbara	1721 Valley Rd	Paxton	IL	60957
Feldman	Francis	809 W Elm	Urbana	IL	61801
Franklin	Melissa	566 W Church	Champaign	IL	61820
Garret	Gerald	1871 Parkdale	Rantoul	IL	61866
Griffith	Oscar	805 W Florida	Urbana	IL	61801
Hall	Robert	102 White	Pekin	IL	61554
Hudson	Henry	892 Bay Ave	Champaign	IL	61820
Irving	Judith	1904 Oliver Dr	Urbana	IL	61801
Jackson	Delbert	1010 W Bridle	Monticello	IL	61856
Jenkins	Alfred	311 Southmoor	Champaign	IL	61820
Jordon	Holly	1311 Grandview	Danville	IL	61832
Kelley	Joyce	142 Hazelwood	Tolono	IL	61880
Knowles	Lesley	1609 W Bradley	Champaign	IL	61820
Lancaster	Terry	805 S Randolf	Champaign	IL	61820
Lee	Kim	135 Cedar	Rantoul	IL	61866
Lowrey	Marcy	407 S Coler	Urbana	IL	61801
Malony	Fred	408 E Main	Tolono	IL	61880
McFall	Ellen	700 W Elm	Rantoul	IL	61866
Mitchell	Dan	909 Crestwood	Urbana	IL	61801
Nelson	Scott	411 E Green	Champaign	IL	61820
Novak	Sandy	3008 Kyle	Urbana	IL	61801
Olson	Roger	305 Briar Lane	Champaign	IL	61820
Owens	Diane	987 W Tremont	Monticello	IL	61856
Pearson	Charlie	605 N Willis	Tolono	IL	61880
Prorok	Brian	111 E Healy	Champaign	IL	61820
Quinlan	Kerry	809 Maple	Rantoul	IL	61866
Reeves	Mike	1507 S Race	Urbana	IL	61801
Russel	Ruby	124 W Park	Urbana	IL	61801
Savage	Julian	114 Edgebrook	Savoy	IL	61821
Skubic	Mike	321 Gregory	Champaign	IL	61820
Spencer	Linda	506 E Oregon	Urbana	IL	61801
Townsend	Laurie	2307 Barberry	Tolono	IL	61880
Tudor	Anthony	100 Kenwood	Champaign	IL	61820
Underwood	Rhonda	1243 W Green	Urbana	IL	61801
Valentine	Paul	1325 Westwood	Monticello	IL	61856
Walden	Roxanne	134 Doddson	Urbana	IL	61801
Weaver	Sally	908 S Oak	Champaign	IL	61820
Willmann	Allison	145 E Hessel	Champaign	IL	61820
Young	Susan	508 N Edwin	Rantoul	IL	61866

Figure 10.17 1-2-3 Data Management

This short mailing list for Kwik Key & Lock is one example of how Lotus 1-2-3 can be used for small data management applications.

secondary key) within each zip code. This might be used to take advantage of reduced bulk mailing rates on advertisement letters grouped by zip codes.

In addition to simple sorting, 1-2-3 has commands that let the user search for records within a data base. For example, with the Data Query Find command and the Data Query Extract command, the Keatings can have 1-2-3 go through their mailing list, pull out all the records of customers who live in Urbana, Illinois, and copy those records to some specified area of the worksheet. Also, some functions available just for data bases let users compute certain statistics. For example, the @DCOUNT function can be used to count how many customers in the data base live in Rantoul. The combination of data base functions and commands allows 1-2-3 to manipulate relatively small (less than 2000) sets of records fairly efficiently. Its relatively modest data management capabilities, however, keep 1-2-3 from being serious competition for more sophisticated data base packages for microcomputers, such as Ashton-Tate's dBASE II and dBASE III.

SUMMARY

Advantages of Using Prewritten Software

Application packages, or collections of prewritten software designed to perform specific tasks, can be of great value to computer users, offering a number of advantages.

Quick Installation   Prewritten packages can usually be put into use as soon as they are purchased.

Well-Defined Function   Users of well-known application packages can more easily determine exactly what they are getting for their money.

Lower Cost   Because software manufacturers expect to sell their products to many customers, the price is less than the cost of developing programs.

Easy Updating and Revising   Established packages are often updated and revised as new technology and techniques are developed.

Familiarity   Employees are more likely to know how to use or want to learn how to use the popular application packages.

Disadvantages of Using Prewritten Software

The major disadvantage of using prewritten software is that it may not do exactly what is needed.

What Makes a Good Package?

Characteristics of a good package are as follows:

Features   The package should provide what the user needs.

Documentation   The package should have adequate user documentation in the form of manuals or on-line help.

Support   Assistance from the manufacturer (preferably by telephone) when unusual problems occur is definitely desirable.

User-Friendliness   An application package should be easy to use and straightforward.

Cost   The price of a package is a major consideration for most consumers.

Flexibility   A package should be adaptable to a wide variety of situations.

Upgradability   Packages that will be revised and updated as new technology and techniques are developed are more useful in the long run.

Types of Application Packages

Application packages have been a major factor in making computers useful and desirable to a great many people. There are a great many types.

Word-Processing Packages Word-processing packages are very popular; they let users easily enter, store, modify, format, copy, and print text.

Electronic Spreadsheets Electronic spreadsheets enable users to perform calculations involving rows and columns of figures.

File Managers and Data Base Packages Free-form indexing and filing programs, file managers, and full-fledged data base management systems allow users to cope with the storage, manipulation, and retrieval of large quantities of data.

Graphics Packages Graphics packages are used to produce visual images, such as graphs and charts, as well as interactive pictures.

Mathematical and Statistical Packages Mathematical and statistical packages perform complex, number-crunching operations.

Modeling and Simulation Packages Packages that do mathematical modeling or simulations of real-life situations allow the computerized representation of complex, inconvenient, or dangerous scenarios.

Business and Financial Packages Business packages handle the accounting needs of firms, and personal finance packages include programs for individuals' budgeting, investment, and tax preparation needs.

Communications Software Communications software enables users' microcomputers to act as terminals in teleprocessing systems.

Software Integration Integrated software packages are all-purpose programs that include applications such as word-processing, spreadsheet, data base, communications, and graphics functions. Software integrators are shells in which users can bundle their own favorite application packages.

An In-Depth Example: Lotus 1-2-3

Lotus 1-2-3 is a very popular integrated software package that includes spreadsheet, graphics, and data management functions.

The Spreadsheet The spreadsheet in 1-2-3 is a fast, powerful feature that contains 2048 rows and 264 columns.

Graphics 1-2-3's graphics function readily allows users to display and print graphs and charts from their worksheets.

Data Management The 1-2-3 package provides a simple data management function that basically allows users to sort and query data-filled worksheets.

COMPUTER CONCEPTS ▬▬▬

As an extra review of the chapter, try defining the following terms. If you have trouble with any of them, refer to the page number listed.

application package 280
upward compatibility 281
help facilities 283
word-processing package 285
electronic spreadsheet 286
cell 286
data base 287

file managers 289
pixels 291
resolution 291
mathematical model 292
simulation 293
linear programming 293
logging on (signing on) 297

software integration 298
integrated software package 298
software integrator package (integrated operating environment) 299

REVIEW QUESTIONS

1. What prompted the development of prewritten application packages?
2. What are some of the advantages and disadvantages for users of prewritten application packages?
3. Why is it important that updated versions of packages be upwardly compatible?
4. List some of the factors to be considered when evaluating an application package.
5. How has the availability of good application packages affected the computer industry?
6. What makes word-processing programs so much more powerful than typewriters?
7. What advantages do spreadsheet programs have over the manual operations associated with calculating rows and columns of figures?
8. How do free-form indexing and filing programs differ from file managers, and how do file managers differ from full-fledged data base management systems?
9. What kinds of things can be done with graphics packages?
10. For what kinds of computers were mathematical and statistical packages originally developed?
11. Why might one want to use a computer to model or simulate real-life situations?
12. Why do most firms use prewritten accounting packages instead of writing their own software?
13. Why haven't home budgeting programs sold as well as business accounting packages?
14. What are some of the tasks a communications package should perform?
15. Why might a user prefer a software integrator package over an integrated software package?
16. What three major functions does Lotus 1-2-3 provide?
17. What kinds of information can be put in the cells of an electronic spreadsheet?
18. How do formulas and functions add power to electronic spreadsheets?
19. What does the cursor do in Lotus 1-2-3?
20. What kinds of graphics can Lotus 1-2-3 produce?
21. What kinds of tasks can be performed with Lotus 1-2-3's data management functions?

A SHARPER FOCUS

Now that you've completed this chapter, you should be able to answer the following questions about the chapter opening.

1. The chapter opening indicates that the advantages of using prewritten software might be balanced by certain disadvantages. What might these disadvantages be?
2. Compare the effectiveness of teaching software with that of on-site training sessions.

PROJECTS

1. Let's say that you have an IBM Personal Computer and that you've been given $1000 with which to buy all the software you'll need as a student. Decide what kinds of application packages you require, and then choose which manufacturers produce the specific packages you want to purchase. Try to be a wise consumer by researching all possibilities and by striving to get the best values for your money. Prepare a report detailing your selections and the reasons behind them.
2. It would seem that the number of different tasks to be done by a word-processing package is fairly small, yet there are dozens, perhaps even hundreds, of different packages available for the most popular microcomputer models. Why? Do they all differ significantly in their features? Investigate this question. Write a report with examples to illustrate your findings, and include a table or chart summarizing them.

3. Small business owners are often told, "Find the application packages you want, and then just buy any microcomputer that'll run them. . . . They're all pretty much the same." What do you think of this advice, and why?

4. Many computer magazines carry monthly listings of the top 10 or top 20 best-sellers in application packages for microcomputers. See what you can conclude about the average life of some of the packages mentioned in this chapter. Relate this to an estimate of what the development and marketing costs for a typical package might be, thereby coming up with an estimate of what sales would have to be to break even or make a profit. Are software packages profitable in most cases, or are they just necessary in order to sell computers?

Operating Systems

▶

FOCUS ON . . . THE SWISS ARMY KNIFE OF SOFTWARE

Work on [UNIX] started back in 1969 because Ken Thompson, 41, a bearded, long-haired programming pioneer who has been known to work 30 hours at a stretch, felt frustrated in constructing a computer game he called Space Travel. The project was an exercise in writing an applications program, and Thompson was dissatisfied with the . . . unresponsiveness of the computers at hand.

Big operating systems of the sort that ran those computers are normally a product of hundreds of systems designers and programmers, and they incorporate many compromises. Thompson decided to strive for simplicity. . . He wanted as much freedom and flexibility for users as possible.

Thompson was soon joined by another Bell Labs programmer, Dennis Ritchie, also bearded and inquisitive, and the two began incorporating into UNIX the best features they could find in various operating systems as well as contributing their own concepts. One of their most brilliant additions was the concept of "pipes," through which one command can be connected to another, allowing the user to create new applications programs by stringing together UNIX "words" into "sentences." The UNIX language provides an unusually large number of preprogrammed commands—more than 200—for sorting data, manipulating text, or searching for information. These "utilities" can be used in thousands of combinations, offering the user a range of instruments of unusual . . . power. "UNIX," one user observed recently, "is the Swiss army knife of software."

A major virtue of UNIX is leverage—a little tapping on the keyboard can bring on a lot of action in the computer. As an example, people at Bell Laboratories point to the set of instructions below. They tell a computer to print out each word in a document, along with the number of times the word occurs, arranging the words in descending order of frequency. That may not be what you want from your computer, but it's a pretty good test of an operating system. A while back, a Bell Labs programmer asked outsiders to estimate how many lines of instructions the task would require—lines, in this sense, meaning commands—and most of the replies fell in the range of 100 to 1,000. With UNIX, just seven short commands do the trick.

```
tr [A–Z] [a–z] I              Make capital letters lower case.
tr –d "(.,;:\"'–_!?\)" I       Delete punctuation.
tr " " "\012" I                Put each word on a separate line.
sed –e "/^ *$/d" I             Delete blank lines.
sort I                         Sort words in alphabetical order.
uniq –c I                      Count occurrences of each word.
sort –nr                       Sort by frequency, in descending order.
```

Where does the leverage come from? Brian W. Kernighan, the Bell Labs programmer who coined the name UNIX, explains that pieces of the job are already done before the user taps a single key. Each of those seven brief directives begins with a general purpose command, such as "tr" or "sort," that is a program in itself. And UNIX is so designed that instructions to modify the general purpose command can readily be "glued on." . . .

We've now covered almost all the basics: from input to output, from hardware to software. We've looked at how just about everything in a computer system works. Logically enough, we've saved for last the element that binds hardware and software together into an integrated, usable whole, capable of doing all the things its parts are designed to do. That element—the operating system—is easily the most important software a computer has. In most cases, the operating system is the first program executed when a computer is turned on and the last program executed before it's shut down. Programmers have a lot of names for this indispensable set of programs, for example, "the traffic cop," "the boss," "the bandleader," and "virtualized interface." No matter what it's called, the operating system is of prime importance.

In this chapter, we'll learn what operating systems do and how they do it, and we'll look at a half dozen of today's most prevalent commercially available operating systems, from Apple's "user-cuddly" system for the Macintosh to IBM's powerful VM for mainframes.

▐▐▐▐ FUNCTIONS OF OPERATING SYSTEMS

What operating systems do

Operating systems are used on all types of general-purpose computers, from micro-computers to supercomputers. They have become such an integral part of the computer that every user should have at least a general understanding of their functions. An **operating system (OS)** can be defined as a set of programs that controls, supervises, and supports a computer system's hardware. The fundamental task of an operating system is to manage the hardware carefully, in order to achieve the best possible performance. This task is accomplished by the operating system's controlling and coordinating such resources as the CPU, other processing units, both primary memory and secondary storage, and all input/output devices. The hardware provides the raw computing power, and the operating system makes this power conveniently accessible to the user.

Providing Services

By handling computer resources efficiently, so that users don't have to worry about every detail of what's happening during processing, the operating system provides several valuable services, including:

How operating systems help users

- *Sharing hardware among users.* In computer systems that can accommodate more than one user at a time, the operating system decides who gets what and when. For example, if there are five users and only one printer, the operating system must be prepared to accept and deal with five simultaneous printer requests. The operating system sees to it that all users eventually get the access they require.

- *Allowing users to share programs and data.* Systems that are accessible to a number of simultaneous users usually include some means by which programs and data can be shared among them. Identical programs and data need not be duplicated for each user. In an airline reservation system, for example, the data base of flights, fares, and available seats, as well as the programs that allow reservations to be made, are shared by all travel agents who have access to the system.

- *Enabling users to protect their data.* Computer systems with multiple users must provide measures by which users can be prevented from accessing or accidentally destroying one another's private data.

- *Scheduling resource use.* Again, if there are several users, a computer's operating system must coordinate the use of all the available resources. A good operating system accomplishes this in the most efficient manner possible.

- *Facilitating input, output, and secondary storage operations.* If a computer had no operating system, every application program would have to specify all the operating details of the input, output, and secondary storage devices. By taking care of such fundamental operations as reading characters from a terminal keyboard, sending them to a printer, and writing records onto a disk, the operating system frees users from having to worry about low-level details.

- *Recovering from errors.* Computer users (especially programmers) have an aptitude for "crashing" computers in any number of imaginative ways. They may write a program that accidentally branches to a memory location containing only garbage, or they may devise an infinite loop. Operating systems usually have the capability to detect errors like these, inform users of their nature, and minimize any damage that could occur to data. A good operating system can save the day in many cases, instead of simply bringing the whole system to a grinding halt.

Acting as an Interface

The operating system functions as an *interface* (a shared boundary or connection) on two levels. First, the operating system interfaces software with hardware. Programs call the operating system to handle most of the details concerned with controlling the computer hardware. This means that programs can utilize the services offered by the operating system without compromising its role as a resource manager. Second, the operating system interfaces users with the computer system. In Chapter 8, we said that a user interface specifies how a person communicates with a program. The operating system defines how users communicate with and control the computer system as a whole.

The operating system as user interface

There are various kinds of users, and each type interacts with the operating system in a slightly different way. *General users*—bank tellers, travel agents, authors, students, and so on—use a computer system in their day-to-day work. They rely on the operating system to run the application programs they need and to handle their storage, input, and output requests. *Computer operators* are responsible for monitoring the operating system. They keep a computer system running smoothly by responding to requests from the operating system and from users and performing nonautomated routine tasks like loading and unloading tapes and disks, putting paper in the printers, and restarting the computer after a system crash. *Application programmers*, whose job we described in the Careers in Technology section of Chapter 8, use the operating system to facilitate the entry, development, translation, and installation of the programs they produce, and *systems programmers* are concerned with installing and maintaining the operating system itself. They tailor it to the particular needs of the facility and modify it to incorporate new types of peripheral devices.

Who uses operating systems

A SHORT HISTORY OF OPERATING SYSTEMS

In Chapter 2, we noted the appearance of the operating system as a significant software development during the third generation of computers. Although primitive operating systems did exist before that, they didn't become a dominant force until the mid-1960s. The earliest computer systems had no operating systems; users had access to computer resources only via machine language programs. Programs were run one at a time by computer operators who manually entered the commands to initiate and complete each one. This pattern of usage wasted a great deal of computer time, since the CPU remained idle between the completion of one task and the initiation of the next.

How and why operating systems evolved

The 1950s were marked by the development of rudimentary operating systems designed to smooth the transitions between jobs (a **job** is any program or part of a program that is to be processed as a unit by a computer). This was the start of *batch processing*, in which programs to be executed were grouped into *batches*. While a particular program was running, it had total control of the computer. When it finished, however, control was returned to the operating system, which handled any necessary finalizations and read in and started up the next job. By letting the computer handle the transition between one job and the next instead of having it done manually, less time was taken up and the CPU was more efficiently utilized.

During the 1960s, operating systems became much more sophisticated, leading up to the development of *shared systems*. These multiprogramming, time-sharing, and multiprocessing systems (which we will define and discuss in more detail later in this chapter) allowed several user programs to be run on a single computer system, seemingly at the same time. Additionally, these systems were the first to allow usage to take place in *interactive,* or *conversational, mode,* in which the user communicates directly with the computer, rather than submitting jobs and passively waiting for their completion. These developments made computer systems more widely accessible and easier to use. Instead of waiting for hours or even days for results from the batch processing of programs, users could get responses from the computer in seconds or minutes. This enhancement was a boon to programmers, who could more quickly locate and correct errors in their programs.

Real-time systems also emerged during the 1960s. These operating systems enabled computers to be used to control systems characterized by the need for immediate response, such as weapons systems or industrial plants. For example, if an oil refinery is being controlled by a real-time system, that system must respond immediately to temperature conditions that could cause an explosion.

In the late 1960s and the early 1970s, there was a trend toward *general-purpose operating systems*. These systems tried to be all things to all users. Often called **multimode systems**, some of them simultaneously supported batch processing, time sharing, real-time processing, and multiprocessing. They were large, expensive, and difficult to develop and maintain, but they helped sell a lot of computers. The prime example of this type of operating system was the one offered with the IBM System 360 family of computers first introduced in 1964. To get one of these monsters to perform even the simplest task, users had to learn a complex **job control language (JCL)** and employ it to specify how their programs were to be run and what resources they would need. Although these systems represented a great step forward, they reached no heights of user-friendliness.

The operating systems from the mid-1970s to the present cannot be characterized by a single, all-encompassing feature. The development of microcomputers and of simple, easy-to-use, single-user operating systems has had a profound effect on the newest systems being developed for all types of computers. The features most in demand are a high degree of user-friendliness and a computing environment that is *menu-driven* (refers to the use of displays and prompts that aid users in selecting functions). Also, operating systems that support on-line processing, computer networking, data security, and distributed data processing are the latest word. Modern operating systems create a **virtual machine**, an interface that relieves the user of any need to be concerned about most of the physical details of the computer system or network being accessed. The virtual machine presented by the operating system lets users concentrate on getting done what they need, without having to be familiar with the internal functioning of the actual hardware.

 ## COMPONENTS OF OPERATING SYSTEMS

What makes up an operating system

An operating system consists of an integrated set of programs, each of which performs specific tasks. These component programs are expressly designed to work together as a team and can generally be categorized as either control programs or

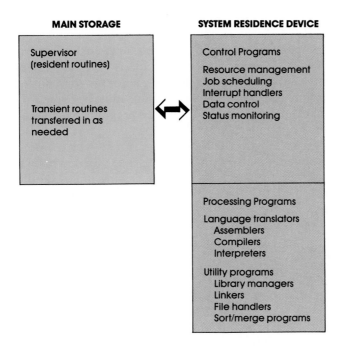

MAIN STORAGE

Supervisor
(resident routines)

Transient routines
transferred in as
needed

SYSTEM RESIDENCE DEVICE

Control Programs

Resource management
Job scheduling
Interrupt handlers
Data control
Status monitoring

Processing Programs

Language translators
   Assemblers
   Compilers
   Interpreters

Utility programs
   Library managers
   Linkers
   File handlers
   Sort/merge programs

Figure 11.1 The Operating System

An operating system is a set of programs, which can be classified as either control programs or processing programs. These programs reside on the system residence device and are transferred into primary memory as needed. However, some of them, the resident routines, are used so frequently they are constantly held in primary memory.

processing programs. *Control programs* direct the operations of the computer system and perform such tasks as allocating resources, scheduling jobs, resolving interrupts, sending messages to users, and managing the fundamental workings of input, output, and secondary storage. *Processing programs* perform functions that aid programmers in the preparation and execution of system and application software.

The collection of programs that makes up an operating system is kept in secondary storage on what is known as the **system residence device**, which is the permanent home of the operating system. The control and processing programs are stored here, ready to be loaded into primary memory and executed whenever they are called on to perform their jobs (see Figure 11.1). In most cases, the system residence device is a disk (which led to the nickname *DOS,* or *disk operating system*); magnetic tape devices and ROM chips are also sometimes used.

Where the system resides

Control Programs

The **supervisor** (also known as the **monitor** or **executive**) is the main control program of the operating system. It is responsible for coordinating the activities of all other parts of the operating system. When the computer is first turned on, the supervisor is the first program to be loaded from the system residence device into main memory. The most frequently used components of the supervisor are kept in primary memory the entire time the computer is on and are referred to as **resident routines**. Portions used less frequently are known as the **transient routines**; they remain on the system residence device and are transferred into primary memory as needed. Tasks performed by the supervisor or by the other control programs it directs include managing system resources, scheduling jobs, handling interrupts, controlling the flow of data, and monitoring system status.

Routines that manage resources, schedule jobs, handle interrupts, control data, and monitor system status

Managing Resources

Control programs that manage computer resources basically govern who gets to use what and when. As we will see, this role is especially important when the operating system is servicing more than one user or program during the same time period. Primary memory and secondary storage must be managed so that they are utilized as efficiently as possible and so that no program destroys another's data. If there is more than one processing unit, control programs must make assignments as to which programs or parts of programs are run on which processors. If there is only one processing unit but more than one user or program to be serviced, control programs must divide up and ration out processing time. Conflicts must be resolved whenever more than one user or program need to access the same input, output, or storage device at the same time.

Job Scheduling

Control programs for job scheduling establish the scheme by which multiple users or programs are serviced. This involves evaluating the resources needed for running jobs, assigning priorities, preparing jobs for execution, directing the flow of jobs through the computer system, and "cleaning up" after jobs are complete (clearing memory locations, resetting input, output, and storage devices, and so on). The performance of these activities may require interpreting job control language (JCL) statements in order to determine the characteristics of a job to be run and which resources it will call for. These statements, prepared by programmers for programs they want to run, are necessary for some operating systems, especially those that function in batch mode.

Handling Interrupts

Since a CPU performs arithmetic calculations much faster than most peripheral devices (tape drives, card readers, printers, and terminals) operate, most computer systems have adopted some form of interrupt scheme to reduce the time the CPU is idle. As we discussed in Chapter 3, an *interrupt* is a temporary suspension of the running of a computer program so that another, higher-priority job can be taken care of immediately. For example, let's say that a particular program does processing on some data that must be read from a tape or disk drive or entered by a typist at a terminal keyboard. Instead of letting the CPU do nothing while this input is acquired, it is put to work on some other processing that doesn't immediately require the requested data. When the data have been successfully read into primary memory, the CPU is interrupted, informed that the input is complete, and put back to work on the original task.

Although this switching back and forth from one job to another may seem like a complicated and hectic way to complete processing tasks, it dramatically increases the amount of work that can be accomplished since it results in more efficient utilization of the CPU's great speed. It's the operating system's job to be constantly ready to respond to interrupts triggered by internal or external events. When interrupts occur, control programs must coordinate the process of saving what is currently being worked on, branching to the routine that resolves the interrupt (the interrupt service routine we mentioned in Chapter 3), and returning to the previous task. This is a very important function of any operating system because interrupts are employed in computer systems of all sizes.

Controlling Data

Programs that control the input, output, and storage of data are an important part of any operating system. Processing tasks such as reading data from input devices, moving data between primary memory and secondary storage devices, and writing data to output devices must be carried out during the running of most application programs. As a result, it's more efficient to have the operating system handle the details of such tasks rather than requiring every application program to specify them internally. This also simplifies the program development process by allowing programmers to avoid starting from scratch every time they must employ a common procedure. Data control programs consist of the low-level routines that drive the input, storage, and output devices. They are sometimes collectively known as the *input/output control system (IOCS)* or the *basic input/output system (BIOS)*.

In addition to directing these low-level activities, the data control programs of an operating system also control the use of such devices as buffers, channels, and spoolers. The concept of buffer storage was introduced in Chapter 3. To restate it in this context, buffers are commonly used for the temporary storage of data in order to reduce the demands on the CPU from operations of input, output, or data transfer. When buffers are used, the CPU can initiate an input, output, or data transfer operation and then return to other processing. After dumping the data to a buffer at high speed, the CPU is free to perform other tasks while the buffer transfers the data to the slower input, output, or storage device.

Large computer systems may utilize **channels** (not to be confused with communications channels): special-purpose microcomputers or minicomputers that control the movement of data between the CPU and input/output devices. Once they have been invoked by the CPU, channels can control several input/output units simultaneously, and independently of the CPU.

Spooling (the word *spool* is an acronym for *simultaneous peripheral operation on line*) is an activity that enables several users to send output to a single printer while input and processing operations are also occurring. Each file to be printed is stored on an intermediate device (usually a disk) instead of being sent directly to the printer. The *spooler* handles the transfer of files from this intermediate storage device to the printer; the printing is carried out with no further involvement of the CPU. Users can continue with other work while their files are being printed via the spooler.

Monitoring System Status

Another important function of an operating system, especially of one for a large computer system, is that of monitoring its own operations. Control routines constantly check for errors or abnormal conditions and resolve these situations as smoothly as possible. A message may be output to the operator or user, or the job causing the error condition may be aborted before a **system crash** occurs. The dreaded system crash is essentially a runtime error in the operating system. A branch instruction to some unintended memory location and an accidental erasure of part of the supervisor routine in primary storage are two of the more common causes. In general, the more complex the operating system, the more built-in safeguards it will have. Crashes do occasionally occur even with the best protected of systems, and their causes may be quite difficult to uncover.

System monitoring routines also notify operators when it is time to take care of manual tasks (such as loading a tape on a tape drive), handle system security (for example, requiring users to log on), and compile statistics about system performance (on the amount of CPU time used by each job, what computer resources are currently in use, how many lines of output have been printed, and so on). These job accounting functions are especially important for large systems that service multiple users who must be correctly billed for the computer services they receive.

Processing Programs

Routines that aid the development and use of software

In addition to control programs, operating systems also include processing programs. By aiding users in their preparation of programs and providing commonly used system functions, the processing programs simplify the development and execution of software. The two major classes of processing programs are language translators and utility programs.

Language Translators

In Chapter 9, we described the three major types of language translators: assemblers, compilers, and interpreters. These programs convert programming language instructions into machine language instructions. Because they're essential to the production of both system and application software, they're considered to be operating system components. The main job performed by language translators is the conversion of source code (instructions in an assembly or high-level language) into object code (instructions in machine language).

Besides the typical language translators like assemblers, FORTRAN compilers, and BASIC interpreters, there are three special types: optimizing compilers, precompilers, and cross-compilers.

Optimizing compilers are translators expressly designed to produce highly efficient object code. Through the use of special techniques, these compilers yield translated programs that execute faster or require less storage than they would if they were translated with ordinary compilers. For the most part, optimizing compilers trade off storage space for execution speed, or vice versa. For example, if a certain program should run as quickly as possible, translating it with an optimizing compiler would, to some extent, make it take up more storage space to gain execution speed. On the other hand, a program could be made to require as little storage space as possible through the sacrifice of execution speed. Once a program has been fully developed and debugged, an optimizing compiler can be useful in cases that require high efficiency.

Precompilers, as their name implies, are translator programs that are employed before using a regular compiler. They translate some shorthand, enhanced, or otherwise modified version of a high-level language into a standard form. The output of a precompiler is standardized source code, which must then be translated by a compiler into machine language. What might be the purpose of introducing this additional step? The answer is that precompilers enable standard languages to be enhanced or customized for particular purposes. For example, before FORTRAN evolved its own built-in structured programming features, RATFOR (RAtional FORtran) was a popular alternative language. RATFOR is similar to standard FORTRAN but has additional features that are compatible with the principles of structured programming. RATFOR precompilers (which in many cases are actually written in RATFOR) are used to convert RATFOR programs into standard FORTRAN programs, which are then translated by FORTRAN compilers into object code.

A **cross-compiler** is a translator that allows a programmer to develop a program on one computer with the intention of actually using it on another computer. With cross-compilers, programmers are able to "cross" their code from one computer to another. For example, let's say that a programmer has to write a complex program for a microcomputer and wants to develop it using a high-level language available only on a mainframe. The program can be developed and debugged using the superior facilities of the mainframe installation and then converted with a cross-compiler into object code that will run on the microcomputer.

Utility Programs

Utility programs (also known as **service programs**) are processing programs that provide users with common necessary functions. Included in this category of operating system components are library managers, linkers, file-handling programs, sort/merge programs, and a number of other programs that perform system "housekeeping" tasks.

Library managers are programs that allow users to build and use their own collections of frequently needed software modules. Such libraries might consist of manufacturer-supplied and user-written subroutines that can be called on by system or application software. By taking advantage of the capabilities of library managers, users can avoid having to rewrite routines they have previously developed. With library managers, users can add to, delete from, and catalog program modules kept in system libraries. Typical program modules kept in a library include those that compute mathematical functions, produce graphics, and interface peripheral devices (such as plotters and speech synthesizers).

Linkers (also called **linkage editors** or **linking loaders**) process the machine language code produced by assemblers or compilers and create the final *executable module,* which is ready to be run by the computer. A linker does this by adding the necessary subroutines from system libraries and by assigning actual storage addresses in primary memory to the components of the object code. In other words, the linker unifies the object code into a completely defined module, ready to be loaded into primary memory and executed by the computer.

File-handling programs perform a number of low-level tasks for users, for example, creating, deleting, moving, copying, and converting program and data files. *Sort/merge programs* enable users to rearrange and combine their data files without having to write their own software for this purpose. Since such file-associated tasks are so frequently required by all types of computer users, general utility programs for performing them are usually included in operating systems.

Finally, various other programs may also be included in operating system software. These perform such tasks as helping programmers debug their code, dumping the contents of memory to a file that can be output for examination, simple text editing, and informing the user as to the current status of the system.

TYPES OF OPERATING SYSTEMS

Operating systems can be classified in a number of ways: by how they organize primary memory, by how many different programs they can execute concurrently, by what kind of secondary storage devices they use for work areas, by the setting in which they are to be used, or by the basic design of their components. We will divide operating systems into six types: serial batch-processing, multiprogramming, time-sharing, multiprocessing, virtual storage, and real-time operating systems. In reality, however, there is some degree of overlap among these categories. For this reason, it is probably better to think of them as being based on certain outstanding characteristics rather than being mutually exclusive groupings. Let's start with the simplest class, the serial batch-processing operating systems.

Serial Batch-Processing Operating Systems

Running one program at a time

A *serial batch-processing operating system* is characterized by its ability to run only one user program at a time. That single program has access to all of the computer system's resources and, once initiated, generally runs to completion before the next program begins (see Figure 11.2). The earliest operating systems for mainframes running in batch mode were of this type, as are many of the current operating systems for microcomputers. Because of their simplicity, familiarity, and natural adaptation to personal computers, serial batch-processing operating systems are the most widespread type. The current popularity of these systems may be waning, however, with the appearance of more complex operating systems for use on the ever more powerful new microcomputers.

Although these operating systems are simple and to some extent do "waste" CPU time, they offer significant advantages when used on single-user computers. Being less complex, a serial batch-processing system is not likely to encounter problems that will immobilize the computer in which it is installed. Since there is only one user at a time, there is no possibility that multiple programs will deadlock the system by requiring the same resource at the same time. Another advantage of this type of operating system is that it allows a computer to be dedicated to a specific use. For example, because the computer has nothing else to do, there's no reason why it cannot be programmed as a powerful calculator, constantly ready for user input. Although the CPU will be idle at times, there are no other demands

Figure 11.2 Serial Batch-Processing Operating Systems
Serial batch-processing operating systems can run only a single job at a time. This diagram shows how each program is run to completion before the next one begins.

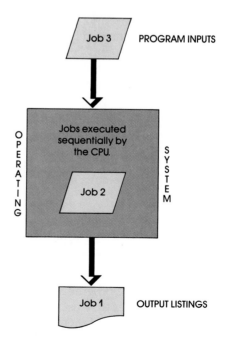

being placed on it by other users, so the "waste" is in fact irrelevant. Therefore, for many small computer systems, serial batch-processing operating systems are an ideal choice. Furthermore, their simplicity makes them easy for beginners and occasional computer users to work with.

Of the operating systems we will be describing in some detail later in this chapter, CP/M, MS DOS, and the Macintosh operating system are serial batch-processing operating systems.

Multiprogramming Operating Systems

Multiprogramming operating systems (also called **multitasking operating systems**) exhibit a characteristic known as *concurrency*, which means that several programs can be executed by the computer system seemingly at the same time. Multiprogramming is similar to what a chef does in the preparation of a multicourse meal. First, one dish is worked on, then it is set aside while another is attended to, and so on until the entire meal is ready at the same time. Note, however, that this type of operating system does not attend to multiple tasks simultaneously (at the same instant), but rather *interleaves* (alternates) the performance of several jobs during a given time frame (see Figure 11.3).

Running several programs concurrently

The primary reason multiprogramming operating systems were developed, and the reason they are popular, is that they enable the CPU to be utilized more efficiently. If the operating system can quickly switch the CPU to another task whenever the one being worked on requires relatively slow input, output, or storage operations, then the CPU is not allowed to stand idle. This means that more can be accomplished during a given amount of time. For example, if a particular program needs to read data from a tape or disk drive, that task can be delegated to a channel

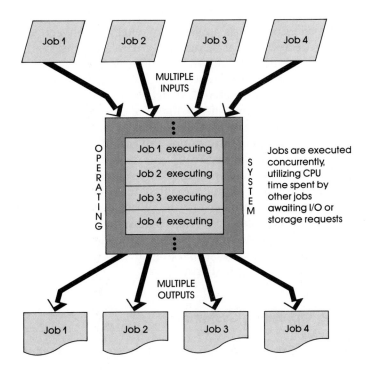

Figure 11.3 Multiprogramming Operating Systems

Multiprogramming operating systems can execute several jobs concurrently by switching the attention of the CPU back and forth among them. This switching is usually prompted by a relatively slow input, output, or storage request that can be handled by a buffer, spooler, or channel, freeing the CPU to continue processing.

and the CPU can be put to work on another program while the data are being read in. Multiprogramming is thus an effective way to keep the fast-working CPU busy with computations while slower input, output, and storage operations are being carried out.

An operating system that supports multiprogramming is necessarily more complex than one that supports serial batch processing because it must recognize events within programs that signal appropriate times to switch jobs. In addition, a multiprogramming operating system must keep track of all the jobs it is concurrently running.

Three of the operating systems we'll be discussing later in this chapter—UNIX, Pick, and IBM VM—can be classified as multiprogramming operating systems.

Time-Sharing Operating Systems

Serving several users concurrently

Time-sharing operating systems function similarly to multiprogramming ones, but they switch among several user programs at fixed intervals of time. As we mentioned in Chapters 2 and 7, time sharing allows multiple users to interact with a single computer—each user is rapidly serviced in turn. Time sharing is a popular feature for computer systems that must interactively serve numerous users. Access to the CPU is given to each active program for a fixed *time slice* (typically a few milliseconds), so that many users can run their programs concurrently. Because the CPU is so much faster than a computer terminal's input and output, the time-sharing operating system gives each user the impression that he or she has the computer's total attention. As long as a computer system isn't saddled with more users than it can handle, its *response time* is quick enough to maintain this illusion. If, however, too many users are active at once, each one will be serviced less frequently, and a noticeable time lag will occur between the entering of a request and the computer's response.

The primary difference between time-sharing and multiprogramming operating systems is the criterion that is applied for switching between jobs. Multiprogramming systems are described as being *event-driven,* and time-sharing systems are *time-driven.* In other words, a multiprogramming system switches from one program to another on the basis of some event (like an input/output request). A time-sharing system, on the other hand, switches to a different job when the clock says to. For example, if the time slice being used is two milliseconds, each job is attended to by the CPU for exactly two milliseconds at a time—and only two milliseconds, no matter what. Furthermore, this round-robin order isn't subject to user control but is completely directed by the operating system. The operating system allocates CPU time by ensuring that all users get their turns. This doesn't mean that every user is equal. Some special-status users (for example, computer operators and system programmers) may be given higher priority; the operating system will give them more turns per cycle. That is, their jobs still get two-millisecond time slices but are allocated more of them (see Figure 11.4).

Of the operating systems we'll be covering later, UNIX, Pick, and IBM VM are frequently used as time-sharing systems.

Multiprocessing Operating Systems

The operating systems we have discussed so far are generally used with computer systems that have one CPU. **Multiprocessing operating systems** are used with

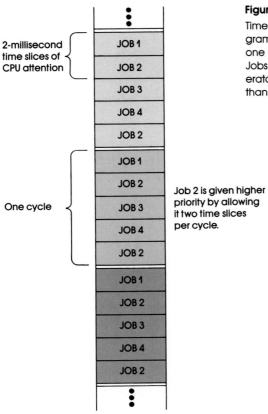

Figure 11.4   Time-Sharing Operating Systems

Time-sharing operating systems are time-driven multiprogramming systems. Each active job in the system is given
one or more fixed time slices of CPU attention per cycle.
Jobs or users with higher priorities (such as computer operators or system programmers) may be allocated more
than one time slice per cycle.

computer systems that contain more than one CPU. *Multiprocessing* is the execution of several instructions in parallel fashion on a single computer system having
several central processing units (see Figure 11.5, page 328). Multiprogramming
and time-sharing systems run jobs concurrently, but multiprocessing systems truly
run jobs simultaneously (at precisely the same instant). The main advantage to
multiprocessing systems is speed; since more than one CPU is available, jobs can be
processed faster than they can with only one CPU. Multiprocessing systems are
high-performance operating systems, implemented almost exclusively on mainframes and supercomputers.

Running several programs simultaneously with more than one CPU

Multiprocessing systems can be subdivided into four general types, all of which
have more than one processor; they are briefly described below and discussed in
greater detail in the special section on supercomputers on page 79.

1. *Homogeneous multiprocessors.*   These systems make use of multiple identical
   CPUs. The operating system coordinates the use of storage by the CPUs so that
   no unresolved conflicts occur. Homogeneous multiprocessors are commonly
   used in general-purpose mainframe computers used for business applications
   of data processing.
2. *Nonhomogeneous multiprocessors.*   These systems make use of special-purpose
   processors in the computing unit, which are actually CPUs in their own right.
   Nonhomogeneous multiprocessors are found in general-purpose mainframe
   computers.
3. *Array processors.*   These systems are composed of a set of identical processors
   (each is called a *processing element,* or *PE*) that are directed and synchronized by
   a single control unit. They are designed primarily for rapidly manipulating

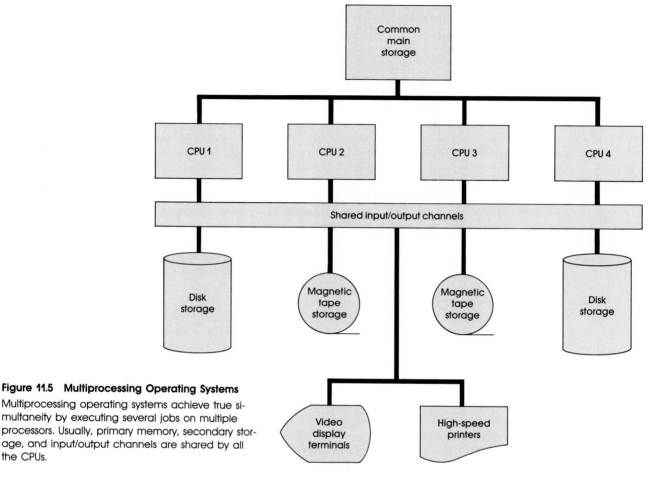

Figure 11.5   Multiprocessing Operating Systems
Multiprocessing operating systems achieve true simultaneity by executing several jobs on multiple processors. Usually, primary memory, secondary storage, and input/output channels are shared by all the CPUs.

highly ordered sets of data, such as are encountered in scientific and mathematical applications.

4. *Pipeline processors.*   In pipeline systems, multiple processors are used to perform different stages of consecutive computer instructions simultaneously. The processors are arranged like a factory production line, allowing several operands to be in different stages of execution at the same time.   Like array processor systems, these systems perform calculations very quickly and so are primarily used for scientific and mathematical applications.

Virtual Storage Operating Systems

Memory management to overcome space limitations

As you know, a program must be loaded into a computer's primary memory in order to be executed. What happens, however, if a program is too big to fit into the available memory or if several programs are competing for space in primary memory? Many operating systems can routinely resolve such situations, without user intervention, through the use of virtual storage techniques. **Virtual storage** (also called **virtual memory**) is a memory management tactic that employs an area of rapidly accessible secondary storage (such as a hard disk) as an extension of primary memory. Portions of programs are swapped into real storage (the actual primary memory) from virtual storage as needed. This gives users the illusion that more primary memory is available than is actually the case. Since this memory management is automatically taken care of by the operating system, users are freed from having to worry about how much memory their programs will require.

Operating systems usually implement virtual storage by making use of segmentation, paging, or a combination of both. **Segmentation** is the process of dividing up a program that is to be run into a number of chunks (or *segments*) of different sizes and placing these chunks in virtual memory wherever they fit. Segmentation is illustrated in Figure 11.6(a). How a program is divided into segments usually depends on its internal logic. For example, a module, subroutine, or function might constitute a single segment. The areas of virtual memory into which the segments of a program are placed are not necessarily adjacent, so the operating system must keep track of where segments are stored by constructing a *segment table*. This table lists the segments and their locations. The operating system transfers segments into primary memory from virtual storage as needed, overwriting any old segments and eliminating the need for an entire program to be in primary memory at once. The price paid for this more efficient use of primary memory is the increased complexity and time it takes for the operating system to keep track of and swap segments into real storage from virtual storage. In addition, the

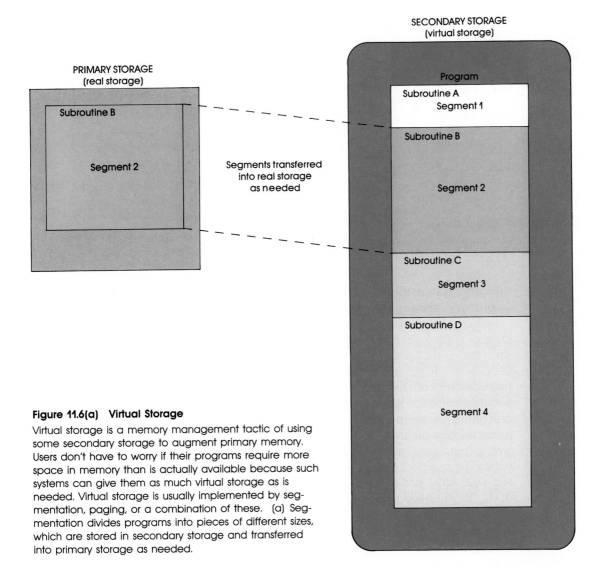

Figure 11.6(a)   Virtual Storage
Virtual storage is a memory management tactic of using some secondary storage to augment primary memory. Users don't have to worry if their programs require more space in memory than is actually available because such systems can give them as much virtual storage as is needed. Virtual storage is usually implemented by segmentation, paging, or a combination of these. (a) Segmentation divides programs into pieces of different sizes, which are stored in secondary storage and transferred into primary storage as needed.

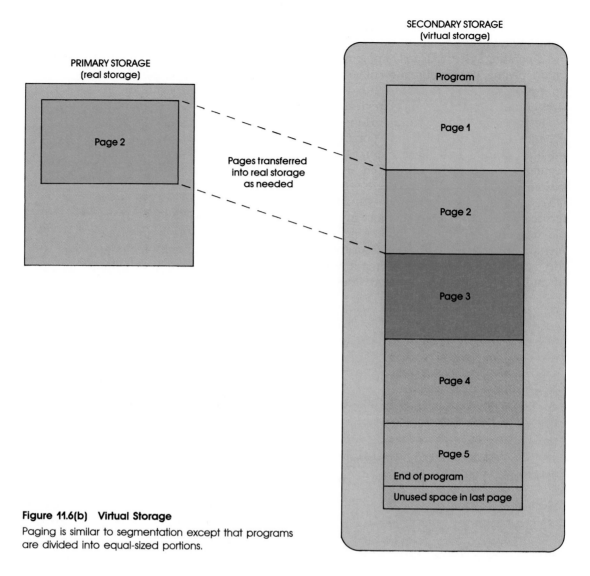

Figure 11.6(b) Virtual Storage
Paging is similar to segmentation except that programs
are divided into equal-sized portions.

operating system must be able to pick out those segments that are presently needed
in primary memory.

The process of **paging** is similar to segmentation except that the program
chunks (called *pages*) are all of the same, fixed size, as shown in Figure 11.6(b).
This means that programs are divided into equal-length pages with no regard for
the program logic. As with segmentation, the operating system keeps track of page
locations by constructing a *page table*. Because of pages' fixed size, the use of
paging can result in less waste of real storage space. Since segments can be of
different sizes, swapping in new segments from virtual storage can leave little frag-
ments of unused space in real memory. By making all program pieces the same
size, paging eliminates this type of waste. However, some memory may still be
wasted because not every program is exactly divisible into fixed-length pages. The
last page may not be completely filled—the program may end before the page
does. The unfilled page will still take up as much space in memory as a full page.

In an effort to combat the inefficiency inherent in both of these processes, a
combination of segmentation and paging is frequently used to minimize the
amount of wasted space in memory. In this combined process, a program is first

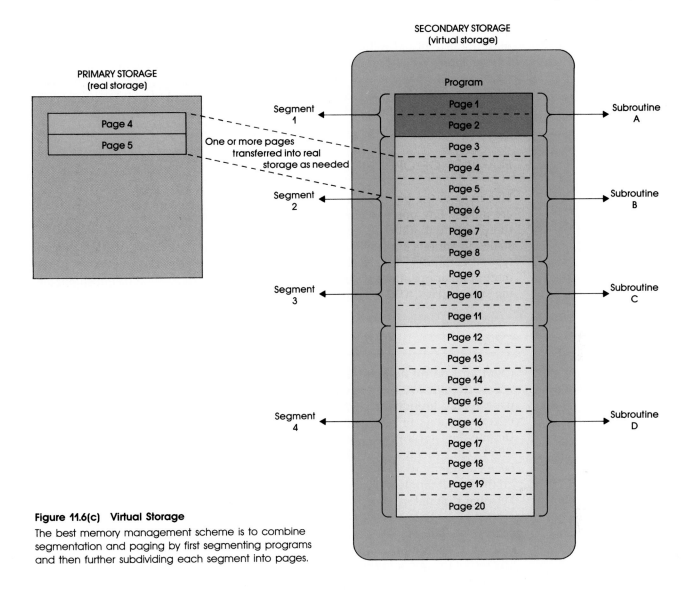

Figure 11.6(c)   Virtual Storage
The best memory management scheme is to combine
segmentation and paging by first segmenting programs
and then further subdividing each segment into pages.

broken into segments, and then the segments are broken into pages, as illustrated
in Figure 11.6(c). Both segment and page tables are needed to keep track of the
various program pieces, which increases the complexity with which the operating
system must deal. The result, however, is that fewer and smaller pieces of primary
memory are left unused, thus increasing the overall efficiency of storage use.

Real-Time Operating Systems

Real-time operating systems control computers that interact with their environments to perform work. There are two major types of real-time operating systems: those that control processes and those that merely monitor processes. **Process control systems** take input data from sensors, analyze them, and then cause
actions to occur that change the processes that they control. **Process monitor
systems** also take input data from sensors, but they merely report this data without actually affecting the processes that they are monitoring.

*Controlling or monitoring
external processes*

Both of these types of real-time operating systems are being used for more and more industrial and military applications; we'll have more to say about them in later chapters. Real-time operating systems are currently being used for such applications as automated environmental monitoring for air and water pollution, microscopic assembly processes, medical analysis systems, air and automobile traffic control, factory production, and oil pipeline regulation.

 ## EXAMPLES OF OPERATING SYSTEMS

Representative operating systems

Like most of the hardware and software available to consumers these days, there are quite a few operating systems to choose from for most computers. Some of those on the market are **generic operating systems**—that is, they can be installed in various kinds of computers. Others are specifically designed for a single type of computer. We've chosen for closer inspection a representative set of the most popular operating systems. They are CP/M, MS-DOS, the Macintosh operating system, Pick, UNIX, and IBM VM.

CP/M

Operating system used on many different microcomputers

CP/M, or Control Program for Microcomputers, is a generic operating system that was written in 1973 by Gary Kildall and is now sold by Digital Research, a company Kildall founded in 1976. CP/M was the first popular operating system for microcomputers to be put on the market by an independent software vendor. Despite the later introduction and rise of other microcomputer operating systems, CP/M is still widely used. Originally designed for 8-bit microcomputers, CP/M has been constantly revised and upgraded. The most recent version, CP/M-86, works on the 16-bit family of microcomputers that followed the introduction of the IBM Personal Computer.

CP/M is characterized by its simplicity and easy adaptability to different machines. Kildall separated all of the machine-specific parts of the operating system and put them into one module, called the BIOS (for Basic Input/Output System). The rest of the operating system is the same, no matter what computer it is running on. This compatibility was a major reason behind the heavy sales of CP/M. Another reason for its popularity was its small size. Conceptually somewhat like a collection of utility programs, CP/M has few commands and functions that the user must memorize. However, because these capabilities were chosen carefully, CP/M is quite powerful. Although it requires users to know a fair amount about its workings, CP/M does perform very strongly at a relatively low cost. Consequently, even though it isn't particularly user-friendly, CP/M has become an industry standard for which a lot of compatible software is available.

MS-DOS

Leading operating system for 16-bit microcomputers

MS-DOS (the full name is Microsoft's Disk Operating System) is the dominant operating system for 16-bit microcomputers such as the IBM Personal Computer. More 16-bit microcomputers come with MS-DOS as their operating system than with any other, and the number of application packages that run with MS-DOS is truly phenomenal. MS-DOS has become the overall industry standard and is by far the most popular operating system in the United States for personal computers.

Conceptually similar to CP/M, MS-DOS also applies some concepts from the UNIX operating system, which we will be discussing shortly. In July of 1981, Microsoft bought an operating system called QDOS (which is short for Quick and Dirty Operating System) from Seattle Computer Products. Microsoft revised the system, renamed it, and licensed it to a number of firms, including IBM. IBM offered it as PC-DOS, the standard operating system on its family of personal computers. When the IBM Personal Computer became a runaway bestseller, MS-DOS rode with it to the top.

Although MS-DOS has the same general "feel" as CP/M, it has benefited from considerable improvements. It is more powerful, easier to use, and handles errors better, and its commands are more logical and straightforward. It has also been continually revised, making it always up to date with the latest hardware developments. However, MS-DOS is not a particularly easy system for a novice to learn, and familiarity with the computer system on which it is installed is generally required before its full power can be realized. MS-DOS is not a generic operating system; it is designed to be used on the 16-bit family of microcomputers that are built around Intel 8088/8086 microprocessors (see Chapter 15). Although it's not well adapted to machines that use other microprocessors, MS-DOS has nonetheless become firmly entrenched as a result of the immense popularity of the 16-bit machines for which it was developed.

The Macintosh Operating System

The Apple Macintosh personal computer, introduced in 1984, utilized a new generation of microprocessor, the Motorola 68000. This 32-bit microcomputer evolved from the earlier Apple Lisa line, was revolutionary in design, and achieved a high degree of user-friendliness. Most of this is due to its specially designed operating system, which has little in common with CP/M, MS-DOS, or any other existing microcomputer operating system. Even though it is a single-user, serial batch-processing operating system, it is large and quite complex, and fully utilizes the capacities of the microprocessor. This advanced operating system has its roots in the Smalltalk programming language developed at Xerox's Palo Alto Research Center in the 1970s (see Chapter 9).

User-friendly operating system for Apple microcomputers

The main idea behind the Macintosh operating system is that the computer should adapt to the user instead of the other way around. It has a user interface that is exceptional in the way it allows the user to perform many tasks quickly and easily. By using a mouse to manipulate graphic objects on the screen, users instruct the computer to perform tasks. For example, to open a file, you "pull down" a menu and select options by pointing to *icons* (small graphic symbols) with the mouse-directed cursor (see Figure 11.7). With a little instruction, users can learn how to operate the Macintosh computer quickly and painlessly. Its user-friendly operating system encourages experimentation and is just plain fun to use.

Despite the rave reviews the Macintosh operating system has received, it does have several problems. For one thing, Apple estimates that it invested more than 200 programmer-years in the development of this operating system and its associated software; therefore, the company plans to protect that investment by not licensing the system to other firms. It is unlikely that computers other than Apple's will ever employ this operating system. Also, to achieve its outward simplicity for the user, the system had to be made so complex internally that independent software vendors have had some problems developing application programs to run with it. The result is that less software is currently available for the Macintosh than

Figure 11.7 The Macintosh Operating System

The user-friendly operating system of the Apple Macintosh personal computer displays icons on the screen to represent system functions. The user selects a function with a mouse-directed cursor.

for microcomputers that employ CP/M or MS-DOS. Finally, some experts have questioned whether the extreme user-friendliness ("user-cuddliness" as one termed it) is necessary or even appropriate for sophisticated users. Since the user interface is implemented at the expense of processing power, other machines with the same microprocessor can do more and do it faster. Even admitting these reservations, however, there is no doubt that the Macintosh operating system has had an enormous influence on the microcomputer industry.

ISSUES IN TECHNOLOGY

The Macintosh operating system offered by Apple has been heralded as the epitome of user-friendliness. However, as we have mentioned, this user-friendliness has been obtained through the sacrifice of a certain amount of computing power. Are ease of learning and ease of use really the most important standards by which operating systems should be judged? Should all operating systems be user-friendly? Or might this hamper the productivity of sophisticated users? What do you think?

UNIX

Portable operating system for micro- and minicomputers

UNIX is a multiuser, multiprogramming operating system developed at Bell Labs and promoted by AT&T. The first version was written in 1971 by Ken Thompson and Dennis Ritchie, both programmers at Bell Labs. Originally designed for use on minicomputers built by Digital Equipment Corporation, UNIX has since been implemented on all kinds of computers from microcomputers to mainframes. UNIX is a generic operating system in every sense of the word. At first found only at colleges and universities (because it was donated to them by Bell Labs), UNIX has become increasingly popular in many scientific and business environments.

UNIX is written in a high-level language called C (see Chapter 9) and is therefore easy to transport to different computers. This portability is one of its major attractions. In addition, UNIX has many other attractive features. Because it is a multiprogramming system, a user can do several jobs concurrently from the same terminal. It is usually set up as a time-sharing system too, so that several users can be accommodated at the same time. Software developers appreciate UNIX because it contains more than 200 utility programs that perform useful tasks and can be easily incorporated into programs being developed. UNIX is so richly endowed

CAREERS IN TECHNOLOGY
Systems Programmer

Job Description Systems programmers create, test, and document software for a computer's operating system and compilers, as well as its sorting and data communications programs. They advise systems analysts who are developing new systems or modifying old ones to meet fresh needs. Systems programmers must sometimes help repair a system that goes down due to a problem with its operating software and must often serve as consultants to in-house users. A systems programmer's work is oriented more toward the computer itself, as opposed to that of an application programmer, who is concerned with what the computer can do. a systems programmer writes and revises the programs that make the computer operate and spends a great deal of time working with the computer's code. Much of a systems programmer's work is done at night and on weekends when the computer isn't in use; emergencies can arise at any (generally the most inconvenient) time.

Qualifications Experience is currently a more important factor than education in qualifying for this position. However, as the job market becomes more competitive, employers are likely to begin setting higher academic standards and requirements for previous employment experience. Basic academic requirements include a bachelor's or associate's degree in computer science with a heavy emphasis on assembly language, compiler design, and operating systems. In any case, a proven technical aptitude and an expertise in systems software gained from at least two years in application programming are the qualifications most frequently sought. Furthermore, a systems programmer must be able to work for long periods of time alone with machines, isolated from other people by the off-peak hours the job requires.

Outlook Largely because the work is demanding and highly technical and the hours and isolation are offputting to many candidates, the employment outlook is good for someone with the particular skills and self-discipline this position requires. Since several years of experience are needed before entering this specialty, prospective systems programmers have plenty of time in which to survey potential openings before making any decision. In other words, the market is larger than the pool of applicants, putting those planning to switch jobs in a strong position. Those programmers who plan on entering the field later in their careers have the advantage of being able to tailor their résumé to fit a goal they have an excellent chance of achieving. Due to continued shortages of qualified people, new openings, and attrition, the outlook for this career is bright.

---

with these utilities in fact that programming sometimes consists of merely stringing together its prewritten program modules.

However, UNIX also has its drawbacks. It isn't particularly easy to learn, although it is flexible enough that the user interface can be modified to make the system more user-friendly. The most obvious disadvantage associated with UNIX is the fact that there are a number of different versions in use, none of which are completely compatible (AT&T itself has several versions). Because most versions of UNIX were developed for teaching and scientific environments, some of them lack features that are important for business use. Finally, application packages to run with UNIX are relatively scarce since most users have traditionally been computer science professionals. Despite these drawbacks, UNIX is more popular every day, and its future seems bright. The demand for programmers who are familiar with UNIX exceeds the supply, and AT&T is expected to continue to put its considerable marketing clout behind UNIX.

Pick

Pick (named after its developer) is similar to UNIX in several respects. It is a complicated multiuser operating system that is rich in utilities and features. However, UNIX was designed primarily as a software development system, but Pick was designed as an information management system. In the 1960s, a government project was started to produce a sophisticated information management tool for an IBM mainframe computer. When the government lost interest, Dick Pick, a programmer on the project, bought the rights and further developed the concept. Pick first appeared commercially on a minicomputer in 1973. Since then, it has been implemented on a number of microcomputers as well as some mainframes. It is a generic operating system, enabling programs that conform to its standards to run on any computer on which it has been installed.

Pick is complex and powerful, yet easy to use. Included in the Pick system are a data base management system, an Englishlike query language, an extended version of BASIC, a spooler for printing, a text formatter, and many other data-handling utilities. *Access,* the query language, is easy to learn and lets even novice users conduct elaborate searches and produce reports. It enables users to concentrate on what they want done instead of thinking about how the computer will do it. The features offered by Pick make it a good operating system for business environments. It works especially well in applications where many people who have little experience working with a computer will require information from a system.

Pick is well developed, with a growing number of enthusiastic supporters. Some of them predict that Pick will surpass UNIX in business use, although most contend that it will be a solid number two among multiuser microcomputer operating systems. Its major disadvantages are its limitation to applications in the information management area and the considerable knowledge that system programmers must have to maintain it.

IBM VM

The IBM VM (Virtual Machine) is a large, complex, multiprogramming operating system used on mainframe computers. A virtual machine, as we mentioned earlier, is an illusion the user has that he or she is working with a real machine. VM can make a single computer appear to be several different computers to different users. Originally developed for the IBM 370 series of mainframe computers, VM has been adapted for use on a number of more recent systems.

VM manages the mainframe computer's hardware to create the illusion for each user operating from a terminal that he or she has an entire computer system, complete with a wide range of input/output devices. VM actually allows several different operating systems to be run at once, each of them creating its own virtual machine. Thus, each user has the choice of running any of several different IBM operating systems or even a customized in-house system. Conventional multiprogramming operating systems share the resources of a single machine among several programs, but VM can simulate several machines by creating virtual processors, storage areas, and input/output devices. Because of this, VM is somewhat difficult to classify since it can concurrently be a serial, multiprogramming, time-sharing, multiprocessing, and virtual storage operating system.

VM offers users more power than any of the other systems we have discussed. This power is, of course, dependent on the power of the mainframe computer on which VM is run. Despite its size and complexity, or perhaps because of it, VM has been quite successful, leading some experts to predict that it will soon become IBM's major large-scale operating system.

SUMMARY

Functions of Operating Systems

An operating system is a set of programs that manages a computer system's hardware by controlling and coordinating such computer resources as the CPU, primary and secondary storage, and input/output devices.

Providing Services Operating systems allow users to share hardware programs, and data; enable users to protect their data; schedule resource use; facilitate input, output, and storage operations; and recover from errors.

Acting as an Interface An operating system interfaces software with hardware and users with the computer system. Users can be classified as general users, computer operators, application programmers, and systems programmers.

A Short History of Operating Systems

Operating systems originated in the 1950s as a means of utilizing CPU time previously lost during job transitions. During the 1960s, more sophisticated operating systems were developed using multiprogramming, time-sharing, and multiprocessing techniques. Real-time systems were also developed in the 1960s, and multimode systems became popular in the early 1970s. Modern operating systems strive for user-friendliness while also incorporating features that allow users to utilize hardware capabilities fully.

Components of Operating Systems

Operating system programs are kept in secondary storage on the system residence device until they are needed.

Control Programs Control programs are the routines that manage resources, schedule jobs, handle interrupts, control data, and monitor system status. The main control program is the supervisor. Resident routines are those that are most frequently used, so they remain in primary memory. Transient routines are transferred from the system residence device as needed.

Processing Programs Processing programs simplify the development and use of software. Language translators and utility programs are the two major classes of processing programs.

Types of Operating Systems

Operating systems can be classified according to certain outstanding characteristics, but some overlap occurs among the categories.

Serial Batch-Processing Operating Systems Serial batch-processing operating systems can run only a single user program at a time. These are simple systems generally used on mainframes that run in batch mode and on single-user microcomputers.

Multiprogramming Operating Systems Multiprogramming (or multitasking) operating systems can run several jobs concurrently by switching between jobs when certain events (such as input/output requests) occur.

Time-Sharing Operating Systems Time-sharing operating systems are time-driven multiprogramming systems that serve several users concurrently by rapidly switching among them.

Multiprocessing Operating Systems Multiprocessing operating systems can execute several jobs simultaneously through the use of more than one processor.

Virtual Storage Operating Systems   Virtual storage is a technique that uses some secondary storage, by employing segmentation and/or paging, to augment primary memory.

Real-Time Operating Systems   Real-time operating systems either control or monitor actual processes and are used in industrial and military applications.

Examples of Operating Systems

The following is a representative set of today's most popular operating systems.

CP/M   CP/M is a widely used microcomputer operating system, noted for its simplicity, small size, and power.

MS-DOS   The leading operating system for 16-bit microcomputers, MS-DOS has many features in common with CP/M and UNIX.

The Macintosh Operating System   Apple's operating system for its family of 32-bit microcomputers is renowned for its power and user-friendliness, but it cannot be used on other computers.

UNIX   UNIX is a popular generic operating system for minicomputers and microcomputers; it has multiprogramming and time-sharing capabilities.

Pick   Originally designed as an information management system for a mainframe, Pick has become a popular operating system for micro- and minicomputers in the business environment.

IBM VM   VM is a large, complex, and powerful operating system designed for use on mainframe computers.

COMPUTER CONCEPTS

As an extra review of the chapter, try defining the following terms. If you have trouble with any of them, refer to the page number listed.

operating system (OS) 316
job 317
multimode systems 318
job control language (JCL) 318
virtual machine 318
system residence device 319
supervisor (monitor, executive) 319
resident routines 319
transient routines 319
channels 321
spooling 321
system crash 321

optimizing compilers 322
precompilers 322
cross-compiler 323
utility programs (service programs) 323
library managers 323
linkers (linkage editors, linking loaders) 323
multiprogramming operating systems (multitasking operating systems) 325
time-sharing operating systems 326

multiprocessing operating systems 327
virtual storage (virtual memory) 328
segmentation 329
paging 330
real-time operating systems 331
process control systems 331
process monitor systems 331
generic operating systems 332

REVIEW QUESTIONS

1. What is the fundamental task of an operating system?
2. What are the key resources managed by an operating system?
3. What services do operating systems provide to users?
4. In what ways does an operating system act as an interface?
5. What general types of users interact with operating systems?
6. What was the basic reason underlying the development of the first operating systems?
7. What are the two general categories of the components of an operating system?
8. What type of storage medium is most often used for the system residence device?

9. What coordinates the activities of all parts of an operating system?
10. What types of tasks are performed by an operating system's control programs?
11. Describe the two major classes of processing programs.
12. List five types of operating systems.
13. What types of computers are likely to have serial batch-processing operating systems?
14. Why were multiprogramming operating systems developed, and why do they remain popular?
15. What is the primary difference between multiprogramming operating systems and time-sharing ones?
16. What enables multiprocessing operating systems to execute several jobs simultaneously?
17. What are the three methods for implementing virtual storage?
18. What are the two types of real-time operating systems?
19. Which of the specific operating systems we've discussed are generic ones?

A SHARPER FOCUS

Now that you've completed this chapter, you should be able to answer the following questions about the chapter opening.

1. Are UNIX's programmed commands examples of control programs or of processing programs? What specific type are they?
2. Do the seven UNIX commands included in the chapter opening seem easy to learn? (Ease of use is one measure of an operating system's power.) Why or why not?
3. Ken Thompson aimed for both simplicity and flexibility in designing UNIX. Is it possible to have both in an operating system? Why or why not?

PROJECTS

1. Choose one of the specific operating systems we've discussed in this chapter and do some research on it. Learn how to use it if you can gain access to a computer system that runs it. Prepare a report that details the features it offers and explains how easy or difficult you found it to use and why.
2. Many popular microcomputers have a variety of operating systems available for them. For example, the Tandy–Radio Shack TRS-80 Model 4 can run TRSDOS, LDOS, CP/M, and several more. Since we've defined an operating system as "a set of programs that controls, supervises, and supports a computer system's hardware" it would seem reasonable to expect that an operating system is a fairly finite set of programs that don't differ much for a given computer system. Is this a reasonable assumption, or are there really wide differences among the various operating systems that can be used on a specific model of machine? Choose one microcomputer model and investigate the various operating systems available for it. Write up your findings as a report, being careful to show your references and to include examples or charts where appropriate.
3. Determine what operating system is in use at your school or company. Also determine if there are additional features the users of the operating system would like to see incorporated into the system. Have there been any system crashes that were traced to the operating system? What was done to resolve these crashes?
4. Determine what system monitoring routines are included in the operating system used at your school or company. How is system security handled? How are accounting and billing handled? Also investigate how the operating system handles the assignment of priorities to jobs. Write a report on your findings, including any deficiencies in the way these things are handled by the operating system.
5. Determine what utility programs are used by the computer center at your school or company. Write a short report covering such aspects as the cost, purpose, and effectiveness of each.

Application Perspective

Starting a Business

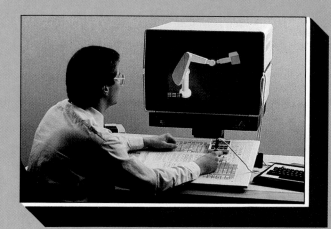

(1) You have an idea. With the moment of inspiration behind you, you work at a graphics terminal in the college where you are taking an evening course in design. With the system's help, your idea evolves into a set of drawings. Now you can derive the manufacturing steps in detail, and soon you can estimate the cost of labor and materials required to put your gadget together.

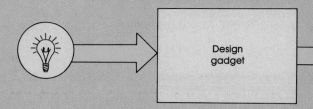

Design gadget

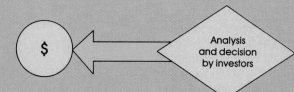

Analysis and decision by investors

$

Smith, Thomas
27 West Elm Street, Apt. 2B
Centerville, Kansas

Number of credit accounts: 2
Number of loans outstanding: 1
Payments over 30 days due: 0
Prior defaults: 0

(4) Your local bank has helped you interest an investor in your business. The bank is a subscriber to a countywide credit reporting service to which it has referred the investor. When the investor checks your credit history, he finds out from this report that you borrow prudently and pay your bills on time. After several meetings with you and a thorough review of your material, he decides that your idea is good and that you're the type of person who can make it work.

(2) Your gadget is an accessory that helps cars with certain types of engines run more economically. You go to the state auto-licensing office, and for a modest charge, you get a computer-generated listing of all cars in your county that can potentially use your gadget. You now have an indication of how large your local market is, and you know something about your typical customer.

Survey market and competition

Generate business plan

(3) You are now ready to use your own personal computer, which you bought at a newly opened store selling used computers. With the estimate of costs and the market projection in hand, you use a spreadsheet program (see Chapter 10) to generate a table of how much money you'll need from investors each month, from the startup to the time when your business is generating enough cash to keep you operating. This information is the heart of your business plan, which you circulate to attract potential investors.

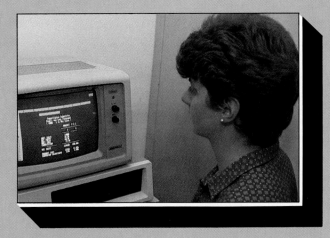

Part 4

SYSTEMS

In Parts 2 and 3, we looked at the two basic components of a computer system: hardware and software. Here, in Part 4, we take up the problem of putting together the right hardware and software to solve problems in business, industry, or any other area in which computers are utilized. The word *system* implies organization, and what is better suited than a computer to organize a jumble of data and functions into a smooth-running, efficient operation?

Chapter 12 introduces the white knights of the computer realm—systems analysts—and describes their pivotal role in the constructive application of technology to what are often complicated and demanding situations. Chapters 13 and 14 provide an in-depth look at three important kinds of computer systems: data base systems, management information systems, and decision support systems.

12

Systems Analysis and Design

IN THIS CHAPTER

▶

FOCUS ON . . . A NEW IRS SYSTEM

The Internal Revenue Service's computer system—the heart of the nation's far-flung tax-collection operation—is on the verge of collapse.

When it was designed 20 years ago, the 11-city network of computers was hailed as a model of decentralized bureaucracy. Now the system is out of date, and breakdowns are common. IRS officials are scrambling to keep the patchwork arrangement from jeopardizing efforts to process tax returns, monitor taxpayer accounts and help agents track down deadbeats. . . .

The IRS has begun a computer-replacement program. But in the meantime, equipment that will be scrapped—and some that won't—is failing with alarming regularity. Problems with collecting back taxes continue to grow, especially in the agency's two busiest processing centers in Austin, Tex., and Fresno, Calif. Tax-return filings have surged in those centers because of migration to the Sun Belt and the West.

In Austin, where breakdowns occur an average of once every five weeks, a General Electric computer recently failed for more than three days. GE quit the computer business years ago, so it took four shipments to get a workable replacement part from another company. Another breakdown delayed the mailing of a warning that a delinquent taxpayer had 15 days before the IRS would attach some property. Because the notice wasn't mailed on time, the agency couldn't act against a taxpayer who clearly owed taxes. . . .

Such computer failures set off a chain reaction of delay through the network of 4,066 data terminals in hundreds of IRS offices nationwide. During Fresno's busiest months, computer inquiries from IRS agents can run as high as 350,000 daily. Without the computers, all the work in these offices, the IRS's biggest, has to be done manually. . . .

When it was installed, the system that monitors account information was designed to handle 700,000 accounts in each IRS center. Today, even with modifications to the system, centers struggle with an average of 1.9 million accounts. Without the cutbacks, though, the Fresno office, for example, would be bursting with about 2.5 million files.

Further complication comes from the many years of patching the system together, which means that about a dozen computer companies are responsible for repairs. . . .

The IRS for years tried to get congressional approval to replace its system with an exotic, $1 billion network that would allow IRS workers anywhere to tap one of the 122 million individual tax-return files. But for security and privacy reasons, Congress balked, and the IRS gave up. Now the agency is making less-elaborate changes that will enable the system to keep pace, at least for a while, with the surge in tax-return filings and the IRS's increasing efforts to beef up tax enforcement.

Once the new system is operating, IRS managers say they won't need so many repair vendors and the agency's $6 million annual maintenance bill will be cut in half.

Phase 2—Systems Analysis	*Find out how the old system works and what the new system must do.*
Data Gathering	*Compile facts about the old system, using written documents, questionnaires, interviews, and observation.*
Data Analysis	*Decide what functions the new system must include, using data flow diagrams, data dictionaries, and black box process descriptions.*
Phase 3—Systems Design	*Specify how to build the new system.*
Review of Project Goals	*Reconsider the objectives of the system project.*
Development of System Requirements	*Detail exactly how the new system should work.*
Presentation to Management	*Summarize once more.*
Phase 4—Systems Development	*Construct the new system.*
Scheduling	*Prepare timetables.*
Programming	*Write the system programs.*
Testing	*Confirm that the system works.*
Documentation	*Explain how the system works.*
Phase 5—Implementation and Evaluation	*Install and appraise the new system.*
File Conversion	*Adapt data files so that the new system can use them.*
Personnel Training	*Teach users and operators how to run the system.*
System Conversion	*Switch from the old system to the new one.*
Evaluation	*Does it fulfill its requirements?*
Maintenance	*Keep the system effective.*

From the beginning of this book, we've repeatedly stressed how computers make this or that process more efficient, how they speed operations and solve the problems that have plagued this or that organization or individual. But the fact of the matter is that an organization can't just bring an Apple or IBM machine back from the local computer store, plug it in, and expect that a bit of fancy keyboard tapping will make all troubles disappear. An organization, large or small, that has a billing or personnel or other system of any complexity will find that its problems and the solutions aren't all that easily isolated and fixed. Furthermore, replacing "the way it's always been done" with something new, strange, and untried, can be a frustrating or even traumatic endeavor.

Here's where systems analysis and systems analysts come into the picture. A whole profession has emerged to develop appropriate solutions to individual problems and to make the transition from the old and cumbersome to the new and efficient smoother and more comfortable. In this chapter, we'll examine the step-by-step process of systems analysis and show how those professional troubleshooters the systems analysts save the day.

This chapter includes a six-part case study about a fictional dentist, Dr. Mary Parkley. As you read about each phase of a systems analysis project, you can refer to the corresponding section of the case study in order to see how the concepts are applied in a real-life situation.

THE SYSTEMS APPROACH

In Chapter 8, we described the process of developing a computer program. Our primary focus was on the program as a single entity, and the effort was mainly presented from the perspective of the programmer. In Chapter 10, we considered some particular software packages from the point of view of the user, who is primarily interested in a specific problem to be solved. In this chapter, we'll open up a broader view of the whole process by answering some crucial questions: Why are programs written? Who instigates the development of new software? Why are programs designed the way they are? What about the elements supporting a particular program, such as the software, hardware, and peripheral devices and the operators and other personnel? How do all of these things come together to produce a successful data-processing tool?

What Is a System?

Defining the concept

Clearly, in answering the kind of questions listed above, we will deal with something much larger than a single program; we must deal with a complete, meticulously planned environment, in other words, with a system. We've used this word dozens of times throughout this book, and it's also one that's used extensively in everyday life. We hear a lot about solar systems, circulatory systems, economic systems, communication systems, and, of course, computer systems. To formally define the term in the context of data processing, we can use the words of the American National Standards Committee: a **system** is "a collection of people, machines, and methods organized to accomplish a set of specific functions." Note that this definition does not necessarily require that a system be computerized. Many small businesses and organizations run their affairs by means of manual systems, that is, without computers.

Whether the paperwork is handled by people or computers, a number of attributes are common to most systems:

- *A system interacts with the environment.* Systems receive input from and transmit output to their surroundings. Because they interact in this way with their environment, they are often called *open systems.*

- *A system has a purpose.* Every system has some aim or objective that is fulfilled by the functions it carries out. For example, the purpose of the human circulatory system is to deliver oxygenated blood to all parts of the body so that life can be sustained, and the purpose of a firm's payroll system is to deliver salaries to employees.

- *A system is self-regulating.* Systems should be able to maintain themselves in a steady state. In other words, they ought to be able to adjust their internal functions to accommodate externally imposed changes. For example, as a person exercises, the heart beats faster to supply the muscles' increased need for oxygenated blood.

• *A system is self-correcting.*   Finally, systems must also be able to respond to abnormal situations that cannot be taken care of by routine self-regulation. Such occurrences should be handled in ways that won't jeopardize the system's whole purpose. Using the circulatory system as an example once more, when a blood vessel is cut or damaged, clotting takes place to minimize blood loss.

Why Systems Change

The necessity for systems analysis and design

We live in a world of constant change. The development of new systems or the modification of old systems may be necessary for any number of reasons. Businesses and organizations must stay abreast of everchanging laws and regulations. The government may change the tax laws or require that businesses provide certain new data about their employees, which will prompt the modification of existing data-processing systems. Equipment currently in use may become obsolete or manufacturers may discontinue repair service and support, which will mean an investment in new hardware. A firm may reorganize, like AT&T did recently, which will bring about a need for new or extensively modified accounting systems. Companies may be faced with increased competition or higher costs, which will compel them to streamline their data-processing systems to save time and money. Users may suddenly require new features and want to incorporate them into current systems. It's obvious that systems aren't static entities but are ongoing processes, constantly being created, updated, and transformed.

How do organizations and individuals cope with change, given that it's so prevalent? Unfortunately, all too often the answer to this question is "not very well." Users of data-processing systems are frequently resistant to change, regardless of whether it will make life easier. People sometimes feel that they will be replaced by computers if a new system is installed. Or they dread the thought of learning how to use a different system, after having invested so much time and effort to master the old one. Users often believe, quite legitimately, that the new system will do no better than the old one and may even do worse. This attitude is particularly likely when system changes are called for by management rather than by the everyday users (who may be as fully aware of the system's deficiencies). Throughout this chapter, we'll pay attention to the role these "people" concerns play in the whole process of studying old systems and designing and implementing new ones.

The Role of the Systems Analyst

What systems analysts do

Systems analysis is the practice of evaluating an existing system to see how it works and how well it meets the users' needs. **Systems design** is the process of planning a new system based on the findings of a systems analysis. **Systems analysts** are normally involved in both of these activities; they are professionals whose basic responsibility consists of translating users' needs into technical specifications for programmers or buyers of software. Beginning with a logical description of the users' needs, the analyst designs a system that solves the problem. This design is then used as a basis for developing the software requirements. A search may be instigated for a software package that fulfills these requirements, or programmers may be given the task of writing new programs to perform the necessary functions. Sometimes software that is purchased must still be tailored to an organization's unique needs. Since computers, programmers, and systems analysts are quite expensive, management has a responsibility to control this whole development process. To an organization's managers, the data-processing system is an investment—the funds expended on it should be spent wisely. Thus, the systems analyst must ensure that the system allows management to exercise control efficiently and effectively.

Systems analysts have a difficult job. They must simultaneously deal with users, technicians, programmers, and managers. Each of these groups of people has different concerns and the expectation that the systems analyst will address them. Users want systems that are easy to work with, powerful, and fast. Technicians want the newest, glossiest, state-of-the-art equipment. Programmers are worried about bits, bytes, data flow, and control structures. Finally, managers are concerned with investment returns, cost/benefit ratios, and development schedules. Systems analysts must perform a juggling act—and do it with a smile. They are concerned not only with the development of software, but also with the hardware, the people who will operate that hardware, the methods of data entry and information output, system security, auditing, and every other aspect of the entire system.

Figure 12.1   The Five Phases of a System Project
A system project is generally broken down into five major phases.

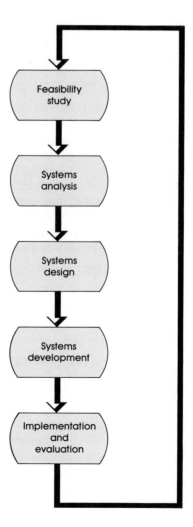

Dr. Mary Parkley has run a successful dental practice in a college town for a number of years. She has about 2000 patients, a quarter of whom are students. On an average day (except during college vacations), she sees between 15 and 25 patients. Billings, including dental insurance claims, average about $15,000 a month.

This might seem to be quite a profitable business, but Dr. Parkley doesn't pocket all the profits, not even a large portion of them. She must pay the salaries of her staff: a receptionist, an office manager, and two dental assistants. Other expenses include rent, malpractice insurance, equipment and supplies, continuing education for herself and her assistants, and, of course, subscriptions to all the magazines in the waiting room.

Until about six months ago, the office was managed by an old friend of Dr. Parkley's named Jerry Douglas. He ran things very smoothly and had become an indispensable employee. The rest of the office trusted him, and he took care of all those details that had to be dealt with to keep the office running efficiently. Unfortunately (for Dr. Parkley), Jerry won $40 million in the state lottery and decided to move to Alaska, where he'd always wanted to live (and which, incidentally, has no state income tax). Dr. Parkley found herself suddenly responsible for all those administrative tasks that Jerry had handled with his efficient, but undocumented, manual system.

Finding Jerry's replacement was difficult indeed. For a while, Dr. Parkley managed the office herself. However, she soon found that the work was too much, and the smooth functioning of the office had become just a pleasant memory. She did learn a lot about the business end of running a dental practice, but she vowed that she'd never again become so dependent on a single employee. Her experience enabled Dr. Parkley to come up with a more explicit job description for the position of office manager than "handling all the financial details," and she hired a recent graduate of the local business college, Elena Velasquez. It was apparent to Dr. Parkley that a business system should be set up so that Elena could follow predefined procedures instead of inventing her own unique ones. In several professional journals, Dr. Parkley had seen articles about the use of computers in dental offices; she thought perhaps a computer was the answer. One of her patients, Tom Washington, had his own firm called Central Systems Specialists (CSS). Dr. Parkley decided to call CSS and seek the help of a professional systems analyst.

The methodology by which systems analysts generally approach their task is the subject of the remainder of this chapter. This procedure is divided into five phases. It is important to note, however, that at any point along the way feedback from users, programmers, or managers may send the analyst back to a previous step. This continuous feedback and looping (see Figure 12.1) are essential to setting up a truly effective system.

PHASE 1—FEASIBILITY STUDY

The first step in any system project must be a **feasibility study** (also called a **preliminary investigation**). The nature and scope of the problem are examined, to determine whether it's worthwhile to pursue the project further.

A look before leaping

Defining the Problem

What's wrong?

Obviously, someone must recognize that a problem exists before a system project can be started. Also, what is the source of the problem? Have users encountered difficulties and asked for help, or has management identified an area of poor performance? Often, the systems analyst is the one who spots the problem. In this initial stage, informal discussions are held to try to reach a point where users, managers, and systems analyst all agree that a problem exists.

Through interviews and conversations, the systems analyst tries to understand the organization, its history, and its current state of affairs. During this time, the analyst prepares a written statement explaining as clearly as possible his or her understanding of the problem. Ideally, this statement is then reviewed in a joint meeting with both users and managers so that obvious errors and misunderstandings can be corrected at an early stage. Although the time it takes to define the problem can be quite brief, perhaps only a single day or less, correctness of the definition is essential. Users, managers, and the systems analyst must agree on a general direction early in the project. If the problem is misunderstood and its definition is incorrect, the final system is almost certainly not going to solve it.

Estimating the Scope of the Project

How hard will it be to fix?

Once the problem has been defined, the systems analyst must estimate how big a job it will be to solve it. The scope of a project is generally a function of the type of problem that must be solved, how much time and money management is willing to spend, and how much change users and managers are willing to accept. This estimation is critical because project schedules and costs tend to expand indefinitely if no firm limits are set at the start. Also, a systems analyst should resist the temptation to recommend an entirely new system if users and managers will be satisfied with relatively simple alterations to the existing one.

What management and users are looking for is the bottom line. That is, how much will it cost and how long will it take? No one expects the systems analyst to predict exactly the final cost and schedule at this early stage, when so much is still unknown. As an expert, however, he or she must be able to come up with ballpark or order-of-magnitude figures. Before management can justifiably commit time and money to a project, it must have some idea as to what the organization is getting into.

Proposing Possible Solutions

What can be done?

After the problem's nature and scope have been determined, a number of solutions may suggest themselves to the systems analyst. This isn't the time to work out the complete solution to the problem, but some preliminary ideas should be proposed. A relatively minor change might be in order, or an entirely new system might obviously be called for. It might be clear to the systems analyst that the functions of some manual system could be more conveniently and economically accomplished using a computer. The systems analyst should offer some suggestions that will basically give users and managers an idea of how much change they are in for if the system project is undertaken.

TECHNOLOGY CLOSEUP
Dr. Parkley's Project—Phase 1

Tom Washington, the senior analyst at CSS, decided he would handle Dr. Parkley's case personally. They met briefly over lunch so that Dr. Parkley could outline her office's history and the problems she was currently having. Washington believed that he could help, and they agreed to go ahead with the first step, a feasibility study.

Later that week, Washington spent the better part of a day at Dr. Parkley's office. He talked to all the employees, but reserved most of his time for Dr. Parkley and Elena. The purpose of this visit was to form a clear definition of the problem at hand. Just what was it that Dr. Parkley hoped to solve? It seemed that generally what Dr. Parkley wanted was to be relieved of the responsibilities of managing her routine office finances. She did, however, want to remain in control and not to become totally dependent on any one employee. Through his conversations, Washington was able to identify two specific problem areas: billing and payroll.

A large part of the billing problem was due to the fact that about 50% of gross office earnings came from dental insurance carriers. Only half was actually paid directly by the patients. Insurance companies must receive completely filled-out forms before they will pay. Even slight errors can delay reimbursement for months. The result of inefficient and inaccurate billing procedures (the sorry state of affairs since Jerry's departure) was a serious cash flow problem. Dr. Parkley had actually borrowed money against her future insurance payments to pay her own bills. The extra money paid in interest on these loans (estimated at about $2500 per year) could have, needless to say, been put to better use. Also, her professional image was being affected by billing errors. Both patients and insurance companies get upset when their bills are wrong.

The other key problem area was payroll. Dr. Parkley's employees trusted Jerry, and he knew the required procedures for figuring, withholding, and reporting income taxes. When Dr. Parkley took over the responsibility for payroll after Jerry left, the employees didn't mind, but it was a nightmare for her. She certainly hadn't learned much about tax law in dental school. Elena, on the other hand, was familiar with payroll procedures, but had not yet gained the confidence of her fellow workers. They all indicated that they would feel better if their paychecks were handled more automatically, say by computer.

Washington prepared a written statement summarizing his understanding of these two problem areas, and it was reviewed by Dr. Parkley. She agreed that he had correctly determined the major sources of her difficulties. She indicated that she might be interested in having CSS solve her problems, if it wouldn't cost too much or disrupt her office. Washington went on to prepare a report describing the scope of the problem as he saw it and suggesting two possible solutions. He estimated that his firm could set up a system for her at a total cost of about $15,000 and that it could be operating in about a month. Both possible solutions involved installing a computer system: the first proposed that CSS develop the required software; the other suggested purchasing a prewritten application package.

At this stage, there may be no apparently satisfactory solution to the problem. For example, it might be that a supermarket chain will just have to live with the fact that a certain percentage of perishable goods will spoil given its distribution system. In such a case, the system project might attempt to minimize particularly undesirable circumstances instead of altogether eliminating them, for example, by fuller utilization of automated equipment and electronic "paper shuffling" to cut down on the time the food spends moving from warehouse to warehouse. In any case, the systems analyst must give management some assurance that something can be done about the problem before the system project can commence.

Reporting to Management

*Summarize for the decision
makers*

The culmination of the feasibility study is the submission to management of a
report summarizing the systems analyst's findings and recommendations. This
report should be a statement of the problem definition, project objectives and
scope, and the preliminary ideas for solutions, along with estimated costs and benefits. The problem may be so simple that no further study is necessary, or it may
require additional examination involving further costs. The central purpose of the
report is to help management decide whether or not to continue with the project.
Once the feasibility study is complete, management is in a better position to estimate if the work that lies ahead will be worth it. Many projects are in fact abandoned at this point; only those promising a good investment return should be
pursued.

Careful consideration is important at this early stage because of the way costs
rise sharply as projects proceed. Consequently, the formal presentation of the report to management marks a critical point in the life of a project. After this point, it
becomes progressively more difficult to scrap the project without incurring significant losses.

If management approval of the project is granted, the feasibility report can
stand as a model of the systems analyst's view of the project and can provide a
picture of how subsequent development is likely to commence

PHASE 2—SYSTEMS ANALYSIS

*How the old system works
and what the new system
must do*

Once management has officially decided to go ahead with the project, the next
phase is systems analysis. This is a logical process that determines exactly what
must be done to solve the problem. The current system is studied in detail to find
out what it does and how it works. This model of the existing system can then be
compared to what users and managers agree the system should be doing. The
process of systems analysis is usually broken down into two major activities: data
gathering and data analysis.

Data Gathering

*Compile facts about the old
system*

For an existing system to be understood, a collection of facts about that system
must be compiled. The analyst must determine the exact inputs, operations, and
outputs of the system. What is being done, who is doing it, how it is being done,
and why it is being done must all be determined accurately. Although the precise
nature of the data that must be gathered and how they can best be obtained will
vary from system to system, analysts frequently use four sources: written documents, questionnaires, interviews, and observation.

Written Documents

Written documents—forms, manuals, charts, diagrams, letters, and any other paperwork used by the organization—can yield insight into how the system works.
Such materials contain a great deal of information about policies, procedures, and
the nature of the relationships among the people in an organization. For example,

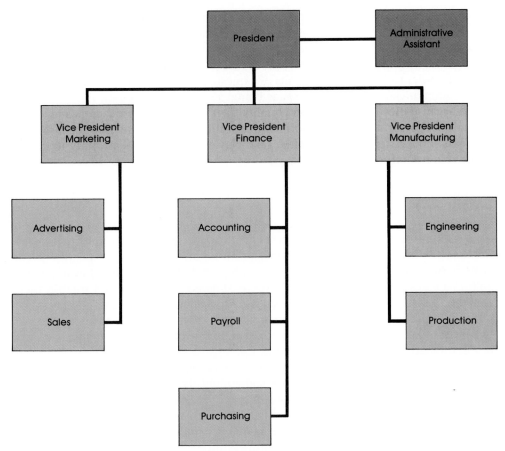

a customer invoice form can reveal many facts about billing procedures. Organization charts can illustrate the formal relationships among personnel and can provide an overview of company operations (see Figure 12.2).

The systems analyst must exercise judgment in the selection of pertinent documents during the data gathering. A large organization will probably produce and/ or process an almost overwhelming volume of paperwork every day. A systems analyst must be skilled at determining which documents tell the most about the workings of a system and which ones have a direct bearing on the problems at hand.

Questionnaires

Systems analysts frequently prepare and distribute questionnaires to the members of an organization as a means of rapidly and inexpensively gathering information. Questionnaires are especially applicable to large or geographically dispersed systems; they also permit anonymous responses. Ideally, a questionnaire consists of inquiries asking for short simple responses, such as checking off "yes" or "no" or rating agreement/disagreement on a scale from 1 to 10. Although not always easy to achieve, a balance should be struck between gathering as much information as possible and keeping the questionnaire easy to complete.

Questionnaires have several disadvantages, however, including the fact that many people will not take the time to fill them out, no matter what the incentive.

In receiving responses only from a certain self-limited group within the organization, the analyst may be getting a biased view of the system. If management makes compliance with the systems analyst's requests mandatory, resentment may color the respondents' replies. Furthermore, some knowledge of statistics is usually required in order to interpret the results of a questionnaire accurately. Finally, many people are critical of questionnaires as being rigid and impersonal; they feel frustrated because they can't clarify and qualify their answers. These factors add to the difficulty of constructing a questionnaire. Psychologists have studied this problem for years, and systems analysts often take classes in order to learn how to create effective questionnaires.

Interviews

Interviews provide a flexibility that questionnaires lack, but they are also more time-consuming. The systems analyst can gather a great deal of information by holding discussions with key personnel in an organization. Some people reveal more in discussions than they would in writing, and others feel that they are better able to express themselves when they are allowed to explain and qualify their answers the way they can in a discussion. Also, the interviewer can observe voice inflections and emphases, which can reveal more than just the words alone would. In a face-to-face talk, the interviewer is free to pursue different lines of investigation if a particularly interesting point comes up.

Interviews, however, also have their disadvantages. Some people are uncomfortable in such situations. Truths are sometimes distorted, or opinions are given instead of facts. In addition, questions or responses can be misinterpreted. Interview results, just like questionnaire results, must be carefully scrutinized. And, like preparing successful questionnaires, effective interviewing is a skill that must be learned. Systems analysts can often acquire or improve interviewing techniques by taking special classes.

There are basically two types of interviews: structured and unstructured. *Structured interviews* include only questions that have been prepared ahead of time. The interviewer asks no other questions. Although they are somewhat rigid, structured interviews are useful when the same set of questions must be asked of a number of people. *Unstructured interviews,* on the other hand, have a general goal and may include some questions chosen in advance, but the interviewer is free to pursue related topics and lines of inquiry if they seem appropriate. This additional flexibility generally requires the expense of more time and means that fewer people can be interviewed. Either type of interview is more than just a chat—an interview is directed toward a particular goal and is further structured by some amount of advance preparation by the interviewer.

Observation

Simply observing the day-to-day operations of an organization is a useful activity for the systems analyst. By noting how data flow through the system, seeing how people and machines interact, and listening to what people say, the analyst can evaluate the accuracy of the information that was gathered via questionnaires or interviews. Furthermore, observation furnishes first-hand experience of what it's like within a system. Although people may at first be self-consciously aware of the analyst's presence and purpose, they usually become more relaxed and act more normally after a short period of time. To facilitate this acceptance by the employees, the systems analyst may temporarily take a part in the activities of the organization. Such *participant observation* can be especially productive if the system under study is a complex one.

Data Analysis

Once information about the workings of the old system has been amassed, this collected data must be analyzed in order to define the logical functions that the new system should incorporate. During this data analysis, the objective is to develop a complete functional understanding of the proposed system. There are, as you might expect, several ways in which systems analysts can tackle this task. One popular structured method calls for the construction of three types of formally defined documents: data flow diagrams, data dictionaries, and black box process descriptions. These documents are then presented to management for an inspection and review.

Decide what functions the new system must include

Data Flow Diagrams

In analyzing the data for a system project, the analyst is concerned with summarizing the proposed system in a way that stresses function rather than physical implementation. In other words, in this phase, the analyst will consider *what* things need to be done instead of *how* they will be done. A **data flow diagram** is a tool that is well-suited to this purpose; it shows the sources, stores, and destinations of data, the directions of data flow, and the processes that transform data. It says nothing, however, about how any of these system elements are implemented. This is in definite contrast with the flowcharts we introduced in Chapter 8. Flowcharts detail how functions are implemented; data flow diagrams show what functions are included and how they relate to one another.

A data flow diagram is constructed using four basic elements: data sources and destinations, data stores, processes, and data flows. In Figure 12.3 (page 358) are shown the symbols for these elements, along with an example of a diagram. *Data sources and destinations* (symbolized by boxes) are the places data come from and go to. For example, in a payroll system, employee time records are a data source, and paychecks are a data destination. *Data stores* (symbolized by rectangles open on one side) are places where data are held for a time; for example, data stores may be files that reside on disk, tape, punched cards, or in primary memory. *Processes* (symbolized by circles or round-cornered rectangles) are steps that change or move data; they can be program modules, whole programs, collections of programs, or even manual operations. Finally, *data flows* (symbolized by arrows) are the movements of data; they indicate how the data move among the other elements of the system.

Data Dictionaries

A **data dictionary** is a collection of information about the data elements of a system. Typically, it contains the name, description, source, format, and use of each major category of data. Data dictionaries help analysts organize information about the data and can alert them to items that were somehow missed in the initial collection. In addition, the data dictionary is quite useful after the analysis phase is complete. It serves as valuable documentation during the succeeding phases of

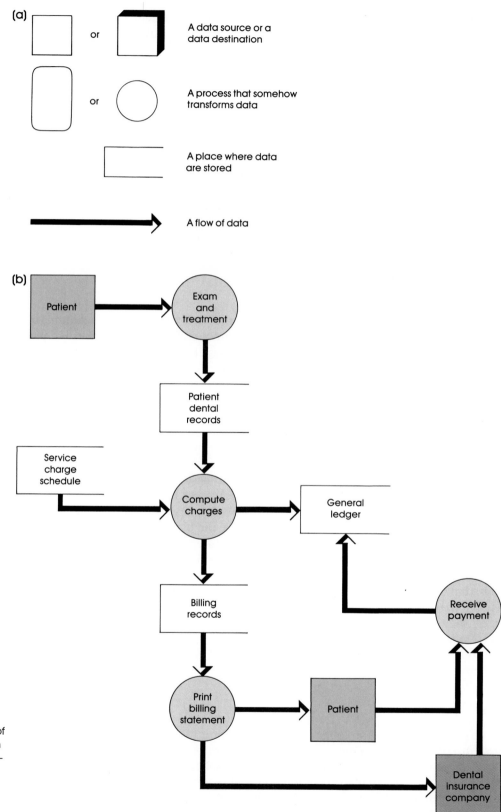

Figure 12.3
Data Flow Diagrams

(a) The four basic symbols of
data flow diagrams. (b) An
example of a data flow diagram for Dr. Parkley's billing
system.

NAME: total-gross-pay

DESCRIPTION: The total pay of an employee before taxes and other deductions have been withheld.

SOURCE: Employee PAYROLL file.

FORMAT: Positive, numeric; maximum value = 99999.00

USE: Printed on checks and used for year-end totals.

NAME: total-federal-tax

DESCRIPTION: The total amount paid by an employee in federal income taxes.

SOURCE: Employee PAYROLL file.

FORMAT: Positive, numeric; maximum value = 99999.00

USE: Printed on checks and used for year-end totals.

NAME: employee-name

DESCRIPTION: An employee's name in the form: last name, first name, middle initial.

SOURCE: Employee timecards, PAYROLL file.

FORMAT: Character

USE: Printed on checks and used for PAYROLL file key.

Figure 12.4   A Data Dictionary
Here are three entries in a sample data dictionary for an employee payroll system.

design, development, and implementation and evaluation by providing a reference source for all who must deal with the system.

At its simplest, a data dictionary can consist of a set of index cards, with one filled out for each data element (see Figure 12.4). There are also a number of commercially available computerized data dictionaries that allow analysts to enter information about data items into a data base. Such systems can be a valuable aid to analysts working on large or complex projects.

Black Box Process Descriptions

We have said that during the analysis phase of a system project the analyst is concerned with what functions are needed, not with how they will work. This means the analyst must have some way to document the processes the system must perform, but only at a functional level. The concept of a black box is frequently encountered in computer science. Simply put, a **black box** is a piece of hardware or software that performs a specific function. How it is to perform this function is not known or is not specified in the context of the discussion. All that is known is that, given certain inputs, the black box will produce certain predictable outputs. A good example of a black box process is the square root function available on many calculators. You probably don't know how this works; all you need to know is that when you enter a number and press the square root key, you get the square root of that number. By viewing and describing system processes as black boxes, the analyst is able to show what should be done without detailing how it will be done.

Primarily through employee interviews, observation, and examining various written documents (like the dental insurance claim forms), Tom Washington gathered data about the present system. Since Dr. Parkley's office was a small operation, organization charts and questionnaires wouldn't be very helpful. Since the old system for billing and payroll was clearly inadequate (without Jerry, that is), it became evident to Washington that a completely new system would have to be prepared to handle both activities. Simply computerizing the current system wouldn't work.

By carrying out a data analysis, Washington established what the new system must do. Since his objective was to gain a complete understanding of the functions needed, he created a data flow diagram (see Figure 12.3), compiled a data dictionary (see Figure 12.4), and wrote black box process descriptions for the proposed new system. Keep in mind that what he did was describe *what* the new system must do, not *how* it was to be done. Systems design, the next phase, would establish the details of how the problem was to be solved.

Washington concluded this phase by submitting a report for Dr. Parkley and Elena to review. Their input was necessary at that point because it would be more difficult to add forgotten features once the actual work on the design had begun. They agreed with what Washington had come up with, and Dr. Parkley gave the go-ahead for the next step, systems design.

Typically, the analyst documents black box processes by writing them out on index cards or sheets of paper (one per process). Inputs and outputs can be sketched in overview, and details can be added later as they become known. Another useful alternative is to use HIPO charts (see Chapter 8, particularly Figure 8.6), filling in minimal information. As the system project moves into the design phase, further details can be added to flesh out the diagrams. This reflects a structured methodology, which is worthwhile since the documentation produced in one step is directly relevant to future steps.

PHASE 3—SYSTEMS DESIGN

Specify how to build the new system

When the analysis phase of a system project has been completed, what must be done to solve the problem is usually known. The next step is to decide exactly how to implement a solution. Alternatives must be considered, and a single set of detailed specifications for the new system must be developed. In addition, the design that is chosen must reflect the previously established goals and scope of the project. Systems design thus consists of reviewing the project goals, developing the system requirements, and presenting a report to management.

Review of Project Goals

Reconsider the objectives of the system project

Throughout the design phase, the systems analyst is responsible for ensuring that the final product will be what users and managers need. In order to do this, the analyst should review the goals and scope of the system project prior to the actual design and should keep these items in mind as all subsequent work proceeds. Furthermore, as the design phase progresses, the systems analyst should consider the effects of certain important factors:

- *The long-range plans of the organization.* Some organizations have plans for the eventual evolution of their data-processing systems. If this is so, the design of the current project must be compatible with these plans.

- *The user interface.* Just as the user interface is an important consideration in the design of programs (see Chapter 8), human factors such as ease of use should be carefully attended to in the design of systems.

- *Economic trade-offs.* Given that there is a finite amount of money and time available for a project, it cannot be perfect. It would be nice if a system were completely flexible, extremely user-friendly, and could recover from every possible error gracefully. However, this state is seldom achieved in an actual system because it would cost too much. Priorities must be set and compromises made if a workable system is to be designed.

- *Availability of prewritten software.* Careful evaluation must be made as to whether any off-the-shelf application package might be suitable. If a workable system can be purchased instead of being developed within an organization, some of the advantages of using prewritten software (which we discussed in Chapter 10) can be realized.

- *Applicability of design methods.* In Chapter 8, we covered methods of designing programs. Most of these are applicable to systems design, as we'll see shortly. Before the design of a system begins in earnest, a consensus as to the general method to use is advisable.

Development of System Requirements

At this point in the system project, the analyst must detail exactly how the new system will work. Just as a program should be completely designed before coding begins, a new system should be comprehensively modeled before actual development work starts. Throughout the design phase, the analyst may employ tools like the program design aids we introduced in Chapter 8. The most popular aids for systems design are data flow diagrams and system flowcharts, but pseudocode, decision tables, structure charts, and HIPO charts are also often used. In addition, the concepts of structured programming, top-down design, modularity, egoless programming, and structured walkthroughs are all frequently employed in systems design.

Detail exactly how the new system should work

The purpose of systems design is to document exactly how a new system should work. In essence, this means preparing a detailed set of specifications for the new system. These system requirements are very similar to the software requirements we talked about in Chapter 8. The design must address the following aspects of the proposed system, usually in this order:

1. Output requirements
2. Input requirements
3. File and storage requirements
4. Processing
5. Controls and backups
6. Personnel and procedures

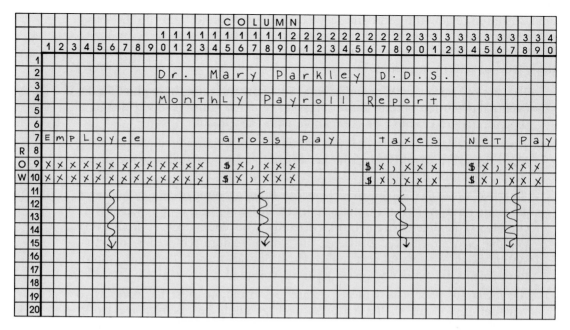

Figure 12.5   A Printer Spacing Chart

A printer spacing chart is used by the systems analyst to specify the format for a printed report.

Output Requirements

Before any other part of the system is designed, the analyst must specify exactly what must be produced, that is, the output. The output is what users and managers are mainly interested in, and it dictates to a large extent how the input, processing, and storage are to be handled.

At the logical level, the analyst must decide what information users need, how detailed it should be, and how frequently it should be presented. At the physical level, the analyst must consider the hardware and media on which the output is to be presented, as well as the exact format. In other words, will the output be presented on a CRT screen, printer, plotter, or microfilm? Exactly how will it look on the output device or medium? The analyst may employ such aids as the **printer spacing chart** (see Figure 12.5), a formatting tool that enables one to plan how a printed report will look.

Input Requirements

After the outputs have been fully specified, the analyst must determine what inputs are necessary for the system to produce them. How the inputs are formatted, how and how often they should enter the system, and what media they will be presented on must all be determined at this time. A systems analyst considers the following questions in order to establish the input requirements of a new system:

- *What data must be collected?*   If a customer billing system is being designed, then the input must include the name, address, and phone number of the customer, the service rendered, the date, the charge, and so forth. These are the basic facts with which the system will work.

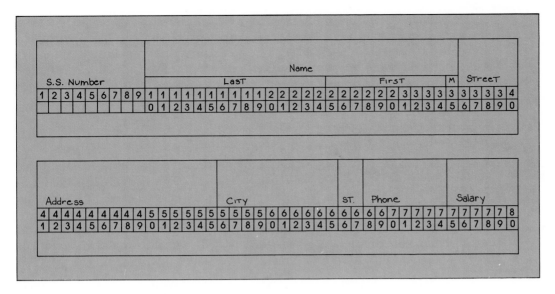

Figure 12.6 A Record Layout Form
The systems analyst can use a record layout form such as the one shown here for
setting up the formats for input and storage file records.

- *How should the data be formatted?*   The analyst has to define how the data will
be arranged so that the system can correctly identify, store, and process the
input. A **record layout form** (see Figure 12.6) may be used to facilitate data
formatting. At this point, the analyst may also have to design forms for people
to fill out if the system will require written input from users. Like questionnaires, forms are not easy to construct well. A lot of thought and planning is
necessary to design forms that are easy for people to use, yet collect the required information in a way that expedites later processing.

- *When are data to be input?*   The analyst must determine whether data have to
be input according to some schedule in order to coincide with processing
needs. For example, if daily inventory reports are required as output, then
daily inputs of inventory levels are necessary.

- *What input media and devices are to be used?*   Punched cards, magnetic disks,
computer terminals, and optical character recognition scanners are only a few
of the alternatives the analyst must consider in deciding what input hardware
and media fit in with the needs of the organization.

File and Storage Requirements

The analyst must describe the data storage needs of the new system in detail. These
include the sizes, contents, organization, media, devices, formats, access restrictions, and locations for all files the system will use. Record layout forms may be
used to describe the content and format of files. Depending on how they are to be
used, files may be organized as sequential, direct access, or indexed sequential files
(see Chapter 5). Storage devices have to be chosen, for example, magnetic tape,
floppy disk, hard disk, optical disk, or some combination of these. Also, a decision
must be made as to which devices are to hold which files and which users should
have access to which files.

Many large systems must interact extensively with data bases (we look at data base systems in Chapter 13). For such systems, the analyst has to decide whether a new data base needs to be established or an existing one can be used. In either case, careful planning of the new system's data storage must be done to ensure compatibility with the organization of the data base.

Processing

The analyst must describe the processing steps that convert inputs to outputs. This involves the use of data flow diagrams and the program design aids covered in Chapter 8 to fully document the operation of the new system. At this time, the analyst should also consider whether any special or new hardware might be required to perform the necessary processing. For example, if the new system is to handle many more computations than the former system did, acquiring a computer with a faster, more powerful CPU may be necessary.

Controls and Backups

Vital to any organization are provisions to ensure the accuracy, security, and privacy of software and hardware resources. *System controls* are instituted to make sure that data are input, processed, and output correctly and to prevent data destruction, unauthorized program modifications, fraud, or any other tampering that might occur. Such controls can be further subdivided into security and privacy controls, accuracy controls, and audit controls.

Security and privacy controls include such things as putting locks and alarms on computers and doors to computer rooms, requiring passwords for access to confidential programs and data, and applying data encryption to disguise secret data (we'll go into more detail about such security measures in Chapter 22).

Accuracy controls are used to ensure that data remain correct and complete from input through output. These measures are similar to software checks to ensure the accuracy of input data (discussed in Chapter 4). The same techniques can be applied at various stages of system processing in an effort to keep errors from occurring.

Audit controls are used to certify that an organization's prescribed procedures are being followed, to check financial operations, and to establish the legitimacy of various external reports. Typically, audit controls trace specific outputs back to the inputs they are based on. In a financial audit, an accounting firm traces a company's business transactions from source documents to final reports to determine how much money has been spent and how much has been earned. Similarly, data-processing systems often employ auditing techniques to make sure everything is going as it should and to trace the source of any problem that arises.

System backups are copies of essential data and program files that are made periodically in order to protect against inadvertent loss or malicious damage. A good analyst cannot overlook this important aspect of system design. An erasure of data might be the result of a power loss, an innocent but inappropriate user command, or a malicious attack by a discontented former employee—in any case, backup copies can save an organization from potential disaster. Imagine the chaos that would result if Social Security or Internal Revenue Service data files were destroyed and there were no backups!

Tom Washington began the design phase with a review of Dr. Parkley's goals in commissioning a new system. Along with considering her long-range plans and how Elena would interface with the system, he gave a lot of thought to whether the required software should be bought or written by his programming staff. He concluded that the software to handle payroll could be purchased right off the shelf because Dr. Parkley's personnel situation was not uncommon. However, her billing needs would have to be fulfilled with customized software—the special college-sponsored dental insurance many of her patients carried required certain additional information and special forms not called for by most other types of dental insurance.

Washington went on to specify the requirements of the new system in detail. He established the output requirements, input requirements, file and storage requirements, processing, controls and backups, and personnel and procedures (what Elena would have to do to operate the system). In this case, since Dr. Parkley's office previously had no computer system, he spent quite a bit of time investigating the hardware components he believed her system should include. Dr. Parkley knew almost nothing about the advantages and disadvantages of the wide array of computer hardware on the market, so this was a very important aspect of Washington's system design.

Before any further time or money was spent on the project, Washington prepared a report of his design recommendations for Dr. Parkley. Because she didn't want her staff to feel uneasy about the upcoming changes, she invited all of them to review this system design report and to offer their opinions in a meeting attended by Washington. Although they came up with a few suggestions that required some minor design changes, the staff was basically satisfied that the proposed system would work. Dr. Parkley was generally impressed with the report, which presented a thorough account of the problem, benefits, design, costs, and schedule of the new system, and she gave her approval for actual development to begin.

Personnel and Procedures

The final aspect of the system the analyst must consider in preparing the design is the people who will make the system work. What personnel (operators, programmers, specialists, and so on) will be needed to run the system? What are the procedures these people will have to follow? A completely effective design must take such human factors into account.

Presentation to Management

Up to this point, the analyst has been making plans for a proposed system but has yet to receive approval from management for the actual development. The considerations and plans of the design phase must be summarized for management in a *system design report* before the project can go any further. This report should contain all the facts management will need in order to make the best-informed decision as to project approval. Specifically, the report should describe:

Summarize once more

- *The problem.* The nature of the current system and the problems it faces should be clearly presented.

- *The benefits.*   Why the new system has been proposed and how it specifically addresses the current system's problems should be explained.
- *The design.*   A design of the proposed system should be presented, but one that isn't overly detailed. Management is interested in the overall structure of the system but will not want to have to wade through highly technical specifications at this point. Relevant diagrams and design aids should be included.
- *The costs.*   An up-to-date estimate of the costs of the new system should be given. Any significant changes in the cost estimates since the completion of the feasibility study should be pointed out.
- *The schedule.*   How long it will take to develop and implement the new system must also be estimated for management.

PHASE 4—SYSTEMS DEVELOPMENT

Construct the new system

Once the final go-ahead has been given by management, the actual development of the proposed system can begin. This phase begins with the design specifications and ends when the system is ready for installation. Four general activities are carried out, to some extent concurrently, during this phase: scheduling, programming, testing, and documentation.

Scheduling

Prepare timetables

The first step of the development phase usually consists of preparing a timetable to ensure that the system will be ready by a given date. Several schedules at various levels of detail may be prepared and further modified as the system development proceeds. One tool frequently used to diagram time spans and deadlines is the **Gantt chart**, or **milestone chart** (see Figure 12.7), a type of bar graph that shows how long it should take to complete various tasks within the complete schedule. The systems analyst typically prepares a Gantt chart showing the projected scheduling of all major development activities. Other members of the development team may construct more detailed Gantt charts covering the subtasks they are responsible for.

Figure 12.7   The Gantt Chart

The Gantt chart is a convenient tool for keeping track of project schedules. This Gantt chart shows some of the project schedule for Dr. Parkley's system.

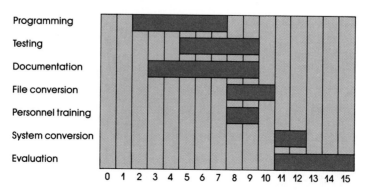

Tom Washington enjoyed this phase of the project the most. Because he'd done his job well in the earlier phases, development was fairly straightforward. Also, he always got excited seeing a new system come together. While he shopped around for suitable prewritten payroll packages, he set his programmers to work on the billing software he'd meticulously designed. Although he was always available in case they had questions, they seldom had anything to ask because his design specifications were so complete. His programmers were happy because they could concentrate on using their skills to produce the best possible software; they didn't have to spend time trying to figure out what Washington wanted.

The first step in this phase was preparing a schedule for the development work. Washington had his programming staff prepare a Gantt chart (see Figure 12.7) for their work, which he merged with one he'd prepared for his software search. Because Dr. Parkley's office required a new computer system, hardware on which the programming staff could develop the software had to be purchased. In addition, Washington needed to have access to the chosen computer so that he could test the payroll software that had to be purchased. In some cases, CSS programmers could write software on the firm's own computers, but the hardware chosen for Dr. Parkley's office wasn't compatible with these. Since they had to have access to the hardware on which the system would eventually run, the programmers had to wait for Washington to assemble it.

Once a suitable hardware configuration was available, the programming began. The programs written by the staff were tested and documented as they were developed, and Washington personally tested the software package he chose for handling Dr. Parkley's payroll. Finally, complete documentation was compiled to facilitate the next and final phase of the project, that of implementation and evaluation.

Programming

We've barely mentioned programming in this chapter, but it does have its place in systems development. Just as coding can be the easiest and least time-consuming part of program development, programming is often the easiest part of systems development—that is, if the system design specifications have been properly prepared. It's essential that programming not be started too early in a system project because that can result in wasted effort (which translates into time and money). If programming commences using incomplete or inadequate design specifications, the end-product is likely to be a system that neither meets user needs nor fulfills management expectations. Given detailed and thoughtfully prepared specifications, the programmer's job is straightforward, and the development of systems programs can proceed in a structured way, as outlined in Chapter 8.

Write the system programs

Testing

Before a system is put into operation, all its component programs must be tested to make sure they work both individually and as a unit. As we mentioned in Chapter

Confirm that the system works

8, desk checking should be done before programs are run on a computer. Comprehensive test data must be created so that programs can be thoroughly debugged. Bugs have a tendency to cost more the longer they are undiscovered, so rigorous testing is always a good practice. Errors caught in the development phase are much easier and less expensive to fix than those that come to light after the system is in daily operation.

Documentation

Explain how the system works

Throughout the system project, documentation has been prepared in the form of reports to management, analysis and design aids, specifications, and charts. In Chapter 8, we pointed out the importance of documentation as an ongoing activity throughout the program development process. In addition to compiling documentation that describes the data and logic of the programs, a systems analyst must also arrange for the preparation of a comprehensive user manual. This manual is especially important for a large system because of the many users who will have to know how to work with it. If user documentation is inadequate or poorly written because it has been prepared in a last-minute rush (which is, unfortunately, often the case), people will need more time to learn how to use the system and may never be able to take advantage of its full potential.

PHASE 5—IMPLEMENTATION AND EVALUATION

Install and appraise the new system

Even after the development phase is over, the system project isn't complete. The new system must be implemented, or installed, in the organization, and its operation must be evaluated to ensure that it fulfills its design specifications. Evaluation gives users another chance to provide constructive feedback. This final phase includes several activities that are necessary to make the new system successful and fully functional: file conversion, personnel training, system conversion, evaluation, and maintenance.

File Conversion

Adapt data files so that the new system can use them

Computerized systems will usually require input data to be in some machine-readable form. This means that data previously handled manually must be entered into the computer system and stored in files. Data entry personnel may be temporarily employed if a large quantity of data must be initially keyed in. Even if the previous system was computerized, a new system may still require that files be modified to accommodate changes in the way in which data are stored or retrieved. Before a new system can be operational, the files it will utilize must be in the formats that will be compatible with its programs.

Personnel Training

Teach users and operators how to run the system

We mentioned that the systems analyst should consider personnel aspects throughout the design phase of the project; however, actual instruction of users usually doesn't occur until implementation. Since the people who will be operating and

When development was complete, the new system had to be installed in Dr. Parkley's office. First, the new hardware had to be moved in and set up. After the hardware was checked out to ensure that there were no malfunctions, the old billing and payroll files had to be entered into the new system. This was a big job since all the records had been kept manually. Tom Washington hired two temporary workers to enter the written records into the new system's storage files and verify them. For this project, file conversion was the most time-consuming of the implementation activities.

Next, Dr. Parkley and Elena were trained to use the new system. Since the other staff members wouldn't be using it, there was no need for them to receive training. Washington continually asked Dr. Parkley and Elena if there was anything they didn't understand or that they thought they'd be unable to teach to someone else. He wanted to make sure that if Elena left, either she or Dr. Parkley could easily train her successor. This pleased Dr. Parkley because she could see that the running of her practice was no longer vulnerable to a single employee's sudden departure. The user documentation proved to be quite easy to follow, and the training was quickly completed.

In this case, converting from the old system to the new system could take place immediately and without any noticeable trauma. Direct conversion worked fine here because there was little risk involved in simply abandoning the old system in favor of the new. During a period of about a month following the conversion, the new system was on probation while it was evaluated by Elena and Dr. Parkley. Its performance was found to be superior to that of Jerry's manual system. Finally, Washington assured Dr. Parkley that his firm would be responsible for the maintenance of the new system. Any as yet undiscovered bugs would be promptly fixed, and future revisions or updates should present no major difficulties.

As Washington and his programmers rode off into the sunset, Dr. Parkley and her staff let out a collective sigh of relief. They could proceed to "drill 'em, fill 'em, and bill 'em," content in the knowledge that things should be running smoothly from then on.

---

using most systems aren't the same people who designed and developed them, training is a key factor in the success of any system project. A well-designed, full-featured system is of little value if people don't know how to use it. User, operator, and programmer manuals are necessary learning and reference aids, which should be prepared for any system of significant size or complexity. In addition, classes and hands-on training sessions are often held to familiarize users with system procedures and capabilities.

System Conversion

The moment of truth eventually arrives—the old system is shut down and the new one is turned on. This event, known as *system conversion,* may be handled in any of several ways. **Direct conversion** takes place when the organization simply stops using the old system and immediately starts using the new one. Somewhat like diving courageously into a cold lake, direct conversion can be risky because it is too late to stop if something goes wrong. **Phased conversion** is like gradually wading in, getting used to the water at each level; all users ease into the new system one step at a time. With **pilot conversion**, only one department, plant, or branch

From the old system to the new

Job Description Systems analysts isolate, analyze, and solve problems in business, science, and engineering and develop methods of applying their findings to data-processing systems. They are not managers or policy makers, but rather problem solvers working at all levels of organizations. Developing a more complete management information system, finding a better way to calculate payroll and benefits, or working out a more cost-effective and labor-efficient manufacturing system— wherever there's a system of any kind that can be improved is where a systems analyst works.

The business systems analyst works on the problems of commercial organizations, for example, inventory control or production efficiency. The scientific systems analyst (or technical systems analyst) performs logical analyses of scientific or engineering problems and formulates a mathematical model, which is made into a program and solved by a computer. System engineers determine what hardware will be necessary to run a particular program or to serve an individual client and also plan how the system should be physically laid out to achieve the most efficient operation.

Although they may specialize in any of these areas, all systems analysts perform some of the same functions. They need to determine what the problem is, what data must be collected, what equipment is required, and what processing steps are necessary. They all use cost accounting methods, sampling procedures, and mathematical models. And they all need to be effective communicators, not only with computers and programmers but with people who know little about computer systems or data processing. Through the use of graphic illustrations and written and oral reports (all of which they must be able to prepare effectively), systems analysts should be able to describe clearly and succinctly the faults of the old system and the benefits and implementation of the new one.

Qualifications Systems analysts must have a bachelor's degree or a certificate in data processing, business administration, or systems analysis. Business specialists need a strong background in accounting, business, economics, and information systems. Scientific or technical analysts must have a degree in physical science, computer science, math, or engineering. Many organizations like candidates to have experience or background in management science or industrial engineering, as well as familiarity with on-line systems design and software. Finally, organizational, management, and communications skills are certainly among the most important assets of a good systems analyst, and a familiarity with computer programming is certainly a plus, since it enables the analyst to understand his or her tools. However, employers seem to be about equally divided on the question of whether management or computer skills are more vital.

In any case, an entry-level systems analyst can expect a salary in the range from $15,000 to $19,000, and the salary range for an experienced analyst is from $20,000 to well over $60,000 a year. Specific salaries, of course, will depend on the analyst's background and the employer's assets and policies.

Outlook As companies acquire their own computer systems, employment of people who can help firms adapt to the new technology with the least trouble is expected to increase. In 1971, there were 93,000 systems analysts; in the early 1980s, there were approximately 250,000. Most projections say that the number of employed sys-

office switches over to the new system, in a kind of trial run, before everyone changes. Finally, **parallel conversion** runs both systems simultaneously for a time until users are satisfied with the operation of the new system. Although it is the most expensive and prolonged approach, parallel conversion is also the safest since it leaves the old system intact until everyone is confident that the new system works.

tems analysts will be greater than 400,000 by 1990. Most of the growth will be in urban manufacturing companies, where most of the changeover to computers is expected to occur. However, wholesale businesses, data-processing services, banks, and insurance companies will also be the source of more job opportunities.

It's important to note, however, that in 1983 more than seven out of every ten job openings for systems analysts were filled by computer programmers moving up the career ladder (see Figure 1 in the Careers in Technology section of Chapter 1). The other three openings were filled by recent college graduates.

Table 1. Outlook Summary: Employment in Systems Analysis.

Job Title	Employment			% Change	Average Number of Annual Openings	Average Entry Salary
	1970	1980	1990			
Systems analyst	93,200	243,000	400,000	+ 65%	30,000	$17,160

Source: U.S. Bureau of Labor Statistics.

Figure 1
Outlook Summary: Employment in Systems Analysis

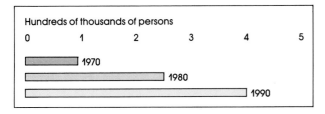

Table 2. Where the Jobs Are.

Industry	1978	1990	% Change
Agriculture, forestry, and fisheries	45	200	344.0
Mining	2,354	5,000	112.4
Construction	1,423	3,000	110.8
Manufacturing	61,915	119,500	93.0
Transportation, public utilities, and communications	8,215	17,700	115.5
Wholesale/retail trade	18,782	35,000	86.3
Finance, insurance, and real estate	14,358	30,100	109.6
Services	59,800	147,500	146.7
Government	21,914	42,000	91.7
Total, all industries	181,998	400,000	119.8

Source: U.S. Bureau of Labor Statistics.

Evaluation

During and after the system conversion, the performance of the new system is appraised to see whether it fulfills all requirements. Basically, the systems analyst will be interested in determining that the system is working the way it's supposed to and that it lives up to the cost and benefit expectations outlined in the system

Does it fulfill its requirements?

design report. If the performance is inadequate in some way, the systems analyst must discover the source of the deficiency and fix it as best as possible. In addition, the entire system project may be evaluated at this time to verify that everything was completed on schedule and within budget.

Maintenance

Keep the system effective

Even when a system is successfully installed and is operating as designed, the project is not quite completely finished. The program development process concludes with the prospect of future revisions, updates, additions, and undiscovered bugs, and newly implemented systems usually require frequent monitoring and periodic adjustment. At some time, these changes may accumulate to the point of being beyond mere maintenance, and the entire systems analysis and design process has to begin anew.

ISSUES IN TECHNOLOGY

The discussion and case study in this chapter have probably given the impression that following a structured approach makes the creation of a new system a straightforward process. Although it is undoubtedly true that most system projects will benefit from this type of approach, admittedly there are situations that defy such a logical procedure. Can you think of any systems problems that might be easier to solve by a less structured, more flexible approach? What alternative methodology would you suggest?

SUMMARY

The Systems Approach

A broader view than the program development process must be taken to produce complex data-processing tools.

What Is a System? According to the American National Standards Committee, a system is "a collection of people, machines, and methods organized to accomplish a set of specific functions." A system interacts with its environment, has a purpose, and is self-regulating and self-correcting.

Why Systems Change Systems may need to change to adapt to new laws, to accommodate new technology, to service a reorganization, to compete more effectively, or to provide newly needed features.

The Role of the Systems Analyst Systems analysts are involved in both the evaluation of existing systems and the planning of new systems.

Phase 1—Feasibility Study

The objective of a feasibility study is to determine if an existing system can be improved at a reasonable cost.

Defining the Problem The first step is understanding and documenting the source of the current difficulties.

Estimating the Scope of the Project The analyst must estimate how big a job it will be to solve the defined problem.

Proposing Possible Solutions A number of potentially workable solutions will be offered by the systems analyst.

Reporting to Management The feasibility study is concluded with the presentation of a report to management; this report explains the findings and recommendations of the systems analyst.

Phase 2—Systems Analysis

If it is decided that a new system is warranted, the existing system is studied in depth so that specific improvements can be suggested.

Data Gathering Facts are collected about the organization and its present system from written documents, questionnaires, structured and unstructured interviews, and direct observation.

Data Analysis The analyst specifies in detail what the new system must do by preparing data flow diagrams, a data dictionary, and black box process descriptions.

Phase 3—Systems Design

In the design phase, the analyst develops the requirements of the new system and maps out its major components.

Review of Project Goals Factors such as the long-range plans of the organization, the user interface, economic trade-offs, availability of prewritten software, and applicability of design methods must be considered by the systems analyst.

Development of System Requirements The output requirements, input requirements, file and storage requirements, processing, controls and backups, and personnel and procedures must all be completely specified.

Presentation to Management A system design report is prepared; it describes the problem, the benefits, the design, the costs, and the schedule of the proposed system.

Phase 4—Systems Development

During the development phase, the new system is actually constructed.

Scheduling Timetables must be prepared to ensure that the system will be ready by a given date. Sometimes these take the form of Gantt, or milestone, charts.

Programming If the design has been properly carried out, programming for the new system is relatively fast and straightforward.

Testing Before a system is put into operation, its various components must be thoroughly tested—alone and together—to make sure that they work as intended.

Documentation Throughout the entire system project, but especially during the development phase, comprehensive documentation must be compiled.

Phase 5—Implementation and Evaluation

The newly constructed system is installed in the organization, and its operation is closely scrutinized.

File Conversion Existing data files may have to be converted to different formats if required by the new system.

Personnel Training Operators and users must be taught to use the new system to its full advantage.

System Conversion The changeover from the old system to the new one is accomplished by direct, phased, pilot, or parallel conversion.

Evaluation The new system is evaluated to see if it fulfills all requirements and lives up to cost and benefit expectations.

Maintenance Even successfully installed systems usually need to be revised, updated, augmented, or fixed at some future time.

COMPUTER CONCEPTS

As an extra review of the chapter, try defining the following terms. If you have trouble with any of them, refer to the page number listed.

system 348
systems analysis 349
systems design 349
systems analysts 349
feasibility study
    (preliminary
    investigation) 351

data flow diagram 357
data dictionary 357
black box 359
printer spacing
    chart 362
record layout form 363

Gantt chart
    (milestone chart) 366
direct conversion 369
phased conversion 369
pilot conversion 369
parallel conversion 370

REVIEW QUESTIONS

1. List several attributes that are common to most systems.
2. What are some of the reasons why systems need to change?
3. Briefly describe what a systems analyst does.
4. Describe the five major phases of a system project.
5. What is the objective of a feasibility study?
6. What are the four sources from which systems analysts most commonly collect data about a system?
7. Describe the three types of documents that are often prepared during data analysis.
8. List some of the factors a systems analyst should keep in mind when designing a new system.
9. What aspects of the system must an analyst be sure to address in the design of a new system?
10. What elements are usually included in a system design report?
11. What are the four general activities making up the systems development phase?
12. List the tasks that must be performed during implementation and evaluation of a new system.

A SHARPER FOCUS

Now that you've completed this chapter, you should be able to answer the following questions about the chapter opening.

1. How is the situation faced by the IRS an example of the necessity for systems analysis and design?
2. How would you define the problem and the project scope?
3. What do you think should be the project goals and system requirements of a new IRS system?
4. What problems can you envision arising in the implementation and evaluation phase of this project?

PROJECTS ▬▬▬▬▬▬▬▬

1. For some system you deal with at school or work, try to identify problems that could be solved by an approach like that outlined in this chapter for systems analysis and design. Perhaps the way classes are graded could be improved, or maybe you could come up with a better system for course registration. Choose some problem and carry out a system "mini project." You don't have to do any system development or implementation; just outline how these might be done. Try to achieve about the same level of detail as in this chapter's case study.

2. People in personnel departments often know little about what qualifications, background, education, or personal characteristics to look for when they are asked to recruit systems analysts, especially among candidates fresh out of school. Prepare some guidelines for a personnel department at a large public hospital. Would these differ from the requirements for a data-processing service? How, and why?

3. Have you ever filled out a state or federal income tax form and wondered who designed it? Systems analysts are often closely involved in activities like the design of forms. What specific recommendations would you make for the federal 1040 form?

4. "Systems development for a microcomputer is different from systems development for a mainframe computer." Do you agree? Why or why not? Thoroughly support any differences you suggest.

5. Outline specific potential consequences that might occur if a systems analysis is poorly done. What parts of a system project do you think are the most critical? Why?

13

Data Base Systems

▶

FOCUS ON ... A "MODEL" DATA BASE

Doug Hopkins is exactly the type of person you'd expect to be piecing together a computer from a Heathkit assemblage. Hopkins is a former college physics major who once worked as a field scientist on a worldwide NASA study of volcanoes. But Hopkins' use of his scientific background and his personal computer only serve to foster his real passion: fashion photography.

Hopkins shoots pictures for magazines such as *Vogue, Mademoiselle* and *Self,* and has corporate clients ranging from Polaroid to Revlon and Clairol. "When I built the Heathkit H-89 four years ago," explains Hopkins, "my goal was to integrate it into the business. I'm a person who doesn't enjoy paperwork, but the computer has organized the business so well that now I have fun doing it." The Heathkit is now used mainly for communications, while a DEC Rainbow "runs my business," he says.

According to Hopkins, the most important function of the Rainbow system is its potential for helping him increase his business. The "Kontax" program is Hopkins' creation; as the name suggests, it is a file of contacts and potential clients. The data base consists of the names of 5,000 art directors, their addresses, and codes describing the kind of work they buy. "These are people who either I or my agent have met with and from our conversations we've concluded how likely they are to hire me." The program was designed to chart the progress of a relationship, providing a record of calls, visits, jobs and letters.

Hopkins designed another program to produce job reports. The program can list everything pertaining to a shoot, including locations, names of models and assistants, type of film used, and the cost of each. The system helps him maintain a running account of expenses. "There are hundreds of messenger receipts, job billings, and model and staff invoices going on simultaneously," says Hopkins, "It's difficult to keep track of it all at once. The computer has made billing a breeze."

By using the computer for his day-to-day operations, Hopkins has learned ways to cut costs. For example, by breaking down expenses, he has learned when to hire a new staff member or employ a free-lancer. Similarly, he has begun to process his own color film, because in the long run it made sense monetarily. "It's important to have a stable foundation in this business. You're always in heavy competition and your ego is a very important part of your work. It's necessary to keep on top of things at all times."

His New York studio houses a large shooting area and a computer room. The latter was originally designed as a dark room. Models and clients are unaware of the computer when they're in the studio. Hopkins is concerned that the mystique of his art might somehow be lessened by the knowledge that behind the screen is a computer. "In some ways I keep the computer invisible to keep a good image. I don't want to make a big deal out of it." Client response has been very positive, though, to the computer's ability to conjure up information. "They know exactly where their money went and have all the photo credit details," Hopkins says.

The more computers are used and the less expensive it becomes to accumulate data in secondary storage media, the greater will be the opportunity for organizations to stockpile vast quantities of data in electronic repositories. Useful as these data may be, they are all too often stored in a disorganized, poorly planned way that may actually cause efficiency to decrease as a result of poor utilization of these resources. Understandably, lowered efficiency is not a desirable state of affairs for any organization. Therefore, it has become necessary to find ways to organize, maintain, and access the various kinds of stored data. By using special software packages called *data base management systems (DBMS)*, random pieces of information can be transformed into convenient, easily accessible files.

In Chapter 10, we learned that a *data base* is a collection of one or more files of related data items that are efficiently stored together for use in multiple applications. In this chapter, we'll study the systems that help people deal with the complicated problem of managing data, systems that accept, organize, store, and retrieve information quickly and efficiently.

BEFORE DATA BASE SYSTEMS

Before the advent and popularity of data base systems, the traditional approach to data storage was to custom-design files for each particular software application. For example, if a business decided to develop a program to handle accounts receiv-

The traditional method of file management

able, the systems analyst or programmer designed the data files that would hold the requisite data. The formats of the items in these files (customer names, addresses, account balances, and so on) were set up specifically for the program being developed. To this point, the traditional approach worked fine. However, suppose that another department in the same business also wanted to develop software that required some of the same data, or that the same department needed another new program that also required some of the same data in the accounts receivable files, for example, a mailing list program for sending out advertisements. Before data base systems, completely new files had to be created or existing ones would be duplicated and restructured to fit the new application. Each department and each software application wound up having its own independent data files. As time passed, it was likely that an organization would accumulate several files holding the same data in different formats.

As you can imagine, this kind of approach results in some overall problems. Organizations that employ software applications that share the same data must deal with data redundancy, updating difficulties, data dependence, data dispersion, and underutilization of data.

Data Redundancy

Duplication of effort

The duplication of files means that the same data are repeated in different files. This represents a waste of storage space and of the efforts of data entry personnel, who must enter new data into several different files. For example, let's say that the various departments of Keyboard Koncepts (the manufacturing company we introduced in Chapter 8) perform their respective data-processing functions without the benefit of a centralized data base. The accounting department maintains its own file of customer names and addresses for its accounts receivable software. The advertising department also keeps a file of active customers so that it can mail out such materials as announcements of new products. Finally, the sales department has yet another file containing the same customer names and addresses so that it can send salespeople to call periodically. Even though they were set up at different times and for different purposes, the three data files hold the same customer names and addresses. Entry time and data storage space are both triple what they would have to be, since each record was typed in three times and is held in three different locations.

Updating Difficulties

Changing every copy

Updating difficulties are related to data redundancy. Having a customer's address in several different files, for example, means that an address change must be reflected in each file. Not only is changing the address several times more work than changing it once, it also increases the likelihood of error. Also, confusion can occur later if the change isn't made in every file (an oversight that occurs all too often). If a customer of Keyboard Koncepts moves, for instance, the accounting, advertising, and sales departments must all be notified so that they can update their respective address files. Obviously, it would be more efficient, economical, and accurate if address changes had to be made only once.

Data Dependence

When data files are intended to be used by particular programs, the programs are dependent to some extent on the data formats and file organization methods used. If the format or organization of the data is changed, the programs that use that data will also have to be changed. Conversely, if a change must be made to an existing program, the format or organization of the data it uses may also have to be changed. This dependence substantially increases the cost of maintaining software.

Intertwining of programs and data

Let's say, for example, that the advertising department of Keyboard Koncepts designed their customer address file specifically for a program that prints out mailing labels. This program is constructed to work with customer records that consist of name, street address, city, state, and zip code. If this record format were changed in some way, then the mailing list program would probably also have to be modified. Or if a new mailing list program were purchased, it might require the data to be in some slightly different format and the customer address file itself would have to be changed. When files are designed specifically for particular programs, the resulting data dependence can cause difficulties if changes must be made to either the programs or the data formats.

Data Dispersion

When data items are stored in many different places and their organization and formats are so intimately tied to the programs for which they are intended, it's difficult for programs to share data. This means that it's hard to tie data together and make cross references. For example, if the sales department wanted to know whether customers who received mailed advertisements subsequently placed orders for the advertised items, this would be difficult to determine. Since the advertising and accounting departments have separate files, each with a different format, answering even a straightforward question such as that one would probably require developing a new, special-purpose computer program. The time and cost required for developing such a specific program would most likely be prohibitive.

Data, data everywhere

Underutilization of Data

Because of data dispersion and the difficulties it causes, full advantage is often not taken of an organization's data resources. The fact that a special new program must frequently be developed means users have little freedom to access existing data in ways not supported by current application programs. They are left with the frustration of knowing that the answers they want are stored in the files but that getting to them is too difficult. Clearly, it is advantageous if all the relevant data stored by an organization can be accessed by anyone needing to. Keyboard Koncepts, for example, would operate more efficiently if department managers could access and make use of pertinent information that has already been collected by other departments. Since writing a specific new computer program is too costly a solution in most situations in which access to data is the goal, some other approach must be used.

Being unable to do all that can be done

THE DATA BASE PHILOSOPHY

In an attempt to address the above problems, software developers in the late 1960s and early 1970s began to design various systems to accept, organize, store, and retrieve data flexibly, quickly, and efficiently. These systems used collections of information, or data bases, organized according to some logical structure. As we said in Chapter 10, a data base consists of one or more files, the basic building block of which is the record. And records are further subdivided into fields. Fields, of course, consist of characters, which are themselves comprised of the elementary units of the computer world, binary zeros and ones. For example, a company's data base might include one file containing information about employees and another file about customers. The employee file might consist of records that hold the name, address, starting date, title, and salary for each employee.

Consolidation of data

The *data base philosophy* is a view of data processing that proposes the use of a single data base for all related information. This data base is controlled by a single software package, rather than having scattered collections of computer files maintained by individual groups of users. The ideals of the data base philosophy are that each piece of information is entered and stored just once and that every authorized user has quick and easy access to any of the stored data. The data are entered, maintained, updated, and accessed in ways that are not dependent on any particular application program.

Of course, any ideal is difficult to achieve, and external factors will have some effect on how closely it may be approached. The data base philosophy isn't practical unless some means exists for quickly accessing a great deal of information. Until the late 1960s and early 1970s, most data-processing installations used magnetic tape for on-line secondary storage, occasionally supplementing it with expensive hard disk systems. Data access times were generally too slow and storage capabilities too limited to allow the creation of truly useful data bases. The further refinement of hard disk systems that improved the speed and efficiency of access to secondary storage and the development of fast, inexpensive semiconductor RAM chips for primary memory made the implementation of practical data base systems feasible.

ADVANTAGES AND DISADVANTAGES OF DATA BASE SYSTEMS

As shown in Figure 13.1, a **data base system** is an integrated set of computer hardware, software, and human users, that is, a working combination of a data base, a data base management system, and the people who use the data base. Given this general view of the data base system, what can an organization expect from one? As usual, data base systems offer both advantages and disadvantages. Their advantages include:

- *Reduction of data redundancy.* Storing most data in one place means less duplication occurs and less space is required.
- *Enhancement of data integrity.* Since data are centralized, fewer updating errors are made and greater accuracy can be maintained.
- *Ensured data independence.* Data are entered, stored, modified, and accessed by methods that are not affected by application programs. Also, changes made

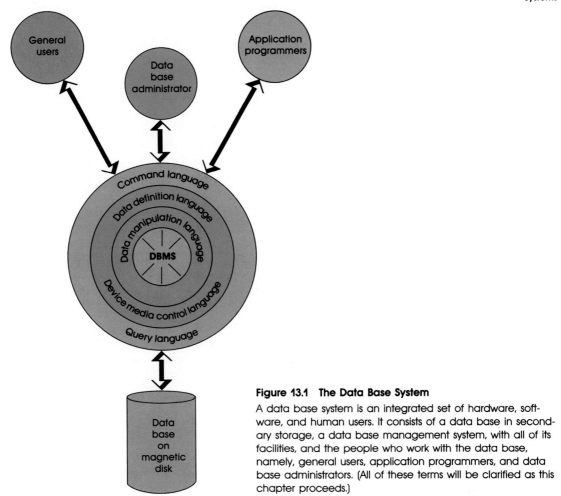

Figure 13.1 The Data Base System

A data base system is an integrated set of hardware, software, and human users. It consists of a data base in secondary storage, a data base management system, with all of its facilities, and the people who work with the data base, namely, general users, application programmers, and data base administrators. (All of these terms will be clarified as this chapter proceeds.)

to data structures usually require no changes to programs that access the data base.

- *Facilitation of data sharing and integration.* Data base systems offer users the ability to combine or to cross-reference data in many different ways.

- *Improvement of access to data.* Data base systems allow users to query the data base directly, without necessarily using an application program.

- *Centralization of security.* It is easier to limit access to information if it is grouped together instead of being kept in several scattered files. Many data bases (see Chapter 22) must be protected and kept private.

- *Reduction of costs.* Data entry, data storage, and the development of new application programs are all made more economical. By eliminating the duplication of data, many organizations can realize substantial savings.

However, they do have certain disadvantages, such as:

- *Complexity.* Data base systems are sophisticated software packages that may require special hardware. They are also difficult and time-consuming to develop.

- *Initial expense.* Primarily because of their complexity and efficiency, data base systems are expensive to develop or purchase.
- *Need for special training of users.* The complexity and the many features offered mean that users must usually receive training before they can work with a data base.
- *Need for a substantial conversion effort.* Changing from a traditional file-oriented system to a data base system can often involve large-scale reorganizations of data and programs. This need can give rise to the user resistance to change we discussed in Chapter 12.
- *Vulnerability.* Data in a data base can be more susceptible to sabotage, theft, or destruction. Although in one sense data bases are protected because of centralized security measures, in another sense they are vulnerable because all the eggs are in one basket. Unscrupulous users who gain access can wreak havoc, and hardware or software failures can possibly destroy vital data.

DATA BASE MANAGEMENT CONCEPTS

The computer programs that are required to create, maintain, and use data bases are called **data base management systems (DBMS)**. That is, they are programs that manage the diverse elements of a data base. Developing such software, even with the help of the latest hardware, is no simple task. Although most operations done on data bases consist merely of searching for or sorting information, the complex data structures and the sheer volume of data can bog down even the fastest computers. For example, a conceptually simple task such as reordering a 5000-name mailing list that is in alphabetical order so that it is in order by zip code instead can take several hours on a microcomputer with poorly designed data base software.

The growth of the market

Originally developed for mainframe computers, data base management systems are now available for machines of all sizes. Users once had to spend between $5000 and $50,000 for minicomputer data base systems and as much as $100,000 for mainframe ones. Now, data base management systems are available for popular microcomputers at prices ranging from $200 to $500. In fact, microcomputer software is the fastest growing segment of the market in data base management systems. Sales of DBMS for microcomputers are increasing by 30%–35% annually and are expected to exceed $900 million by 1988. Although fewer than a third of all microcomputer users currently own data base software, some market analysts predict as many as half of them will own such programs by 1990.

Since data base management systems are so important a part of today's computer scene, let's take a closer look at what they do and how they work.

DBMS Objectives

What a good DBMS should do

The designers of data base management systems are faced with a number of challenges. Their software must provide users with concrete and worthwhile benefits to justify the expense and effort associated with installing it. Ideally, a DBMS should exhibit the following attributes:

- *Efficient use of resources.* A DBMS should function efficiently given the current or projected computer resources of the installation. It should not require the user to add expensive new hardware or software to make it work, and it should not waste storage space or processing time in the performance of designated tasks.

- *Speed.* A DBMS must run fast enough to provide replies to users' questions within an acceptable time frame. Many systems are now interactive (the user types in a query and expects an immediate response), so speed is a primary objective.

- *Compatibility.* A DBMS must interface smoothly with existing hardware, software, and data if it is to be installed successfully. If an organization has to buy a lot of new computer equipment or new software or have all its data reentered, it has probably chosen the wrong DBMS. Although some conversion of data and software is often required, it should be kept at a minimum.

- *Updatability.* A DBMS must allow for the quick and efficient addition and deletion of data records and categories. It must also be flexible enough to handle changes to or rearrangement of the data in its data base.

- *Accessibility.* DBMS users should find it convenient to interrogate the data base. Most systems have an easy-to-learn query language (first described in Chapter 9) that allows users to ask a wide variety of questions about the data without having to prepare specially designed application programs. For example, a sales analyst in a company's home office who was using Artificial Intelligence Corporation's query language REFLECT could key in a question such as "WHICH SELLERS HAVE THE LOWEST PERCENT OF QUOTA IN THE WESTERN REGION?" instead of a series of program codes.

- *Data integrity.* Since the data base is the one place the information is stored, a very important quality of a DBMS is how well it safeguards data integrity. In case something goes wrong (a power failure, for example), the DBMS should have backup measures to ensure that valuable data remain intact. Furthermore, the DBMS should prevent users from making potentially disastrous mistakes. For example, requiring users to reconfirm data deletions can help to avert accidental erasures.

- *Privacy and security.* One of the major concerns about data bases (which will be addressed further in Chapter 22) is the privacy and security of the information they contain. Medical records, bank records, credit files, and military information are but a few examples of the types of sensitive or confidential material kept in data bases. A major objective of any DBMS is to limit access to authorized users. Features such as passwords and access codes are often utilized to restrict unauthorized individuals from changing or viewing data.

ISSUES IN TECHNOLOGY

Between 1971 and 1974, a subcommittee of the U.S. Senate Judiciary Committee conducted a survey and compiled a list of 858 data bases kept by 54 federal agencies. These data bases contained 1.25 billion records, and it was estimated that there were many more data bases that the survey had failed to uncover. At least 29 of the uncovered data bases contained disparaging or sensitive information about citizens (such as their passing of bad checks, poor credit ratings, or sexual habits). Over half of the data bases studied had no explicit authority for their existence, yet federal agencies regularly exchanged data about individuals, who seldom even knew they were on file. Do such possible abuses outweigh the great benefits offered by data base systems? What do you think?

Data Description

Every data base management system must provide procedures that allow users to describe information for the purposes of storage and display. This activity is called **data description**, or **data definition**, and it is often done by data base administrators at large installations (see the Careers in Technology section at the end of this chapter). Data description involves organizing how information will be stored in the data base so that accessibility, efficiency, and security are maintained. If you think of a data base as a filing cabinet, data description is like deciding how many folders are needed and what labels they should have and then arranging the empty folders in the drawers.

In any case, data description requires some careful thought about the best ways to organize information for storage and retrieval. In general, there are two ways of perceiving storage in a data base: as physical storage and as logical storage.

Physical Storage

Views of data storage

One way to think about how data are arranged in a data base is the **physical storage** (or **external storage**), which refers to how the data are actually placed on the secondary storage device, usually a magnetic disk. This physical arrangement is, for the most part, a concern of the designers and developers of the DBMS. It is at too low a level and is too machine-oriented to interest the users and programmers who normally access the data base. Data base administrators, on the other hand, should have a basic understanding of how data are physically arranged in storage so that they can better comprehend the system's workings and cope with problems that arise.

Logical Storage

Physical storage in a data base can be contrasted with **logical storage**, the users' view of how the data seem to be arranged. Logical storage is much more abstract and usually has nothing to do with how data are physically stored. For example, let's say that you want to access a company's data base to extract the names and addresses of recent customers so that you can construct a mailing list for sending out advertisements. In this situation, it is most convenient for you to think of customer names and addresses as being stored together. Your *logical view* is that customer names and their full mailing addresses are stored in close proximity. In reality, the physical locations of these pieces of data may be anywhere on a magnetic disk, determined in some creative way so the DBMS can handle updating, minimize storage space, and facilitate access. However, as long as the DBMS does its job in accessing the correct information, how or where the data are actually kept in storage doesn't matter. The DBMS acts as an interface between the logical view the user employs and the true physical arrangement of the data in storage.

Many data base systems use different terms for the elements and concepts of logical storage, but there are a few common ones worth noting here. A **data base record** (sometimes called a **segment**) is essentially the same as the traditional file record in that it consists of a collection of related fields. A **set** is a collection of records that have at least one attribute in common; in other words, they exhibit a *one-to-many relationship*. For example, for each customer record in a company's data base, there may be a set containing one or more invoice records. These invoice records, each of which describes a purchasing transaction, are related by the fact that they all pertain to one customer.

At a more abstract level, the logical storage for a data base is often defined in terms of a **schema**, a global description of the conceptual organization of an entire data base. The organization of a specific portion of a data base is described by a **subschema**. Subschemas usually define cohesive subsets of the schema, such as all the data to be used by a specified group of programs or users. Subschemas are particularly useful for maintaining data base security and limiting access to authorized individuals. For example, in setting up a customer mailing list, you would only need data from an accounts receivable subschema. You would have no business looking at and would be denied access to records concerning fellow employees' salaries (which would probably be in a personnel subschema).

Data Description Tools

Data base management systems have various features that allow data base administrators or users to set up data descriptions. Many systems utilize a data dictionary for this purpose. Recall from Chapter 12 that a data dictionary contains information about the data elements of a system. A data dictionary facility in a DBMS lets user define fields, records, files, sets, schemas, and subschemas.

Setting up the data base

Another popular tool employed by users of DBMS is a **data definition language (DDL)**. This is a set of commands with a formal syntax that enables users to create logical descriptions of the contents of a data base. However, not all DBMS include a data definition language, and the ones that do exist vary significantly from each other. Another facility, most often employed by data base administrators, may be included in a DBMS to allow the definition of how data are to be physically stored. A **device media control language (DMCL)** can help data base administrators customize data base systems so that they work with the hardware at a particular installation.

DATA MODELS

A data base system can be designed in many different ways. Computer scientists have devoted whole careers to developing data base theories, and programmers have written hundreds of data base management packages. All data base systems are characterized by the way they structure, organize, and manipulate data items and by the relationships among the items. These design elements are reflected differently in the various **data models**, of which three are currently the most popular. Most modern data base systems are structured according to the hierarchical model, the network model, or the relational model. Which of these three is the best is a fiercely debated issue. In fact, it depends on the situation, and, in practice, most systems combine features from each of the basic approaches.

Approaches to data organization

The Hierarchical Model

The **hierarchical model** was developed in the 1960s and has been used almost exclusively for data base systems for large mainframe computer installations. It works best with data that fall naturally into some hierarchy; that is, groups of data items that can be arranged according to some ranking, as in the organization chart of a company. In a hierarchical data base system, such as the IBM Information Management System (IMS), information is expressed as a series of one-to-many

Ordering data by rank

relationships. Each item can have many subordinate items but at most only one item directly above it in the hierarchy. Graphically, the hierarchical model resembles a series of upside-down trees (see Figure 13.2). Subordinate items are often called *children,* superior items are called *parents,* and parents of parents are called *ancestors.* In this model, a parent can have many children, but each child can have only one parent. For example, as shown in Figure 13.2, each part can have several suppliers, but each firm supplies only one part.

Figure 13.2   The Hierarchical Model

The structure of a simple hierarchical data base illustrated by a parts data base for the fictional company Keyboard Koncepts. Three types of records are used: (1) *PART records* containing part number, part name, and cost;   (2) *SUPPLIER records* containing supplier number, name, address, and phone number; and   (3) *SHIPMENT records* containing how many units were shipped. The data are arranged in treelike structures in which PART records are the topmost items and SHIPMENT records the lowest.

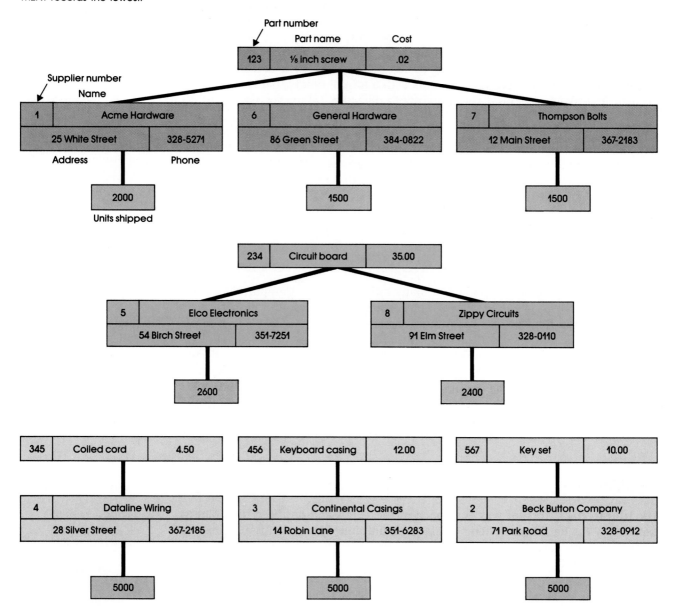

The hierarchical model has the advantage of being relatively simple to implement, understand, and use, but it's not very flexible. Applications that aren't strictly hierarchical may be awkward to represent or may result in duplication of data. For instance, if a supplier is the source for more than one part, a SUPPLIER record will be required for each part furnished. Furthermore, because of the strict hierarchical ordering of the data, certain types of queries aren't handled very efficiently. Since every record can only be accessed through its parent, such activities as finding out the total number of parts shipped by all suppliers, in this case, would require going through every record in the data base. To access each SHIPMENT record, the DBMS would have to follow a path through all of its ancestors, which can be a rather time-consuming process.

The Network Model

The more general **network model** for data base systems consists of a set of records (also called *nodes*) and the links, or associations, between those records. It is most applicable if there are *many-to-many relationships* among the records in a data base (see Figure 13.3). The lines that represent links not only lead from parent to child, as they do in the hierarchical model, but also connect any two records in any direction. In other words, a given record may have any number of immediate superiors as well as any number of immediate subordinates. When drawn out as shown in Figure 13.3, the records and their links form a *network,* or an interconnected system of nodes. *Interconnecting structures*

A common restricted form of the general network model, called the *CODASYL model,* is based on a set of standards established in 1971 by the Conference on Data System Languages (the model's name was taken from that of the conference), a group of computer industry and academic professionals that has been studying data base management systems since the late 1960s.

Network data base systems have been used extensively with mainframes and minicomputers but rarely with microcomputers. Since a hierarchical data base can

Figure 13.3 The Network Model
In this network model for the Keyboard Koncepts parts data base, as in the hierarchical model, the data are represented by connected records. However, this model is more general because a given record may have any number of subordinates as well as any number of superiors. Thus, it allows for the fact that suppliers provide more than one part and for the horizontal linking of records of the same type. The basic record categories and contents are the same as those shown in Figure 13.2.

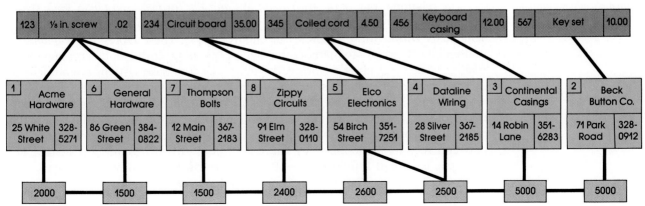

be thought of as a restricted network with only single links between parents and children, the hierarchical model is often seen as being a special case of the network model.

Although more complex than the hierarchical model, the network model has the advantage of also being more general and thus applicable to a wider range of situations. For instance, the network model works better for the Keyboard Koncepts parts data base since several suppliers do provide more than one part (many-to-many relationships). Furthermore, because sideways links are possible in a network data base, users aren't limited to accessing every record only through its ancestors, as is true with a hierarchical data base. Again, in our example, since all of the SHIPMENT records are connected by sideways links, the DBMS can access them without having to go through all of the SUPPLIER and PART records. In many cases, records can be accessed quite efficiently with a network data base system.

Although the interconnecting links in a network data base allow quick and fairly flexible access to information, insertion and deletion of records are somewhat complicated by the fact that any new or broken links must be correctly updated. This means that network data base systems are best used when the relationships between records will remain relatively stable. For example, data bases for inventory and order entry are typically accessed in pretty much the same ways over a period of years. Because the data items and the relationships between them are well defined from the start, there will be few occasions when the network structure will need to be changed.

The Relational Model

The **relational model** was developed by E. F. Codd, a mathematician working at IBM, in the early 1970s and was slow to gain popularity. Only a few relational data base systems were implemented during the 1970s on mainframe computers. However, by the early 1980s, relational data base systems for microcomputers were flooding the market. Today, nearly every DBMS for microcomputers is based on the relational model, and the model is also being increasingly applied to systems for minicomputers and mainframes. dBASE II, dBASE III, Condor 3, and Sequitur are examples of popular data base systems for microcomputers that employ the relational model. The relational data base system has become the latest rage, having been described as the ideal, problem-free, and almost mythical DBMS. These glowing descriptions represent views of loyal advocates, but they all have some basis in fact.

Mathematically manipulated tables

The relational model organizes all data into *flat* (or *two-way*) *tables*, each made up of rows and columns. The rows represent data records, and the columns represent fields within those records (see Figure 13.4). These tables (or *relations*, in mathematical terms) are manipulated by the DBMS in storing and accessing information. The operations performed by relational data base systems are all defined in strict mathematical terms, based on the theory proposed by Codd.

In Figure 13.4, we've organized the data about parts, suppliers, and shipments into three tables according to the relational model. The significance of this model is not that data are arranged in tables. The really important thing is that relationships between records are implied by the data values stored in common fields. For example, each part listed in the PARTS table is associated with its supplier in the SHIPMENTS table. That is, the relationship between part and supplier is implied

PARTS TABLE

Number	Name	Cost
123	⅛ inch screw	.02
234	Circuit board	35.00
345	Coiled cord	4.50
456	Keyboard casing	12.00
567	Key set	10.00

SHIPMENTS TABLE

Supplier No.	Part No.	Quantity
1	123	2000
2	567	5000
3	456	5000
4	345	5000
5	234	2600
6	123	1500
7	123	1500
8	234	2400

SUPPLIERS TABLE

Supplier No.	Name	Address	Phone
1	Acme Hardware	25 White Street	328-5271
2	Beck Button Company	71 Park Road	328-0912
3	Continental Casings	14 Robin Lane	351-6283
4	Dataline Wiring	28 Silver Street	367-2185
5	Elco Electronics	54 Birch Street	351-7251
6	General Hardware	86 Green Street	384-0822
7	Thompson Bolts	12 Main Street	367-2183
8	Zippy Circuits	91 Elm Street	328-0110

Figure 13.4   The Relational Model
By arranging records into tables, the relational data base provides a more flexible structure than do the other two data models. Since there are no parents or children, relationships among records aren't predetermined by the data base structure. Here the Keyboard Koncepts parts data base is structured as three tables: a PARTS table, a SUPPLIERS table, and a SHIPMENTS table.

by the common field, Part Number. Part number 123 is also a field in a record in the SHIPMENTS table. This shows that its supplier is number 1, and from the SUPPLIERS table we see that this number refers to Acme Hardware.

How does the user access a relational data base? The DBMS provides the user with a set of commands to manipulate data tables. The two most important of these commands are *JOIN* and *PROJECT*. The JOIN command combines two tables to produce a third table. For example, you could use JOIN to combine the PARTS and SHIPMENTS tables to form another table containing part number, part name, cost, supplier number, and quantity. The PROJECT command extracts columns from one or more tables to produce a new table. You could use PROJECT to extract the supplier numbers from the SHIPMENTS table, the supplier names from the SUPPLIERS table, and the part names from the PARTS table to form a new table including supplier numbers and names and the parts they furnish. By using JOIN, PROJECT, and other mathematical operations, it is possible to manipulate or extract any information in a relational data base.

The relational model has some very appealing characteristics. It is conceptually quite simple; most people find it natural to organize and manipulate information in tables, since they have many uses in everyday life. In a relational table, there are no parents or children. This means that relationships among records in different tables aren't predetermined by the structure of the data base. Instead, they are specified by the user when data are retrieved. Consequently, relational data base systems provide a high degree of flexibility and data independence. There is no need to know in advance what questions users might ask about information in the data base. Data files can be designed and set up and then perhaps used for purposes that hadn't been considered. Relational systems, in contrast to network and hierarchical systems, are therefore ideally suited for situations in which the types of user queries cannot be prespecified.

USING THE DATA BASE

As we've pointed out, data base management systems vary in their designs and in the features they offer. However, most of them provide users with several basic functions. We've already discussed one of these, data description. Other common DBMS facilities are data entry and updating, command and query languages, data manipulation languages, and report generators.

Data Entry and Updating

Inputting and modifying data

Every DBMS must obviously include some means for entering data. There are several different ways in which data entry can be accomplished. The most common method is direct entry from a terminal keyboard. Data base systems may have built-in text editors to facilitate the data entry. Or, after the data descriptions are complete, the system might successively prompt users for each field of the input records (see Figure 13.5). Once all the fields have been filled with data, the entire record is usually displayed, giving the user a chance to correct any errors. When the user indicates that the record is correct and complete, it is entered into the data base and the same prompts appear for typing in the next record.

Many data base systems allow users to design their own formats for data entry. Such systems have procedures that enable users to set up blank forms, which appear on the screen and are filled in with data. In Chapter 10, we saw that this feature is included in many file management application packages (see Figure 10.5

```
Enter Last Name: Keaton

Enter First Name: Patricia

Enter Street Address: 1404 Glendale Drive

Enter City: Champaign

Enter State: Illinois
```

Figure 13.5 Prompting Data Entry
Many data base systems prompt users for data entry after the data descriptions are complete. In this representation of a typical series of data entry prompts, the information typed in by the user is highlighted.

for an example of a data entry form). User-created forms can smooth the data entry process by customizing the way input information is typed in and displayed on the screen.

Every DBMS must also allow users to reaccess a previously entered record and to update, or make changes to, any of its fields. In addition, some systems provide a method for simultaneously changing a certain field of selected records in the data base. With such a feature, for example, you could simultaneously decrease the price of every item in an inventory data base by 10% for a storewide sale.

Command and Query Languages

Once information has been entered into the data base, there must be some means for instructing the DBMS to perform manipulations, comparisons, and operations. A **command language** consists of all the procedures for issuing orders to the system. A query language (introduced in Chapter 9) is a subset of a command language and consists of rules for specifying the criteria by which to perform operations. Many modern data base systems employ *nonprocedural command and query languages*. Instead of giving step-by-step instructions to the DBMS on how to perform operations (as is necessary when using a traditional high-level programming language), the user tells it what to do by simply choosing items from a *menu*, typing in Englishlike commands, or filling in blanks in response to prompts. Most data base systems for microcomputers make some use of menus, which are just lists of possible options from which to choose (see Figure 13.6).

Telling the system what to do

Figure 13.6   A DBMS Menu
Many data base management systems have menus from which users can choose operations. This is a typical menu from the Sequitur relational data base system that is available for IBM Personal Computers.

```
DATABASE: a:example


                        Press <F1> for help

These are Sequitur's basic commands
+==========================================================================+
|  Databases              Set Commands            Copy Commands            |
|    CHOOSE database         SELECT from table       COPY table            |
|    CREATE database         MANUAL select           APPEND to table       |
|                            JOIN tables                                   |
|  Table Entry              SORT table             Maintenance             |
|    EDIT table                                      COMPACT database      |
|    ADD to table           UNION                    DUMP to file          |
|                           INTERSECTION             LOAD from file        |
|  Table Output             DIFFERENCE               REMOVE rows           |
|    SHOW table             UNIQUE rows                                    |
|    PRINT table            DUPLICATE rows           EXIT Sequitur         |
|    REPORT generator                                                      |
|    FORMS generator                                                       |
+==========================================================================+
    Command:
```

Here are some examples of things you could tell a DBMS to do using command and query languages:

Compile a list of all employees who have been absent from work more than five days this past year.

Sort a list of customers by name.

Prepare a mailing list.

Find out if any customers who have placed new orders have not yet paid bills for past orders that are more than 30 days past due.

Subtract all payments made this week from customer balances owed.

Data Manipulation Languages

Accessing data bases from application programs

A **data manipulation language (DML)** is an interface between a programming language and a data base management system. It allows application programmers to access data bases from within programs they write. Data manipulation languages are employed to write programs that work with data base management systems but do not do so through the interactive command and query languages. They allow the full power of some high-level programming language (like COBOL, FORTRAN, or Pascal) to be used in conjunction with the functions of a DBMS. Data manipulation languages are especially useful at large computer installations, where a staff of programmers may be employed to write customized software.

Typically, a DML consists of a set of commands that can be included in a user program to perform such common manipulations as creating, storing, accessing, changing, deleting, and sorting records in a data base. For each programming language that is to be used, a different DML is usually necessary. For example, a FORTRAN DML for a particular data base system will look different from a Pascal DML for the same system. Although the same functions will be included in both, the forms of the commands will be different, reflecting the differences between FORTRAN and Pascal.

Report Generators

Printing out the results

Finally, all data base management systems must include certain features for outputting information. After selecting, sorting, combining, comparing, or otherwise manipulating items in a data base, a user frequently wants a printout of the results in an easy-to-understand format. Most data base systems provide a *report generator* that allows users to produce hard copy formatted according to their own design. Also, a report generator is often able to perform a few functions on its own, such as computing and printing out summary calculations.

Sometimes included in a DBMS package and sometimes sold separately, report generators vary greatly in their power and ease of use. A good report generator should be able to do the following:

Print titles, headings, footers, and page numbers.

Select, arrange, and rename fields for output.

Set margins, page length, line spacing, etc.

Calculate and print counts, subtotals, averages, and grand totals.

CAREERS IN TECHNOLOGY
Data Base Administrator

Job Description Because of the proliferation of public and private data bases, there is a growing demand for people who can operate and monitor them. Such people are data base administrators. Note that the data base administrator usually plays no part in the design and development of the data base management software. Although they may participate in selecting software, data base administrators usually take over once the system has been installed at the organization. In addition, they are responsible for the data base's security and for the scheduling and coordination of user access. They advise management, including various department heads, as to which data should be included in the data base, how long the data should remain, and how the data should be organized. Along with the security specialist (see the Careers in Technology section in Chapter 22), the data base administrator prepares backup files, secure procedures for access, and emergency recovery plans. Finally, data base administrators must compile and analyze statistics on use and efficiency and must write periodic reports for higher management.

Qualifications This is a management position, requiring five to ten years of experience with data processing in both technical applications and business (systems design and analysis or programming). A B.S. in computer science is generally necessary, and an M.B.A. is increasingly valuable. Management skills—leadership capabilities, written and oral communication skills, organizational abilities, and the ability to delegate authority and responsibility effectively—are vital. Requests for access to a data base will often be simultaneous, conflicting, and equally urgent, meaning that the data base administrator must be able diplomatically to negotiate workable compromises among equally insistent department heads.

Outlook As both their ability to adopt data base systems and their need for them grow, companies will also need more people to administrate them. Considerable potential exists for advancement into upper-level management positions or consulting work.

DISTRIBUTED DATA BASES

Throughout this chapter, the data base has been referred to as if it were in one place on a single computer. However, just as computer systems can be arranged as distributed data-processing networks (see Chapter 7), data bases can also be distributed. In other words, a particular data base can be accessible to several computers concurrently. This may be accomplished by having the data base reside in a centralized host computer that is accessible to outlying computer sites. Another possible arrangement could have parts of the data base stored in different computers in a network, or a complete copy of the data base can exist at each remote location.

Accessibility to more than one computer

Distributed data bases offer the advantage of being available to more users; but as a result of this increased accessibility, they must deal with *concurrent access*, which occurs when more than one user tries to access the same data at almost exactly the same time. Suppose, for example, that two travel agents are using a distributed data base to book flights for a commercial airline. If they both access the data base at nearly the same time and see that a particular seat is available, they may sell it to two different customers, which is certainly a problem. In addition, if one user is updating or deleting a record while another is trying to access it, entirely unpredictable results may occur. To deal with such situations, distributed data base systems usually have a feature that enables authorized users to "lock out" other users while certain operations are being performed.

SUMMARY

Before Data Base Systems

Traditionally, data files were custom-designed, created for specific software applications.

Data Redundancy   Data might often be repeated in more than one file.

Updating Difficulties   Keeping all the files up to date can be problematic.

Data Dependence   Programs may be dependent on the data formats and file organization methods used.

Data Dispersion   Scattered data are difficult for programs to share.

Underutilization of Data   Dispersed data cannot usually be used to full advantage.

The Data Base Philosophy

The data base philosophy is a view of data processing that proposes the use of a single data base for all related information.

Advantages and Disadvantages of Data Base Systems

Data base systems reduce data redundancy, enhance data integrity, ensure data independence, facilitate the sharing and integrating of data, improve the access to data, centralize security for the data base, and reduce overall costs. However, they are complex and expensive to develop and set up, require special training of users and a substantial conversion effort, and are vulnerable to sabotage and intrusion (largely because of their centralized security).

Data Base Management Concepts

A data base management system is a set of programs that manages the various elements of a data base. Originally developed for mainframes, data base management systems for all types of computers have become widespread.

DBMS Objectives   A DBMS should make efficient use of computer resources, be fast, interface smoothly with existing facilities, be updatable, provide easy access to authorized users, preserve data integrity, and ensure the privacy and security of data.

Data Description   The arrangement of data in a data base may be viewed in terms of physical or logical storage. Data descriptions are set up using such tools as data dictionaries, data definition languages (DDLs), and device media control languages (DMCLs).

Data Models

Data base systems are characterized by the way in which they structure, organize, and manipulate data items and by the relationships among these items.

The Hierarchical Model The hierarchical model arranges data according to some ranking, in a series of one-to-many relationships. Graphically, hierarchical data base systems resemble a series of upside-down trees. Data are divided into parents, children, and ancestors. Such systems are simple to implement, but somewhat inflexible.

The Network Model The network model is often used when the data exhibit many-to-many relationships. More flexible than the hierarchical model, the network model can be applied to a broader range of situations. But the large number of complex interconnections means that these systems do not allow for easy alteration of data.

The Relational Model The relational model organizes data into mathematically manipulated tables containing rows and columns. These systems are flexible and easy to use.

Using the Data Base
Most DBMS include the following features.

Data Entry and Updating Data base systems may employ text editors, prompts, or user-designed forms for data entry.

Command and Query Languages Command and query languages allow users to instruct the data base system as to what they want it to do.

Data Manipulation Languages Data manipulation languages allow programmers to access data bases from their application software.

Report Generators Most data base systems provide a report generator that allows users to produce formatted hard copy.

Distributed Data Bases
Some data base systems are set up so as to be accessible to several computers concurrently.

COMPUTER CONCEPTS

As an extra review of the chapter, try defining the following terms. If you have trouble with any of them, refer to the page number listed.

data base system 382
data base management
    systems (DBMS) 384
data description
    (data definition) 386
physical storage
    (external storage) 386
logical storage 386
data base record
    (segment) 386

set 386
schema 387
subschema 387
data definition
    language (DDL) 387
device media
    control language
    (DMCL) 387

data models 387
hierarchical model 387
network model 389
relational model 390
command language 393
data manipulation
    language (DML) 394

REVIEW QUESTIONS

1. What was the traditional approach to data storage before data base systems were commonly used?
2. List the overall problems that are due to this traditional approach.
3. What is the data base philosophy?

4. What role did the refinement of hard disk systems play in the development of data base systems?
5. List some of the advantages and disadvantages of data base systems.
6. For what type of computers were data base management systems originally developed?
7. What attributes should a good DBMS exhibit?
8. What does the process of data description involve?
9. Contrast the physical storage of data in a data base with the logical storage.
10. What features do data base management systems commonly offer to enable users to set up data descriptions?
11. Evaluate the three major data models. In what situations would one be better than the others, and why?
12. What are some of the facilities for data entry into a DBMS?
13. What means is usually used to tell a DBMS what to do?
14. What enables application programmers to utilize data base management systems?
15. What kinds of things should a DBMS report generator be able to do?
16. What problem must distributed data bases anticipate?

A SHARPER FOCUS

Now that you've completed this chapter, you should be able to answer the following questions about the chapter opening.

1. In what ways does Doug Hopkins' data base reflect the data base philosophy?
2. Does it meet the DBMS objectives listed in the chapter?
3. Would a command language be appropriate for Hopkins' system?
4. How might his system work as a distributed data base?

PROJECTS

1. Imagine that you are the data base administrator for your school's or company's mainframe computer system. How would you set up the data description for the data base? What information would you store about students, faculty, and classes or about employees and business activities? What would the data formats be? What security and privacy policies would you enact?
2. Consider the data base supporting a typical motel reservation system. Assume the motel is a chain, with facilities in a number of cities. Do you think a hierarchical, network, or relational data base structure would be best for this application? Why?
3. The company you work for is considering the installation of a data base system and has asked you to produce a detailed cost/benefit analysis. Since it is so difficult to put a specific price tag on many of the benefits of a data base system (such as improved customer service), how would you go about "selling" the data base concept to the company's executives?
4. Your bank has "Kwik-Kash" automatic teller machines all over town, which are operated by a data base system. One day, you stop at one and insert your card, intending to withdraw $100. What you don't know is that your spouse is doing the same thing, at the same time, at a mall on the other side of town. You both hit the ENTER button at the same time, both trying to withdraw $100 from an account containing only $125. What happens? What can the bank do to prevent this sort of problem from happening?

5. Assume that approval has been given for the installation of a data base system at your school or company, but you know that the new system will not be greeted enthusiastically by everyone. Where can you reasonably expect user resistance to come from, and what forms might it take? What are some typical barriers facing such a change?

6. What criteria can you propose to be applied in the evaluation of a distributed data base? (You might begin by looking at the advantages and disadvantages of both a distributed data base and a centralized data base.)

14

Management Information and Decision Support Systems

▶

FOCUS ON ... TEACHING MANAGERS TO USE AN MIS

The head of a Fortune 500 company often spends 10 to 12 hours a day at his job and lugs home a briefcase full of work at night. Finding spare time to teach himself a new technology is almost impossible. So, most chief executives who use a personal computer began the learning process by attending an intensive hands-on class or by having a tutor available. . . .

Larry Burden, now the corporate vice-president of management information services at Firestone, has helped two CEOs [chief executive officers] through the initial stages. His first experience was with Ben Heineman, head of Northwest Industries. "Late in 1976, Heineman's assistant approached me with the idea of getting his boss and other lay executives at Northwest the ability to do financial analyses directly at a computer CRT," recalls Burden, then with Northwest. "I put together a prototype DSS (decision support system) for Heineman and three other senior executives. . . ."

With the system in place, Burden and other members of his management information staff acted as tutors on call. The prototype later became a formal system and many other executives at Northwest were trained. In the process Burden developed a programmed approach to teaching. "We hired people right out of MBA programs who understood financial analysis and showed a propensity for coaching," he explains. "We taught them to use the DSS system and made them available all day long to the CEO and other top executives." Heineman's usage flourished in the coaching environment and today he is an avid user of personal computers. . . .

His approach worked so well at Northwest that Burden used it again at Firestone. The only real differences were a full-day course he ran the executives through after an initial period of coaching, and the use of IBM Personal Computers from the beginning.

The first door Burden had to walk Firestone's CEO through was one labeled "Fear," he says. "Like most first-time users, John Nevin was afraid he was going to break the machine or destroy a file. The coaching helped him get past this computer mystique."

Fear of the machine is also the biggest problem Jim Alfaro faces in teaching CEOs. . . .

To break down the initial apprehensions, Alfaro starts his four- to eight-hour seminar with some simple financial routines that give the executives immediate screen successes. Each executive works at his own personal computer. "It's like teaching someone how to drive a car," he says. "You'd better start in a parking lot where the students won't get in an accident and they can forget about their fears by getting involved in something they can relate to." . . .

In the final analysis, teaching the CEO to compute is very much like teaching any other high-level executive, except his time is even more limited and his ego has to be treated a little more gingerly. Having someone on call for him who understands his very special needs and can still entice him forward is probably the single most important ingredient in a successful teaching program.

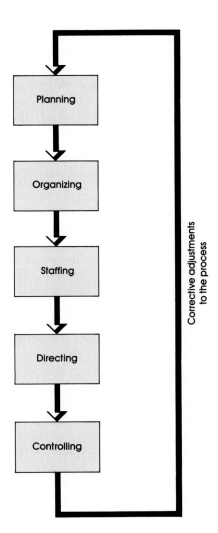

Figure 14.1   Functions of Managers
Note that managers' functions don't make up a
rigid sequence but rather a process that involves
feedback and flexibility.

order to plan, they must forecast future conditions, set objectives, develop strategies, establish priorities, construct budgets, set procedures, and define policies.

2. *Organizing.* Managers establish the organizational structures for utilizing resources to implement their plans. They must first identify and try to locate all of the resources needed to carry out their plans. Organizing can include, for example, setting up new departments, determining the chain of command, assigning responsibilities, and specifying divisions of labor.

3. *Staffing.* Managers acquire the necessary resources to achieve their goals and objectives. Although staffing usually refers to the selection, orientation, and training of personnel, it is also used in a less limited sense to mean the acquisition of all required resources. Thus, staffing can include recruiting personnel, purchasing materials, raising capital, and procuring other necessary goods and services.

4. *Directing.* Managers coordinate the actual execution of planned activities. As leaders, managers must ensure that resources are utilized in an efficient and cooperative manner. Directing includes delegating responsibility, as well as communicating with and motivating subordinates. Because of this, directing is sometimes described as getting things done by other people.

5. *Controlling.* Managers compare actual performance with planned performance and initiate actions to correct any shortcomings. Thus, controlling includes establishing a reporting system to monitor activities, developing performance standards, measuring results, rewarding good performance, and making corrective adjustments, which may mean starting a project over again from the planning stage.

Levels of Management

Three levels with distinct responsibilities

The five management functions just discussed are rather general, as they are intended to apply to managers of all kinds. But just what kinds of managers are there? One approach to viewing the composition of management is based on a hierarchy in which management is traditionally organized into three levels: top, middle, and first-line. Of course, the actual number of managers in an organization depends on its size and complexity. A very small firm, such as a gas station, may have only a single manager (the sole proprietor). On the other hand, the largest corporations, such as General Motors, have thousands of managers. Regardless of the number of managers in an organization, the three levels of management still apply. In a gas station, all three are embodied in the single owner; in General Motors, there are many managers at each level. The distinctions among the three levels can be explained in terms of their characteristic concerns and duties (see Figure 14.2).

Top management is concerned with long-range, strategic plans. This level of management is oriented toward the future of the organization and oversees the performance of the key personnel (middle management) who will carry out the plans. The duties of top management primarily involve planning the firm's activities for five or more years into the future, coordinating the overall efforts of the firm, establishing major policies, and dealing with external organizations and events. Examples of managers at this level are the chief executive officer, the president, the vice-presidents, and the heads of major divisions.

Middle management is concerned with short-term, tactical plans. Managers at this level are involved with what the organization will be doing from one to five years into the future. They oversee the performance of first-line management and

Figure 14.2 Management Levels
Management is usually organized into three hierarchical levels, reflecting different responsibilities, concerns, and needs for information.

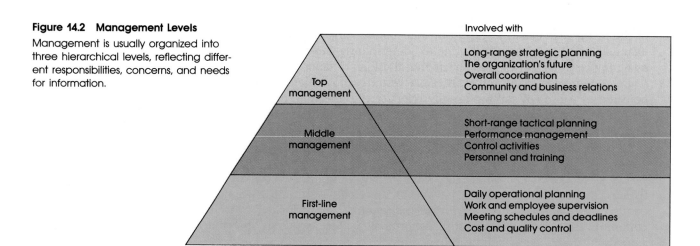

control the activities that move the organization toward the goals established by top management. Middle management is typically responsible for such matters as plant layout, employee training and other personnel considerations, equipment and material acquisition, product improvement, and research and development. Top management is mainly concerned with planning, but middle management's role is characterized by a fairly equal mix of planning and controlling. Examples of middle managers include plant managers, regional managers, directors of research laboratories, and retail managers.

First-line management is concerned with day-to-day, operational plans. This is the largest group of managers in a firm. First-line management is essentially supervisory and is more familiar with the technical skills of employees than either top or middle management. First-line managers' job is to ensure that employees follow established procedures in their work activities, that schedules are kept, and that deadlines and quality and cost control standards are met. Since first-line managers are closest to the workers and to the daily activities of the business, they also have the important task of providing feedback to the higher levels about how things are going "in the trenches." First-line management's main concern is with control; planning is performed on a very limited scale. Examples of first-line managers include department heads and plant supervisors.

INFORMATION NEEDS OF MANAGERS

Information—the output of an MIS—is of vital importance to an organization's managers. It is essential for the achievement of short-term, intermediate, and long-range goals. Given adequate information, management can rely on deductive and analytical methods rather than on guesses and intuition, which are all that's possible if relevant facts are missing. Even though intuition based on experience can certainly be of value, many disastrous decisions have been based on insufficient or inaccurate information. As we have already noted, information is one of the key resources of any organization. Many proficient managers believe that sound information is a major source of competitive power. It allows them to outmaneuver their rivals at critical times, such as when introducing new products or services. If managers don't have the information they need, they cannot effectively perform any of their functions. The result might well be an "out-of-control" firm that can neither gain the lead nor recover from setbacks.

Given the importance of information to management, just what kinds do the different levels need? Figure 14.3 shows the general needs of the three management levels.

A key resource

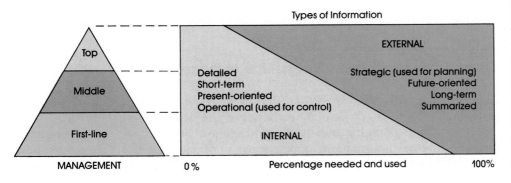

Figure 14.3 Information Needs of Managers

Managers at different levels have information needs defined by their characteristic activities. In this diagram, the general types of information needed and used by managers at the three levels are indicated. For example, top management needs a higher percentage of external information than does middle or first-line management.

Strategic Information for Top Management

Help in making long-range plans

Just as managers at different organizational levels have different concerns, they also have different information needs. **Strategic information** is that which is used by top management in its long-range planning. It usually consists in large part of material derived from or relating to areas of knowledge outside the organization. Sources of such *external information* can include governmental legislation, customer feedback, supplier reports, competitor announcements, labor union statements, and economic trends, forecasts, and indicators. This external information is used by top management for planning purposes and for analysis of organizational problem areas.

Some strategic information is also derived from inside the organization. Such *internal information* typically includes forecasts and projections from various departments. Furthermore, it must be in summarized form—top management can't be concerned with every detail of the organization's operations.

In most cases, strategic information is used to determine *why* rather than what, how, or where; it forms the basis of an organization's objectives, priorities, strategies, and policies. Examples of strategic information might be projected financial statements for the next five years, estimates of long-term capital need, present and projected personnel requirements, suggestions of potential new product lines and markets, long-range evaluations of research and development efforts, and investigations of alternative supply sources.

Tactical Information for Middle Management

Help in making short-term plans

Tactical information is that used by middle management for relatively short-term planning (up to about a year in the future). This type of information is needed by middle management to implement the strategic plans made by top management and to allocate resources properly to attain organizational objectives. Unlike strategic information, tactical information is typically used by a large number of people in an organization. Also, tactical information is a fairly equal mix of summarized information for planning and detailed information for control; strategic information, on the other hand, is mainly directed toward planning activities. Thus, tactical information consists of roughly equal amounts of external and internal information.

As we mentioned earlier, the types of decisions made by middle management are likely to concern such areas as plant layout, personnel problems, product improvement, and research and development. Examples of tactical information include budget reports, shipping schedules, evaluations of sales department performance, periodic inventory summaries, engineering progress reports, research and development progress reports, and short-term market forecasts.

Operational Information for First-Line Management

Help in controlling routine activities

Operational information is that used by first-line management to control the structured, repetitive, day-to-day activities of the organization. Since it is little concerned with planning but mostly with control, it consists predominantly of detailed internal information. Operational information is used by the greatest number of people in a company, that is, by first-line managers and many nonmanagerial employees. Operational information makes it possible to measure actual performance against predetermined objectives and enables first-line managers to see how operating standards and policies can be improved. This feedback from the workplace keeps higher levels of management aware of both favorable and unfavorable operating conditions.

Operational information is used to ensure that specific tasks are implemented in an effective and efficient manner. As a result, it consists almost entirely of detailed material describing current conditions. Examples of operational information include personnel records, sales orders, engineering specifications, manufacturing orders, inventory records, purchase orders, shipping routes, and payroll and cash flow records.

Characteristics of Useful Information

As any student, businessperson, or professional knows, information overload is a very real problem in our fast-paced, computerized world. The necessity of having information is well recognized; however, it's not how much information one has that's important, it's how good that information is. Managers can easily be swamped by the deluge of information at their disposal. The management information system must not provide just any information. To be truly an asset, an MIS must provide quality information. Generally, information that exhibits accuracy, timeliness, relevance, completeness, and conciseness is the most valuable.

Evaluating the quality of information

Accuracy

Accuracy refers to how correct, true, or precise information is, that is, whether the information represents the situation or event as it really is. Sometimes accuracy is expressed as a ratio (or a percentage) of correct information to total information during some period of time. For example, if 1000 payroll checks are produced each month and 980 of them are correct, the accuracy of the monthly payroll production is 0.98 (or 98%). The accuracy level that is acceptable depends on the activity and on an organization's standards. Issuing inaccurate checks to 20 employees each month is probably not acceptable; but if an inventory of inexpensive parts is 98% accurate, that might be good enough. As you can imagine, the accuracy of information is of paramount importance.

How true information is

Timeliness

Timeliness refers to how current information is. The most accurate information is of little value if it is obtained too late to influence important decisions. The quicker managers can receive the information they need, the better will be their ability to help their firms compete in the marketplace. Minimum acceptable response times from management information systems will vary, however, with the kind of information being provided. Some requests must be answered immediately, such as those for stock market figures, which can change hourly. On the other hand, some information, such as employee payroll reports, is only needed at certain regular intervals. Another important factor determining response time is that it costs more in terms of computer resources to produce immediate information. Therefore, response times must be balanced against costs to ensure that information is obtained in time but not at excessive expense.

How up-to-date information is

Relevance

How pertinent information is

Relevance refers to how applicable information is to a given decision-making or problem-solving situation. A management information system cannot simply dump everything it has in a manager's lap—that leads back to the problem of information overload. The information that is provided should directly and conclusively pertain to the specific, well-defined issue. For example, if a manager is trying to determine whether to hire more people in the near future, he or she has no need to see every employee's personnel record. The relevant information in this case would be summary reports of present and projected personnel requirements.

Completeness

How comprehensive information is

Completeness refers to whether information tells all that is currently known about the subject at hand. Although managers can't afford to wade through reams of irrelevant material, they should have enough pertinent information to make good decisions. If, after reading a report, a manager has a number of unanswered questions, the report is incomplete. For example, a research and development report that simply outlines current areas of investigation without summarizing the progress made so far is incomplete. Even though it is often impossible to achieve total completeness, information should be as complete as possible.

Conciseness

How succinct information is

Conciseness refers to how compact information is. As we have said, information should be relevant and complete, but it is also desirable that it be expressed as succinctly as possible. Extraneous and misleading detail should be omitted. If a report that could take up five pages can be condensed to one or two pages, the shorter form is preferable. In many cases, graphs and charts can be used to present information in a more concise and dramatic manner. This is one of the reasons why computer-generated graphics have recently achieved such phenomenal popularity in the business community.

Output of Information

How an MIS presents information

By now, you should have a fairly good idea of what makes information useful to management. However, we must still discuss *how* information is presented to management by an MIS. The output of management information systems generally takes one of two forms: reports or responses to inquiries.

Reports

Types of printed summaries

Reports are the primary means by which an MIS presents information. They are usually classified according to how often they are output, how detailed they are, or the purpose for which they are used. In general, reports are produced more or less in batch mode. They fall into five general categories:

1. *Periodic reports.* Also called *scheduled reports,* these are produced at regular intervals (daily, weekly, monthly, etc.) and show routine information in detailed or summarized form. Examples include sales reports, financial statements, inventory records, and payroll reports.

2. *Demand reports.* Sometimes called *unscheduled reports,* these are produced only when called for (or on demand). Demand reports satisfy known, but not regularly recurring, information needs. They aren't prepared unless a manager makes a specific request. For example, a demand report listing employees' job skills might be requested by the personnel director when a vacancy must be filled.

3. *Exception reports.* These are automatically generated by an MIS when certain exceptional situations occur that require managerial attention. Exception reports are usually triggered by unsatisfactory or unusual conditions, for example, if actual costs are significantly greater than budgeted costs or if production falls below levels that have been predetermined to be acceptable.

4. *Special reports.* These are prepared to satisfy unanticipated informational needs. Special reports are requested as a result of some significant but totally unforeseen turn of events. For example, the discovery of a hazardous substance in a manufacturing process might prompt managers to request a special report listing absenteeism and medical claims by personnel who have been exposed to the substance. Special reports differ from exception reports in that they aren't generated automatically by the MIS.

5. *Predictive reports.* These are prepared using techniques of statistical analysis, simulation, or modeling (see Chapter 10). Predictive reports attempt to forecast future trends. Examples are projections of personnel requirements, estimates of long-term capital needs, and projected financial statements.

Responses to Inquiries

As an alternative to reports, most management information systems also allow *Fast answers* users to submit on-line requests for information, or *inquiries.* Similar to the data base queries described in Chapters 9 and 13, MIS inquiries enable managers to request information directly in interactive fashion. Since, as we'll discuss later in this chapter, a data base system is an essential component of any MIS, addressing questions directly to an MIS is very similar to querying a data base.

Inquiries are answered in a matter of seconds or minutes, as opposed to the longer time periods usually associated with report generation. Even if quick response isn't critical, inquiries are attractive because they allow greater freedom of expression on the part of the MIS user. Since inquiries are usually formulated in nonprocedural query languages (which we discussed in Chapter 9), little or no training is generally needed before managers are submitting requests for information. Inquiry submission allows managers to experiment with different ideas, to follow up interesting answers with additional questions, and to utilize more fully their human capabilities of creativity, organization, analysis, and synthesis.

In contrast to reports, which often take up voluminous amounts of paper, inquiry responses are frequently limited to a size that will comfortably fit on a CRT display screen. Inquiries tend to be quickly formulated questions that can be answered by a few lines or a page or two of displayed text. Sometimes responses will include charts and graphs if the MIS software and hardware have graphics capabilities. If an inquiry is such that it requires a very long or overly specialized response (calling for hard-copy graphs, multiple copies, or wide-paper formats), then a special report would probably have been more appropriate.

Inquiry responses are used primarily to support planning and organizing, although their flexibility makes them applicable to most management functions. One reason that inquiry responses are not generally relied on to support the directing and controlling of activities is that those functions are already well serviced by report generation. Even though managers' use of inquiries is increasing dramatically, it is virtually certain that inquiry responses will never completely replace reports.

The ability to pose follow-up questions interactively is especially beneficial to the planning function. Planning is the least structured of all management functions, which means that managers are rarely able to completely anticipate all of the information that will be required to develop a plan. As plans begin to take shape, it often happens that additional information needs arise. A manager's planning abilities could be seriously impaired if information were available only in report form, or if applicable information were not considered simply because it would take too long to obtain.

In organizing, managers typically review many past and present situations in search of activities similar to those planned for the future. This process is greatly aided by inquiries, which can direct the MIS to search large volumes of data and select those elements that meet certain criteria. For example, a manager at an automobile plant who is organizing the production of a new model can ask the MIS to locate and present all previous cases of, say, front wheel disc brake assembly operations. This type of focused data gathering is extremely difficult and time-consuming to do manually, but quite easy to do via inquiries to an MIS.

COMPONENTS OF AN MIS

What an MIS is made of

It's rather difficult to describe management information systems in clear and unambiguous terms. Systems vary from one organization to another, reflecting different purposes, characteristics, information needs, and resources. We wouldn't expect the MIS of a large bank, for example, to be exactly like that of a major military installation. Also, management information systems are difficult to characterize because they are largely conceptual rather than physical. The information flows, functional relationships, and managerial decision-making processes central to such systems are less tangible than their computer hardware counterparts.

An MIS can't be reduced to a collection of connected computer hardware or an application package. You can't go to your friendly neighborhood computer store and buy a management information system. Unlike a DBMS, an MIS is not a discrete set of specially designed programs that are documented and packaged as a unit. Instead, an MIS consists of both computerized and noncomputerized parts, both hardware and software. The hardware can be almost any combination of those elements already covered in Part 2 of this book: a computer as well as input, storage, output, and communications devices. Consequently, we will say almost nothing about the hardware components of management information systems. We will concentrate on the data management and functional subsystems that make up the typical MIS (see Figure 14.4).

To illustrate these subsystems, we've constructed a six-part case study about the MIS used at Keyboard Koncepts, the fictional firm we introduced in Chapter 8. As you read about each subsystem, the corresponding part of the case study should give substance to the discussion. Although both the company and the MIS are fabricated, the example reflects what is found in the typical manufacturing firm.

The Data Management Subsystem

*Methods of information
storage and use*

The purpose of an MIS is to provide quality information to all three levels of management. Because this information is usually derived from massive quantities of

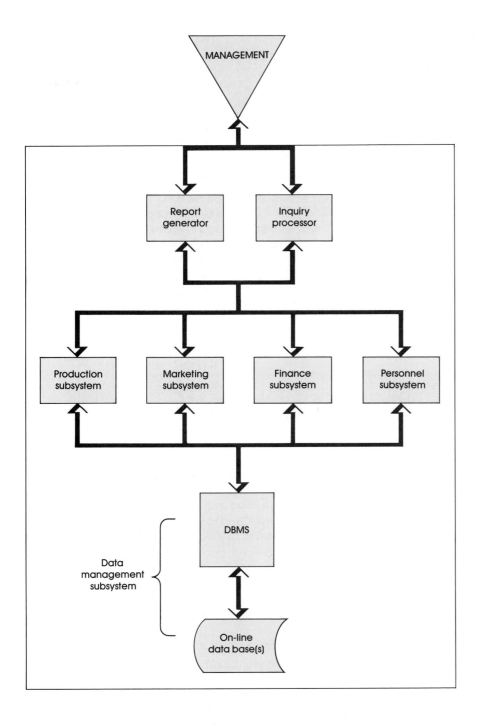

Figure 14.4 Components of a Typical MIS
The conceptual components of a management information system for a typical manufacturing firm.

stored data, the maintenance and use of data bases are central to all the activities of an MIS. Therefore, the data management subsystem of an MIS consists of one or more data bases and a data base management system (see Chapter 13). This subsystem is perhaps the most important component of an MIS because proper data management is vital to the success of any computer-based system.

As a matter of fact, it's not uncommon to confuse the concepts of the MIS and the DBMS; in many instances, these two terms are treated as synonyms. However, even though the two types of systems are clearly related to each other, they are still

TECHNOLOGY CLOSEUP
An MIS for Keyboard Koncepts

Keyboard Koncepts manufactures various models of electronic keyboard for both microcomputers and computer terminals. It has no retail outlets but sells its products to computer manufacturers using a network of sales personnel. It has three warehouses (in New York, Chicago, and Los Angeles) and one factory (in Chicago), where all the keyboards are produced. Keyboard Koncepts has a central computing facility at its corporate headquarters (also in Chicago), which is used by the factory, warehouses, and sales personnel.

In many ways, Keyboard Koncepts is a typical manufacturing company. It advertises, solicits, receives, and fills orders, maintains warehouse inventories, manufactures its products to meet demand, carries out research and development, bills its customers, collects payments, and pays its employees, its suppliers, and its taxes. All these activities are documented in the detailed records maintained by the centralized computer system. Vice-presidents in charge of marketing, finance, and manufacturing (production), along with their subordinate managers, must be able to access these records in order to run the company effectively. The management information system helps them do this.

distinct. A DBMS is concerned with the storage, updating, and retrieval of data; an MIS concentrates instead on the *meaning* of those data. Management information systems obtain appropriate data from data bases and process them to produce information that is meaningful to users. Thus, the DBMS provides the data, and the MIS provides the *meaning* through processing those data. An MIS selects the informational content for inclusion in reports and responses to inquiries; the DBMS provides that content. A DBMS is not the same as an MIS, but it's a central element of one.

Functional Subsystems

An MIS component for each department

There are any number of ways in which systems can be conceptually broken down into subsystems. For example, an organizational system could be divided into subsystems based on the flow of resources: labor, money, and materials. Management information systems, however, are typically viewed as collections of *functional subsystems*. This means that organizational activities (such as those of production or manufacturing, marketing, finance, and personnel) are grouped together into departments, with each department forming a subsystem. Not all organizations exhibit the same functions, of course, but the basic principles of functional organization apply in any case. For example, although a manufacturing firm typically has production, marketing, finance, and personnel subsystems, a governmental agency will have a different set of major departments. The discussion here will take the manufacturing firm as its basis.

Data Management at Keyboard Koncepts

Keyboard Koncepts has a central mainframe computer system, which it uses to maintain a single, fully integrated relational data base system (see Chapter 13). The DBMS includes a nonprocedural query language that lets users ask questions interactively. In addition, the DBMS has a data manipulation language and a report generator that are used by the functional subsystems of the MIS. By organizing its data with such a system, Keyboard Koncepts can realize all the advantages associated with the use of a data base. Since the MIS gets all the data it needs from the DBMS, it is free to concentrate on producing the necessary answers and reports, without maintaining data files itself. The data base system is truly a central element of the MIS for Keyboard Koncepts.

The Production Subsystem

Production, or manufacturing, involves the conversion of resources (inputs) into goods or services (outputs). For example, an automobile manufacturer converts labor, capital, and raw materials into new cars. The most important production activities are

Inventory management ensures that raw materials are on hand when they are needed and that enough finished goods are on hand to meet customers' demands.

Scheduling attempts to achieve the most efficient use of production facilities.

Operations are the processes by which the resources are actually converted into goods.

Engineering is responsible for the design of products and facilities.

Shipping and receiving carry out shipping instructions from the finance department and process invoices from vendors.

Purchasing involves the procurement of resources from suppliers.

Quality control ensures that product standards are being upheld.

The production subsystem of an MIS serves these functions by supplying reports concerning such items as production schedules, inventories, suppliers' bills, customers' orders, forecasts of consumer demand, budgets, product specifications and designs, invoices, prices of materials, and quality control limits.

The production subsystem of the MIS for Keyboard Koncepts provides managers with various reports concerning the conversion of raw materials (keyboard casings, key sets, cords, circuit boards, screws, etc.) into finished products (fully assembled and tested keyboards). Inventory reports list the quantities and locations of both components and assembled keyboards in each of the firm's three warehouses. Production schedule reports show how many finished keyboards are being made each day, week, month, and year. Engineering reports give details about the design and specifications for each keyboard model the company offers. Order reports summarize how many of each type of keyboard will be needed to fill customers' requests. Purchasing reports show what raw materials must be ordered from what suppliers to fulfill production quotas. Finally, quality control reports indicate how successful the assembly line is at turning out keyboards that meet the design specifications.

The Marketing Subsystem

Since the early 1950s, the marketing function has become increasingly important for companies. In very narrow terms, marketing consists of advertising and selling. However, marketing can also be defined as the performance of those business activities that direct the flow of goods from producer to consumer. Thus, it serves the two important functions of satisfying customer needs and accomplishing company objectives. Some of the key activities that come under the heading of marketing are

Market research attempts to find out what the public wants and how much they are willing to pay for it.

Product development is the link between market research and engineering, the translation of consumer preferences into product specifications.

Pricing involves assigning an appropriate, competitive price to each product made by the firm.

Promotion, one of the most important marketing activities, makes the public aware of products through advertising and other means.

Sales management involves the administration of sales personnel.

The marketing subsystem of an MIS supports these activities by providing information on consumer preference surveys, product comparison tests, observations of buying habits, product warranties, competitors' prices, production costs, sales personnel performance ratings, sales budgets, and estimated sales figures.

The Finance Subsystem

The finance function comprises those activities that are concerned with the management of a firm's money. Since computer systems and data-processing techniques have been used in these areas for years, it's not surprising that the finance subsystem is often the most extensive subsystem of an organization's MIS. These are some of the most important finance activities:

Budgeting makes possible managerial planning and control of the firm's financial resources.

Cost accounting involves the determination of where money has actually been spent.

Funds management ensures that enough money is available to meet the firm's ongoing financial obligations while maximizing the return on investments.

Financial accounting is the classification, recording, and summarizing of monetary transactions for investors, creditors, and the government.

Accounts receivable is the set of activities by which customers are billed and their payments processed.

Accounts payable is the set of activities by which payments to vendors for materials are processed.

The finance subsystem of an MIS keeps managers on top of these activities by providing information such as projected cost and income figures, actual expenditures, investment opportunities, interest rates, balance sheets, income statements, and summaries of orders and invoices.

The finance subsystem of the MIS for Keyboard Koncepts is the largest, most heavily used, and most indispensable of its subsystems. It processes the data and generates the reports that are used to manage the firm's financial resources. Cost accounting reports show exactly how much money is spent and where it goes. These reports are extremely important to the managers involved in budgeting for payroll and the purchase of materials and new assembly line equipment. Asset holdings and mar-

ket analysis reports help funds managers to keep Keyboard Koncepts in the black by providing the information needed to ensure that there's enough liquid capital to pay the bills. Financial accounting reports are generated to show investors, creditors, and the IRS how much money Keyboard Koncepts makes and spends. Finally, routine processing for both accounts receivable and accounts payable is completely handled by the finance subsystem of the MIS for Keyboard Koncepts.

The Personnel Subsystem

Large organizations generally operate more economically if they maintain computerized personnel records. An additional benefit is that, when job openings occur, appropriately skilled individuals can often be found among current employees. Activities that fall under the personnel function are

Labor relations is the interface between the firm and its employees.

Personnel actions are such activities as hiring, promoting, keeping track of vacations and sick leave, and administering medical and life insurance programs.

Record maintenance involves the constant updating of all necessary data on all employees.

Payroll is the process by which employees receive their wages.

The personnel subsystem of an MIS supplies information about the above activities in such forms as employee contracts, wage scales, allowable fringe benefits, training provisions, wage rates, tax deductions and withholdings, paychecks, earnings statements, and payroll summary reports.

 ## DECISION SUPPORT SYSTEMS

Helping management make decisions

One of the most recent developments in computer-based information systems attempts to specifically address the decision-making needs of the various levels of management. A **decision support system (DSS)** helps managers by giving them quick answers to interactively asked "what if" questions. Decision support systems provide a basis for judging situations analytically; they do so by applying statistical and mathematical models and simulation. Decision support systems are

Like most companies with a lot of employees, Keyboard Koncepts has computerized its personnel operations. Records concerning the work history, job performance, skills, education, pay rate, accrued vacation time, benefits, and hours worked of each employee are kept in the centralized data base (subject to strict security measures). This information is used to process the payroll automatically and issue regular paychecks. The personnel subsystem of the MIS produces summary reports from these records and also helps to match up current employees with new positions that have opened up within the firm. By ensuring that payroll is accurately and rapidly processed and by pinpointing advancement opportunities for people already within the company, the personnel subsystem benefits both Keyboard Koncepts and its employees.

intended to *help* managers make decisions, not to make decisions for managers. Furthermore, decision support systems are generally oriented toward dealing with relatively unstructured problems such as those concerning new products, policies, company mergers, and acquisitions.

Decision support systems build on as well as complement management information systems. Typically on-line and fully interactive, decision support systems primarily are designed for problems for which little or no precedent exists. Management information systems, on the other hand, are generally oriented toward collecting, organizing, and summarizing information to help managers deal with well-structured problems (such as where to locate plants and warehouses or the preparation of budgets, cost analyses, accounts payable, and payroll).

To be more specific, decision support systems are usually characterized by ten essential qualities:

1. *A broad-based approach to the support of decision making.* Decision support systems must directly relate to the goals and objectives that form the basis of corporate strategies. By providing flexible financial planning and budgeting models, for example, decision support systems encompass a broader view of organizations than management information systems typically do.
2. *Interaction between person and computer in which the person retains control over the decision-making process.* The DSS is only a tool to be employed by managers in evaluating alternatives so that effective decisions can be made.
3. *Support for all types of decisions.* Although decision support systems tend to be directed toward unstructured problem-solving, they can also be used for well-structured problems.
4. *Utilization of appropriate statistical and mathematical models.* Decision support systems apply abstract models to approximate the real world so that inferences can be made about the effects of various courses of action.

5. *Output directed to all levels of organizational personnel.* Effective decision support systems provide decision-making aids to managers at all levels, as well as to other operating employees.
6. *Interactive query capabilities.* Decision support systems must allow on-line access so that users can obtain information on request.
7. *Integrated subsystems.* All related functions must be well integrated into the overall system to allow management to retrieve and manipulate information for decision making.
8. *A comprehensive data base.* As with management information systems, a complete data base and a DBMS are central to decision support systems.
9. *Ease of use.* The hallmark of an effective decision support system is its user-friendliness. Decision support systems should be natural extensions of the users' decision-making processes.
10. *Adaptability.* An effective decision support system must allow for change over time. It should be a highly adaptive system that not only helps users to confront new problems but can be modified to accommodate changing conditions.

The real key to the difference between decision support systems and management information systems is the second characteristic listed above. This interaction between person and computer, or the *human/machine interface* as it's sometimes called, represents a step beyond the typical management information system in that it allows users to react immediately to the output. The decision maker can interact with the DSS by getting answers to a series of "what if" questions. That is, the DSS is geared toward fostering learning, creativity, and evaluation. More specifically, an MIS primarily helps managers quantify aspects of a problem, solve the problem, and produce output to aid in the decision-making process. In contrast, a DSS allows the decision maker to look inside a problem, discover previously hidden aspects, isolate certain parameters, and ask a series of "what if" questions involving these selected parameters. This interplay between decision maker and computerized system helps to uncover the essence of problems and often yields new ways of arriving at answers.

The following example should help to make clear the basic difference between the typical MIS and DSS. A certain manager depends on an MIS in scheduling and controlling the day-to-day operations of a manufacturing plant. Although the system generally works well for these routine planning and controlling purposes, there is a problem in that special orders are frequently received. These special orders request relatively small quantities of items that must be custom-designed and manufactured. Relying on the MIS, the plant manager has little choice but to decline these orders if the factory is busy because it would be too difficult to find out how each one would affect the existing production schedules. With a DSS, however, the manager can quickly and easily use a mathematical scheduling model to work out on a CRT terminal the effect of accommodating special orders. The human/machine interface makes it possible to establish the feasibility of accepting special orders by asking "what if we try to handle those orders?" Via the mathematical model, the manager is able to find out if shipping dates for regular orders can still be met and if the special orders can be profitably filled. Also, the DSS makes it possible to offer counterproposals to customers who place special orders, for example, if higher prices must be charged or if a later shipping date will be necessary. In this example, the DSS gives the plant manager complete control over the acceptance of special orders, an option that would be impossible with the typical MIS.

CAREERS IN TECHNOLOGY
Project Leader

Job Description A project leader (also known as a project director or project manager) oversees programming projects from inception through completion, prepares and enforces schedules for those projects, and organizes training sessions. Other duties include preparing budgets for the programming department and periodic progress reports for upper-level management. This is a first-line managerial position with substantial supervisory responsibility. A project leader in a large company may be responsible for supervising the work of up to 30 programmers or systems analysts, making sure that projects stay on schedule and within budget.

Qualifications A B.A. in business administration, with a solid background in programming, business systems analysis, and accounting, is required. A project leader isn't a programmer, but must have sufficient skills to understand the work being done and to propose alternative ways to increase efficiency. Supervisory and managerial skills of communication, leadership, and organization are vital to a project leader's successful interaction with users, management, programmers, systems analysts, and operators.

Outlook This job market is highly competitive, in part because outside applicants must compete with experienced workers within a company who are moving up the supervisory/managerial ladder. The competitiveness is also due to some extent to the growing number of graduates in business administration, who are seeking jobs in an already crowded field. Excellent credentials and relevant experience are a big help, and a personal contact in the industry can be invaluable.

ISSUES IN TECHNOLOGY

In this chapter, we have naturally emphasized managers' use of information. However, the most important resource with which managers work is people. Most managers would agree that dealing with and motivating employees is a major part of their job. A great deal of qualitative information is gathered by managers through interacting with their subordinates. Does the availability of an effective MIS encourage managers to spend less time in such interactions? Might a good MIS therefore create managers who are *less* in touch with the organizational atmosphere? What do you think?

DESIGN AND IMPLEMENTATION OF MIS AND DSS

You have probably realized by now that designing and implementing management information and decision support systems is a tremendous challenge for systems analysts. The many issues that must be addressed and the difficult problems that must be solved to develop an effective MIS or DSS have been the subject of many recent articles and books. To give you an idea of what some of the important design and implementation questions are, we'll briefly consider a few specific ones.

Planning the MIS or DSS

Should a top-down or bottom-up design approach be followed? In Chapter 8, we defined top-down design as a hierarchical, divide-and-conquer approach. In the design of an MIS or DSS, this means first studying organizational goals and the types of problems managers face to develop a picture of how information flows through the firm. From this, the design specifications can be developed. Top-down design has the advantage of being a sensible way to solve such a big problem because it facilitates the integration of the various system elements. The disadvantage is that it's difficult to define goals and decision-making activities precisely enough so they can be translated fairly directly into detailed design specifications; the possible result is the building of an expensive yet ineffective system. The bottom-up approach to design, on the other hand, begins with low-level, day-to-day activities like processing transactions and maintaining the data base. Higher-level modules are then built and added on to support managerial functions such as planning, controlling, and decision making. The advantage of this approach is that smaller pieces of the whole are developed in detail, minimizing the likelihood of developing a complex but inadequate system. The disadvantage of bottom-up design is that it's difficult to produce the overview type of information managers need, when systems are built up starting from low-level operational activities. Consequently, most systems designers use some combination of the two approaches.

How many data bases should be created? The designer of an MIS or DSS is faced with the problem of deciding on the organization of the data base(s). Should there be a single data base for all three levels of management, or should each level have its own? Or, should there be a separate data base for each functional subsystem? Since each management level has different information needs, it may be justifiable to have separate data bases to support the production of strategic, tactical, and operational information. Different functional subsystems also need different information, although there is usually a lot of sharing of data among departments. How the data items themselves are arranged is determined by the DBMS that is to be used, but the nature and number of data bases for the MIS or DSS must be decided by the designer.

How can external information be incorporated into the system? As we've already pointed out, the higher the managerial level, the greater is the need for information about matters external to the organization. Internal information is produced by the organization itself, so incorporating it in a system is much less problematic. The systems designer is responsible for determining the methods by which information from external sources can be accessed and brought into the firm's data bases. It may be necessary to arrange for the purchase of machine-readable data from outside organizations or for direct access to outside data bases.

ADVANTAGES OF MIS AND DSS

Although they are usually expensive and often difficult to implement, management information systems and decision support systems offer several significant advantages to managers who use them:

How an MIS or DSS can help

- *Helping to diagnose problems and recognize opportunities.* By providing them with current internal and external information, these systems better equip managers to catch potentially troublesome conditions early and to spot ways to further organizational goals.

- *Saving time.* By summarizing mountains of data, these systems enable managers to spend more time performing high-level activities such as planning and organizing and less time searching through irrelevant material.
- *Clarifying complex relationships.* By providing quality information, these systems can help managers evaluate possible alternatives in complicated situations. For example, complex economic relationships can be more easily identified using these systems, which better equips managers to make their firms competitive in the marketplace.
- *Helping to implement plans.* By providing up-to-the-minute information, these systems help managers direct and control activities so as to implement their plans.
- *Centralizing decision making.* These systems help to centralize decision making and thus authority by providing timely information that is effectively summarized.

SUMMARY

What Is an MIS?

A management information system is an organized means of providing managers with the information they need to do their jobs effectively.

What Is Management?

Management's job consists of converting resources in order to accomplish some desired results and doing so profitably.

What Managers Do Managers basically plan, organize, staff, direct, and control.

Levels of Management Management is traditionally organized into three levels: top management is concerned with long-range plans; middle management is concerned with short-term plans; and first-line management is concerned with controlling day-to-day activities.

Information Needs of Managers

Without information, managers cannot effectively do their jobs. Different management levels have different information needs.

Strategic Information for Top Management Strategic information helps top management make long-range plans and consists primarily of external information, along with some internal information.

Tactical Information for Middle Management Tactical information helps middle management make short-term plans and implement the strategic plans made by top management and consists of fairly equal amounts of internal and external, detailed and summarized information.

Operational Information for First-Line Management Operational information is used by first-line management to control the structured, repetitive, day-to-day activities of the organization.

Characteristics of Useful Information To be valuable, information must be accurate, timely, relevant, complete, and concise.

Output of Information Management information systems generally provide output in the form of printed reports (periodic, demand, exception, special, or predictive) or on-line inquiry responses.

Components of an MIS

An MIS consists of both hardware and software.

The Data Management Subsystem   Central to all the activities of an MIS are one or more data bases and a DBMS.

Functional Subsystems   Management information systems are typically viewed as collections of functional subsystems, which correspond to organizational departments (for example, production, marketing, finance, and personnel).

Decision Support Systems

Decision support systems help managers by giving them quick answers to interactively asked "what if" questions.

Design and Implementation of MIS and DSS

Issues that must be addressed in planning an MIS or DSS include whether a top-down or bottom-up approach should be used, how many data bases should be created, and how external information can be incorporated.

Advantages of MIS and DSS

MIS and DSS help to diagnose problems and recognize opportunities, save time, clarify complex relationships, implement plans, and centralize decision making.

COMPUTER CONCEPTS ▬▬▬

As an extra review of the chapter, try defining the following terms. If you have trouble with any of them, refer to the page number listed.

management information system (MIS) 403	tactical information 408 operational information	decision support system (DSS) 418
strategic information 408	408	

REVIEW QUESTIONS ▬▬▬

1. What is the purpose of an MIS?
2. In general, what do managers do?
3. What distinguishes the three levels of management?
4. How do managers' information needs vary as a function of their organizational level?
5. What characterizes useful information?
6. What are the two basic forms of MIS output?
7. List and briefly describe the five types of MIS reports.
8. What advantages do inquiry responses offer?
9. What component of all management information systems is perhaps the most important?
10. List the functional subsystems that would be found in an MIS for a typical manufacturing firm and briefly describe what they do.
11. What are some of the questions that must be considered in planning an MIS or DSS?
12. How can MIS and DSS help managers?
13. What are the ten essential characteristics of decision support systems?
14. What's the basic difference between an MIS and a DSS?

A SHARPER FOCUS

Now that you've completed this chapter, you should be able to answer the following questions about the chapter opening.

1. Is it absolutely necessary that managers learn to gather their own information using a personal computer? What are some possible advantages and disadvantages of such an approach?
2. Is the use of an MIS via a personal computer more appropriate for certain levels of management than for others? Which ones, and why?
3. Does the information obtained by managers through the use of personal computers fulfill the characteristics of useful information given in this chapter?
4. Is it possible to have a true DSS that runs on a personal computer?

PROJECTS

1. Managers encounter two basic types of decision-making situations. The first type is routine in nature and recurs regularly, and is often called a *programmed decision situation*. The other type is nonroutine, nonrecurring, and might be encountered only once, and is referred to as a *nonprogrammed decision situation*. Investigate how management information systems and decision support systems can be used to assist managers in both these types of situations. Which system might be better for each type of situation, and why?
2. Management information systems are usually identified with large-scale computer systems. Consequently, many people think that an organization must own a mainframe computer to have an MIS. Investigate the feasibility of an MIS for an organization with a small computer. Is an MIS workable in such an environment? Do any management information systems exist for small computers? What might be the problem (if any) of using smaller computers?
3. Investigate some large businesses and organizations to find out if they have an MIS. Periodicals like *Computerworld* and *MIS Weekly* might be good places to start looking. Also, you can ask any people you know who work for such organizations. Write a report listing the organizations you uncover, and include whatever details you obtain about their systems.
4. Try to become familiar with a computer-based information system. Perhaps your school or company has such a system. Consider what would happen if a computer wasn't used in that particular case. What sacrifices would have to be made in the types of information that would be available? What time delays would result? Be as specific as possible.
5. What role has the developing computer technology played in the recognition of data as a corporate resource? Write an essay expressing your views.
6. "Management information systems often fail because the typical manager prefers face-to-face communication with people to dealing with the output of a machine." Do you agree or disagree with this statement? Defend your position.
7. Many people believe that management information and decision support systems are much too rigid, that they don't alert managers to trends, one-of-a-kind situations, or the possible need to change organizational goals and objectives. What do you think about this opinion? Support your statements.

Application Perspective

Buying a New Sweater

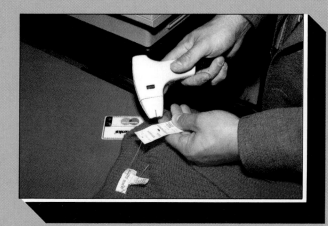

(1) You select a nice sweater and bring it to the check-out counter, where the clerk uses a wand to read the item number and price from its tag into the computer. Your credit card is inserted in the terminal, and the information is read and transmitted to the computer.

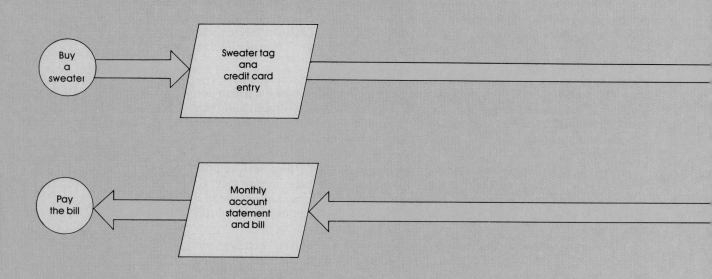

Buy a sweater → Sweater tag and credit card entry

Pay the bill ← Monthly account statement and bill

(4) In some places, the money to pay for the sweater can be immediately deducted from your checking account and credited to the store's account directly from the POS terminal. Most frequently, though, the computer generates a monthly bill showing each of your purchases, the total amount due, and the various available credit options. You then send off a check (which starts the sequence of data-processing transactions represented in the Application Perspective at the end of Part 1).

(2) The status of your credit card account is okayed. Also, your card number is checked against a list of those reported lost or stolen. Appropriate information from your credit card and from the sweater's tag is printed on the sales slip. The clerk doesn't have to enter anything manually.

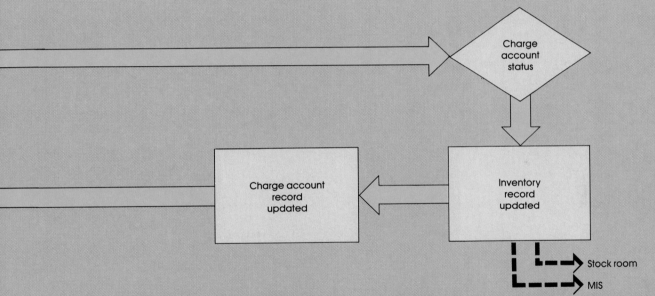

Charge account status

Charge account record updated

Inventory record updated

Stock room

MIS

(3) Information from the sweater's tag is used automatically to reduce the inventory level of that type of sweater. A program prints a message on the terminal when more of those sweaters need to be brought out onto the floor. Records are also kept that automatically trigger reordering of goods from suppliers. In addition, reports to management are generated, showing how well or how poorly different items are selling. The information from your credit card and from the tag causes the necessary billing data to be generated to update your account.

Part 5

THE MIRACULOUS MICRO

Microcomputers and microprocessors—today, in the world of computer technology, the maxim seems to be the smaller the better. If computers still relied on vacuum tubes, the personal computer that fits on a desk would fill a house and some of its backyard as well. But this isn't the case, thanks to the developments in miniaturization during the third generation (which we described in Chapter 2). Today, the microprocessor has made possible not only computers the size of phone books but such novel applications as singing greeting cards and robot helpers.

In keeping with its subject, Part 5 contains a lot of information within a small space. Chapter 15 is a guide to the personal computer, and Chapter 16 is an overview of contemporary microprocessor applications. You'll come away from this part well versed in the capabilities of this small but mighty modern workhorse.

15

The Personal Computer

IN THIS CHAPTER

FOCUS ON . . . THE ON-LINE FAMILY

What started as a childhood fascination with the flashing, beeping computers of science-fiction movies has evolved into a practical way of life for Fran De l'Aune. At last count, she, her husband, Bill, and their five children were sharing their big Victorian house in southern Connecticut with no fewer than nine personal computers—technology so integral to their daily routine that it's as though the family were living not in 1984 but in 2000.

The De l'Aunes depend on their microcomputers, acquired over the last four years, for everything from their growing computer-consulting business to their home-based schooling program for the two youngest children. So far, the De l'Aunes have invested nearly $37,000 in computers—four Apples, two Timex/Sinclairs, a Morrow Designs, a Texas Instruments TI and a NEC, plus accessories ("peripherals"). The micros are ensconced on all three floors of the family's 14-room house. Next to the china cupboard, for example, there is a computer in the pantry. The master bedroom holds another, along with a large heavy-duty printer. There is even a micro inside the cabinet of a gutted upright piano, in a cozy room complete with rocking chair.

It was Fran's infatuation with technology that sparked the purchase of the family's first computer in 1979. But beyond being captivated by the machine's "sexy" allure, she planned to give the children, who now range in age from 6 to 17, an educational advantage and the computer-programming skills to help earn their college tuition. . . .

But in the beginning, things didn't go quite as Fran had envisioned. The children weren't using the computer because Bill, ironically, had taken it over. . . .

The only solution was to buy a second computer—for the children. But soon Fran herself became heavily involved in learning programming, and two machines just weren't enough. So another micro was added. More computers were installed in 1980, shortly after Bill accepted a free-lance assignment to write a series of programs for the Veterans' Administration. . . .

The VA project generated a deluge of word-of-mouth referrals, and by the following year, Fran began to take on programming jobs, too. With an ever-expanding client roster, Fran officially launched Rochel Consulting Service in 1982. . . . Work is shared by Fran, who is president, Bill and son William, Jr., 17.

Another major move that brought more computers into the household was the decision almost two years ago to educate the youngest children, 11-year-old Michael and 6-year-old Christian (known as Chrissy), at home. "I'm disappointed in the school system and had always considered home education," says Fran. "I thought I could do at least as good a job, if not better. Plus we wanted to give our kids the advantage of computers. They're coming into the schools very slowly, and I saw an opportunity to jump the gun."

As far as Fran is concerned, virtually no one's too young to tackle a computer. Chrissy, 2 years old and scarcely out of diapers when the first Apple arrived at the De l'Aune home, quickly began turning on the machine and running programs on his own.

According to a number of predictions, more than half of all homes in the United States will have some sort of microcomputer by 1990. These machines will be used for figuring taxes, storing recipes, keeping track of household finances, doing homework, playing games, shopping, voting, and working. The amazing microprocessor chip was the start of this boom. The development of an 8-bit microprocessor chip, the Intel 8080, led to the introduction in 1975 of microcomputer systems for the hobbyist market. The first commercially available personal computer was the Altair 8800, originally sold in kit form for about $400 by MITS, a small electronics firm in Albuquerque, New Mexico. However, MITS was unable to survive in the marketplace against the onslaught of mass-market companies such as Tandy–Radio Shack, Apple, and Commodore Business Machines, which, by 1978, had developed their own less hobbyist-oriented personal computers and captured most of the market. Soon, even established mainframe manufacturers such as IBM, Digital Equipment Corporation, Burroughs, and Hewlett-Packard entered the field, and today it seems that a great many firms either make microcomputers or want to. The personal computer is proving to be an indispensable invention; this chapter discusses its impact and its many applications.

WHAT IS A PERSONAL COMPUTER?

The Center for Futures Research at the University of Southern California defines a **personal computer** to be "an essentially stand-alone, general-purpose computer system, containing one or more microprocessors, which is purchased or operated by an individual or small group of individuals (say, two to ten)." The definition goes on to say that personal computers are used interactively for many purposes, including recreation, education, and business. An important characteristic of such systems is that the cost is low enough that an individual can justify purchasing one on the basis of personally received benefits, financial, recreational, educational, or other. Thus, just about any general-purpose microcomputer system that sells for less than $15,000 can be considered to be a personal computer.

The basic elements that make up a microcomputer, or personal computer, system are essentially no different than those that make up minicomputer or mainframe computer systems; personal computers just have less computing power, or smaller memories, or fewer attachable accessories. (Interestingly, many of today's personal computers have more computing power than did the mainframes of 10 or 15 years ago.) Let's look a bit more closely at the hardware components, different types of personal computers, and the most commonly used software for personal computer systems. We've covered the topics of hardware and software in general in Parts 2 and 3 of this book, but now we'll take a more focused view of some of their aspects in the context of personal computer systems.

HARDWARE COMPONENTS OF PERSONAL COMPUTER SYSTEMS

The characteristic parts

Discussing microcomputer hardware is somewhat like discussing stereo or home video equipment. Novices are confronted with a bewildering assortment of models, components, specifications, terms, and abbreviations. It's common to be intimidated or to feel hopelessly lost. However, when it comes right down to it, the average computer user doesn't really need to know all that much. Of course, any sophisticated electronic system like a microcomputer will have many complex and unfamiliar parts, yet the typical user only has to be concerned with a few of the most important, characteristic ones. These are the microprocessor, primary storage or memory, secondary storage, the interfaces, the keyboard, display devices, printers, and other peripherals.

The Microprocessor

The microprocessor, the CPU on a single silicon chip, is the "brain" of the microcomputer. Since it does the calculating, logical decision making, and controlling of the processing, the microprocessor is the major determinant of the computing power and speed of the system. Although several types of microprocessors are commonly used for microcomputers, they can be categorized fairly straightforwardly according to word size. In Chapter 3, we said that a computer's word size is equal to the number of bits that are most often manipulated and stored as a unit. So, for example, an 8-bit microprocessor has a word size of 8 bits and handles data in 8-bit chunks. Virtually all of the microcomputers sold today utilize 8-bit, 16-bit, 24-bit, or 32-bit microprocessors.

In general, the larger its word size, the faster, more powerful, more complex, and more expensive is the microprocessor. By manipulating larger chunks of data, a microprocessor can do more work in a given amount of time, but the hardware needed to back it up is also necessarily more sophisticated. We don't have the space in this book to provide detailed discussions of all the microprocessors found in microcomputers, but a few of the most commonly used chips are the following:

Commonly used chips

Zilog Z80. This 8-bit microprocessor, one of the most widely used, is a direct descendant of the Intel 8080 chip used in the first microcomputers. The Zilog Z80 is used in some Kaypro, Tandy–Radio Shack, North Star, Epson, and DEC microcomputers.

MOS Technology 6502. This 8-bit chip, although not as powerful in some respects as the Zilog Z80, has been used in some popular and economical microcomputers produced by Apple, Commodore, and Atari.

Intel 8086/8088 family. These 16-bit microprocessors have conquered the microcomputer world since the 8088 was chosen by IBM in 1980 for its original Personal Computer model (see Figure 15.1). The chips that make up this family are similar to each other in many ways, differing mainly in speed and how many bytes of data at a time are transferred to and from the outside environment. In addition to IBM, companies that use these chips in their computers include Columbia, Compaq, Corona, DEC, Eagle, Grid, Hewlett-Packard, Sanyo, Sharp, Texas Instruments, Wang, and Zenith. (The 24-bit Intel 80286 microprocessor is an advanced member of the 8086/8088 family and is used in the powerful IBM Personal Computer AT.)

Motorola 68000. This 32-bit microprocessor is a very fast and powerful chip that may eventually give the Intel 8086/8088 family serious competition. The Motorola 68000 is found in Apple's user-friendly Macintosh, as well as in new machines from Atari, Commodore, Hewlett-Packard, Sinclair, Cromemco, Altos, and Pyramid.

Figure 15.1 A Popular Microprocessor Chip

This 16-bit microprocessor chip, the Intel 8088, is one of the most popular CPUs for microcomputers. It's used in the IBM Personal Computer as well as a host of IBM-compatible machines.

In addition to the main microprocessor, some microcomputers contain a second microprocessor chip to perform specialized tasks. Such chips are called **coprocessors** and are often employed for mathematical calculations involving floating-point numbers (also called real numbers; see Chapter 3). For example, owners of IBM Personal Computers can purchase and install an optional Intel 8087 Math Coprocessor chip to enable their machines to more quickly perform such calculations.

Primary Storage

Built-in RAM and ROM

In Chapter 3, we explained that random access memory (RAM) is used for computer primary storage because data kept at any location can be directly read or written in the same amount of time. We also said that read-only memory (ROM) is a type of nonvolatile storage that is written to only once, usually when it is manufactured. After being written, the data stored in ROM can only be retrieved; it cannot be altered. Most microcomputers have primary storage composed of both RAM and ROM semiconductor chips.

RAM

A computer's capacity to hold programs and data is measured by the amount of RAM it has. You'll recall that the amount of RAM is usually expressed in units of 1024 bytes, called kilobytes and abbreviated K. The more RAM a computer has, the larger the programs it can run and the greater the quantities of data it can handle without having to access secondary storage. Thus, a microcomputer's maximum RAM is a good indication of its power and speed. The maximum amount of RAM a microcomputer can utilize is directly dependent on what microprocessor was installed and what operating system is used. For example, the Kaypro 10 microcomputer with an 8-bit Zilog Z80 microprocessor running the CP/M operating system (see Chapter 11) can utilize a maximum of 64K RAM. As another example, the IBM Personal Computer AT with a 24-bit Intel 80286 microprocessor can utilize as much as 640K of RAM if it's running the MS-DOS operating system. If it's running the XENIX operating system (a version of UNIX), however, the AT can utilize up to 3 megabytes (3000K) of RAM. As you can see, today's personal computers exhibit a wide range of RAM capacities, from about one kilobyte in the smallest hand-held models to several megabytes in the more powerful desktop ones.

ROM

As we've said, ROM chips are manufactured with data permanently written in each memory location. Microcomputers may utilize these chips to store parts of operating systems, entire operating systems, built-in language interpreters, or other specialized and frequently used permanent programs. Since ROM chips are inexpensive, simple, nonvolatile, and fast, they are especially well suited for use in microcomputer systems. Most microcomputers contain one or more ROM chips as part of their primary storage. For example, the IBM Personal Computer AT uses a 64K ROM chip to store fundamental input/output routines, some hardware self-testing routines, and a complete BASIC interpreter.

Secondary Storage

Because RAM is wiped clean every time the power is switched off, some type of secondary storage is a necessary part of every microcomputer system. In Chapter 5, we covered in detail the most commonly used secondary storage devices. Microcomputers typically employ one or more of the following types of secondary storage: cassette tapes, ROM cartridges, floppy disks, and hard disks.

Tapes, cartridges, and disks

Cassette Tapes

Some inexpensive personal computers designed for home use utilize ordinary cassette tape recorders to store programs and data on tapes. The use of cassette tapes as a secondary storage medium was much more common in the early days of personal computing when floppy disk drives were rather expensive; cassette tape storage is gradually being phased out. Although such tapes are quite inexpensive, they are also very slow, must be sequentially accessed, and have a limited capacity. Consequently, most contemporary microcomputers are equipped with floppy disk drives, even though many still have the capability to utilize cassette tapes for storage. For example, the Atari 1200XL, the Commodore 64, and even the IBM Personal Computer can use cassette tape recorders as secondary storage devices.

ROM Cartridges

Some microcomputers use ROM cartridges for the secondary storage of such application programs as games, word processors, and electronic spreadsheets. Although ROM cartridges are inexpensive and fast, and are almost impossible to illegally copy, they provide users with little flexibility since their contents cannot be changed. You'll remember from Chapter 5 that ROM cartridges are small plastic boxes that house one or more ROM chips on which are permanently written programs. The cartridge is simply inserted into a slot in the computer, and the program is activated by turning on the machine or by typing in a special command. Microcomputers that use ROM cartridges are usually machines intended for home use, for example, the Atari 800XL.

Floppy Disks

Floppy disk drives, which we discussed in Chapter 5, are the most common secondary storage device for microcomputers. Floppy disks are the most widely used medium for storing programs and data, as well as the primary medium for the sharing, distribution, and transfer of prewritten software. The most common sizes used in microcomputers are the standard $5\frac{1}{4}$-inch diskette and the $3\frac{1}{2}$-inch microfloppy. Although some microcomputers (such as the Commodore 64) have external floppy disk drives, many machines (the IBM Personal Computer for one) now come with at least one built in.

Hard Disks

Hard disk (or Winchester disk) drives, as we mentioned in Chapter 5, have become increasingly popular for microcomputer systems. In fact, many of the more expensive and sophisticated models (such as the IBM Personal Computer AT) are sold with a built-in hard disk drive as standard equipment. As the cost of hard disk systems has decreased, manufacturers have been quick to take advantage of their great speed and storage capacity. Many microcomputer models not originally designed to employ hard disks can now be modified by add-on Winchester disk systems (internal or external). An internal hard disk drive (and the printed circuit board that controls it) can directly replace an existing floppy disk drive, increasing the microcomputer's on-line secondary storage capacity by 30 times or more. By having both floppy and hard disk drives, the microcomputer becomes an extremely powerful and easy-to-use machine. The most common storage capacities for microcomputer hard disk systems are 5, 10, and 20 megabytes.

Interfaces

Connections to the outside world

An **interface** is a connection between a computer's CPU and a piece of equipment operated under its control. Such pieces of equipment, or *peripheral units*, perform

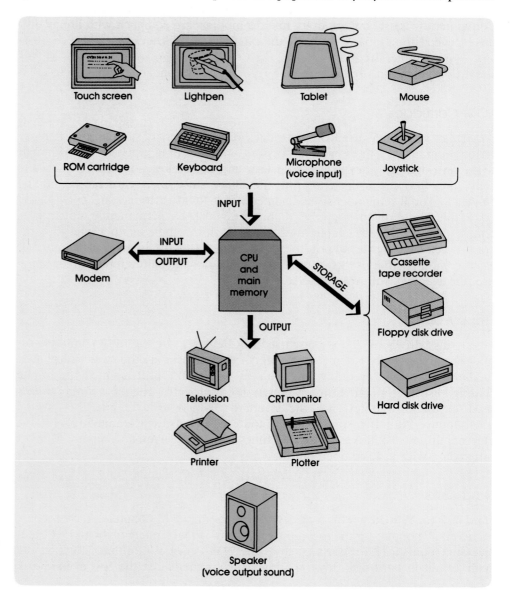

Figure 15.2 Interfaces

Interfaces make it possible to connect a wide variety of peripheral units to a microcomputer.

input, output, and storage functions. Disk drives, keyboards, monitors, printers, plotters, modems, and graphic input devices are all examples of peripheral units commonly connected to microcomputers. In Figure 15.2, the interfaces between the peripheral units and the CPU are symbolized by arrows. All microcomputers marketed today have the capability of utilizing at least some of the devices pictured in Figure 15.2. The desirability of general interfaces and the versatility that they afford are apparent. What isn't so obvious is just how such a wide range of different devices can be connected to the same computer. Three hardware components of the microcomputer—the bus, the serial interface, and the parallel interface—make it possible.

The Bus

A **bus** is a group of wires that connect all of the various internal and external components of a computer system to its CPU (see Figure 15.3). This group of wires is divided into three subgroups: address lines, data lines, and control lines. Address

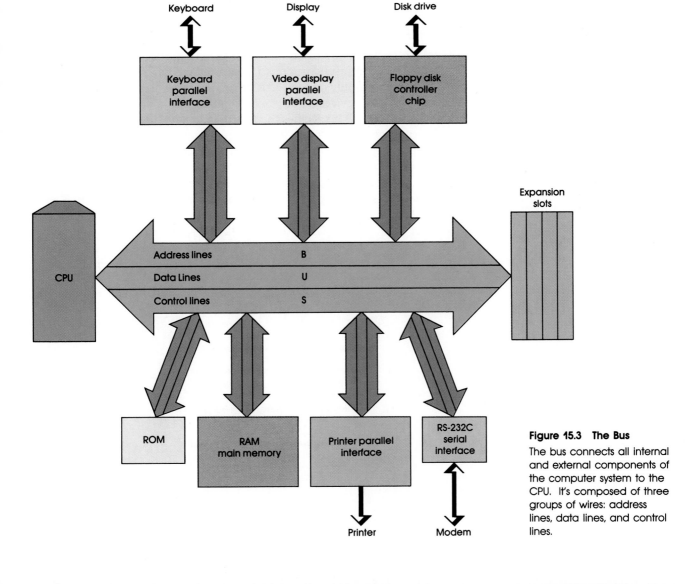

Figure 15.3 The Bus

The bus connects all internal and external components of the computer system to the CPU. It's composed of three groups of wires: address lines, data lines, and control lines.

lines carry signals indicating which memory locations are to be read from or written to. Data lines carry instructions and data to and from primary memory. Control lines convey such things as which operation (read or write) is to be performed in memory.

In many microcomputers, the bus is accessible to a series of connectors, or **expansion slots**, that accept plug-in circuit boards with extra components. The IBM Personal Computer AT, for example, has eight such expansion slots that allow users to add boards containing additional disk controllers, more RAM, or extra serial and parallel interfaces or boards controlling color graphics monitors, modems, or a host of other optional hardware devices.

Some microcomputers have all their components arranged on a number of circuit boards that plug into a set of closely spaced, identical slots. A set of slots like this, in which the bus has been incorporated, is known as a **motherboard**. Such a design is what identifies the *S-100 bus* family of microcomputers, all of which utilize a standard bus of 100 wires with predefined functional and electrical characteristics. The Altair 8800, the first commercially available microcomputer, was an S-100 bus computer, as are contemporary microcomputers made by CompuPro, Cromemco, and North Star.

The Serial Interface

A **serial interface** transmits bytes of data from the computer to some peripheral unit one bit at a time in an asynchronous fashion, as we described in Chapter 7. Serial interfaces are commonly used to connect computers to modems, printers, and graphic input/output devices. The *RS-232C standard* is a serial interface used with many microcomputers. It specifies the functions and voltage levels of 25 lines attached to pins on a plug. Since the RS-232C interface is designed for the serial movement of data, only one wire is actually used to move the data bits in each direction. Some of the other lines are used to send **handshaking signals**, electrical impulses that are sent back and forth between computer and peripheral unit indicating readiness to send or receive data. One of the lines is always used as a ground (electrical reference) line to carry the computer's signal that it is about to transmit a byte of data. All 25 wires of the RS-232C standard are rarely used by any one device; many are left open for future applications. Figure 15.4 shows how a computer and a modem are connected with an RS-232C serial interface.

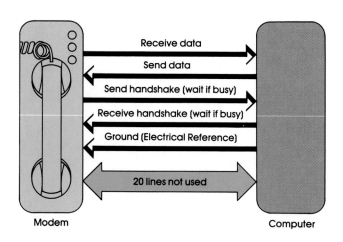

Figure 15.4 A Serial Interface

A serial interface transmits bytes of data a single bit at a time. The most common type of serial interface used with microcomputers is the RS-232C standard, whose 25 lines can be used as shown here to connect a computer and a modem.

Receive data

Send data

Send handshake (wait if busy)

Receive handshake (wait if busy)

Ground (Electrical Reference)

20 lines not used

Modem

Computer

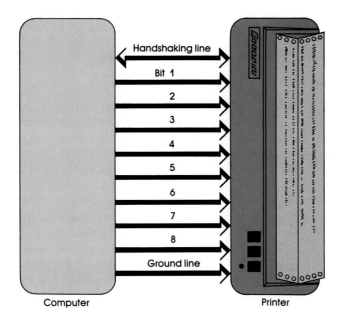

Figure 15.5   A Parallel Interface
Parallel interfaces transmit data one byte at a time and are commonly used as shown here to connect a printer to a microcomputer. Note that ten lines are required to send data in parallel: a ground line, a handshaking line, and a line for each bit in a byte.

The Parallel Interface

A **parallel interface** transmits data from the computer to some peripheral device one byte at a time. Eight bits are sent simultaneously, with a single wire carrying each bit. Parallel interfaces, most commonly used to connect printers to microcomputers, work much faster than serial interfaces, but are also usually more expensive. Ten lines are needed to send data in parallel: one for each of the eight bits in a byte, a ground line, and another handshaking line. Figure 15.5 shows the connection of a computer and a printer with a parallel interface.

Two commonly used parallel interfaces are the *Centronics standard* and the *IEEE-488 standard*. (The IEEE, or Institute for Electrical and Electronic Engineers, is the principal professional society for electronic engineers.) The more widely adopted Centronics interface is based on the connector used in the printers manufactured by Centronics Data Computer Corporation. All of the models of the IBM Personal Computer family, for example, use an 8-bit Centronics standard parallel interface to connect to the dot matrix IBM Graphics Printer. The IEEE-488 interface, although used as a connection between a computer and a printer, is more often used to connect laboratory equipment and instruments to a computer. It is more complex and more versatile than the Centronics interface.

The Keyboard

An essential component of any personal computer is the keyboard—it's the primary means by which the user inputs data and tells the computer what to do. Most keyboards have all the alphabetic, numeric, and mathematical symbols and punctuation marks found on ordinary typewriters, with the exception that some very small or inexpensive personal computers may not have lowercase letters. The similarities among keyboards end there, however, since virtually every personal computer model has a keyboard that is in some way significantly different from

The primary means of user input

those of its rivals. Often, there may not even be consistency among the keyboards of different models from the same manufacturer. IBM, for example, uses different keyboards for some members of its Personal Computer line.

Keyboard Construction

An important consideration concerning personal computer keyboards is the type of construction. A small, inexpensive system is likely to have a touch-sensitive *membrane keyboard* consisting of a flat plastic surface on which the locations of keys are printed. These keyboards, which are somewhat like the control panels on many microwave ovens, are durable and resistant to spilled food and drink. But they are difficult for touch typists to use since both well-defined key surfaces and the familiar key movement when keys are pressed are absent. For this reason, the membrane keyboard is much less popular than the *raised keyboard,* which has individual keys made of plastic or rubber. One type of raised keyboard used for small, inexpensive systems is often called a *chiclet keyboard* because the individual keys look like a type of chewing gum tablet. Chiclet keyboards tend to feel stiff to touch typists. Most users prefer the type of personal computer keyboard called a *full-travel keyboard* because the keys move when pressed, like the keys on an electric typewriter.

Keyboard Layout

Most personal computer keyboards have the alphabetic typewriter keys in the usual places. However, keyboards also have anywhere from a few to many special-purpose keys in various locations. There is no definitive standard. Many keyboards have an auxiliary *numerical keypad* at the right of the main keypad, which is used to facilitate the entry of numerical data. Another option is a set of keys marked with up, down, left, and right arrows, which are used for moving the cursor, the lighted line or box that indicates a position on the display screen. Additional **function keys**, sometimes called **user-definable keys**, may be available to reduce certain often-used commands to a single keystroke.

Special-purpose keys vary widely among computer systems and have different functions based on what software is used, so we won't go into details here. However, the physical attributes of the number, size, and placement of these keys contribute to the differences among keyboards. For this reason, feel, key placement, and personal preference are generally the criteria users apply when judging the layout of a computer keyboard. Although some vendors do offer alternate keyboards for certain personal computer models, most models are manufactured and sold with a single standard keyboard design. Through concentrated effort, most users can eventually adjust to the idiosyncrasies of any personal computer keyboard.

Display Devices

The primary means of microcomputer output

Every personal computer must have some type of display device in order to present output to the user. Displays are the primary way people receive information from their computers. Since it's not uncommon for a user to spend hours at a time staring at a computer display, its performance and appearance can have a profound effect on attitudes toward working and playing with the personal computer. Some personal computers (especially portable models) have built-in display devices, but in many cases the display device is a separate unit called a *monitor*, which we discussed in Chapter 6. The types of display units used by personal computers include flat-panel screens, black-and-white or color television sets, and monochrome or multicolor CRT monitors. Some personal computers can support more than one of these types. For example, with the appropriate extra plug-in circuit boards, a user can hook up both a monochrome and a multicolor CRT monitor to an IBM Personal Computer and switch back and forth between them at will.

Flat-panel screens (see Chapter 6), in the form of liquid crystal displays or electroluminescent displays, are usually found only in expensive portable personal computers because of their high cost. Many inexpensive personal computers can use an ordinary television set as a monitor. Although this alternative keeps the price of the system down, since most people already have at least one television at home, the video image tends to be poor, especially for text. Monochrome CRT monitors, specially designed to present text in green, white, amber, or black, are common in personal computer systems and sell for as little as $100. They are preferred by users who spend long sessions working with text, for example, doing word processing or programming, because they produce sharply defined characters. More expensive multicolor CRT monitors, whose prices range from about $300 to $1500, have also become popular since so many personal computer systems now support color graphics. These monitors dramatically enhance the presentation of graphs, pictures, and charts. However, except on expensive models, ordinary text often does not appear as sharp as it does on monochrome monitors.

Printers

Although often postponing the purchase as something that can be put off until later, almost every personal computer owner eventually realizes the need for some type of printer to provide hard-copy output. By far the most common printers designed for personal computer systems are dot matrix printers (see Chapter 6), but daisy wheel printers, thermal printers, inkjet printers, and, recently, even laser printers are also available. The marketplace has a huge array of character printers of all sizes, speeds, capabilities, and prices, but a good example of an "average" model is the IBM Personal Computer Graphics Printer. This unit prints 80 characters per second, uses ordinary 9-by-11-inch fanfold paper, plugs into a Centronics standard parallel interface, costs about $300, and can produce dot graphics if special programming is done.

Peripherals to produce hard copy

Other Peripherals

Thanks to expansion slots, serial and parallel interfaces, and the ingenuity of hardware manufacturers, there is a dazzling array of other peripherals that can be purchased and attached to personal computers. Most of these hardware items can be attached by simply plugging them in and perhaps running special software provided by the manufacturer. Some of the more common types of other peripherals are

Commonly used external devices

> *Modems.* These devices, which we discussed in Chapter 7, allow personal computers to be used to access information networks and mainframe computer facilities via phone lines. Some modems are external units that plug into an RS-232C serial interface, and others are constructed on a circuit board that slips into an expansion slot.

Plotters. In Chapter 6, we introduced plotters as computer-controlled drawing machines. Pen, inkjet, flatbed, and drum plotters have been designed especially for personal computers.

Game controls. Commonly used with personal computers to play video games are graphic input devices such as paddles, joysticks, and trackballs.

Other graphic input devices. Other graphic input devices such as mice, digitizers, and light pens are available for many personal computers. In addition, voice input systems, bar code readers, and magnetic strip readers can be purchased for some personal computers.

Speech and music synthesizers. Relatively inexpensive devices that enable personal computers to talk or make music are becoming fairly commonplace.

Videodisk controllers. One of the newest types of peripheral units are devices that allow personal computers to be connected to videodisk players and color televisions. This hardware and its accompanying software give the user the ability to program which scenes are to be played, when to play them, how fast they should be played, and whether they should be played forward or backward.

TYPES OF PERSONAL COMPUTERS AND THEIR APPLICATIONS

The tremendous variety of personal computers available in the marketplace is indicated by the wide price range for these machines—from about $100 to $15,000. Of course, personal computers can be classified according to any of a number of characteristics: size, use, speed, memory capacity, microprocessor, bus structure, operating system, or price. A natural and obvious choice is a classification by size, or how easy a personal computer is to pick up and carry around. To some extent, this criterion produces the same groupings as price and use since computers of a given size tend to have a characteristic price range and similar applications. Although some models are hard to classify, most personal computers fall obviously into one of the following size categories: hand-held, briefcase, portable, and desktop.

Hand-Held Computers

Machines that work anywhere

Less than ten years ago, science fiction writers were concocting stories with references to seemingly outlandish appliances like computers you could hold in your hand. The first real hand-held, or pocket, computer commercially available was the Tandy–Radio Shack PC-1, introduced in 1981. This little wonder, actually manufactured by Sharp Electronics, was smaller than a paperback book and weighed less than seven ounces. With a base price below $100, the PC-1 sold hundreds of thousands of units. Since the PC-1, more advanced hand-held computers have been marketed by Tandy–Radio Shack (the PC-2, PC-3, and PC-4), Sharp (the PC-1250), Casio (the FX-702P and FX-802P), Panasonic (the RL-H1500), and Hewlett-Packard (the HP-75).

Unlike pocket calculators, hand-held computers have a complete alphabetic keypad as well as a numeric keypad and a few other keys for controlling computer functions (see Figure 15.6). They have single-line, liquid crystal displays capable of presenting 12 to 64 characters at once, usually have less than 24K of available

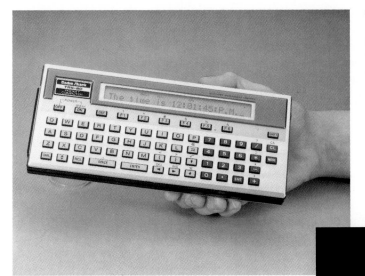

Figure 15.6 A Hand-held Computer
Hand-held computers, such as this Tandy–Radio Shack
PC-2, are battery-powered and small enough to fit in your
pocket yet have complete alphabetic and numeric keypads and one-line LCD screens.

Figure 15.7 A Briefcase Computer
Briefcase computers, such as this Data General One,
weigh between 4 and 12 pounds and are small
enough to fit in an average briefcase.

memory space, and run on built-in rechargeable batteries. Most can be programmed in BASIC or can utilize prewritten, ready-to-run application software
sold separately by the manufacturer. Peripheral devices for some models include
printers, plotters, and modems, and cassette recorder interfaces, television or video
monitor interfaces, and RS-232C serial interfaces are also available. The cost for an
entire hand-held computer system can be as little as $190 or as much as $1000.

Hand-held computers are ideal for on-the-go engineers, businesspeople, and
students who need more computing power than pocket calculators provide. However, the minimal memory capacities and small screens of hand-held computers
mean that they can't handle sophisticated text manipulation, data base operations,
electronic spreadsheets, and many other common personal computer applications.
They are most frequently used for personal and business finances, statistics, engineering math, and simple games.

Briefcase Computers

Briefcase computers, also called laptop computers, are the latest rage in the ever-
changing personal computer industry. In general, these machines weigh from 4 to
12 pounds and have a liquid crystal or electroluminescent flat-panel display presenting 40 or 80 columns of 8, 16, or 24 lines (see Figure 15.7). They are usually

Sleek traveling companions

equipped with a typewriterlike keyboard that has reasonably large keys, but only a few may be dedicated to special functions. With available memory capacities ranging from 8K to 512K, briefcase computers come close to the primary storage range of full-sized personal computers. Some but not all briefcase computers have built-in disk drives, usually accepting $3\frac{1}{2}$-inch microfloppies. Still others use magnetic tape cartridges or bubble memory chips to store data and built-in ROM cartridges to hold installed software. Most have a built-in modem or serial interface for sending data to and receiving data from other computers. In addition, the serial interface may also be used to drive nonportable peripherals such as full-sized CRT monitors, printers, or floppy disk drives (for $5\frac{1}{4}$-inch diskettes).

This class of personal computers was designed to provide computing performance comparable to that of the desktop models in a package that can be used almost anywhere. Consequently, most briefcase computers have a built-in rechargeable battery, or perhaps an external battery option. With prices ranging from $399 for the economical Tandy Model 100 to $7995 for the high-performance Grid Compass II Model 1139, these computers fit into almost any user's budget. Other popular models include the Data General One, the Texas Instruments Pro-Lite, the Hewlett-Packard Portable, the Sharp PC-5000, the Epson Geneva/PX-8, the NEC PC-8401, and the Tandy 200.

Although a wide variety of mobile professionals use briefcase computers, it's still a relatively small group. The most natural application of these little machines is their use by people who spend most of their time in the field. For example, the internal auditing staff of the Singer Company uses Data General Ones during their visits to different facilities throughout the world. Briefcase computers are handy because they can easily be taken on airplanes. Television executives and producers who travel a lot find these computers useful for taking notes at shooting locations and transmitting electronic mail back to the home office. Some realtors have their agents use briefcase computers to access a mainframe computer to get pertinent data on homes that meet the customers' requirements. It seems that these personal computers are finding their natural role in performing certain specialized tasks where mobility is essential.

ISSUES IN TECHNOLOGY

The concept of a truly portable, yet fully functional, personal computer that can fit inside a briefcase has great appeal for many people. It seems a new model appears every few months or so, as evidenced by the glossy photographs of the sleek, low-profile machines splashed across the covers of monthly computer magazines. They look beautiful, but how useful do the people who buy them actually find them to be? The debate rages: Are they novelties good only for limited or specialized jobs? Or are they truly useful, full-fledged personal computers? What do you think?

Portable Computers

Machines that are movable

Of course, the hand-held and briefcase computers we've been considering are portable in the sense that they're easily carried about, but the term *portable computer* has come to mean personal computers that are more or less the size of a suitcase (see Figure 15.8). Weighing from 20 to 35 pounds, these rugged machines are designed to be moved but not to be used in transit. They aren't battery-powered, so they can be used only where they can be plugged into an electrical socket. They provide users with the full range of personal computer features, including small CRT monitors with 24 lines of 80 characters, as much memory as the given microprocessor and operating system can handle, at least one floppy disk drive, expansion slots, serial and parallel interfaces, and even internal hard disk drives. In short, a portable computer is a complete personal computer system that you can fold up and take with you, just as you can a portable electric typewriter.

In general, the portable computers on the market have proven to be well-designed machines that are as useful as their desktop relatives. As long as you don't have to carry one too far and if you don't mind peering at a 9-inch screen rather than a 12-inch one, a portable may be just the thing if you like to take your work home at night or away for the weekend. The prices of portable computers are very reasonable, for the most part lower than or approximately equal to comparably equipped desktop models. Popular portables include the Kaypro II (26 pounds), IBM Portable PC (30 pounds), Compaq Portable Computer (33 pounds), Hyperion (22 pounds), Columbia (32 pounds), and Seequa Chameleon (28 pounds).

Desktop Computers

In the last size category are the machines that most people think of as personal computers. This size of computer originally gave rise to the term *personal computer* by being small enough to fit on top of a single table or desk and thus convenient for one user (see Figure 15.9). Some desktop computers are all-in-one units, while

The original personal computers

Figure 15.8 A Portable Computer
Portable computers, for example, this IBM-compatible model by Compaq, weigh about 30 pounds and are about the size of a suitcase when folded up.

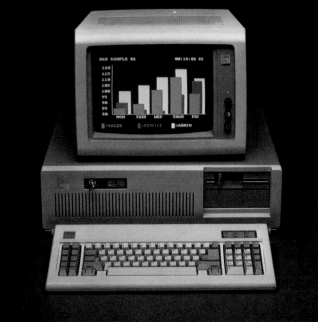

Figure 15.9 A Desktop Computer
Desktop computers, such as this top-of-the-line IBM Personal Computer AT, are the most common type of microcomputer.

others have computer, keyboard, monitor, and disk drive as separate components. Commonly used for home, business, research, and educational applications, desktop computers are complete, independent microcomputer systems. Desktop computers offer a broad range of capabilities and prices. Some high-performance desktop computers have even been christened **supermicros**. Equipped with powerful, yet inexpensive 24-bit or 32-bit microprocessors, the supermicros are machines that can service more than one user and that approach the speed and storage capabilities of many minicomputers at a fraction of the cost.

SOFTWARE FOR PERSONAL COMPUTERS

What makes the hardware useful

Personal computers, just like their larger counterparts, would be quite useless without quality prewritten software. In fact, software availability is especially crucial in the personal computer market since most users are neither professional programmers nor employers of a data-processing staff. Fortunately, there are many entrepreneurial individuals and companies eager to produce software to meet this intrinsic demand. Their ingenuity, skills, and drive for financial reward have resulted in an almost unbelievable variety of programs for sale. Although no one knows for sure just how many different software packages for personal computers are currently being marketed, estimates range from thousands to hundreds of thousands. And new applications are being developed every day.

Obviously, we can't even list all of the different programs that can be purchased for personal computers. We have, however, already covered several of the most important classes of system and application software in Chapters 10 and 11, and the majority of these are available for personal computers. In this chapter, we'll briefly present some of those types of software most intimately associated with personal computers. (Integrated software, electronic spreadsheets, and graphics packages, which are common applications for personal computers, were covered in sufficient detail in Chapter 10, with its in-depth section on Lotus 1-2-3.)

System Software

Operating systems and languages

Every personal computer comes with some system software. At the very least, a machine is sold with an operating system. As we said in Chapter 11, the most common operating systems for microcomputers are CP/M, MS-DOS, and the Apple Macintosh operating system. Recently, versions of UNIX have been installed in some top-of-the-line personal computers, for example, IBM's Personal Computer AT and AT&T's PC 7300. Although some personal computers allow the user to make a choice, many can run only one operating system. For example, the IBM Personal Computer can run either MS-DOS or CP/M-86, but the Apple Macintosh can run only the user-friendly operating system designed especially for it.

A second important type of system software for personal computers is language translators. Although not necessary for many applications, given the availability of prewritten software, translators are required by users who want to learn about programming so they can create their own software. As we noted in Chapter 9, BASIC is the most popular language for microcomputers, and a BASIC translator is often included along with the operating system as part of a package when a personal computer is purchased. Virtually every personal computer can run some sort of BASIC interpreter or compiler. In addition, many users expand their horizons to take in other popular high-level languages, including Pascal, FORTRAN, C, COBOL, Forth, LISP, and LOGO. More technically oriented users can even purchase assembly language translators so that they can write efficient and compact low-level programs.

Entertainment and Games

Recreation is one of the most common uses to which personal computers are put, particularly the more inexpensive models aimed at the home market. Computerized entertainment has come a long way since Atari's original Pong game, with its beeping luminous dot bouncing around a two-dimensional video tennis court. Well over a thousand computer games have been marketed, and many have hit the lists of best-selling software. This exciting type of software tends to make liberal use of the more flashy capabilities of personal computers, such as color graphics, graphic input, and sound generation.

Fun for all

Among the large population of game programs, several clear categories have become evident over recent years:

Arcade-type games. These games test players' reflexes and stamina by providing fast-moving challenges of the shoot-em-up, dodging, or maze-running variety. They are often scaled-down versions of the coin-fed diversions found in video arcades. Popular arcade-type games include Star Wars, Space Invaders, Crossfire, and Pac-Man (the most famous and most imitated video game ever).

Strategy games. Requiring cunning, problem solving, thought, and imagination more than quick reflexes, these games emulate military campaigns (such as the battle of Gettysburg) or traditional board games (such as chess, backgammon, Scrabble, and Monopoly).

Adventure games These computerized fantasy stories provide would-be heroes with spine-tingling adventures as they seek treasure or attempt to survive in an alien environment filled with hidden dangers. Adventure, Dungeons & Dragons, Zork, and King's Quest are popular examples in this category.

Simulations. These game programs use the personal computer to mimic exciting or dangerous experiences in the comfort and safety of the home. Examples include Flight Simulator, Air Traffic Controller, and Decathlon.

Music synthesizers. Musical prodigies can use these sophisticated programs to compose music, duplicate the sounds of traditional instruments, or create totally new electronic sounds. MUSICALC, Music Machine, and Music Maker are just a few of these entertaining and creative programs.

Word Processing

If you use a personal computer at all, chances are you use it for word processing. As we mentioned in Chapter 10, word-processing packages are one of the most popular types of software for personal computers. In fact, a recent survey by the Consumers Union of 22,000 personal computer owners indicates that word processing has overtaken game playing as the most frequent application for a computer in the home. That's not too surprising, since the survey also indicated that half of

The most common application

those owners use their personal computers exclusively or partially as an occupational tool.

In addition to job-related writing, the combination of a personal computer and a word-processing program is also widely used in the home for composing notes, letters, and school reports. Word-processing programs make it easy to fix typing errors on screen, before a single character is printed. They are especially appreciated by two-finger, hunt-and-peck typists, who once composed with pen and pad and then tried to pound out a clean copy on a typewriter. Even the simplest word-processing program allows correction, reorganization, and revision as a document is entered. More complex programs include extra facilities oriented toward business and professional use: merging documents together, setting up unusual formats, producing customized printing, and automatically checking for spelling errors against a stored dictionary of words. In Chapter 17, we'll be discussing word processors in more detail to give you a better idea of what it's really like to use one.

Education

Programs that teach

Among its many talents, it seems that the personal computer is a versatile teacher. Educational software is changing not only the way students are taught, but also *what* they're taught. Schools at all levels are buying microcomputers at an astonishing rate; there are at least a million personal computers in our nation's schools, and this figure does not include those individually owned by students or their parents. Millions of parents are convinced that personal computers can enhance both their children's and their own education. A recent Gallup poll found that 42% of personal computer owners use their machines as a learning tool. Millions of educational computer programs are purchased each year, and the market is still growing.

Educational programs exist in almost any subject area imaginable, but parents, students, and teachers are also realizing the importance of learning about the computer itself. In the future, all but the most menial jobs will require at least some familiarity with computers. Our society depends on a highly technological and information-oriented economy, and thus knowledge of the computer is essential. Educational software helps students understand how to deal with computers and what to expect from them.

Communications

Talking to other computers

One of the most entertaining and most widely utilized applications of personal computers involves communicating with other computers. We discussed communications software in Chapters 7 and 10, and we mention it again here because many people also see it as one of the most practical and beneficial applications of personal computers. There has been a recent emergence of a grass-roots network of personal computers that extends all across the nation. People are using their computers to communicate with each other and to access vast quantities of information in on-line data bases. By becoming familiar with today's communications software, users are coping with the present information explosion and preparing for technological innovations yet to come.

Communications software such as Smartcom II or Crosstalk XVI allows personal computer owners to send data to and receive data from other computers.

This capability lets them utilize the many services offered by on-line information networks such as The Source and CompuServe. In addition, communications software also makes it easy for many people to work for a company at home, or to *telecommute*. They can stay at home and yet use the resources of their employer's mainframe or minicomputer via telephone lines. There's also a wide variety of special-interest electronic bulletin board systems that can be accessed using a personal computer. In short, communications software can lessen the isolation of the personal computer user while preserving individual control.

Personal Management

Organizing your activities

Need help balancing your checkbook, keeping a household budget, planning vacations, analyzing mortgages, and maintaining records of credit accounts, appliance warranties, doctor bills, and magazine subscriptions? The marketplace is full of programs to help users organize their homes and personal lives. Although most of the packages in this category are aimed at personal money management, there's a wide variety of other interesting programs. How about a genealogical data base manager, an electronic Rolodex, an automated appointments calendar, an exercise and diet planner, or a cookbook on a disk? The list goes on and on, and more personal management programs come out each day. Some of the best-known of these programs are Dollars and Sense, Your Personal Net Worth, Micro Cookbook, and Home Budget.

Despite the novelty and variety of personal management software, it has its critics. Many people are skeptical of how helpful such programs can be. Personal and home management applications aren't the most efficient use of computer capabilities; in some cases, it's easier to just do the tasks by hand. However, for those who border on the obsessively organized, who have extremely complex or extensive financial holdings, or who just want to have some fun or impress their friends, there's bound to be a suitable personal management program.

Home Control

Watchdog software

Imagine living in a home in which mundane chores are taken care of, in which automatic adjustments are made to regulate daily use of heat, light, and electrical appliances, in which a computer watches out for fire, flood, and theft and uses the phone to call for help in an emergency. Is this a picture from science fiction or the twenty-first century? No, microprocessors and the personal computer make these and other automatic functions a present reality. A typical home control system consists of a personal computer acting as a controller that communicates with remote receiver modules to switch lights and appliances on and off. Other peripherals such as sensors (for temperature, water, smoke, sound, and movement), speech synthesizers, voice recognition modules, and even personal robots can usually be added to a system. How much do home control systems cost? Without the personal computer, a basic system to control lighting and appliances, with simple thermostatic and anti-intruder security features, costs about $1000.

Many families feel that the convenience, security, and energy savings provided by a sophisticated home control system are worth the price. Several companies offer a variety of home control devices. For example, Compu-Home Systems manufactures a well-planned system called Tomorrowhouse II that connects to any computer with an RS-232C interface. Sensors for temperature and humidity allow the computer to control up to eight different heating and cooling zones in a single large house. Hypertek's Homebrain is another example of a complete home control system that accepts input from as many as 32 remote sensors to monitor smoke and burglar alarms as well as light, temperature, and humidity levels.

OVERVIEW OF THE INDUSTRY

Since its birth in 1975, the personal computer industry has grown so rapidly that it's mind-boggling. It's difficult to discuss the personal computer without also examining to some extent the industry that ushered in this gold rush of new technology. In this section, we'll take a look at some of the companies that led the way in the manufacturing of personal computers and in the development of application software.

Personal Computer Manufacturers

The machine builders

There are, as we said earlier, a great many firms that manufacture and sell personal computers. Although innovative ideas and valuable contributions have come from many of these companies, a small group stands out among the crowd.

IBM

It's no coincidence that IBM is first on this list. Founded in 1911, IBM is currently the world's largest seller of data-processing equipment. With annual sales exceeding $40 billion, it makes more profit than any other corporation in the world. Even though it had been a leading manufacturer of mainframes for years, IBM didn't enter the personal computer market until 1981. Its first model, the IBM Personal Computer, soon captured a substantial portion of the microcomputer market and then became the best-selling, industry standard. By having other companies provide much of the hardware, software, distribution, and service for the Personal Computer, IBM entrenched the new line in the marketplace. Hundreds of companies popped up to produce parts and programs that work on various models of the Personal Computer. In addition, several firms developed PC "clones"—machines that worked just like (or in some ways a little better than) the original IBM one and usually sold at a lower price.

Even though microcomputers account for only a small fraction of IBM's total sales, the company has made a firm commitment to lead the industry. In fact, it is reasonable to classify all personal computers into two groups: those that are IBM-compatible and those that are not. IBM's extremely solid reputation as a hardware manufacturer ensures that it will continue to set the standards for tomorrow's microcomputers as well. Besides the basic Personal Computer, IBM's other well-known microcomputers include the PC XT, the recently discontinued PCjr, the PC Portable, and the powerful PC AT.

Apple

You've probably heard the rags-to-riches story of how Apple Computer, Inc., was formed in 1977 by Steven Jobs and Stephen Wozniak, who built their first prototype in a garage for $1300. Even the first Apple computers had none of the complicated switches and lights of earlier hobbyist-oriented computers like the Altair 8800. Instead, Apple offered a simple single-unit machine with keyboard, aimed primarily at home users. Apple also encouraged other companies to make compatible hardware and software. Less than five years after its birth in that Silicon Valley garage, Apple Computer, Inc., made the Fortune 500, a feat no company had achieved so quickly before. And Jobs and Wozniak became folk heroes in the computer world for starting "the company that started it all." Jobs is no longer chairman of Apple, and Wozniak left the company in 1984 to work on new projects of his own.

If IBM is the Goliath of the personal computer industry, then Apple is David, bravely battling the giant. The Apple II series dominated the personal computer market from 1977 to 1982, when the IBM Personal Computer took over. By mid-1983, after the unenthusiastic reception of Apple's two new models, the Lisa and the Apple III, market analysts began to wonder if Apple would survive. Amid corporate infighting, Jobs himself took over the division of Apple that was building its last, best hope—the entirely new Macintosh. Released in early 1984 to the accompaniment of a $20-million advertising scheme that billed it as a computer "for the rest of us," the Macintosh was hailed as an extremely user-friendly machine. Even though some people criticized it for being too much of a toy and not suitable for serious business use, Apple has been producing 40,000 units a month. Even though it's somewhat dated, the Apple II is still selling; the Lisa line has been dropped but replaced with a 512K Macintosh. Also, Apple sells a seven-pound portable, the Apple IIc.

Tandy–Radio Shack

Originally a leather goods manufacturer, Tandy diversified in 1963 by merging with the Radio Shack chain of electronics stores for hobbyists. One of the pioneers of the microcomputer industry, along with Apple and Commodore, Tandy–Radio Shack had great success with its first machine, the TRS-80 Model I. Somewhat unusual in that it sells under its own name products produced both internally and by other manufacturers, Tandy–Radio Shack has the broadest line of microcomputers in the world. From powerful business systems (such as the TRS-80 Model 16) to IBM-compatible machines (such as the Tandy 1200 HD) to pocket-sized computers (such as the TRS-80 PC-4), the company has a model to fill every user need. A major reason for the firm's steady success is the exceptional distribution provided by its more than 8800 full-line, retail electronics stores. By also making available application software, product support, and service through its stories, Tandy–Radio Shack can offer customers the convenience of having most of their personal computer needs met in one place.

Commodore

Founded by Jack Tramiel in 1954, Commodore Business Machines began as a typewriter repair shop that also sold adding machines. In the early 1970s, Commodore became one of the major contenders in the booming market for hand-held electronic calculators. When Texas Instruments, Tramiel's major supplier of semiconductor chips, decided in 1975 to sell calculators themselves, Commodore was almost driven out of business. To survive, Commodore bought its own chip supplier, MOS Technology, the original manufacturer of the 6502 microprocessor used in the Apple II computers. The acquisition of MOS Technology put Commodore into the computer business.

Commodore's first computer, the PET, was a huge success after its introduction in 1977. Aiming at the low end of the home and education markets, Tramiel followed up the PET with two more powerful models, the VIC-20 and the Commodore 64. In 1983, Commodore sold over a million of these inexpensive computers in the final three months of the year (ironically, driving Texas Instruments as well as Mattel and Timex out of the home computer market). Commodore has since added to its line the even more powerful Commodore 128, the five-pound LCD Lap Computer, and the new Amiga Personal Computer.

AT&T

AT&T, the communications giant, is a perennial source of inventions and advances (for example, the transistor and the UNIX operating system) that have profoundly affected the computer industry. It's been designing and building computers for the world's largest telecommunications network for more than 20 years, but was precluded by antitrust laws from retailing computers until its divestiture of the Bell System telephone companies in 1982. Free to enter the computer business, AT&T established its Information Systems division and quickly set about marketing microcomputers.

Its first personal computer, the PC 6300, is an IBM-compatible machine that was introduced in 1984. The PC 6300 is a solid, well-engineered microcomputer but isn't particularly innovative. Its real significance is that, in a market dominated by IBM, AT&T is seen as one of the few companies that can offer Big Blue serious competition. Even without the Bell System, AT&T is a huge corporation that has several of the qualities that make IBM such a formidable contender: size, a name that is a household word, and a reputation for quality products and service. As one of the most recent newcomers to the personal computer industry, AT&T must fight for market share and recognition against well-established adversaries. Although it's still too early to tell how well AT&T is doing against IBM, many analysts predict an imminent showdown. In addition to the PC 6300, AT&T also sells the advanced PC 7300, which runs a version of the UNIX operating system and is intended as an alternative to IBM's Personal Computer AT.

Software Vendors

The program peddlers

There are even more software developers than there are manufacturers of personal computers. Many are quite small and may offer just a single best-selling package, while others produce a broad line of programs. The five biggest names in the software arena are Microsoft, Lotus, MicroPro, Digital Research, and Ashton-Tate.

Microsoft

Founded in 1975 by Bill Gates and Paul Allen, Microsoft Corporation is the largest developer of software for personal computers in the United States. Based in Bellevue, Washington, this company with 620 employees sells well over $100 million in software annually. Gates, still the driving force behind Microsoft, has been described as "the Thomas Edison of software." His company has emerged as the leading software designer in the industry, supplying the operating systems, pro-

CAREERS IN TECHNOLOGY
Computer Sales Personnel

Job Description The field of computer sales covers such job titles as computer salesperson and marketing representative (also known as a customer support representative). A computer salesperson in a retail showroom needs to know more than just the price of a personal computer and whether or not there's one in stock. He or she needs to understand how a variety of very different systems operate, what their strengths and weaknesses are, and which ones are compatible. Salespeople also have to be able to answer more formal requests for proposals (or RFPs) from potential large-scale clients (corporate or individual users) who are planning to make a significant investment in computers. The salesperson must be able to put together the most reasonably priced and best-suited system for a particular client, while at the same time ensuring a maximum profit for his or her own company. Salespeople must be able to comprehend a client's specific needs and must know the computer market well enough to match those needs with the appropriate systems. They also need to be familiar with the available manuals, documentation, journals, software, and accessories.

Marketing or customer support representatives are highly trained salespeople who travel around a geographical region giving sales presentations to potential customers and visiting current clients to offer advice, encouragement, and suggestions. They work for computer manufacturers rather than for retailers. Market representatives must also be able to offer proposals to potential clients and must have a strong understanding of the technical aspects of their company's equipment.

Both retail salespeople and marketing representatives work mostly on a commission basis; that is, they are paid a minimum base salary, but the bulk of their income derives from receiving a percentage of each sale, which can conceivably add up to hundreds of thousands of dollars a year. Companies set annual sales quotas (generally expressed in points, with, say, 10 points given for a disk drive and 30 points for a laser printer) and offer bonuses or vacations as incentives.

Qualifications Marketing representatives must generally have a B.S. in computer science or electrical engineering, with a strong background in business and marketing, or a B.A. in marketing with considerable training in computer science. Requirements vary from company to company. Salespeople in retail stores, whether local branches of the Computerland chain or manufacturers' outlets like the Radio Shack stores, don't necessarily need a college degree. What they do need are a basic knowledge of data processing and a sound technical proficiency gained either from college and vocational courses or from hands-on experience with a variety of systems. Communication and selling skills are clearly essential, and, again, either direct experience in sales or substantial marketing coursework is often required. Most organizations offer their own training courses for sales personnel, however.

Outlook The job prospects in the field of computer sales are excellent, although competition is increasing and standards are getting higher all the time.

gramming language translators, and application programs that make all kinds of personal computers useful to a great many people. More than 2 million computers are currently running Microsoft-developed software. From the operating system chosen by IBM for its Personal Computer family (MS-DOS) to the best-selling, award-winning Flight Simulator program, Microsoft software has had a profound influence on the entire personal computer industry. Other popular Microsoft packages include Windows, Word, Multiplan, Olympic Decathlon, Adventure, and translators for BASIC, Pascal, FORTRAN, and C.

Lotus

Even in the fast-paced world of personal computer software, Lotus Development Corporation has had a meteoric rise—from nonexistence to manufacturer of the best-selling business software in a single year. Started by Mitch Kapor in 1982, Lotus sold over $53 million worth of software by the end of 1983. The star product, of course, was the 1-2-3 package (see Chapter 10). Introduced in the fall of 1982, at COMDEX, a major personal computer industry convention, Lotus 1-2-3 sold 60,000 copies by July of 1983. With the introduction of its second package, Symphony, in the summer of 1984, Lotus solidified its position as the industry leader in the integrated software market. By combining an electronic spreadsheet with graphics, word-processing, data base management, and communications capabilities, Symphony has earned rave reviews as a worthy encore to 1-2-3.

MicroPro

MicroPro International, founded in 1978 by Seymour Rubinstein, developed and sold WordStar, the most popular program in the early history of personal computers. This perennially best-selling word-processing program fueled MicroPro's growth since its introduction in mid-1979. Although it's had severe competition lately from several easier-to-use programs, WordStar has sold over 1.25 million copies (and has been illegally copied an untold number of times). MicroPro had $67 million in sales in 1984 alone. MicroPro's other popular packages include MailMerge, InfoStar, SpellStar, and WordStar 2000 (a redesigned version of the original).

Digital Research

Gary Kildall, inventor of the landmark CP/M operating system, founded Digital Research in 1976. Although CP/M was at first considered by IBM in 1978 for its soon-to-emerge Personal Computer line, Digital Research was beaten out by its arch rival Microsoft. Despite the fact that MS-DOS now outsells CP/M by a wide margin, Digital Research still has annual revenues in excess of $40 million. Digital Research has built a reputation for supplying high-quality products, especially language translators and educational software such as C-BASIC, Pascal/MT, and DR Logo.

Ashton-Tate

Ashton-Tate was founded in 1980 by George Tate and Hal Lashlee. (There was no Ashton; that name was coined by advertising man Hal Pawluk, who thought it sounded good with Tate.) In January of 1981, the firm marketed a data base management system called Vulcan, which was developed by Wayne Ratliff, an engineer who had worked at NASA's Jet Propulsion Laboratory. Vulcan was renamed dBase II, and it sold very well because of its exceptional versatility. By the end of 1983, Ashton-Tate had sold over 200,000 copies of dBASE II, making it one of the hottest software products in the personal computer marketplace. In May of 1984, Ashton-Tate introduced dBASE III, a successor to its top-selling program. Later that same year, it released Framework, an integrated software package designed to compete with Symphony (by Lotus). With annual sales of about $40 million, Ashton-Tate is the fifth-largest independent supplier of personal computer software.

SUMMARY

What Is a Personal Computer?

A personal computer is a stand-alone, general-purpose, microprocessor-based computer system used by an individual or small group of people for recreation, education, business, or other applications.

Hardware Components of Personal Computer Systems

The most important characteristic parts include the following:

The Microprocessor   The microprocessor is the component that determines the computing power of a microcomputer. Commonly used microprocessor chips include the 8-bit Zilog Z80 and MOS 6502, the 16-bit Intel 8086/8088 family, the 24-bit Intel 80286, and the 32-bit Motorola 68000.

Primary Storage   A microcomputer's primary storage is composed of RAM, or user memory, and ROM chips to hold built-in operating system components.

Secondary Storage   The most commonly used secondary storage devices for microcomputers are cassette tape recorders (which, however, are being phased out), ROM cartridges for permanently stored software, and floppy and hard disk drives.

Interfaces   Interfaces allow external, peripheral units to be plugged into a microcomputer. The bus connects all internal and external components to the CPU and may allow for expansion slots that accept additional components. Many peripherals are plugged into serial interfaces (which transmit data a bit at a time) or parallel interfaces (which transmit data a byte at a time).

The Keyboard   The keyboard allows the user to tell the computer what to do. Various types of construction and layouts are found among personal computer keyboards. Common constructions are membrane, raised, chiclet, and full-travel keyboards. Keyboard layouts often include special-purpose keys, a numerical keypad, cursor movement keys, and function (user-definable) keys.

Display Devices   Display devices present output to personal computer users and are usually flat-panel screens, television sets, or CRT monitors.

Printers   Dot matrix, daisy wheel, thermal, inkjet, and laser printers are used in personal computer systems to produce hard-copy input.

Other Peripherals   Other peripherals for personal computers include modems, plotters, game controls such as joysticks, other graphic input devices such as mice or light pens, speech and music synthesizers, and videodisk controllers.

Types of Personal Computers and Their Applications

A wide range of machines and uses are available.

Hand-held Computers   Hand-held computers are tiny, battery-powered units with complete keypads, small LCD displays, and up to 24K RAM.

Briefcase Computers   Small enough to fit in a briefcase, these computers weigh from 4 to 12 pounds and have 40-column or 80-column flat-panel displays.

Portable Computers   About the size of a suitcase, portable computers have all the power of full-sized personal computers.

Desktop Computers   Most personal computers fit comfortably on top of a table or desk. High-performance desktop computers are called supermicros.

Software for Personal Computers

Prewritten software is especially crucial in the personal computer market since most users aren't programmers.

System Software Every personal computer system must have an operating system and some language translator programs.

Entertainment and Games Recreational software includes arcade-type games, strategy games, adventure games, simulations, and music synthesizers.

Word Processing Word-processing programs are one of the most popular types of personal computer software.

Education Educational software can turn the personal computer into a learning tool to approach almost any subject.

Communications Communications programs are practical and beneficial because they allow personal computers to communicate with other computers.

Personal Management A wide variety of personal computer software is available to help with everyday organizing and planning activities.

Home Control Some personal computer software can control devices to regulate home energy use and detect emergency situations.

Overview of the Industry

The most important companies in the personal computer industry include the following:

Personal Computer Manufacturers Leading manufacturers of personal computers include IBM, Apple, Tandy–Radio Shack, Commodore, and AT&T.

Software Vendors The leading software developers are Microsoft, Lotus, MicroPro, Digital Research, and Ashton-Tate.

COMPUTER CONCEPTS

As an extra review of the chapter, try defining the following terms. If you have trouble with any of them, refer to the page number listed.

personal computer	expansion slots	parallel interface
coprocessors	motherboard	function keys (user-
interface	serial interface	definable keys)
bus	handshaking signals	supermicros

REVIEW QUESTIONS

1. Describe what is generally meant by the term *personal computer*.
2. List the most popular microprocessors used in today's microcomputers and give their word sizes.
3. What is a microcomputer's RAM used for?
4. What do many microcomputers store in ROM?
5. List the most commonly used secondary storage devices for microcomputers.
6. What three types of lines make up a computer bus?
7. Give an example of a serial interface that is used in many microcomputers.
8. What are parallel interfaces usually used for and how do they differ from serial interfaces?
9. What are some of the different types of keyboard constructions found in personal computers?

10. What kinds of display devices are usually used in personal computer systems?
11. What kinds of printers are often found in personal computer systems?
12. List some other peripherals often connected to personal computers.
13. Briefly describe the differences among hand-held, briefcase, portable, and desktop computers, and give an example of each type.
14. What types of system software must every personal computer have?
15. What general categories of game programs are available for personal computers?
16. Why are educational programs for personal computers popular?
17. What are communications programs used for?
18. What are some of the things personal management software can help a user do?
19. How can personal computers be used to automate some household functions?
20. What are the major manufacturers of personal computers?
21. What are the biggest names in personal computer software development?

A SHARPER FOCUS

Now that you've completed this chapter, you should be able to answer the following questions about the chapter opening.

1. Should the De l'Aunes have tried to maintain compatibility among their personal computers? Why or why not?
2. Do you think home-based education employing a personal computer is feasible today? Will it be more feasible in the future?
3. Is there such a thing as too much computer use in the home?

PROJECTS

1. After reading the special section on pages 461–467, imagine that you have $4000 to invest in a complete personal computer system. What would you want to use it for? What software would you get? What kind of computer would you get? Be specific about your choices concerning the microprocessor, memory capacity, kind of secondary storage, display device(s), and other peripherals. After you've specified your system, do some actual shopping. Look in computer stores, department stores, and the mail-order ads of computer magazines to compare prices. Prepare a report detailing your choices, reasons, and price comparisons.

2. An owner of a small business is confused by the different operating systems he might run with his personal computer. Prepare a list or table summarizing the advantages and disadvantages of UNIX, Pick, MS-DOS, and CP/M for him.

3. An often-heard statement suggests "home computers have become the 'crockpot' of the 1980s" because there are a lot of them that were probably purchased for Christmas, used briefly, and now just sit on the closet shelf. Do you know any people who have a personal computer but don't use it? Sample the people in your neighborhood, at your job, or at your school to formulate some picture of this phenomenon. Also, see if you can suggest the real reasons why the computers were purchased and then either not used at all or used much less than was expected.

4. Many computer programs are available to help people prepare for all kinds of examinations: for example, the SAT, the GRE, and entrance exams for most of the professional schools, including law school and medical school. What can you find out about the advantages and disadvantages of these programs? What do they cost? Do they really help?

5. This chapter mentioned two on-line information networks (The Source and CompuServe). Prepare a table of the costs associated with using these two services. Also

note any differences in the services offered. Are there any special hardware considerations the user needs to keep in mind? (Do they require a certain transmission rate, certain brand of computer, minimum memory capacity?)

6. Many large companies have discontinued certain models of personal computers, including the Texas Instruments TI 99/4a, the IBM PCjr, the Timex Sinclair, the Apple Lisa, and the Coleco Adam. Why? Was there something about each of these machines that couldn't be fixed, that forced its exit from the marketplace? These are large companies. Didn't they do their market research correctly?

7. This chapter reported that the IBM Personal Computer very rapidly captured a substantial portion of the microcomputer market, but there are several "clones" that are more powerful or have features that the IBM Personal Computer doesn't have. Prepare a report outlining what a user can get (other than a lower purchase price) by buying one of these "clones."

8. Although the IBM Personal Computer has become the industry standard—especially for the small business market—there are a number of things that users don't like about it. Research this subject and write a short report entitled "What's Wrong with the IBM PC."

9. What computer user groups and clubs are established in your city or town? What machines do they support, or are they for all users? At what level (new users, experienced programmers, game-players) are the members, or is the membership composed of all levels? If you live in a large city, you might include just those organizations within a reasonable radius of your home.

Selecting a Personal Computer System

Choosing the right computer, peripherals, and software is no easy task. The explosive growth of the personal computer industry leaves the poor consumer facing an overwhelming number of possibilities. In this special section, we'll review with you some of the important factors you should consider when selecting a personal computer system.

SELECTION CRITERIA

The decision to buy a particular computer system will be based on many factors, but there are three that should have top priority:

1. What you want to *use* the computer for.
2. How much *power* (speed and memory) you need.
3. How much *money* you have to spend.

To develop a clear picture of what you want to use a personal computer for, you must know what such machines can and cannot do. Reading Chapter 15 should have given you a pretty good idea of the kinds of tasks personal computers can perform. An honest evaluation of your needs is the next step, to determine if a personal computer could really be of help. If it could, then perhaps the best way to approach the selection process starts

with determining what software you want to use. Do you primarily want to do word processing, or are you looking for a machine to run computer games? Do some research on the software available for microcomputers and decide what programs you want to run. Picking out the software first will mean you'll be sure about exactly what you want to use the computer for.

Once you know what programs you want to run, you can then limit your consideration to hardware systems that can execute this software. You'll need a system that is fast enough, has enough memory, and has versions of your chosen programs specifically designed for it. By selecting your software first, you're more likely to end up with a machine well-suited to your needs, not one that is too powerful or too limited.

Finally, the bottom line is, of course, your budget. Which computer you get or even if you get one at all is ultimately dependent on how much money you have to spend. But, as we've said, there's a wide price range in today's market.

THE COMPATIBILITY ISSUE

Besides the three basic questions we've just covered, another inevitable decision facing today's computer shopper is whether to purchase an IBM-compatible system. Currently, the whole class of personal computer systems can be boiled down to three major categories: IBM and IBM-compatible machines, the Apple Macintosh family, and all others. Not to belittle any of those others, but the industry is quite simply dominated and obsessed by the first two categories. What then is the compatibility issue all about?

In general terms, compatibility refers to how well two devices or a piece of hardware and a piece of software work together. In the case of the IBM Personal Computer, the industry has accepted three clearly defined compatibility levels:

1. *Operationally compatible.* These machines, sometimes referred to as "IBM clones" or "IBM look-alikes," will run virtually any software the IBM Personal Computer will run and will accept plug-in expansion boards and other hardware peripherals designed for the Personal Computer. Examples include the popular Compaq, Columbia, and Corona personal computers.
2. *Data-compatible.* These computers can read information from floppy disks written by the IBM Personal Computer, enabling the easy transfer of data back and forth. The Texas Instruments Professional, DEC Rainbow 100, and Wang PC are examples of machines that are data-compatible with the Personal Computer.
3. *MS-DOS–compatible.* These systems are related to the IBM one only in that they run the same basic operating system. In other words, they can run those MS-DOS programs that have been translated to their own particular floppy disk formats. In this group are the NEC Advanced Personal Computer, Grid Compass, and Hewlett-Packard HP 150.

The advantages offered by being compatible with the IBM Personal Computer are due to the multitude of hardware and software products that have been developed for it. For any item that can be plugged into or run on a personal computer, chances are there's a version for the IBM Personal Computer or an IBM-compatible machine. The Personal Computer has become the de facto standard in the 16-bit personal computer industry, and going along with the crowd assures a user of access to help, services, and products from similarly equipped others. The disadvantages of owning an IBM-compatible machine lie in the possibility of passing up some new state-of-the-art features that can be realistically implemented only on noncompatible machines or in having to pay a premium price for power that may not be needed. So, as you can see, deciding whether or not to go with IBM compatibility is one of the crucial user choices.

MARKET OUTLETS

Personal computers have become so popular that there are many different places where computers, peripherals, and software can be purchased. Independent or national computer stores, regular department stores, and mail-order houses are the biggest outlets. Since each of these offers both advantages and disadvantages, the wise personal computer shopper should consider all the possibilities before buying.

Computer Stores

Retail outlets such as the Computerland chain offer a wide selection of brands and models because they specialize in sales of computer hardware and software. Knowledgeable salespeople are usually available to offer advice, help you try out products, and assist in your decision. And although computer store prices tend to be relatively high, these outlets usually offer local service and maintenance, that is, without having to ship products back to the manufacturer.

Department Stores

Department stores, such as Sears and K-Mart, can often sell computers and peripherals at low prices because they buy in volume. Low price and immediate availability are advantages of buying from mass merchandisers, but there are also significant disadvantages. Department stores often carry just one or two low-end brand names and a limited supply of accessory hardware and software. In addition, salespeople are usually not computer experts and may be able to offer only very limited technical advice. Finally, most department stores can neither fix nor maintain the computer products they sell, and so you may have to wait weeks for any necessary factory service.

Mail-Order Houses

For knowledgeable computer shoppers or those who know exactly what they want, mail-order houses can be an economical alternative to local stores. These firms advertise in all

the major computer magazines, offer an extensive choice of products, and often quote very low prices as a result of low overhead. Although a few computer mail-order firms have been known to offer deals more spectacular than those they actually deliver, most in the industry are quite reputable. Many sell products they develop themselves or can service the merchandise they sell that is manufactured by other companies. Technical advice and assistance can be somewhat hard to obtain, however, and dealing through the mail usually means waiting days or weeks for orders to be received.

 ## LEARNING MORE

In general, acquiring more knowledge about specific hardware and software will help you be more successful in both selecting and utilizing a personal computer. Fortunately, there's a wealth of easily accessed information out there that can make your involvement with a computer much less frustrating and more interesting.

Books

Go to a local bookstore, library, or computer store; it's highly likely you'll find an impressive collection of recent books about personal computers. The reason is, of course, that such books are selling like hotcakes. Books have been written that cover practically every aspect of personal computer use. Although some are quite technical, a large percentage were written especially for the novice. There are books about particular computer models, software packages, and even peripherals such as printers. Other popular topics include word processing, data base management, business applications, games, graphics, computer music, philosophical and sociological concerns, circuitry, and programming in BASIC, FORTRAN, Pascal, and other languages.

Periodicals

Magazines and newspapers are the best way to keep tabs on the constantly changing world of the personal computer; they can also fill in the gaps left by poorly written manuals and uninformed salespeople. Although books serve to present overviews or treatments of specialized topics, they're usually somewhat out of date by the time they're published, so they don't let you know what's happening in the marketplace *now*. Computer-oriented periodicals, some of which are published weekly, are filled with articles about the newest hardware and software products, along with a multitude of advertisements. In addition, many magazines instruct their readers by presenting hints, advice, and informative articles by everyday users. A comprehensive library of recent information about a particular type of personal computer could be built up by subscribing to one or two periodicals.

In 1975, there were only two magazines devoted to personal computers. Today, there are at least 450 titles to choose from, some available at newsstands and others only by mail. No matter what your special interest or personal computer model, there's probably a magazine that can teach you more about it. Popular periodicals include *Infoworld*, *Byte*, *Personal Computing*, *Computers and Electronics*, *Family Computing*, *PC*, *PC Week*, *Computer World*, and *Macworld*.

Disk Magazines

An exciting new information source for personal computer owners has been gaining in popularity. Disk magazines are publications issued on floppy disks and aimed at the owners of particular computer models. Some provide subscribers with fully documented, tested, guaranteed-to-run programs for business, education, personal management, and recreation; others more directly imitate printed magazines. Both kinds are fully self-contained and supply users with valuable software. Programs are often solicited from subscribers, with offers of payment or reduced subscription rates, giving average users the chance to contribute software they developed themselves. Since putting out a disk magazine requires a far smaller labor force than publishing a regular magazine, the price of an issue is often not too much more than the retail cost of a blank diskette. Popular disk magazines include *A+ Disk Magazine* for Apple II users and *PC Disk Magazine* for IBM Personal Computer users.

Organizations

Contrary to the media image, computer users are a very sociable lot. At intervals of a month or so, thousands gather in societies, clubs, and user groups to share experiences, problems, and software. Although most people don't join until after they buy, several benefits can be realized by becoming involved with such a group before purchasing a personal computer system. Many groups are organized around a particular model or product line. If you join before you buy, club members can offer advice on where to get the best deals or may even be able to let you in on group discounts. If you join after you buy, an organization can bring you into contact with people who have the same equipment—a valuable resource because they may have already solved the problems you're just encountering.

User groups offer camaraderie, support, and answers to those tricky questions not addressed in any manuals. Quite a few have been established since the advent of personal computers. For example, there are over 300 groups serving Apple computer users in the United States, Canada, England, Ireland, Australia, and New Zealand. Although some groups have remained local and small, like the Lincoln (Nebraska) Microcomputers Club with its 45 members, others have grown quite large. The Boston Computer Society, for example, was founded in 1977 and today has 7000 members, holds 25 monthly events, has 23 special-interest subgroups, and puts out its own bimonthly newsletter, *Computer Update*.

Classes, Seminars, and Camps

Other popular ways to learn more about personal computers are to take a class, attend a seminar, or go to a computer camp. Many classes, covering all kinds of topics concern-

ing personal computer hardware and software, are offered by universities, community colleges, computer stores, and private individuals. Seminars and conferences, usually aimed at busy professionals, promise to provide thorough instruction within a few hours or days. Their topics include how to use popular operating systems and application packages, fundamentals of microcomputer data communications, and setting up and using local area networks. Finally, computer camps offer children a high-tech alternative to more traditional summer camps. By providing instruction in computer programming, instead of or in addition to canoeing, tennis, and horseback riding, these camps give interested youngsters a few weeks of exploration, learning, and fun. And why should kids have all the fun? Some plush resorts offer computer-study retreats to adults in locations such as Jackson Hole, Wyoming; Guadeloupe, Mexico; and the Bahamas.

Embedded Microprocessors

▶

FOCUS ON . . . SMART GREETING CARDS

A year ago the first generation of electronic greeting cards could perform relatively simple feats, like beeping *Jingle Bells* and humming *Joy to the World.* Now the second generation can play complex melodies and harmonies, blink lights, and even wish recipients Christmas greetings in a scratchy voice. The technology behind the small but growing number of brainy cards comes from the Far East, and they are sold by several card companies, including the big three: Hallmark Cards, American Greetings, and Gibson Greeting Cards. Retailing for $4 to $7.50, the cards include a microchip, speaker, and battery; can run for 12 hours; and operate when the cards are opened, much like a music box.

Card companies are making substantial investments in new technologies, including laser printing and holography. Hallmark is constructing a $20-million Technology and Innovation Center, where engineers, craftsmen, and artists will work side by side dreaming up and refining new products, from cards to the gifts and paraphernalia the companies have started selling in recent years. Industry executives estimate that electronic cards represent less than 1% of U.S. card sales ($3.2 billion in 1984) and doubt they will ever replace traditional cards in any big way. "We believe that printed paper products will be here for a long time," says Kurt Pfahl, Hallmark's director of technical research and engineering. "But new generations of people are growing up with video games, and we'll have to find out what the impact on the market is likely to be."

Eyes for Your Personal Computer	A scanning wand connected to a personal computer for reading printed, bar-coded programs.
And Little Friends	A line of microprocessor-controlled recreational robots.
Smart Cars	Improving an existing product.
Engine Controls	Microprocessor-based electronic controls to achieve the highest gas economy and lowest emissions.
Displays	Displays that provide more information and are easier to read.
Diagnostics	Help with finding and preventing problems.
Comfort and Safety	Adjusting the suspension to the load. Testing and using the air bag. Preventing skids caused by wheel-lock.

Although it may seem that we've said about all that can be said about the microprocessor chip, we haven't. When it is surrounded by a given set of RAM, ROM, secondary storage, and peripheral equipment, it is the "brains" of one of the varied microcomputer systems that we just studied in the last chapter. But the same microprocessor chip that is a personal computer's CPU can also be used to augment a whole catalog of devices that aren't computers at all. Many familiar modern products, for example, telephones, photocopiers, cameras, toys, and automobiles, depend on the high-tech microprocessor to extend their functions and/or improve their efficiency.

In this chapter, we'll look at some of the newest and most significant (or just plain interesting) applications of microprocessor technology—a first step in making the transition from studying *how* computers work to appreciating the scope of *what* they do.

THE EMBEDDED MICROPROCESSOR CHIP

Store shelves are piled high today with so-called **smart products**: any appliance, tool, gadget, or knick-knack that contains an **embedded microprocessor**, which is a microprocessor chip that can accept input data but that you don't have to program. For example, the embedded microprocessor in a video game responds to input from joystick or keypad by causing preprogrammed movements of symbols on a screen. An embedded microprocessor in a new car responds to input in the form of the position of the accelerator pedal by controlling the amount of gas fed to the engine. For these and other examples we'll study, the program embedded in the chip is written by the product's manufacturer and stored in ROM (read-only memory), and is as integral a part of the product's design as its switches and gears. The user of the smart product is simultaneously the user of this prepackaged program.

Before the development of the microprocessor, electronic controls were built out of individual transistors or low-level integrated circuits. These individual components were assembled and interconnected on printed circuit boards. A small,

The basis for a new class of smart products

Before programmed microprocessors

assembled printed circuit board with a handful of parts on it could cost as much as several hundred dollars to manufacture. Even though a typical microprocessor chip contains thousands of individual transistors, it costs just a few dollars when purchased in large quantities. Moreover, improving the performance of or correcting an error in an embedded microprocessor only involves reprogramming the ROM, not redesigning and remanufacturing the whole device. (Note that only the memory contents need be changed if the ROM is programmable, that is, if it is a PROM.) Not only are microprocessor-based controls more economical, more reliable, and easier to alter than printed circuit boards, but they are inherently more flexible. The elevator controls in an office building, for example, can be programmed to respond to the differing patterns of demand at various times of the day and to adjust waiting times accordingly.

Flexible and reliable

We'll see in Chapter 20 how medical instrumentation in hospitals and laboratories has been revolutionized by smart products and in Chapter 21 how microprocessors have been embedded in weapons systems. In this chapter, let's examine a select group of smart products for businesses and consumers in order to get some idea of the growing impact of this application of computer technology.

 ## SMART PRODUCTS FOR BUSINESS AND INDUSTRY

Generating, recording, and communicating information with greater speed and reliability is the function of a new class of smart products, inside and outside the office.

The Very Smart Telephone

A microprocessor in a telephone

Smart telephones do more than connect person to person; they connect computer to computer as well, streamlining business functions and making communications instantaneous rather than delayed. They have their own microprocessors, memories, and keyboards, and can interleave data and voice over the same line. This means that individuals in different parts of the country can send *screen mail* to each other and converse while viewing the same information on their computer screens—all by touching a couple of keys. This desk-to-desk teleconferencing is just like handing a contract draft or a sales report across a conference table, except no one has to fly anywhere to do it.

A smart phone isn't just a jazzed-up modem, however. It has its own embedded microprocessor, which allows it to be more than simply a passive data transmission device. Electronic mail can be entered and stored during business hours, then transmitted at night when phone rates are lower. Incoming mail is stored in the phone's memory or on a diskette in a personal computer until the recipient arrives. Correspondence can be routed to distribution lists, forwarded to others, filed, or pitched, as in any office. Programmable telephone directories, automatic dialing and redialing (for when the line is busy), paging, and message taking are features that make the smart phone an increasingly attractive business asset.

Shown in Figure 16.1, Communications CoSystem, manufactured by Cygnet Technologies, is an example of a smart phone with all the functions we've just described. In addition, an individual working with an application package such as Lotus 1-2-3 or WordStar can temporarily stop working to send or receive mail, and then pick up again wherever the application program was stopped. The system

(a)

(b)

(c)

Figure 16.1   The Cygnet Technologies Communications CoSystem

In April 1982, Cygnet Technologies was founded; in August 1983, it introduced its Communications CoSystem. (a) Federico Faggin, codeveloper of the first microprocessor, tests the CoSystem communications link from his new firm, Cygnet Technologies. (b) The CoSystem matches the personal computer's ability to process information with a telephone system's ability to gather and distribute it. The CoSystem works as a separate but equal partner to a personal computer; it has its own microprocessors, memory, and keyboard. (c) Note that since the memo is confidential, the user must type in a password to access it. The user can then call up an electronic mail editor to compose an immediate reply.

will transmit files created by those or other programs, using sophisticated techniques for checking errors in transmission. This capability means that users can also send programs to one another. (An error in transmitting a program will result in the recipient not being able to run it.) The CoSystem includes a 400-name personal telephone directory as well as a calendar and reminder service (using a blinking red indicator light and a beep), which is integrated with a personal time-scheduling and record-keeping system.

Intelligent Copiers

It used to be that copiers just had to make copies. Today, they enlarge, reduce, collate, count, control the release of chemicals to maintain uniform image quality, and diagnose their own troubles when they're broken. And, of course, they have to do all of this more rapidly and less expensively than ever before.

The Mita copier, for instance, shown in Figure 16.2, uses a 4-bit microprocessor to control the reduction or enlargement size, the document source and paper feeds, an automatic exposure device that adjusts for the different degrees of contrast in the original documents, storage of the desired number of copies keyed in by the

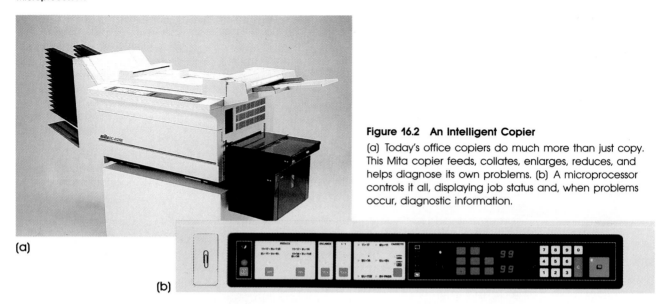

Figure 16.2   An Intelligent Copier
(a) Today's office copiers do much more than just copy.
This Mita copier feeds, collates, enlarges, reduces, and
helps diagnose its own problems. (b) A microprocessor
controls it all, displaying job status and, when problems
occur, diagnostic information.

(a)

(b)

*Microprocessors in office
copiers*

user, and the display panel that communicates the machine's overall status. The
microprocessor also allows a user to interrupt an ongoing job to make higher-priority rush copies by pressing an interrupt key, which stores the number of copies
remaining to be made and other preset values from the first job along with the total
count for the new job. When the rush job is completed, another touch of the
interrupt key recalls the stored values so the first job can be continued.

Is human intervention soon to be completely unnecessary for copiers like this,
which self-feed and self-collate in addition to all their other features? Probably not;
however, the microprocessor does control the display of job status while such a
copier is operating and, if a malfunction occurs, displays a trouble indicator signaling for human help. The cause of the malfunction is given by a displayed numeric
diagnostic code, which assures that the service personnel will arrive with the right
parts to set things straight. The microprocessor also controls a simulation-and-test
mode used to check the copier's systems during routine service and repair. For
example, cleaning out paper jams is made easier because the machine automatically displays the place in the system at which the problem occurred.

Help for the Meter Reader

After years of dealing with unfriendly dogs, locked gates, and annoyed homeown-
ers fresh out of the shower, meter readers can now do their job without leaving
their vehicles, thanks to embedded microprocessors. In fact, they can read meters
on both sides of a street while cruising by at up to 20 miles per hour. This improvement in the quality of life for meter readers (and for utility customers and their
dogs) was made possible by Engineering Optics, Inc., of Las Cruces, New Mexico,
which developed the Infrared Meter Access (IRMA) system. A circuit containing
an 8-bit microprocessor is installed in a standard electric meter (see Figure 16.3).
This circuit not only keeps track of total power consumption (which is what a
standard meter does) but also monitors variations in consumption during any time
periods specified by the utility, usually peak periods when generation is more

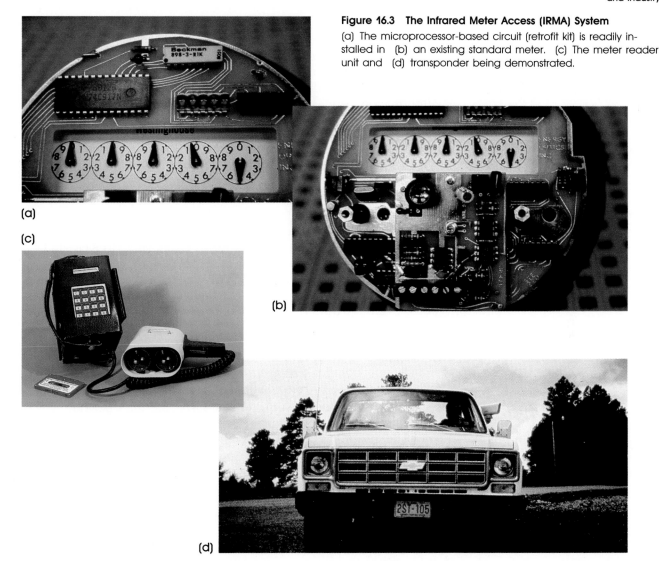

Figure 16.3   The Infrared Meter Access (IRMA) System
(a) The microprocessor-based circuit (retrofit kit) is readily installed in   (b) an existing standard meter.   (c) The meter reader unit and   (d) transponder being demonstrated.

costly. This permits billing rates to reflect more directly the power company's actual costs, as dictated by consumer demand.

The circuit in the meter is connected to an infrared *transponder,* a receiver-transmitter that transmits the stored data automatically on receipt of the appropriate signal. The reason this system utilizes infrared transmission is that radio frequencies are becoming increasingly saturated with signals and are fully regulated by the Federal Communications Commission. Light frequencies, on the other hand, including those in the infrared range, are virtually unused and completely unregulated. For the relatively short distances involved in this meter-reading application, infrared transmission is a low-cost and reliable method. The transponder can be mounted at the meter or nearby, for example, under the eaves of the house or on a utility pole. The meter reader, sitting in a vehicle, simply points a device like a "ray gun" in the general direction of the transponder and pulls the trigger. This signal to the transponder establishes instant two-way communication. In less than two-tenths of a second, the information is read from the meter; it is then

Remote meter reading

recorded on a cassette tape attached to the gun. An audible beep signals the successful completion of each reading. Back at the utility company, the contents of the cassette tape, which can store over a thousand meter records, are automatically read over onto the input medium required by the company's billing and record-keeping system. The meter reader can also remotely reprogram a meter's circuit to collect new information on power consumption, perhaps during certain specified days or hours.

SMART PRODUCTS FOR THE CONSUMER

Microprocessors help close high-rolling business deals, keep expensive photocopiers operating efficiently, and make it easier for the power company to read our meters and set their rates. But these are commercial applications of this versatile technology—there are an amazing number of more personal ones as well. In fact, there are more consumer products containing embedded microprocessors than we could possibly describe here: everything from VCRs and clock radios to dishwashers and birthday cards. We can't discuss all the numerous consumer-product applications, but we can at least look at a few of the most interesting.

Clever Cameras

The *single-lens reflex (SLR) camera* is the longstanding choice of serious photographers. In a traditional SLR camera, a mirror at a 45-degree angle behind the lens reflects the image-forming light rays from the lens onto a viewing screen at the top of the camera. The mirror lies directly between the lens and the film. When the user presses the button to take a shot, the mirror swings out of the way, the shutter opens, and the film is exposed. In other words, what you see on the viewing screen is what you get back from the developer. Non-SLR cameras generally have the disadvantage that there is some degree of difference between the image seen in the viewfinder and the image recorded on the film.

A truly automatic camera   As helpful a tool as SLR cameras are, however, certain factors governing the quality of shots still depended on the person with his or her finger on the button—until now. One of the latest automatic SLR cameras, the microprocessor-equipped Nikon FA, senses the brightness of five areas of the viewing frame instead of just the center, as is traditional (see Figure 16.4). Its microprocessor then computes both shutter speed and aperture (how long and how far the shutter is to remain open to admit light) for perfect exposure. The combination of multiple zones for light sensing and the computational facility of the microprocessor makes it possible to get fine shots automatically, even in the most difficult conditions. Diehard traditionalists are, of course, able to override the microprocessor and do things manually. However, according to informed reports, it takes some doing to better the smart camera's photographic skills.

Eyes for Your Personal Computer

Magazines aimed at microcomputer users and amateur programmers, such as *Byte* and *PCM,* frequently feature long, printed programs for their readers to use. If you've ever tried to key a program listing into a computer, you know what a

(a)
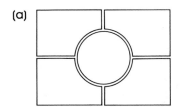

(b)

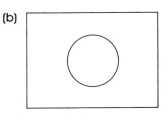

**Figure 16.4
The Nikon FA**

This SLR camera offers the option of automatic operation based on sensing light in (a) five zones or (b) the traditional single center area.

tedious, time-consuming, and error-prone process it is. Now Tandy–Radio Shack offers a small scanning wand as an accessory for its TRS-80 Model 100. A joystick or mouse can be used to call up a program already in memory, but this wand has an embedded microprocessor to interpret the bar code so that external programs can be entered quickly and accurately. It lets users read bar-coded BASIC program listings directly from the pages of *PCM* into the Model 100.

The scanning wand, shown in Figure 16.5, connects to the Model 100's standard interface for a bar code reader. The wand is passed smoothly over each line of

(a)

Figure 16.5   A Bar-Code Reader

Light from a light-emitting diode (LED) in (a) the tip of the scanning wand is reflected from the white (uninked) areas of the bar-coded strips. The inked areas (bars) don't reflect. This provides a pattern of signals to a detector in the wand, and a microprocessor decodes them into (b) the BASIC program statements. (b) © 1985 by Falsoft, Inc. Reprinted from PCM—The Personal Computing Magazine for Tandy © Computer Users. P.O. Box 385, Prospect, KY 40059.

(b)
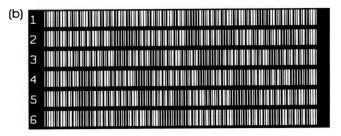

the bar code; the encoded BASIC statements are first converted into a pattern of electrical signals by light from a light-emitting diode in the tip of the wand. A light detector responds to the reflected pattern of light and dark like any standard UPC-reader (see Chapter 4), and the microprocessor decodes the pattern into the BASIC program statements that are entered into the computer's memory.

A scanning wand for reading printed programs

Although many computer-oriented publications offer their featured program listings for sale on diskettes or cassette tapes, these are often fairly expensive. The wand with its embedded microprocessor represents a one-time investment (of about $100) that may well be worth the price. It allows the user to take advantage of the convenience and economy of the printed page, which contains information about the program and how to use it, while providing an immediate way to load the program and run it.

And Little Friends

The day when clever little computer-companions will follow us around to clean up, make dinner, and rescue us from dreaded enemies is far off in the future. For the most part, today's robots are industrial (as we'll see in Chapter 18)—utilitarian and not at all cute. There is, however, a new crowd of so-called *recreational robots,* high-tech toys of varying sophistication and even more varying usefulness. Neiman-Marcus, the sophisticated Texas-based department store, offers its ComRo line of housekeeping robots for around $20,000, but they are of limited practical usefulness. Most of the other robots currently available are for amusement only, such as Tomy Corporation's trio of toy ''droids,'' none of which are likely to rescue you from the darker corners of the universe. A family portrait is given in Figure 16.6.

Recreational robots

DINGBOT, to start with, stands all of five inches high and skitters along the floor, ''reading'' a map and bumping into things. At each encounter, it stops, chatters to itself, shakes its head, and moves on.

The second member of Tomy's product line is VERBOT, a voice-activated robot that responds only to its owner's voice speaking preprogrammed commands, which are entered via a wireless, remote-control microphone transmitter. VERBOT can be programmed to perform eight functions; on the appropriate verbal

Figure 16.6 Recreational Robots
The Tomy line of toy robots are (from left to right): DINGBOT, VERBOT, and OMNIBOT.

command, it will move forward or backward, turn left or right, pick up a small object and carry it or set it down, or stop. When ordered to smile, VERBOT's eyes light up and it emits a cheerful clicking sound.

The top of the Tomy line is OMNIBOT. Standing nearly two feet tall, it is a preprogrammable robot complete with microprocessor, cassette tape player, remote control transmitter, digital alarm clock, built-in microphone, and a "hand" that can grasp objects. OMNIBOT moves forward or backward, turns left or right, and stops on command. Using the remote control transmitter, an owner can program OMNIBOT to repeat up to seven different programs at designated times, as far ahead in the future as seven days. OMNIBOT can be programmed to perform by remote control or from its memory. As a result, it can deliver a note held in its hand or recite a pretaped message via its on-board tape deck or serve as a butler, delivering snacks on its little serving tray. It can bring in the newspaper and then retreat to a corner of the room and play music from a cassette tape, or it can come into a room at a preprogrammed time in the morning with a recorded wake-up call. OMNIBOT is battery-operated and both rechargeable battery and recharging unit are built in.

ISSUES IN TECHNOLOGY

Are "fun" computer applications (like a toy programmed to react to bumping into furniture) okay, or should technological advances be taken more seriously? The ancient Romans developed the steam engine but used it only to power little toy carts for children; a leap forward in human progress might have occurred if they had harnessed steam more seriously. Does our own casual and commercial attitude toward technology represent a similar deterrent to real progress?

SMART CARS

As their cost continues to decrease and their performance continues to improve, it's natural that microprocessors will be increasingly used not only as the basis for new products, like those we've just discussed, but also as a means of making existing products cheaper and better. Nowhere is this trend better demonstrated than in the automobile industry, where microprocessors are being applied to yield radical alterations in subsystems that have traditionally been mechanical. Some people have described this changeover as a quiet revolution in an industry whose economic importance is paramount. As we discuss the specific automotive subsystems in which microprocessors are found, it will be apparent that their incorporation has been due to a range of causes, from the need to meet federally mandated environmental standards to the drive to improve safety and economy of operation.

Improving an existing product

Engine Controls

The 1984 model year marked a milestone in the automobile's history: nearly all the cars sold that year contained microprocessor-based electronic engine controls. The principal cause behind this achievement was the need to meet the federal Environmental Protection Agency's mandates for emission and fuel economy levels.

*Increasing gas economy and
lowering emissions*

Generally, an engine microprocessor receives input from sensors that communicate such data as the mass of intake air, temperature, pressure, throttle position, and the operating load and speed. With these inputs, the microprocessor controls the recirculation of exhaust gases, air and fuel injection, and spark timing, in order to achieve the greatest economy and lowest emissions. Some recent microprocessor-based engine control systems are precise enough to eliminate much of the usual emission-control hardware, thereby simultaneously reducing costs and improving engine performance. Since 1980, automobile fuel economy has increased by more than 25%, and the 1980 figures were already vastly improved over those of the previous decade. Since 1970, emissions have been reduced by factors of from three to seven for those pollutants of major concern.

Displays

As display technology continues to develop rapidly, driven largely by the demand for low-cost, rugged displays for personal computers and computer terminals, the automobile will be a beneficiary. The current trend is toward flat-panel displays and the judicious use of voice messages. Chrysler introduced the latter in 1983 and made them more specific and briefer in 1984, when it also added a turn-off option.

A state-of-the-art display is shown in Figure 16.7. This microprocessor-controlled instrument cluster, which is standard on the 1985 Buick Somerset Regal, uses a *flat fluorescent display tube*. The tube has layers of fine wires embedded in it so it can be illuminated in any desired pattern. Other auto manufacturers use very similar display technologies. The purpose of such a display is to provide information whenever requested by the driver, but to provide automatically only what is important for the driver to know. Information that is automatically displayed includes messages to warn of malfunctions (such as low oil or brake pressure) and oversights (such as a key left in the ignition or headlights left on).

*Displays that provide more
information*

Figure 16.7   The Microprocessor-Controlled Instrument Panel of the 1985 Buick Somerset Regal
An 8-bit microprocessor and memory chip does the calculating and provides the storage for maintaining an image, which is updated every 1.6 milliseconds. A switch changes the display mode for the speedometer, odometer, and trip odometer from miles to kilometers. Another switch, for the multifunction gauge, alternates from tachometer to voltage, to oil pressure, to temperature, and back to tachometer. The fuel gauge can be switched from full scale (empty to full) to quarter scale when gas is low and greater accuracy is desired.

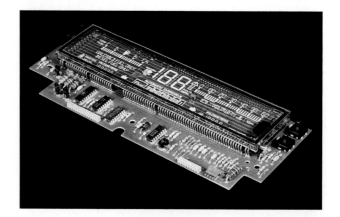

In previous chapters, we've given you a great deal of general information about careers in data processing. But where can you go for more detailed, "real-world" information? To answer that question, we'll use this Careers in Technology section to give you a list of some of the leading employers of computer professionals. These are fifteen of the largest manufacturers of computers and peripheral equipment. We're also including corporate addresses, so that you may write to any of these firms for information on their products, employment practices, and personnel requirements.

Apple Computer
20525 Mariani Avenue
Cupertino, CA 95014

Burroughs Corporation
Burroughs Place
Detroit, MI 48232

Control Data Corporation
8100 34th Avenue South
Bloomington, MN 55440

Data General Corporation
4400 Computer Drive
Westborough, MA 01580

Digital Equipment Corporation
146 Main Street
Maynard, MA 01754

Hewlett-Packard Company
1501 Page Mill Road
Palo Alto, CA 94304

Honeywell, Inc.
Honeywell Plaza
Minneapolis, MN 55408

IBM
Old Orchard Road
Armonk, NY 10504

Memorex Corporation
San Thomas at Central Expressway
Santa Clara, CA 95052

NCR
1700 South Patterson Boulevard
Dayton, OH 45409

Sperry Rand
1290 Avenue of the Americas
New York, NY 10019

Storage Technology Corporation
2270 South 88th Street
Louisville, CO 80027

Texas Instruments, Inc.
P.O. Box 225474
Dallas, TX 75265

3M
3M Center
St. Paul, MN 55101

TRW, Inc.
23555 Euclid Avenue
Cleveland, OH 44117

Wang Laboratories, Inc.
One Industrial Avenue
Lowell, MA 01851

As long as we're on the subject, here are the addresses of ten manufacturers of automobiles, aircraft, and electronic equipment. These are some of the largest employers of computer professionals outside the computer industry.

American Motors, Inc.
Franklin Road
Southfield, MI 48024

Bendix
Bendix Center
Southfield, MI 48037

Ford Motor Company
The American Road
Dearborn, MI 48121

General Dynamics Corporation
P.O. Box 81127
San Diego, CA 92138

General Motors Corporation
3044 West Grand Boulevard
Detroit, MI 48202

Grumman Corporation
1111 Stewart Avenue
Bethpage, NY 11714

Lockheed Electronics Company
U.S. Highway 22
Watchung, NJ 07060

RCA Corporation
Building 202-2
Cherry Hill, NJ 08358

United Technologies Corporation
United Technologies Building
1 Financial Plaza
Hartford, CT 06101

Western Electric
P.O. Box 25000
Greensboro, NC 27420

Interesting new uses for microprocessor-controlled displays are being researched by all the auto manufacturers. Some intriguing possibilities for the near future are discussed in Chapter 23.

Diagnostics

There is currently a major effort to develop on-board microprocessor-controlled systems that assist in fault diagnosis, repair, and routine maintenance, in addition to alerting the driver to potentially dangerous problems. On some 1985 Cadillacs, a total of 43 malfunction codes can be displayed on the instrument panel. An

Finding and preventing problems

owner or a mechanic interrogates the *electronic control module (ECM)*, which controls engine functions, by pressing the appropriate buttons. When this is done, the ECM switches from control mode to diagnostic mode and displays the malfunction codes. These codes furnish diagnostic information about the 19 principal engine subsystems. A *body control module (BCM)* controls the body-related subsystem: heating, ventilation, and air conditioning. It detects malfunctions and stores corresponding codes in memory. Again, in diagnostic mode, these codes are displayed. Comparable systems are available on top-of-the-line models from other manufacturers.

Auto manufacturers' provision of on-board systems that give definitive and comprehensive diagnostic information is paralleled by the manufacturers of the increasingly automatic equipment used in the auto repair shop. Most maintenance systems—from the complex ones used for engine tune-ups to those that do dynamic wheel balancing—incorporate microprocessors. The Coats 460, for example, compares actual data for the engine of the car being serviced with the manufacturer's specifications, which are stored on floppy disks. The floppy disks are updated when new car models make their appearance. It performs a large battery of tests and prints out the results, flagging significant discrepancies between actual performance and the manufacturer's design standards. Such automatic comparisons and the accompanying analysis are particularly useful for state auto inspections, since the examination is quick, detailed, accurate, and objective. Figure 16.8 shows a computer-based automobile systems tester being used.

Comfort and Safety

As cars are built lighter, to bring down the price and increase the fuel economy, the maintaining of a comfortable ride gets more difficult. In a heavy car, the coil springs can accommodate to the full range of loads, from a single driver to a full load of passengers and luggage. But with lighter cars, this load range represents a greater percentage of the total weight (car plus load). A spring hard enough to handle the full load gives the driver of the empty car too hard a ride.

Adjusting the suspension to the load

On some of its models, Ford has introduced an electronic air suspension system that uses microprocessor-controlled, adjustable air springs. Adjusting the suspension system to the load provides not only a more comfortable ride, but also a safer one. Because the system automatically changes the car's front and rear road clearance to allow for the load distribution, its leveling feature keeps the headlights aimed properly and results in more stable handling. General Motors has a similar system.

Testing and using the air bag

Ford has also made an air-bag restraint system available on some of its 1985 models. The system consists of an air bag, a special steering column and wheel, sensors that detect when to deploy the system, and microprocessor-based diagnostic and control electronics. When a deployment-level impact is sensed, the microprocessor unit ignites a gas generator, which produces the nitrogen gas that fills the bag before the occupants can be seriously injured by the jolt. The unit also monitors the readiness of the system, detecting any of eleven possible disabling faults.

Preventing wheel-lock skids

Lincolns for 1985 have an optional system that helps prevent the wheels from locking when the brakes are applied, particularly on slippery roads. Separate speed sensors on all four wheel hubs send continuous signals to a microprocessor. If one

Figure 16.8   An Automated Tester in the Repair Shop

wheel begins to slow more rapidly than the others during braking (an indication of imminent wheel-lock) the microprocessor takes over the system and pulses the brake pressure (releases and reapplies the brake in a sequence of quick taps) to that wheel. The antilock system monitors itself; if it detects a fault, it returns the braking operation to normal manual mode and lights an indicator lamp.

SUMMARY

The Embedded Microprocessor Chip

When augmented by primary and secondary memory and peripheral equipment, the microprocessor is the CPU of a microcomputer system. But microprocessors are also the basis for a new generation of smart products, in which the chip provides the program and the user the input. Embedded microprocessors are inherently more reliable and more flexible than the specialized, more costly circuit boards that they have largely displaced.

Smart Products for Business and Industry

The beginning of an avalanche of new products makes information-handling simpler and more reliable.

The Very Smart Telephone   Smart telephones, attached to personal computers, provide instant networking capability. They have their own microprocessors, memories, and keyboards, and can interleave voice and data on a single line. Electronic mail (with on-line filing) and teleconferencing are among their uses.

Intelligent Copiers   The capabilities to interrupt and later resume large jobs, to copy from different originals to any of several selected copy sizes, to control copy quality automatically, and to give assistance in locating troubles are copier characteristics that result from microprocessor control.

Help for the Meter Reader   The meter reader can read meters remotely, from a moving vehicle, if the meters have been fitted with the IRMA system. A microprocessor-based circuit installed in an existing meter stores the consumption information, and a specialized communications system allows the remote read-out of the stored data.

Smart Products for the Consumer

There are many consumer-product applications of embedded microprocessors.

Clever Cameras A microprocessor automatically calculates the best exposure (shutter opening size and duration) for each shot by the newest single-lens-reflex cameras.

Eyes for Your Personal Computer A scanning wand for the TRS-80 Model 100 allows the input of bar-coded listings of BASIC programs directly from the pages of the magazine *PCM*.

And Little Friends A line of recreational robots by Tomy Corporation performs entertaining and somewhat useful actions.

Smart Cars

Microprocessors are the basis not only for entirely new classes of products, but also for the improvement of existing ones, especially the automobile.

Engine Controls Using information from sensors monitoring air, temperature, pressure, and throttle position, a microprocessor controls the engine to produce the highest operating economy and the fewest emissions possible.

Displays Flat-panel displays provide information that was previously unavailable in a format that is readily read and understood by the driver.

Diagnostics Troubles are avoided, but also located if they do occur, with the help of on-board microprocessor-based diagnostic systems augmented by sophisticated electronic systems in the repair shop.

Comfort and Safety Electronically controlled air suspension systems adjust to the weight and distribution of the automobile's load; a too-hard or too-soft ride is avoided, and handling is improved; air bags are kept in readiness and deployed only when needed. All of these are controlled by a microprocessor-based system. A microprocessor also prevents dangerous wheel-lock and skidding.

COMPUTER CONCEPTS ▬▬▬

As an extra review of the chapter, try defining the following terms. If you have trouble with either of them, refer to the page number listed.

smart products 471   embedded microprocessor 471

REVIEW QUESTIONS ▬▬▬

1. Microprocessors are most common as CPUs for personal computers. How else are they used?
2. What form did electronic controls take before microprocessors were developed?
3. Describe a typical teleconference using a smart telephone.
4. What electronic mail functions does the smart telephone provide?
5. What copier functions are controlled by an embedded microprocessor? How does it help to maintain the copier?
6. What are the three basic parts of the IRMA system? How do they operate?
7. How does the embedded microprocessor in an SLR camera help you get the best shot possible under given lighting conditions?
8. How does the Tandy–Radio Shack scanning wand work to read bar-coded information? What are the advantages of using a scanning wand to input a BASIC program?
9. What are OMNIBOT's principal subsystems? How are they used?

10. What factors have been most important in advancing the use of microprocessors in the automobile?
11. What sensors provide inputs to the microprocessor-based electronic engine controls? What does it control? What is the result?
12. What results are achieved by microprocessor-controlled automobile dashboard displays?
13. What are the diagnostic functions of the electronic control module (ECM) and the body control module (BCM)?
14. Describe the operation of the Coats 460. Where does it store and update manufacturers' specifications?
15. What does the microprocessor of the electronic air suspension system control?
16. Explain the operation of an automatic air-bag restraint system.
17. How does the wheel-lock prevention system work?

A SHARPER FOCUS

Now that you've completed this chapter, you should be able to answer the following questions about the chapter opening.

1. Would you call the new greeting cards "intelligent"? Why or why not?
2. Singing greeting cards, like recreational robots, are one of the less serious applications of embedded microprocessors. How might they evolve into a more serious application?

PROJECTS

1. Describe some microprocessor-based products not mentioned in this chapter, focusing on some specific product area, such as office products, communications products, or recreational products.
2. Go to an automobile showroom. For one of the top-of-the-line new models, and with the help of the sales and service personnel, see whether you can enumerate and describe the functions of its microprocessors.
3. One group of consumer products that is often overlooked, but in which there has been a tremendous amount of microprocessor use, is electronic musical instruments. Visit a store that sells electronic organs, and have a salesperson show you what's inside the fancy wooden cabinet. Write a report summarizing your findings.
4. Small robots are available from several other well-known companies besides Tomy. Investigate the characteristics and limitations of one of these products, and prepare a report describing the tasks around your house that you could (realistically) program such a robot to do.

Application Perspective

A Quiet Evening at Home

Voici une belle
plage de la Martinique.

PRESS [RETURN] TO CONTINUE_

① You've been dreaming of a trip to the French-speaking Caribbean island of Martinique for several years. Now, this is the year! You bought a French-teaching program to get ready. During a quiet evening at home, you're learning a little French when a thought suddenly hits you: Can I really afford this trip, or am I just kidding myself? Who's going to take care of everything while I'm away?

What'll I do tonight? → Study French in preparation for trip

Relax by simulating a flight to NYC → Go to sleep

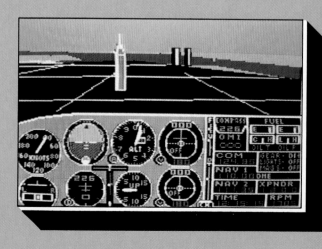

④ You're reassured that your vacation plan is realistic, you've informed those who depend on you of your intended absence, and you're ready for a little relaxation before you turn in. You load the flight simulator game and take off in your Cessna to fly to New York City. Tired but triumphant after a safe touchdown, you turn in.

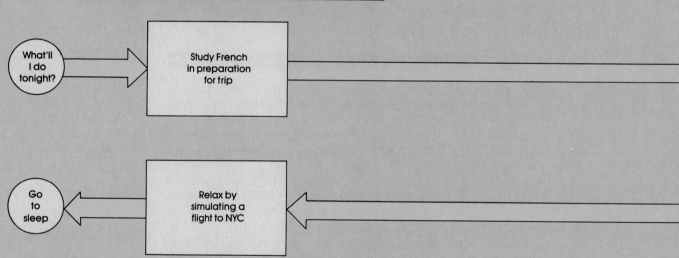

② You insert the spreadsheet program that you use to plan your expenses by quarter. Your inspection shows that you aren't saving as much as you had forecasted but that by cutting back modestly on a few items you'll still be able to save the money you need for your trip by the end of the year.

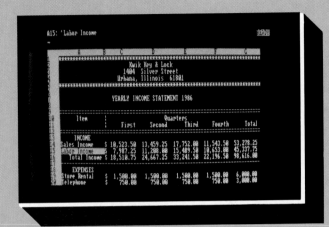

Can I really afford to go?

Notify those who need to know of my travel plans

③ You next retrieve a file of people who must be notified about your upcoming absence. You compose a general letter using your word-processing program. Most of the letter is done only once and serves for all the recipients; you then personalize each person's with a little note that relates only to that recipient.

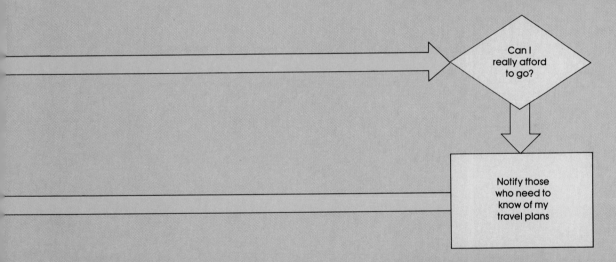

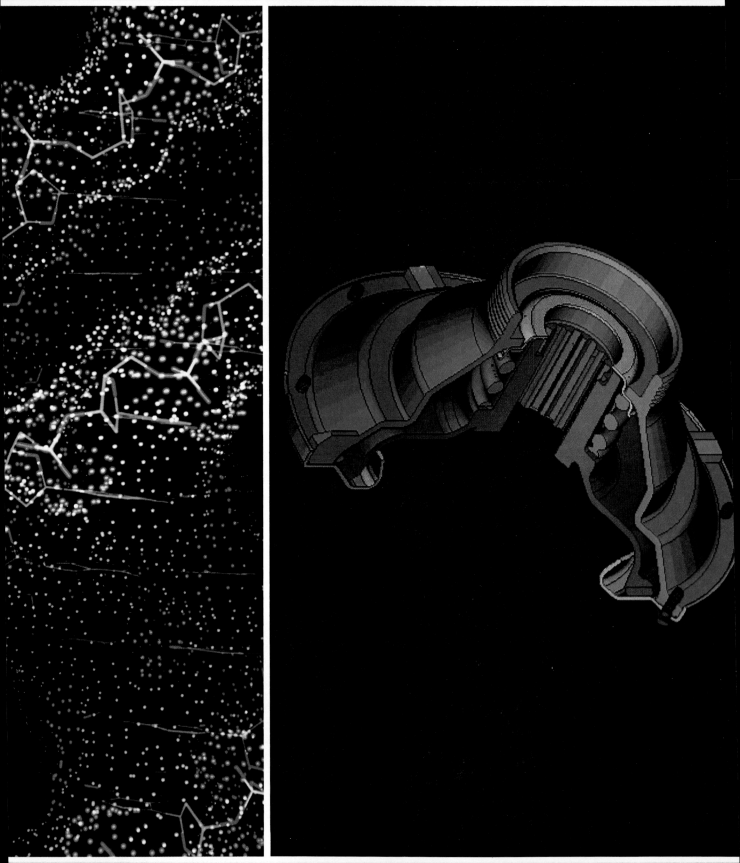

Part 6

APPLICATIONS

Backed by a thorough understanding of computers—their history and hardware, software and systems—we can now turn our attention to the various ways they perform useful, vital, and intriguing work for us. These applications are the fruits of technology, the benefits that make computers worthwhile.

Chapter 17 explores the role computers are playing in modern offices, in everything from word processing to networking. Chapter 18 introduces the "steel-collar worker" that is appearing in research laboratories and on assembly lines as major industries increasingly turn to computers for help in all areas of design and manufacturing. Chapter 19 presents an overview of computers in the business world, exploring their applications in the commercial realm. Chapter 20 turns from the world of high finance and big business to the world of learning and creativity: education, the arts (notably music and movies), and science. Finally, Chapter 21 reports on the reliance of local, state, and federal governments on computers, from the highway patrol and the IRS to new defense systems in space.

17

Computers in the Office

IN THIS CHAPTER

▶

FOCUS ON . . . THE DOWNSIDE OF THE COMPUTERIZED OFFICE

People have been discovering the hard way that there is more to modernizing an office than simply replacing each typewriter with a video display terminal (VDT). . . .

The more suddenly an organization tries to make the changeover from ink to electrons for information processing, the more unsettling that change may be for the workers who have to participate. Children and computer hobbyists find it easy to fall in love with these new machines; they can learn at a comfortable pace how the machines behave, and the learning process itself is a form of play for them. The situation is different if your boss just took away your beloved electric typewriter and told you that from now on you'll spend your days staring at the phosphorescent glow of a CRT screen. When computers are forced on you, there's nothing playful about them.

Working with "soft" information on a screen is fundamentally different (both for better and for worse) from working with "hard" information on paper. That difference permits greater efficiency and productivity but also presents an entirely new set of possibilities for accidents, errors, and loss of information. It would be surprising if people didn't feel insecure while adapting to a new situation in which pressing the wrong button can wipe out a whole day's work, "crash" the program, or maybe cause the whole computer to explode in smoke and flying sparks. (Everybody has seen it happen in movies and TV shows. How can you be sure of its impossibility?)

One of us (Mitchell) reports that though he used to dismiss VDT stress as irrational and silly, he changed his mind after driving a friend's expensive new car through the city. "Normally I enjoy snaking my old jalopy smoothly through Boston's notoriously competitive traffic," he reports, "but driving the new car was a miserable experience because of the responsibility and tension involved. Getting out of that car and back into my familiar old junker brought a feeling of relief that seemed as much physical as mental." Conclusion: Even seemingly irrational fears deserve to be treated with respect, because they can be just as debilitating as a concrete physical threat.

Bob Cratchit, Ebenezer Scrooge's clerk in "A Christmas Carol," scribbled away more than 12 hours a day, entering figures in ledgers and copying correspondence by the light of a candle in a cold, dim backroom. Perched on a backless stool before a tiny desk, he's a well-drawn illustration, only somewhat exaggerated, of the office conditions under which most people worked in Dickens's London. Things were much the same in this country during the nineteenth century. The lighting was bad, the workload enormous, and the staffing, for the sake of economy, as small as possible. The clerk, a sort of combination photocopier, secretary, and accountant, had too much to do, and most of it was laborious, dull, and time-consuming. Imagine making 20 copies of this chapter by hand, each one identical, legible, and without scratch-outs, smudges, or erasures—and you've begun to imagine working in the old-style office.

By 1900, the typewriter was in general use. Its adoption in the workplace took place very much like the more recent integration of computers into the office, and the effect of its appearance was just as revolutionary. In the first half of the twentieth century, the office changed. Volume and productivity became the watchwords. The office was transformed into a giant manual processing system, and the clerks' cubbyholes gave way to warehouse-sized rooms full of rows of desks, with telephones, typewriters, and adding machines producing a deafening racket. This sea of mechanized people, cogs in a giant paper-pushing machine was significantly brighter and more efficient than the Victorian office but little more pleasant.

In this latter part of the twentieth century, the office has changed again. This chapter examines the rise of the information age and its impact on how, and where, white-collar work is done.

 ## THE DIMENSIONS OF OFFICE AUTOMATION

Computers in the white-collar workplace

This chapter is about how computers are being used to improve the productivity and general environment of the modern office. This process, which has been going on since the early 1960s, has been called a number of colorful, although somewhat misleading, names, including *office automation, office information systems, the office of the future, the electronic office, the paperless office, the integrated office,* and *office support*. Although none of these terms is universally accepted to describe the application of new technology in the office, **office automation** is perhaps the most widely used. In general, it refers to the use of computer, communications, and office equipment technologies to support the many activities that occur in the business environment. After discussing the importance of the office in our society and detailing what is actually done in offices, we'll describe some of the specific applications of computers in these white-collar workplaces.

The Information Age

Coping with paperwork and change

Basically, an office is a place where information is processed; it's a text, data, and decision factory. The growing importance of such places in today's society is at least partly due to the fact that we've been experiencing an information explosion for the past two decades. More and more people are now working in the information sector; the United States has progressed from having primarily an industrial economy (in which tangible goods like steel and automobiles are produced) to an information economy (in which data are processed into information). The salaries paid to office workers comprise a large percentage of many organizations' expenses, and it tends to increase every year. The application of new technology is one way in which existing staff can be made more productive while the chronic overflow of paperwork is reduced. In the information age, computers become more than just valuable; they are essential for handling vast quantities of data and keeping costs down to manageable levels.

ISSUES IN TECHNOLOGY

It's been said that office workers and managers are drowning in data but starving for real information. Because computers *can* easily process so much data and output so many reports, they're often programmed to regurgitate information in every possible way. A central issue concerning office automation from its start has been the question of whether introducing computers dampens or accelerates the so-called information explosion. Do automated offices generate information for no real reason except that they're capable of doing so? Do all those fancy computer-based machines encourage the production of nicely formatted but worthless documents? What do you think?

Office automation has also been necessary to cope with the ever-increasing rate of change in today's world. Organizations that don't utilize new office technologies aren't able to keep up with accelerating technological advances and find it more difficult to compete in the marketplace. In addition, as the rate of worldwide change increases, an organization's environment becomes more unstable. To combat this uncertainty, an organization must process still more information with still greater efficiency. Finally, proponents of office automation claim that it can help workers achieve more satisfying, less stressful, and more prestigious jobs by reducing the tedium of performing mindless, repetitive tasks. Whether or not this is the case, there is great potential for allowing office personnel greater freedom in terms of when, where, and how they do their jobs.

ISSUES IN TECHNOLOGY

Recently, Working Women, a national association of office workers, took a survey among women employees who work with computers and word processors. The survey asked individuals to describe what they like and don't like about their work. The findings indicated that these employees enjoy social contacts with others, variety in their work, opportunities to advance, and the acquisition of new skills and of knowledge about their company and industry. Not surprisingly, they dislike a lack of respect from their supervisors, the prospect of no advancement, and low pay. Furthermore, the study also found that although many of these employees admit that computers and word processors helped them increase their productivity, their organizations didn't necessarily reward them for this efficiency in terms of higher pay. One conclusion that can be drawn here is that some workers don't see office automation as benefiting them at all; on the contrary, they see it as *worsening* their work situation (less variety, fewer social contacts, lower relative pay, and routine jobs). Is the automated office just a high-tech sweatshop?

Office Functions

In order to see how computers are being applied to office procedures, we need to start from some point of agreement about just what these functions are. This isn't as obvious as it might seem. Offices serve a variety of purposes, many of which aren't especially well defined. There are vast differences among the offices of various kinds of organizations, and modern offices in general are in a state of drastic change. Since the advent of data communications, it may not even be valid to impose geographical boundaries on offices. The activities and functions normally attributed to the office no longer necessarily have to occur in any particular location; they can be widely dispersed. There are, however, a few generalizations we can make about the nature of the office.

What goes on in the office

As we've already noted, and as almost everyone would agree, offices process and handle information. Beyond this, there are diverse but overlapping views of exactly what goes on in an office. In general, however, the following functions are performed by the managers, professionals, and clerical staff who work in offices:

- *Generating information.* Office workers, especially managers and professionals, produce information in the form of letters, memos, reports, and other documents.

- *Modifying information.* In most offices, information that is stored must be periodically changed or updated. For example, business offices that handle customer accounts must process payment transactions to update their records.
- *Gathering information.* Often, data must be amassed about some aspect of the general environment to fulfill an organization's purposes. Governmental offices, such as those of the Census Bureau, the Social Security Administration, and the Internal Revenue Service, collect vast quantities of information from and about citizens.
- *Filing (or storing) information.* Information that is generated or gathered must be held somewhere. For a small business office, this function might be fulfilled by keeping some folders in an ordinary filing cabinet. The Internal Revenue Service, on the other hand, maintains massive stores of information on magnetic tape kept in vaults.
- *Retrieving information.* Accessing stored information is an important function in almost every office. The activities of generation, collection, and storage are of little use if information cannot be retrieved when needed.
- *Analyzing information.* Most offices that gather information must analyze or process it in some way. The Internal Revenue Service, for example, processes tax returns to verify them, to issue refund checks, and to conduct audits.
- *Communicating information.* Office communications involves the transfer of messages both within an organization and to and from the outside world (most often via telephone and mail). This function also includes the output and distribution of information in the form of reports and publications.

The New Technology

The future is already here

The term *office of the future* is a misnomer, of course, because, although most offices haven't integrated all of the parts, the technology for full office automation is currently available. Full office automation doesn't mean that human workers won't be needed, but rather that many of the office's traditionally repetitive, time-wasting tasks can be minimized or eliminated. A lot of the hardware and software described throughout this book is being applied to improving office conditions, efficiency, and productivity. The major areas in which office automation is bringing about notable changes in the white-collar workplace are word processing, office communications, office output, and ergonomics (which we'll discuss in Chapter 22).

 ## WORD PROCESSING

Writing with a computer

Simply defined, *word processing* is writing with a computer. Text is entered on a keyboard, and it appears on a screen. A *word processor* (referring to the computer hardware and/or software) lets the user insert, delete, edit, rearrange, format, and merge textual material until a document appears exactly as it should. At that point, the document is ready to be stored, printed, copied, and distributed. In addition, any stored text can be easily revised at any time. Some word-processing systems can also merge stored text and other data (to produce personalized form letters, for example), perform simple computations, generate output for typesetting machines, accept input from optical character recognition devices, and communicate with other word-processing systems.

Some type of word-processing system is found in virtually every modern office. As the cornerstone of office automation, word processing is used in government, education, business, the communications industry, and the majority of other large organizations. In addition, word-processing programs are very popular application packages for personal computers, as we noted in Chapters 10 and 15. Writers, students, teachers, lawyers, editors, and computer scientists are but a few of the people for whom word processors are helpful tools. In short, wherever documents are routinely prepared, word-processing systems are likely to be found.

The Problem with Conventional Typing

As we mentioned at the start of this chapter, the introduction of the typewriter significantly affected the nature and productivity of office work. For most of this century, the typewritten document has been the primary vehicle of business communication. Yet, as important as it still is, analysts have long recognized that conventional typing has several inherent shortcomings:

Constant retyping and introduced errors

Repetitive text—such as the contents of form letters, report headings, standard contracts, and similar "boilerplate" material—must be retyped over and over again to produce multiple originals. Such retyping is time-consuming. Also, it carries with it the potential for introducing new errors each time and thus the necessity of proofreading each duplicate document.

Even the most highly skilled typists make some keystroking errors. The usual correction methods (erasing, "whiting-out," or starting over) interrupt the typist, take time and may deface the document.

Minor revisions or simple format changes often require typing an entire document over again. Many documents—such as technical reports, proposals, and legal briefs—must be routinely revised as a result of content changes and/or rearrangements. Again, each time a document is retyped, the possibility exists for entering errors in portions that were typed correctly in the first place.

These shortcomings contribute to degraded work, low clerical productivity, and increased costs for document production. The major advantage of word processing as compared to conventional typing is that the operator doesn't have to retype corrected documents. Errors can be detected and easily corrected before documents are printed. Finished documents can be stored, and as many identical copies made as needed. If modifications are necessary, there is no need to retype the entire document; the stored text is readily retrieved, altered, and reprinted.

A Brief History of Word Processing

Word processing is essentially the application of computer technology to the input, editing, merging, storing, formatting, and printing of text. It evolved as a means to facilitate these tasks and overcome the limitations associated with conventional typing.

From typewriters to mainframe-based systems

In the early 1960s, automatic typewriters such as the Friden Flexowriter and the American Autotypist simplified the task of repetitious typing by storing keystrokes on punched paper tape that could be played back to create multiple typewritten originals. The era of word processing, however, actually began in 1964 with the introduction of IBM's Magnetic Tape Selectric Typewriter (MT/ST). This device, the first of its kind, recorded keystrokes simultaneously on paper and on an easily removable magnetic tape. Besides automatically producing typewritten copies of stored documents, the MT/ST made it easy for typists to correct errors and make changes in previously entered text. Although it seems crude by today's standards, the MT/ST set the stage for the use of computer technology and magnetic storage media in automated word processing.

The next major development was the introduction of CRT display screens, which allow operators to see and edit what they enter before it is printed onto paper. As word processing became a common and useful office practice, computer-based systems involving microcomputers, minicomputers, and mainframes were developed. Today, several categories of word processors are in widespread use.

Types of Word Processors

Although some overlap exists among the categories, word-processing systems can be divided into four types: electronic typewriters, dedicated systems, personal computer systems, and shared systems. Keep in mind that word processors really form a continuum, with the electric typewriter at one extreme and the mainframe-based system at the other. With more sophisticated word-processing systems, differentiating them from computers is difficult. In fact, word processors are computers that have special software and sometimes special keyboards, displays, and printers.

Electronic Typewriters

Computerized typewriters

Electronic typewriters are electric typewriters with embedded microprocessors (see Figure 17.1). These machines allow users to make corrections, insertions, and deletions before the text is typed on paper. Special keys are usually included to center, justify (make even) the right margin, print in boldface, and underscore words. Electronic typewriters most often have a removable ball or daisy wheel printing element.

Figure 17.1 An Electronic Typewriter
The electronic typewriter is an electric typewriter with an embedded microprocessor. Most models have at least a one-line display screen, and some can store text on magnetic tapes, cards, or disks.

Figure 17.2 A Dedicated Word Processor
The dedicated word processor is a specialized microcomputer system with a CRT display, a keyboard, one or two floppy disk drives, and a printer. Its sole function is word processing.

These machines are "intelligent" in that they have a memory that can store at least one line of text before it's typed. Some advanced models use magnetic tapes, cards, or disks to hold multiple pages of text that can be played back to make corrections or additional copies. Text is usually previewed, before printing or storage, on a small light emitting diode (LED) or liquid crystal display (LCD) screen that may show from one to several complete lines. Electronic typewriters are well suited to repetitive jobs that don't require extensive editing. They're particularly useful for secretarial and clerical workers, who tend to be good typists. For such users, electronic typewriters supply extra power and can significantly speed up their work. Since they offer more functions and are generally more reliable, electronic typewriters have replaced ordinary electric typewriters in many organizations.

Dedicated Systems

Dedicated word processors are the most familiar and heavily marketed of all word-processing systems. Also sometimes called a *stand-alone*, or *single-purpose, word processor*, such a system essentially consists of a microcomputer with a large CRT display screen, a full keyboard, one or two floppy disk drives, and a letter-quality printer (see Figure 17.2). Even though these dedicated systems include microcomputers, their sole function is word processing. Some have extra hard disk storage and built-in communications devices. Dedicated word processors are single-user systems primarily designed for medium to large offices. They're generally housed in handsome, well-designed consoles and usually come with well-prepared instructions and documentation.

Single-purpose microcomputer systems

Text is typed in at the keyboard and appears on the CRT display. Entered material is stored in the microcomputer's primary memory and can be viewed on the screen and edited before being sent to disk storage or to the printer. Some systems can communicate with other word processors via phone lines or send and receive electronic mail. A dedicated system is run by built-in word-processing software that usually can't be replaced or supplemented by other prewritten software. Since they're fully integrated systems designed purely for effective word processing, dedicated systems differ from general-purpose microcomputers in being unable to run other application packages (such as electronic spreadsheets, graphics packages, or educational software). However, dedicated systems do what they were designed to do very well; as word processors they tend to be very powerful, fast, and easy to use.

Figure 17.3 The Personal Computer as Word Processor

Any single-user personal computer system becomes a word processor when it's running a word-processing application package.

Personal Computer Systems

The familiar personal computer

As we've already seen in Chapters 10 and 15, a personal computer can be used as a word processor if a prewritten software package for word processing is run on it. The basic hardware components of a personal computer system are essentially the same as those in a dedicated word processor: a single-user microcomputer, CRT display, keyboard, one or more disk drives, and a printer (see Figure 17.3). The software, however, is not built-in but must be purchased from an independent software vendor. As we mentioned in the preceding section, the definitive difference between the dedicated word processor and the microcomputer as word processor is that the latter can be used to run other applications.

Although microcomputer-based systems are usually less expensive than dedicated word processors and are not limited to a single application, they tend to lack the convenience, full spectrum of features, and excellent instruction and documentation materials typical of dedicated word processors. Nevertheless, word-processing packages for personal computers are extremely popular, being especially common in small offices. The selection of such packages is large, and the personal computers can also be used to run other application software.

Shared Systems

Multiuser time-sharing systems

Word processing can also be done on powerful, multiuser minicomputer and mainframe systems (see Figure 17.4). Such **shared word processors** (or **clustered word processors**) can serve several users at once on a time-sharing basis. Since large computers are already used in many offices for data processing, it's often economical to purchase word-processing packages from manufacturers or independent software vendors and run them on the existing computer facilities. Although they're not as popular as dedicated word processors, the market for shared systems has been growing faster recently because of the ever-increasing power of new hardware and software.

With a shared system, a number of terminals are often designated to be used only as word-processing **workstations** (places with input and output hardware set up for individual users). The operating system of the computer is programmed to recognize these terminals solely as word-processing units. In this way, file secu-

Figure 17.4 Shared Word Processors
The shared word-processing system utilizes a powerful time-sharing computer, word-processing software, and multiple workstations to serve several users at once.

rity can be maintained. This security is important since most shared systems allow users to manipulate and employ files that were originally created and stored by other users of the computer system (sales reports and customer accounts, for example).

Although they often aren't as convenient for the individual user (because of slower response times or fewer features), shared word processors do have several advantages over dedicated word processors. Expensive peripherals such as letter-quality printers or high-capacity hard disk drives can be shared by several users. Documents to be printed can be routed to a centrally located, high-quality printer, eliminating the need to have a printer at each workstation. More and longer documents can be processed and stored because of the faster speeds and larger memories of powerful time-sharing computers. In addition, time-sharing systems can be set up so that people can do word processing from many remote locations (even at home) through the use of terminals, modems, and communications channels.

Components of a Word Processor

Even though characteristics and capabilities vary greatly, some elements are common to virtually all word processors.

Keyboard

Every word processor has a keyboard as its primary input device. The keyboard layout is similar to the familiar typewriter arrangement, but there are usually some extra, special-purpose keys. The keyboard is often designed with the user's comfort in mind and thus may have a flat, low profile. It may be built into or attached to the display screen console or linked only by a flexible cable so that its height and angle can be adjusted to suit the individual. Word processor keyboards are much quieter than those of traditional typewriters. They can be designed to work almost without any sound at all, but many of them emit a reassuring little click when a key is pressed to satisfy those who want to "hear" what they type.

In addition to keys for the traditional letters, numbers, and punctuation marks, there may be a number of keys for special symbols or functions, just like those

Where text is typed in

found on many personal computer keyboards (see Chapter 15). A separate numeric keypad may be present to facilitate the entry of numbers. There's sure to be a RETURN (or ENTER) key analogous to the carriage return on a typewriter; it tells the word processor to process the line just typed in. Control (CTRL) and alternate (ALT) keys are often present; they are used in combination with other keys to achieve certain functions. On many systems, for example, pressing the CTRL key and S key at the same time tells the word processor to stop scrolling the document so that it can be more easily read. Command keys such as HELP (to display information about system operations), INSERT (to insert text), DELETE (to delete text), and PRINT (to send a finished document to the printer) make it easy for the user to invoke facilities that are frequently required. Finally, screen management keys (for example, HOME, END, PAGE-UP, PAGE-DOWN) and arrow keys (left, right, up, down) are usually present to let the user move around within a document.

Display

What you see is what you get

As we said earlier, a word processor accepts characters typed in from a keyboard and presents them on some sort of display screen. The display usually consists of a CRT on which scrolling is possible; the user only sees a piece of the document at a time but is free to roll the image forward or backward. Some more advanced systems utilize windows (see Chapter 10) to display parts of more than one document at the same time. The size of the typical computer display screen is 24 lines of 80 characters each, but several word processors have larger displays that can present a full page of text (66 lines of 80 characters). Although most word processor screens have a black background with white, green, or amber characters, some are white with black characters so as to appear more like a paper page of text.

On a typewriter, text originates where the type element strikes the ribbon and paper. As characters are typed, the carriage moves to the left or the type element moves to the right, and the text becomes visible. On a word processor's display screen, text appears at the *cursor,* the little box or underscore that flashes on and off or appears in reverse video. As characters are typed into a word processor, the cursor automatically moves to the right. One of the great advantages of word processors is that the cursor can very easily be moved with the screen management and arrow keys to any particular place within a document for inserting, editing, and deleting. Some systems have a mouse, touch-panel screen, joystick, or other input device that can also move the cursor. In addition, the cursor can usually be moved by command or control keys. For example, most word processors have keystroke combinations to move the cursor to the beginning of a line, the end of a line, the next word to the right, the next word to the left, the beginning of a paragraph, and the end of a paragraph.

Menus and Commands

Telling the word processor what to do

Obviously, word processors must be told what to do by their users. For example, actions such as creating a new document, editing an existing document, saving an entered document on a disk, deleting an old document, and printing a finished document must be explicitly requested. There are two main ways users tell word processors what to do: by choosing options from menus and by issuing commands. A *menu* is a presentation listing the available choices of functions and how to invoke them; it may be a fixed part of the display or temporarily "pulled down" by pressing some control key or a button on a mouse. The user selects from the menu, performs the appropriate action (for example, pressing a certain key or pointing with the mouse), and the function is invoked. A command, on the other hand, is a typed-in directive that causes a given function to be performed. The major difference is that the user must remember the command or look it up in a manual.

Although menus are generally considered to be easier for novices to use, commands tend to be faster (once the user has learned them) and don't take up screen space. Word processors that primarily use menus are said to be *menu-driven*, and those that heavily employ commands are called *command-driven*. In fact, most word processors use some combination of both.

Storage

Central to every word processor is its ability to store the text that the user types in. Semiconductor primary memory is used while documents are being entered and edited, but some type of secondary storage is necessary for holding permanent files. Floppy disks and hard disks are the most common secondary storage media for word processors.

Saving text

Printer

The ultimate purpose of any word processor is to produce printed documents. With the exception of electronic typewriters, all types of word-processing systems include some type of printer. Because they produce print that looks just like that from electric typewriters, daisy wheel printers are perhaps the most popular for word-processing systems. However, letter-quality dot matrix printers and, more recently, laser printers are also commonly used.

Producing the final hard copy

Features of Word Processors

Word processors facilitate the production of documents by having features ordinary typewriters don't have. It would, of course, be impossible to describe every feature of every word processor on the market, but we can outline the major categories of available features. Although there are many differences among individual systems, a general similarity of function exists among all word processors. Most of the important functions of word processing fall into one of the following categories: text entry, text editing, text formatting, text management, text printing, and advanced features.

Text Entry

Just as data must be input before they can be processed into information and then output by a computer, text must be entered before it can be processed into documents and printed by a word processor. Initial entry of text into a word processor is fairly straightforward (basically, it is simply keyed in), but any of the following features can facilitate the input process:

Typing in the text

- *The communications area.* Most word processors reserve a small space at the top or bottom of the display to present information about the current session. For example, the communications area may include a *ruler*, or *format line*, which shows the margin and tab settings being used, and a *status line,* which gives details about the current document, such as its title, and where the cursor is currently located by page, line, and column number.

- *Help menus.* Even word processors that are billed as command-driven usually have some on-line help facility. This feature frequently takes the form of menus that list commonly used commands and options so that users (especially beginners) don't have to be constantly referring to manuals.

- *Word-wrap.* Most word processors automatically perform a carriage return when the text being entered starts to extend into the preset right-hand margin. When a word overflows into the marginal area at the end of a line, it's "wrapped around," or moved to the beginning of the next line. This feature allows the user to type continuously without worrying about where to end each line. Some word processors even perform automatic hyphenation of long words so that the right margin of the text looks fairly even.

Text Editing

Arranging the document

Text editing is the process of inserting, deleting, modifying, and viewing the characters that make up a file. *Text* can be anything composed of printable characters: letters, memos, briefs, reports, or even computer program source code. Some pre-written packages are known as **text editors**. They preceded word-processing software and are more limited, since they usually can't do interactive text formatting, which word processors can do. For example, a word processor "knows" how to structure a document and does it automatically when it starts a new line, starts a new page, hyphenates a word, or numbers a page. Text editors generally cannot do these things and are better suited for entering and editing computer programs and data files. Word processors have more powerful editing capabilities and are easier to use than text editors.

Word processors offer different editing features, of course, but the following are almost always available:

- *Insertion.* Inserting new material into existing text is a frequently used editing feature. The process typically consists of moving the cursor to the place where the new text is to be inserted, pressing a control key to signal insertion, typing in the new material, and then pressing the same or another control key to signal that the insertion is completed. Sometimes there's a distinction between, and different commands for, the insertion of a single character and the insertion of an entire line or more.

- *Deletion.* Sometimes portions of existing text must come out; deleting text is the opposite of inserting it. Usually, the cursor is moved to the first character to be removed, a control key is pressed, the cursor is moved to the last character to be removed, and another key is pressed to perform the actual deletion. The deleted portion disappears, and the surrounding text "closes up" the gap. There may be specific commands for deleting a single character, a word, a line, a paragraph, a block, and a page of text.

- *Correction.* Errors can often be corrected by changing existing characters. This is usually done by simply moving the cursor to the desired place and typing new characters over the old ones.

- *Manipulation.* It's often useful to be able to move an existing section of text from one place to another or to copy a certain section of text in another location. Almost all word processors offer *cut-and-paste* and *copy-and-paste options* to facilitate these text manipulations. Typically, the block of text is delimited, or marked, by moving the cursor to the beginning and hitting a special key, then moving it to the end and hitting another key. The cursor is then moved to the place where the marked block is to be moved or copied, and a move or copy command is issued. A move (cut-and-paste) removes the block from its original location, and a copy (copy-and-paste) simply reproduces it in the second location.

- *Search and replace.* It can be a real plus for a user to be able to find a particular word or phrase (a name, for example) in a long document without having to read through the whole thing. Most word processors have a *search function* to perform this task. The search command is issued, and the user is asked to provide the piece of text that is to be located. The word processor scans the document and positions the cursor at the first instance (if any) of that word or phrase. The *replace function* goes a step further by allowing the user to specify new text to replace the searched-out piece. This replacement activity can be carried out repeatedly and is especially valuable for automatically fixing consistently misspelled words throughout an entire document.

- *Proofreading.* Many word processors have limited proofreading capabilities, the most common being a *spelling checker.* This feature causes the word processor to examine the words in a document and compare them to an internally stored dictionary. If a word is not in the dictionary, it is somehow pointed out to the user; it may be misspelled, or it may be a proper name or simply a term not included in the dictionary. The user then decides whether the word is to be changed or left alone. Most spelling checkers let users add new words to the internal dictionary, so they improve with use. Some can even do simple, obvious corrections automatically (like changing "teh" to "the") or can suggest the word that may have been intended.

- *Undoing.* Most word processors have a feature for canceling a mistakenly entered editing command. If, for example, you delete the next line instead of the next word, the *undo feature* can recover that line. In addition, many word processors make a backup copy of an existing document before any editing functions are performed so that an original version remains intact. Then, if you accidentally mess up on a larger scale (by inadvertently deleting an entire page, for example), you can start over again without losing any of the original text.

Text Formatting

Text formatting involves structuring the textual material in a document so that it will present a suitable appearance when printed. This feature allows the user to establish specifications for the entire document, such as print size (pica or elite), line spacing, margin settings, the number of lines per page, tab positions, headings and footers, paragraph indentation, page numbering, and justification (varying the space separating words in a line so that the right margin is even). Also, functions for character enhancement allow the user to underline, boldface, italicize, superscript, and subscript selected words or parts of words within documents.

Getting ready for printing

Since there are so many text-formatting options (we've listed only a few of the most common ones), a word processor is usually preprogrammed for a group of *default parameters,* or standard selections for the available settings. The word processor will automatically put these settings in effect unless the user specifically changes them. For example, a word processor might have default parameters calling for pica type, single line spacing, 54 lines per page, one-inch margins on all four sides, and a page number printed at the bottom of each page. If, however, you would rather have double line spacing, you're free to explicitly set that yourself. Once these text-formatting functions are set, they are performed automatically. The user doesn't have to think about such things as whether there's enough room on the page for one more line; the word processor takes care of all of them.

Text Management

Organizing stored documents

After a document is entered and edited, it will most likely be stored in a file on a disk, just like programs and data are. Text management is a feature that supervises this electronic filing, usually via commands to maintain and use document directories. Such a directory lists the name, size, date of creation, and location of the files created with the word processor, which is helpful for managing the many files that tend to accumulate. For example, a document directory can show at a glance that three different versions exist of a letter sent out over a month ago (although only one was actually mailed, the two earlier drafts were never erased). Besides wasting disk space, this duplication can eventually cause confusion as to which version was in fact sent. Old backup files and documents no longer needed can be erased or moved to some other off-line storage device. The text management feature greatly facilitates the organization of document storage.

Text Printing

Getting text on paper

Most word processors have features that control various aspects of the actual printing of documents on paper. Facilities for text printing allow users to specify such things as which pages of a document to print, how many copies to make, what kind of paper to use (continuous fan-fold or single sheets), whether to pause between pages, how fast to print (if the printer has more than one speed), which print quality to produce (*draft* for quick, lower-quality printouts; *letter-quality* for final versions), and which printer to use (if more than one is connected to the system).

Advanced Features

Extra options

Some word processors offer other features above and beyond the typical ones. Some of these advanced features are as follows:

- *Numerical tabulation.* The production of charts and tables containing columns of numbers is much easier with numerical tabulation features. These enable users to arrange numbers in neat columns that are aligned on the decimal point or at the right or left. Columns may be deleted, exchanged, moved, or copied. Arithmetic facilities permit the computation and placement of horizontal and vertical totals.

- *Record processing.* Some word processors can manipulate files in which each line of text represents a record, for example, a telephone directory or a mailing list. Record-processing facilities enable users to sort, delete, add, modify, merge, and otherwise manipulate the items in such files.

- *Mail-merge facility.* Many word processors have a **mail-merge facility** that allows them to merge a file of names from a mailing list with a form letter, for example, to create a whole batch of seemingly personalized letters. The letter is composed with the places where the names are to be entered left blank but marked in some special way. The word processor then produces each individualized copy of the letter by filling in the blanks with a name from the mailing list.

- *Electronic mail.* Although this topic is covered in more detail in an upcoming section, it's worth pointing out here that many word processors have the capability of sending messages and documents to other word processors through the use of communications hardware and software.

- *Optical character recognition.* We saw in Chapter 4 how optical character recognition devices can "read" printed material on paper. Some word processors can accept input from such devices, enabling them to incorporate text directly from printed documents.

- *Computer output microfilm.* Organizations that produce a great deal of textual material often find it economical to output their documents on microfilm or microfiche (see Chapter 6). Some word processors can send their output to microfilm recorders instead of (or in addition to) printers.

- *Typesetting.* Materials that require high-quality printing, such as books, newspapers, and magazines, are usually produced with computerized phototypesetting equipment. Some word processors can send output directly to these machines, eliminating the need for the text to be reentered.

OFFICE COMMUNICATIONS

Information is of little value if it isn't transmitted to those who have a use for it. The information that's generated, gathered, and analyzed in an office must also be distributed to various people, both inside and outside the organization. The methods and technologies of office communications are in a state of rapid evolution. Although handwritten memos, intercoms, ordinary telephones, and messengers are all still employed, a whole array of more advanced means of communication, including electronic mail, voice mail, facsimile transmission, local area networks, and remote conferencing, is gaining a foothold in many of today's offices.

Distributing information

Electronic Mail

Electronic mail systems are a fast, reliable, distance-independent means of moving information from one place to another. Relying on computers and telecommunications channels (see Chapter 7), they can transmit messages that would otherwise be sent by messenger, telephone, or the postal service. Electronic mail is nonsimultaneous communication; transmission and reception occur at different times, unlike a telephone call, for example. Also, unlike many other forms of communication, electronic mail automatically creates a permanent computer record of each transaction.

Sending messages between computer users

The cost of electronic mail systems has been steadily decreasing, and their popularity in the business community has been increasing. Both trends are likely to continue. One important reason for the proliferation of these systems is their superiority in certain respects over traditional channels for business communication. The postal service can be slow, letters are sometimes lost, and the mail usually takes longer the farther apart two places are. Telephone calls require both sender and receiver to be on the line at the same time or someone to take a message. Handwritten memos are dependent on some internal distribution process and are easily lost in the shuffle of paper. Electronic mail is free from all of these drawbacks.

An electronic mail system allows an authorized user to send a typed message to a specified recipient on the first try, at any time of day or night. The message is held in the recipient's private *mailbox* (a sort of electronic in-basket) to be reviewed at his or her convenience. Passwords are issued to users when they first join the system to ensure that access is limited to those authorized. Messages can be sent to one person or to a group of people, who may or may not be using the computer system at the moment. Terminals used for electronic mail are often located in communications centers or sometimes placed on the desks of office personnel. The recipient can view incoming mail items on the CRT screen or have them printed out. After reviewing messages, the recipient can acknowledge their receipt, reply to them, store them for later action, forward them to others, or simply delete them. Messages can usually be sent and received from any remote terminal, even ones in homes, or from portable terminals. Some information services (such as Compu-Serve and The Source) provide electronic mail functions to widely distributed users of different computer systems.

Voice Mail

Recorded oral messages

Voice mail, sometimes referred to as *voice store and forward,* is an electronic message-transmitting system similar to electronic mail, except that the messages are vocal ones. Since most people find it easier to speak a message than to type it out, voice mail has one inherent advantage over electronic mail, at least from the users' standpoint. Users of voice mail systems can simply call one another at any time and leave a spoken message, which is stored digitally on a magnetic disk until it's retrieved and replayed by the recipient. The disadvantages of voice mail systems are that they tend to be more complex, more difficult to implement, and more expensive than ordinary electronic mail systems.

In fact, voice mail systems can do more than just record and replay messages on demand. Since they're computer-based and they store messages in digital form, voice mail systems give users capabilities not found on basic telephone-answering machines. For example, a user can record a single message and distribute it to any number of recipients, request that the system confirm delivery to each recipient, and alert recipients if the message is urgent. Like electronic mail, voice mail can be sent from remote locations at any time of the day or night.

On the receiving end, users of a voice mail system can employ ordinary touch-tone telephones to call in to find out how many messages they have waiting and if any have been tagged as urgent. Routine messages can be held to be listened to later; once messages have been heard, they can be saved or discarded as desired. Messages can even be forwarded to others, as is or with additional comments appended. Each user has a confidential password to ensure security, and some systems even use voice prints to confirm each caller's identity.

Facsimile Transmission

Sending pictures and text via phone lines

Facsimile transmission (or **fax**) is a process by which text and fixed graphic images (such as documents, pictures, maps, charts, and newsprint) are optically scanned, converted into electronic signals, transmitted over communications lines, and reproduced at a remote location. It was invented in 1890 by Alexander Bayne, who developed a technique for sending pictures over telegraph lines. Today, much more sophisticated facsimile-transmitting devices apply computer and communications technology to perform high-quality, high-speed, reliable image reproduction.

Conceptually, a *facsimile transmitter* can be thought of as a copier that photoelectrically digitizes an image and sends the resulting zeros and ones to some remote location. On the other end of the communications channel (usually a telephone line), the *facsimile receiver* accepts the transmitted stream of zeros and ones, generates the image, and prints it on paper using the electrostatic, thermal, or inkjet method. Usually, both transmitter and receiver are built into a single machine known as a *facsimile transceiver*. Offices equipped with compatible transceivers can send any documents back and forth at will.

The advantage that facsimile transmission offers over ordinary data communications and electronic mail is that the contents of any page can be transmitted, including text, drawings, photographs, charts, and even handwriting. Only black and white reproductions can be made. No keyboard entry is required; the physical operation consists solely of feeding the original sheet into the facsimile transmitter.

Local Area Networks

If the diverse individuals and devices found in modern automated offices are to communicate with one another, they must be interconnected. The rapid proliferation of personal computers within organizations and the development of local area networks have resulted in the widespread potential for such interconnection. In Chapter 7, we saw that local area networks allow individual computers and peripheral equipment to be linked together without employing modems or telephone lines. More and more offices are using local area networks as a communications facility for the implementation of electronic mail and the sharing of expensive computer resources, such as high-speed printers and high-capacity hard disk drives. Some local area networks have even implemented voice mail and facsimile transmission. In addition, offices are using local area networks to connect word processors and personal computers to one another, and to carry information transferred from shared files and data bases.

Linking office equipment

Local area networks are well suited to the office environment. Since a local area network can be completely owned and operated by a single organization, it can help reduce the dependence on and the expense associated with an outside service like the telephone company. Furthermore, local area networks are designed to operate within the confines of a relatively small geographic area, a single building or closely placed group of buildings. They allow very high rates of data transmission, are relatively inexpensive to install and maintain, and provide an effective interconnection for a large number of computers and computer-based devices.

Remote Conferencing

Organizations often have problems getting key members together for important conferences. Full work schedules, travel costs, and conflicting outside appointments make face-to-face meetings difficult to arrange for many managers. Computer conferencing and teleconferencing have recently emerged as viable alternatives to meeting or working together in person. Usually easy to arrange on short notice once the systems are in place, computer conferences and teleconferences are particularly useful for crisis situations and the coordination of large and decentralized projects and in fast-moving markets and places that are isolated and difficult to travel to.

Computer Conferencing

On-line meetings

As we learned in Chapter 7, computer conferencing refers to the use of distributed computers and data communications networks to conduct on-line discussions among persons in remote locations. The participants don't even have to be on-line at the same time. Messages can be stored and later displayed for any participant to see and respond to. Because everyone doesn't have to be participating at once, there's usually time for responses to be researched and carefully prepared before being entered on the system. Computer conferencing removes barriers of time and geography, allowing individuals to work at their own pace without the interruptions and digressions characteristic of conventional meetings.

Computer conferencing is frequently used to facilitate communication among groups of scattered individuals who must work together, such as researchers, scientists, and engineers working jointly on projects, editors and reviewers working on journals and books, and committee members drafting proposals.

Computer conferencing is also valuable for employees working at home (or telecommuting, as we described in Chapter 7). With access to computer conferencing facilities, some employees are able to work just as well at home as at an office. Many job activities can be performed practically anywhere on remote or portable terminals. Computer conferences can link distributed workers so they can report on their progress or on problems they're encountering. Although it's similar in many ways to the use of electronic mail, telecommuting via computer conferencing is production-oriented rather than communication-oriented. Its purpose is getting a particular job done rather than transmitting routine messages.

Teleconferencing

Audio and video meetings

The term **teleconferencing** is usually applied to the holding of audio and video meetings by electronically linking geographically dispersed participants. This communications technique has been used successfully by such well-known organizations as IBM, AT&T, the Bank of America, and NASA. Teleconferencing is becoming a widespread business tool; at least 80% of the Fortune 500 companies have plans for the installation of some sort of teleconferencing system.

Audioconferencing in its simplest form is the conference call option offered by the telephone company by which several people in different places can talk to one another on the phone. More complex systems require special conference rooms equipped with microphones and loudspeakers. Although audioconferencing is quite economical and convenient, the lack of face-to-face interaction and the inability to transmit visual images such as graphs, charts, drawings, or photos limit its appeal and usefulness.

Videoconferencing is holding a meeting via live television. It provides the face-to-face, visual interaction that audioconferencing and computer conferencing lack. However, videoconferencing requires that the conference rooms be studios equipped with highly sophisticated and expensive video and communications equipment, and sometimes also facsimile transceivers and electronic chalkboards. Because of the high cost, most organizations can't afford to have their own videoconferencing studios. To meet the demand, therefore, some common carriers, such as AT&T, maintain videoconferencing facilities in larger cities, which they rent out by the hour.

OFFICE OUTPUT

The information processed by offices can be presented or output in any number of ways. All of the forms of computer output we covered in Chapter 6 are used in offices. A few special categories are worth a separate look here.

Presenting information

Business Graphics

Business graphics, which consist of all kinds of bar and line graphs and pie, contour, and three-dimensional charts, can greatly enhance the communication of complex relationships and statistics (see Figure 17.5). Visual images in more than one color are more exciting and often more comprehensible than tables of dry figures. The advent of personal computers, business graphics software, and color graphics output devices has made the production of professional-looking graphs and charts easy, fast, and economical. The three graphs produced with Lotus 1-2-3 that were shown in Chapter 10 reflect how easy it can be for virtually any office worker to construct helpful graphics, given the right hardware and software.

Graphs, charts, and drawings

Also, interactive drawing or painting programs (see Chapter 10) have recently been gaining popularity in the automated office. Not only can office workers plot data and insert graphs into reports, they can also design new sales forms, sketch office layouts, draw logos, and create diagrams. The new breed of personal computers that support these kinds of individualized graphic endeavors (the Apple Macintosh, for example) promises to do away with the need for pencil-and-paper drawings (as well as reduce the burden on in-house art departments).

Micrographics

Micrographics is the area of information processing that's concerned with the production, handling, and use of **microforms**, or very small photographic images

Document reduction and storage

Figure 17.5 Business Graphics
Graphics hardware and software are increasingly used in the automated office environment to produce all types of graphs, charts, and drawings.

Figure 17.6   Microforms
Microfilm and microfiche are the two most common types of microform; they offer an alternative means for storing large quantities of information.

that are used to store both text and graphics (see Figure 17.6). In Chapter 6, we introduced the two most commonly used types of microform: microfilm and microfiche. Other types include film cartridges and aperture cards. The *microimages* contained on microforms are created either by reducing photographs taken of paper source documents or by producing computer output microfilm (see Chapter 6).

The use of micrographics can solve a significant problem in many offices, that of where to store large masses of paper documents. By replacing some of the paper and thereby greatly reducing the space required for storage, microforms provide a cost-effective means for keeping long-term or very voluminous records. Whether used alone or in conjunction with other office equipment, micrographic devices can significantly increase the productivity of information processing in the office.

We briefly described the devices used in the production of computer output microfilm in Chapter 6. Other basic types of micrographic devices are microform recorders, microform retrievers, and microform readers. *Microform recorders* are similar to copying machines, except that they produce tiny microform replicas instead of full-sized paper copies. Source pages are fed in, photographically reduced, and developed to form microimages on film. *Microform retrievers* locate and fetch desired images from stored microforms through the application of computer-assisted retrieval (CAR) techniques. Finally, *microform readers* are used to magnify microimages and project them onto display screens so that they can be easily viewed.

Reprographics

High-quality document reproduction

Reprographics is the area of information processing that's concerned with the reproduction of documents, mainly at or near full size. Two major types of office equipment are classified as reprographic: copiers and phototypesetting machines. Although such devices have been commonly used since the 1960s, continued technological advances have enlarged their role in the modern automated office.

Copiers

It's virtually impossible to manage information in an office without a copier or access to one. Documents that must be distributed and stored must be copied, and photocopying machines make it easy to reproduce them.

Although over 20 different copying processes have been successfully used in office applications, the xerographic variant of the electrostatic process, developed by Xerox Corporation in the early 1950s, is currently dominant. In this process, a bright light, a lens, and a drum coated with photosensitive material are employed to transfer electrically charged toner particles to ordinary paper in order to reproduce images.

Chapter 16 introduced a new breed of copier, known as the *intelligent copier*, that has recently been developed for use in offices. These machines, which are controlled by embedded microprocessors, can function as copiers and as printers linked to computer or word-processing systems. They can usually print in several different fonts and can make high-quality photographic reproductions. Some can produce enlarged, reduced, or multicolored copies. Eventually, intelligent copiers are expected to have facilities for formatting text, correcting spelling, and printing color photographs, as well as collating, stapling, or binding the final copies. Since intelligent copiers can be directly linked to local area networks or distributed data-processing networks, they may ultimately replace facsimile transceivers.

Phototypesetting Machines

Documents produced by typewriters, word processors, and computer printers are adequate for most office applications, but for publications such as annual reports, catalogs, and newsletters, typesetting is usually required. Such printing (like the text of this book) can include several different sizes and styles of type and is undeniably more attractive and more impressive than typewritten or dot matrix printed text. It's also more economical when very large numbers of copies are needed. **Phototypesetting machines** accept text input and produce output on film or on special photographic paper, which is then chemically processed to produce a plate from which pages can be printed (see Figure 17.7).

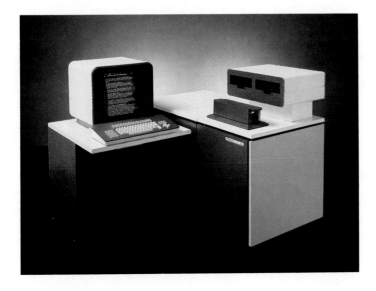

Figure 17.7 A Phototypesetting Machine
The phototypesetting machine accepts input text and produces printing plates from which very attractive, high-quality documents can be produced.

CAREERS IN TECHNOLOGY
Computer Service Technician

Job Description Also known as a field engineer or a customer engineer, the computer service technician is responsible for working on hardware in need of scheduled or unscheduled maintenance. IBM had the first service representatives, who wore suits and ties on their visits to offices, and they set standards that still apply to this position.

Although computer service technicians must be able to perform relatively simple repairs such as adjusting, lubricating, and cleaning mechanical and electromechanical parts, they also must have sufficient knowledge to check interconnections and to locate and identify defective components and circuitry. They must have the technical and analytical skills to diagnose the often mysterious causes of equipment failure. Besides screwdrivers, pliers, and wirecutters, their tools are voltmeters, ohmmeters, oscilloscopes, and soldering equipment. They are also called on to run diagnostic programs, lay cables, hook up connections between machines, and install new equipment. If a systems analyst designs a new configuration for a company's computer system, the service technician must set it up.

Most service technicians work for firms that provide maintenance and repair services or for manufacturers of computer equipment who offer such services to their customers. Generally, a technician is assigned a specific geographical area and is responsible for answering all repair calls from clients within that zone. Since it's more efficient to run a computer around the clock, calls can come in at any time of the day or night. A 40-hour week, perhaps with somewhat irregular hours, is normal, however.

Qualifications A computer service technician must have a high school diploma, and two years of post–high school study of basic electronics and electrical engineering at a college or vocational school or in the military. Good hearing (to identify and locate "funny" noises) and color perception (to differentiate color-coded wiring) are essential physical attributes. Finally, computer service technicians must possess good communications skills, since they need to describe problems, answer questions, and offer maintenance advice, generally to office workers or other people who are likely to be unfamiliar with technical jargon.

A newly hired technician should expect to enter a three- to six-month period of course work in computer theory, math, circuitry, and electronics, followed by from six months to two years of on-the-job apprenticeship. Entry-level technicians earn salaries around $15,000, and experienced technicians can expect to receive at least $25,000 a year.

Outlook In 1971, there were 30,000 computer service technicians. By 1980, that number had increased to over 83,000. By 1990, the number of computer service technicians is expected to reach nearly double that, or 160,000, as a result of the proliferation of small systems. Experience and training, however, are still vitally important. Only about three out of every ten job openings are filled

As we mentioned in an earlier section of this chapter, some phototypesetting machines can receive input text from a word processor through a hardware or software interface. By eliminating the need for retyping the text, this direct transferral avoids additional typographical errors, saves significant amounts of time, and reduces costs. Although there are some difficulties associated with such interfacing, most of the problems have been worked out well enough to successfully link selected word processors to many phototypesetting machines. However, as intelligent copiers and laser printers (which already produce very attractive text) become even more sophisticated, fewer offices will need to utilize phototypesetting machines.

Table 1 Outlook Summary: Employment in Computer Service.

Job Title	Employment 1970	1980	1990	% Change	Average Number of Annual Openings	Average Entry Salary
Computer service technician	31,708	83,000	160,000	+93%	20,000	$14,000

Source: U.S. Bureau of Labor Statistics.

Figure 1 Outlook Summary: Employment in Computer Service

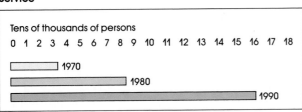

Tens of thousands of persons

0 1 2 3 4 5 6 7 8 9 10 11 12 13 14 15 16 17 18

1970
1980
1990

Table 2 Where the Jobs Are.

Industry	1978	1990	% Change
Agriculture, forestry, and fisheries	5	10	100.0
Mining	87	210	141.4
Construction	95	200	110.5
Manufacturing	15,914	44,000	157.6
Transportation, public utilities, and communications	816	1,580	93.6
Wholesale/retail trade	18,737	46,000	145.5
Finance, insurance, and real estate	527	1,300	146.7
Services	25,132	66,000	162.6
Government	1,683	3,700	119.2
Total, all industries	63,001	160,000	154.0

Source: U.S. Bureau of Labor Statistics.

by recent graduates in electronics from two- or four-year colleges. Most of the openings are filled by experienced technicians who have done equipment maintenance and repair in noncomputer industries, by apprentice/trainees, or by veterans who received electronics training during their military service. Your best bet is to get the necessary academic training and then apply to corporations that have in-house training or apprenticeship programs.

Multifunction Intelligent Workstations

The ideal of office automation, the fully integrated information system, is manifested in the **multifunction intelligent workstation** (also known as the **universal workstation**). This is a computer terminal or locally linked personal computer with an associated set of input, communications, and output devices (see Figure 17.8). It is designed to serve the needs of executive, managerial, professional, secretarial, and clerical staff with equal ease.

The multifunction intelligent workstation is a single functional unit that incorporates most existing desktop tools: telephone, calculator, word processor, com-

Integrating the office information system

Figure 17.8 A Multifunction Intelligent Workstation

The multifunction intelligent workstation fully integrates the automated office by providing access to a wide range of desktop tools and shared office equipment.

puter terminal, mailbox, dictaphone, in-basket and out-basket, calendar, notepad, etc. The user can easily switch from one tool to another and can carry on more than one activity at the same time. In addition, the multifunction intelligent workstation serves as a command center from which users can access many of the facilities described in this chapter. Although no single system currently sold includes every feature discussed here, multifunction intelligent workstations are available that have many of them.

SUMMARY

The Dimensions of Office Automation

Office automation refers to the use of computer, communications, and office equipment technologies to support the activities of the white-collar workplace.

The Information Age Our economy is based primarily on the processing of information. Office automation is necessary for coping with the glut of information and the state of rapid change.

Office Functions The office is a place where information is generated, modified, gathered, filed or stored, retrieved, analyzed, and communicated.

The New Technology The automated office of the future is already possible today.

Word Processing

Word processors let users insert, delete, edit, rearrange, format, and merge textual material until a document appears exactly as it should. Various types of word processors are used in all kinds of organizations to store, print, copy, and distribute documents.

The Problem with Conventional Typing Conventional typing often requires that material be retyped if more than one copy is needed or if revision is necessary. Typical methods of correcting inevitable typing errors leave much to be desired. The results are worker frustration, low productivity, and high costs.

A Brief History of Word Processing   Word processing began in 1964 with the introduction of the IBM MT/ST automatic typewriter, which stored text on a magnetic tape. Further developments incorporated CRT displays and other advances in computer technology.

Types of Word Processors   Electronic typewriters are electric typewriters with small display screens and embedded microprocessors. Dedicated word processors are single-purpose microcomputers with a keyboard, CRT screen, one or more floppy disk drives, and a letter-quality printer. Personal computer systems can run word-processing software and thus become word processors. Shared word processors depend on powerful minicomputer or mainframe systems to provide word-processing functions to several users at once on a time-sharing basis.

Components of a Word Processor   The basic components of a word processor are a keyboard with some special-purpose keys, some type of display device, menu-driven or command-driven control, magnetic storage, and a printer.

Features of Word Processors   Common word-processing features facilitate text entry (the communications area, help menus, and word-wrap); text editing (insertion, deletion, correction, manipulation, search and replacement, proofreading, and undoing); text formatting (print size, line spacing, margins, page length, indentation, pagination, justification, headings, and footers); text management (organizing stored documents); and text printing. Advanced features include numerical tabulation, record processing, mail-merge facility, electronic mail, optical character recognition, computer output microfilm, and typesetting.

Office Communications

Information must be communicated to be useful; a wide range of modern office equipment is available to help distribute it.

Electronic Mail   Electronic mail systems use computers and communications channels to provide a fast, reliable, distance-independent means of transmitting text messages.

Voice Mail   Voice mail is similar to electronic mail except that the messages are vocal and are stored digitally on magnetic disk.

Facsimile Transmission   Facsimile transmission is a process by which text and fixed images can be transmitted over ordinary telephone lines between facsimile transmitters and receivers, or transceivers.

Local Area Networks   Many offices are creating local area networks to connect diverse office equipment.

Remote Conferencing   Computer conferencing refers to the use of distributed data-processing networks to conduct on-line meetings. Teleconferencing refers to the holding of an audio or video meeting by electronically linking geographically dispersed participants.

Office Output

An important function of the office is the preparation of information for effective presentation.

Business Graphics   Business graphics are used to present all kinds of information as graphs, charts, and drawings.

Micrographics   Micrographics is concerned with the production, handling, and use of microforms, mainly microfilm and microfiche.

Reprographics   Reprographics is concerned with the high-quality reproduction of documents, primarily by copiers and phototypesetting machines.

Multifunction Intelligent Workstations   Multifunction intelligent workstations serve to integrate the automated office by providing common desktop functions as well as access to a wide range of computer-based office equipment.

COMPUTER CONCEPTS ▰▰▰

As an extra review of the chapter, try defining the following terms. If you have trouble with any of them, refer to the page number listed.

office automation 494

electronic typewriters 498

dedicated word processors 499

shared word processors (clustered word processors) 500

workstations 500

text editors 504

mail-merge facility 506

voice mail 508

facsimile transmission (fax) 508

teleconferencing 510

micrographics 511

microforms 511

reprographics 512

phototypesetting machines 513

multifunction intelligent workstation (universal workstation) 515

REVIEW QUESTIONS ▰▰▰

1. What is meant by "office automation" and what are some of the other terms used to describe it?
2. Why is office automation necessary in today's economy?
3. List the functions performed in offices and indicate how automation can help each of them.
4. What advantages does word processing have over conventional typing?
5. What was the first word processor and when was it introduced?
6. List and briefly contrast the four basic types of word processors.
7. What are the major components of a word-processing system?
8. What are some of the most common features found in word processors?
9. What kinds of advanced features are sometimes found in word processors?
10. Why has electronic mail become so popular?
11. What's the difference between voice mail and ordinary telephone answering machines?
12. What does a facsimile transceiver do?
13. How are local area networks used in offices and what makes them so well suited to this environment?
14. Give some examples of the use of computer conferencing.
15. What advantage does videoconferencing have over audioconferencing and computer conferencing? What are its disadvantages?
16. How can business graphics be used in the office?
17. What office problem can the use of micrographics help solve?
18. Enumerate some of the capabilities of intelligent copiers.
19. What are some reasons for interfacing word processors to phototypesetters?
20. How do universal workstations help to integrate information processing in the automated office?

A SHARPER FOCUS ▰▰▰

Now that you've completed this chapter, you should be able to answer the following questions about the chapter opening.

1. Is "VDT stress" still a valid concept, or are office workers becoming accustomed to computers in their midst?
2. How might an organization overcome the natural resistance to change that occurs when an office is computerized?

PROJECTS

1. Visit an office at your school or company and ask to see the word-processing system that is used. Try to find out why that particular system was chosen and what it can do. Is it connected to devices for optical character recognition or computer output microfilm or to a phototypesetting machine? Can it send electronic mail to word processors in other offices? How much did it cost? Most importantly, try to talk to the office workers who actually use the system on a daily basis; find out how they like it. Write up your observations as a short report.

2. We briefly stated the basic differences between command-driven and menu-driven word-processing software. Explore this topic further. Try to find product reviews of word processors in computer publications such as *InfoWorld, Byte,* and *ComputerWorld.* See how the reviewers feel about the advantages and drawbacks of each type. How do novices feel about having to remember or to look up commands? How do experienced users feel about having to spend time and waste keystrokes traversing menus? (You may be able to try out a word-processing package or two yourself.) Prepare a report contrasting these two approaches or showing how many of today's word processors combine them.

3. Is electronic mail used at your school or company? If the organization has a time-sharing mainframe computer or a local area network of personal computers, it's likely that some kind of electronic mail system is installed. If so, try to find out how it works. Are passwords required? How do you go about sending a message to one or ten people? How do you know if there's a message in your mailbox, and how can you read it? How many people use the system and for what purposes? Write up your findings as a short report.

4. This chapter has assumed that office workers will leave their homes and go to the office to work. What if, however, the office worker chooses to work at home instead? Consider the various functions performed by office workers and the various pieces of available hardware and software, and write a report about the factors associated with telecommuting. Mention not only the pros and cons, but also any special equipment and capabilities that would be needed. What sorts of office tasks would lend themselves to this environment? What couldn't be done? How would the work of at-home employees be controlled? What additional issues do you think should be raised about such an environment?

5. What are the characteristics of a fax application? In other words, what conditions do you think have to be present for facsimile transmission to be a viable technique? After carefully researching and thinking about your list of conditions, develop a list of specific applications for such a process.

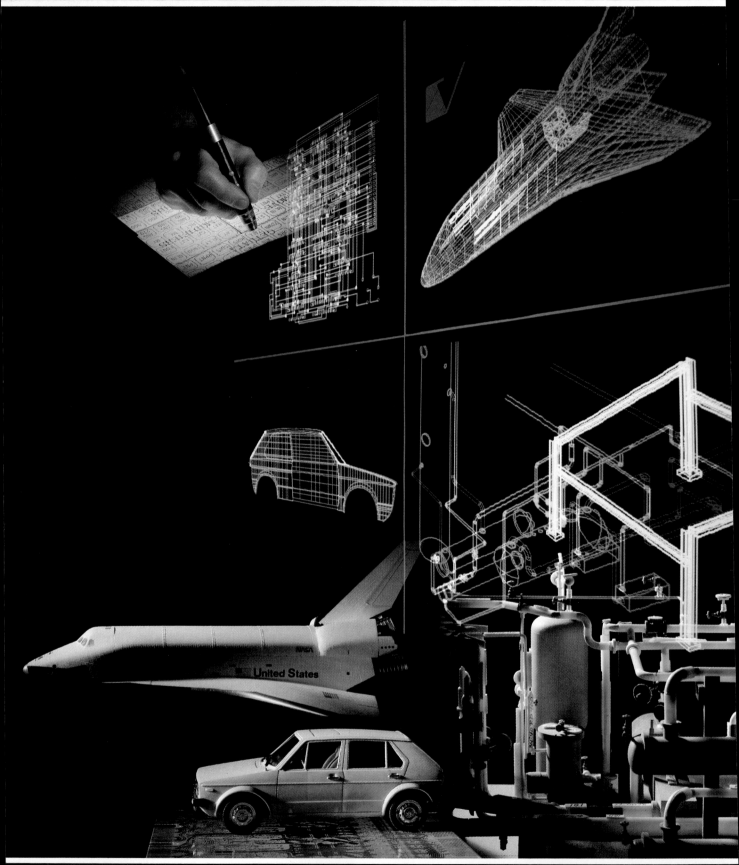

18

Design and Manufacturing

▶

FOCUS ON . . . CARS BY COMPUTER

Nowhere was the impact of the assembly line as profound as in the manufacture of automobiles. For nearly a century, those creeping conveyor belts that Henry Ford borrowed from the meat-packing industry have symbolized Detroit. But that technology may be reaching the end of the road. Just as Ford Motor Company's assembly line became the mainstay of U.S. industry, General Motors Corporation's new Saturn subsidiary may pave the way for the elusive "factory of the future."

GM's Saturn subsidiary is a $5-billion bid to do nothing short of revolutionize automobile manufacturing. The details are still being ironed out, but GM is trying to pull together the most advanced manufacturing technology possible. By replacing the assembly line with a fully computerized production system that extends from the dealer to the factory floor, GM is betting that it can close the estimated $2000-per-unit gap between its production costs and those of its Japanese competitors.

Saturn will tie together GM's collection of advanced technology, robots, machine vision, and computers that the company has assembled over the past few years. GM, which has long been frustrated in trying to get its myriad computer systems to communicate, has already taken a leadership position in developing the procedures that will enable all of its computers to exchange data. EDS is building a network that will hook together computers working in such diverse areas as design, engineering, and purchasing—even hooking up with those of individual dealers.

Saturn's major departure from traditional auto making will be in bringing component production and assembly together on one site. To cut down on transportation and warehousing costs, the Saturn complex will include at least a half-dozen component manufacturing plants and an assembly plant. This setup will make it possible to create a fully integrated line that could, for example, cast engine blocks, machine them, and assemble the engine.

Robots will play a far greater role in the process than ever before. Saturn "is going to advance significantly the state of the art in automated assembly," says Jimmy L. Haugen, vice-president for automotive assembly systems at GMFANUC Robotics Corporation, the joint venture of GM and Fanuc Ltd., a Japanese robot maker. "It will be the most robotized of any GM plant—and probably any plant in the world."

Robots with limited functions are widely used now in auto assembly plants for such repetitive tasks as welding and painting, but GM plans to take advantage of robots that "see," employing them in a far broader range of tasks on the factory floor. Saturn is expected to use robots to position the sheet metal for car roofs so that other robots can weld it. Robots will also install windshields and possibly rear windows. GMFANUC is working with Saturn on a robot with machine vision that will install car doors. Robots will probably put on the wheels, install the seats, and install the modules in the car.

When the Saturn production lines are up and running in 1988 or 1989, GM expects to be able to deliver one of the new compact cars just days after it is ordered. A dealer ordering a car today typically must wait six to eight weeks.

Programmable Industrial Machines	*Numerically controlled machine tools: turning rough stock into high-precision products. APT programs: defining the product's geometry and the required cutting path. Industrial robots for boring or hazardous work environments and programmable production lines.*
Process Monitoring and Control	*Process monitoring: open-loop control, from the process to the computer. Automatic process control: closed-loop control for continuous production processes.*
Manufacturing Support	*Software-oriented applications to manufacturing. MRP: producing schedules that result in higher profits.*
Computer-Integrated Manufacturing	*Group technology: organizing part descriptions for easy retrieval and, with MRP, forming a basis for CIM.*

Before we get into this chapter's topic—the computer's applications in both new and old industries—let's consider the three main motivating forces behind the idea of industrial automation. The first and most basic motivation has been a desire to increase the productivity of labor. Since the Industrial Revolution's introduction of steam-powered machines into processes that had previously relied totally on human and animal muscle, increased productivity has been the primary goal. Today's computer-based automation takes a step farther toward that basic goal by being applied not only to physical labor, but also to certain jobs considered white collar—engineering, design, and project management.

The second motivation is quality. No one doubts that a bulldozer can move dirt faster than a person with a shovel, but emotions enter the picture when we try to judge the comparative quality of the work. Although the machine's path may be uniform, the human's may be more precise or more aesthetically pleasing. Whether we're talking about construction or automobile assembly or even the design of VLSI chips, the issue ultimately boils down to just what sort of quality is most profitable.

Finally, competition is a pressing reason for automation. If Company A switches over to an automated assembly line and produces a greater number of wooden boxes for a lower cost, then Company B may feel compelled to abandon its line of hand-crafted boxes and get its own machines, just to keep up. Jobs are lost and jobs are gained through automation (social issues that we'll consider in Chapter 22), but with the days of guaranteed markets over and the United States no longer the undisputed industrial leader it once was, the computer-based theories and practices we'll examine in this chapter may no longer be just another option.

THE DESIGN/MANUFACTURING CYCLE

Until a few years ago, a more or less clear distinction existed between engineering and design. For one thing, engineering was done by engineers, and design was usually done by non–degree-holding designers or designer/draftspeople. For example, an electrical engineer would describe the components to be used in a circuit and would provide a rough sketch or description of how they were to be connected, but with no indication of the wiring pattern needed to produce the desired connections on the printed circuit board. A designer or designer/draftsperson would then carefully draw the components and their connections to scale and, by a trial-and-error process involving many redrawings, move them around until either an acceptable wiring pattern was produced or the problem was given up as unsolvable. In the latter case, it was time for a conference with the engineer to find another approach. Another good example is the engineering of an automobile. Teams of engineers would first design the subsystems to meet the product requirements for cost, performance, operating economy, weight, and safety. It would then be the job of designers to try to combine them all under the hood, which would sometimes mean redesigning them so they could all fit into the allocated space. The same sort of division between engineering and design existed in civil, industrial, and most other engineering fields.

One continuous process

Today, particularly in electronics, the dividing line is blurred. The computer-based *engineering workstation* now fills the engineer's need for a sketch pad, calculator, and computer while at the same time its graphics software either directly converts sketches into precise final-design artwork displayed on its high-resolution screen or produces the input for specialized computer-based layout systems that do so. The engineering workstation is a manifestation of a trend toward **computer-aided engineering (CAE)**, which is the application of computer programs that simulate complex electrical or mechanical systems to the design and development of products. It is simultaneously a manifestation of a similar growth in **computer-aided design (CAD)**, which is primarily the application of interactive computer graphics to product design and drafting. The modern engineer's working environment now includes the hardware and software of both CAE and CAD systems. We will treat both of these applications in the next section and reduce the terminology overload by referring to them collectively (as is generally done) as computer-aided design.

Computer-aided manufacturing (CAM) can be straightforwardly characterized as the application of shared data bases and computers to all aspects of production, including the design of special tools and dies, the programming and use of computer-controlled machines, the monitoring and control of manufacturing processes, and the overall coordination of the manufacturing facility. Computer-aided manufacturing is the subject of this chapter's third main section.

Figure 18.1 is a diagram showing the place in the product cycle of CAE, CAD, and CAM.

COMPUTER-AIDED DESIGN

Linking of design and manufacturing

The two principal objectives of computer-aided design are (1) to increase the productivity of product designers and (2) to produce the information—graphical, numerical, and textual—required to manufacture the product. Achieving the first goal involves using the computer to simulate product designs so they can be analyzed and tested. We've already looked at the use of simulated aircraft flight to train pilots in Chapter 10, and we'll consider the scientific foundations of simulation in Chapter 20. Here we want to improve our understanding of how computers are used to achieve CAD's two goals.

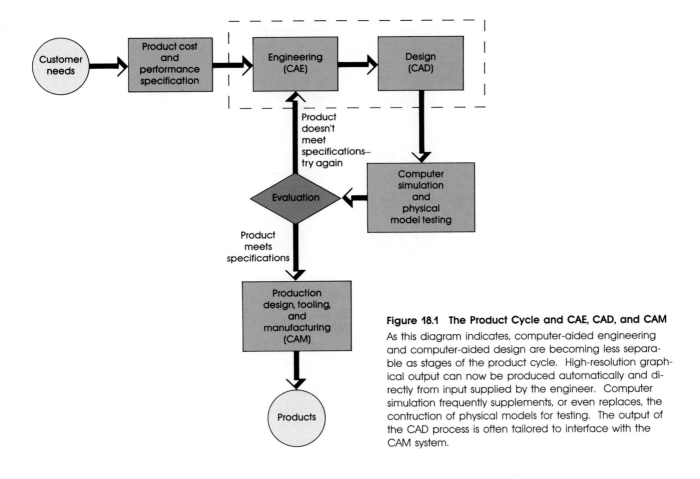

Figure 18.1   The Product Cycle and CAE, CAD, and CAM
As this diagram indicates, computer-aided engineering and computer-aided design are becoming less separable as stages of the product cycle. High-resolution graphical output can now be produced automatically and directly from input supplied by the engineer. Computer simulation frequently supplements, or even replaces, the contruction of physical models for testing. The output of the CAD process is often tailored to interface with the CAM system.

Interactive Graphics: The Geometric Model

In Chapter 4, we saw how users can input graphic information to computers from terminals. We learned how the digitizer, light pen, joystick, mouse, and touch panel work with the keyboard and screen in accomplishing this. In CAD, an engineer uses one or more of these means to create a *geometric model* of a product on a terminal screen. This model consists simply of a picture and an accompanying descriptive computer file, which together indicate all the constituent points, curves, and shapes. Curves may be lines, arcs of circles, or more complex curves; shapes may be two- or three-dimensional. Software then fills in these elements and connects them. It's becoming routine practice for the designs of all kinds of structures, from buildings to battleships, to go through a phase as a computerized geometric model. In fact, some architects now go directly from such a geometric model to building plans.

Letting the engineer see and manipulate the product

    Although we'll concentrate here on areas of broader general concern, on the strong interactions between computer-aided design and manufacturing, it is important to note that once any geometric model exists in computer form, it has great potential to be of assistance in the design process. For example, an engineer can manipulate the model: enlarge or reduce parts of it, and move the pieces around. Three-dimensional images of geometric objects can be created on the display screen, with perspective, shading, and color automatically provided by the graphics

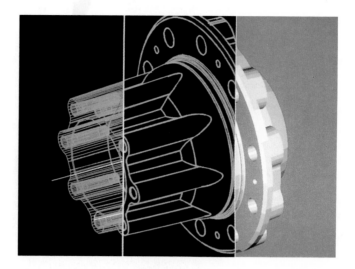

Figure 18.2 Three-Dimensional Geometric Models Created Using CAD Systems

software and hardware. These "solid" models can be "handled" by the engineer almost as if they were real. They can be turned about any axis or viewed from the back side. Obtaining each new view prior to the advent of computerized model-building might have taken weeks of drafting to produce a picture of comparable quality and value to the engineer. Figure 18.2 shows an example of the images that can be created with interactive graphics.

The final result of this part of the CAD process, produced with a smaller invest-ment of time and effort than was previously possible, is much more than a pretty picture. First, the product or part is not only clearly pictured for the engineer but also permanently stored in computerized form. It can be retrieved at any time and modified for some different use or incorporated in a different assembly. In other words, it remains part of a design data base, which can be searched when new parts are needed in the future. Moreover, this data base serves as ready input to the next part of the CAD process, analysis and testing.

Analysis and Testing

Evaluating the computer model

Using the geometric model, the design can be subjected to a variety of simulated tests using prepackaged or custom software. For example, structural analyses can be performed. Since all the dimensions of the product are completely specified and the properties of the materials of which it will be made are known, the way it will respond to stresses can be determined. A *static analysis program* is used when the part will be in an environment in which the forces or loads on it are either constant or change very slowly with time. A *dynamic analysis program* is employed when the loads on the part will vary with time, as is the case for an aircraft in flight.

Using a CAD system, an engineer can retrieve a geometric model from the design data base, alter it if desired, specify the loads to be applied in a static or dynamic analysis, and then use the results to modify the geometric model before trying again. The engineer can accomplish in hours or days a job that only a few years ago involved many different skilled people (including designers, draftspeople, and model builders) and took weeks or months to complete. Computerized analy-sis and testing is being applied in the design of products from simple tools and appliances to ships, aircraft, and buildings.

Figure 18.3   A "Driver" Tests a New Design

Here a computer does dynamic analysis interactively. A "driver" controls the simulated automobile by manipulating a joystick. With such a system, the performance effects of a new design can be tested without the cost and delay associated with building and assembling the parts. Only the most promising designs are actually built.

As an example, significant improvements in the performance and comfort of automobiles as well as in their fuel economy and engine emissions have resulted from the use of a dynamic analysis and testing system. For an automobile with electronic engine control, a major programming system in use at the Ford Motor Company simulates the interactions between the engine, the drive train (the mechanics that transmit the motion from the engine to the wheels), the electronic engine controls, and the driver (see Figure 18.3). Models of the various subsystems and their interactions are represented by subroutines, which are linked together by the overall program. This arrangement allows the engineers to alter an existing subsystem or insert a new subsystem without having to revise the overall program. The responses of the simulated driver can be programmed on the basis of known data about how drivers manipulate the gas and brake pedals to accomplish a desired change in speed. Alternatively, a person acting as "driver" may interact directly with the simulation program, using a joystick to simulate the pedal action.

Various aspects of the automobile industry related to the application of computers continue to concern us throughout this book: in Chapter 16, we looked at what microprocessors are doing under the hood; we mention automobiles here and in the section on computer-aided manufacturing; and in Chapter 23 we'll preview the role of the computer in relation to the automobile of the near future. In a recent article in *Science,* E. J. Horton and W. D. Compton state, "If all this doesn't sound to you like a declining smokestack industry, you're right. The U.S. auto industry has, since 1982, spent more on research and development than any other industry in the United States." It is, in fact, a major developer of CAD and CAM systems.

Now let's look at how the results of computer-aided design are used as inputs to the manufacturing process, particularly to computer-aided manufacturing.

The Manufacturing Interface

References to CAD/CAM are common. This combined form is suggestive of a single integrated process extending from the design to the manufacture of a product. And that is becoming the case, as we'll see in the next section on computer-aided manufacturing. For now, we'll simply observe that one of the most important

TECHNOLOGY CLOSEUP
The Design and Manufacturing of Electronic Chips

Specialized workstations for the computer-aided design of electronic circuits are a recent technological advance. These powerful and relatively expensive systems (around $50,000 each) should not be confused with either personal computers or simple terminals attached to a larger machine. These systems help engineers design circuits that are built up by interconnecting standard memory, logic, or arithmetic chips on a printed circuit board. Some of the latest of these workstations actually aid in the design of entirely new semiconductor chips that may, in turn, incorporate existing chips.

The first function of such a system is to help the engineer develop a circuit diagram on a high-resolution CRT. This diagram identifies the chips that are to be incorporated from the data base and indicates the desired connections between them, as illustrated in Figure 1.

Once the workstation holds a complete description of the circuit, it can invoke simulation programs that de-

termine whether the circuit actually performs the function intended by the designer. Beyond this, it can run other programs of its own or furnish the required interfaces to programs that are run on other machines in order to analyze electrical properties of the circuit, such as its speed of operation.

Some workstations provide output to systems that mathematically establish the best pattern of printed circuit board conductors to interconnect the chips. Output from these systems, in turn, drives high-precision flatbed plotters (see Chapter 6) that draw these patterns on the

Figure 2   Automatic Artwork Generation

Until recently, it was necessary to draw and check all the circuits on a chip manually. New workstations interface directly with high-precision plotters so that most of this work can be done automatically.

Figure 1   Circuit Connections as Displayed on the Work Station's High-Resolution CRT

Labels such as are shown at the left identify chips; the red and green lines represent the wiring determined by the system to accomplish the interconnections specified by the designer. The white dots indicate connections.

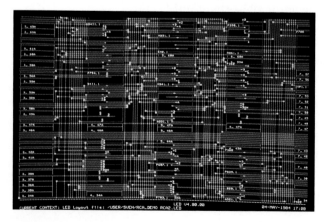

actual artwork used to manufacture the printed circuit boards. It used to be necessary to produce this artwork by hand at many times actual size, so that it would have the necessary precision when photographically reduced. Making corrections and changes was a demanding and time-consuming job. And, as exact as the precision requirements are for the conductors on printed circuit boards (a thousandth of an inch or so is typical), they are much more stringent for the artwork used to fabricate the chips themselves (currently a millionth of an inch and decreasing regularly). In fact, some artwork is "drawn" with a computer-controlled electron beam in order to achieve the desired precision. Figure 2 shows the scale of the artwork when it is manually prepared. It is ultimately reduced to the size of a tiny chip.

The next step, after the artwork has been generated and reduced to chip size, is to transfer it onto a glass *mask*, as shown in Figure 3. This mask is one in a series of

perhaps ten or more that are necessary to manufacture a chip. Each mask characterizes a layer of the multilayer chip structure. The image on the mask is transferred to a silicon wafer, which has previously been injected with minute quantities of other elements to give it the appropriate electrical characteristics. The transfer process is shown in Figure 4. The wafer is then dipped in an acid, which removes protective material from the pattern areas so that access into them is possible during further processes that give them their unique characteristics.

The pattern transfer and dipping process is repeated for each required layer. When the processing is complete, the wafer is tested. If the circuit is a new one, very few, if any, of the chips will work. After the bugs have been worked out, perhaps half or more of the chips on a wafer are generally good at this point in the manufacturing cycle. Next, the wafer is sawed, with fine diamond saws, into the individual chips. These are then packaged in plastic or ceramic packages, with each chip electrically connected to the metal pins on a package by tiny

Figure 3
One in a series of masks used to transfer patterns from artwork to semiconductor wafer.

Figure 4 Transferring a Pattern to the Wafer
With the silicon wafer under the mask, the image is transferred to the wafer photographically, by means of a photosensitive coating applied to it.

gold wires. The assembly package undergoes a final test performed by a computer-controlled, multiprobed tester, like the one shown in Figure 5.

The whole package is subsequently connected to a printed circuit board in some product, by soldering its pins to the conductors on the board.

Figure 5   Automated Chip Tester
Automated testers are used to make as many as thousands of tests on each chip after it has been bonded into a package that permits its connection by soldering to printed circuit boards.

CAD output as input to CAM

features of computer-aided design is that, when it is well done, its output includes the data needed to get the product into the manufacturing process, as illustrated in Figure 18.4. When this is the case, there is no need for the traditional costly and time-consuming separate phase in which engineering drawings and documentation are translated into detailed manufacturing plans. The CAD systems that are used to design mechanical parts, for example, greatly facilitate the programming of the automatic cutting tools that manufacture the parts, as we'll also see in the next section. The transition from CAD system to CAM system is even more direct in the production of electronic chips. The Technology Closeup on pages 528 and 529 describes this process, in which CAD and CAM are rapidly becoming inseparable.

 ## COMPUTER-AIDED MANUFACTURING

Two types of automation

It's common practice to distinguish two types of manufacturing automation: *Detroit-type automation,* an assembly line set up to achieve high-volume production of a single product, possibly with some limited range of variations; and what has come to be called **programmable automation**. In the first type, everything is geared for volume production at low cost. Production runs are assumed to have a reasonably long life; in Detroit, it is typically a year or more between major changes. The production process is relatively fixed, and changeover requires a major effort. Programmable automation, on the other hand, is aimed at handling a

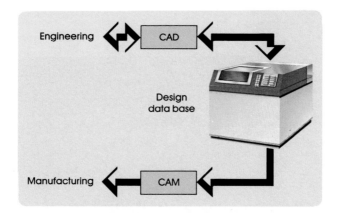

Figure 18.4   The Interface Between CAD and CAM

The results of the CAD phase are computer-analyzed and -tested products, represented by geometric models in the design data base. These models provide the inputs from which the detailed manufacturing plans are made.

more varied product environment. It employs tools that can be reprogrammed quickly and whose economic advantages can be secured over relatively short production runs. It is carried out primarily by numerically controlled machine tools but increasingly involves industrial robots, and we will discuss both these types of devices shortly.

Our primary interest is naturally in programmable automation, where the computer's role is clearly defined from the outset, and therefore this will be the subject of the next section. In a later section about manufacturing support, however, we will look at the computer's application to aspects of planning, management, and operation that are common to either type of manufacturing automation and, in fact, to nonautomated production as well. And, of course, the computer's role in manufacturing doesn't end with its *doing* work; it also monitors and supervises work. Computers are widely used to observe production processes; the data gathered are displayed to humans who, based on the information provided, act to maintain or improve the state of the process. A separate section on process monitoring and control describes this application. Another upcoming section looks at the computer's growing role as an integrator, around a single data base, of the entire design and manufacturing process, extending from product definition and design through manufacturing to final test and shipment—an application that is referred to as *computer-integrated manufacturing*.

Monitoring, control, and integration of the manufacturing process

Programmable Industrial Machines

Turning a roughly shaped piece of metal into a precisely machined part, for an aircraft or earth-mover engine, for example, was until the 1950s exclusively the job of highly skilled and experienced machinists. Today, less than 35 years after the first programmable industrial machine was developed at MIT, more than 15% of the machine tools employed in U.S. industry can be programmed to grind, drill, shape, and, in general, work metal automatically. These are the numerically controlled machine tools we'll discuss next. Although they are more costly than their manually operated counterparts, they can be quickly and economically reprogrammed and, of course, will operate 24 hours a day under environmental conditions that a human worker couldn't tolerate.

Cousins to these programmable machines that work material are the programmable industrial robots that handle material and operate tools. These adaptable

Types of programmable industrial machines

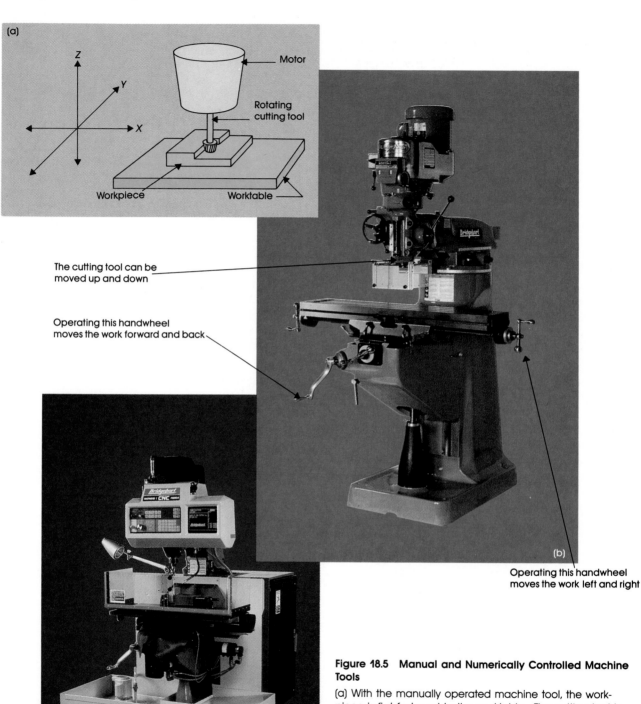

The cutting tool can be moved up and down

Operating this handwheel moves the work forward and back

Operating this handwheel moves the work left and right

Figure 18.5   Manual and Numerically Controlled Machine Tools

(a) With the manually operated machine tool, the workpiece is first fastened to the worktable. The cutting tool is driven by a motor and can be lowered to the desired depth in the workpiece. The worktable (and with it the workpiece) is moved by turning the handwheels shown in (b), thereby cutting away metal to obtain the precise shape. (c) In the numerically controlled version, the worktable is moved not by manually operated handwheels but by special precision motors that are controlled by a tape in the electronic control unit at the right of the machine.

machines are used mostly in assembly operations, but also do such jobs as welding and spray painting; they can be programmed using the same general kinds of techniques as are used for machine tools. This programming of machines is quite similar to working with machine-level computer languages. Unlike computer-controlled machine tools, however, a robot can often be directly "taught" to do a job by being moved through the desired sequence of operations, which it stores in its memory.

Numerically Controlled Machine Tools

A **numerically controlled (NC) machine tool** is a power-driven mechanical device whose actions are determined by a program that describes, in detail, each step in the sequence of operations required to transform a piece of metal stock (the *workpiece*) into a finished, high-precision, machined product.

NC machine tools

To understand what this definition really means, it's best to start with a basic understanding of how a machine tool is manually operated and then contrast this with numerically controlled operation. Figure 18.5 shows the same basic machine tool in a manually controlled and a numerically controlled version. A skilled machinist, by turning the handwheels, can cut curved shapes with a precision of a thousandth of an inch. Numerically controlled machine tools are designed to do the same thing. The path of the cutting tool is programmed in individual steps of a thousandth of an inch to match the precision of a human operator.

In the early days of numerical control, these descriptions of the workpiece motions required to produce the part, collectively called the *part program*, were drawn up separately, one step at a time, from an engineering drawing. A numerical code representing each step was then punched on a paper tape. This tape, inserted in the electronic control unit, issued the sequence of instructions to the tool. As you can imagine, this process was tedious and error-prone. A few years after the first numerically controlled machine tool was developed, a high-level programming language was created that greatly simplified part programming. Called APT (for Automatically Programmed Tools), it and its many related off-shoots still dominate the field of programming industrial machines. An APT program consists of two sections. The first contains special geometric statements—for example, those defining points, lines, and circles—that describe the shape of the part. Then the motion required to cut out the part is described, using a sequence of motion statements that refer to the part's geometric layout. Motion statements in an APT program look like these:

Defining the product's geometry and the cutting path

```
FROM/STPT
GOFWD/L1
```

These translate to "from the starting point, go forward to line 1." Both the starting point and line 1 must be defined in earlier geometric statements. An APT program is compiled and the control tape is generated by a computer. The entire process of producing a part in this fashion is summarized in Figure 18.6.

Another simplification, similar in spirit to what we described in our discussion of the interface between computer-aided design and manufacturing, has recently been made in this production process. Engineers are using workstations where, with interactive graphics, they can create the geometric data base that describes a part. Then an engineer, or a part programmer, uses a light pen to trace out the cutter motion. After visually checking to see that the program produces the correct

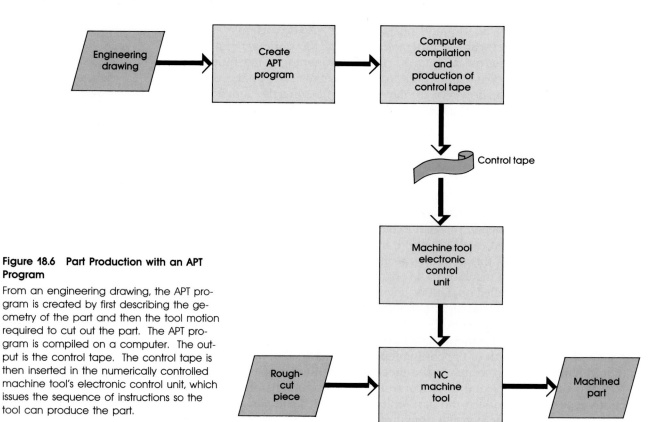

Figure 18.6 Part Production with an APT Program

From an engineering drawing, the APT program is created by first describing the geometry of the part and then the tool motion required to cut out the part. The APT program is compiled on a computer. The output is the control tape. The control tape is then inserted in the numerically controlled machine tool's electronic control unit, which issues the sequence of instructions so the tool can produce the part.

part, the control tape is created. Some programmable tools are controlled directly by a computer, eliminating the need for the tape, and some computers can control groups of such machines.

The basic principles of numerically controlled machine tools apply generally to controlling motion in two or three dimensions. The technology has been applied to build automatic plotters, wiring machines, drills, and numerous other devices.

ISSUES IN TECHNOLOGY

To be a machinist is to be a practitioner of an old and respected craft. As is the case with all true crafts, great satisfaction results from turning out an excellent piece of work using one's hands directly. Does a comparable satisfaction result when the work that is "crafted" is an APT program? What determines a person's level of job satisfaction? In the case of working with machine tools, what has changed? What has remained the same?

Industrial Robots

An industrial robot is a fairly general-purpose, programmable machine that has found a niche in a number of manufacturing processes. The number of industrial robots in current use is just beginning to become a significant part of the labor picture; there are about 60,000 worldwide and the population is increasing rela-

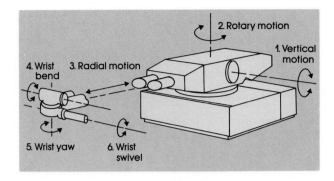

Figure 18.7 An Industrial Robot's Range
The six program-controlled motions of which
the typical industrial robot is capable. These
robots can also be fitted with a variety of
specialized "hands." [From Dan T. Moore, Jr.
"Will Robots Save Democracy?" *The Futurist* 15
(August 1981): 17. Reprinted by permission of
the publisher, World Future Society, 4916
St. Elmo Avenue, Washington, D.C. 20014.]

tively rapidly. Almost all of these robots can only blindly repeat a task that they've
been programmed or "taught" to do. That is, they can neither sense nor adjust to
their environment; they don't have any means of observing the effect of their
work. A robot will go on painting a fender even if, by some mistake, it isn't there.
Figure 18.7 shows the set of movements of which the typical industrial robot is
capable. In Chapter 23, in our discussion of artificial intelligence, we will examine
much "smarter," more advanced robotic systems that are currently in various
stages of research and development.

Robots are most frequently used for the following kinds of jobs: long sequences
of absolutely repetitive mechanical tasks; work in an environment that presents
health hazards such as high temperatures or fine paint or chemical sprays; work
that must continue at all hours; or work that involves lifting awkward or especially
heavy loads. Such jobs include spray painting, welding, parts handling, and tasks
on an assembly line.

*Industrial robots for boring
or hazardous work*

As we mentioned earlier, a robot may be either programmed or taught to do a
job, that is, to execute a precise sequence of the motions of which it's capable.
Programs are usually written in a high-level language furnished by a robot's manufacturer. Although each manufacturer has its own proprietary language, all these
languages are rather similar, at least semantically. Newer robots have memories
that can hold more than a thousand steps. Teaching a robot means using an auxiliary device called a *teach pedant*, which allows the robot to be taken manually
through a sequence of moves and to store the data describing the physical aspects of
each move so that the sequence can be repeated.

Robots can also be grouped to form reasonably flexible production lines for
assembly or other operations. Figure 18.8 (page 536) shows a robot line used in
the manufacturing of automobiles. A robot line that paints automobiles or that
does auto-body welding need not be set up all over again from scratch because of
a moderate change in body style. Nothing more may be required than the reprogramming (or reteaching) of a few of the line's robots.

*Programmable production
lines*

As we said at the beginning of this section, the market for industrial robots isn't
a large one yet by U.S. standards, but it's experiencing reasonable growth. It was
$240 million in 1983 and reached approximately $375 million in 1984. Production and sales of robots are much higher in Japan, stimulated in part by government financing and labor retraining programs. Recently, however, the commitment of U.S. manufacturers to robot production and use seems to be increasing.
This, coupled with the research and development activity in the United States in the
advanced robots described in Chapter 23, is encouraging for the future of this
young industry.

Figure 18.8   A Robot Line
Unimate robots doing welding on an automobile production line.

Process Monitoring and Control

In the last section, we discussed the use of computers to operate the programmable machines that actually do manufacturing work, the numerically controlled machine tools and industrial robots that turn raw materials into products. In this section, we turn our attention to computers that are "observers" of what goes on in the industrial trenches.

When a computer is used solely to observe, record, and display the state of a manufacturing system, it is called a **process monitor**. The information flow is one-way—from the process to the computer. A human operator reviews the displayed information and takes any required action to maintain or change the state of the process. This type of control is called **open-loop control** because there is no direct feedback from the computer to the process; the human operator provides the necessary link (see Figure 18.9).

Open-loop control, from the process to the computer

Automatic process control, on the other hand, operates without human intervention. The computer program, acting through specialized peripheral equipment, assesses the state of the process and operates controls so as to maintain it or, if it has gotten out of the desired state, to bring it back into line. Feedback moves both from process to computer and from computer to process, forming a closed loop, and giving the name **closed-loop control** to this type of process control.

Closed-loop control for continuous production processes

The devices used to measure such parameters in a system's state as temperature, pressure, and electrical or chemical values are known as *sensors*. They are available in varying accuracies and at a range of costs to measure practically any parameter and provide digital values to a computer. *Actuators* are controls, such as switches and valves, that operate the production system. A wide assortment of actuators that accept digital values and respond appropriately (for example, a valve that shuts off completely when it receives a zero and opens fully at a one, with a range of intermediate states) are also available.

Computer-based systems for process monitoring have some unique advantages. Even though a computer isn't being used to control, it can be programmed to increase the frequency with which it records certain conditions. This facility for extra vigilance is particularly useful for situations that threaten equipment or personnel because a detailed history leading up to the unsafe conditions can be recovered and the knowledge gained can be used to help prevent a recurrence. Of

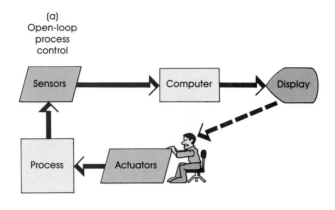

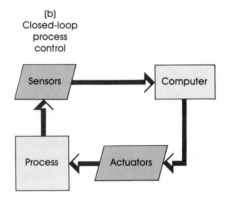

Figure 18.9   Types of Process Control
(a) The computer displays the status of the process to an operator, who assesses the situation and responds by manipulating the actuators to maintain the process or bring it to a desired state. This is open-loop control. (b) In closed-loop control, the assessment is made by the computer program, which controls the process directly.

course, monitoring systems can and do display dangerous conditions, as well as indicating the appropriate steps to be taken by operating personnel. Monitoring systems are often used to track items through the manufacturing and testing stages. Pharmaceutical firms, for example, are required by federal law to keep records of materials used and products manufactured. By means of identification codes, batches can then be tracked automatically when needed, to determine which products used which inputs and to which customers they were shipped. Also, equipment is monitored to assess its reliability and performance, and the testing of products is monitored to assist in operation management and planning as well as quality control.

Automatic process control is generally, but by no means exclusively, associated with continuous production processes such as electric power generation, petroleum refining, and bulk production of chemicals and foodstuffs. As the incident at Three-Mile Island demonstrated, nuclear generation of electrical power can give rise to situations in which events move too rapidly to be handled by solely human assessment of conditions and manual response. The general trend in power production systems seems to be toward the incorporation of more automatic safety features in the context of increasingly automated process control. And it isn't only in massive power plants that automatic process control is important. Food producers, for example, have relied on these production techniques for years. Even many of the most traditional food products, such as cookies and bread, are produced under a regime of automatic control. Daily or seasonal variations in the supplies of input materials and the demand for products are taken into account by computer programs that calculate the product mix that will produce the greatest profit at a given time. The bakery (or refinery or feed mill) is then controlled to produce that mix.

Manufacturing Support

So far, our discussion of computer-aided manufacturing has emphasized its hardware aspects, by concentrating on the tools and robots that actually work materials into products. Even though these machines are programmable, the output of the programs is the direct operation of this hardware that does the production tasks. The hardware aspect of computer-aided manufacturing is still in the foreground when the computer is used to control, or even to monitor, production machinery. The computer in such a case is physically attached to the machinery through sensors to which it directly responds.

Software-oriented applications to manufacturing

In contrast, manufacturing support, to which we now turn, is a predominantly software-oriented application. The hardware involved is primarily of the standard data-processing variety we already studied, rather than being industrial machinery. **Manufacturing support** systems are used mainly to assist in the functions of production planning and control. One of the most important of these functions is that of managing inventories of raw materials or purchased parts. The appropriate software can be immensely helpful in determining when to order and how much to maintain on hand in order to minimize the risk of shutting down a line because needed items are unavailable while, at the same time, not tying up cash and space by holding more inventory than is reasonably required. This procurement activity must be closely coordinated with production scheduling, which establishes when and where the given items will be needed and in what quantities. Production scheduling, in turn, is based on knowledge of the time and material requirements for each step in the production process. Gathering this data may involve doing time and motion studies for manual tasks and estimating or measuring the time required for the tasks that are to be performed automatically by machines. If past data are already on hand for some of the steps in the process, analyses of them may yield helpful information.

When the time, material, equipment, and space requirements are known for each of the individual steps, it is possible to carry out the simulation of production flow. We've already noted the importance of computer simulation to computer-aided design, and it is also important in computer-aided manufacturing. Just as it's far less costly, in every way, to detect an aircraft design flaw in a computer simulation than to discover it in the sky, it's also less costly to uncover a production bottleneck with a simulation program than to do so on the active production line. Production simulation systems run models of the production situation, sometimes incorporating information from statistical studies of the performance times of both humans and machines on given tasks. They help determine the mix of labor skills required to maintain a smooth flow in the production process.

The organization of any production process that involves the manufacturing and/or assembly of many different parts into more than one product presents so many possibilities that it is generally impossible to determine an optimal, or most profitable, production plan. For continuous processes such as petroleum refining or bulk chemical production that have relatively small numbers of material inputs and product outputs, it is possible to apply optimization techniques such as linear programming. For the typical factory situation, an acceptable plan can fall short of

CAREERS IN TECHNOLOGY
Fabricator

Job Description A fabricator generally works on an assembly line, putting together a computer's hardware: securing components on a circuit board and wiring, testing, and packing the various parts of a system prior to shipment. Other fabricators process chemicals or are engaged in quality control supervision throughout the product assembly process. Even though much of this work is automated, fabricators are needed as "step workers" between automated stations, where they check a machine's work or perform jobs that machines can't. The fabricator's job consists of repetitive and detailed work in a cool, sterile environment.

Qualifications Most manufacturers require only a high school diploma and some technical credits in electronics from a vocational school. Patience, good eyesight,

and manual dexterity are the principal physical qualities required for this job, along with a willingness to work.

Outlook Wherever computers are being produced, there is a need for people to assemble their components—at least until robotics penetrates this industry as it has others. For the foreseeable future, however, there are many job openings, mostly in the southwestern and northeastern regions of the United States, in a booming industry that offers good salaries and benefits. But remember, this job is closely tied into the industry itself. Recent slowdowns, even factory shutdowns, by Apple, Wang, and IBM had an adverse effect both on their own fabricators and the general employment market for these positions.

the best possible combination of labor, machines, and products, as long as it eliminates the major sources of delay and reduces inventory costs to a tolerable level.

A widely used computerized method for preparing production plans that work quite well is one that was introduced by IBM in the late 1960s. The method is called **manufacturing resource planning**, or **MRP**, and its technique is to begin with the required completion or delivery date for assembled products and to work back from there. When provided with all the necessary inputs concerning the time and materials requirements for individual production steps, MRP produces schedules for labor, machines, and materials. It is estimated that more than 10,000 manufacturing sites currently use MRP and have mostly achieved higher profitability as a result.

Producing schedules that result in higher profits

Computer-Integrated Manufacturing

In describing the design/manufacturing cycle at the beginning of this chapter, we emphasized the blurring of the boundaries among CAE, CAD, and CAM. Subsequent sections of the chapter have focused on the growing numbers of applications of computer programs to the design/manufacturing cycle: from highly analytical ones that do dynamic simulation of product designs to those that produce the instruction sequences that drive the numerically controlled machine tools and industrial robots that manufacture products. An important trend is the utilization by many of these programs of a common data base.

Organization of part descriptions for easy retrieval

This concept is best illustrated by a recent development called *group technology*, which is essentially an information storage and retrieval system in which part descriptions are organized into files according to similarities in their geometries and in the sequence of machining operations required for their fabrication. New parts, and their corresponding manufacturing sequences, need not be designed completely from scratch every time. The data base can readily be searched for the description of an existing part that is similar enough to be merely "edited" to meet the somewhat different new requirements. The revisions in the manufacturing sequences are developed as part of the "editing" process. As a result, developmental lead times and costs are greatly reduced.

A basis for CIM

When group technology is used to provide input data to an MRP system, the application approaches the ideal of **computer-integrated manufacturing (CIM)**, a process in which a common data base serves the needs of all the computer programs that are involved in any part of the design/manufacturing cycle—from new product definition and design through the setup and management of manufacturing operations.

SUMMARY

The Design/Manufacturing Cycle

For many classes of products, the separations among engineering conception (CAE), design (CAD), and detailed specification and drawing are breaking down. Engineering workstations are accelerating the merging of these parts of product development into one continuous process whose output feeds directly into the manufacturing process.

Computer-Aided Design

The main objectives of computer-aided design are to increase the productivity of product designers and to produce the required interface to computer-aided manufacturing.

Interactive Graphics: The Geometric Model The engineer creates a geometric model of a product on the screen of an interactive terminal, utilizing any of a variety of input means. The product can then be viewed from different angles and "handled" almost as if it were real. The computer file describing the product also serves as input to analysis and testing programs.

Analysis and Testing Structural and other types of simulated analyses can be performed on a geometric model. Analysis programs can accomplish in hours or days what used to take weeks or months to complete. In addition to saving time and money, this software allows many more design alternatives to be investigated.

The Manufacturing Interface CAD systems automatically produce much of the data required to manufacture a product.

Computer-Aided Manufacturing

Detroit-type automation is geared to the high-volume production of a single product over a relatively long period of time. Programmable automation, using computer-based numerically controlled machine tools and industrial robots, is aimed at increasing the efficiency of more frequently modified or shorter production runs. A major use of the computer in all types of industry, whether automated or not, is in the planning, management, and operation of manufacturing.

Programmable Industrial Machines   Numerically controlled machine tools work rough stock into precisely machined parts.   Industrial robots do assembly operations as well as such jobs as welding and spray painting.   In numerically controlled machine tools, computer-controlled motors move the material past a cutting tool.   The sequence of motions required to cut a given shape is derived from a program written in the specialized high-level programming language APT.   Industrial robots can execute a large repertoire of motions and are used for a variety of repetitious, unsafe, or difficult tasks.   Robots can be programmed using special languages.   They can also be "taught" to do a sequence of operations by moving them manually through the desired sequence.   In many applications, robots are grouped into flexible, completely automated production lines.

Process Monitoring and Control   When a computer is used as a process monitor, information flows only one way, from sensors measuring physical characteristics of the process to the computer.   The computer simply displays information concerning the state of the process, and a human operator takes any necessary action.   In automatic process control, which is used mainly in continuous production processes, no human intervention is required.

Manufacturing Support   Manufacturing support is a primarily software-oriented application of computer technology in the areas of production planning and control.   Inventory management and production scheduling are two main functions that are supported.   Computers are sometimes used to simulate production flow in order to detect potential bottlenecks.   MRP is a widely used computerized method for generating manufacturing plans; it works backwards from desired completion dates, providing detailed production schedules.

Computer-Integrated Manufacturing   Many industries are employing group technology to store and retrieve descriptions of parts, so that new needs can, as much as possible, be met by the relatively quick and economical revision of existing parts.   When group technology is coupled with MRP, computer-integrated manufacturing, or using a common data base to drive the entire design/manufacturing cycle, is almost realized.

COMPUTER CONCEPTS ▬▬▬

As an extra review of the chapter, try defining the following terms.   If you have trouble with any of them, refer to the page number listed.

computer-aided
  engineering (CAE) 524
computer-aided design
  (CAD) 524
computer-aided
  manufacturing (CAM)
  524
programmable automation
  530

numerically controlled
  (NC) machine tool 533
process monitor 536
open-loop control 536
automatic process control
  536
closed-loop control 536
manufacturing support
  538

manufacturing resource
  planning (MRP) 539
computer-integrated
  manufacturing (CIM)
  540

REVIEW QUESTIONS ▬▬▬

1. What is the primary goal of automation?
2. What are the effects of automation on the cost and quality of products?
3. What is the basic distinction between product engineering and design? How is this affected by engineering workstations?

4. What are the two principal objectives of computer-aided design?
5. What is a geometric model? How is it created? How is it used?
6. What is the difference between dynamic analysis and static analysis?
7. Describe the overall structure of Ford Motor Company's automobile simulation system.
8. How does computer-aided design interface with the manufacturing process?
9. Distinguish between Detroit-type automation and programmable automation.
10. What are the two most important types of programmable industrial machines? What is the basic difference in the ways they are used?
11. Why are most common types of industrial robots referred to as "blind"?
12. What is the main function of a machine tool?
13. How is a numerically controlled machine tool programmed to cut out a shape?
14. Describe the movement capabilities of the typical industrial robot.
15. In what two ways may an industrial robot be programmed?
16. What are the advantages of a robot-operated production line?
17. Distinguish between process monitoring and automatic process control and between open-loop control and closed-loop control.
18. With what type of production process do we associate automatic process control? Give some examples.
19. What are the major applications of computer-based manufacturing support?
20. How is simulation used in the design of a production system?
21. How does MRP work? Does it produce optimal plans?
22. What advantages are offered by a group technology system?
23. What characterizes computer-integrated manufacturing?

A SHARPER FOCUS

Now that you've completed this chapter, you should be able to answer the following questions about the chapter opening.

1. How will the Saturn complex make use of computer-aided manufacturing?
2. Describe how the automotive assembly system planned for Saturn is an example of computer-integrated manufacturing.

PROJECTS

1. Radio Shack currently sells an inexpensive toy version of an industrial robot, called Armatron. If you have access to one of these machines, write a "program" to accomplish some task, perhaps choosing something involving the small plastic pieces that come with the machine. Note that each of the two "joystick" controls has six different placements, making a total of twelve movements available. You might assign a number or letter to each of the movements and then determine how you'll define the length of a movement—perhaps in seconds or inches. Also, devise a way to document your program. The following instructions might help you get started:

```
10 0.125   'WRIST UP .125 SEC
07         'CLOSE JAWS
12 6.000   'ARM UP TO 6 INCHES
```

2. Once a firm has installed a CAD/CAM system and achieved the anticipated productivity improvement, what does it do next? What do you think the next step(s) might be?
3. What criteria should be used to determine whether or not a potential CAD/CAM application should be implemented? Identify some applications in design and manufacturing

Projects

that do *not* lend themselves to CAD/CAM. Can you identify a common set of characteristics in these applications?

4. How would you conduct a cost/benefit analysis for a specific CAD/CAM application? Identify not only the various factors you'd consider, but also the relative importance of each. Would your factors and/or their relative importances differ for different applications in the same industry? Is it possible that your factors and/or their relative importances might differ for the same application in different industries?

5. What criteria should be used to determine if a CAD/CAM application will be beneficial to an organization? Who should evaluate CAD/CAM performance? Will the criteria be different for different applications in the same company or for applications in different companies in the same industry?

19

Computers in Business

IN THIS CHAPTER

▶

FOCUS ON . . . MILK, BUTTER, CHEESE, AND PCs

A marquee-size computerized sign heralds the approach to Stew Leonard's "World's Largest Dairy Store" in Norwalk, Connecticut. Next to the sign is a petting zoo. Roaming the 500-car parking lot and handing out candy to children is a 6-foot cow! (It's really a 6-foot man in a cow outfit.) A realistic plastic cow guards the entrance, ushering you into the one wide—and crowded—aisle that winds its way through the entire store. . . .

Stew Leonard, originally a milk deliveryman, opened the dairy store in 1969 and he has expanded his building 22 times to its current 100,000 square feet. It remains a family-owned, single-store operation. Over 100,000 people visit each week, purchasing 1,000,000 cartons of yogurt, 10 tons of cottage cheese, and more than 36,000 pounds of butter each year. The *New York Times* has called Stew Leonard's "one of the most remarkable success stories in American food retailing."

Although the supermarket industry is beginning to explore the use of PCs, it should come as no surprise to anyone familiar with Stew Leonard's that the store was one of the first to buy them. "Stew Leonard is a progressive thinker and very innovative," says Jeff Pirhalla, the store's data processing manager. Leonard's was the first supermarket in the state of Connecticut to install a scanning system back in 1976. Before the year is out, the store will be able to boast a network linking the store's 30 cash registers to a mainframe and to several PCs. . . .

. . . Leonard uses the store's PCs for corporate planning, budgeting, and forecasting. One of the first things he did along these lines was to enter the weekly and daily sales figures for a 3-year period into the 1-2-3 spreadsheet. Currently, Leonard manually plugs in sales and customer count figures taken from hard copy that is generated by the company's minicomputer.

Using 1-2-3, Leonard can compare sales figures for any week with those of the same week the previous year. His sales goal this year is a 20 percent increase over 1983 sales—which he claims the PC is helping him meet. One column of the spreadsheet lists the projected sales for 1984 based on the 20 percent increase. Once daily sales figures come in, the PC calculates the actual percentage change from last year. If sales are down, management asks whether the decline was caused by a holiday, or whether another store ran a big special. If sales have increased, perhaps an ad or special was particularly effective. . . .

In addition to charting sales for the entire store, the PC breaks out sales totals for each of the store's seven departments—grocery, dairy, ice cream, meat, deli, produce, and bakery. The breakouts help department managers plan their sales strategies and clue in Leonard on departments needing closer attention. . . .

The company now has 400 employees, about 100 more than in 1983, but graphs of wages and overtime reveal the same peaks and valleys for both years. . . . The company is currently developing a program for the PCs that will chart hourly customer count to help schedule its workers.

Business Application Packages	*Software that contributes to growth and profitability.*
Accounts and General Ledger	*Doing an accountant's job.*
Payroll and Labor Analysis	*Paying and evaluating the workforce.*
Tax Planning	*Paying the government.*
An Example: Business and the Computer	
Point of Sale	*Systems to speed up retail transactions.*
Inventory	*Instant performance of a tedious job.*
Order Processing	*Electronic restocking.*
Sales and Marketing	*Analyzing the market and developing new advertising strategies.*

Let's call it the commercial network, even though that may seem a somewhat fancy label for that familiar thing known as business. Unlike the word *business,* the concept of a network of commerce accurately describes what's going on out there. A business can be anything from a shoe store to a multinational corporation or a public utility; a network is a complex and interwoven system of buying and selling, shipping and receiving, manufacturing and storing, investing and banking, profit and loss.

A retractable ball point pen, for example, has parts made from plastic and steel and contains a pigmented liquid (ink). It comes to a store bubble-wrapped in another plastic and attached to a card made from wood products. In a half dozen different places, workers in mines, forests, mills, factories, and labs created the pen's various parts. Engineers invented it, designers laid out the packaging format to be executed by printers, and an ad agency prepared newspaper and magazine copy about its unmatched qualities. Store owners placed orders for it, and trucks, trains, and jets brought its parts together and then delivered it to shops. When you bought it, your check went through an intricate system of local and regional banks, the Federal Reserve System, and the post office. Your check itself used to be part of a tree somewhere; it passed through another system of paper mills, designers, printers, warehouses, and transportation before it ended up in your checkbook. The whole network is amazingly interwoven, and hundreds of seemingly disassociated parts are in fact vital to one another's operation and success. And perhaps the most incredible thing is that this whole enormous, tangled, complicated network is really very personal—it leads inevitably to you, your neighbors, and your friends, the consumers who enjoy its products.

The person who can understand and deal effectively with such a network is the person who will be a success in business. Those who try to do that— businesspeople—are discovering that they have an electronic helper who promises to make things simpler, more direct, faster, and much more profitable. What better device for harnessing the diverse and detailed information generated by the commercial network than the computer?

▌▌▌ COMPUTER APPLICATIONS

The commercial network is composed of a number of different general business concerns, whose smooth running has become more and more dependent on computers. Conservative estimates suggest that businesses will have spent some $270 billion on office automation by the end of 1985, although other predictions place such expenditure as high as $600 billion. Let's look in general at how computers are used in some major commercial areas.

Manufacturing

Computers in manufacturing, from quality control to the office

Manufacturers, those industries that produce the goods that move about in the commercial network, use computers for a variety of tasks. You saw in the last chapter how computer-aided design and manufacturing are revolutionizing the design and production of goods, and Chapter 14 described the use of management information and decision support systems. Let's briefly review these manufacturing applications.

Computers are used for **production control**, the constant monitoring of labor, production standards, and performance (including quality control). In **production scheduling**, computers are utilized to determine the best start-up dates for production orders, the most efficient allocation of materials, and the least costly adjustment of inventories. Finally, in **production planning**, computers help managers develop long-term projections of how much they are able to manufacture as well as how much they can *afford* to manufacture, based on forecasts of sales, orders, costs, and expenses. These forecasts are also made in large part with the help of computers. On the basis of a production plan, manufacturers can develop labor and hiring schedules; prepare orders for parts, equipment, and materials; and determine how to put their facilities to the most profitable use.

Banking and Finance

The flow of personal and corporate money

Banking is a $15-trillion-a-year industry in the United States, and the Federal Reserve's computerized Fedwire system moves money around the country at a rate of $100 million per second. Aside from basic administrative operations, such as payroll and personnel, banks use computers for on-line savings and automation of check processing by means of MICR and OCR devices (as we discussed in Chapter 4, and as we saw demonstrated in the Application Perspective at the end of Part 1). Savings accounts are automatically updated when deposits or withdrawals take place, and interest is compounded electronically (a source of possible criminal tampering, as we'll see in Chapter 22). Statements and analyses of loans, trusts, and investments are prepared with the help of computers. And one of the fastest growing applications of computers in banking is the use of the **automatic teller machine (ATM)** (see Figure 19.1). Today, more than 3000 financial institutions, mostly banks, have installed over 27,000 of these remote terminals, from which customers can make withdrawals or deposits in airports, grocery stores, or on the street, 24 hours a day. By 1989, there will be at least 100,000 automatic teller machines in the United States.

Every year in the United States, some 40 billion checks, representing more than $8 trillion, are passed around among businesses, governments, and individuals. In fact, 90% of all financial transactions in this country are handled by check, and if

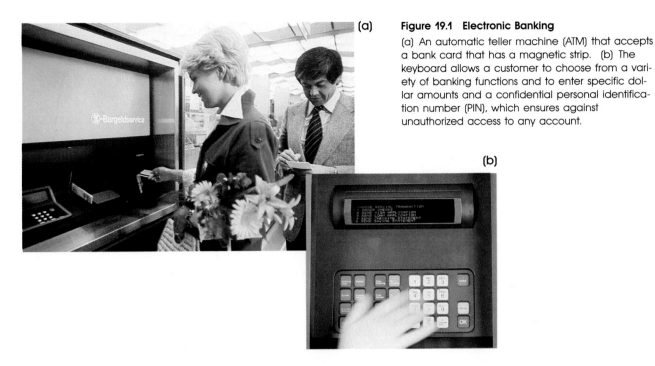

(a)

(b)

Figure 19.1 Electronic Banking

(a) An automatic teller machine (ATM) that accepts a bank card that has a magnetic strip.   (b) The keyboard allows a customer to choose from a variety of banking functions and to enter specific dollar amounts and a confidential personal identification number (PIN), which ensures against unauthorized access to any account.

there were no computers to help process them, as much as half of the entire population would have to work at it, just to shuffle all the paper around to the right places. And the number of checks keeps rising; from 1940 to 1970, it increased by more than 1000% and has risen steadily at about 7% each year since then.

The enormous problem of moving the mountain of paper represented by all those checks and the somewhat smaller mountain of cash and coin may one day disappear. A vision of the future that has begun to seem more realistic is that of the *cashless society,* in which plastic cards with magnetic strips or even microcircuitry will replace money (see Figure 19.2). Credit cards were in the vanguard of the

Plastic cards and electronic tellers

(b)

Figure 19.2 Smart Cards.

(a) This *smart card* contains a microprocessor and memory embedded in the lower right hand corner. Similar cards can be used for banking, shopping, and even making telephone calls from specially designed *card phones* such as the French model shown in (b).

(a)

cashless society, and the bank cards that are fed into automatic teller machines are the current stage in the evolution toward a time when all financial dealings are handled by **electronic funds transfer (EFT)**.

Insurance

Managing and analyzing insurance data

Insurance companies use computers for figuring out premiums, billing, investment analysis, policy approval, keeping track of policyholders' records, and processing claims. Computers are used to set premium rates on the basis of *actuarial tables,* statistical analyses of the risks involved in insuring various groups (statistics on life expectancies or automobile accidents, for example). The data bases required to store and utilize this mass of data efficiently and effectively are necessarily enormous, and computers have become vital in the insurance industry.

Utilities

From billing to simulations

Public utilities—power, water, gas, and communications companies—use computers not only for running and monitoring the equipment that generates, distributes, and carries their commodities, but for billing, record keeping, and accounting. Rate schedules are set and state and local taxes are calculated with the aid of computers. Utilities also use computers to create **operational simulations**, models that project how a company's equipment will function under any of a number of hypothetical situations. A power company might want to know whether its generators could hold up at peak demand times during a long heat wave, or a long distance telephone company might want to know how many of its lines and switches are likely to be required on Mother's Day. Such computer simulations enable utilities to be prepared to meet their customers' needs.

Transportation

In the air and on the ground

Airlines, bus companies, car rental agencies, trucking companies, and other businesses concerned with moving people and products from place to place also depend on computers. Rate calculations, tariff and regulation analyses, reservation systems, vehicle scheduling, purchasing and maintenance budgets, analyses of traffic patterns, and route selection are some of the tasks to which computers are applied.

Airline pilots and dispatchers get accurate and up-to-date information about the weather, fuel consumption, and the flight plan from computers in the cockpit (see Figure 19.3). Also, *autoland computers* programmed with detailed data on airport locations and runway positions guide jumbo jets to safe "instrument" landings during periods of poor visibility. On the ground, air traffic controllers rely on computers to monitor scheduled landings and takeoffs, current flight locations, weather, and runway conditions. In the terminal, airline clerks use computers to make and cancel reservations, to assign seats and print tickets, and to keep track of special dietary, seating, or facility requests, such as kosher meals or wheelchairs.

In the nation's travel agencies, which represent a $20-billion-a-year service industry, computers are used to make hotel, train, bus, ship, and rental car reservations. For example, American Airline's SABRE system provides travel agents with the rates, flight schedules, and seating availability for most airlines and destina-

Figure 19.3 Computers in the Air
Electronic controls play a vital role in the flying of high-tech commercial aircraft such as the Concorde.

tions. American's own flights, of course, are displayed in the first positions of every listing.

Hotels

Hotels and motels use computers (Holiday Inn's Holidex and Inn-Scan systems, for example) to make advance reservations within the chain, bill customers, and keep inventories. Computers also help schedule maid service, monitor room schedules, and keep track of special requests for cribs, room service, wake-up calls, messages, and forwarding addresses and phone numbers. A subsystem of the Inn-Scan housekeeping system, Motorola's Maid-Aid, was designed specifically to streamline the cleaning of rooms. A maid simply calls the computer on the room telephone once a room has been cleaned, and the computer adds the room to the "open" list for the reservation system.

Electronic innkeeping

The Stock Market

Brokerage houses, investment firms, banks, and other organizations that have major funds invested in the stock market have been using computers in their activities for some time. The classic glass-domed ticker-tape machines have been replaced by CRT displays in brokers' offices, and city streets are littered with punched cards and the edge strips from fan-fold paper rather than ticker tape after parades. On the floor of the New York Stock Exchange and on nearly 10,000 display boards worldwide, computers keep traders informed about international buying and selling activities as nearly 70 million shares are traded every day. Besides day-to-day reporting applications, another way in which computers are employed is as links in financial information networks, which can provide instant data on the current financial condition of almost any company. Such electronic information services are offered to amateur and professional investors alike by Dow Jones News/Retrieval, Standard and Poor's Compustat, Wharton Econometric, and Data Resources, Inc. (DRI). Financial news is available from UPI, *The Wall Street Journal*, *Forbes*, and *Barron's*, as well as from a number of sources in specific industries.

Brokers, investors, bankers, and the SEC

Figure 19.4   EDGAR

As well as providing an important data base for businesses, the Security and Exchange Commission's Electronic Data Gathering And Retrieval (EDGAR) system allows on-line preparation and filing of periodic financial reports.

The Securities and Exchange Commission (SEC) handles over 6 million pages of quarterly, annual, and other reports from companies every year. Information on a company's filings, earnings, or estimates of growth is vital both to brokers and investors and to the SEC, which examines the documents for discrepancies and adherence to various laws and regulations. Every business day, express delivery trucks line up for blocks around the SEC's Washington, D.C., headquarters. In an effort to reduce the confusion and to streamline a cumbersome but essential regulatory process, the SEC introduced the EDGAR (Electronic Data Gathering And Retrieval) system, which allows companies to file their reports directly to the SEC, from computer to computer (see Figure 19.4). In addition to eliminating a great deal of paper, the system has established a very valuable data base, in which up-to-date information is available without the usual delay experienced with most financial data bases.

Printing and Publishing

From first draft to the bookstore

The printing and publishing industries annually produce countless newspapers and magazines, books and pamphlets, brochures, posters, and blank forms. In many printing houses, bulky and noisy linotype machines have been replaced by compact computerized phototypesetting equipment and trays of lead type by a few floppy disks. Newspaper reporters and magazine writers no longer tap away at typewriters, but instead key in their copy at word processors. As illustrated in Figure 19.5, editing, layout, and typesetting functions are increasingly handled with computers, which also perform circulation, media, and market analyses. Many large newspapers have transferred their *morgues* (all their past articles carefully clipped and cataloged in huge rooms of filing cabinets) to computer files, making it much more convenient for reporters and researchers to access background and historical materials.

Architecture

Computer-generated blueprints and models

Architects can use computer models to run stress tests for buildings they're designing and computer graphics to create complete exterior and interior blueprints and sketches. Figure 19.6 (page 554) shows the exterior view of such a computerized

Figure 19.5 Electronic Publishing
Computers are used by publishers (a) for writing and editing text; (b) for layout and composition (choosing typefaces and the way the text is arranged on a page); (c) for phototypesetting; and (d) for producing final camera copy.

model. Such computer graphics can even be animated so clients in the sales office can see what the building will look like as they walk around its base, fly around its upper stories, or stroll down a hallway. A computer can simulate and/or analyze earthquake resistance, the effects of wind, rain, snow, temperature, and age, and energy efficiency. Modifications can be made instantly. A single change in any

Figure 19.6 Architectural Graphics
Programmers and animators at Omnibus Computer Graphics created this animated conception of Scotia Plaza, a building under construction in Toronto. Based on detailed architectural input, the images were generated in order to attract companies to buy office space in the uncompleted building.

part of a blueprint can have effects on the dimensions anywhere else, and subtle changes that a human might miss can be caught by the computer. The overall process of developing a building plan from generalized schematic sketches to detailed scale drawings can be shortened from three weeks to a day or two.

 ## BUSINESS APPLICATION PACKAGES

Software that contributes to growth and profitability

The cost of buying a small computer, peripheral devices, and accounting software is minimal in comparison with the cost (for salary, benefits, and facilities) of maintaining an accountant or two. Furthermore, the speed and convenience of keeping the books in-house using a computer far outweigh the difficulties of farming the job out to a CPA firm. A small business will spend only about $10,000 for a computer system that can handle most of its financial operations—an expenditure most small companies can afford. In fact, one South Carolina contractor's modest investment in computer technology saved his company $35,000 annually, paid for itself within four months, and increased his company's profit margin by 15%.

As the cost of computerizing financial functions falls within the reach of more medium and small businesses, it's becoming apparent to them that they're losing money by *not* buying their own computers. Once a company has made the investment in hardware, the use of the appropriate software in the form of *business application packages* enables it to make drastic reductions in the amount of time and resources spent on mundane but crucial tasks, thus streamlining its operations.

Accounts and General Ledger

Doing an accountant's job

Accounts payable are simply the amounts of money that a company owes to others, suppliers, for example. *Accounts receivable* comprise what is owed to the company. Computers, with their quickly accessible memories and their ability to hold and organize vast quantities of data, are ideally suited to the task of keeping track of accounts, bills, and invoices. Efficient management of accounts helps ensure that customers are billed promptly, that credit is extended prudently (thus avoiding bad

(a)

```
                        ACCOUNTS RECEIVABLE

    DATE 12-16-88
    --------------------------------------------------------------

    --------------------------------------------------------------
    CUSTOMER  CUSTOMER                     +30    +60   CREDIT   EXCEEDS
    NUMBER    NAME      BALANCE  CURRENT   DAYS   DAYS  LIMIT    LIMIT

    14332   ACRES INC    457.34   322.10  135.24              600.
    16734   BOOK CELLAR 1329.80   455.00  437.40  437.40   1500.
    23864   DELFI-CRAFT  152.00    27.00   96.       29.     100.    &
    39000   FITZ/TGNCO  5860.33  2257.00 3423.33             8000.
    57213   HART-PERM     22.00    22.00                     5000.
    78823   MERRICK INC 7833.25   568.20 5620.12  1644.93  6000.    &
    98652   SONDERBELT   745.23   700.00   45.23             1000.
    99455   INTERWHEEL   927.88   365.12  413.      149.76  2000.
    --------------------------------------------------------------
```

(b)

```
                   HYTEK-DATAFLO  CORPORATION  (HDF)

                      SUMMARY  LEDGER  REPORT

                            2/14/89
    --------------------------------------------------------------
                              ACCOUNT BALANCE    YEAR TO DATE
    ACCOUNT  DESCRIPTION         THIS YEAR        LAST YEAR
    --------------------------------------------------------------
    CASH ON HAND & IN BANKS      344,584,904.32   253,452,143.60
    ACCOUNTS RECEIVABLE (NET)    655,473,321.08   527,004,321.97
    INVENTORIES                  344,733,211.95   130,892,021.80
    LAND                             548,000.00       520,000.00
    BUILDINGS                    123,894,992.00       864,389.00
    EQUIPMENT/MACHINERY        1,448,993,406.00   894,600,000.00
    SALES                      5,945,652,870.00 1,236,772,345.00
    COST OF SALES GOODS          432,975,346.00   844,987,235.00
    --------------------------------------------------------------
```

Figure 19.7 Accounts and General Ledger Reports
(a) A computer-generated accounts receivable balance sheet and (b) a general ledger summary report.

debts), and that invoices are paid on time (thus maintaining a good reputation with suppliers).

A *general ledger package* can assemble balance sheets, income statements, and reports that compare this year's financial situation with last year's (or with projections for upcoming months) and also provide accurate and detailed breakdowns of all the significant information. Figure 19.7 shows a typical computer-generated accounts receivable balance sheet and general ledger summary report.

Payroll and Labor Analysis

A *payroll analysis package* works with information such as pay scales, hours worked, tips, commissions, piecework done, and vacation and leave time owed. It calculates local, state, and federal taxes to be withheld. And it subtracts automatic deductions for Social Security payments, union dues, insurance, and charitable contributions, while simultaneously adding bonuses for holidays and profit-sharing

Paying employees

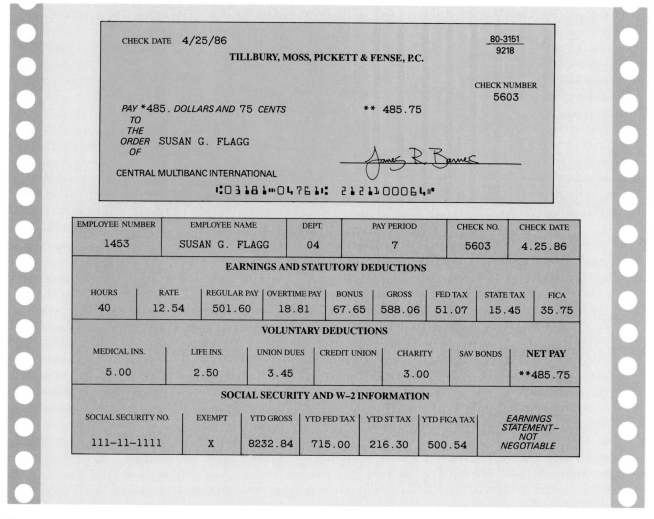

Figure 19.8   Computerized Payroll
A computer produced this employee paycheck and earnings statement.

Evaluating the workforce

or incentive programs. It even prints out paychecks and earnings statements, like the one in Figure 19.8. All the payroll data can be incorporated into accounting programs that perform year-end calculations for tax filing and financial reports.

A *labor analysis package* is useful for examining worker productivity and cost-effectiveness to determine whether a company's workforce should be expanded or diminished and how workers should be distributed throughout the business at any given time. By combining analyses of payroll and labor with information regarding sales volume and customers, an employer can determine the exact cost of providing some service to a customer and can therefore allocate employee time more efficiently.

Tax Planning

Paying the government

Information for tax forms, such as a company's quarterly estimates to the IRS and W-2 forms for employees, can also be calculated and then printed on the appropriate forms fairly easily by means of specialized business application packages. At one company, the adoption of a personal computer system saved managers three months' time and the cost of hiring an outside accountant—just in figuring out the year-end taxes. Programs for tax planning and preparation offer businesspeople the opportunity to enjoy the benefits of professional tax consultants without the costs. Such programs can project up to four years of alternative tax plans and can demonstrate how a particular deduction or other situation will affect the bottom line of profitability. Suppliers of tax planning software generally sell updated versions that incorporate all the changes in federal and state tax laws for the past year, thus ensuring that businesses can take advantage of any beneficial new laws and avoid any accidental illegality. And since all financial data are stored in the computer's memory, the company has ample evidence of its preparations in case of an audit by the IRS.

ISSUES IN TECHNOLOGY

It seems that computers in business are only as good as the businesspeople who run them. A number of studies have shown that in many companies the use of popular business application packages and expensive computer systems resulted in *lower* profits. The reason is that the companies were weak to begin with, and their management practices failed to keep up with the technology. In these cases, computers only served to make poor business practices worse, and did it with the same dramatic efficiency with which they can help sound practices work better. Is there a risk that businesses will expect computers to solve all their problems, will interpret manufacturers' promises of increased profitability as meaning "just plug it in and watch it go"? How can this risk be avoided? What kind of retraining or restructuring is necessary if management is to avoid the perils of GIGO?

BUSINESS AND THE COMPUTER

Now let's consider some business applications of the computer in the context of a typical situation in which many of them are actually put to use. The following example should give you a better perspective on how important computers are in everyday business activities. The story is summarized graphically in Figure 19.9.

"We're primarily a campus supply store," says Nancy Ebert, the owner and general manager of The Book Cellar, "carrying textbooks, stationery, paper, pens, sweatshirts, souvenirs, three-ring binders—things like that—for the faculty and students of Northcentral College. Our sales pattern and volume is closely tied to the school calendar and enrollment statistics. That is, there's a lot of demand in the fall, when students first arrive and want to buy all new supplies. Then there's a mini-boom in the spring for second semester. But it fluctuates. It used to be that either we were caught short on everything or we were overstocked for five or six months. One semester I had boxes of notebooks stored in my office, in my apartment, in my car—I thought I'd never get rid of them all. That was before we had the computer, though. It's certainly made things easier."

Assume you are a student at Northcentral College. In the middle of taking notes for your Introduction to Data Processing class, your pen runs out of ink. You manage to make it through the last 15 minutes by borrowing a broken pencil stub and a piece of green chalk. Between classes, you run across the street to The Book

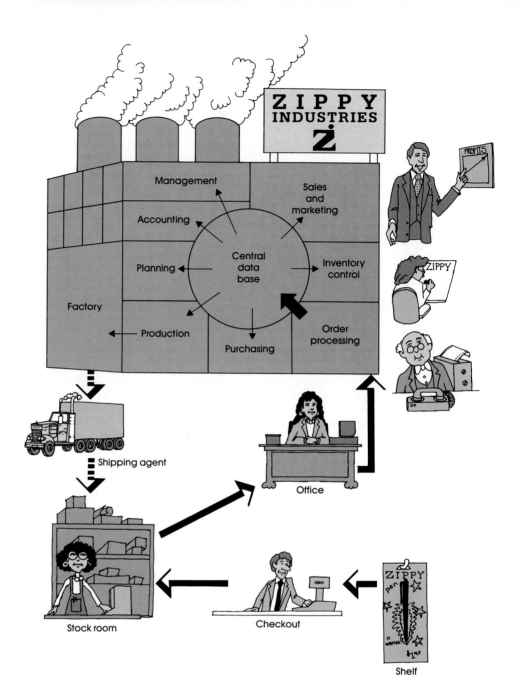

Figure 19.9 Business and the Computer

The role of the computer in the commercial network as exemplified by The Book Cellar and Zippy Industries.

Cellar and quickly choose a medium-point Zippy Pen with blue ink. Without thinking of the commercial network that brought you and new pen together, you shell out $1.95 plus tax and hurry back, late, to your next class.

Point of Sale

Systems to speed up retail transactions

In 1984, there were 20,000 point-of-sale (POS) systems in the United States; in 1985, there were more than 50,000. By 1990, there will be more than 140,000 of such systems in operation, performing—according to the American Bankers Association—more than 13 billion transactions each year. A POS system consists of one or more terminals connected either to a local minicomputer or to a storage unit that transmits data to a large central computer located somewhere else. Data are entered at the terminal through a keyboard very similar to a cash register's or through OCR or MICR devices, such as hand-held wands or the optical scanners used in many grocery stores (these devices were introduced in Chapter 4).

At The Book Cellar, many of the school supplies sold, including pens, have Universal Product Code (UPC) bars printed on their packages. Tom Poser, the check-out clerk who rang up the sale when you bought your pen, simply ran a pistol-like device over the UPC symbol printed on the card in which the pen was bubble-wrapped. The wand emitted a beam of light that was reflected off the black and white stripes, converted to electrical signals, and transmitted to The Book Cellar's minicomputer in the storeroom. The computer quickly translated the signals into an inventory number for a medium-point Zippy Pen with blue ink. The minicomputer matched the code to a stored price list, figured the tax, and sent this information (along with the time and date) back to Tom Poser's terminal, where it appeared on the display and was printed on the receipt you threw away as you ran out the door.

"I really like the POS terminal," says Tom Poser. "It's fast and it's accurate, which is mostly why I think it's so great. The first year I worked here we didn't have the computer, and it took me a long time to learn the register. And I made mistakes sometimes. I overcharged people, which made customers mad, or undercharged them, which made Nancy Ebert mad. Even if I caught the mistake, everything had to stop while someone from the office came over to initial the receipt so that the bookkeeper wouldn't get mad. I think everyone's a lot happier now, with the computer."

Nancy Ebert is also pleased with the POS system. "Look," she says, "our store's not very big, but we do a very high volume of business during about half the year. Before we got the computer, we had four check-out lanes and they took up a big chunk of our floor space, which we really need for merchandise. The POS system is four times faster than conventional registers, so we reduced the number of check-out lanes by half, and our sales volume rose simply because we can make more sales in a day. Also, of course, the reduction in check-outs meant that our overhead dropped, since we didn't need four full-time check-out clerks any more. We can get along fine with just part-timers like Tom. On the management side, that means lower costs in wages and benefits."

Although POS terminals cost between 20% and 25% more than conventional cash registers, transactions that take nearly three minutes on those registers are completed in less than 40 seconds with a POS system. POS systems are more accurate and more convenient for customers (aside from their speed, they produce detailed receipts) and cut employee training time in half. The installation of POS systems also allows the number of check-out stations and personnel to be reduced by 25%–50%.

Inventory

"Not only does the computer read UPC symbols and store current prices," continues Nancy Ebert, "it handles our inventory records, too. Lucia Green, our stock manager, keys in all the pertinent data—such as delivery date, quantity, price, and UPC code. That's all stored in the minicomputer downstairs. The computer can automatically supply the correct price for any item and can also automatically keep track of how many, say, deluxe Hejhogg backpacks have been sold, how many are left, and when we need to reorder." (See Figure 19.10.)

"The reorder point varies from item to item. We determined those points with the computer's help, based on enrollment patterns at the college for the last five years and the time it takes to process orders and deliver the items. We also input estimated enrollment projections for the next two years. All of that was used to determine how many of each item we should keep on hand at any given time. When the stock reaches that point, the computer prints out an 'inventory alert' to Lucia and displays it on my desktop terminal. I look at our forecast for the next few months, and how we're doing financially, before I make the decision to go ahead and reorder. There are some things we *always* need, like paper clips. The computer regularly reorders things like that (there are only a few of them) from the supplier, computer-to-computer. Most things fluctuate, though, so those decisions always come down to me."

Instant performance of a tedious job

Before there were computers, stores would close down for a day or two to take inventory, that is, to go through the store and stockroom and count how many of each item were there. The process was costly (since the store would lose two days' sales), time-consuming, and subject to error. Furthermore, since it was only an annual or semiannual event, the numbers weren't current enough to be useful much of the time. With POS systems, stores keep track of their inventories with up-to-the minute accuracy, and current data are available to managers whenever they need them. Hand-held OCR wands can be used to enter inventory counts and also to change prices of items electronically. The printed bar codes remain the same, but the computer's interpretation of a code is altered—a much more efficient process than changing thousands of price tags.

Figure 19.10 Computerized Inventory at The Book Cellar
In this detailed inventory control report, the first three columns show stock number, item description, and the number of items last ordered (and when that order was placed). The next four columns show how much of the order has been received (and when), how many have been sold, how many are left, and at what point a new order should be made. The last five columns are for planning; they show the annual number of units ordered for each item, the cost of a unit and of the annual order, the total current sales for that item, last year's sales as of the same time (YTD means year-to-date), and the computer's projected sales for this year.

STOCK NO.	DESCRIPTION	ORDERED	+RECEIPTS	−ISSUE	= ON HAND
10446	KWIK−ZAP ERASER	150 [2/10]	20 [2/20]	144	26
11397	ZIPPY PEN	40 [3/7]	40 [3/15]	19	21
24465	NOTE−O−PAD	450 [5/18]	380 [6/20]	286	194
46773	PENCILETTE	25 [2/8]			
58832	STIKY TAPES−IT	90 [5/18]	50 [6/1]	20	30

ORDER POINT	ANNUAL UNITS ORDERED	UNIT COST //TOTAL	ANNUAL SALES CURRENT	LAST YTD	PROJECTED
75	1000	.06//6.00	144	120	980
20	120	.78//93.60	19	28	120
225	2000	1.50//3000.	286	220	1900
10	100	3.20//320.	0	22	87
60	1500	.85//1275.	20	20	1450

Job Description Once a systems analyst has determined which equipment and software are most appropriate for a business, the EDP manager must take responsibility for the purchasing, installation, and administrative control of the new electronic data-processing center. An EDP manager is an administrator whose responsibilities include hiring and scheduling operators, ensuring efficient running of the facility, keeping track of maintenance schedules, and dealing with equipment and personnel emergencies as they arise. The EDP manager is also responsible for informing personnel outside of the data-processing department of the capabilities and limitations of the facility, establishing standards, and reporting to his or her superiors (most likely the general office manager) about the strengths and weaknesses of the system as an integral part of the company.

Qualifications A college degree isn't necessarily required for this position, but an academic or applied background in business, computer programming, and systems analysis is considered highly useful. Some previous experience as a supervisor or personnel manager is indispensable. A thorough understanding of hardware and software technology, office operations, and management principles is also extremely important.

Outlook As a growing number of companies acquire computer systems, there will be a corresponding need for people to supervise and manage EDP centers. Banks, large law firms, insurance companies, data-processing services, and the administrative offices of wholesale and retail stores are just a few of the places in which large number of EDP managers are currently employed.

Order Processing

Interestingly enough, the one Zippy Pen you bought brought the stock level to the reorder limit for that item. So, even as you dashed out the door, a message was printed out by the minicomputer down in the stockroom, and Lucia Green informed Nancy Ebert that there was an inventory alert. At her terminal, Nancy Ebert called up the report, and the information shown in Figure 19.11 was immediately displayed.

Electronic restocking

Lucia Green's printout simply told her that the item was out of stock. Nancy Ebert's CRT display gives her detailed information on how many pens were in stock before the last reorder (under OPENING BALANCE), how many were shipped and when they were received (under +RECEIPTS and DATE), a day-by-day list of the number of pens sold (under −ISSUE), how many are currently in stock (under +ONHAND), and what the reorder point is (under REORDER POINT). It even gives her the address, phone number, and contact person at the supplier. With this information, Nancy Ebert can consult her sales projections to determine what to do. She notices that more than half the stock was depleted in the first half of the month and decides to double the regular order for this time of year, to order 40 rather than 20, even though it's the "slow time of year." A professional's business sense and good judgment are still necessary, even in this age of computerized business systems. The computer provides the information; the manager still makes the decisions.

```
┌─────────────────────────────────────────────────────────────────────┐
│                                                                       │
│   4/14 2:07:43 PM REORDER ALERT        To: NE From: SYSTEM            │
│  ┌──────┬──────────┬─────────┬──────────┬────────┬────────┬────────┐ │
│  │STOCK │          │OPENING  │          │        │        │ORDER   │ │
│  │NO.   │  ITEM    │BALANCE  │+RECEIPTS │ -ISSUE │+ONHAND │POINT   │ │
│  ├──────┼──────────┼─────────┼──────────┼────────┼────────┼────────┤ │
│  │11397 │ ZIPPYPEN │   18    │   40     │4/02 4  │››20‹‹  │  20    │ │
│  │      │ M OR BLU │         │  DATE    │4/05 15 │        │        │ │
│  │      │ $ .78 EA │         │  3/15    │4/06 11 │        │        │ │
│  │      │          │         │          │        │        │        │ │
│  │      │ ($1.95 EA)│        │          │4/08 5  │        │        │ │
│  │      │          │         │          │4/13 2  │        │        │ │
│  │      │          │         │          │4/14 1  │        │        │ │
│  └──────┴──────────┴─────────┴──────────┴────────┴────────┴────────┘ │
│                                                                       │
│   ORDER FROM:                                                         │
│   ZIPPY INDUSTRIES                                                    │
│   407 ZIPPY PLAZA                                                     │
│   RIGLYVILLE, PA 54321     CONTACT: I. PHILIPPS                       │
│                                    ORDER PROCESSING                   │
│   333 333-3333             DEPT 33                                    │
│                                                                       │
└─────────────────────────────────────────────────────────────────────┘
```

Figure 19.11 The Book Cellar's Inventory Alert

A more detailed report than that in Figure 19.10, the inventory alert shows the wholesale and retail price of the item, detailed sales data, and the information necessary for reordering.

The rest is handled by two computers: Nancy Ebert's at The Book Cellar and the one at Zippy Industries. Nancy Ebert fills in half of an order form on her computer screen and, using a modem, electronically mails it to Isaac Philipps, her contact person at Zippy Industries. He will fill in the rest when the shipment goes out. When he receives the order, he notifies the inventory control department, where the company's stock is monitored, letting them know that one of their customers needs 40 Zippy Pens.

"When I enter an order into our system here," says Isaac Philipps, "the data are automatically coded and stored in the central data base. All the departments in the company have access to it. Accounting needs to know what our orders are, so they can figure out how much money we're making. The planning office keeps track of general sales patterns, in order to tell purchasing how much it can spend. Purchasing works through suppliers, who gather materials from various sources for processing and assembly in our factory, where much of the manufacturing is also computerized. The production department schedules operations in the plant, and they need to know what production levels have been set. That's done by the general manager, the top boss who uses data from all our offices to make policy and production decisions. Since we've gone over to computers, Mr. Ziparelli—the boss— gets all the data he needs as soon as he wants it. Everything has an impact, even a single order from a small store." Even the purchase of a single pen.

Sales and Marketing

Analyzing the market and developing new advertising strategies

Alec Pozarnov and Carla Perez are heads of the sales and marketing departments at Zippy Industries. Alec Pozarnov is the company's sales manager, and he explains the role of computers in his job: "It's up to me to analyze incoming orders and the performance of our sales personnel to see how these figures compare with our past sales levels and our projections. I have to determine which markets are drying up and which ones we should pay more attention to. Then I develop profit, growth, and sales reports for Mr. Ziparelli. The raw data come in from all over the country, all year long. I couldn't do my job as efficiently and accurately as I do without computers."

Carla Perez, the marketing director, also relies on computers for her work. "Once Alec has made his reports and projections," she says, "Mr. Ziparelli wants to act. I need to develop advertising campaigns and sales promotions that not only will achieve Alec's projections, but will do it in the most cost-effective way possible. To do that, I need to carefully select media and methods and to consult market research studies that tell me who's buying which products, in what quantities, and when. Market research shows what sorts of customers we have and what they like. Computer analyses of our own sales data and the results of consumer behavior studies give me accurate profiles of our current buyers and potential customers. On the basis of that information, I know whether to aim our advertising and packaging designs toward older or younger people, men or women, students or professionals, liberals or conservatives. I can even develop campaigns on the basis of what kind of music customers like and what food they eat. Market research gathers data from every imaginable corner of the country, like Alec's raw sales data. Computers make the process of gathering, organizing, and interpreting that data faster and more complete."

Nancy Ebert's doubling of her usual order catches the attention of Alec Pozarnov and Carla Perez, and they conduct a careful computer-assisted analysis of the Northcentral College area. They decide that The Book Cellar would be an ideal store in which to test-market the new, improved Zippy Pen 2. A few months later, the signs go up in The Book Cellar's big front window. And at about that time, your Zippy Pen runs out of ink.

SUMMARY

Computer Applications
Computers are vital to the smooth functioning of a variety of industries.

Manufacturing In addition to computer-aided design and manufacturing, computers are used for production control, production scheduling, and production planning.

Banking and Finance On the money side of the commercial network, computers are not only increasingly convenient, but increasingly necessary. Automatic teller machines (ATMs), which provide basic banking services at diverse locations, and electronic funds transfer (EFT) systems, which allow even wider computer application in financial transactions, may well be the start of the cashless society.

Insurance Insurance companies have huge data bases, containing premiums, policies, actuarial tables, and a host of other statistics, which require the help of computers.

Utilities Running and monitoring equipment, billing, record keeping, rate setting, and operational simulation are some of the principal computer applications that public utilities rely on.

Transportation Rate calculations, reservation systems, and route selection are some of the important tasks to which computers are put by airlines, bus and trucking companies, and car rental agencies. In the airline industry, computers are especially important for in-flight control and air traffic control.

Hotels Hotels and motels use computers to streamline reservations, billing, inventory, housekeeping, and special services.

The Stock Market Brokers, investors, and banks use computers when they invest funds in the stock market. The SEC's EDGAR system delivers complete, up-to-date financial data on companies. Electronic information systems provide financial news and market performance information.

Printing and Publishing Computers have replaced typewriters and mechanical typesetting machines in the publishing industry. Books, newspapers, and magazines are frequently written, edited, layed out, and typeset with the help of computers.

Architecture Architects use computers to run stress tests, design buildings, produce blueprints, and sell their designs to customers using computer-generated (sometimes animated) graphics.

Business Application Packages

Computerizing a business can greatly reduce expenditures, but software is necessary to make a system work. It is largely through the use of business application packages that businesses save time and money.

Accounts and General Ledger Computers help companies keep track of money they owe and money owed to them. Efficient account management ensures prompt billing and payments. A general ledger package uses sales, profit, loss, and expense data and assembles it into coherent records and reports.

Payroll and Labor Analysis Working with such data as pay scales, hours worked, tax rates, and payroll deductions, payroll analysis packages produce paychecks, earning statements, and accounting documents. A labor analysis package can help raise productivity and lower costs by evaluating a company's workforce.

Tax Planning Tax planning programs calculate a company's tax payments by taking profits, expenses, deductions, and tax laws into account. They can prepare the forms and the appropriate documentation.

Business and the Computer

From the factory to the check-out aisle, computers help move products, money, and ideas throughout the commercial network. Even the smallest purchase has a significant impact.

Point of Sale POS systems help stores complete sales transactions more quickly and accurately and reduce overhead costs significantly.

Inventory Some of the benefits of a POS system are that it keeps accurate, updated inventory records, can place reorders automatically, and can keep managers informed of the current status of their stock.

Order Processing The detailed information produced by a POS system lets managers make informed decisions on what, when, and how much to reorder. Suppliers and manufacturers use computers to process and fill orders.

Sales and Marketing Analyses of sales and projections of volume, profit, and productivity are accurate only if they are based on large quantities of current data. Computers are well suited to the organization and analysis of masses of data. Market research and consumer profiles are also prepared with the help of computers.

COMPUTER CONCEPTS ▬▬▬

As an extra review of the chapter, try defining the following terms. If you have trouble with any of them, refer to the page number listed.

production control 548
production scheduling 548
production planning 548

automatic teller machine
 (ATM) 548

electronic funds transfer
 (EFT) 550
operational simulations
 550

REVIEW QUESTIONS ▬▬▬

1. How are computers used to help manufacturers?
2. What is the cashless society, and how do ATMs and EFT bring it closer?
3. What kinds of things are in a typical insurance company's essential data base?
4. How can operational simulations assist utilities?
5. What are some of the major applications of computers in the transportation industries?
6. What did the SEC do to bridge the gap between the regulator and the regulated?
7. What capabilities are enjoyed by architects who use computers?
8. Define the following business applications, and tell how computers are used for them: accounts payable and receivable, general ledger, payroll and labor analysis, and tax planning.
9. What is a POS system? What are its advantages? How does it make the inventory and ordering processes easier?
10. What do sales managers do, and how can computers help them?
11. Tell how computers can be useful in market research.

A SHARPER FOCUS ▬▬▬

Now that you've completed this chapter, you should be able to answer the following questions about the chapter opening.

1. Is there any question that Stew Leonard's personal computers will pay for themselves? How?
2. What other computer applications might there be at Leonard's store? (There *are* applications that aren't specifically mentioned in the chapter opening.)
3. What advantages does the "World's Largest Dairy Store" enjoy over other, similar operations that don't use computers? What are the possible effects of these advantages?

PROJECTS ▬▬▬

1. How many of the business applications of computers discussed in this chapter can you locate in your community? Prepare a brief report in which you document the locations and functions of as many different business applications as you can. Also, suggest what the advantages of each application might be for managers, employees, and consumers.
2. Describe the various points at which computers and a traveler might intersect during a long vacation. Begin with planning an itinerary. Consider the possibilities raised in this chapter—travel agencies, hotel reservations, and car rental, for example—as well as any other computer contacts you can think of, such as automated subways in large cities or computer-based amusements at tourist attractions like Epcot Center. Prepare a chart illustrating all the intersection points.
3. Two students are talking. One says, "Why should *I* have to learn anything about data processing? I'll be going to work for my father in our funeral parlor." The other replies, "I know. My mom and dad are farmers, and I'm going to work on their farm once I get my degree in agriculture—what've computers got to do with *me?*" Are they right? Do some businesses have nothing to gain from adapting a computer to their operations? Can these two students avoid learning about data processing and still expect their businesses to thrive in today's environment? Support your answer with careful research and cite your sources.
4. Consider your church, fraternity, sorority, or other similar nonprofit organization. How could it, as a sort of "small business," benefit from a microcomputer? What software packages would you suggest be used, and how would you go about choosing them?

20

Computers in Education, the Arts, and Sciences

▶

FOCUS ON . . . COMPUTER CATCH-UP

One way or another, students in the Soviet Union often adopt, belatedly at least, Western fads. By turning to the thriving black market in Moscow and other cities, many Soviet teens manage to spend their spare rubles on imported designer jeans or bootleg tapes of Michael Jackson and Boy George. But Soviet youth have so far missed out completely on one craze that is sweeping much of the West: the computer boom. Most Soviet teens have never touched a personal computer, much less spent hours hacking away happily at a keyboard.

Soon, however, the U.S.S.R. may have its own generation of computer kids. The Kremlin has decreed that in September computer classes will begin "on a large scale" for the 8 million ninth- and tenth-grade students in the Soviet Union's 60,000 high schools. Said a statement issued by the Politburo: "All-round and profound mastering by young people of computers must become an important factor in speeding up the scientific and technological progress in the country." While computers are widespread in American high schools, most Soviet students have no chance to learn about the machines until college . . .

The Soviets will be hard pressed to have the high-school computer program in full swing by the Politburo's September deadline. Western experts doubt that enough computers will be available to equip all the schools. Even if the machines arrive, there will probably be shortages of computer textbooks and teachers who know how to use them. "There are still many obstacles," admits an article about the new computer program in *Pravda*, the official party newspaper.

The biggest questions are what kinds of computers will be used and where they will come from. Personal computers first appeared in the U.S. in the mid-1970s, but the Soviets did not produce one until 1983. That maiden model, called the Agat, a shortened form of the name Agatha, is a crude copy of the Apple II, one of the first personal computers sold in the U.S. . . .

Technological progress and strong economic growth in such industrial nations as the U.S. and Japan have been spurred by the swift spread of information made possible by computers. If the Soviet Union maintains restrictions on their use, it might not come close to realizing the full economic potential of computers. Says Loren Graham, a professor of the history of science and a Soviet expert at M.I.T.: "We may be about to learn that the Soviet system is not designed for the information age."

There are those who contend that the world is neatly divided between the scientists and the artists: that a person either has an analytical, logical mind dedicated to concrete problem solving and the uncovering of clear physical truths or else is romantic, irrational, impractical, and completely emotional. A great deal has been written on the conflicts between the "two cultures," but such black-and-white rules rarely stand up in fact. It is in part the broad application of computers throughout our society that is rapidly breaking down this longstanding myth. The same tool, in various incarnations, is used by both artists and scientists for what are ultimately, in their own ways, creative efforts: spacecraft navigation systems and CAT scanners, rock music and special effects.

In this chapter, we'll look at some applications of computer technology that bridge the "gap" between the "two cultures." We'll begin with a common starting point for all types of people—education—and then turn to the fascinating, ground-breaking, and creative applications of computer technology in the arts and sciences. Throughout, we'll be emphasizing those applications that have a direct relationship with your everyday life.

COMPUTERS IN EDUCATION

There are more than 100,000 computers in U.S. schools, helping administrators keep track of the business of education, helping teachers improve their students' progress, and helping students learn not only about computers but also about math

Improving students' performance

and science and medieval history. Computer manufacturers are finding that worthwhile tax breaks and other incentives are available from federal, state, and local governments in return for the donation of computers to financially stressed public schools. As a result, the number of educational applications of computers is likely to increase significantly.

Educators, once wary of their electronic teaching assistants, are finding computers are not threats to their own jobs but rather are valuable learning tools for students. In an age increasingly affected by computer technology, the absence of terminals in a school may prove to be as devastating to a student's potential as would be the absence of instruction in reading or arithmetic. Studies have revealed that students in high schools where computers are available score from 13 to 16 points more on the SAT exam, particularly on the math part, than students in computerless schools.

The advantages of computers aren't limited to high school juniors and seniors; a variety of computer applications spans all grade levels. In experiments across the country, teachers are using computers with remarkable success to teach children in kindergarten how to read. An IBM computer displays a picture of an object, accompanied by the phonetic and dictionary spellings, and ''speaks'' the word. The child says the word with the computer, and then spells it out on the keyboard. If the child's spelling is correct, he or she receives hearty electronic encouragement and goes on to the next word. Children using these Writing to Read programs have scored higher on achievement tests in reading than most first graders (see Figure 20.1).

In special education classes, teachers are discovering that computers can improve the reading skills of learning-impaired children by more than 70% and that physically and mentally disabled students are able to use computers to manipulate their environment in ways they never could before. Students with cerebral palsy, for example, who can't use their hands to draw on paper, can create pictures on a computer screen by keying in a program. That such activities perform an instructional and therapeutic function is obvious. That computers have opened up careers previously closed to the disabled, such as architecture and design, is perhaps less apparent, but no less appreciated by educators. In all classes, computers have demonstrated convincingly that they are an asset, not just a distraction.

Figure 20.1 Computer-Assisted Instruction

Learning to read isn't just a simple matter of opening books anymore. Here, a young reader is learning to spell *elephant*—with the help of a voice-recognition system and computer graphics.

Computer-Assisted Instruction

Computer-assisted instruction, or **CAI**, is the use of computers to assist in the process of learning. CAI is derived from the work in *behavior modification* done by B. F. Skinner. Educators were quick to see the possible classroom applications of his theories of reward and punishment. If students receive immediate positive response to their work, they will tend to learn material more rapidly and retain information longer. Although instant feedback can be virtually impossible for one teacher faced with 30 students, it's a piece of cake for a computer. Thus the development of computer-assisted instruction.

Helping teachers provide individualized attention

Initially, computer-assisted instruction consisted of quizzing, or "drill-and-practice," routines. The computer presented a question to the student, who responded. If the student's answer was correct, the computer displayed "yes" or some similar positive message and went on to the next question. If the student was wrong, the computer indicated that, gave the right answer, and presented another question similar to the first. Although such simple formats are still in use today, for example, in the kindergarten reading program we described above, more intriguing and sophisticated educational uses of computers are being developed every day. Computers are used for foreign language drills (in which the student and computer engage in a Spanish or French or German dialogue), tutoring (in which concepts are explained and wrong answers are corrected at length), and problem solving in physics and higher mathematics. Computers can provide students with realistic decision-making scenarios (as we'll see in a later section of this chapter on physician training) or engage them in complex *Socratic dialogues* (interchanges in which questions and answers, from both student and computer, run along a logical line to a clear conclusion). In history classes, students can refight the Battle of Gettysburg or rule a feudal manor, in which case the computer will inform them of the effects of their decrees on the economy, agriculture, or political climate of their fiefdom.

Math teachers have found that computers perform a doubly valuable role in their classrooms, since writing a program to solve a problem requires that a student be completely comfortable not only with programming techniques but also with the basic mathematical concepts represented by the problem. Some high school students have become such practiced programmers that they have produced customized software for their teachers in geography, economics, calculus, and history. One of these precocious programmers made over $40,000 his first year out of high school by writing a game for an Apple computer.

Some colleges and universities, such as Carnegie-Mellon, Boston College, and Dartmouth, require some or all of their entering students to purchase a personal computer along with their textbooks and notepads. More and more college libraries are installing computer systems to replace bulky and unmanageable files of index cards. Shelf location and whether or not the book is in circulation can be accessed by keying the book's title, call number, or author. Systems in some libraries feature subject searches as well. College-level CAI applications—such as the PLATO instructional system developed at the University of Illinois, which stores over 8000 hours of course material in every area from physics to Swahili—are increasing every day. College departments across the country are participating in programs in which professors are loaned personal computers that they can keep if they develop an application appropriate to their discipline. The benefits are threefold: increased production of home-generated software for colleges, innovative course material for students, and free personal computers for professors.

Computer-Managed Instruction

Monitoring students' progress

All CAI applications represent ways in which computers are used primarily to help students. **Computer-managed instruction**, or **CMI**, on the other hand, is the use of computers to help teachers. Although they are different, CAI and CMI are often used together. CMI systems allow teachers to monitor students' progress in CAI programs and to diagnose their strengths and weaknesses. CMI systems can graphically display a student's performance over a given period, illustrate overall progress, or output detailed breakdowns and analyses of problem areas. In addition, as a sort of electronic attendance-keeper, the CMI system can keep track of how often and for how long each student was at the terminal, which lets the teacher know whether students have been conscientious about their assignments and reveals whether more or less computer-assisted instruction is called for.

ISSUES IN TECHNOLOGY

What happens to students who attend financially strapped inner-city or isolated rural schools that can't afford to purchase expensive computer equipment? Manufacturers can't be expected to donate computers to every school in the country, but schools that can get computers have a clear advantage. Might our democratic public education system soon begin to produce two distinct "classes" of students: the computer literate, who have higher test scores and a clearer shot at success in a high-tech job market; and the computer illiterate, who are as unfairly deprived of a complete education as if they were denied math books? What is the answer, if any?

Administration

The business side of education

The people who run the schools, the educational administrators, can also benefit from computer applications. Computers can help administrators to compile and produce class lists and schedules, to organize and evaluate testing and counseling, and to order books and supplies. Accounting, budgeting, and payment of bills and salaries can be accomplished in a more orderly way. Detailed records can be kept of all of these activities, which is always an asset in a well-run business. All student and personnel records can be efficiently stored and readily accessed, streamlining the complicated business of keeping a school running smoothly.

The school cafeteria is another area in which a computer can help, not so much in food preparation but in the compiling of nutritional, cost, and delivery information into a logical system that ensures that a school cafeteria doesn't end up with too much caviar and not enough chicken soup.

In short, nearly all of what teachers, students, and administrators do in school—teach, supervise, plan, analyze, evaluate, learn, and eat—can be traced back to a computer.

 ## COMPUTERS IN THE ARTS

The word *arts* encompasses a far broader range of endeavors than we'll be able to discuss here. However, whether the field is literature, dance, sculpture, painting, photography, cinematography, or even the language arts, computers are playing an ever expanding role in all kinds of creative expression.

Theater

Writing, casting, and performing a play

A playwright writes a play with her word processor. Her agent uses his personal computer to locate likely investors and to figure out his percentage. A casting agency employs its computer to scan quickly through a file of actors to find tall, pale, sinister-looking ones who might portray the villain. Tickets are sold through computer networks like Ticketron, which allow customers nationwide to choose the play they want to see at the time they want to see it, and even to choose where they want to sit. In the theater, the lighting for the performance is controlled by a computer program that dims the houselights and changes the stage lighting at the appropriate times; a synthesizer generates the "orchestral" accompaniment (as one did on Broadway for *The Pirates of Penzance* and *Amadeus*); and a POS system in the lobby keeps track of how many glasses of white wine are sold at intermission. The next morning, after the reviews are out, the playwright goes back to her word processor to revise a few rough spots in the dialogue. Shakespeare would be amazed.

Music

Computer-generated music and computer-assisted composition

For a computer to produce music, just as for a computer to do anything, its input must be converted to numbers, processed, and then converted into human-understandable output. Since music's tonal and rhythmical qualities are mathematically based (it was the Greek mathematician Pythagoras who, in the sixth century B.C., invented the seven-tone *diatonic scale* still used in Western music), converting a melody's "formula" into computerese is a fairly straightforward operation. Electronic music is the result when this conversion is made through **pulse code modulation (PCM)**. Simply stated, pulse code modulation is the assigning of binary values to tonal input, so that B-flat becomes, for example, 00001101. The musical notes can be computed; their tonal qualities can be read as numerical quantities. A **digital-to-analog converter (DAC)** is a device that translates the binary word representing a sound into a voltage signal (for example 00001101 means 0.06 volt), and a *filter* smoothes the computer's "stair-step" sound wave into a curve, which is then amplified through a speaker so it becomes audible sound. Figure 20.2 (page 574) illustrates this process.

The first song actually played on a computer was "A Bicycle Built for Two" at Bell Laboratories in 1932, and computers have, in effect, been humming away ever since. Computers are used in the composition and performance of music by a diverse group of artists, from serious modern composers such as John Cage, Morton Subotnick, Iannis Xenakis, and Karl-Heinz Stockhausen, to popular performers such as Vangelis, The Electric Light Orchestra, The Human League, and the Eurythmics (see Figure 20.3, p. 575). In between the avant-garde and the pop are musicians like Wendy Carlos, who uses computers and synthesizers to duplicate traditional instruments in recordings of compositions by Bach, the Beatles, or Scott Joplin.

As we mentioned, the use of the computer goes further than performing music. Writing music is also aided by the use of computer hardware and software. Composers can use Polywriter, Xerox's Mockingbird, or similar systems produced by Yamaha, IBM, Apple, and dozens of smaller companies, to compose music at a keyboard; the notes they play are displayed on a screen in standard sheet-music format. The composition can be edited, the notes can be printed on sheet-music paper, and the musical data can be stored on diskettes. A software-driven synthe-

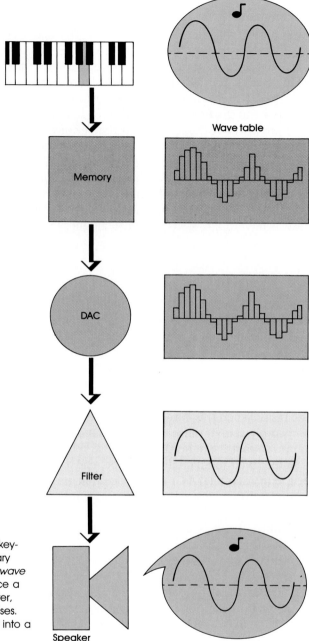

Figure 20-2 Pulse Code Modulation

A computer produces sound by matching each keyboard instruction (or note) to a sequence of binary numbers stored in its memory. The sequence, a *wave table* representing a sound wave that will produce a musical note, goes to a digital-to-analog converter, where it is changed into a series of electrical pulses. This "stair-step" wave is then smoothed by a filter into a wave that can drive a speaker.

sizer will play back the composition for the composer, simulating as many as 100 different musical instruments from French horns to kazoos. Figure 20.4 shows some of the components of a computerized music system.

Also, a number of actual musical instruments, from a Yamaha piano to electric guitars, are equipped to play back music diskettes. A *musical instrument digital interface (MIDI)* acts as a modem to link the computer with a synthesizer or electronically compatible instrument. With this link, any such instrument can become the "output speaker" of the pulse code modulation process. Then music can be

Figure 20.3 Electronic Music
As computer-based electronics flood the music world, it's becoming increasingly difficult to tell the performers from the engineers. For this musician, the piano keyboard and the computer keyboard are equally important instruments.

composed at a computer keyboard, stored on a disk, and played back on a high-quality instrument.

With music software and a synthesizer, composers can alter a work's rhythm and tempo at will. The computer automatically stores the input notes according to the desired time, regardless of the speed at which the musician plays them. Melodies, harmonies, and intricate variations can be mixed and altered with a few simple commands. Many popular musicians can't read music, but such musical computer systems allow them to compose "by ear" as well as to produce hard copies of their musical creations so other musicians can perform them. Computers may thus serve to "democratize" music by opening up composition and performance to people who lack the natural talent or the years of training traditionally required.

The Movies

Of all the fine arts, film is the most modern, the most mechanical, and the most dependent on technological advances. A piece of charcoal and a fairly clean cave wall are the only necessary components of painting, but film is a new and essentially technological art form. Before Thomas Edison and William Dickson invented the *kinetograph* around 1890, there simply were no movies. Since then, whenever

A technology-dependent medium

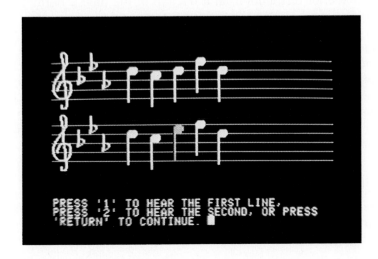

Figure 20.4 Music System Components
An Apple music composition system.

an applicable technological advancement was made, whether it was sound recording (also an Edison invention) or cameras that could take pictures in existing light, it was quickly embraced by the movie industry. Computers are no exception. Their application in two areas of film making, editing and special effects, is particularly significant.

Editing

That two-hour movie you go to see at your local theater was recorded on more than 10,000 feet of celluloid held on six reels; more than 1000 individual still pictures (or *frames*) are required for each minute of action. The movie was composed of an average of 2000 separate pieces of film, strung together, resorted, and respliced during many months of work until those assorted bits of celluloid wound up telling a particular story. The film editor works with the director to make a coherent movie out of a jumble of individual scenes.

Traditionally, an editor sits at an *editing table,* or *Movieola,* on which are mounted several film reels, a splicing device, sound mixing controls, a speaker, and a small viewing monitor. The editor has to look at each segment of film, at versions of the same shot from different angles or with different lighting, and then put all the shots together, combining and remixing the film and soundtrack into various sequences until the best arrangement is found. It's a painstaking process that often takes as long, or sometimes longer, than the actual filming. These editing decisions are very important, since the way the shots are combined determines what the movie will look like on the screen. As much as half of the film shot for a movie can end up "on the cutting room floor."

By capitalizing on the speedy and efficient organizational and cataloging abilities of computers, film makers can both shorten and improve the editing process. At the Lucasfilms headquarters of *Star Wars* director George Lucas in northern California, an advanced editing computer called EditDroid scans unedited film with a video camera and transfers the celluloid images to video disks. The editor sits by EditDroid's controls and scans through these disks just like a film buff with a Betamax. He or she can "mark" the beginnings and ends of sequences and move them around in the same way blocks of text can be moved with a word processor. EditDroid also has a large, high-quality screen, which lets the editor see instantly what the edited footage will look like on the theater screen. The original celluloid is then marked and edited according to the editor's final disk version, and copies are quickly made for distribution, in a fraction of the time it normally takes.

EditDroid's sound-mixing counterpart is the *audio signal processor.* It converts sound into binary digits (in the way we described in the preceding section on music), thus streamlining the tedious and detailed work of mixing together all the sounds that go with the visual images. Sounds can be made louder or softer, stretched out or shortened; speech and other sounds can be synthesized. Since a single scene in a movie may require more than 60 separate sounds, from background music and dialogue to glasses clinking in a restaurant, this is no small task. The ratio of sound editors to film editors working on *Return of the Jedi,* for example, was four to one.

Special Effects

Perhaps the most stunning computer application in film making is in the area of *special effects:* the production of visual images that don't normally occur in nature. Computers can guide cameras around a model, can control and vary film speeds to enhance an effect, and can simulate changes in perspective. The traditional back-bone of special effects in films is the **matte effect** (pronounced "mat"), which is illustrated in Figure 20.5. In the past, achieving this effect was a time-consuming and complicated process, and the results were not always altogether convincing. Technicians often ended up producing shadowless, out-of-proportion images with tell-tale blue rings around their silhouettes, which signaled audiences that a matte image, whether it was a spaceship, a monster, or a seventeenth-century London skyline, was being used. This represented a distinct dramatic disadvantage, since audiences were more aware of the technique itself than of the action it was supposed to support.

(a)

(b)

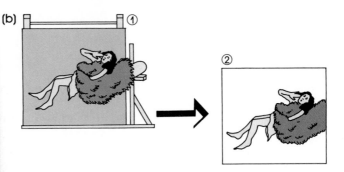

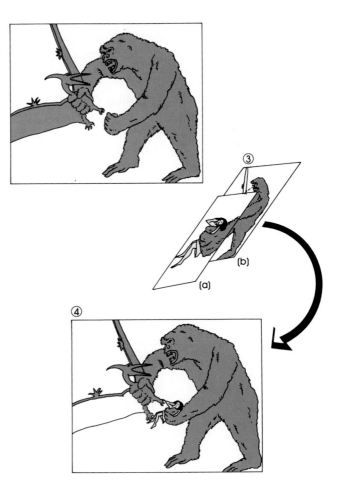

Figure 20.5   The Matte Effect.

(a) The matte effect was used extensively (along with other manually-produced photographic effects) in movies such as 1933's *King Kong*. In this still, the ape and pterodactyl, the woman, and the background were all filmed separately, then combined.   (b) Traditionally, a matte effect is achieved by (1) filming an image in front of a blue screen, then (2) photo-graphically reprocessing the image to remove the blue ele-ments, leaving only a figure on a transparent field. When that print is physically overlaid onto another (3), the result is a matte image (4). The first image blocks out part of the sec-ond, and the two appear to be in the same place. Exact synchronization of camera and model movements, as well as a steady, expert hand in the photo lab, are vital if the effect is to be convincing.

Figure 20.6 More Mattes
Modern computer imaging techniques allow the production of special effects, like this scene from 1983's *Return of the Jedi*, that far surpass the quality of earlier films. Computerized matte effects are precise, convincing, and virtually unlimited in application.

A computer, however, simply scans the film and reads the images as numerical values. It can then remove all the blue (or red or green) values of a particular shade and replace them, precisely, with values from the desired background or object, thus eliminating all potential for sloppy lab work, human error, or simple physical mismatching of mattes. The resultant image is as precise as numbers can be (see Figure 20.6). The *Star Wars* movies, *Close Encounters*, *The Last Starfighter*, *Ghostbusters*—virtually any recent movie that contains special effects relied on computer-imaging techniques to achieve its breathtaking moments.

Creative Graphics

That the picture in Figure 20.7 was produced by a computer may not surprise you, but that the vase and teapots in Figure 20.8 are also computer-generated images may be harder to believe. In fact, that realistic still life is the product of Lucasfilms' revolutionary graphic simulator, Pixar. We've already seen some applications of computer graphics to video games, product design, and business presentations. Now we consider the use of the computer by artists who create original images for films and television, and simply for art's sake.

Like computerized special effects, computer images can not only mimic reality but also create original images, impossible and other-worldly pictures and scenes, with a startling realism and mathematical precision. It shouldn't be forgotten that computers can deal only with numbers, and the production of graphics is no exception to that rule. The delicate Japanese teapots in Figure 20.8 are simply the end-product of complex mathematical equations to the computer that created them. They result from calculations just like those performed by a hand-held calculator, only many degrees more complicated.

Analyzing and manipulating pixels to generate art

A graphic simulator "sees" and reproduces the world as a sort of jigsaw puzzle of *pixels* (or *picture elements,* which we learned about in the section on graphics packages in Chapter 10), each of which represents one tiny segment of the whole picture. It isn't only computers, of course, that break images up into pieces. Look closely at a newspaper picture—it's actually just a collection of shaded dots, a form of pixels. There are about 25,000 dots in a 2-by-3-inch newspaper photograph. A

Figure 20.7   A Computer-Generated Line Design
This is what most people generally associate with the idea of "computer art." Complex as the production of this line design may be, however, computers are capable of generating far more spectacular graphics.

Figure 20.8   A Computer-Generated Still Life
Developed and produced by a Lucasfilm computer, with some help from programmer Alvy Ray Smith. Using a process called ray tracing, the computer "traces" an imaginary ray of light from each pixel point on its screen to an "object," the objects surrounding it, and finally to the light source. By thus "tracing" a ray of light backward, the computer collects detailed data on the object's color and reflective properties, as well as the location, brightness, and color of the light source. Painstaking and strange, the process results in astoundingly realistic images, such as the teapots here.

television picture is also a collection of pixels, about 281,000 on a 19-inch screen. The 35-mm motion picture film used for most movies has about 9 million pixels per frame. The more pixels there are in a given amount of a picture's area, the better will be the picture's clarity, or *resolution*.

For a computer to generate graphic images, it first reads an artist's program, which mathematically describes the dimensions, shape, and configuration of the image to be generated. In an alternative method, analog-to-digital conversion hardware (similar to the digital-to-analog converters we described in the section on music) scans photographs or drawings and converts the images to binary digits, which the computer can store and which can be called up later for alteration or printing. A third method involves the use of a special graphics tablet, or digitizer, and a light pen (introduced in Chapter 4), with which the artist directly inputs the lines forming the image into the computer.

In any case, the picture is transformed into pixels, which the computer then fills in. First each pixel is assigned a multidigit code. This code describes the shade of the pixel's color and the intensity with which it reflects light (which determines the material out of which the object will appear to be made) and is based on knowledge of the laws of optics stored in the computer's memory. Then each pixel is compared with all the others, which can number from 9 million to more than 100 million, to achieve the proper relationships of shape and texture, light and shadow, color and reflection.

An image composed of 9 million pixels can take a computer nearly 20 hours to generate. When this technology is applied, whether commercially or artistically,

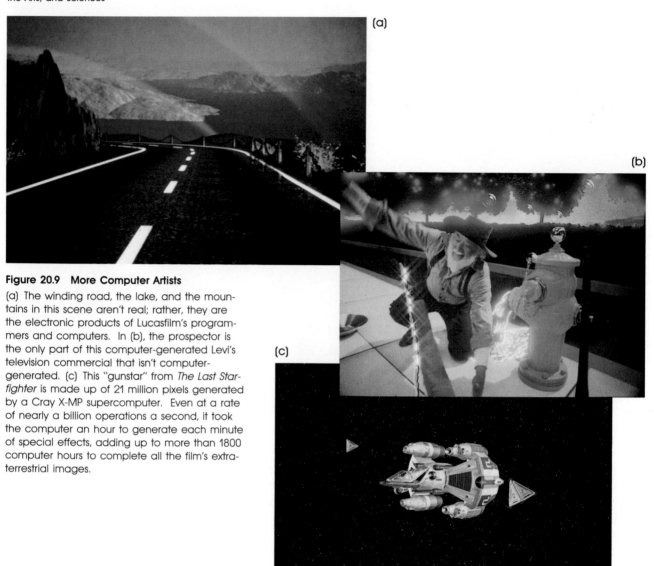

Figure 20.9 More Computer Artists

(a) The winding road, the lake, and the mountains in this scene aren't real; rather, they are the electronic products of Lucasfilm's programmers and computers. In (b), the prospector is the only part of this computer-generated Levi's television commercial that isn't computer-generated. (c) This "gunstar" from *The Last Starfighter* is made up of 21 million pixels generated by a Cray X-MP supercomputer. Even at a rate of nearly a billion operations a second, it took the computer an hour to generate each minute of special effects, adding up to more than 1800 computer hours to complete all the film's extra-terrestrial images.

the entire process can take months to complete. But all the time, effort, and expense required to produce "computer art" hasn't dissuaded artists, film makers, advertising agencies, television networks, and a wide variety of others striving for striking visual presentations from turning to computers for artistic assistance (see Figure 20.9).

Literature

Word processing and computer poets

Word processing is currently the major computer application in the world of letters. An increasing number of writers, from novelists to ex-Presidents, have discovered that word processors are ideally suited to the basic task of writing—the manipulation of words. Writers use computers, then, more or less as sophisticated typewriters.

No best-selling books have been written even in part *by* computers, in the way that popular movies such as *TRON* or *The Last Starfighter* contain many images produced by computers. On the other hand, there is computer-generated poetry:

The sunset is leaving, shouting but silent
Singing or crying its joy or anger
The sun's whim was this afternoon's season:
Beautiful, cruel, worldly, now forgotten, now cherished,
Sometimes feared, sometimes invented, always grasping
As we were demanding earths and legs and continents of orchids
And the intention and the life of our own raucous blood;
For this sunset is ours, our curse, our home,
Rushing but staying, enduring time glacial and quick.

This poem, called ''Diary Excerpt: Emeritus,'' was composed by a computer at Allegheny College in Pennsylvania for a class called ''BASIC Poetry.'' Professor Alfred Kern, who wrote the program that produced the poem, uses computers to demonstrate to students the mathematical properties of classical poetic forms such as the sonnet and the villanelle. Armed with a list of 600 words and instructions on grammar, syntax, line length, meter, and stanza forms, the computer randomly selects words from its dictionary and assembles them into the appropriate format. Whether or not a PC will ever take its place beside Shakespeare and T. S. Eliot, though, is quite another question.

SCIENTIFIC COMPUTING: SIMULATION

We have stated many times that computers deal only with numbers. Numbers can, however, represent a great many things: among them, words, pictures, and complex relationships. The variety of systems and situations that can be represented numerically, and thereby be made grist for the computer mill, is virtually endless.

Computers generally simulate reality by executing programs that incorporate not a physical but a mathematical model of some real situation or system. This is what lies at the heart of scientific computing. But computers are also perfect instruments for the application of a much older process called the *scientific method* (see Figure 20.10), in which scientists first make observations of whatever system they are trying to understand. The next step is writing mathematical relationships that describe their observations as accurately as possible. This depiction is the *mathematical model*. The model is then used in attempts to calculate outcomes that reproduce the observed results and also situations that have *not* been observed. (For example, the celebrated relationship between mass and energy, $E = mc^2$, was written down by Einstein long before there was a chance to confirm its validity through experiments.) When a model fails to duplicate the values that are observed, the model is revised. Sometimes the instruments for making measurements are improved or the precision of the calculation is increased, and the cycle goes around again.

The scientific method, by which scientists try to increase our understanding of our surroundings, hasn't really changed at all during the past few centuries. What has changed, and dramatically, is that the computer now allows scientists to apply the method successfully to much more difficult problems. Computers can handle

Mathematical models and computer simulation

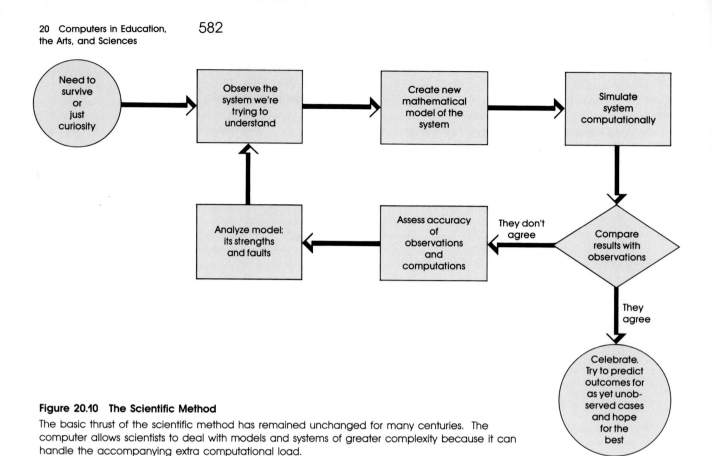

Figure 20.10 The Scientific Method
The basic thrust of the scientific method has remained unchanged for many centuries. The computer allows scientists to deal with models and systems of greater complexity because it can handle the accompanying extra computational load.

models of great complexity, perform the tremendous numbers of calculations involved in their simulation, and reproduce the behavior of the actual systems with unprecedented exactness.

Biological Systems

Simulating patterns of population growth and molecular structure

Perhaps the simplest *biological model* (a mathematical model of a biological system) is the exponential law of population, an equation that describes the growth or decline in the population of a single species in terms of the numbers of births and deaths per year. The exponential law of population is a simple mathematical model of an aspect of the behavior of real biological systems. Computers aren't necessary to simulate this behavior; a calculator will do. But, considering our own species, suppose a scientific study is undertaken to estimate births and deaths during a census year, simultaneously examining some additional hypotheses (that is, refining the mathematical model), such as whether births and deaths vary in some predictable way according to income, health, or education. This kind of problem requires a highly intricate and involved statistical and mathematical effort.

When biologists try to model the populations of several interacting species of animals, the situation grows even more complicated. Even the relatively straightforward case of two species, one of which sustains itself exclusively by eating the other (an interaction known as a predator-prey system), produces population phenomena that can't be described with a simple equation. Both population levels can fluctuate: the predator population will grow until it consumes nearly all the prey, and then it starts starving out, which gives the prey population time to recover.

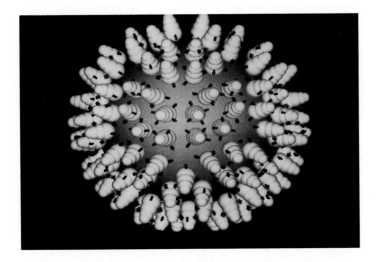

Figure 20.11 Molecular Structure on a High-Resolution Display

High-resolution displays are used in research by biochemists attempting to determine molecular structures and their relation to biological functions in a living organism. The displayed image results from the combination by the computer of mathematical models of the relations that must be obeyed by the groups of atoms in the molecule and sophisticated graphics packages; these results are presented graphically so that they can be observed and manipulated by the researcher interactively.

Eventually, when there are again ample prey, the predator population begins to increase. This sort of cyclical behavior is qualitatively very different from simple exponential growth or decay and can be described accurately only by a very complex mathematical model. In dealing with any sort of real ecosystem, with its many interacting species of plants and animals, scientists are faced with incredible levels of complexity; attempts at the simulation of such systems can stress even the largest computers. However, even though predicting human or animal populations accurately is still a very problematic endeavor, the techniques that the computer has allowed scientists to employ can produce valuable insights into interactions between species.

The computer plays a significant role in all the biological sciences, from the study of species population interactions down to the investigation of the molecules that constitute individual cells. Studies of how molecules "fit" together and how their chemical structures relate to their biological functions make extensive use of mathematical models, computer simulation, and computer-controlled instruments. Figure 20.11 illustrates the use of a high-resolution graphics terminal to display the structure of a molecule of DNA, which serves to encode the particular genetic information common to all body cells of a given species.

Economic Systems

Economic systems have long been the subject of intensive efforts at mathematical modeling. Perhaps the best known of the more recent attempts is the *input-output model* (not the same as the data-processing terms) of Wassily Leontief, for which he was awarded the Nobel Prize in economics in 1973. The model gets its name from the way it describes the relationships between the various sectors that constitute an economy. If, for example, it requires three cents worth of coal to produce one dollar's worth of steel, then the relationship between the coal and steel sectors is described by the number 0.03. That is, the model uses numbers that express the value of the input from one sector that is required to produce a dollar's worth of output from each of the others.

Economists who use the Leontief model to study the economy make use of sophisticated scientific computer programs to solve the large systems of equations (sometimes more than a thousand) required to describe the relations among all the

Studying the relations among an economy's sectors

sectors of the U.S. economy. What would be the effect on U.S. industry if our oil supply were drastically curtailed? Could the other energy sources such as coal and nuclear power make up for the loss? What are the economic effects of the transition from chromium to aluminum in the automotive sector? What are the effects on employment of the shift from blue-collar to service-oriented industries? These are just a sampling of the important issues studied by government and private economists using computer models of the U.S. economy.

Flight Control

Simulating the forces acting on aircraft and spacecraft

From the microscopic bases of life to social and economic interactions, to the exploration of outer space—the applications of scientific computing are virtually limitless. The navigational controls of aircraft and space vehicles are computerized to a significant degree. Whenever an aircraft or spacecraft executes a maneuver to maintain its course, it is being guided by a computer that issues commands on the basis of a mathematical model that takes into account all the influences on the vehicle's course. The inputs to the computer may come from an on-board *inertial measurement unit,* which senses the positions of sensitive gyroscopes in order to determine the direction in which the vehicle is heading and its orientation. For a space vehicle, the commands will be directed to the engines, which will fire in a certain sequence and for definite durations to accomplish the desired course alteration. For an aircraft, the computer causes adjustments of the aerodynamic surfaces to accomplish the necessary result. Computers on the space shuttle can do both, since it is an air- and spacecraft.

In the earth's atmosphere, a vehicle's motion is significantly affected by the aerodynamic lift and drag on its surfaces. These surfaces can be manipulated automatically by a computer or manually by a pilot to produce desired changes in direction and altitude. The model used by the computer in this case is based on a set of equations called the *fluid dynamic equations,* the fluid being the atmosphere. These equations describe the effects that result when the motion of a body in a fluid is affected by both the resistance of the fluid and the motion of the fluid.

A vehicle-borne computer may be in communication with backup computers on the ground to assess where a spacecraft is and what course corrections are required for it to reach its destination; the ground-based computers might receive independent data on vehicle location from radar systems monitoring the flight. The spacecraft computer will do a simulation based on star sightings (which were also used by the voyagers of old) and a model of the gravitational influences on the vehicle's course. If the vehicle is, for example, midcourse on a lunar flight, its path will be influenced by the gravitational attraction of the earth, moon, and sun, and, to a lesser extent, nearby planets. Computing the resulting gravitational force on the vehicle requires solving equations that Isaac Newton wrote down in the seventeenth century but that couldn't be solved in any useful way until the computer age.

THE SUPERCOMPUTER'S ROLE

As far as computational speed is concerned, the supercomputer is the top of the line. Because of their tremendous computing power, supercomputers have had a profound impact on science and technology.

Image Processing

We've all seen several types of computer-processed images: CAT scans, which we'll discuss in the upcoming section on medicine; the fascinating computer-enhanced composites of the earth taken by orbiting satellites; and the unique pictures of Jupiter and Venus beamed to earth from distant spacecraft in the form of streams of pixel values reconstructed by NASA computers. In applications such as these, the computer is programmed to distinguish between **signals** (pixel values that really are part of the image) and **noise** (spurious values caused by electrical disturbances in the atmosphere or by equipment malfunction). The computer can also be used to bring out the contrast between parts of a scene. One easy way this can be done is by having the printer print the pixel values corresponding to the low-contrast colors of blue and green as high-contrast black and white so that a land-water boundary shows up more clearly.

Sharpening images and recognizing objects

Although they are conceptually simple, these image-processing techniques require enormous computer resources for their practical application. The sheer volume of image data returning from space motivated NASA to develop the supercomputer MPP (Massively Parallel Processor), a centrally controlled array of 16,384 individual processors in one system. As another example of how demanding these applications can be, even with the use of its Cray X-MP to execute the special effects for movies such as *The Last Starfighter*, Digital Productions in Los Angeles (one of the major film industry sources for scene simulations) estimates that it can produce no more than 12 minutes of film per month. Even just the realistic portrayal of action scenes involving real (photographed) and synthetic (animated) objects tests the limits of the fastest supercomputer.

The requirements for computing power become even more demanding when computers are used to identify images—that is, to determine what is being shown rather than simply showing it. In the applications we've discussed so far, a computer works on sequences of pixels without "knowing" what the overall image is. The still-emerging field of **pattern recognition** is concerned with efficiently using computers to describe and/or identify pictorial objects. Applications of the techniques of pattern recognition are beginning to find a place in the automation of manufacturing. Recently developed robots have the ability to "see" machine parts on assembly lines and then act on the basis of what they observe, for example, in performing some rudimentary inspection functions (see Chapter 18 and the section "Vision and Advanced Robotics" in Chapter 23).

One class of pattern recognition techniques, particularly useful in classifying satellite images of the earth, is statistical in nature. With these **clustering methods**, pixels are grouped together if their values (colors) are statistically similar, according to some predefined criterion. These groups of pixels are then classified by their characteristic colors into land-use categories. Such methods have been applied successfully to identify different crops and to distinguish among pasture, forest, cropland, desert, and urban settlement for large areas of the earth, some of them never previously mapped. One often previously mapped area is classified by these means in Figure 20.12.

Oil Exploration and Recovery

Techniques similar to clustering methods are employed to map the earth's mineral resources. As these resources become scarcer, the supercomputer's role in helping

Aids to exploration and recovery

Figure 20.12 Automatic Land-Use Classification

(a) A computer-generated color composite of a NASA LANDSAT satellite image of Lake County, Illinois. Such images are available for all of the United States and much of the rest of the world. (b) A clustering method devised by the Laboratory for Remote Sensing at Purdue University was used to obtain this land-use map of the area shown in part (a). The pioneering program was written at the University of Illinois and run on the supercomputer ILLIAC IV at the NASA Ames Laboratory in California in the late 1970s. The map's coding is as follows:

COLOR	LAND USE
Yellow	Agriculture and open space
Dark blue	Heavy urban
Light blue	Light urban/suburban
Dark green	Forest
Light green	Pasture (grass)—improved open space
White	Water
Medium gray	Wetland (marsh)
Red	New development

to locate and recover them is correspondingly more important. The resource that best exemplifies this situation is oil.

Since the early 1920s, oil companies have been using *seismic prospecting* to determine the underground structure of areas being explored for oil and to locate the layers most likely to contain oil or gas. In seismic prospecting, small explosive charges are set off at selected locations in the exploration area. The frequency and intensity of the resulting vibrations, or seismic waves, are measured by seismometers and recorded as *seismic traces* (as shown in Figure 20.13). Most major oil companies now use supercomputers to solve the complex systems of equations that are involved in the process of analyzing these traces to determine whether there are likely oil- or gas-containing layers at a given location. A significant industry has developed to supply smaller oil companies with this kind of computational sup-

Figure 20.13 Seismic Prospecting
Seismometer measurements of the frequency and intensity of the vibrations produced in the vicinity of a small explosion result in seismic traces as shown here. From these traces, supercomputers can characterize the layered underground structure as far down as several kilometers, including the depth of each layer, its angle of inclination, and its physical properties. These results are used to determine whether oil and gas are likely to be present.

port. The oil industry, as a whole, uses about 10% of the nation's total supercomputer capacity.

Removing the "easy" oil that is driven to the surface by underground pressure reduces the pressure in the reservoir to the point where the oil no longer comes to the surface by itself (primary recovery). But as much as two-thirds of the total volume remains in the reservoir at that point, and some oil deposits are tightly bound to the surrounding rock. These circumstances have led to a number of so-called secondary and tertiary recovery techniques. Water or gas can be pumped into the well to build back up the pressure that was lowered by removing the oil, or steam may be injected to help get the remaining oil to flow more easily. Fires may even be started to burn off part of the oil to make the rest easier to recover. These more complicated and costly recovery schemes require a more precise knowledge of the subsurface structures. In the past, time-consuming, expensive, and often inaccurate drilling tests were the only method available for finding elusive deposits, and "dry holes" were common. Now, calculations for *reservoir simulation,* done on CYBER 205 and Cray X-MP supercomputers, are beginning to supplement actual drilling tests and will perhaps ultimately replace that costly trial-and-error method.

The Weather

In 1948, a group of meteorologists from around the world took up residence in Princeton in order to gain access to von Neumann's IAS computer. They were interested in **numerical weather prediction**, the computer simulation of the weather based on a mathematical model of the atmosphere's motion. The economic value of timely and accurate weather forecasts is incalculable for agriculture (in deciding when to plant, harvest, apply chemicals, or cut hay, for example), the oil industry (in deciding how much heating oil or gasoline to refine), commercial

One of the first supercomputer applications

INITIAL

48 HR. FORECAST

48 HR. VERIFICATION

Figure 20.14 Weather Prediction

Supercomputers generate weather forecasts on the basis of current meteorological data applied to a mathematical model. Here, the computer's printout of the current (initial) conditions (top), the forecast (middle), and the actual weather pattern as it developed (bottom).

airlines, and a host of other endeavors in which weather is a factor, from satellite launches to ski resorts. Although receiving less attention than fusion energy research or high-tech defense systems, attempts to compute weather forecasts have been one of the driving forces behind the development of more powerful supercomputers.

While we all have a tendency to remember the bad forecasts that left our picnic drenched by an unexpected downpour, the fact remains that weather prediction continues to improve in accuracy. Today's 48-hour forecasts are about as reliable as the 24-hour forecasts of a decade ago, largely because of increasingly powerful supercomputers that can incorporate in the models with which they work more details of the atmospheric physics that govern weather patterns. These supercomputers perform calculations at more points on the globe and do so with greater precision than was possible before. Figure 20.14 shows a recent computer-generated forecast.

Just as a flight simulation program needs data about where an aircraft is at any given time in order to compute where it will be later, an atmospheric simulation program needs data on the present state of the atmosphere in order to compute its future state. The atmosphere's condition, however, is by no means easy to measure. Continued improvement in the quality of numerical weather prediction depends not only on the development of more powerful supercomputers but also on the improvement and extension of atmospheric measurements on and above the ground.

MEDICINE

The cost of health services in the United States is in excess of $300 billion annually. This is more than the defense budget or the cost of all food sold at the retail level; it's about 10% of the annual gross national product. Computers play a significant and growing part in virtually all aspects of the health services industry. Although they contribute positively to the quality of medical education, instrumentation, diagnosis, and treatment, they may also contribute to the increased cost of health care. In this section, we'll study the role of the computer in medical advances from the points of view of both patient and practitioner and try to bring this role into perspective.

Physician Training

Even before they become M.D.'s, today's medical students are exposed to computers. At New York University's School of Medicine, for example, computer-generated graphics allow students to "operate" repeatedly on a simulated patient, practicing different techniques and surgical strategies that would otherwise require hundreds of cadavers. A three-dimensional perspective can be viewed from any angle; unexpected (but preprogrammed) complications can arise; and the healing process takes place in minutes, allowing the prospective surgeons to observe their success.

Simulating the patient's response to treatment

At the University of Illinois Medical Center in Chicago, students practice diagnosis with the help of a computer-simulated "patient." Students ask questions in conversational English and receive responses. They can call up stored medical records concerning the case and consult with programmed "specialists" before diagnosing the problem and prescribing a cure. The result of a diagnosis is provided immediately, letting the students know if the treatment was successful. If they get it wrong, they can try again—an option that won't necessarily be open to them in real practice, of course.

Patient Histories

Numerous systems have been developed to take histories from patients at interactive terminals. The most sophisticated of these are driven by programs with a branching structure that permits them to follow different sequences of questions stored in their data bases as different diagnostic possibilities emerge during the session. Such programs vary according to whether they are designed to gather general information or to narrow down the set of reasonable diagnostic alternatives. After the initial history has been taken, there are corresponding provisions for entering follow-up data. (One of the positive side effects of the use of these systems has been an increased trend toward the standardization of medical nomenclature.)

Obtaining and managing patient data

A beneficial consequence of increasing the health care data base is the ability to use specialized data base management systems to conduct searches that, for example, create a list of all patients who had a given disease during a certain period of time. A widely used system of this type is MUMPS (Massachusetts General Utility Multi-Programming System). As the use of such systems becomes more widespread throughout the health service system, the National Center for Disease Control in Atlanta is better able to do its job of detecting disease outbreaks early and alerting the appropriate medical communities.

Medical Instrumentation

From chemical tests to patient monitoring

A vital part of the patient data used in making diagnoses, and in prescribing and monitoring treatment, comes from laboratory instruments. Analyses of blood cells, blood serum, and coagulation times, urinalysis, and tests for disease-linked chemical changes are all aided by computers that monitor instruments, analyze data, and screen the results for error. Although the majority of diagnostic lab tests must be performed by people, computers help ensure the accuracy of the results of the 60,000 performances of 500 different tests done in the average hospital lab every day, and they store those results efficiently. They also speed things up—a blood test that normally takes four and a half hours can be completed in under an hour and a half. Faster results mean shorter stays for patients, which in turn saves money for both patients and hospitals.

The computer's role doesn't end, however, with collecting, storing, and providing access to information from patients and medical instruments. Electrocardiograph (ECG) equipment is used to trace changes in electrical potential during heartbeats. For many years, these traces were used only by experienced physicians to spot abnormalities in the heart muscle. Manufacturers of ECG equipment now offer software systems that automatically analyze and interpret this data. Some of these systems also digitize and store the ECG data in efficient digital format and can compare a patient's current electrocardiogram with past ones, looking for diagnostically significant changes.

Direct patient-monitoring systems (DPMs) in a patient's room act as round-the-clock nurses. They monitor and display a patient's vital signs—heart rate, breathing, brain waves, and temperature—and alert hospital staff if anything begins to go wrong. The data collected by these monitoring systems provide doctors with continuous records of their patients' physical condition, an analysis of which could detect minor changes or subtle trends. Such continuous monitoring may sometimes be clearly called for, especially if a patient's condition is critical.

That brings us to the most demanding of hospital environments: the intensive and critical care units. Computers in some of these units now do the complete job of managing patient data: they monitor ECGs for disturbances in rhythm, take blood pressures, and monitor blood flow through the body. Utilizing such information, they can even administer medication with high-precision pumps, adjusting dosages by closed-loop control based on the monitored results.

Decision Making

Since the late 1950s, there have been ongoing attempts to use medical data bases to make diagnoses by relating sets of symptoms to specific diseases through the use of

CAREERS IN TECHNOLOGY
Technical Writer

Job Description From writing instruction manuals and documentation for personal computers to generating sales reports and press releases for software manufacturers, individuals who combine writing skills with a comprehensive understanding of computer technology are increasingly in demand. Technical writers prepare original technical, procedural, and instructional materials, training aids, and technical reports, as well as revise technicians' writing into "human-readable" prose.

Qualifications A technical writer needs exceptional communication and organizational skills, coupled with some familiarity with software design, data processing, and computer systems. Some colleges offer specific degrees in technical writing, although a degree in Eng-

lish, rhetoric, or journalism combined with some technical or scientific coursework (or even courses in business with a computer emphasis) is also a valuable asset for would-be technical writers.

Outlook Because new applications for computers are constantly springing up, largely in nontechnological environments like living rooms or offices, the need can only increase for people who can clearly explain difficult computer concepts in a way that makes the new conveniences accessible to *all* users. In addition, the proliferation of computer-interest magazines and professional trade publications provides a constantly expanding market for computer-oriented articles and reviews.

---

various inference techniques. (Some of these techniques can be classified as artificial intelligence, which we'll discuss in Chapter 23.) The largest of these systems is the University of Pittsburgh's CADUCEUS (formerly known as INTERNIST), a program that cross-indexes 500 disease profiles with more than 3000 separate symptoms. Provided with medical records and current complaints, it can diagnose a patient's problem, recommend further tests (including a consideration of cost and discomfort factors), and suggest treatment. The program was designed to follow the diagnostic strategies of an eminent physician at the university and has passed the board examinations in internal medicine. Similar programs are Stanford's MYCIN, which diagnoses blood infections, and PUFF, which analyzes data from breath samples to diagnose cardiopulmonary problems.

Medical Imaging

The medical applications we've discussed so far work with data that consist of either alphanumeric text or digitized (one-dimensional) curves, requiring no more than several thousand bytes of storage for each record. Now we turn to the two- and three-dimensional images produced by medical imaging systems. To begin with, there are the more than 20,000 traditional X-ray machines in use in the United States. There are another 10,000 fluorographic X-ray units. Some hospitals currently digitize X-ray films by a variety of available means and maintain them in a computer-accessed data base. Since an average X-ray machine produces

X-rays, CAT scans, ultrasound, and other imaging techniques

50 films per day, and each digitized film requires a million bytes of storage, this is no small job. Another problem is that the digitizing methods aren't uniformly good at preserving the high resolution required for making difficult diagnoses.

It seems entirely possible that conventional X-ray machines will, over the long run, be displaced by recently developed units that produce digital images directly. A conventional X-ray machines works by exposing a film plate to a beam of X-rays. A new system, developed by Fuji, exposes a phosphor plate to the X-rays. When scanned by a laser, this plate produces light output that can be digitally recorded. The phosphor plates are packaged in cassettes of the same size as the film cassettes that fit into the existing machines. Moreover, they require shorter exposure times. This new system, as well as other direct digital X-ray techniques, is currently being evaluated at several major U.S. hospitals.

A complicating factor in X-ray diagnosis is that the more dense a region of the body, the higher is its rate of absorption of X-rays. As a result, all dense regions show up on X-ray images as shadows, and it's often hard to distinguish overlapping structures, particularly when they have comparable densities. *Computerized axial tomography (CAT) scanners* solve this problem by taking X-rays through the body at many different angles. The various images obtained this way are then recombined by a sophisticated computer program, which is an integral part of the system, into images of horizontal sections of the body. These "slices," when stacked up, show the internal structures in three dimensions. There are more than 2000 CAT scanners currently installed in the United States.

A comparable imaging technique currently in wide use employs ultrasound; this technique is like radar in the sense that it reconstructs information on the basis of the returning echoes of transmitted pulses. These pulses, however, are at ultrasonic rather than radio frequencies. Ultrasound systems primarily employ analog computers for the reconstruction and storing of images on videocassette recorders. They are particularly safe to use since they use acoustic radiation, and they are also low in cost. As a result, more than 10,000 of these systems are installed in the United States.

Other computerized imaging techniques are positron emission transaxial tomography (PETT) and nuclear magnetic resonance (NMR) scans. Doctors who want to avoid exploratory brain surgery can employ PETT or NMR scans to observe chemical reactions and metabolic functions in the brain to locate tumors or discern brain damage. PETT scans use a radioactive substance that is injected into the patient's brain. NMR scans represent the newest technology in imaging. They are carried out not with X-rays or with radioactive injections, but with magnetic fields produced by a large circular magnet that surrounds the patient. A radio-frequency energy source is coupled with this magnetic field to create a computer-generated image more accurate than that of a CAT scan. While doctors watch, the NMR scanner can produce "motion pictures" showing the movement of blood or the reaction of a tumor to treatment.

An excellent example of the merging of computerized medical imaging techniques with advanced computer display systems is shown in Figure 20.15.

Prosthetics and Beyond

Microprocessor-driven systems to replace injured limbs and organs

Microelectronics has brought amazing advances to the field of prosthesis (the replacement of limbs and organs with artificial devices). Over 100,000 electronic

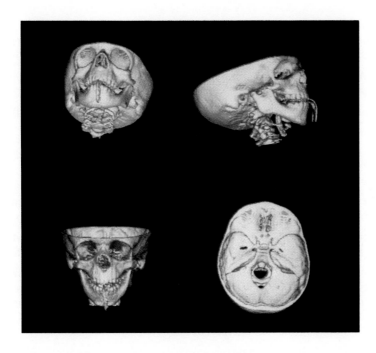

Figure 20.15   Computerized Axial Tomography
Data from a CAT scan or NMR scan can be manipulated, in real time, by the examining physician. Using controls such as track balls and cursors, they can be rotated or cut away to show what lies beneath.

pacemakers are implanted every year in the United States alone. Researchers at the Illinois Institute of Technology have invented a microelectronic system by which artificial limbs can be moved by the brain's own electrical impulses, just like natural limbs—a sort of "thought control." Electrodes convert neural signals into electricity, which a microprocessor in the artificial limb interprets to activate an electromechanical movement system. Not to be outdone, researchers at the Massachusetts Institute of Technology are working on reversing the process to provide artificial limbs with a simulated sense of touch. Similar systems are used to exercise and control paralyzed limbs.

Computers can also simulate auditory and optical nerve signals, allowing the deaf to hear and the blind to see. Artificial hearts controlled by microprocessors can prolong life (the first kept Dr. Barney Clark alive for 112 days in 1983), and computers that perform fetal monitoring can warn doctors of health problems in patients still unborn. Computerized devices that detect brain waves are accepted in many states as the final authority in pronouncing death. From *before* the cradle to the grave, physicians now rely on computers to help them observe, analyze, monitor, treat, and cure their patients.

SUMMARY

Computers in Education
When computers are introduced into the educational process, students' interest, comprehension, and test scores have been shown to rise considerably. Computers also open up new possibilities for disabled students.

Computer-Assisted Instruction   Computer-assisted instruction has grown from simple quizzing routines to an interactive educational tool, involving students in individualized instructional efforts.

Computer-Managed Instruction   Computer-managed instruction helps teachers keep track of students' progress, maintain class records, and pinpoint problem areas.

Administration   Student records, financial data, and all the other businesslike aspects of education can be managed more easily with the help of computers.

Computers in the Arts

Computers are assisting artists of all kinds in their creative expression.

The Theater   From a playwright's first draft through casting and production, computers play a useful role in the theater.

Music   Music is a mathematical art form, perfectly suited to computers. Musicians can compose, revise, orchestrate, print, and perform their works with help from computers.

The Movies   Film making is essentially a technological art form and has made extensive use of new developments since its inception. By converting sound and images to machine-readable binary digits, editing machines cut the time and costs involved in assembling scenes into a movie. And computerized mattes and computer-generated graphics are dramatically changing movies' special effects.

Creative Graphics   By breaking a picture down into pixels, a computer can generate, alter, and create images for movies or television commercials, or simply for art's sake.

Literature   For novelists and other writers, word processing is a significant computer application. Some computers can generate poetry, too.

Scientific Computing: Simulation

Computers create simulations of reality based on mathematical models. Using the scientific method, comparison of simulated results with observed values furnishes the basis for revising and improving on the model.

Biological Systems   The mathematical model of population increase or decay can be replicated on the computer.

Economic Systems   Leontief's input-output model of an economy is one important scientific computing application.

Flight Control   In the atmosphere, a vehicle responds mainly to aerodynamic effects; in space, it encounters only gravitational forces. Both of these situations are modeled and simulated to control aircraft and spacecraft.

The Supercomputer's Role

Because of their extremely high speed and accuracy, supercomputers are at the center of scientific computation in a variety of fields.

Image Processing   Digitized pictures are processed in a variety of ways to enhance their quality. Pattern recognition identifies the objects in a scene.

Oil Exploration and Recovery   The likelihood that costly test drilling will be unsuccessful is reduced by seismic prospecting, or computer processing of the seismic traces that result from small explosive charges. Reservoir simulation is used to select the most efficient recovery method.

Weather Forecasting   Numerical weather prediction, or the simulation of weather, was among the first applications of supercomputers. It remains among the most important forces behind the continuing quest for greater computer power.

Medicine

Computers play a vital part in medical education, instrumentation, diagnosis, and treatment, as well as contributing to the costs of modern medical care.

Physician Training Simulation systems permit medical students to practice their skills and observe the effects of their treatment on a varied group of "patients."

Patient Histories The principal diagnostic tool is information provided by the patient. Getting, storing, updating, and presenting it can be more efficiently accomplished with the computer's help.

Decision Making Data base systems and the inference techniques of artificial intelligence are being combined to computerize diagnosis.

Medical Instrumentation Laboratory test data are obtained using computer-based instruments. Electrocardiograms may be automatically interpreted and vital signs may be monitored by computers.

Medical Imaging Two- and three-dimensional images of the interior of the body are produced by computer-driven X-ray units, CAT scanners, PETT scanners, and NMR scanners. They are already an indispensable part of the diagnostic process.

Prosthetics and Beyond Microprocessors are being used to provide complex interfaces between the brain and artificial limbs and organs.

COMPUTER CONCEPTS

As an extra review of the chapter, try defining the following terms. If you have trouble with any of them, refer to the page number listed.

computer-assisted instruction (CAI) 571
computer-managed instruction (CMI) 572
pulse code modulation (PCM) 573

digital-to-analog converter (DAC) 573
matte effect 577
signals 585
noise 585

pattern recognition 585
clustering methods 585
numerical weather prediction 587

REVIEW QUESTIONS

1. In what areas of education are computers particularly valuable?
2. What is the theory behind computer-assisted instruction? What were its initial applications, and what is it like today?
3. What are the advantages of computer-managed instruction for teachers and for students?
4. How are computers used by the administrators of a school?
5. Describe the ways computers may be involved with a theatrical production.
6. How do computers aid composers?
7. What is the traditional method of editing a movie, and how have computers changed it?
8. Describe a matte. How are computers involved in achieving matte effects?
9. Explain how a computer generates an image.
10. How does a computer write poetry?
11. Distinguish between a mathematical model and a simulation.
12. Describe the scientific method and how computers lend themselves to its use.
13. What is the computer's role in the control of aircraft and space vehicles?
14. How are computers used to enhance the quality of images?

15. What is the main goal of the field of pattern recognition?
16. What is the role of supercomputers in exploring for oil and in recovering oil?
17. What is required to improve the quality of numerical weather prediction?
18. What are the advantages of using simulation systems in medical education?
19. What are the advantages of having computer-based patient records?
20. What functions are performed by the software systems available with ECG equipment?
21. What is a direct patient-monitoring system? What are the advantages of its use?
22. What does the CADUCEUS system do?
23. Contrast the operation of the new Fuji system with that of a conventional X-ray machine.
24. How does a CAT scanner work?
25. How is ultrasound used to produce images?
26. Contrast PETT and NMR scans.
27. What is the role of the microprocessor in a prosthetic system?

A SHARPER FOCUS

Now that you've completed this chapter, you should be able to answer the following questions about the chapter opening.

1. The U.S.S.R. has produced its own sophisticated supercomputers and computer-guided weaponry. Can it maintain a level of technological excellence without providing computer instruction for young people? Why or why not?
2. How will computer education fare in the U.S.S.R. in the face of a lack of top-notch microcomputers?
3. What have microcomputers such as the Apple Macintosh and the IBM PC done for computer education in the United States?
4. What might a growing population of ''computer kids'' do to the concept of security in the U.S.S.R.?
5. What contradictions (and dangers) does an essentially information-based technology pose for a society in which access to information is strictly controlled?

PROJECTS

1. Visit the placement or career guidance office at your school, and investigate its use of computers. Do they use computerized ability testing or have access to employment opportunity databanks? See what other computer applications you can uncover in the administration of your college, from word processing to student information files. Write a report on your findings.
2. Choose a rock group or other musician who uses a computer-based electronic instrument of any sort (instruments are often identified on album covers). Find out more about the particular instrument by consulting retailers, manufacturers' literature, or publications such as *Modern Recording and Music*. Prepare a report describing the instrument, its properties and capabilities, its cost, its sound quality compared to that of other similar instruments, and its role in a particular piece of music.
3. Do computer-generated ads for television and magazines really do a better job of selling products than more traditional methods do? Prepare a detailed answer to this question, in which you (a) define *computer operated* and *traditional*, (b) compare the relative cost and cost-effectiveness of the two methods, and (c) provide specific examples of products that have been represented by computer-generated advertisements. In your research,

you might consult marketing journals, teachers in retail and marketing fields, advertising agencies, and computer graphics production companies.

4. Interview the weather forecaster for a local radio or television station. Find out what sources are used for forecasts. Ask for the forecaster's opinions about the trends in the accuracy of weather forecasting and for the reasons behind those opinions. Find out about the special forecasting services used by pilots and farmers. What private and public sector groups are involved in weather forecasting?

5. Visit your local hospital. List the computer applications you find. Discuss their costs and benefits with hospital personnel. You might choose to concentrate just on imaging systems. Prepare a report on your findings.

21

Computers in Government

▶

FOCUS ON . . . HIGH-TECH TRAFFIC CONTROL

As seething motorists and impatient pedestrians have long suspected, Washington's traffic lights are frequently on the blink.

So the city is going to spend $25 million over the next five years to transform its aging signals into a computer-controlled network of lights that can be programmed to ease rush-hour congestion and improve traffic flow . . .

"The project is a citywide effort to connect the 1,300 signalized intersections that are located throughout the Washington metropolitan area into an integrated, centrally supervised, digitally controlled computer system," says H. Nathan Yagoda, president of Computran Systems Corp., the company that will be providing the computer expertise.

What American Telegraph & Telephone Co. does for phones, the proposed system here would do for traffic lights. The new system would link the city's traffic signals in a giant computer network that could monitor each signal and program it to display red or green depending on the intensity of traffic . . .

The system will help maximize the effectiveness of "green time" to reduce congestion on the busiest streets, says Computran's Yagoda. . . .

The District now relies on a 30-year-old system from Motorola that is teetering on the edge of collapse. The signals, which can be radio-controlled, rely on electromechanical timers, much like egg timers, that constantly fall into disrepair—to the dismay of the city's traffic controllers and the outrage of its roughly 600,000 daily commuters. What's more, there's no technical way to monitor whether the lights are working or not . . .

The real flexibility of the new system, says [traffic controller George] Schoene, will be seen in the variety of new traffic signal patterns the new technology allows. Schoene says the city has amassed considerable data about how traffic moves in various parts of the District. The problem is, the existing system isn't sophisticated enough to allow traffic engineers to apply that knowledge. The new system could calibrate traffic lights in a sequence down to the precise second and make the difference between a steady flow of traffic and the fits and starts familiar to most of Washington's motorists today.

Similarly, the new system would allow the District's traffic engineers to customize traffic patterns to meet special situations. During the times just before and after school, for example, traffic lights by neighborhood schools can be programmed to favor the pedestrians—presumably young children—over the automobiles.

Similarly, as traffic patterns change, the timing sequences and patterns at key intersections can be modified to assure that the signals can accommodate the change without creating unnecessary congestion.

The Political Machine	*Computers in the electoral process.*
Defense	*Computers in battle.*
Missile Guidance Systems	*Computer-based weaponry.*
C³I System	*A vital military information network.*
Space	*Satellites for reconnaissance and communication.*
The "Star Wars" Computers	*A computer-based defense system.*
Civilian Satellites	*Private projects on government rockets.*

More than 100,000 local, county, and state government bodies in the United States use computers to do everything from counting votes in school referenda to capturing criminals. On the national level, more than 4 billion personal files are stored in computer systems by the federal government—15 or 20 files on each and every citizen, not just on spies and thieves. The information is vital to the government's ability to provide benefits from the whole range of social programs, for the enforcement of tax laws, and for letting legislators know just what the voters want. Computers in state, local, and federal governments work together in areas such as welfare and taxation, saving time, money, and mountains of paper. In the area of law enforcement, all levels of government have combined facilities, data, and resources to create an electronic dragnet ("just the data, ma'am") to track down suspects and felons. Computers that orbit the earth monitor both the environment and potential military threats. The governmental applications of computer technology are as extensive as the bureaucracy itself, their software and circuitry working tirelessly, night and day, to preserve and protect.

In this chapter, we'll consider this pervasive role of the computer in our government institutions.

STATE AND LOCAL GOVERNMENTS

Although the use of computers by state and local governments is widespread, their application has by no means reached its full potential. Computer systems are used in large part simply to streamline the bureaucracies that sustain most governing bodies. They are used to manage reports, statistics, records, payrolls, taxes, and assessments; that is, they are used in the same way as they are in business. Computers help city planners develop highways, parks, public services, and traffic control systems as well as plan equitable and economical zoning ordinances. Computer models can project, for example, how the development of a downtown mall will affect the environment of nearby neighborhoods through which traffic will be re-routed, how parking revenues will be affected, and whether the overall economic impact will be good or bad. Budgets are set and systems of taxation are planned using computers. In addition, local medical services, food and shelter

Figure 21.1   Emergency Services
Computers are used to make emergency services available more quickly and efficiently to the people who need them. Here, New York City fire department officials show Mayor Ed Koch (right) one of the local teleprinters used in the city's computerized fire-fighting system. A signal or spoken message is sent from an alarm box to a central computer that transfers the alarm data to a teleprinter in the firehouse nearest the blaze.

Figure 21.2   Computers in Public Transportation
San Francisco's elaborate Bay Area Rapid Transit System (BART) relies heavily on computerized control centers, such as this one, to ensure its efficient operation.

programs, and family counseling programs are organized, budgeted, and kept current with the help of computers. In a number of cities in which tourism is a major industry, computers in travelers' assistance centers are used to access quickly such useful data as hotel vacancies, the locations of convenient car rental agencies and restaurants, and the hours that attractions are open. Of course, all this can be done without computers, but only at the expense of more time and money and with the loss of considerable efficiency and accuracy.

Figures 21.1 and 21.2 show two important applications of computers by local government agencies.

Law Enforcement

Finding and capturing criminals

Many of the newest computer applications in government are in law enforcement. The Want and Warrant System of Los Angeles County, the Law Enforcement Information Network (LEIN) of the Michigan state police, and the New York Statewide Police Information Network (NYSPIN) are just three examples of the increasing use of computer networks by the police. By storing criminal and arrest records and crime reports in computers, law enforcement personnel can more readily identify stolen property and suspected criminals. When local computers are linked with county and state data bases, and when states or regions cooperatively set up computerized dragnets, law enforcement becomes much more efficient. In most major cities, police squad cars are equipped with portable computer terminals for quickly checking license plates, car registrations, and driver's licenses against a central data base (see Figure 21.3). In New York, a hand-held computer called SIDNEY (short for Summons-Issuing Device for New York) helps traffic police identify drivers who habitually neglect to pay their parking tickets. When an officer enters the license plate number on SIDNEY's tiny keyboard, a small printer strapped to his or her belt prints the ticket, and SIDNEY's screen displays any prior unpaid violations. The car can then be towed away.

Suppose that a local police officer in a tiny Iowa town stops a speeding auto. The officer, before leaving his car, routinely radios the license plate number to the state police, who check with computers at the National Crime Information Center (see next section). In two minutes, the police officer approaches the stopped car cautiously, with his gun out, because he knows that the car's license plates were stolen in Nebraska, the car was stolen in Florida, and the driver is a man on the FBI's most-wanted list for murder in Kentucky. Before the advent of computer-assisted law enforcement, the driver might have simply paid his fine and gone free.

There are less dramatic but equally effective examples. For example, the California Department of Social Services collected the names of 117,000 parents from all over the state who had neglected to make child support payments. These names were sent to the tax board, and $10 million in tax refunds due to those persons were held back to offset the costs to the state of supporting their dependents. The whole process required such enormous quantities of data—legal records, tax returns, and addresses—and such immense requirements of time and energy that it would have been an impossible task without computers.

In New York State, the Bureau of Controlled Substances Licensing operates a computerized clearinghouse for information on all prescriptions written by doctors. State, federal, and local law enforcement officials can monitor this data to prevent illegal distribution or use of pain-killers and tranquilizers. (We'll consider the potential problems raised by such sharing of data among government bodies in Chapter 22.)

Figure 21.3 Computers on Patrol

In Chicago, and on the streets of many other cities as well, police cars come equipped with their own on-board computers. These mobile systems allow officers instant access to car and driver registration records, arrest histories, and the FBI's National Crime Information Center computers.

Monitoring prisoners

After criminals are captured and convicted, applications of computers and microelectronics are still in evidence. The state district court in Albuquerque, New Mexico, is experimenting with a *house arrest device* that will allow people convicted of minor but imprisonable offenses to keep their daytime jobs and be "locked up" in their homes at night and on weekends. Many states have work-release systems, but the Albuquerque court's experiment lifts a considerable burden from already overcrowded prisons. Derived from a gadget a judge saw in a *Spiderman* comic book, the house arrest device consists of a small transmitter that is strapped to the person's leg like an ankle bracelet. If the wearer ventures more than 150 feet from home on evenings or weekends, a central monitoring computer alerts authorities. If the device is unstrapped or removed, the computer notifies the police that an "escape" has occurred. In other parts of the country, prisons are currently trying out a guard-robot that may eventually patrol many prisons, keeping an electronic eye on inmates with infrared, microwave, motion, and odor sensors. Although hardly a replacement for a human guard, such a robot would provide a supplemental monitoring service for under $2000 a year.

The National Crime Information Center

The core of a central crime data base

Established in 1967, the FBI's **National Crime Information Center (NCIC)** is a central data repository used by law enforcement agencies all over North America and in Europe. Its computers store over 8 million active records, which are accessed by local police more than 275,000 times every day. NCIC's responses are sent back in less than two seconds and result in roughly a thousand arrests or returns of stolen property daily (see Figure 21.4).

It's interesting to see how NCIC measures up with the rest of the FBI's records. The FBI holds 77 million fingerprint cards and identification sheets in its criminal files. There are 93 million fingerprint cards and identification sheets in its civil files, mainly of federal employees and military personnel. That's 320 million files of hard copy sitting around in filing cabinets, and taking considerably longer than two seconds to access. However, the FBI is currently working on "digitizing" fingerprint cards for storage in the NCIC computers, which should lead to faster assistance for local law enforcement agencies.

Figure 21.4 NCIC
The records contained in the FBI's National Crime Information Center computer system provide police departments across the country and around the world with fast, up-to-date information on crimes, criminals, and investigations. Such sharing of information helps law enforcement agencies do their job more effectively.

The Legal System

Once computers have helped police and government agents arrest suspected criminals, their role in law enforcement still hasn't ended. Suspects need lawyers, and those lawyers need computers. More and more, computers are being used by attorneys and judges to turn the wheels of justice more smoothly. Computers help lawyers arrange their schedules and bill their clients, as well as access files, legal precedents, and court records. Word processors make the preparation of briefs, standard forms, contracts, wills, trusts, and correspondence much easier. Computers assemble lists of jury candidates from voter rolls and arrange "batches" of potential jurors for selection. Also, records of legal documents are often kept in computer files in the courthouse.

Making the practice of law more efficient

Most law work is research. Attorneys must cite long lists of cases that set legal precedents supporting their arguments, and for some arguments precedents are hard to find. Most of an attorney's time isn't spent in dramatic courtroom drama but rather plowing through dusty volumes in search of arguments in favor of their client's side. Three computerized services are available that can help cut down the amount of time lawyers spend on research, however, freeing them to move their clients through the judicial system more efficiently while ensuring that each client's case is comprehensive and complete.

WESTLAW is a computerized subscription service of the West Publishing Company, which publishes textbooks for law students and volumes of case histories. Subscribers have access to abstracts (short summaries) of all the company's published material from the past 20 years and the text of over 380,000 court decisions. **LEXIS**, one of the largest electronic data bases in the country, is a service of Mead Data Central, Inc., and contains nearly 500,000 court decisions, administrative rulings, trade regulations, and securities and tax laws from the past 60 years. Mead also offers **NEXIS**, a computer-based text-search system covering more than 100 legal and commercial publications.

These systems operate similarly. A user can enter the system and retrieve the desired document if he or she knows its title (the name of a case, such as *Brown* v. *Board of Education,* or the title of a law or regulation, such as section 1343 of Title XVIII of the U.S. Code). Or (with LEXIS), a series of words can be entered, such as "horse W/7 thie! OR robbery." This entry would result in the computer's displaying or printing out all the cases in the system's files in which the words *horse* and *thief* (the exclamation point instructs LEXIS to also search for related forms, such as *thievery*) or *horse* and *robbery* appear within 7 words of each other (the user can specify that the desired words be anywhere from 1 to 255 words apart). Even taking into account the potential for receiving long lists of inappropriate responses, an hour or two with the computer can replace weeks of research. In fact, the average search time on LEXIS is 15 to 20 seconds, which is considerably quicker than conventional library research methods. All of this translates into lower costs and speedier, fairer trials.

THE FEDERAL GOVERNMENT

The Internal Revenue Service

The Internal Revenue Service is the federal government's largest computer user. The IRS uses computers to record and store the information sent in by taxpayers on their returns and to send out forms and notices (see Figure 21.5). Its tax return

Collecting taxes

Figure 21.5   The IRS
Recently famous for its embarassing (and expensive) breakdowns, the IRS's computer system is nonetheless one of the most complex, extensive, and efficient in the country. At tax time, operators such as those shown here enter virtually unimaginable quantities of data into the IRS's regional and national computers.

files, over 95 million individual returns annually, are stored on 1500 reels of magnetic tape. The average taxpayer's complete tax history for the last five years takes up only about a quarter inch of such tape.

Computers are involved in all stages of the tax-paying and tax-collecting process, beginning with the calculator or personal computer you use in preparing your return. When a 1040 form arrives at an IRS regional center, it is sorted by bar code readers that can handle 30,000 returns an hour. The form then passes through human sorters, who write special codes on it that stand for tax bracket, exemptions and deductions claimed, and other key information. The codes are entered into another computer, which checks them for legal and mathematical consistency and then transfers the data to magnetic tape. The tape eventually ends up at the IRS National Computer Center in Martinsburg, West Virginia, where yet another computer compares the return's data against the information supplied by banks and employers (for example, on a W-2) and determines such things as whether or not a refund is due or whether the check enclosed does in fact represent the correct amount of tax owed.

Since the IRS needs to know who does and doesn't owe taxes, who should and shouldn't pay, and whether or not anyone has neglected to pay in the past, the volume of paperwork used to be (and, to a large extent, still is) mind-boggling. Computers have become absolutely essential to the maintenance of the huge data bases on which the functioning of the tax system depends.

Another interesting application of computers by the IRS is its Taxpayer Compliance Measurement Program (TCMP). Since 1962, the IRS has annually selected a random sample of 30,000 taxpayers for intense 200-question audits. The TCMP computer analyzes the answers and projects, on the basis of income and region, the statistical probabilities that any taxpayer will commit fraud. IRS auditing policies and decisions are made on the basis of this computer model. By 1990, the IRS hopes to have new computer systems installed (with all the bugs worked out) in a dozen regional centers that will be capable of performing instant audits on *all* returns, thus further increasing the Service's efficiency while discouraging tax-payers from cheating.

It should be noted, however, that the IRS doesn't use computers only to spot fraud by the public. Its Audit Information Management System (AIMS) is used to monitor the honesty and productivity of its 87,000 employees.

Other Agencies

There are, as we've said, over 4 billion files stored in computer systems by the federal government; these are distributed among its many bureaus, agencies, services, and divisions. Besides that of the IRS, the largest computer systems in the federal government, containing some 500 million files each, are those operated by:

Computers throughout the federal government

- The Social Security Administration, which keeps track of 200 million workers and 36 million retirees.
- The Civil Service Commission, the main "personnel office" for all federal employees.
- The Department of Health and Human Services, which administers food-stamp, Medicare, and similar social programs.

Other enormous data bases are maintained by the Department of Commerce, the General Services Administration, the Department of Defense, the Congressional Budget Office, and the Department of Justice. The Veterans Administration's TARGET system has streamlined the distribution of some $14 billion in compensation and benefits to more than 30 million veterans. VA employees in 57 cities use 3000 terminals to process more than 200,000 transactions every day, answering simple questions and straightening out mix-ups concerning benefits.

The U.S. Soil Conservation Service also uses computers. In cooperation with the National Weather Service, it collects data on the water content, weight, depth, and temperature of winter snowfall from 500 different points in the western United States. The data are then added to a computer model that also incorporates satellite and ground observations, as well as historical observations concerning seasonal melting and runoff. Actions taken as a result of this processing save billions in flood damage each year.

The Legislative Branch

In Congress, computers are becoming an increasingly valued tool for expediting the legislative process (see Figure 21.6). There are 44 terminals in the House of Representatives which help members to vote on legislation when they are in committee or otherwise unable to come to the chamber. When a representative inserts his or her identification card, which is like the ones used with automated teller machines, the terminal screen shows the issue, the current count for and against, and the time remaining for the member to go to the chamber and cast an electronically registered and computer-tallied vote.

In the halls of Congress

The **LEGIS system** stores and displays information on the contents of all bills proposed in Congress and their current status—whether they're still in committee or nearing a vote. SOPAD (Summary of Proceedings and Debates) gives members up-to-the-minute information on all legislative activity in the House and Senate—

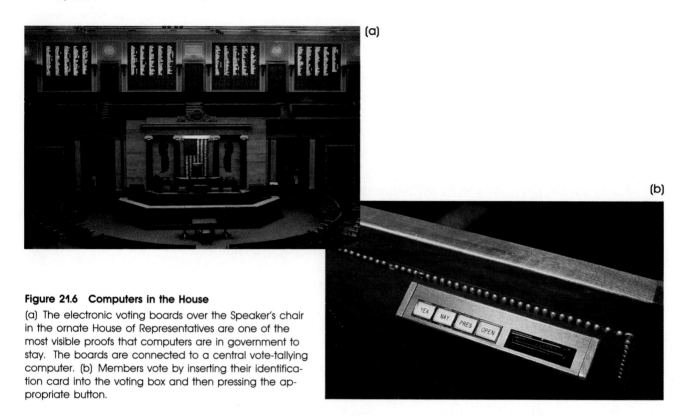

Figure 21.6 Computers in the House
(a) The electronic voting boards over the Speaker's chair in the ornate House of Representatives are one of the most visible proofs that computers are in government to stay. The boards are connected to a central vote-tallying computer. (b) Members vote by inserting their identification card into the voting box and then pressing the appropriate button.

votes, debates, committee meetings, and so on. And FAPRS, the Federal Assistance Program Resource System, provides members with information about any assistance programs that are available to their constituents, which makes serving the interests of the people back home much easier. Finally, computerized mailings keep constituents informed about their elected officials' voting records, positions, and activities.

ISSUES IN TECHNOLOGY

Does the installation of computerized voting systems in Congress present any potential problem with legislators not having to be in the House or Senate chambers during a vote? What complications might this system create for the Senate minority whip, for example, whose job is to ensure that votes are cast along the correct party line, since senators could be anywhere in the Capitol building, in their offices, or conceivably (some day) in their home districts? What if the system had a bug, or the power failed? Find out how the legislature plans to cope with such problems, and add suggestions of your own.

The Executive Branch

The high-tech presidency

Computers have also taken up permanent residence at 1600 Pennsylvania Avenue (see Figure 21.7). There are nearly 200 IBM Display Writers and PC/XTs linked to

Figure 21.7   Computers in the Executive Branch
Computers have become a vital part of the presidency. Here,
White House Deputy Press Secretary Larry Speakes works at the
word processor in his office.

a mainframe computer in the White House, a system that is the result of $1.2 million spent in the last few years in order to provide high-technology assistance to the President and his staff. Word processors produce speeches, executive memos, policy statements, itineraries, reports, and all the other documents required by an Administration. An electronic mail system zaps such material from office to office in a few seconds. With the help of computers, 5000–7000 letters are processed daily, meetings are scheduled, legislation is tracked, and special graphics for briefings and speeches are produced.

In the past three years, the Executive Office of the Presidency Computer Center (EOPCC) has quadrupled in size. It now includes ten major systems, two IBM 3083s, and an IBM 4341, for a total of more than 48 million bytes of memory. A Xerox 9700 laser printer produces official documents at a speed of two pages per second. In 1984–1985, $9.1 million was budgeted for the operation of and software development for the EOPCC.

The Political Machine

Before they're elected, many candidates for public office use computers in their political campaigns. The popular political software package Campaign Manager produced by Aristotle Industries allows candidates to utilize IBM or Apple II microcomputers to organize their schedules and print petitions, income disclosure statements, and to file requests for federal matching funds in formats that comply with Federal Elections Commission requirements. Computers can also analyze opinion polls and voter registration data, identify potential volunteers or contributors, and print letters. The hardware and software packages to do these things can cost $10,000 or more, but their versatility and long-term cost-effectiveness are making such electronic campaign managers increasingly popular.

Computers in the electoral process

The Republican party's REPNET system, first used during the 1980 election, includes such specialized computer-based operations as ADONIS (Automated Donor Information System), which locates potential contributors; MAIL CALL, which generates mailing lists; UNICORN (Universal Correspondence and Word Processing), which prints "personalized" letters, envelopes, postcards, and position papers; and CPA (Computerized Political Accounting), which helps handle all the required reports and disclosures that must be submitted to the Federal Elections Commission. The Democrats have a similar system. Campaign Manager is within the budget of most independent candidates and small parties.

Through computer-orchestrated **geodemographics** (the statistical study of populations by geographical region), mass mailings can be tailored to address issues of interest to specific regional, economic, and social components of the electorate. As a result, voter turnout has been increased by as much as 11% in some areas.

The 1980 Presidential election marked the first widespread use of computers in political campaigns. By the 1984 election, the two major parties were relying heavily on electronic assistance. Most polling analysis is performed by powerful mainframes, and scheduling, budgeting, management, and keeping track of the opponent's itinerary and positions are the principal functions of personal computers. (During the 1984 campaign, the Mondale organization used Compaqs, and the Reagan campaign relied on Coronas and IBM PC/XTs.)

At the 1984 Republican and Democratic national conventions, computers were in widespread use. Candidates kept track of their delegates through a complex computer network linking the candidate's trailer with floor managers, delegates, and key platform committees. At the Democratic convention, a sophisticated new computerized vote-tallying system was supposed to be used during the official roll call for nominating a candidate for the Presidency, but the state delegations demanded that they be allowed to announce the totals from their particular "great state" live on prime time television. The votes were counted, but not quite as quickly as they could have been. And, of course, the television, radio, and newspaper correspondents came equipped with computers for word processing their reports, generating patriotic graphics, and compiling statistics on how many people named Smith were in attendance (see Figure 21.8).

Figure 21.8 Electronic Elections
Computer-generated graphics such as the elephant and logo pictured here figured prominently in television's coverage of the 1984 presidential campaign.

On election day, computers in many areas count votes, generate voter profiles, and project winners on the basis of results in selected precincts. Although this processing is certainly faster and more accurate than having a roomful of people laboriously counting each ballot by hand, there can be problems. In the 1983 gubernatorial election in Illinois, for example, a large number of the punched-card ballots used in Chicago (a city known for election irregularities even in low-tech times) somehow got wet and had to be draped over radiators, baked in ovens, and otherwise dried out before they could be counted by the computer. Untested software, faulty tabulation programs, and equipment failures are other potential sources of trouble.

Defense

Since they were first developed, computers have played a key role in national defense. Supercomputers are a principal tool in the design of new weapons and are also vital to military intelligence activities. But *all* types of computers are becoming more prominent in the nation's defense plans. Tanks, missiles, jets, submarines, and satellites are all essential links in the defense effort, and all of them rely on computers, super and otherwise.

One recent military application of computers is the M-1 tank. It weighs 60 tons, costs $2.7 million, and uses computers and laser beams to fire its 105-mm cannon at targets a quarter of a mile away—and it hits them even in darkness or heavy fog. Other on-board computers help soldiers accurately locate both themselves and the target, monitor fuel consumption and mechanical operations, and perform other indispensable functions. But perhaps the computer's most significant military application occurs mostly off the ground, in missiles and satellites.

Missile Guidance Systems

The **Terrain Contour Matching (TERCOM) System** developed by McDonnell-Douglas weighs only 82 pounds yet can guide a Cruise missile to within about 60 feet of its target. The TERCOM computer is a specialized image-processing system. The images it deals with are elevation maps of areas that the Cruise will fly over en route to its target. Each pixel on a map represents the elevation of one of the small squares into which an area is divided, as illustrated in Figure 21.9. The computer's memory contains the elevation of each square. A radar altimeter aboard the Cruise constantly reports the altitudes of the areas beneath. As the missile enters one of the mapped areas, the computer recognizes the pattern of elevations, identifying them with a particular map in its memory, which also contains the desired course through that area. The sequence of elevations it is flying over gives its actual course. It is a straightforward matter to compute and execute the corrections required to restore the missile to its planned flight path. The computer provides the means to transform a collection of low-cost subsystems into a high-precision weapon. Each Cruise missile costs only $750,000, which is a bargain compared to the enormous costs of the fleets of "look-down" radar planes and long-range intercept aircraft required to defend against it.

Matching observed real terrain against a set of stored elevation maps, as the Cruise does, is one example from a general class of image-matching techniques used to guide weapons to their targets. **Template matching** is the technique of

Computer-based weaponry

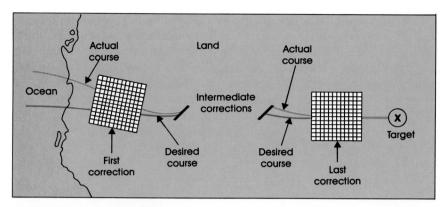

Figure 21.9 The TERCOM System

When the Cruise missile gets over land, the TERCOM computer starts comparing the patterns of elevations observed beneath to its stored landfall maps. When the pattern matches, it checks to see if the current course is correct and computes any needed correction to bring the missile back to the desired flight path. It repeats this process periodically over successive mapped areas. The computer accurately guides the Cruise missile to its target, despite the lack of precision of its low-cost subsystems.

comparing what's actually there against a predefined pattern, in this case a specific arrangement of pixels that define the target. When the target is matched, the weapon is directed against it. This same pattern-recognition technique forms the basis for numerous nonmilitary industrial applications.

Another application of computer technology to missile guidance is found in MIRVs (Multiple Independently Targeted Reentry Vehicles). Guided by an on-board computer, the "MIRVed" missile—that is, a missile equipped with several nuclear warheads—can release its smaller bombs with deadly accuracy. An on-board guidance computer makes adjustments in the course, speed, and direction of each warhead, allowing for wind resistance, terrain, and weather conditions, and sends them directly to their assigned target.

C³I System

A vital military information network

The **Command, Control, Communications, and Intelligence (C³I) System** is an integrated network of computers, telecommunications systems, Airborne Warning and Control Systems aircraft (or AWACS, which are the "look-down" radar planes mentioned in the preceding section), satellites, ground radar, and flying command centers on board modified 747s. The U.S. government spends more than $1 billion annually to maintain this huge system, employing more than 90,000 people just to keep the equipment operational. The system gives the National Command Authority (the President, Secretary of Defense, and chief cabinet and Pentagon officials) direct control of all strategic forces at all levels, enabling them to receive intelligence information, issue commands, and keep up to date on the situation. In an age of complex, accurate, and very fast weapons, such a computer-centered network is essential to maintaining control of the defense efforts. Without computers, such control would be impossible.

The National Security Agency (NSA) is the U.S. government's electronic intelligence arm. Among its responsibilities are *signal intelligence* (the interception of foreign communications carried over telephone, telegraph, radio, and microwave) and the provision of secure communications channels for the nation's diplomatic, military, and intelligence services. The NSA has huge dish antennas set up in various places, from Washington, D.C., to Australia, to listen in on Soviet pilots and Chinese missile tests. Its *Ferret* satellite was used by the British to listen to Argentine commanders during the 1982 war in the Falkland Islands.

A 1982 court case concerning the NSA's intelligence-gathering methods (in which they were found to be not illegal), disclosed how its dish antennas in West Virginia, Maine, Washington, and California routinely record conversations beamed off international communications satellites. NSA computers sort through these masses of data, tagging and printing out conversations that contain certain flagged words, such as *Qaddafi* or *nuclear*. NSA personnel can then choose whether or not to investigate further. Such monitoring inhibits the activities of foreign agents. Communications secrecy for U.S. agents and diplomats is assured through the use of codes and equipment developed by the NSA (see Chapter 22).

Space

On October 4, 1957, the Soviet Union launched *Sputnik.* Like the Wright brothers' first flight at Kitty Hawk, it wasn't much in itself, but it certainly got things started. In the last 30 years or so, there has been a total of more than 11,000 satellites whizzing around the globe for a variety of purposes. Roughly 10,000 have fallen from orbit, but about 1500 remain up there and more are being launched every week.

Satellites for reconnaissance and communication

About all *Sputnik* did was emit a little beeping noise that let everyone know it was there. The first experimental communications satellite was launched by the United States in 1958. It was passive in the sense that signals from the ground were simply bounced off its mirrored surface to receiving antennas elsewhere. The first commercial communications satellite was *Intelsat I,* which could transmit 240 telephone calls or a single transatlantic television broadcast.

The first reconnaissance satellite was *Discoverer,* launched by the United States in 1960. From a high altitude, it took photographs with a high-powered telephoto lens and then ejected its film cartridge, which dropped from space into a net carried by an Air Force plane below. Computers on board today's reconnaissance satellites convert images into electronic signals, which are interpreted and enhanced by computers on earth, and then output on paper for human analysis.

The "Star Wars" Computers

On March 23, 1983, President Reagan announced his plan for the federal government to undertake a program he called the **Strategic Defense Initiative (SDI)**, a research and development project that would surpass, both in cost and in the production of new technology, the Manhattan Project of the 1940s and the Apollo space program of the 1960s and 1970s. He budgeted $26 billion for SDI through 1988, and the estimated total cost of the program could exceed $1 trillion by the turn of the century. Because of its reliance on space-based weapons and yet to be developed computer technology, SDI quickly became known as the "Star Wars" program.

A computer-based defense system

The system is still largely theoretical and is currently in the very early stages of research. The basic idea is that as many as 2000 satellites, each with a mirror 30 feet in diameter, would be launched into geosynchronous orbits. Reconnaissance satellites would spot enemy ICBMs being launched, and ground-based supercomputers would instantly analyze the missiles' size, payload (whether they were MIRVs or carried single warheads), speed, trajectories, and targets. The computers would alert and aim defense *killer satellites,* which would generate high-energy beams (reflected off the 30-foot mirrors) to harmlessly destroy the missiles as they rose over the North Pole high above the atmosphere. Missiles that made it through the satellite defenses would be attacked by computer-piloted drones (interceptor aircraft) and *smart rocks,* which are self-guided projectiles launched from bombers to crash into enemy missiles (or defensive satellites) with destructive velocity (see Figure 21.10).

Every phase of this controversial defensive system relies on computers, from the detection of a missile launch to the identification of decoys, the assignment of targets, the aiming, firing, and guiding of the drones and projectiles, the verification

Figure 21.10   The Strategic Defense Initiative

(a) A reconnaissance satellite in geosynchronous orbit spots the start of an attack and beams the data to (b) a central command computer. (c) As the missiles leave the earth's atmosphere, killer satellites generate powerful beams that destroy most of them in space. (d) Another reconnaissance satellite tracks the surviving MIRV, which has released (e) its payload of armed and decoy warheads. The central computer (f) directs armed drones and smart rocks toward their incoming targets and (g) keeps Washington informed of developments.

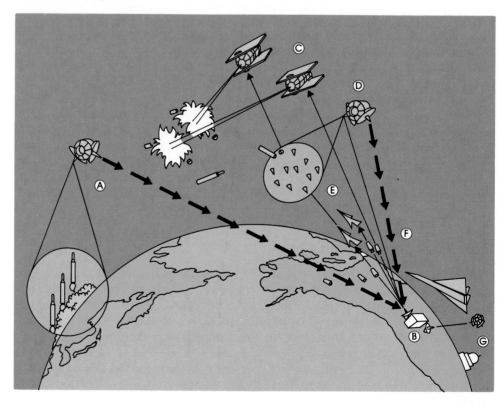

CAREERS IN TECHNOLOGY
Government Work

Job Description Almost any computer-related job in the private sector, from data entry operator to programmer and systems analyst, is also performed in the public sector by employees of federal, state, and local government agencies.

Qualifications Government requirements for computer workers are generally the same as private industry's, but they may also call for passing a test or getting on a register of qualified applicants. Operators, however, are required by the federal government to have either a high school diploma *or* specialized training and experience, rather than both. Earnings are a slightly different matter. All the stories about overpaid government workers aren't entirely true: annual salaries for entry-level computer professionals in the federal government average about $4000 less than in private industry, and government benefits and retirement plans do not always compare favorably with those offered in the private sector. On the other hand, equal employment policies are strictly enforced by government agencies, promotional paths are clearly stated, the experience is transferable to private jobs, and the government bureaucracy is very unlikely to go out of business.

Outlook The Bureau of Labor Statistics recently estimated that the government (that is, local, state, and federal agencies) would experience an 80% increase in employment of computer professionals by the end of the 1980s. As systems expand from revenue collection and payroll and insurance processing into wider and more complex applications, there will be a greater need for programmers, systems analysts, and computer operators. In fact, about 2000 new programmers, 20,000 new systems analysts, 52,000 new operators, and 2000 new service technicians will be needed by 1990. These people all do exactly what their counterparts in private industry do.

The greatest number of openings for computer professionals will be in federal public administration—in the Internal Revenue Service, the Department of Health and Human Services, and the Department of Transportation, in particular—largely due to the adoption of major computer systems and the development of large data bases. For those interested in the more exotic aspects of the government, the CIA, FBI, Department of Defense, and NASA all make extensive and intriguing use of computer technology and are often on the cutting edge of research and development. All of them are actively recruiting programmers, systems analysts, operators, and engineers for entry-level positions.

of strikes, and the operation of communications and command systems. The analysis of virtually unimaginable amounts of diverse data, as well as the split-second speed with which it must be done, are well beyond the capabilities both of humans *and* of existing supercomputers. The SDI requires a whole new generation of machines, using programs ten times longer than the biggest ones today—containing as many as 100 million lines! The programs themselves would have to be written and debugged by artificial intelligence systems still to be invented. State-of-the-art image-analyzing computers, such as NASA's Massively Parallel Processor (MPP) (which was used to convert the signals from the Viking probes into pictures), can perform 6.5 billion operations per second. Such computers only anticipate SDI's minimum requirements.

Civilian Satellites

In addition to their numerous military applications (surveillance, tracking, reconnaissance, and detection of communications signals, military activity, and weapons testing), satellites have a wide variety of peaceful applications. But the government is still closely involved when private enterprise goes into space. Most obviously, the launch vehicles that lift commercial and experimental satellites into orbit are still almost exclusively government-owned and -operated, although a fledgling private rocket-launching industry is slowly developing. As the commercial applications of satellites increase, however, it is likely that the government's role will diminish and the number (and success rate) of private rocket entrepreneurs will grow.

In general, nonmilitary satellites are employed to:

- aid sea and air navigation,
- map the atmosphere as input to numerical weather prediction,
- provide economical telephone links for long-distance voice or data communications,
- relay television signals,
- map the earth's resources, and
- monitor crop and environmental conditions

It is even conceivable that satellites 25 miles wide will one day convert solar radiation into microwave energy, which could be transmitted to earth and turned into electricity. There are more than a billion dollars' worth of commercial satellites in orbit, and probably more than that amount of military satellites. When you talk to someone overseas on the telephone or when you watch Alpine skiing or network news on television, you are on the receiving end of signals that were transmitted via satellite. Satellites use computers to receive and transmit signals, to analyze data, and to maintain or alter their orbital paths.

Intelsat (short for International Telecommunications Satellite), for example, is part of an international network linking more than 100 nations and 20,000 telephone circuits. Two-thirds of the world's transoceanic communications travel across the seas by being bounced off the Intelsat satellite. Intelsat, like all other communications satellites, is in geosynchronous orbit at an altitude of 22,300 miles.

Other satellite systems, Landsat and Thematic Mapper, locate water and mineral deposits and monitor soil erosion and pollution. They are used for mapping, evaluating crop and soil conditions, and monitoring snowfall and flooding.

We saw in Chapter 7 how satellites are used to link distant computers with each other. That application is becoming more and more important as computers become more and more numerous. On New York's Staten Island, 17 dish antennas 25 feet in diameter have been erected. The purpose of this Teleport, as its developers call it, is to access 24 existing and projected communications satellites, making the Teleport a sort of international telecommunications switchboard. Connected to an underground network of fiber optic cables, the $300 million Teleport will link computers all over New York City. Eventually, its developers plan to install similar facilities in two dozen other cities, linking banks, businesses, and homes into an international computer network.

SUMMARY ━━━━━━━━━

State and Local Governments

Most state and local governments use computers to streamline bureaucracy, manage paper-work, plan development, and distribute services.

Law Enforcement Most government computer applications are in the area of crime control and law enforcement: criminal record clearinghouses and crime information systems.

The National Crime Information Center The FBI's National Crime Information Center, a central national data repository containing more than 8 million records, is accessed by police from all over the world.

The Legal System Computer-based information systems such as LEXIS help attorneys research cases more quickly. Many law firms now use word processors to prepare correspondence, legal papers, briefs, wills, and contracts.

The Federal Government

The Internal Revenue Service The Internal Revenue Service is the federal government's largest computer user. Tax returns are processed and audited, reports are compiled, and taxpayer histories are updated by IRS computers.

Other Agencies The Social Security Administration, the Civil Service Commission, the Department of Health and Human Services, and the U.S. Soil Conservation Service are some of the larger government users of computer technology.

The Legislative Branch In Congress, computers play a valuable role in keeping legislators informed about current issues, upcoming votes in both houses, and their constituents' concerns.

The Executive Branch The Executive Office of the Presidency Computer Center, along with a network of word processors in the White House, expedites the production of Presidential paperwork, tracks legislation, and coordinates schedules.

The Political Machine Computers play an important role in elections, from producing voter profiles to selecting likely contributors and printing letters, position papers, speeches, and reports.

Defense Computers are vital elements of such modern weapons as the M-1 tank. The Cruise missile uses a TERCOM computer to guide it to its target, turning low-cost subsystems into a high-precision weapon. Computers are, in general, indispensable to the rapid assessment and action demanded in battle.

C^3I Perhaps more important than the weapons themselves is the computer's role in the Command, Control, Communications, and Intelligence System and in the National Security Agency's collection of intelligence and surveillance data.

Space Satellites transmit images to earth for many uses, from military intelligence to monitoring crop conditions. The earliest satellites were passive; today's are active participants in military reconnaissance and civilian communications.

The "Star Wars" Computers The Strategic Defense Initiative (or "Star Wars" program) depends on the development of futuristic computerized satellite weapons and the computers that would control them.

Civilian Satellites Communications and experimental satellites produced by private industry still largely depend on the government for launching.

COMPUTER CONCEPTS ▬▬▬

As an extra review of the chapter, try defining the following terms. If you have trouble with any of them, refer to the page number listed.

National Crime
   Information Center
   (NCIC) 604
WESTLAW 605
LEXIS 605
NEXIS 605

LEGIS system 607
geodemographics 610
Terrain Contour Matching
   (TERCOM) System 611
template matching 611

Command, Control,
   Communications, and
   Intelligence (C^3I)
   System 612
Strategic Defense Initiative
   (SDI) 613
Intelsat 616

REVIEW QUESTIONS ▬▬▬

1. What are some of the ways in which local governments use computers?
2. What are the advantages to law enforcement of systems such as SIDNEY and the NCIC?
3. How are computers used by lawyers and judges?
4. Describe the use of computers in the processing of a typical income tax return. How else does the IRS use computers?
5. Computers are used in Congress and the White House. What are the functions of these computers, and how might they be affecting the way those branches of government operate?
6. How are computers used during elections?
7. How does the TERCOM System work? How does the computer transform low-precision subsystems into a high-precision weapon?
8. How does the National Security Agency use computers to monitor international telephone transmissions?
9. List some military uses of satellites.
10. What are the components of the "Star Wars" defense system?
11. What communications functions are performed by satellites?
12. How do satellites help monitor the earth's resources?

A SHARPER FOCUS ▬▬▬

Now that you've completed this chapter, you should be able to answer the following questions about the chapter opening.

1. How might computerized traffic control affect a city government's budget?
2. What alternatives to computer-controlled traffic lights might have been tried before this system was possible?

PROJECTS ▬▬▬

1. Contact your local police department and ask if they use the NCIC network. Find out from them what they think of the application of the computer in law enforcement, and how technology has helped or hindered them.

2. Talk to an attorney who uses the LEXIS or WESTLAW system in his or her practice. Prepare a report detailing your findings.

3. The computers that are a part of most weapons systems are usually special-purpose, as opposed to general-purpose, computers and can't usually be separated from the weapons systems. Software for these systems has to be created from scratch for each new weapon, adding greatly the cost of development for new computerized weapons. What is being done by the Department of Defense to reduce these costs and the time frames associated with such special-purpose program development? Write up your findings as a fully referenced report.

Application Perspective

Computers and Your Car

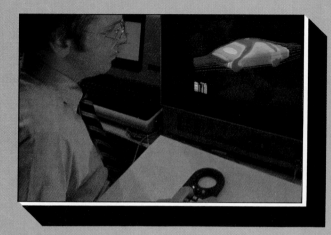

① We've discussed some of the ways in which computers, from microprocessors to supercomputers, are used in the design and analysis phase of automobile manufacturing. The continuing increase in automotive sophistication makes the role of computer-aided design increasingly more important to the industry.

Consumer Needs → Design and analysis

Consumer satisfaction ← Maintenance

④ When your car needs maintenance, you bring it to the repair shop, where a computer-driven diagnostic tester puts its engine through hundreds of tests to check whether it is operating within the manufacturer's specifications. Perhaps it was an on-board, computer-driven tester that let you know in the first place that your car ought to go to the shop.

(2) Computers control the robots that assemble new cars on this line. Computers either directly control or prepare the control tapes for the numerically controlled machine tools used to make many of the parts that are being put together here. All aspects of manufacturing procurement and scheduling are planned by still other computers.

Manufacture

Operation

(3) Ford Motor Company's fourth-generation electronic engine control system (EEC-IV) is used in most Ford vehicles for engine control. Of its components, MROM is the read-only memory that stores the program and data. KAM (keep-alive memory) is a low-power, read-write memory that maintains its needed information even when engine power is off. Driver controls fuel injection, and QDD controls the car's many small electric motors. The CPU runs the whole show. All this computer hardware and associated electronic devices—with more power than two UNIVACs— help you operate your car!

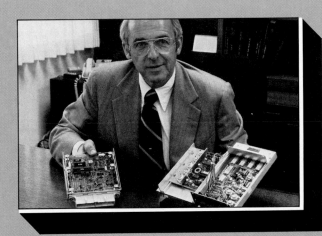

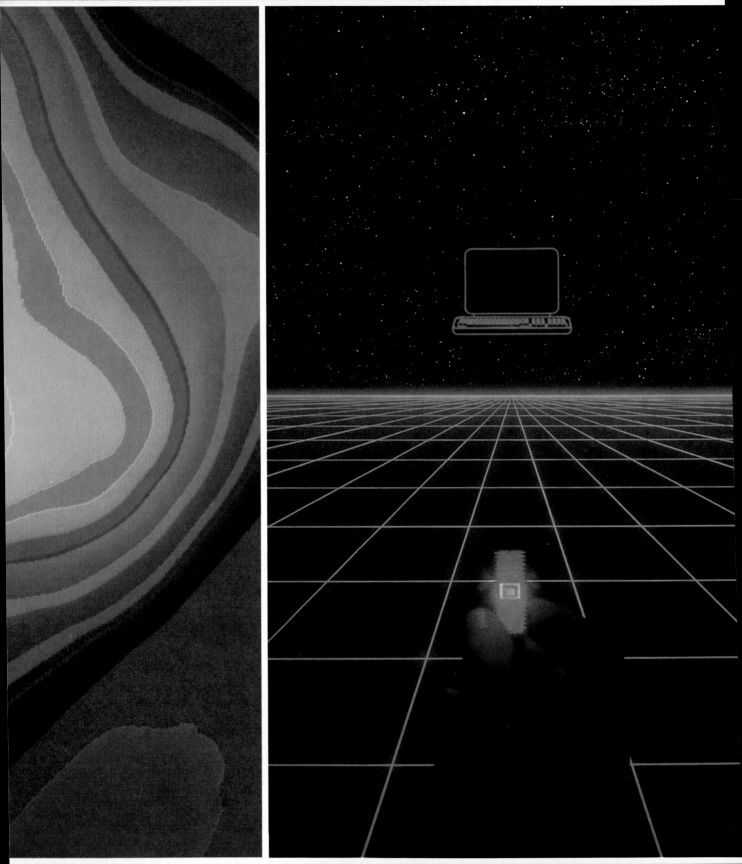

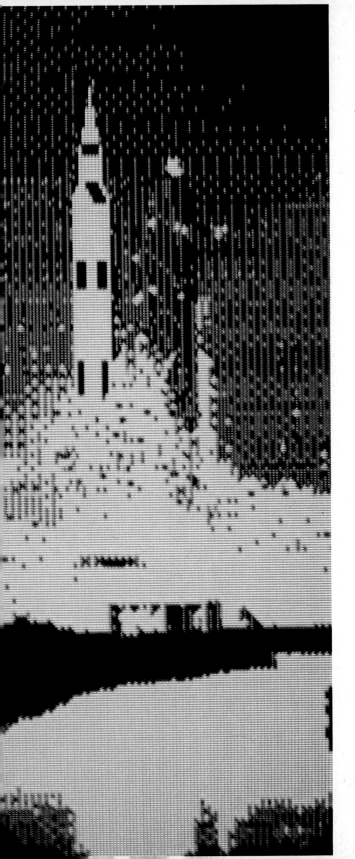

Part 7

IMPLICATIONS

What are the possibilities, good and bad, raised by the technology we've been studying? Just because we ask that question here, near the end of this book, doesn't mean that the answer is somehow of secondary importance, a footnote, or something to be treated lightly. In fact, what better time to question the impact of facts than once those facts are all finally understood?

In Chapter 22, we'll cover the major areas of social unease related to the computer applications we've already discussed, looking at some very real problems and suggesting possible solutions. The point of Chapter 22 is that change is not only essential, but unavoidable. Chapter 23 picks up on that point, to take a realistic look at the inevitable changes that will occur during the next twenty years in the way we live and work.

22

Privacy, Security, and Other Concerns

FOCUS ON . . . SELLING SOFTWARE ON THE HONOR SYSTEM

A trio of software publishers are combating the piracy problem by simply giving away their programs with a request that satisfied customers send in a voluntary payment. Enough customers have ponied up to launch the three in full-time business.

Jim Button, 42, claims he's netting more money from his ButtonWare Co. than he earned in his former job as a systems engineer for IBM. With the help of his wife, Helen, and sons Stephen, 14, and David, 10, Button's high-tech cottage operation in Bellevue, Washington, is clearing $100,000 a year. Button's 7,000 customers range from his former employer, IBM, to the Internal Revenue Service and Yale University.

The honor system strategy is the brainchild of Andrew Fluegelman, 40, editor-in-chief of *PC World* and *Macworld* magazines and owner of Headlands Press, a software company in Tiburon, California. He decided that instead of warning customers not to pirate a program, as most software companies do, he would urge them to make copies for friends. The recipients would pay only if they liked the program.

Fluegelman got the idea while listening to a fund-raising promotion for a public TV station. He figured people would make a contribution for quality software as readily as for quality television. "I started it as an experiment in economics, and it's definitely been a success," he says. Fluegelman says Headlands Press brings in revenues comparable to those of Button and the third honor system publisher, Bob Wallace, 35, of Seattle.

Wallace, a former programmer for Microsoft, runs a company called Quicksoft. He has added a new wrinkle to the honor system: customers get a $25 commission for each $75 program their friends buy.

The three publishers each offer a product with a popular function. ButtonWare sells PC-File III for data base management, Headlands sells PC-Talk, a program for communicating with other computers, and Quicksoft has PC-Write, a word-processing program. All three are comparatively simple to learn and use. Another reason for their popularity surely lies in the unusual selling strategy. "We encourage people to copy so they won't feel guilty," says Button. Indeed, the honor system gives copiers an opportunity to feel noble.

Securing the System

 Controlling Personnel   *Avoiding unauthorized use.*

 Passwords   *Guaranteeing authorized access.*

 Cryptography   *Disguising data via ciphers.*

Hazards and Safeguards

 Heat   *Guarding against overheating and moisture.*

 Smoke and Steam   *Damage to magnetic storage media.*

 Electricity   *Protecting against power failures.*

 Wildlife   *Insects and mice can raise havoc.*

 Earthquakes   *Seismic catastrophes. The importance of disaster recovery teams.*

 Electromagnetic Pulse   *Computers and nuclear war.*

Health

 Radiation and VDTs   *Public concern about radiation leakage from terminal screens.*

 Physical Complaints   *Aches and pains from poorly designed workstations.*

 Ergonomics   *A science to answer workers' complaints.*

 Stress   *Psychological consequences of overwork.*

 Isolation   *Telecommuting and social isolation.*

Ethics and Responsibility   *A new sense of professional responsibility.*

The Displacing Technology   *The new technologies both create and destroy jobs.*

Technology has always aroused controversy. In early nineteenth-century England, the Luddites tried (without much success) to stop the Industrial Revolution by breaking into factories and smashing machines. They believed the new devices threatened their jobs, their health, and their accustomed way of life. Later in that century, there were similar movements in the United States, as industrialization spread unchecked. Recent technological advances—especially machines that seem somehow to think for themselves—have stirred up similar fears and concerns.

A general computer-anxiety is evident everywhere. Newspaper and magazine articles warn of health hazards; best-selling books describe the computer's threat to privacy; headlines announce the most recent outrageous computer crime. From the half-mechanical Darth Vader and the ominously high-tech Empire of *Star Wars* to the uncontrollable supercomputer of *WarGames,* frustrations and fears of our modern age are all over the movie screens as well.

This chapter will examine the most controversial questions raised by this new technology in order to encourage a healthy awareness of the dilemmas that face us.

PRIVACY

Maintaining privacy in the information age

In Chapter 21, we learned that the federal government maintains an average of 17 separate computer files on each of the 234 million U.S. citizens, or 4 billion files. More than 200,000 times every day, one credit company based in southern California supplies a client with the name, address, telephone number, place of employment, salary, marital status, and credit history of one of the 86 million individuals recorded in its computer files. Nearly half of the nation's population is included in the computer records of only five credit companies.

If you're married, a marriage license bureau somewhere has a record of the occasion. If you're not, you may be on file with a computer dating service. Your doctor may have your health and payment record on disk, and your hospital's computer stores a history of your visits. Hotels and stores have your name, address, and credit card numbers; telephone companies know whom you called and how long you talked; and mail-order houses use computers to send you innumerable one-time-only opportunities. If you pay taxes, drive a car, vote, own a gun, or travel abroad, there are computer records about you. Little wonder that nearly half of all U.S. citizens say they are concerned about violations of their personal privacy.

Matching

Computers' speed and accuracy, and the ways in which they shorten lines, hasten deliveries, organize inventories, and improve product quality are well known and generally appreciated by now. Certainly no one is bothered by their convenience. What does bother some people is that personal information kept in computer systems can be so quickly retrieved, so widely accessed, and so easily cross-referenced with other personal data to paint a potentially damaging portrait.

When government agencies share data

In the 1960s, during the Kennedy and Johnson administrations, there was talk of creating a national "central data bank" that would consolidate all the information held by various government agencies. The public outcry against this project was so loud and the task itself so enormous that it was never undertaken. During the late 1970s and early 1980s, however, in the Carter and Reagan administrations, comparisons of federal computer files were widely used to detect fraud in government programs. **Matching**, as this practice is called, is simply a process by which a computer is used to compare records from government or private information systems to find individuals who are common to more than one set. This simple procedure has an enormous number of diverse applications. Social Security employment records, for example, can be compared with food-stamp rolls to find people who are earning more than the minimum allowed. Tax returns can be matched to student assistance records to find those graduates who have neglected to repay their loans. Alimony cheaters and draft dodgers can also be located through computerized matching.

A special committee was established by President Reagan to encourage such data matching by federal agencies, since the Department of Labor estimated that the government could retrieve "billions of dollars every year" previously lost to fraud or error. A public outcry was raised again, however, when it turned out that a number of people were removed from welfare and child-support rolls on the basis of incorrect income data.

Legal Protection

U.S. citizens are not guaranteed a right to privacy by the Constitution—those words simply don't appear. Many legal experts have concluded that the right is implied in the document, but opinions differ. The Fourth Amendment protects citizens against "unreasonable searches and seizures" of "person, house, papers, and effects," but whether or not those effects include credit ratings and checking account histories is problematic. The best protection against unwarranted distribution of computerized personal information or against the perpetuation of damaging misinformation lies outside the Constitution, in four acts of Congress.

Legislation for privacy

The Fair Credit Reporting Act of 1970

The Fair Credit Reporting Act of 1970 guarantees your legal right to have free access to your credit records. If you find some mistake, you also have the right to challenge the accuracy of the data. The credit agency may charge a fee for access and correction unless you've been denied credit for any reason, in which case you have the right to examine your records free of charge.

The Freedom of Information Act of 1970

The Freedom of Information Act of 1970 guarantees citizens the right of access to all personal data gathered by any agency of the federal government. Any government agency, from the Department of the Navy to the IRS, the FBI, or the CIA, if requested in writing, must turn over copies of any records they are keeping, unless that information is vital to the national security or represents an invasion of someone else's privacy.

The Crime Control Act of 1973

The Crime Control Act of 1973 requires that when arrest histories are distributed (by agencies such as the FBI, through the NCIC, as we saw in Chapter 21), the data must show not only that an arrest took place, but whether or not prosecution and conviction followed. It also provides that "an individual who believes that information concerning him [*sic*] in an automated system is inaccurate, incomplete or maintained in violation of this [Act]" has access to the records "for the purpose of challenge or correction." Since arrest records can be very damaging, it is especially important that they be accurate.

The Federal Privacy Act of 1974

The Federal Privacy Act of 1974 limits the activities of the federal government in gathering information about its employees to "relevant and necessary" information that is obtained, whenever possible, directly from the person being investigated. The subject must be informed of why the information is needed, how it will be used, and what legal right the government has to ask for it. All these requirements are intended to protect people from mysterious interrogations or surveillance based on gossip, hearsay, and false reports.

    The Computer Systems Protection Act, introduced in 1977, would have provided further protection. It declared unauthorized access, alteration, or destruction of computers, programs, and data a federal crime punishable by fines and imprisonment. The bill, however, was never passed.

 COMPUTER CRIME

*Unauthorized access for
unlawful purposes*

There are those against whom the laws and protections set up to secure privacy have little effect. The average **computer crime**—that is, the unauthorized manipulation of computers, computer programs, or data for inappropriate or unlawful purposes (generally for personal profit)—nets its perpetrator about $500,000. Compare that with the $15,000 taken in an average armed bank robbery, even with the $25,000 from the average embezzlement, and you can see why computer crime is on the increase. It has been estimated that anywhere from $100 million to $5 billion are lost every year to computer-related crimes.

Methods

How it's done

There are four common procedures used for committing a computer crime. The **trapdoor** is a set of program instructions that allow the perpetrator to bypass the computer's normal internal security systems. The **Trojan horse** is named for the hollow wooden horse in which invading Greek warriors hid. The perpetrator, usually a computer programmer, develops a useful program which is installed in the system and used by other employees to conduct legitimate operations, for example, a program that computes interest for a bank. Embedded in the program, however, is a set of instructions (an electronic Greek soldier) that can detect when a "privileged" user (the criminal) is running the program and that can provide access to otherwise inaccessible data. Once "in," the criminal can sack the data at will—changing balances, transferring interest to his or her own accounts, and otherwise disrupting the normal course of business.

A variant on the Trojan horse is the **time bomb**, used by computer criminals not so much for personal gain as to damage data or to cover their tracks. A time bomb is a coded section of a program that initiates some event C after other events A and B have occurred. For example, for two years Paula X has been using a Trojan horse to alter her company's financial records for her own profit. She adds a time bomb to the program and gives a week's notice, saying she's found a new job. A week later, her name is deleted from the company's active personnel list (event A). Two weeks after that, her final paycheck is processed and her name is taken off the payroll (event B). Then the time bomb goes into effect. Its "fuse" slowly burns away over a week's time, and then the bomb "explodes," destroying incriminating data, crashing the system, and leaving no evidence of itself. Paula has been gone for three weeks.

A slower, less direct method of committing computer crime is via the **salami slice**, in which small amounts of money are diverted during normal processing to a separate place; for example, fractions are "sliced" off all the accounts in a bank file every time interest is compounded. The pennies, or even fractions of pennies (the tenths of a cent deleted in rounding off), are transferred from many thousands of accounts to a dummy account which the criminal later closes out as if it were legitimate. In 1975, a computer programmer "sliced" fractions from employees' accounts in a company investment plan and ran off with $385,000, which had automatically accrued for him while he went about his normal business.

Industrial Espionage

There is another sort of computer crime, in which a computer or software manufacturer, rather than an individual, is the victim. **Industrial espionage**, the cloak-and-dagger spying activities between corporations intent on stealing one another's ideas, designs, or trade secrets, is becoming more common as the computer and software industries become not only more lucrative but also more fiercely competitive. In 1971, the plans for IBM's 330 disk file system were stolen by a group of IBM employees. The plans were worth $160 million to competitors, who wanted to produce identical or compatible products of their own. The thieves were caught in 1973 and charged with felony theft of trade secrets, receipt of stolen property, conspiracy, and offering or accepting inducement to steal trade secrets.

Competition leading to spying and theft

In 1983, two Hitachi employees paid $622,000 for the plans of a then-experimental IBM computer, the 3081. Unfortunately for them, they paid the money to an FBI sting operation and were charged with industrial espionage. Hitachi settled with IBM out of court for $300 million, and Mitsubishi Electrical Corp., which was also involved in the theft, was fined $10,000. An American company, National Semiconductor, which markets Hitachi's IBM-compatible products through its subsidiary, National Advanced Systems, was accused by IBM of conspiring with the Japanese companies to obtain trade secrets. Although denying the charges, National Semiconductor settled with IBM in January of 1984 for $3 million.

In 1984, Congress passed the Semiconductor Chip Protection Act, which makes it illegal to reproduce any chip pattern for ten years after the design is registered with the Library of Congress. The law imposes fines of up to $250,000 for copyright infringement. However, *reverse engineering* (taking something apart to see how it was put together) is allowed as long as the intention is to improve the chip, not just reproduce it.

Software Piracy

If any industry is growing more rapidly than the manufacturing of computer hardware, it's the production of computer software. In 1982, total software sales totaled $1 billion. By the end of 1983, that figure had more than doubled, and the industry enjoyed sales of over $5 billion in 1985. But analysts and software companies suspect that for every program purchased there are as many as ten illegitimate copies. Just as the cassette recorder crippled the record industry and home videotaping poses a serious threat to Hollywood, piracy of software may be equally dangerous to the software industry. A 1984 Supreme Court decision that home videotaping of copyrighted materials for personal use was not illegal did not calm the software manufacturers' fears. They saw a clear similarity between copying a studio's movie or a network's television show onto a blank videotape and copying computer programs onto blank diskettes.

Users who copy rather than buy

With no clear-cut legislation on their side, software makers have had to be more creative in protecting their intellectual property against theft. One way they do this is by "hiding" essential program segments in unpredictable locations on a disk—placing sector 305 in the middle of sectors 1 through 7, for example. Another protection is to use **software licensing**, rather than selling the product outright. That is, the disks are sealed in plastic, with labels stating that once the seal is broken, the purchaser has entered into a legal and binding contract that gives

IBM Program License Agreement

YOU SHOULD CAREFULLY READ THE FOLLOWING TERMS AND
CONDITIONS BEFORE OPENING THIS DISKETTE(S) OR CASSETTE(S)
PACKAGE. OPENING THIS DISKETTE(S) OR CASSETTE(S) PACKAGE
INDICATES YOUR ACCEPTANCE OF THESE TERMS AND CONDITIONS.
IF YOU DO NOT AGREE WITH THEM, YOU SHOULD PROMPTLY
RETURN THE PACKAGE UNOPENED; AND YOUR MONEY WILL BE
REFUNDED.

IBM provides this program and licenses its use in the United States and Puerto Rico. You assume responsibility for the selection of the program to achieve your intended results, and for the installation, use and results obtained from the program.

LICENSE

You may:

a. use the program on a single machine;

b. copy the program into any machine readable or printed form for backup or modification purposes in support of your use of the program on the single machine (Certain programs, however, may include mechanisms to limit or inhibit copying. They are marked "copy protected.");

c. modify the program and/or merge it into another program for your use on the single machine (Any portion of this program merged into another program will continue to be subject to the terms and conditions of this Agreement.); and,

d. transfer the program and license to another party if the other party agrees to accept the terms and conditions of this Agreement. If you transfer the program, you must at the same time either transfer all copies whether in printed or machine-readable form to the same party or destroy any copies not transferred; this includes all modifications and portions of the program contained or merged into other programs.

You must reproduce and include the copyright notice on any copy, modification or portion merged into another program.

YOU MAY NOT USE, COPY, MODIFY, OR TRANSFER THE PROGRAM, OR ANY COPY, MODIFICATION OR MERGED PORTION, IN WHOLE OR IN PART, EXCEPT AS EXPRESSLY PROVIDED FOR IN THIS LICENSE.

IF YOU TRANSFER POSSESSION OF ANY COPY, MODIFICATION OR MERGED PORTION OF THE PROGRAM TO ANOTHER PARTY, YOUR LICENSE IS AUTOMATICALLY TERMINATED.

TERM

The license is effective until terminated. You may terminate it at any other time by destroying the program together with all copies, modifications and merged portions in any form. It will also terminate upon conditions set forth elsewhere in this Agreement or if you fail to comply with any term or condition of this Agreement. You agree upon such termination to destroy the program together with all copies, modifications and merged portions in any form.

LIMITED WARRANTY

THE PROGRAM IS PROVIDED "AS IS" WITHOUT WARRANTY OF ANY KIND, EITHER EXPRESSED OR IMPLIED, INCLUDING, BUT NOT LIMITED TO THE IMPLIED WARRANTIES OF MERCHANTABILITY AND FITNESS FOR A PARTICULAR PURPOSE. THE ENTIRE RISK AS TO THE QUALITY AND PERFORMANCE OF THE PROGRAM IS WITH YOU. SHOULD THE PROGRAM PROVE DEFECTIVE, YOU (AND NOT IBM OR AN AUTHORIZED PERSONAL COMPUTER DEALER) ASSUME THE ENTIRE COST OF ALL NECESSARY SERVICING, REPAIR OR CORRECTION.

Continued on inside back cover

Figure 22.1   License Agreement

This license agreement accompanies IBM's Easywriter software. Like other software licensing agreements, it stipulates that only the purchaser is entitled to use the software under a contract that is "signed" by breaking the package seal. The contract is terminated only if the original program and all copies are destroyed. This is one way software manufacturers provide themselves with legal protection. (Reproduced by permission of IBM.)

the purchaser alone the right to use the software (see Figure 22.1). If copies are made, a contract has been broken, and the user can be sued in court.

A case of software piracy was settled out of court in 1984. Lotus Development Corporation, makers of the 1-2-3 package (see Chapter 10), sued a company called Rixon, Inc., for $10 million. Rixon, it seems, had made copies of 1-2-3 and distributed them to its branch offices. Rixon agreed to pay an undisclosed settlement and to return all the illegal copies to Lotus.

Computer Vandalism

Most computer crimes that get publicity are not robberies or espionage but rather are a serious sort of high-tech vandalism. Four 13-year-old students in New York tapped into the Telenet data network and accessed the data bases of 19 different Canadian companies (including PepsiCo, Honeywell, and Bell-Canada) in an attempt to have a few free cases of Pepsi delivered to their school. At one company alone, 20% of its data were destroyed. A 17-year-old student in California gained access to U.S. Leasing's computer system and filled the files with obscenities, which came streaming out of printers every time inventory was called up. Also in California, 26 college students used Cal Tech's IBM 370/158 to print up 1.2 million entry forms for a McDonald's contest and won $40,000 in prizes. And recently, a reporter for *Newsweek* magazine found that his credit card numbers, as well as his address, phone number, and wife's name, had been stolen from a credit company computer and his telephone and power service were being tampered with by young *hackers* (computer programming enthusiasts) across the country who'd been annoyed by an article he'd written exposing their antics. Once they'd managed to get access to his credit card and utility account numbers and post them on electronic bulletin boards, there was virtually no limit to the damage they could do to his credit rating, finances, and peace of mind.

Hackers' pranks as serious crimes

In the early 1980s, there was a flurry of reports about hackers accessing commercial, Department of Defense, and NASA computers. Although the stories of large quantities of sensitive data being blipped out of existence like Space Invaders are mostly fictional and greatly exaggerated, this kind of unauthorized and malicious access is a bothersome problem, certainly irresponsible, sometimes criminal, and in any case a disturbing suggestion of the possibility of more sinister tampering (see Figure 22.2).

Often the search for computer vandals is so expensive that companies prefer simply to take their losses. In the Telenet case, the search for the four schoolboys cost $250,000, and no charges were filed against them. The obscene inventory file at U.S. Leasing cost that company $60,000 to repair plus $200,000 to find the culprit, who was then subject only to charges of making an obscene phone call.

This type of computer tampering is so new that there is some problem with making the old laws effectively fit the new crimes. According to the FBI, where only 1 agent in 40 has any formal training fighting computer crime, there is currently no federal law against unauthorized entry into computers, although Congress is currently considering such legislation. Most computer vandals are prosecuted under section 1343 of Title XVIII of the U.S. Code, which forbids unlawful use of telephone lines. However, laws specifically governing computer crime have been enacted in a number of states. In 1984, for example, a 19-year-old college sophomore in Los Angeles used his $200 home computer to break into the Department of Defense's communications network. He was caught and charged with

Old laws, new crimes

Figure 22.2   "Syscruncher" and "Vladimir"

In 1980, hackers calling themselves "Syscruncher" and "Vladimir" invaded the computer system at Chicago's DePaul University. They locked out authorized users, accessed the school's master account file, and crashed the entire system twice. Two high school students were eventually arrested on charges of "theft of services" and were sentenced to a year's probation, despite their mothers' pleas that they were just "exuberant, innocent pranksters." It took nearly 200 hours to repair the damage they'd caused. (Donn B. Parker, excerpted from *Fighting Computer Crime.* Copyright © 1983. Reprinted with permission of Charles Scribner's Sons.

```
**LOGOFF E110 1218 #20
**LOGON  B999 1218 #18
03  HELLO, THIS IS THE 'SYSCRUNCHER'   (REMEMBER ME? I BROUGHT YOUR SYSTEM
03  DOWN LAST WEEK?)
**LOGOFF  D204 1219 #05
03 ATTENTION.......................................................
03 IS THERE ANYONE THERE, I WANT TO TALK TO YOU N O W !
**LOGON  D204 1219 #05
03 €€€€€€€€€€€€€€€€€€€€3333333333333333333###############>>>>>>>>>>>>>>>>
03 AAAAAAAAAAAAAAAAAAAAAAAAASSSSSSSSSSSSSSSSSSDDDDDDDDDDDDDDDFFFFFFFFFFFFF
03 >>>>>>>>>>>>>>>>>>>(((((((((((((((((((.....................//////////
03
03 IF YOU GIVE ME A LISTING OF YOUR 'MIX' ASSEMBLY PROGRAM, I WILL
03 LEAVE YOUR SYSTEM ALONE
03 HELLO, ARE YOU THERE
03 YOUR ATTENTION PLEASE
03
03 BEEP      B E E P
03 BBBBBBBBBBBBBEEEEEEEEEEEEEEEEEEEEEEEEEEPPPPPPPPPPPPPPPPPP
03 I WILL BE BACK A LITTLE LATER TO TALK TO YOU, OR EVEN BETTER,
03 IF YOU LEAVE ME A PHONE #, I'LL CALL YOU INSTEAD
03 BYE NOW
03
03
03                          SYSCRUNCHER
**LOGOFF M209 1224 #04
**LOGON  M209 1224 #04

PLEASE LOG IN
HELLOO--X999,XXX999
ILLEGAL FORMAT
BYER
PLEASE LOG IN
BYE
PLEASE LOG IN
BYE
PLEASE LOG IN
HEL-X999,XXX9999
ILLEGAL ACCESS
HEL-D200,320

WELCOME TO VLADIMIR'S NEWLY CONQUERED
HP 2000 TIMESHARING SYSTEM. IF YOU
WANT TO CONTACT VLADIMIR, PLEASE LEAVE
A MESSAGE ON PBBS PHONE #359-9450
```

```
203:                        CAVEMAN DAVE
204:                        ALIAS: THE GAME PLAYER
205:
206: JAMES T. KIRK
207: VLADIMIR
208: DE PAUL
209: SEP. 25, 1980
210: VIRGIN
211: VLAD: CONGRATULATIONS.  WE MUST GET TOGETHER TO DISCUSS
212: HOW YOU ACCOMPLISHED THE GREAT DEED.  BEING DISGRUNTLED
213: WITH THIS             UNIVERSITY MYSELF. I GOT A BIG KICK
214: OUT OF HAVING IT BROUGHT TO ITS KNEES.  GET BACK TO ME.
215:
216: VLADIMIR & SYSCRUNCHER
217: JAMES T. KIRK
218: DE PAUL
219: SEP. 26, 1980
220: ORBY
221: HI ! THIS IS SYSCRUNCHER
222: ACTUALLY, VLAD HAD VERY LITTLE TO DO WITH THE DOWN FALL
223: AND EVENTUAL DESTRUCTION OF YOUR MIGHTY (COUGH) HP (SNICKER!)
224: IT WAS V E R Y SIMPLE TO READ YOUR PASSWORD FILE ON A000
225: ESPECIALLY SINCE THE FILES ITSELF WAS LOCKED, AND
226: THERE JUST HAPPENED TO BE A LOCKED FILE READING PROGRAM
227: ALSO ON A000.  THEN IT WAS A SIMPLE MATTER TO EXE*OUT=* THE
228: FILE PROGRAM SO IT WOULD PRINT IT INTO THE FILE. I DID THIS
229: SINCE THE LINES IN THE FILE WERE 250 CHARACTERS ACROSS
230: I THEN READ THE FILE AND B I N G O ! THERE WERE YOUR PASSWORDS
231: WE USED A OSI MICRO TO GET A000 SINCE YOU NEGLECTED TO PLACE
232: IT IN A FILE. AFTER WE KNEW THE FORM OF YOUR PASSWORDS
233: (3 LETTERS) IT WAS SIMPLE !!!
234: DO NOT FEEL BAD, ESPECIALLY SINCE YOURS IS NOT THE FIRST
235: SYSTEM TO FALL BEFORE ME, NOR WILL IT BE THE LAST !
236: THE SYSTEMS TO MY CREDIT ARE:
237: D211
238: D214
239: DE PAUL
240: GAMEMASTER
241: AND OTHER LESSER SYSTEMS THAT NEED NOT BE MENTIONED
242: IF YOU NEED HELP IN RESTRUCTURING YOUR ID SYSTEM, LEAVE
243: ME A MESSAGE. OTHER WISE, WATCH OUT,
244: SYSCRUNCHER IS ALIVE AND WELL !!!
245:
246: VLADIMIR
247: JAMES T. KIRK
248: DE PAUL
249: SEP. 26, 1980
250: 0
251: HELLO THERE!! I THOUGHT SOMEONE WOULD
252: APPRECIATE MY DEED, I'M A SENIOR IN HIGH SCHOOL
253: AND HAVE SOME QUESTIONS ABOUT YOUR SYSTEM.
254: I WOULD LIKE TO CONTACT YOU BUT IF YOUR ON THE
255: STAFF
256: MY NUMBER IF YOU REPLY.
257: DESTRUCTIVELY YOURS
258: VLADIMIR
```

12 felony counts of "malicious access to a computer system" and 1 count of receiving stolen property (the data he'd removed). Those charges could lead to six years in prison.

ISSUES IN TECHNOLOGY
A number of computer vandals have claimed that they were actually performing a valuable public service by revealing weaknesses in computer security systems, which could be exploited by people less honest and responsible than themselves. In light of what you know about computer crimes, does this plea hold any water? What really compels such wayward hackers to invade computer systems and destroy or steal valuable or sensitive data?

SECURING THE SYSTEM

Computers themselves are not without defenses against theft and vandalism, to keep vital personal information from being stolen or destroyed. There are a number of measures that can be taken to ensure the integrity of computer systems and protect them from improper access.

Controlling Personnel

Avoiding unauthorized use

Since many invasions of data files and abuses of computer systems are performed by the people who are employed to work with them, limiting access to a few carefully screened and authorized individuals is one measure that can improve security. If programmers are also computer operators, then they can not only write illegitimate programs but conveniently run them as well. If programmers work in their offices and operators in the computer room, and management knows who's where and what they're up to, opportunities for covert electronic embezzlement decrease significantly. Such separation of functions is, of course, easy for a firm with a large data-processing staff but may be impossible for a small company with only two or three computer professionals, who must each handle several overlapping jobs. In any case, careful screening of job applicants—checking their references and looking closely at their backgrounds—is vital to any system's security. Needless to say, if someone lies on a résumé or has a history of committing computer crimes, that person is definitely not a good risk. A great deal of information about our activities is available in computers, and a legal screening of an applicant's background can be easily and quickly accomplished.

Figure 22.3 shows two devices used to physically limit access to computer systems to authorized personnel.

Passwords

Guaranteeing authorized access

Passwords and **access logs** are two means of ensuring that all users are identified before they can enter the system. Supplying the correct password gets a user into the system, and an access log keeps track of who "passed" in, when they entered, and when they left. Frequent examination of programs and access logs by profes-

Figure 22.3   On-the-Job Security
(a) At this factory, only authorized workers are able to enter a particular area. The security system functions as a guard against improper access, and as a time clock, recording who entered, and when. (b) These security terminals, manufactured by SecuraKey, help organizations keep certain areas "off limits." The stand-alone ENTRACOMP 2100 access control computer (left) can keep up to 8000 authorized card numbers in its memory, and can print out the date, time, and card number of each attempted entry. The Data Logger L-2 (right) sounds an alarm if an unauthorized entry attempt is made. (c) Fingerprints can be digitalized and used as an effective and secure means of worker identification.

sional auditors is another commonly used security method. If there has been a great deal of activity on the computer system during what should be off-hours, an auditor who simply inspects the log thoroughly may be able to stop a computer crime before it starts.

The idea behind the use of passwords or account numbers is to provide access to the computer only to authorized users. If Sam, a bona fide computer user, can gain access to the system by simply entering his name, there is nothing to stop an unauthorized person who knows that Sam has access from keying in SAM and entering the system. Instead, Sam can use something like his dog's name, or part of his license plate number: they're easy for him to remember, and it's unlikely that another person will guess them.

Cryptography

Cryptography is the practice of transcribing a message from its *plaintext,* or original form, into a secret code or cipher from which the original meaning can supposedly be recovered only by an authorized recipient who holds the *key,* or system of

Disguising data

retranscription. With a *code*, some predetermined substitution is made for words, phrases, or other meaningful parts of a sentence. A **cipher**, on the other hand, makes a substitution for each letter (or sometimes each fixed group of letters). That is, each letter in the plaintext is replaced by a different letter or symbol. The sentence *Eagle buys the laundry* is a code in which *Eagle* stands for Agent X, *buys* for steals, and *laundry* for the secret plans. Enciphered, with its letters altered and regrouped into new blocks, the same message might read *DZB.FH KJXHMF ?ZKJRFJ.*

In 1977, the National Bureau of Standards (NBS), in cooperation with IBM, designed the **Data Encryption Standard (DES)**, a standard public cipher for senders and receivers of data. The National Security Agency (NSA) has endorsed this cipher, which the NBS claims would cost over $200 million and take more than 3000 years to crack (or 571 years if, with the help of a supercomputer, one attempt were made every microsecond). The DES is a *block cipher;* that is, it breaks up the text to be coded into groups (or blocks) of 8 bytes (64 bits) and uses a 7-byte key to transform those blocks into new 8-byte groupings. There are over 70 quadrillion (70,000,000,000,000,000) possible combinations of digits. Here's an example:

Plaintext: THIS IS A SECRET MESSAGE

DES cipher: I,R.[-C.*Q=W,.S9GE9.3---N.,!.3,[

Inexpensive commercial software packages (such as Standard Software's The Protector or K & L's N-Code) designed solely to encrypt microcomputer programs are also available. Although all ciphers, like rules, are made to be broken, the enciphering of programs provides substantial protection against invasion.

HAZARDS AND SAFEGUARDS

Of course, people aren't the only serious threat to the security of a computer system's data. A variety of environmental perils creates serious problems for computers—everything from fire and water to cockroaches and nuclear war.

Heat

Overheating and moisture

Computer rooms must be kept cool because a computer's circuits can generate enough heat to keep several offices warm. (In fact, the home office of the Hartford Insurance Group saved over 81,000 gallons of oil the first year it used its computer facilities as a heat source.) As was mentioned in Chapter 3, computer components that get hot fail more often than ones that remain cool, which has prompted computer manufacturers to install fans in many of their units, even in small desktop computers that use only about 100 watts of power. Larger (and therefore hotter) computer systems come equipped with liquid refrigeration units (you've no doubt noticed that computer rooms are often very chilly).

Smoke and Steam

Damage to magnetic storage media

Steam, or even just very high humidity, can short out circuits, and the particles suspended in smoke and dust can scratch and permanently damage the magnetic

surfaces of tapes and disks or clog ventilation systems. For example, the fine vol-
canic ash from the 1980 eruption of Mount St. Helens brought down a number of
computer systems in the state of Washington. Filtered ventilation systems and
moisture detectors are common safeguards in computer rooms.

Electricity

A common computer-related concern is that if the electricity surges or fails, all
human knowledge (or at least our bank accounts) could be lost. To some extent,
this concern is justified; a loss of electricity, even for a sixtieth of a second, can
cause the destruction of data. As a rule, however, most major systems have banks
of batteries that can sustain the power supply long enough (usually only for a few
minutes) to unload the contents of all volatile memory onto nonvolatile magnetic
storage media. If a computer's function is so vital that it simply can't be left sitting
idle until power is restored (air traffic control computers, for one example), large
diesel- or gas-powered generators are employed to provide emergency power. For
microcomputers, there are dozens of surge-protection devices that sell for
under $50 and small stand-by generators that cost between $300 and $500.

Protecting against power failures

A less dramatic form of electrical threat is caused by static electricity, which can
damage tapes and disks. Grounded wire woven into the computer room carpeting
or special anti-static slippers worn by computer operators help prevent the generation of static electricity.

Wildlife

Finally, on an even smaller scale, mice can nibble the insulation around wiring or
even gnaw through live cables (which tends to crash both computer and mouse).
Insects and small animals have, from time to time, managed to block off ventilation
ducts with their nests, causing dust and overheating in computer rooms. Even a
tiny insect on a disk represents an enormous obstacle to a read/write head. Clearly,
those in charge of maintaining the computer's environment must occasionally be
prepared to go on safari.

Problems with wildlife

Earthquakes

In 1985, there was a large earthquake in Mexico City and dozens of computer
systems were down for several days. Most of the damage was caused not by gaping
cracks in the earth, but by hardware units crashing into each other. Anchoring
cabinets and consoles is a simple precaution against that kind of damage.

Seismic catastrophes and disaster recovery

Earthquakes have secondary effects, though, including fires and smoke, steam
from broken pipes, power failures, debris, and even the complete destruction of the
facility itself. The establishment of a **disaster recovery team** can help keep
damage to a computer system at a minimum. Particularly common in earthquake-
prone regions, a team composed of systems analysts, disaster recovery experts, and
employees, carefully plans which programs are most essential and need to be reinstalled immediately after the disaster. They decide what equipment, facilities, and
supplies will be required right away and which employees are essential. Dry runs
and drills keep the plan operational, but the adoption of new equipment, software,

or management objectives can send the team back to the planning stages. Cooperative agreements are often worked out with competing companies nearby to share personnel and facilities in the event of a disaster. Off-site storage of spare parts, copies of data and programs, and even backup hardware can also help soften the blow.

Electromagnetic Pulse

Computers and nuclear war

There is, however, one further threat to computer systems. A single megaton nuclear warhead, detonated in the upper atmosphere over the United States, would create an *electromagnetic pulse (EMP)* like a giant bolt of lightning, effectively blacking out all computerized communications systems for several hours, days, or even longer. In the event of a nuclear war, the difficulty of placing a long-distance call might seem minor, but consider the more serious effects. Conventional military command, control, and communications systems; incoming warhead detection; and television, radio, and civil defense communications would also be silenced. Organization of coordinated relief and rescue efforts would be made very difficult since no one would be able to talk to anyone else over any distance. The Department of Defense has studied the potential effects of EMP and ways to avoid its consequences, but its findings are classified. The mobile and largely airborne C^3I System discussed in Chapter 21, however, is considered one possible safeguard against such catastrophic disruption.

HEALTH

In its April of 1983 issue, the *Health Letter* of the Harvard Medical School divided the health problems associated with the use of computers, specifically with the use of CRTs and other *video display terminals (VDTs)*, into four categories: radiation-linked problems, visual disturbances, musculoskeletal difficulties, and stress. Radiation emission has been widely discussed in the popular media and deserves first attention.

Radiation and VDTs

Public concern about radiation

Within a year after the installation of VDTs in the editorial offices of *The New York Times,* two editors developed cataracts. Since 1980, there have been reports of clusters of miscarriages and birth defects in the United States and Canada among females who operated VDTs for long periods of time. These and similar reports have given rise to concerns that VDTs emit radiation that causes cataracts, birth defects, sterility, blindness, cancer, or other less specific complaints. But in fact there have been no epidemics of cataracts or birth defects, as might be expected after the widespread adoption of VDTs. The March of Dimes Birth Defects Foundation observed that the increased numbers of women who work with VDTs has itself raised the statistical probability of "chance clusters" of problem pregnancies.

Public concern, however, prompted extensive studies by the Food and Drug Administration's Bureau of Radiological Health (FDA-BRH), the Occupational Safety and Health Administration (OSHA), the National Institute of Occupational Safety and Health (NIOSH), and the Canadian Radiation Protection Bureau, all of which found no detectable radiation hazard from VDTs. (In Canada, however, VDT operators who become pregnant are now regularly transferred to other duties.) In the FDA-BRH study, for example, 125 different VDT units were examined under worst-case conditions, and only eight emitted more X-ray radiation than is allowed for televisions. Those eight models were withdrawn from the market.

Physical Complaints

But the extensive tests for radiation uncovered other problems with VDTs in the workplace. Eyestrain, neck pains and backaches, and fatigue were common operator complaints. The source of these physical problems was clear: traditional office design and furniture simply do not comfortably accommodate the new technology. Glare, flickering images, heat, noise, and poor posture are frequently the causes of discomfort among VDT operators.

Aches and pains from poorly designed workstations

To alleviate such problems, NIOSH made a number of recommendations for safer, more comfortable workstations (see Figure 22.4):

Screen hoods to block glare from light sources

Antiglare filters on screens

Indirect lighting in offices

Recessed work-area lighting fixtures with downward (rather than outward) deflectors

Adjustable blinds or curtains on windows to block glare from direct sunlight

Screen brightness of 500–700 *lux* (or luminous flux, the international unit of illumination)

5 × 7 dot matrix to form characters 2.6 mm to 4.2 mm high

Keyboard home-row height of 720 mm and 790 mm ($28\frac{1}{4}$ inches and 31 inches), that is, at about elbow height

Screen at 10°–20° below the horizontal plane of the operator's eyes, at a distance of 450–500 mm ($17\frac{3}{4}$–$19\frac{3}{4}$ inches)

Upright copyholders

Adjustable chairs with lower back rests

A = 10° to 20°
B = 19¾"
C = 31"

Figure 22.4 Operator Posture

NIOSH recommended that the center of the VDT screen should be no more than 10°–20° below the operator's eye level, at a distance of no more than 19¾ inches. The keyboard's home row should be no higher than 31 inches from the floor.

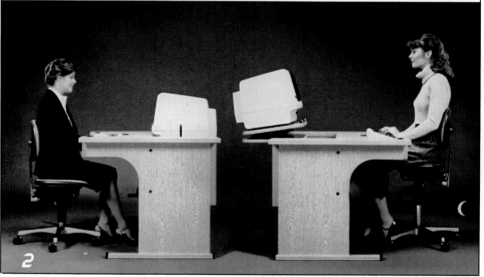

Figure 22.5 The Ergonomics Industry

A whole new business has grown up around the need to adapt the workplace to the new tools, as this advertisement for the Biotec line of office equipment demonstrates. It emphasizes the timeliness, decreased health risks, greater worker productivity, and the aesthetic appeal of the work stations.

Furthermore, the "reassuring click" of keyboard keys and the clatter of printers could become an annoyance, and the office environment should be closely monitored to prevent the heat generated by desktop computer hardware from becoming uncomfortable.

Ergonomics

A science to answer workers' complaints

Ergonomics is the study of how people's living and working conditions can be adapted to the technology around them, whether it's making tractor seats more comfortable or computer workstations more pleasant. It is closely related to **biotechnology**, which is that aspect of technological research concerned with the problems posed by the interaction of human beings and machines. Studies such as those conducted by NIOSH (which was an ergonomic study, since it was aimed at adjusting the working environment to the workers' requirements) have resulted in a number of intriguing changes in the workplace. Several companies have begun to market "ergonomically designed" workstations and office furniture (see Figure 22.5). Swiveling or tilting terminal bases, recessed keyboards, adjustable chairs, wrist rests, convenient and compact storage devices, and **acoustical enclosure units** (cabinets that muffle printer noise) are only a few of the specially designed furnishings available from ergonomically minded manufacturers.

Stress

The technological improvement of work conditions, however, can lead to another problem for VDT operators—stress. A person working at a word processor can produce as much as twice the material he or she could type on a typewriter. This potential gain in productivity has made many employers expect greater efficiency from their operators. Also, since material can be called up, assigned, corrected, stored, printed, and forwarded from one unit, social isolation can become another problem (see Figure 22.6). An operator may begin to feel pushed or harassed by the seemingly insatiable computer, separated from his or her coworkers, and generally overworked, and morale may decline. The very tools brought in to increase productivity have proven in a number of organizations to be the source of increases in tardiness, absenteeism, slow-downs, and errors.

Psychological consequences of overwork

On the other hand, word processors and other electronic equipment in the office are far more often greeted with delight and relief by office workers. The speed and efficiency they bring to formerly time-consuming and monotonous typing and filing chores generally make secretarial and clerical functions lighter and more pleasant. Most typists, for example, have found that the opportunity to be trained on and work with high-tech equipment improves not only their job performance but also their opportunities for advancement.

Many European and American companies, as a result of either management initiative or union contract, have set specific limits on the amount of time their

Figure 22.6 Worker Isolation

As fewer and fewer people are needed to operate increasingly self-sufficient computers, the potential emotional problems created by worker isolation and lonely, sterile working conditions must be faced.

workers should spend operating VDTs, and have taken advantage of higher productivity to upgrade and expand workers' other administrative and clerical responsibilities. As a result, computers in such workplaces have led to higher morale and greater feelings of self-esteem, as well as reducing "intensity anxiety," or stress caused by feelings of being overworked. The FDA-BRH report mentioned earlier found "that efforts expended to reduce stress would also reduce the adverse impact on health," and other studies have found that positive attention to the ergonomics affecting office workers can increase their productivity by 13%–15%. Everybody gains from a comfortable, healthy environment.

Isolation

Telecommuting and social isolation

The advent of personal computers that can be linked to large central systems has offered employers the option of enlarging a workforce without expanding facilities. There is no longer any reason why a number of jobs, particularly some secretarial and clerical work, can't be performed just as efficiently at home as in the office (see Figure 22.7). As many as 30,000 people telecommuted in 1983, and the University of Southern California's Center for Futures Research estimates that 10 million people will work at home with computers by the year 2000. (Chapter 7 introduced telecommuting, and Chapter 17 examined its impact on the traditional office.) However, many of those workers whose job functions are well suited to telecommuting, particularly women, are afraid that they will become trapped in the home. Their concern is that at-home workers will be paid less and have fewer benefits than full-time office workers and will miss out on the social aspects of the office environment while working away in a twilight zone between housewifery (or househusbandry) and career. Others, however, welcome the opportunity to be a full-time parent or housekeeper and a wage earner as well, while saving money on day-care and commuting.

But isolation in the workplace isn't the only concern. There is a growing fear that as society becomes increasingly linked together by computers, people will hide away by themselves, endlessly tapping away at keyboards, living their lives by computer. A similar fear, interestingly enough, was expressed following the invention of the telephone: that people would no longer talk face to face but would instead converse exclusively over wires. Conversation has only increased in the

Figure 22.7 Home Work

The advent of the personal and portable computer has made it possible for much office work to be done at home. While working at home may be attractive for some, isolation, lack of benefits, and less than ideal working conditions are drawbacks to such arrangements that need to be considered.

CAREERS IN TECHNOLOGY
Security Specialist

Job Description   It is the job of the security specialist to prevent the sort of improper access discussed in this chapter by developing a variety of safeguarding measures, from physical barriers such as electronically locked doors or turnstiles to program controls for limiting access or detecting intruders.   The security specialist's ongoing job is to monitor and test existing security systems to ensure their continued effective operation, to work with auditors to prevent managerial fraud (such as the alteration of data to show false profits or losses), and to supervise the creation of duplicate files and backup equipment in case a power loss or natural disaster threatens the data or facility.

Qualifications   Some experience in programming, systems analysis, and EDP management (see the Careers in Technology section in Chapter 19) is useful, and a strong general understanding of the equipment, techniques, and technology of data processing is essential.   Continuous research and study to keep up with both hardware and software advances as well as state-of-the-art computer crime is vital.

Outlook   Because large systems handling sensitive data are the ones most likely to be "hit," security specialists work mostly for banks, credit companies, and major data-processing services.   Computer consulting companies often employ field security specialists to work on the individual problems of their client organizations.   As the rate of unauthorized intrusion rises, and as more sensitive data are stored in computers, the need for people to guard and secure that information will undoubtedly rise.

years since Bell's invention, and the more people talked, the more lingering nineteenth-century social barriers were broken down. It is likely that computer linkage may have a similar effect, opening new avenues of communication among more people.

ETHICS AND RESPONSIBILITY

Most professions have codes of ethics or ethical guidelines, a set of general principles by which the people in a given profession are expected to behave. The doctor's Hippocratic Oath and the legal profession's Canon of Ethics are two such standards, and doctors or lawyers who violate them are subject to reprimand, suspension, or expulsion from their profession. With so many sensitive issues facing professionals in the fields of computer science and data processing, it seems reasonable to expect some standard for their behavior, some list of dos and don'ts. In fact, there are several. The *American Federation of Information Processing Societies (AFIPS)* is an umbrella organization including most computer societies, such as the Association for Computing Machinery (ACM), the Data Processing Management Association (DPMA), and the Institute of Electrical and Electronic Engineers (IEEE). It recognized a need for a formal code of ethics in 1970. Since then, many of its affiliates have developed standards of ethical behavior for their members.

A new sense of professional responsibility

After five years of work experience in the computer field and after passing a five-part examination on data-processing equipment, management principles, accounting, finance, mathematics, statistics, and systems analysis and design, a candidate receives the **certificate in data processing** and can put **CDP** after his or her name. A CDP (which is to data processing what CPA is to accounting) represents professional recognition of a person's experience and competence, and certifies that he or she has met the ethical standards set by the *Institute for Certification of Computer Professionals (ICCP)*, which oversees the certification process. Many candidates have passed the examination but have been denied a CDP because they failed in some way to meet the ICCP's ethical requirements. Examples of unethical activities by computer professionals that violate professional standards are such things as falsifying data, using a company computer for personal projects on company time, taking advantage of a known vulnerability in the system to gain unauthorized access, and obtaining records or data without authorization.

 THE DISPLACING TECHNOLOGY

Technological development: creating and destroying jobs

The Congressional Budget Office estimated that in 1984–1985 almost 8% of those unemployed—or between 450,000 and 750,000 people—lost their jobs because of technological advances. A private study commissioned by the W. E. Upjohn Institute for Employment Research found that, by 1990, from 100,000 to 200,000 more jobs will be eliminated because of technology, largely in the auto industry. The same study projected that from 32,000 to 64,000 new jobs will be created in robotics, but the new jobs will be for highly skilled workers—not for the displaced semiskilled ones. Finally, researchers at Carnegie-Mellon University estimate that 4 million manufacturing workers could be displaced by robots by the turn of the century. By 2025, they say, it is conceivable that nearly all current blue-collar workers could be displaced.

The ideal future has us all freed by technology from repetitive and heavy labor, with plenty of leisure time on our hands. It's not that simple, though. Working is simply too important to the way we live and think and to the way we respect ourselves and others. "What do you do?" is a common conversation starter; it reflects the significance of work in our lives. "Nothing" is not an acceptable answer. Furthermore, there are serious personal and social ills associated with forced leisure, ranging from depression and illness to drug addiction and violence. If we are in fact on the verge of a laborless leisure culture, we must prepare for it now, and not wait until tens or hundreds of millions of unemployed people in industrialized nations suddenly need something to do.

Part of the answer lies in extensive (and expensive) **retooling** programs to retrain industrial workers in technologically useful skills. In the future, we all may work part-time at two or three different jobs in order to make room for each other, which in turn means practically life-long education and training for everyone. Dramatic changes in our whole society may very well be inevitable. And technology won't stand still. The computer and electronics industries are undergoing rapid changes, and today's high-tech professionals will need to retool themselves as the tech gets higher. We're all going to have to face a lot of change, and job displacement will not be limited to the old industries.

SUMMARY

Privacy

We are becoming increasingly dependent on the wide dispersal and easy accessibility of personal data. Greater convenience and efficiency may lead to greater intrusions into personal privacy.

Matching   The idea of matching different data bases dates from as early as 1960. The practice is now commonly used to spot fraud and mismanagement, particularly in welfare and tax evasion, saving taxpayers billions of dollars every year.

Legal Protection   Although there is no clear constitutional guarantee of a "right to privacy," the Fourth Amendment may apply. Four acts of Congress definitely do: the Fair Credit Reporting Act of 1970 (free access to credit records); the Freedom of Information Act of 1970 (free access to personal data gathered by the U.S. government); the Crime Control Act of 1973 (arrest histories must be kept current and complete); and the Federal Privacy Act of 1974 (investigations must be justified).

Computer Crime

Computer crime is the unauthorized manipulation of computers, computer programs, or data for inappropriate or unlawful purposes.

Methods   The four most common methods for committing computer crime are the trapdoor, the Trojan horse, the time bomb, and the salami slice.

Industrial Espionage   As the computer and software industries become more lucrative and competitive, it becomes more tempting to engage in cloak-and-dagger spying activities.

Software Piracy   Software manufacturers need to take precautions to protect themselves against the pirating of copies of their merchandise. "Hidden" program segments and software licensing agreements with customers are two precautions used.

Computer Vandalism   High-tech vandalism by hackers destroys data, creates inconvenience, and costs money. The high cost and low probability of locating computer vandals make many companies unwilling to pursue them. Laws are only recently being written or updated to apply specifically to computer vandalism.

Securing the System

A number of measures can be taken to ensure the integrity and security of computer systems.

Controlling Personnel   Screening employees and limiting access to computer equipment are examples of worthwhile security measures.

Passwords and Access Logs   The use of secret user codes and accurate access logs is a comparatively simple technique for securing data against unauthorized intruders.

Cryptography   The use of enciphering can protect sensitive data from unauthorized access or use. The Data Encryption Standard (DES) developed by the National Bureau of Standards may be the most secure cipher.

Hazards and Safeguards

Perils other than those posed by criminals threaten the security of data.

Heat   Computer circuitry converts most of the electricity it consumes into heat, and the warmer the circuitry, the greater is the chance of malfunction. Built-in fans and cooling systems and air-conditioning of facilities are solutions to overheating. Excess humidity can short out circuitry, so moisture detectors are also needed.

Smoke and Steam High levels of smoke, dust, or ash may scratch and damage tapes and disks or clog vents. Filtered ventilation systems and smoke detectors are common in computer rooms.

Electricity Power surges and failures are protected against by surge-protection devices and backup sources of power such as batteries or generators. Static electricity can be controlled by grounded carpets and special slippers.

Wildlife Mice and insects can be a problem. They can gnaw through wiring or nest in vents, causing shorts, fires, dust, or overheating.

Earthquakes Earthquakes' primary hazard is that unanchored hardware units can crash into each other. Their secondary effects—fire, smoke, steam, power failures, and debris—can also be devastating to an organization. Disaster recovery teams are established to create and implement workable plans for returning to normal operation following such a disaster.

Electromagnetic Pulse An electromagnetic pulse from the detonation of a nuclear warhead would black out computerized communications systems nationwide. Airborne communications centers may be one possible safeguard.

Health

Health problems associated with the use of computers, specifically with the use of video display terminals, are radiation-linked problems, visual disturbances, musculoskeletal difficulties, and stress.

Radiation and VDTs Despite concerns about the incidence of cataracts, miscarriages, birth defects, sterility, and cancer, studies by the U.S. and Canadian governments and private research groups have found no link between VDT radiation and disease.

Physical Complaints Studies have shown that computer users may develop eyestrain, neck pains and backaches, and fatigue as a result of a poor working environment. Such workstation improvements as screen hoods, filters, indirect lighting, adjustable chairs, and specific screen brightness, character size, and keyboard height can alleviate these problems.

Ergonomics Ergonomics is the study of how living and working conditions can be adapted to technology; biotechnology is research into the problems posed by the interaction of humans and machines. The need for better working environments has resulted in the marketing of specially designed furniture: adjustable chairs, terminal bases, wrist rests, and acoustical enclosure units.

Stress Since computers are so fast, VDT operators may feel compelled to work faster. Tension, isolation, and pressure can sometimes result in decreases in productivity and morale. Some companies limit the amount of time their workers will spend operating VDTs.

Isolation Although computer networks and personal computers may make life more efficient, their impact on the overall quality of living may not be entirely positive. Loss of job benefits and isolation of telecommuters are some of the issues that will need to be faced.

Ethics and Responsibility

Ethical standards adopted by the affiliates of AFIPS and by the ICCP for its requirements for the certificate in data processing (CDP) are designed to guide the professional ethics of computer professionals.

The Displacing Technology

With the possibility of 1 million people being out of work by 1990 due to technological advances, and 4 million more jobs eliminated by 2025, our society faces some serious questions about how it will change and what all those people will do. Retooling, retraining, and job sharing are possible solutions.

COMPUTER CONCEPTS ▬▬▬▬

As an extra review of the chapter, try defining the following terms. If you have trouble with any of them, refer to the page number listed.

matching 628
computer crime 630
trapdoor 630
Trojan horse 630
time bomb 630
salami slice 630
industrial espionage 631
software licensing 631

passwords 636
access logs 636
cryptography 637
cipher 638
Data Encryption Standard (DES) 638
disaster recovery team 639

ergonomics 642
biotechnology 643
acoustical enclosure units 643
certificate in data processing (CDP) 646
retooling 646

REVIEW QUESTIONS ▬▬▬▬

1. Name some of the different places in which computer files on an individual may be kept.
2. How is matching used, and what are the arguments for and against such a practice?
3. What are the guarantees and limitations of the Fair Credit Reporting Act of 1970, the Freedom of Information Act of 1970, the Crime Control Act of 1973, the Federal Privacy Act of 1974, and the Computer Systems Protection Act?
4. How does computer crime differ from conventional crime?
5. Why are industrial espionage and software piracy serious crimes?
6. What is meant by "computer vandalism"? Is the term appropriate? Why or why not?
7. What are some of the possible penalties for various computer crimes?
8. What are the ways computer systems can be safeguarded against unauthorized intrusion?
9. Explain the effects of each of the following on computer systems: heat, humidity, smoke, dust, earthquakes, mice, and an EMP. How can computers be protected from each?
10. What are the health problems associated with the use of VDTs? What are the causes? What are the "cures"?
11. What does "ergonomically designed" mean, and what is the goal of such designs?
12. How do computers cause stress in the workplace? Are there any ways to relieve such stress?
13. Describe the disadvantages of telecommuting.
14. List some common ethical problems faced in the computer industry.
15. How does the technological ideal of the future compare with that suggested by current employment and social realities? How might the problem of displacement be solved?

A SHARPER FOCUS ▬▬▬▬

Now that you've completed this chapter, you should be able to answer the following questions about the chapter opening.

1. Do you think that selling software on the honor system encourages or discourages piracy?
2. Is this a better way of protecting software than licensing it as described in the chapter?

PROJECTS

1. Find out more about one of the computer crimes described in this chapter. How (and why) did the perpetrators do it? What did they get? Where are they now?

2. Laws and penalties for computer crimes vary from state to state. Some states have very specific and very strict laws; others attempt to apply existing laws to computer crimes. Find out about the laws regarding computer crime and the privacy of computerized data that have been enacted or are under consideration in your state. When were they passed, what do they say, and what are the possible penalties? If your state has no specific law on computer crime, should it, or is the current arrangement sufficient? Finally, find out if any computer crimes have been committed in your state.

3. Talk with the appropriate official in your school's computer center or in a local company. How is the system safeguarded against unauthorized access? Find out if there have ever been any successful attempts to gain access. What was done to prevent future penetration of the system?

4. Perform an ergonomic study of places in which VDTs are in use in your school, library, offices, or home. Determine, as best you can, whether or not the work areas comply with the NIOSH recommendations. If they don't, find out (by visiting an office supply store or writing to an office furniture dealer) how much it would cost to improve the conditions.

5. Security analyst Donn B. Parker led a workshop on Ethics and Values in Science and Technology for the National Science Foundation. Computer professionals, lawyers, and experts in ethical philosophy took part. The following are based on some of the scenarios they discussed, as taken from Parker, *Fighting Computer Crime* (New York: Charles Scribner's Sons, 1983), pp. 196–226. Consider the various ethical issues raised in each, and formulate your own code of professional standards to address the issues. Prepare a report on the issues, their complications, and your solutions.

   - A university's director of computer services announces that any student who can manage to illegally access the system will be given a reward. There are hundreds of attempts made, and all fail. One student, however, succeeds, and reports the security breach to the director. While he is given his reward, nothing is done to correct the security flaw. The student continues to use it to access the system.

   - An executive in computer service firm A resigns to work as a private consultant. He takes with him the password to the firm's large computer system. When he returns to A to offer his consulting services (to find security flaws in the computer system) he is turned down and told that the system is secure. He uses the password to access A's system by telephone and extracts copies of sensitive client data. The consultant plans to use the data as evidence that A does in fact need his help. Turned down again, he sells the password to computer service firm B and the data to the competitors of A's clients.

   - The manager of a computer operations department of a large company handles data preparation and entry, system security, and report generation. The top executives are engaged in a massive fraud against stockholders and investors, inflating the company's reported assets to cover up improper financial activities such as illegal investments and embezzlement. Evidence of the fraud is in the computer's data files, and the manager is aware of the existence of the fraud. She carefully avoids being exposed to its details, however, and just carries out orders and does nothing.

   - A computer scientist at a struggling university develops a system that can carry on convincing conversations with people for extended periods of time. She unveils the computer to the news media, and gives a lengthy press conference to detail the mechanics of her revolutionary device. She asks the reporters to let her review their reports for accuracy before publication, but they refuse and the stories are wildly inaccurate, sensational, and distorted. The publicity, however, brings the university much-needed prestige and lucrative research contracts, and the scientist enjoys lavish speaking engagements, television appearances, and honors. Although her articles in technical journals are strictly accurate, she never attempts to publicly correct the misleading popular reports.

23

The Next Twenty Years

▶

FOCUS ON . . . HAZARDOUS-DUTY ROBOTS

A new breed of robots is being devised in laboratories around the world to tackle hazardous chores such as cleaning up nuclear power plants and chiseling rock deep inside coal mines.

The aim: to come up with "steel collar" workers that can either perform chores quicker than their human counterparts—or handle dangerous duties that people won't carry out at all.

Until recently, robots have been primarily confined to the factory floor. There they haven't been much more than mechanical arms, carrying out simple repetitive tasks in a predictable environment.

But the new generation of machines would be fitted with rudimentary sensory and intelligence capabilities, allowing them to adapt and react to their environment to some degree. This would open a host of new jobs they could do in factories. It would also make them suitable outside the manufacturing plant.

Getting robots to replace hard-hat workers won't be easy, though, nor in most cases is such change likely to come soon. For one thing, the machines will have to be mobile. This requires complex technologies—for instance, sensors that will allow them to dodge obstacles. As yet, virtually no robot can open a door. They will also have to be rugged: Consider what dust and rocks could do to a robot in a mine alone.

Nevertheless, efforts are under way in Japan and the United States to develop machines for a host of dangerous duties. Japan is spending $100 million over eight years to develop third-generation robots, some of which would carry out tasks in hostile environments, such as rescuing disaster victims or toiling deep under water.

One Japanese company has hatched a lumberjack robot fitted with a chain saw. British researchers have devised a robot that helps repair sewer pipes beneath city streets. Some U.S. police have used, with mixed success, remote-controlled robots to dispose of bombs.

Among other specialized areas where machines now—or someday might—stand in for man:

- *Nuclear power plants.* Japan has devised the most novel mechanical aid here: an experimental snakelike robot designed to inspect the remote areas of power plants. Dubbed the "elephant's nose," the seven-foot device has eight joints and is equipped with touch sensors and a tiny television at the tip. . . .

- *Mining.* Coal miners probably don't have to worry about stepping aside for smart robots for 5 to 10 years yet, if then. But one advance that might be applied to mining has recently come out of Carnegie-Mellon University. . . . In March, researchers tested an autonomous vehicle—a robot that propels itself—in a mine in the rumpled hills of western Pennsylvania. . . .

- *Construction.* The Japanese have developed prototype robots that help lay concrete, spray fireproofing material on steel girders, and bore tunnels. Relatively little construction robotics work has been done in the U.S. so far. But some experts think it will soon come.

Predicting the future isn't very difficult: just sit down and dream up some sleek, high-tech scenario out of a science fiction movie, and call it "A Look Ahead" or even "The Next Twenty Years." On the other hand, it's much harder to predict the future *correctly*. A world exposition in the early part of this century tried predicting life in the 1960s and came up with four-mile-high skyscrapers, with businesspeople ferried between them in biplanes and gliders. In the early 1950s, another prophetic exposition foresaw cities full of moving sidewalks, wheelless cars that floated above the streets on a cushion of air, and buildings that looked more like plumbing fixtures than architectural structures—all samples of what life would certainly be like in 1980. George Orwell and H. G. Wells made their predictions several decades ago; Arthur C. Clarke and Isaac Asimov do so today. And here we go again.

Of course, we can't predict the future with any certainty, and trying to predict the way people will live twenty years from now is a hopeless undertaking. After all, there are so many variables in effect besides technological innovation: political, economic, social, commercial, and artistic. What we can do is try to take a look ahead at what is *reasonably* likely to happen within a *reasonable* period of time. All through this book we've been considering today's technology. Here, we'll look at what today's developments seem to suggest for the near future, somewhere around the middle of the first decade of the next century. Don't look here for colonies on Jupiter or human-looking robots running for President; rather, you'll see what changes your home, or your children's home, may undergo during the course of the next two decades. We'll discuss artificial intelligence, advanced robotics, and the fifth generation, but we'll also talk about newspapers and cars and work. In short, what we're looking for here is the *real* future, the possible future, the future whose foundation we're building today.

Before we look at some ways computers will change our lives, let's look at how the machines themselves will be changing over the next twenty years.

ARTIFICIAL INTELLIGENCE

For application after application, we've seen how difficult it is to distinguish what computers produce from what humans produce. And we've learned that all any

Computer simulation of human intelligence

computer really does is a very long and highly branched sequence of operations on binary numbers. Nonetheless, despite all that we know, the results can be astonishing. If computers can so accurately perform basic humanlike operations, from calculation to welding, are there any limitations to their ability to simulate the products and processes of human intelligence? This is the question pursued by researchers in a field called **artificial intelligence (AI)**. Two approaches have characterized this 20-year-old field. One is to imitate human thought processes as closely as possible in the hope of producing intelligent results; the other is to try, by whatever means, to produce those results.

But where, exactly, is the dividing line between a machine that simply does what a program specifies and one that very clearly demonstrates those qualities we associate with intelligence? Debate rages over whether or not machines are capable of crossing that line. The British mathematician Alan Turing, who made lasting contributions to theoretical computer science, suggested a neat answer to this question. He proposed that a human submit typed questions to a computer and to another human, both unseen by the questioner. The human's responses would be typed back in such a way as to most convincingly demonstrate his or her human identity, while the computer would be programmed to do as convincing a job as possible of answering as a human would. Turing said that the machine would demonstrate intelligence if the questioner had a 50:50 chance of guessing the identities of the two respondents incorrectly, that is, of being fooled by the computer half the time. Think about the complexity of the program: for a chess-playing computer to "converse" about chess is quite an achievement; for a computer to be able to chat in an unstructured, humanlike way about recent movies, favorite restaurants, quantum physics, and its best bowling score is an almost unimaginable programming feat.

Alan Turing's test

Knowledge-Based Systems

We are confronted every day with decisions that must be made without the benefit of precise mathematical algorithms:

> "Do I have a cold or is my allergy acting up?"
>
> "Is that my bus coming?"
>
> "Should I put my money in a savings account or a money market, or spend it all on software?"

We apply experience and intuition to such problems, perhaps of greater or lesser importance, many times each day. We may seek the advice of experts about the more important ones; but, although we feel our decisions are better for having their advice and we often act on it, we don't expect it to be absolutely correct all of the time. This is true for a wide range of problems, from medical diagnosis and financial advice to deciding where to drill for oil. Computers involved in artificial intelligence research often employ heuristic algorithms to simulate human thought processes. **Heuristic algorithms**, like humans, employ intuition and common sense to solve problems. They don't necessarily produce perfect solutions, or even the best possible ones. Rather, these algorithms rely on strategies that select good or adequate solutions from a huge, unwieldy set of possibilities.

Just as we don't expect a physician to make a diagnosis without adequate knowledge of symptoms, treatments, and cures—a specific decision environment called *domain knowledge*—we can't expect a computer to be of help in problem solving unless a similarly adequate knowledge base is available. And such a knowledge base, unlike the conventional data bases we've discussed previously in this book, must include diverse kinds of knowledge, for example, knowledge about objects and processes, about goals and actions, and about cause-and-effect relationships. Such knowledge will often involve intuition or common sense, judgment which is, in general, difficult to represent in a satisfactory way in a computer system. For this reason, researchers in AI are deeply concerned with the subject of *knowledge representation* as it pertains to **knowledge-based systems**, which are attempts to program computers to make deductions from a stored base of facts and experience, rather than to execute a precise algorithm that is mathematically guaranteed to solve a problem.

Systems that simulate intuition and common sense

AI researchers are also concerned with the closely related questions of how to manipulate stored knowledge: how to draw inferences, how to deal with incomplete knowledge, and how to extract the knowledge of human experts to set up a knowledge base. The programming language that most AI researchers currently prefer to use in dealing with such questions is called PROLOG. Using PROLOG, one can express both information and rules for making inferences based on the information. The information that John likes Mary, for example, is represented as

PROLOG's rules for making inferences

$$\texttt{likes(John, Mary)}$$

The information that Mary is very popular can be expressed as

$$\texttt{likes(y, Mary)}$$

where y is anyone. Rules in PROLOG have the form

$$P_1 \text{ if } (P_2 \text{ and } P_3 \text{ and } P_4)$$

where P_1, P_2, P_3, and P_4 are items of information, such as that John likes Mary. If we want to state the rule that children like their mothers, we first express that z is the mother of y by writing

$$\texttt{mother(z, y)}$$

Then we write the rule

$$\texttt{likes(y, z) if mother(z, y)}$$

The rule that John likes anyone who likes him is written

$$\texttt{likes(John, x) if likes(x, John)}$$

where x is anyone.

PROLOG can be used to determine new inferences from given information and rules or to verify if some assumption is consistent with a given set of rules and facts. It has been used to develop many expert systems.

Expert Systems

Expert systems are frameworks that allow for the incorporation and organization of the knowledge of human experts in specific subject areas. They are used much like human experts are—to render assistance in fields as diverse as medicine and

Figure 23.1 CADUCEUS
Interactive expert systems use a series of questions to solve problems. Here, two doctors use the CADUCEUS medical expert system to help them quickly diagnose a patient's illness.

Rules and relationships applied to specific subject areas

mineral prospecting. Such systems are beginning to emerge from academic research centers into the commercial software marketplace. As they do, AI researchers have found that it is frequently more important to amass a sufficiently large knowledge base than to discover and incorporate more complex rules and relationships. This finding has led to a recognition of the real importance of human experts in developing expert systems. First, there must be reasonable agreement about who is and who isn't an expert. Second, the experts must be able to communicate their decision methods and the knowledge on which those decisions are based.

Furthermore, many investigators have found that systems using only simple PROLOG-type rules for making inferences don't necessarily produce the best results. When empirical information, acquired from the experience of experts, is the only information available, basing a system on such rules is a useful and practical alternative. However, when causal or functional relationships are known, their inclusion will improve the results. In Chapter 20, we mentioned three expert systems currently used in medical diagnosis: MYCIN and PUFF, which deal with relatively narrow areas of knowledge about specific diseases, and CADUCEUS. CADUCEUS achieves its great generality (it can deal with about 500 diseases) by incorporating some knowledge beyond empirical rules: it uses a model of the human body and the relationships between its organs to construct inferences. It also makes inferences on the basis of the timing of symptoms as a disease progresses. CADUCEUS, like many expert systems, is interactive; that is, the user works with the system actively to solve a problem through a series of questions, the answers to which lead to further questions, and ultimately to a solution. A physician communicates with CADUCEUS using a special vocabulary, as shown in Figure 23.1.

The rapidly growing list of areas in which expert systems are already available includes electronic circuit design, mineral prospecting, chemical analysis, computer system configuring, robotics, and, naturally, the design of expert systems. Later, when we discuss the Japanese fifth generation computer project, we'll consider the powerful hardware that expert systems require for their operation. First, we'll continue our discussion of AI by considering researchers' efforts to endow computers with the power of speech, sight, and the admirable human ability to master complex board games.

Chess

In Eastern European cities, subway riders on their way to work avidly read news-paper accounts of yesterday's chess matches with the same passionate concern many of us experience when we read about baseball or football games. For over a thousand years, chess has enjoyed a unique place among intellectual recreations, and almost since the beginning of AI research, it has been one arena where results can readily be measured against human performance. These results clearly dem-onstrate both the progress that has been made in developing artificial intelligence and the distance yet to go.

The classic test of progress in artificial intelligence

The numerous chess-playing programs, past and present, have at one time or another used all the AI techniques: heuristic and nonheuristic algorithms, knowl-edge bases containing move-by-move example games, and learning schemes that improve the program's play on the basis of both winning and losing experience. The complexity and variety of the possible moves make chess particularly challeng-ing for programmers. Figure 23.2 will give you an idea of exactly how challenging chess is by examining a much simpler game's programming structure.

Among the techniques used to develop good to excellent chess-playing programs are combinations of knowledge bases, including stored actual games (to avoid moves that have previously resulted in losses and encourage those that pro-duce wins); heuristic algorithms that apply numerical scores to board positions and produce good, if not optimal, moves; and schemes for projecting a few plays ahead (to avoid making moves that can lead to vulnerable positions).

How good are chess programs? The best of them, running on supercomputers, play very respectable games. The United States Chess Federation groups players

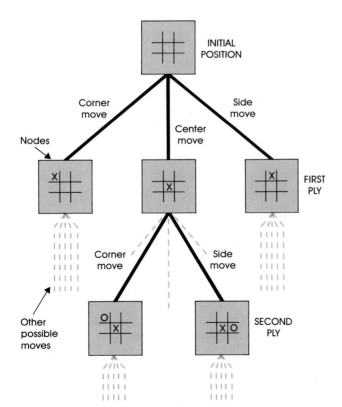

Figure 23.2 Game Tree for Tic-Tac-Toe

Many games are best represented for com-puters as treelike data structures. The set of game positions that can result from the pos-sible moves at a turn is called a *ply*. The branches of the tree are the moves, and the leaves (called *nodes*) are the resulting game positions. The game tree for tic-tac-toe can't be any deeper than 9 plies (since there are only nine squares in the game), and cover-ing the 3 basic moves (corner, center, and side) brings the total number of possible game positions to about 300. This number of alternatives can be easily searched by a program to select the move at each turn that will lead to a win or a draw. It isn't that easy with chess, however. An average game between good players involves about 45 moves for each, or 90 plies. For each posi-tion on the board, there are an average of 35 possible moves, which means that the bottom ply of the game tree for chess con-tains 35^{90} nodes—a number of alternatives far too large for any current computer to consider in a reasonable amount of time.

into categories, with point ranges for each category. International grand masters, the top category, range from 2600 to 2800 points. International masters range from 2300 to 2600 points, American masters from 2100 to 2300, expert players from 1900 to 2100, and average to strong amateurs from 1400 to 1800. The best chess programs have just broken into the American master range. And it seems that not only can some computers play chess better than many humans, they are increasingly able to talk about it, too.

Speech

Speaking to machines

Artificial intelligence is concerned with other things besides simulating the results of the "processing" function of the human brain, such as game playing or problem solving. AI research has, since its inception, been equally active in trying to achieve more natural human communication with computers. The recognition of speech by machines remains a high-priority objective for computer scientists in this field.

Although unquestioned progress has been made and some machines can be directed by humans using restricted vocabularies and speaking with special emphasis (see the sections on voice input and voice output in Chapters 4 and 6, respectively), the goal of a machine that accepts and transcribes natural speech remains distant.

When you speak into a telephone, your voice causes a diaphragm to vibrate. This produces a corresponding variation in an electric current, that is, an analog waveform. At the receiving end, the current flows through an electromagnet; as the strength of this magnet varies with the magnitude of the current, so does its attraction for a steel diaphragm, which vibrates accordingly to produce sound.

Many developments have resulted from the digital revolution in telephone communications. Transforming speech into binary digits rather than just analog waveforms made many new functions possible. Speech may be more readily "compressed" to reduce the storage space required for messages, and improved security is made possible through encryption. Vocalized words and phrases that have been stored are readily manipulated by computers to produce the familiar recorded messages, from time-and-temperature reports to directory assistance, talking registers in grocery stores, and chatty Coke machines. Spoken messages can be stored and forwarded at a time specified by the caller. These and many other now-routine digital speech-processing functions have also helped pave the way for AI investigators working on the automatic recognition and understanding of speech.

As we've noted, considerable progress has been made in getting computers to recognize special vocabularies of isolated words. As their label implies, these are words that are surrounded by pauses or intervals of silence. The computer is thus not faced with the formidable job of distinguishing the individual words among the continuously spoken phrases of normal speech. No computer will be able to do that in the near future unless progress takes place at an unforeseen rate. However, even computers' current capability with isolated words is producing a growing

Applying speech recognition

number of significant applications. For example, an existing limited-vocabulary system permits physicians to call in 24 hours a day to match organs with transplant recipients. Executive telephone terminals that can, via speaker phones, respond to a set of voice commands such as "Call Henry" or "Call Dad" have been developed. It is unclear, however, whether there is any market for such devices. Of more commercial interest, perhaps, are the automated airline information and reservation systems currently being researched, which would allow individuals to plan and schedule their trips over the phone or at automated ticket centers set up in shopping malls.

Vision and Advanced Robotics

In Chapter 18, we discussed the current generation of industrial robots, almost all of which are insensate; that is, the locations of all components and subassemblies must be controlled very accurately so that the "blind" robots can find them exactly where they're supposed to be. This requirement can add considerably to the cost of industrial automation. More than 20 years ago, AI scientists began research aimed at producing more flexible robots that could sense important aspects of their environment. As a result of this work, a few robots with limited vision and tactile feedback to their computer controls have made their commercial debut. These sensor-based robots are at the center of much of the excitement and promise of the next generation of robots, promising to revolutionize not only manufacturing, but space exploration, undersea mining, and the development of entirely new classes of prosthetic devices.

Robots that sense their environment

A welding robot being tested at General Electric's Evandale, Ohio, aircraft engine plant, welds together the curved edges of two steel plates. A vision subsystem consisting of a laser illumination source and a video camera monitors the position of the path to be welded, feeds out the proper amount of welding wire, and controls the welding torch. In robot systems such as this, the vision subsystem is necessary because the pieces being worked on are large and heavy, and consequently difficult to position accurately. The robot must be able to make the required adjustments and also to execute different welding paths for pieces of different shapes. The General Electric robot does high-quality work at speeds about twice those of an average human operator, using image-processing techniques such as those described in Chapter 20.

While moving ahead rapidly in the automation of work done with heavy pieces in difficult environments, robotics has been making very slow progress in jobs of light assembly, jobs such as those done in electronics manufacturing, where the most important requirements are speed and dexterity. Meaningful robot penetration into this area can only result if there is substantial simultaneous progress in the development of more sophisticated and less costly manipulators, vision sensors, and controls.

The Fifth Generation

In 1980 and 1981, Japan announced two major national objectives: first, to develop a supercomputer greatly more powerful than any yet built; second (and perhaps more significant), to create an entirely new type of machine, based on AI principles, that would excel at reasoning, that is, at making inferences. The latter type of machine, dubbed the **fifth generation** of computers, would handle problems difficult or impossible for conventional, numerically oriented machines and also would be very simple to program and communicate with.

The AI-based machine, the fifth generation, is our main focus here, but let's first digress briefly to clear up some confusion about Japan's two objectives that

Supercomputers and intelligent machines

occurs in the popular media (and even occasionally in the computer trade press). The first project, to develop enhanced supercomputers, concerns the use of numerically oriented machines to tackle complex scientific problems. Two such supercomputers, built by Fujitsu and Hitachi, were delivered in 1984, and seem to be comparable in computing power to machines currently built by U.S. companies. However, the Fujitsu and Hitachi machines are IBM-compatible (they can run programs written for IBM computers); the Cray and CDC machines built in the United States are not. It's unlikely that IBM will sit by and watch competitors, whether foreign or domestic, offer its customers compatible systems that might be more cost-effective, megaflop for megaflop. Thus the Japanese entry will almost certainly bring IBM back into the supercomputer competition after more than 20 years on the sidelines.

Goals for upcoming Japanese and U.S. supercomputers are roughly comparable, and there is no reason for alarm that the United States has "lost out" to Japan. In fact, real competition has developed quite suddenly in a field that from its beginning was dominated by U.S. machines.

Goals of the fifth generation project

Now let's get back to the business of this section: the fifth generation. The Japanese fifth generation project is predicated on major progress in every significant area of computer science—from VLSI circuit design and manufacture to system architecture, from higher-level programming languages to software design. The schedule calls for some sort of working system by the late 1990s. At first glance, the proposed system might appear to represent a mere juxtaposition of every new concept in computing—and there are those who think this is at least partially true. The project calls for the development of a new inference and knowledge-based programming language called Fifth Generation Kernel Language, or FGKL, which will extend the knowledge processing and AI capabilities of PROLOG. A language called FGKRL, for Fifth Generation Knowledge Representation Language, will manipulate data in the knowledge base which is to be a relational data base (see Chapter 13). Early versions of this fifth generation machine will contain 1000 processors operating simultaneously, with later versions incorporating more advanced architectural techniques. Memory size will be on the order of 100 billion bytes, and the overall rate of instruction processing will be approximately 1 trillion instructions per second. Applications of the fifth generation machine are expected to reach into all aspects of society: from the planning of resource use to science, medicine, manufacturing, and office automation.

Response to the Japanese project has been worldwide. Great Britain, France, the Soviet Union, and Germany have all felt compelled to accelerate their own AI research. In the United States, the Defense Advanced Research Projects Agency (DARPA) initiated its Strategic Computing and Survivability (SCS) Program in 1983 to develop a new generation of intelligent machines that will have humanlike capabilities to assess, reason, plan, and even supervise the actions of military systems in the field (and we saw in Chapter 21 the necessity of new computer technology to the Strategic Defense Initiative). The budgets of the DARPA and the Japanese projects are both set at about $500 million over five years. These sums are certainly very large, but when viewed from the perspective of IBM's *annual* research expenditure of $3 billion, the likelihood that these national efforts will dominate the future computing scene seems smaller.

Although AI is certainly an important field, it isn't exactly the mainstream of computing. Rather, it is an intellectually exciting and portentous area of research that will undoubtedly produce a significant share of the developments and debates within the computing world well into the next century. Now, though, let's consider a few of the day-to-day changes the near future will bring.

THE COMPUTER EXPLOSION

From the beginning of the world until 1980 or so, there were maybe a million computers. Since then, more than that have been sold every year—some 20,000 Apple units alone have been delivered each month. By the end of this decade, computers may be selling at the rate of nearly 11 million a year. According to a 1984 study by the U.S. Commerce Department, worldwide sales of software alone could reach $55 billion by 1987—representing a 30% *annual* increase since 1983. International Data Corporation estimates that there will be 400 million computers in the United States by the turn of the century. Despite periodic setbacks (in a single week early in 1985, IBM ended production of the failed PCjr, Apple temporarily closed down its Macintosh production facilities due to massive overstocks, and Wang also declared a one-month halt in production), growing sales and expanding markets seem inevitable.

A boom in sales and use

That optimistic view is a matter of simple economics: as the price of something desirable gets lower, the volume of its sales increases as the number of people who can afford it becomes larger. The computer industry's costs are dropping rapidly: in 1982, a 64K chip wholesaled for $10; by 1985, its price was less than $2. And the savings are, as they say, passed on to the consumer.

A hand-held computer cost over $150 in 1980, about $75 in 1985, and will cost about $20 in 1990. By then, a tiny but powerful programmable computer, costing less than a clock-radio, could be connected to equally inexpensive peripherals to form the core of a home computer system. With such a system, less expensive than the average stereo-television console of today, cable TV subscribers could access their bank's electronic banking service to pay bills, make rent or mortgage payments, make deposits and withdrawals, or secure loans. Users could "thumb through" store catalogs on their video monitor, order items and arrange deliveries, even "window shop" whole malls to make price comparisons, to search out special sales, or to look for gift ideas. Newspapers, magazines, sports scores, and financial news could all be accessed directly from the average middle-class living room.

THE IMPACT ON DAILY LIFE

This isn't just idle conjecture. New York's Citibank plans to have more than half its 2.5 million account-holders on-line by 1995. Major retail chains like J. C. Penney's are experimenting with at-home shopping systems, and computer-based news, sports, and entertainment services such as QUBE and Teletext are already available. A shopping mall near Washington, D.C., offers shoppers a "window shopping" service accessible through a modem. The service lists sales and specials in a store-by-store index. Users can call up price comparisons of particular items, place orders, and request gift suggestions for women, men, children, pets, older relatives, secretaries, or a variety of other recipient categories.

Trends that will shape the future

The wide availability of inexpensive computers could have a dramatic impact on our society. Sociologists once worried about the American culture becoming rootless and too mobile; the personal computer might well bring everyone back home. It isn't unreasonable to suggest that 10 million people may be telecommuting full-time from their homes by the turn of the century, and that another 25 million could be telecommuting half of each week and spending the other half in the office. Men and women could pursue domestic and professional careers simultaneously; parents could spend more time with their children. Working and playing together more may very well produce new stresses in family life, but with computers completely taking over some mundane and repetitive household chores and expediting many others, there will be increased time to work things out.

Don't be surprised to find future store shelves stocked with smart blow-dryers, toasters, and toothbrushes (which may remind you to brush up and down rather than from side to side or warn you of impending cavities while simultaneously scheduling your next appointment with the dentist). Don't laugh: a few years ago, it would have been silly to suggest that microprocessors could be put in greeting cards to sing happy birthday or Christmas carols, but it happened in 1983.

It's now undeniable that computers are going to become increasingly embedded in the least computer-like aspects of our day-to-day existence. We've mentioned many of the applications we'll be looking at here in previous chapters, and many of these systems and devices have been recently introduced. But numbers are the important thing in constructing any adequate view of the future. As the number of users grows, and as access to these applications becomes virtually unlimited, these now-isolated examples will cease to be merely interesting anecdotes or conveniences for a privileged few. It's at that point, when navigation systems in cars and computers that run whole households have become as common as pocket calculators or telephones, that our look at the future begins.

At Home

Computer-based systems for the home

Computer-based systems that "run" certain household functions, such as General Electric's remote-controlled HomeMinder system (Figure 23.3), are currently avail-

(a)

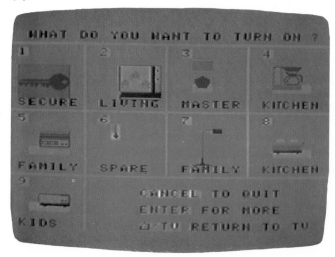

Figure 23.3 Today's Computer-Based House

General Electric's HomeMinder system is the latest step toward computerized housekeeping, turning the home's electrical wiring into a computer-controlled network. (a) The family television serves as the central command point, displaying HomeMinder's functions and locations around the house. (b) At the left, the adaptor wall plugs that link appliances and the computer (center). On the right, the hand-held keypad onto which commands are entered.

(b)

able. Heating, air-conditioning, lights, stereos, VCRs, and kitchen appliances can be monitored, controlled, and timed by the computer to ensure safe, convenient, and energy-efficient operation. Not only do such systems lower utility bills, but their vigilance also reduces the hazards of fire or explosion. Sensor devices at doors and windows, activated by unauthorized pressure or the breaking of a beam of light, can alert the local police station of a break-in, while at the same time sounding a general alarm.

In future homes, terminals could be built into the kitchen (for controlling appliances, storing recipe files, planning nutritionally balanced meals, ordering groceries, and keeping a busy family's activities organized), in the family room (for playing games, monitoring news, sports, and entertainment networks, and printing out publications and correspondence), in the study (for telecommuting, working on budgeting and finances, and word processing), and in children's rooms (for homework and recreational programming). It is unlikely, on the other hand, that domestic robots will be anything but a novelty until well into the twenty-first century.

Appliance manufacturers have already started creating the automated home. Microprocessors are found in dishwashers, food processors, washing machines, dryers, color televisions, and microwave ovens. A new refrigerator by Whirlpool adjusts its interior temperature when food is added or the kitchen warms up, and General Electric's 24E refrigerator boasts "brilliant little microchip computers" that beep if the door is left open (and probably ensure that the light goes out inside). Dryers containing moisture sensors that end the cycle when the clothes are dry and dishwashers that alert users when the drain is clogged and can display specific mechanical failures requiring a service call are currently available as top-of-the-line models. A more mundane application in widespread use is the embedding of microprocessors to control appliances' mechanical parts to increase their efficient use of energy. In the developmental stages are microwave ovens that respond to voice commands and washing machines that sense how dirty the clothes are and measure the precise amount of detergent needed to clean them.

As part of an automated home, such appliances could dramatically streamline household chores and routines. Imagine that it's the middle of a cold winter 15 years from now. You order groceries using your personal computer, and they're delivered to your home (delivery is inexpensive, since home shopping has eliminated many of the costs of maintaining attractive, service-oriented supermarkets, which have given way to low-cost, mechanized warehouses). When you place an order, the store's computer enters the items' bar code data into your personal computer via microwave transmissions received by the dish antenna on your roof (see Figure 23.4). Billing and payment are also of course done through your home computer.

The bar code contains not only price and inventory data, but also cooking instructions for frozen and packaged foods. You read the OCR code number from a gourmet frozen dinner to your microwave oven in order to call up the instructions, pop the dinner in, say "defrost," and the oven sets the correct time and temperature. If you feel more ambitious, you can put a duck in your gas-microwave oven, announce the product code, and work at your word processor while the duck is microwaved to perfection, then gas-flamed to a crispy brown. When cooking is complete, the oven gently tells you so. If you prefer a more exotic recipe than that included in the product code, you can simply replace it with the appropriate code from your personal computer's recipe file. You'll still have to peel potatoes, but a large part of the work of cooking will be done for you.

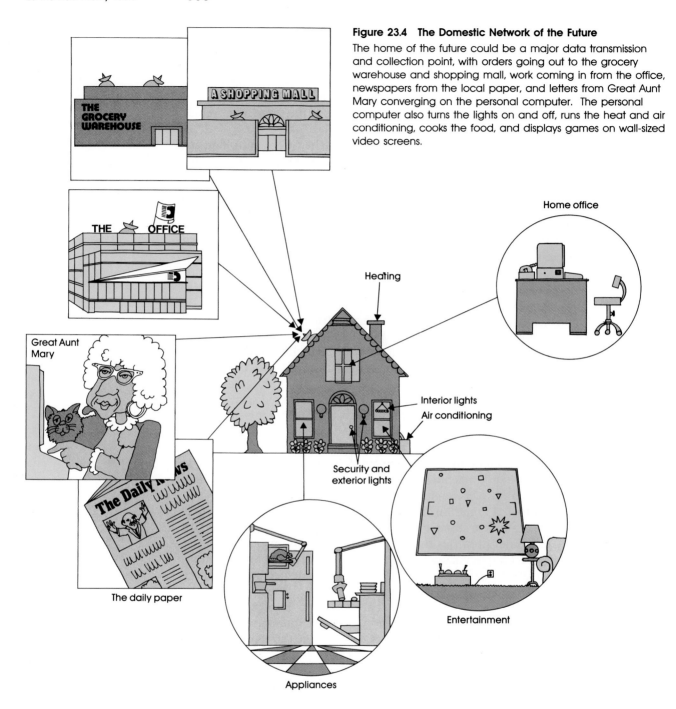

Figure 23.4   The Domestic Network of the Future
The home of the future could be a major data transmission and collection point, with orders going out to the grocery warehouse and shopping mall, work coming in from the office, newspapers from the local paper, and letters from Great Aunt Mary converging on the personal computer. The personal computer also turns the lights on and off, runs the heat and air conditioning, cooks the food, and displays games on wall-sized video screens.

After dinner, while you and your friends relax, a small robot arm in the kitchen looks at the dirty dishes you've stacked on the counter and loads them into the dishwasher. Then it sprays the countertop with cleaning fluid and wipes it dry. This was one of the first domestic applications of industrial robotics, and your friends already call you old-fashioned because you don't have similar robots for putting food in the oven and cleaning the bathroom. You do have a new computerized video system that lets you put yourself into the movies you watch on your wall-sized television (so *you* can say "Play it again, Sam"). Your personal computer is a master chess player and not bad at Trivial Pursuit. Optical sensors brighten or dim the panels of your ceiling lights depending on how much light is coming in the window, where in the room you're sitting, and what you're doing— providing more light for reading, dimmer and less direct light for word processing, and a soft amber glow first thing in the morning.

In Newspapers

The spread of computers in the home will most likely not cause the demise of the newspaper, despite videotext systems. It's more likely that newspapers will change, but not disappear. Classified ads and stock market prices will probably be available in a videotext version of *The New York Times* or *Chicago Tribune,* as paper becomes more costly and computer-accessed versions more popular with their sub-scribers. The telephone didn't eliminate letter-writing, and there is a similar charm and convenience to reading a newspaper that simply isn't matched by watching words slide up a screen. Some information is well suited to being accessed with computer (classified advertisements, stock quotations, sports scores, personals, as-it-happens wire service links). However, as the several videotext services that folded in 1985 discovered, specialized data services may be popular with profes-sionals, but long articles and soft features aren't necessarily attractive as on-line items.

Reader-edited newspapers

As a result of the proliferation of inexpensive, high-quality printers, however, it is certainly possible that newsstands and delivery people will become outmoded. The daily newspaper may be printed out in each subscriber's home. An option that will probably be available to newspaper readers in the future is selectivity. If you are accessing the newspaper via your computer, there is no reason for you to print out anything but what you want to read. By the turn of the century, it's likely that newspaper subscribers in major cities will be constructing their own versions of the local daily. Based on an initial table of contents, they could either have the whole paper printed up (in an $8\frac{1}{2}$-by-11 format, of course) or select the most appealing articles (from their headlines), favorite comic strips, and best columnists (see Figure 23.5). In a busy, time-pressed society, such personally tailored papers could be-come highly popular, actually increasing the circulation, of at least some parts of a paper. As more and more people come to own personal computers, on-line news-papers will be taken for granted.

On (and Off) the Road

When you leave your home in the not-so-distant future, driving may be a lot easier. Today, microprocessors scan a car's major systems and alert the driver to problems as they develop (as we saw in Chapter 16). Automobile manufacturers plan to expand their applications of computers and are already testing systems that not only monitor interior temperature shifts and adjust the heat or air conditioning accordingly, but also operate defrosters, demisters, and windshield wipers. The prototype Buick Questor (see Figure 23.6) periodically projects speed, mileage, and engine data onto the windshield in the driver's line of sight. Other automotive systems in development include an automatic transmission controlled by touch-sensitive spots on the steering wheel and voice-activated ignition systems, door locks, trunk and hood latches, and lights. The latter systems will increase both convenience and security—the days of lost or locked-in keys will end, and voice-print security systems will ensure against theft.

Smart cars

```
           SAN DIEGO UNION  ***    April 2, 2006      Final

            --- On-Line "SelectNews" Subscriber Menu ---

   *** The UNION and VOX Data Entry Systems now
       offer "SelectNews" subscribers a voice input
       option. See AdPage 1 for details.

   *** Please Note: Weekender magazine will be
   transmitted in four colors starting this Sunday.
   Subscribers with three-color printers will not be
   affected.

                        Output Options
   [A]   MONITOR ONLY
   [B]   PRE-PRINT MONITOR REVIEW & EDIT OPTION
   [C]   PRINTER ONLY

   >>   C
```

```
                     Printer Only Options

   [P] PRINT PER PROGRAM
   [A] PRINT ALL SECTIONS
   [B] PRINT SECTION 1 (NEWS) + ADPAGES ONLY
   [C] PRINT SECTION 2 (SPORTS/FEATURES) + ADPAGES
   ONLY
   [D] PRINT SECTION 3 (BUSINESS/CLASSIFIEDS)
   + ADPAGES ONLY
   [E] PRINT "SELF-EDIT" SELECTIONS + ADPAGES ONLY

   >>   E              "Self-Edit" Headline Menu

   *** PAGE 1   X = PRINT

   President to Ride Next Space Shuttle Mission—X
   King Charles Plans San Diego Visit—
   Giant Insects Threaten Wheat Harvest—X
   New User Tax on PC's Passed by House—X
   TV Star Denies Charges, Sues Paper—
   Mr. Silicon to be Crowned at Pageant Tonight—X
   Weather Round-Up—X

   XX to CONTINUE XX
```

Figure 23.5 The Self-Edited Newspaper

You get home from work and are informed by your desktop terminal that the daily paper is ready for "delivery" to your printer. A menu like the one shown here appears on the screen. If you don't want to be bothered with making selections, you can leave instructions to have the whole paper printed by the time you get home.

Other systems being developed include obstacle-detecting radar connected to computer-controlled brakes and electronic navigation systems. One such system, called the Navigator, can generate street maps of all major cities in the United States. Provided with the car's current location and destination, the Navigator can chart the best course, illustrate the car's location on it at all times, and detect wrong turns. If tied into the computer systems of local traffic control and emergency authorities, such navigating devices could keep drivers updated on road and traffic conditions and could alter suggested routes to avoid traffic jams, icy patches, or construction. Drivers could also override the normal selection criteria by request-

Figure 23.6   The Buick Questor
(a) Buick's prototype car of the future, the Questor, is equipped with all of today's high-tech options, from electronic engine and monitoring systems to pushbutton controls centered on the steering wheel (b). (c) The Questor's Navigation Center generates street maps and finds the best route from here to there.

ing scenic drives in the autumn or sight-seeing routes in historic cities. General Motors will offer the Navigator as an option (costing about $1400) on several of its 1987 models, and Honda is also planning to introduce a similar system. Chrysler's experimental navigation system, called Class, uses signals from navigation satellites to compute the car's location and stores maps on a digital laser disk.

For longer trips, you might someday take a train that runs by **magnetic levitation** (or **maglev**). Today, the world's fastest trains are the French TGV and the Japanese bullet train, or *skinkansen,* both of which depend on computers for navigation and control as they speed along at 125 miles per hour. Maglev trains, however, could leave them far behind. A system of charged electromagnets mounted on the rails and on the train provides a frictionless propulsion that can produce speeds of over 250 miles per hour while treating passengers to a silent, vibrationless ride. At such speeds, trackside signals and conventional controls are rendered obsolete: the signals would be blurs, and the operator's reaction times too slow to be effective. Instead, on-board computers will control speed, guidance, and the electrical current to the magnets to maintain the proper gap between rail and train. The maglev train's "engineer" will be a computer that monitors weather, position, and track conditions, operates acceleration and braking devices, and lowers the train gently onto the tracks at the station. All along the route, the train's computer will be constantly communicating with a central routing computer that will ensure that schedules are kept and safety requirements met. Experimental maglev systems are currently being developed in the United States, the Soviet

Magnetic levitation

Union, France, Germany, and Japan. Routes between Frankfurt and Paris and along the Boston–Washington, D.C. corridor are planned to be operational by 1990.

Computerized air traffic control

Computerized air traffic control has already been tested in several airports, resulting in a lower incidence of near-accidents. Computers on the ground, linked with computers in planes, combine with radar and sonar devices to keep track of where each plane is at all times and how fast it's flying. A human air traffic controller can watch only one flight closely at a time, but a computerized system can monitor all incoming flights essentially simultaneously. The increased use of computers to do those things in which human error is both possible and disastrous can free humans to exercise their professional judgment and to do other things that computers—for now at least—can't do.

At School

The classroom of tomorrow

The U.S. Department of Education estimates that one-third of U.S. schools have at least one computer, which means that two-thirds don't have any. Distribution of computers among schools *is* unequal. In some school districts in the rural South and in northern inner cities, for example, there are no computers at all. In Minnesota, however, 95% of students have access to instructional computers. The results of this inequity could be socially harmful over the next twenty years, making the future pretty bleak for some of today's grade schoolers. With the current public concern for raising educational standards, the increased willingness of parents to pay higher taxes or tuitions for better "service," and manufacturers' large-scale donations of computers to schools, the statistics recently show definite signs of improving.

Ten years ago, computers in schools were only found in the math labs of the most affluent high schools. Today, they're used in all areas of the curriculum, and they'll soon be just one more of the basics. Imagine, for example, a high school English class in the early twenty-first century. Because of the increased emphasis placed on teaching and the quality of education throughout the 1980s, the class is small and the room is technologically sophisticated. Half of the 12 students are in the back of the classroom, revising their essays at word processors. The machines make editing and revision so easy that the young writers are able to make a number of experimental drafts: moving sentences and paragraphs around to alter the chronology of the narrative, doing global search-and-replaces to change verb tenses or correct spelling errors, and doing dozens of other things that would have taken hours, even days, to do by hand, assuming they were done at all. The computers compensate for the patience most of us lack and help bring out the story-telling skills we all possess.

In the front of the classroom, most of the other students are watching a computer-based interactive video of a sequence from *Tom Sawyer*. After watching the whole presentation, the group can experiment with altering the story. At key points, a microprocessor stops the action, and the students can choose from a number of possible alternatives and then watch the resulting changes in the story line. As they "rewrite" Twain's novel, the students learn about narrative logic, characterization, and the consistent use of symbols, and can discover why the author made the decisions he did. Far from allowing them to avoid the substance of a novel, this type of exercise actually helps them more fully appreciate the book they are currently reading.

As three-quarters of the class use computers, a couple of students work in the library on an independent-study project, and a third discusses his grammar difficulties with the teacher, who has the time to devote nearly a full hour to a single student's problems. The next day, the word-processing and video groups switch places, and the rest of the week is spent in more traditional pursuits such as discussion, reports, and lectures. The effect of computers on the classroom will not be to turn everyone into typists, but to open up fascinating new discoveries for the students and to personalize, rather than mechanize, teaching.

In colleges and universities, computers are already important teaching and learning tools, and there is every reason to expect this importance to continue to increase dramatically in the near future. The growing acceptance of **courseware** (software programs developed specifically for use in particular classes) suggests that academics are becoming more inclined to accept the computer as a useful instructional tool. As we said in Chapter 20, more and more colleges are requiring (or at least encouraging) students to purchase personal computers, often offering grants, loans, or special prices from manufacturers (students at Dartmouth and other schools in a special consortium can pick up a Macintosh for about half its regular price). Many students, in fact, are buying their own computers before college, regardless of requirements. Most colleges (large and small) are increasing the numbers of microcomputers and computer facilities available to students. And the students are using them for a variety of courses, ranging from English to business. The result of all this will be not only the computerization of a college education but also the spread of computer ownership throughout our society.

Prestigious graduate business schools, such as those at Harvard, Stanford, and Carnegie-Mellon, are also increasingly aware of the present and future importance of computers to their students, who will use them every day to make important management decisions. Extensive programs are currently being developed to combine traditional business studies with computer modeling, decision-making computer "games," and computer networks. The networks will link various student "industrial groups" who will interact in complicated, long-term, simulated situations ranging from financial and tax problems to labor relations and the day-to-day operation of a multinational corporation. Such advanced learning tools offer students the chance to grasp basic concepts early, so they can devote the remainder of their time to learning how to cope with more complex and realistic situations. These current educational applications are preparing future businesspeople who will be both comfortable and creative with computer resources.

At the Office

A future day's work

The manager of the future is coaxed awake by her alarm clock, which also automatically triggers her shower, the coffee maker, and the toaster. In the study, the front page and business section of the morning paper start printing, followed by an agenda of the day's activities and a memo from the company's vice-president. After breakfast, she puts the dishes in the dishwasher and turns it on. The machine senses the weight and distribution of the dirty dishes and releases the precise amount of detergent required.

She gets into her car and tells its navigational computer the address of the downtown parking lot nearest her office. Because of a stalled car on the freeway, the computer charts the best alternate route through town, adjusting the car's speed to the timing of the city's computerized traffic light system. Arriving at her office building just on time, she announces her floor to the elevator, which takes her there, where she says good morning to the receptionist. Meanwhile, a voice-recognition device in her office senses her in the lobby and turns on the lights, adjusts the blinds, and activates the computer terminal on her desk, which immediately displays the vice-president's memo—just in case she hasn't read it yet.

Down the hall, the 3 operators in the word-processing room are already at work. This same room used to house 7 of the company's 15 typists; now it holds 3 operators and several laser printers, and twice the workload is handled in a fraction of the time it used to take. The machines print out clean copies quickly, with errors in spelling and grammar all corrected. Every two hours, each of the operators takes a 45-minute break in the gym, working through exercise routines designed by a computer to meet that individual's health needs. The computer monitors these sessions and prints out a daily report on calories burned, repetitions performed, and general progress over the past months. Other breaks are taken in the coffee room, but in either case productivity remains high. The other clerical personnel, as well as the managers, also take an exercise break during the day in addition to lunch. While they're out, their desktop computers work on compiling statistics, organizing data, or printing reports and correspondence.

The manager has to make several decisions based on data from a number of field offices. Her computer gathers the material, then produces five different practical alternatives for solving the problem. She selects one, and the computer shows her that it will have a slightly negative impact on the company's profits for the next five years but will broaden its base of customers and streamline production. She instructs the computer to print out the data in the form of colorful bar graphs, which she will incorporate into a presentation for the president.

The rest of her day's work involves reading the daily reports from the field offices, which she can just as easily do at home. By 2:30 in the afternoon, she's back in her own apartment, wearing comfortable clothes. As the daily reports come into her office via the Intelpost electronic mail network (set up in the early 1980s by the U.S. Postal Service), they are retransmitted to her personal computer. Her machine reads them aloud to her as she tidies the house and starts cooking the dinner she's planned for a little party that evening.

Clearly, not everyone's professional life will be as high-tech as this example, and there's no guarantee that all computer applications will be this humane—there's always the potential for isolation and overwork, for lower benefits and the exploitation of telecommuters (as we discussed in Chapter 22). But all the technology we've described exists to some degree in offices today. The only things missing are its unified application and the existence of the necessary complex networks. And as computers become less expensive, easier to use, and more vital to the successful operation of businesses, the more likely it is that they will become as much of an everyday fixture in most offices as a coffee machine is now. Once that happens, once computerized contact among clients, competitors, field workers, managers, and support staff is as easy and as accessible as it is via telephone now, an amazing variety of work schedules, office designs, and professional relationships will be possible. The end result for everyone will be a streamlined, more pleasant, more productive place to work, with the opportunity not only for advancement and success but for increased leisure time as well.

SUMMARY

Artificial Intelligence

Artificial intelligence is the computer simulation of human intelligence. The research in it includes the study of knowledge-based systems, which use inference rules to provide assistance in applications for which exact algorithms are not known or not computationally practical. Applications of knowledge-based systems to specific fields are called expert systems.

Knowledge-Based Systems Knowledge-based systems simulate the results of human intuition and common sense; knowledge representation is a key element. The computer language PROLOG is the basis of many current efforts to create rule-based systems.

Expert Systems Expert systems provide frameworks for the incorporation and organization of the knowledge of human experts about specific subject areas. Commercial systems exist in a growing number of fields, including medicine, circuit design, mineral prospecting, chemical analysis, and robotics.

Chess Chess programs have been the historic testing ground for progress in artificial intelligence, since they rely on knowledge bases and learning schemes. The best chess-playing programs currently play at the level of American masters.

Speech The understanding of human speech by machines is a principal goal of research in artificial intelligence. Developments were hastened by the representation of speech in digital form for telephone communications.

Vision and Advanced Robotics AI research is concerned with robots that can sense some aspects of their environment, principally through the use of vision subsystems. Such robots, now in the development stage, don't require the precise positioning of parts to do their tasks, making their application more flexible.

The Fifth Generation Japan's fifth generation project is an attempt to apply AI principles to develop a new type of computers manifesting new programming languages, architecture, and VLSI circuits. The Japanese effort has stimulated research activities in many other countries, including the United States.

The Computer Explosion

More computers have been sold every year since 1980 than were sold in the whole history of the world until then. As the cost of computers drops, their role as permanent, everyday fixtures in our lives increases dramatically.

The Impact on Daily Life

The future is approaching with surprising speed, as the growing numbers of personal computers and microprocessor applications have dramatic effects on our society.

At Home Microprocessors embedded in appliances are already a reality; linked into a home computer system, they'll help relieve domestic life of much of its drudgery. Computer-based systems such as GE's HomeMinder will use a central computer to control the lights, heat, air conditioning, and appliances and coordinate home entertainment, telecommuting, housekeeping, shopping, information, and correspondence functions.

In Newspapers A significant application of computers in the next two decades will be the advent of on-line newspapers: dailies offering subscribers a menu of the day's news, features, sports, and business articles, as well as classified ads. Computer owners will be able to select any or all of the features and either view them on a monitor or have them printed out.

On (and Off) the Road Cars of the future will feature a variety of computerized systems, including electronic navigation systems. Maglev trains will make extensive use of computers for safety, guidance, and other functions as they travel at high speeds. Computer-assisted air traffic control will further reduce accidents and near-misses.

At School Computers can provide students with opportunities to enhance their own skills and help in comprehending difficult concepts. Schools and colleges are already emphasizing computer study as an essential part of a student's training for the real world, producing a new generation of people who are comfortable and skilled with computer technology.

At the Office Computer technology can link the workplace and the home, blurring the distinctions between the two. Clerical work is faster and more efficient when computers are employed, and managers can benefit from extensive information regarding their business decisions. If used wisely, computers can make work more pleasant as well as faster and more efficient, resulting in healthier, more productive, and happier employees who have more leisure time.

COMPUTER CONCEPTS

As an extra review of the chapter, try defining the following terms. If you have trouble with any of them, refer to the page number listed.

artificial intelligence (AI) 656
heuristic algorithms 656
knowledge-based systems 657

expert systems 657
fifth generation 661

magnetic levitation (maglev) 669
courseware 671

REVIEW QUESTIONS

1. What was Alan Turing's proposed test for whether or not a computer system possessed intelligence?
2. What are the two different approaches taken by AI investigators?
3. What is the basic structure in the programming language PROLOG? Give an example. To what is this language applied?
4. Name four fields in which expert systems currently exist. In what new fields might you expect to see them applied? Why?
5. What is the importance of the game of chess to AI research?
6. Make a game tree for a simple game. (It should be a *very* simple game or you will learn first-hand about the proliferation of possible moves faced by chess programmers.)
7. How good are the best chess-playing programs today?
8. What has resulted from the digital revolution in telephone communications?
9. Describe two systems that accept spoken input.
10. Distinguish between insensate robots and robots that provide feedback to their computer controls about their environment.
11. What jobs can robots with sensors do that insensate robots can't do? Why?
12. How does Japan's fifth generation project differ from their supercomputer project?
13. In which areas will progress be required if the fifth generation project is to be successful?
14. What is the result of the declining cost of computer components?
15. Describe some likely future applications of computer technology in the home.
16. What might newspapers be like in the twenty-first century?
17. What functions do electronic navigation systems perform for automobile drivers?
18. Describe some of the potential applications of computers in rail and air transportation.
19. What uses of computers in the classroom will be likely to expand?
20. What is the potential impact of computers on home and office life?

A SHARPER FOCUS

Now that you've completed this chapter, you should be able to answer the following questions about the chapter opening.

1. To what extent do you think the various aspects of artificial intelligence can be integrated in the new industrial robots?
2. What sensory capabilities will robots need in order to function in unpredictable hazardous environments?
3. Which are better suited to work on bomb squads and in nuclear plants: humans or robots? Why?

PROJECTS

1. Read one or two of the many books that outline future developments in computer technology and applications. John Naisbitt's *Megatrends* is a recent example, and Christopher Evans's *The Micro Millenium* (1979) and Alvin Toffler's *Future Shock* (1970) provide earlier perspectives. You might also look for data-processing textbooks from the 1960s and read their chapters on the future. Do these projections seem to be based more on actual developments or on wishful thinking? Have some of their examples of long-term developments already come and gone? How accurate can such predictions be? Why?
2. If you were called on to take part in one of Alan Turing's experiments as a questioner, how would you prepare? Make a list of ten questions that would let you tell the difference between a computer's response and a human's. Explain why you think your questions would trip up the machine.
3. A large number of high school and college math teachers have complained that the introduction of the pocket calculator "destroyed" mathematics. They believe that today's students can't do even simple arithmetic problems without consulting their calculators. Do you agree? Why or why not? Think about what might be the result of the introduction of an inexpensive textbook-sized computer with a word processor and a grammar and spelling checker. Would this similarly "destroy" other disciplines? What do your teachers think?

APPENDIX
An Introduction to BASIC Programming

The goal of this appendix is to provide enough information to enable you to write simple programs in the programming language BASIC. There are seven major steps in programming computers (which were introduced in Chapter 8). This appendix discusses how to perform the step of writing, or coding, programs. It explains BASIC's more common features and capabilities. Unfortunately, there are a number of different dialects of BASIC. Within this appendix, all the examples have been carefully chosen to avoid most of the pitfalls encountered when programs must be transferred to a different machine. The features that are presented are a subset of those available on the MicroSoft BASIC interpreter. All the examples have been run on an IBM Personal Computer.

The first version of BASIC (an acronym for Beginner's All-purpose Symbolic Instruction Code), was unveiled in 1965 at Dartmouth College by its co-creators, professors John Kemeny and Thomas Kurtz. They created it to provide a simple language for students to use. It was available on a large (for those days), time-shared mainframe computer. BASIC proved to be popular with students because it was simple to learn. In the following years, its popularity spread to computer manufacturers, who found it simple to implement on their computers and well received by their nontechnical customers. The first implementation of BASIC for a microprocessor was made in 1975. Many of the limitations currently found in BASIC result from its once being forced to exist within the confines of extremely small machines. In 1975, the typical microprocessor system had between 8K and 16K of primary memory. In contrast, current microcomputers have up to 500K or even 1000K memory locations. Today, millions of microprocessor systems later, BASIC reigns as king of the microcomputer world.

Communicating with BASIC

Computer programming 30 years ago was a solitary practice—one person against one machine. The memory of the machine was meticulously loaded, one storage location at a time, using toggle switches. This obviously error-prone method was soon replaced by the use of off-line program entry techniques. Punched cards (see Chapter 4) were encoded on relatively inexpensive, totally mechanical equipment. Off-line program preparation was important because only a few computers existed and access to them was a privilege.

The BASIC Interpreter

Most of you will be using a program called a BASIC *interpreter*. BASIC programs are entered into a computer using the letters of the alphabet, numbers, and a few punctuation marks and special symbols. An interpreter then extracts the essential information out of this human-readable input and stores it in a compacted binary form in memory. As shown in Figure A.1, no information is lost. In fact, certain commands in BASIC perform the reverse translation; compact binary is displayed as the original text, the form in which the program was created. The translation into a compact form is much easier than the task carried out by another type of program, the BASIC *compiler*. Compilers translate computer languages directly into machine code.

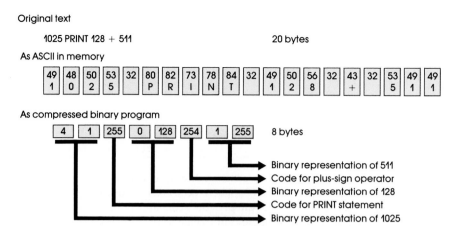

Figure A.1   Compression of Text by the Interpreter for More Efficient Storage and Faster Execution

When the interpreter executes a BASIC program, it consults internal storage to determine which operations to perform. The use of a compact internal form, rather than machine language, may make the initial translation easier, but it slows the actual execution of a program. A compiled program may execute 100 times faster than an interpreted one. Fortunately, this slowdown is barely noticeable for many programs because of the high speeds of modern computers.

When the BASIC interpreter is in charge of a computer's resources, it performs three distinct tasks. First, the user enters a program with the help of BASIC's text-editing capabilities. Second, a group of high-level commands can direct BASIC to do certain housekeeping tasks such as recording the program on a diskette. Finally, the program is brought to life through execution of the lines of the program statements entered previously. Crossing over from any of these different operational modes to another is tightly controlled. Therefore, it is nearly impossible for any BASIC program (malfunctioning or not) to modify information that was typed in via the text editor.

Keystrokes and Correcting Mistakes

Computers are often programmed to accumulate one line of data before processing that input. The complete line of input is sent on its way to further processing steps when the user presses a key usually labeled RETURN (short for carriage return, a name carried over from typewriters). Depending on the model of computer, the label on the key may also be ENTER or a special arrow ←. While a line of input is being entered, special keys (and combinations of keys) can be used to make corrections. For example, the BACKSPACE key deletes text, working backward from the last character entered.

Although the user can correct typing mistakes by laboriously backspacing to the leftmost error and reentering the corrected information, other editing keys facilitate such corrections by allowing the user to save the good parts of an input line while modifying the bad. Cursor positioning keys can move the character insertion point to any position in a line, not just the end. Other command keys tell the computer to replace the character at the insertion point or to scoot the rightmost part of the line over one character for every one entered. Unfortunately, just as there is variety in the label for RETURN, each computer has its own set of editing keys and capabilities. Anyone who expects to write more than a few BASIC programs will find it worthwhile to learn all the editing shortcuts built into the machine that is to be used.

Entering Programs

Every line of a BASIC program consists of two parts: a *line number* and a *program statement*. Line numbers are simply integer numbers. However, the number of digits that can be used in a line number is limited. Confining line numbers to the range from 1 to 30000 will ensure that programs are compatible across a wide range of BASIC interpreters. The line numbers serve two functions: they mark each program statement for future editing, and they determine the order in which statements are executed. Program lines may be entered in any order. They will, however, be executed in ascending numerical order.

Program lines may be changed by reentering the number of the line that is to be changed, followed by the revised program statement. The program statement previously associated with that line number is destroyed. Therefore, entering only a line number is a quick way to delete statements. Unfortunately, when a program is changed in this manner, there is no warning that a piece of the program is being deleted. Because most programs eventually require modification, it is good practice to use 10 as the first line number and to increment by 10 for all subsequent numbers so that additional lines can easily be inserted if the need arises.

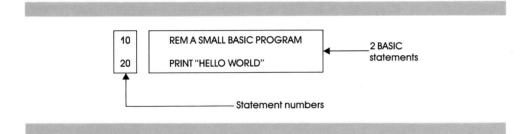

Annotating a Program

The simplest of all BASIC statements is the REM (for REMark) statement. All the remaining characters of program lines that open with REM are ignored and are not processed as part of the program. Remarks are comments directed to any other person who may read a program. They should tell what a program (or a piece of a program) does, what its limitations are, and where the reader should look for additional information. However, the use of too many comments can be considered too much of a good thing. Because comments consume storage space and sometimes actually slow the execution of programs, the information included in them should be carefully selected. For large (or important) programs, a separate computer file should be used for recording the bulk of the comments about the program's construction and its operational characteristics.

```
10  REM DEMONSTRATION BASIC COMMENT LINE
20  REM NUCLEAR ANALYSIS WRITTEN BY E. TELLER
30  REM REFER TO FILE "EXAMPLE.DOC" FOR MORE INFORMATION
40  REM ******************************************
```

Table A.1 Common System-Level Commands

Command	Meaning
LIST	Displays a program
SAVE	Records a program on a secondary storage medium
LOAD	Reads a program into primary memory from secondary storage
RUN	Executes a program
EDIT	Allows program statements to be changed
AUTO	Directs BASIC to automatically assign line numbers
NEW	Erases the program currently in memory
DELETE	Deletes blocks of program lines
RENUM	Reassigns line numbers

System-Level Commands

System-level commands are instructions that are given directly to the BASIC interpreter. They can't be entered as part of a program. The commands in Table A.1 are available in most dialects of BASIC. There may also be others, such as commands to list the contents of a diskette and to delete disk files.

LIST

The LIST command causes the program currently in memory to be expanded from its compressed binary form and displayed on the computer's screen. Computers with printers also have a variation of the LIST command that creates a hard-copy printout of the program. Entering only the keyword LIST causes the entire program to be presented. Part of the program can be listed by specifying starting and ending line numbers.

In all the highlighted examples in this appendix, italic type is used for words that are placeholders in a BASIC command or statement. Everything else is entered into the computer just as it is shown. The explanation of a command's format and function may indicate that certain placeholders are optional. Leaving them out of a statement will generally cause the interpreter to rely on internal reference values for those placeholders. Those internal values are often called *default values*.

Command: LIST *StartingLine#* − *EndingLine#*

Both *StartingLine#* and *EndingLine#* are optional. If the minus is the last character in this command, all the lines from *StartingLine#* to the end of the program are listed.

Examples: LIST 30–100   Lists lines from 30 to 100

LIST 330   Lists only line 330

LIST 330–   Lists from line 330 to end of program

LIST   Lists the entire program

SAVE AND LOAD

Primary memory is volatile; that is, the program residing in memory disappears as soon as power is removed. Any program in memory can be transferred to secondary storage, however, with a SAVE command and can be retrieved with a LOAD command. Information is stored on secondary storage media in a *file*. Each file has a file name that is used to identify it. The exact format for the file names that can be used with the SAVE command is dependent on the model of computer. Also, there are sometimes additional commands that deal with the differences in saving a program on various storage media, for example, floppy disk and cassette tape.

Command: SAVE *"Filename"*
The BASIC program currently in memory is transferred to a file in secondary storage. If the *Filename* used in a SAVE command already exists, the old file is deleted before the current program is saved. The program in memory is not altered by the SAVE command.

Example: SAVE "GAME"

Command: LOAD *"Filename"*
The LOAD command deletes the program currently in memory before loading the one specified by *Filename*.

Example: LOAD "HOMEWORK"

RUN

The RUN command starts the execution of a program. If you enter just the keyword RUN, execution begins at the statement with the lowest line number. When initially developing a new program or debugging an old one, you may want to start execution somewhere other than the first statement. Entering a line number following RUN will cause execution to start at that point.

Command: RUN *StartingLine#*
StartingLine# may be omitted. If it is not present, then execution begins at the lowest numbered line of the program.

Examples: RUN   Executes the program beginning with the first line

RUN 130   Starts executing the program at line 130

EDIT

The EDIT command lets you change a line of a program without having to reenter the whole thing. After you type EDIT and a line number, the computer will display the line you requested and then wait for you to make your changes. The line may be changed with any of the editing keys, such as the backspace key. The entire line is reprocessed when you press RETURN. Therefore, if you don't change the line number of the statement, pressing RETURN will completely replace the statement in the program that previously had that number. However, if you change the line number, the original program statement will be left unchanged. Changing only the line number is a way to duplicate a program statement.

Command: EDIT *Line#*

     The computer displays the indicated line and allows the user to employ the normal text-editing facilities to make changes.

AUTO

Reusing a line number destroys the program statement that was previously stored with that number. To allow for added lines in the future, it is good practice to give the original program line numbers that are multiples of 10 (or more). The AUTO command starts a program entry mode in which the interpreter supplies successive line numbers. When the AUTO command is used, the interpreter watches the program statements already in memory. An indication is given if a new line number will replace a statement already included in the program. AUTO entered by itself generates line numbers starting at 10 and incrementing by 10 for each successive line. You may choose other values better suited to your programming style by specifying both the starting line number and the increment to be used. Obviously, having the computer generate the line numbers is a time-saving advantage when a long program is being entered.

Command: AUTO *StartingLine#, Increment*

     Both *StartingLine#* and *Increment* are optional. Both have a default value of 10.

Examples: AUTO 100, 25   Generates line numbers 100, 125, 150, . . .

           AUTO   Generates line numbers 10, 20, 30, 40, . . .

NEW and DELETE

Entering just a line number deletes any statement associated with that line number. The NEW command erases every line of a program. A slightly less drastic command is the DELETE command. Just as with the LIST command, typing a range of line numbers with DELETE causes only the statements on those lines to be erased.

Commands: NEW

                DELETE *StartingLine# − EndingLine#*

     The NEW command erases the entire program from primary memory.

     DELETE selectively erases portions of the program. The *− EndingLine#* component is optional.

Examples: NEW   Erases the entire program

           DELETE 130–190   Removes seven lines (if numbered in increments of 10)

RENUM

After debugging and subsequent program editing, your program's line numbers probably won't start at 10 and march up in the orderly progression 20, 30, 40. The RENUM command makes order out of chaos. Entered by itself, RENUM renumbers the entire program to the standard pattern of 10, 20, 30. If you need to open up a "hole" in a program, RENUM can be told to start in the middle of a program and use an increment other than 10. Obviously, renumbering the entire program makes old listings out of date. Avoiding this is the reason for originally entering a program with line numbers increasing by 10. Then a small number of additional lines can easily be tucked in the space between two statements.

Command: RENUM *First#, Start#, Increment*

All numbers are optional. Commas may also be omitted if they are at the end of a line. *First#* and *Increment* default to 10 (become 10 unless otherwise specified). *First#* will be the first line number of the new sequence. *Start#* tells where in the original program the renumbering should start. *Increment* specifies how much should be added each time to form the line numbers for subsequent lines. (The important thing to notice about RENUM is that it not only changes line numbers but also makes corresponding adjustments to the program statements where necessary, as in line 200 below.)

Example:

```
LIST
10 PRINT "HELLO FOR THE"; COUNT; "TIME."
20 LET COUNT = COUNT + 1
30 GOTO 10

RENUM 100,,50
LIST

100 PRINT "HELLO FOR THE"; COUNT; "TIME."
150 LET COUNT = COUNT + 1
200 GOTO 100
```

Summary

The BASIC interpreter processes input lines in two different manners. Program lines, which consist of a line number followed by a statement, are recorded in memory as they are entered. System-level commands are acted on immediately.

The LIST command displays the current program on the computer's screen.

The commands LOAD and SAVE are used to move programs from main memory to secondary storage and back, respectively.

The RUN command executes the current program.

Several commands assist in the tasks of entering and maintaining programs. EDIT allows changes to be made to existing program lines. NEW erases all of the program currently in memory. DELETE selectively removes one or more lines.

The AUTO command speeds program entry by having the computer provide line numbers automatically. RENUM reassigns the line numbers at the start of each program statement so that they fall into an orderly sequence and also simultaneously updates any line numbers referred to within statements.

Exercises (Exercises marked with an asterisk require a computer.)

1. What would be printed if you entered the following program?

```
10 PRINT "GOOD"
30 PRINT "MORNING"
20 PRINT "CLASS"
```

*2. Create two programs, one that prints your name and another that prints the name of your school. Save the programs on a floppy disk (or whatever secondary storage medium is available). Reload each program and run it once.

*3. Enter this program:

```
10 PRINT "NUMBERS"
30 PRINT "THE END"
AUTO 20
```

Now enter additional PRINT statements to output the numbers 1, 2, 3, and 4 on separate lines. Did you get any error messages? If so, what were they and why were they printed?

 ## WORDS IN THE BASIC LANGUAGE

In English, letters make up words, words are combined into sentences, and sentences form paragraphs. Unlike natural languages, with their myriad constructs and ambiguities, programming languages have rigid structures and very limited vocabularies. This section describes some of the properties of the words used in BASIC.

Six types of words are recognized in BASIC. They are numbers, strings, variable names, reserved words, operators, and illegal words. Unlike natural languages such as English, the BASIC language has no dictionary that contains all its valid words. Instead, there are rules that determine the category of each word. Before beginning an investigation of BASIC words, we need to review some terminology concerning characters. The letters from A to Z are called the *alphabetic characters*; 0 to 9 are the *numeric characters*. Combining these two sets gives the *alphanumeric characters*.

Numbers, Strings, and Variable Names

Numbers

Ordinary numbers are written in BASIC just as you would expect, for example, 1234 and 4.5. Numbers that don't contain decimal points are called *integers*. There are a few places in BASIC where only an integer can be used; for example, line numbers must be integers. Commas cannot be used within numbers in BASIC.

Scientific notation is often useful when very large or very small numbers must be entered. With scientific notation, numbers are formed from two numbers separated by the letter E (see Figure A.2). The second number is called the *exponent* and indicates what power of 10 the first number is multiplied by. The exponent must be an integer but can be a negative integer. In that case, division by the specified power of 10 is done rather than multiplication.

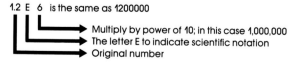

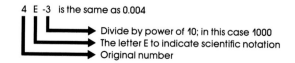

Figure A.2 Expressing Numbers Using Scientific Notation

Strings

A sequence of characters can serve as data in a program. Such sequences are called *strings* and are indicated by enclosing the characters within quotation marks (''). Any of the 96 printing characters from the ASCII character set may be entered as part of a string. All of the following are strings; the last one is a string with no characters in it:

```
"THIS IS AN EXAMPLE OF A STRING"
"THIS IS A STRING WITH 35 CHARACTERS"
""
```

Variable Names

The previous two types of words, numbers and strings, are sometimes called *constants*. The value of a constant will not be changed by the execution of a program. To store data that changes during the execution of a program, a special section of memory is used. A machine accesses all of its memory locations using numeric addresses. BASIC allows programmers to make up names of their own for accessing memory. Those names are called *variable names*. Variable names always start with an alphabetic character. Names that are longer than one character can contain any of the alphanumeric characters. However, the last character of a variable name may be a special character such as a dollar sign ($). It is that final character in a name that determines what kind of data may be stored in the variable. Standard BASIC has only two kinds of variables: numeric and string. String variables always end with a dollar sign.

To achieve faster, more efficient processing of programs, some BASIC interpreters allow other special characters as the ending character of a variable name. For example, MicroSoft BASIC uses a percent sign (%) to signify variables that may contain only integer quantities whose values fall in the range from −32000 to +32000. Microcomputers perform arithmetic calculations much more rapidly when working solely with integer values. Because of the guaranteed limited range of these integer variables, less storage space needs to be reserved for them. For the range above, only two bytes of memory are required to hold a variable's value.

In Table A.2, the two illegal variable names are incorrect because the first does not start with an alphabetic character and the second contains a nonalphanumeric character, the ampersand.

Many BASIC interpreters don't distinguish between upper-case and lower-case letters used in variable names. Because your programs may one day be run with an interpreter that does, however, it is best to use exactly the same characters for a variable each time you write it. The number of characters that can be used in a variable name is limited. Interpreters discard trailing characters that exceed the limit they are prepared to remember. The first edition of BASIC in 1965 set the limit at two characters. That low limit still remains in many interpreters. Although there are interpreters with a limit of more than 20 letters, the programmer should choose variable names that can be differentiated by their first two characters.

Reserved Words

All of the possible combinations of alphabetic characters aren't available for variable names, however. Certain names are *reserved words* that have special meanings. The number and

Table A.2 Valid and Invalid Variable Names

Integer	Numeric	String	Illegal
INDEX%	AVARIABLE	TITLE$	1776POPULATION
AGE%	CATCH22	X$	NEAR&FAR

Table A.3　Reserved Words of BASIC Used in This Appendix

AND	FOR	MID$	RESTORE
AS	GOSUB	MOD	RETURN
ASC	GOTO	NEXT	RIGHT$
CHR$	INKEY$	ON	RND
CLOSE	IF	OPEN	SIN
COS	INPUT	OR	SQR
DATA	LEFT$	PRINT	TAN
DEF	LET	RANDOMIZE	THEN
DIM	LEN	READ	TO
ELSE	LINE	REM	WEND
END			WHILE

names of reserved words vary among different versions of BASIC. (There are more than 150 in the version of BASIC for the IBM PC, for instance.) In this appendix, we will discuss the reserved words listed in Table A.3.

Operators

There are other characters besides the alphanumeric ones. We have already seen uses for the percent sign, dollar sign, period, and quotation marks. Many of the remaining available characters (from among the 96 printing characters defined as ASCII characters) are used alone or in combinations to form words called *operators* (see Table A.4). Operators, when appropriately combined with variables, numbers, and strings, make BASIC statements.

Illegal Words

Any characters on a computer's keyboard that don't appear in Table A.4 may have special-ized uses with a particular BASIC interpreter or may be illegal outside of a string. If any of these characters are used outside of a string, the words they appear in are known as *illegal words*.

Summary

There are six categories of words used in BASIC:

1. *Numbers* are written in decimal or scientific notation.
2. *Strings* consist of a sequence of ASCII characters.
3. *Variable names* start with an alphabetic character that can be followed by several alphanumeric characters.
4. Some words that could otherwise be classified as variables are *reserved words*.
5. *Operators* consist of nonalphanumeric characters and are used in building formulas.
6. Other characters may appear on a computer's keyboard. They may be used only within a string. If they are used elsewhere, they form *illegal words*.

Exercises
1. Can a reserved word be used as a variable name?
*2. Determine how many characters can be used in variable names on your computer.
*3. Determine the largest number that can be recorded in a numeric variable (an answer within a factor of 10 is acceptable). (*Hint:* Use scientific notation.)
4. Can a string contain an operator, for example, a plus sign (+)?
5. Can the exponent part of a number expressed in scientific notation contain a decimal point?

Table A.4 Nonalphanumeric Characters Used in BASIC

Operator	Action or use
=	Assignment, comparison for equality
< >	Comparison for inequality
<	Less than
>	Greater than
< = or = <	Less than or equal to
> = or = >	Greater than or equal to
/	Division
*	Multiplication
^	Exponentiation
/	Integer division
( )	Parentheses (used in formulas)
+	Addition
−	Subtraction
#	File descriptor
,	Comma (used in lists)
;	Semicolon (used in PRINT statements)

SIMPLE BASIC STATEMENTS

Creating Output: The PRINT Statement

The PRINT statement is used to output information. In many of the examples in this appendix, a simple PRINT statement is used to display information on the computer's screen. More complex PRINT statements are available to control precisely the format in which the information is output (the number of blanks used, where commas appear, and so on).

Statement: PRINT *Value Separator Value Separator . . .*
  Separator can be either a comma (,), to arrange the values into columns, or a semicolon
    (;), to put little or no space between values.
  Value can be anything from a simple constant to a string or a complex formula. You
    may use as many values and separators as will fit within one program line.
  PRINT automatically performs a carriage return after printing the information unless the
    last item in the statement is a separator (see line 50 below).
  PRINT entered by itself results in a blank line.

Example:

```
10 PRINT 1, -2.0, 3.14159, 1.3E3
20 PRINT 3; 4; -5; 1.3E20
30 PRINT "HEL";  "LO"
40 PRINT
50 PRINT 6;
60 PRINT "STUDENTS ARE AWAKE"
```

Computer Output:

```
1             -2            3.14159      1300
3   4 -5   1.3E20
HELLO
6 STUDENTS ARE AWAKE
```

When commas are used to separate the values listed in a PRINT statement, the output values are aligned in vertical columns. The number of columns and the width of each column depends on the number of characters that can fit on the computer's screen. Usually each column is between 14 and 20 characters wide. A number can be output in three different ways depending on its actual value. If the number has no fractional part and its value is small enough, the number is simply printed. If there is a fractional part, and the number doesn't take up too many print positions, it is printed in decimal notation. Any numbers that don't fit the above definitions, either because their values are too large or too small, are printed in scientific notation. The PRINT statements in lines 10 and 20 above produces the three types of numeric output.

Semicolons direct the BASIC interpreter to place one space after a number but no space between strings. Also, positive numbers have a space printed before them, and negative ones have a minus sign. This effect is demonstrated by the output from lines 20 and 30 in the example on the PRINT statement. Semicolons are useful when composing sentences that describe the information being output.

Additional lines are used if the information being output takes up more spaces than are available on one line on the screen. When the last item in a PRINT statement is a separator, only a partial line is output. Then the next PRINT statement will start generating output somewhere in the middle of the screen rather than at the left margin. Lines 50 and 60 show the result of using a semicolon at the end of a PRINT statement.

To print blank lines, you can enter PRINT without any additional parameters. Blank lines can dramatically improve the readability of printed reports. To completely erase the screen, you could repeat PRINT enough times to blank out every line, but most dialects of BASIC have a quick way to do just that. The MicroSoft BASIC CLS statement both clears the screen and sets the cursor to the top-leftmost position.

Statement: CLS
    Clears the screen and places the cursor at the top left of the screen.

Arithmetic: Building Formulas with BASIC

Data are manipulated through the use of formulas, and formulas in turn are built from constants, variables, and operators. There are different kinds of formulas, each type being determined by the operators and variables that are used. This section starts with a description of numeric formulas, those that generate numbers as their values. In BASIC, the operators that stand for addition and subtraction have the usual symbols of plus (+) and minus (−). The arithmetic operators are summarized in Table A.5.

Each arithmetic operator combines two values, sometimes called operands, into a single numeric result. When there is more than one operator in a formula, BASIC decides which one to evaluate first by applying certain rules. First, the operations are performed in the order shown in Table A.5. Negation is done first; exponentiation is done next, and so on. When performing operations that are in the same group (such as multiplication and division), BASIC proceeds from left to right through the formula.

Table A.5   Arithmetic Operators

Order	Operators	Actions
1	−	Negation
2	^ or **	Exponentiation
3	* and /	Multiplication and Division
4	MOD	Remainder
5	+ and −	Addition and Subtraction

Example:

```
10 PRINT 1 + 2 * 3,    4 - 5 - 6 + 1
20 PRINT (1 + 2) * 3,    4 - (5 - (6 + 1))
30 PRINT (52 * 51 * 50 * 49 * 48) / (5 * 4 * 3 * 2 * 1)
40 PRINT 2 ^ 16 - 1
50 PRINT  X, -X, 1 - X
60 PRINT 10 MOD 3
```

Computer Output (assuming that the variable X has the value 1776):

```
7              -6
9               6
2598960
65535
1776          -1776          -1775
1
```

All the arithmetic operators, except for negation, require two operands, and are therefore called *binary operators*. However, line 50 in the box above shows a unique characteristic of the minus sign; it may be used with either one or two operands. When used with only one operand, the minus is given a special name, the *unary minus*. (In this context, minus means to negate or subtract from zero.)

Line 10 in the example above prints two numbers. The first value is generated by multiplying 2 by 3 (because multiplication is done before addition) and then adding 1 to that product. The order of evaluation of operators can be changed by using parentheses. A section of a formula inside a pair of parentheses is boiled down to a single number before the program proceeds to evaluate the final answer. If that section of formula has another set of parentheses within it, that innermost formula is evaluated first. Therefore, the second value in line 20 in the box above is calculated by first adding 6 to 1, then subtracting the result from 5, and finally subtracting the result from 4.

Line 30 in the example above illustrates another use of parentheses. The first group, (52 * 51 * 50 * 49 * 48), is evaluated the same with or without the parentheses. They are there solely to aid the programmer in understanding the expression. This formula computes the number of different five-card poker hands. It could also have been written as follows:

```
30 PRINT 52 * 51 * 50 * 49 * 48 / 5 / 4 / 3 / 2 / 1
```

Its meaning is much easier to grasp with the parentheses.

Exponentiation is a way of expressing repeated multiplication. Line 40 above computes the largest integer that can be stored in a 16-bit memory cell. Exponentiation in this case is equivalent to multiplying a total of 16 twos (2 * 2 * 2 * ... * 2) and finally subtracting 1.

The operator MOD calculates the remainder when the first operand is divided by the second.

A pair of strings can be joined into one larger string (*concatenated*) with the plus sign operator. The box below assumes that another BASIC statement has *initialized* (or given a value to) the string variable NAME$. When a program first starts executing, all of its numeric variables are set to zero and all of its string variables are set to the empty string. A program statement that gives the first value to any variable is called an *initializing statement*. Using any of the other operators besides the plus sign with string operands will result in an error message, such as SYNTAX ERROR or TYPE MISMATCH. An error will be noted if you try to use the plus sign to combine a string and a numeric value and the program will stop executing.

Operator: Plus sign used for string concatenation (assume that the variable PROF$ contains the value "SLOTNICK")

Example:

```
10 PRINT PROF$
20 PRINT "GOOD MORNING, MR. " + PROF$ + "!"
```

Computer Output:

```
SLOTNICK
GOOD MORNING, MR. SLOTNICK!
```

Assignment: The LET Statement

Variables are used to hold information while a program is being processed. As we have seen, BASIC has two kinds of variables, numeric and string. One way information is placed in a variable is by a LET statement. In later sections, we will look at some other ways of getting information into variables (the READ, INPUT, and FOR statements).

Statement: LET *VariableName* = *NumericFormula*
            LET *StringName$* = *StringFormula*
     A formula is evaluated and its result saved in a variable. The keyword LET is optional in many versions of BASIC.

Example:

```
10 LET X = 5
20 LET WHO$ = "JOHN DOE"
30 LET DAY = 60 * 60 * 24
40 LET AUGUST = DAY * 31
50 PRINT "WELL "; WHO$; ", THERE ARE"; DAY; "SECONDS IN A DAY AND"
60 PRINT AUGUST; "SECONDS IN THE MONTH OF AUGUST."
```

Computer Output:

```
WELL JOHN DOE, THERE ARE 86400 SECONDS IN A DAY AND
 2678400 SECONDS IN THE MONTH OF AUGUST.
```

The formula used in a LET statement, of course, can consist of a single item, such as another variable name, a number, or a string as in the second line numbered 10 in the summary above. The only restriction placed on the formula is that its result be of the same type as that of the variable name. Therefore, formulas that produce strings can be assigned only to variable names ending with a dollar sign.

BASIC programs tend to contain a fairly high percentage of LET statements. Many versions of BASIC make the keyword LET optional. If LET is optional, it should be left out of most statements; its use should be restricted to those situations where you wish to emphasize a processing step. (This is how we will handle LET in this appendix.) For example, using the keyword LET is appropriate for indicating where important variables are being initialized.

Example:

```
1 AGE = 17
10 PRINT "YOU WERE"; AGE;
20 AGE = AGE + 1
30 PRINT ", BUT NOW YOU'RE"; AGE
```

Computer Output:

```
YOU WERE 17 , BUT NOW YOU'RE 18
```

The LET statement is processed in two steps. First, the formula is evaluated to yield a single result. Next, that value is placed into the memory cells associated with the variable name, replacing any previous value.

Summary

The PRINT statement sends information to the computer's display screen.

PRINT can be used to output several values on one line of the computer's screen. The separators used between the values in the PRINT statement may be either commas or semicolons. Commas produce columns of output. With semicolons, the information is displayed with little or no space between adjacent items.

BASIC computes the value of a formula by performing arithmetic operations in a defined order. The minus sign is used for both negation and subtraction; negation is always performed first. Exponentiation, symbolized by either a pair of asterisks (**) or a caret (^), is performed next. Then multiplication (*) and division (/) are performed. Finally, addition (+) and subtraction (−) are done.

Within a formula, calculations are done from left to right. The order of calculation can be altered by the use of parentheses.

The addition operator (+) can also be used to concatenate two strings into one.

The LET statement is used to store the result of a calculation in a variable.

Exercises

*1. The number of spaces used to form columns of output with the PRINT statement varies among different computers. How many spaces does your computer use to make columns?

*2. Using the LET statement, determine whether your computer distinguishes between upper-case and lower-case letters in variable names. If it does so, are the keywords PRINT and print both acceptable?

3. What would the following PRINT statements display?

```
10 PRINT 1,
20 PRINT 2
```

4. What is the value of each of the following formulas?
   a. 3 − 4 − 5   e. 1 / 2 * 3
   b. 3 − (4 − 5)   f. (((3)))

c. 2 ^ 3   g. 2 + 2 ^ 1 + 1
d. 5 MOD 2   h. "ABC" + "XYZ"

*5. What error message is given when you try to concatenate a string and a number?

*6. Is the reserved word LET optional on your computer?

*7. What error message is given when a number is assigned to a string variable?

*8. Write a program that will show what happens when you use PRINT with a string variable that contains more characters than can fit on one line of the computer's screen.

CONTROLLING THE ORDER OF EXECUTION OF STATEMENTS

Comparison: IF-THEN Statements

Computer programs call for the machine to make decisions. The simplest BASIC statement that makes a decision is an IF-THEN statement. An IF statement conditionally executes a portion of a program. The condition is based on the value of a certain kind of formula called a *boolean expression,* which evaluates to one of two values: TRUE or FALSE. Of course, TRUE and FALSE are simply a pair of numbers that BASIC uses to represent a condition.

Statement: IF *BooleanExpression* THEN *Statement*

Boolean expressions are constructed using comparison operators and logical operators. *Statement* is executed only if the boolean expression is true.

Examples:

```
10 IF TEMPERATURE < 212 THEN PRINT "WATER DOESN'T BOIL."

20 IF HOURS > WORKDAYS * 8 THEN OVERTIME = HOURS - WORKDAYS * 8
```

Comparison operators are evaluated after all the arithmetic operators have been evaluated. BASIC provides six comparison operators, all of which are shown in Table A.6.

In addition to comparing two numeric formulas, boolean expressions may also be used to compare strings. Strings are compared using the alphabetical ordering of the ASCII character set. For the alphanumeric characters, numbers come first. They are followed by capital letters; lowercase letters come last. When comparing strings, the less-than operator is interpreted as "comes before," and greater than as "comes after." If two strings are of different lengths, and the smaller string is identical to the initial characters of the larger string, then the smaller string comes before the larger. Note the difference between comparison of strings and comparison of numbers as illustrated by the last two examples below.

All these boolean expressions are true.

```
"ALPHA" < "OMEGA"

 "DATA" < "DATABANK"

  "810" > "1101"

    810 < 1101
```

Table A.6   Comparison Operators

Comparison Operator	Meaning
=	Equal to
<	Less than
>	Greater than
> = or < =	Greater than or equal to
< = or = <	Less than or equal to
< > or > <	Not equal to

Some algebraic formulas give unexpected results when programmed literally in BASIC. For instance, this expression won't always yield what you'd expect:

```
IF 3 <= X <= 4 THEN PRINT "IN BETWEEN"
```

The reason for the discrepancy lies in how the values TRUE and FALSE are stored in the computer's memory. For example, MicroSoft BASIC uses 0 for FALSE and −1 for TRUE. The subexpression $3 <= X$, which is evaluated first, has an outcome of either 0 or −1. That result is always less than 4! To arrive at the correct result, it is necessary to rewrite the boolean formula into two separate parts. The parts are joined with the reserved word AND, one of BASIC's *logical operators*.

```
IF 3 <= X AND X <= 4 THEN PRINT "IN BETWEEN"
```

The operator AND combines two boolean expressions and yields an answer of TRUE only if both expressions are true. OR is another logical operator; it returns an answer of TRUE if either of the boolean expressions is true.

The GOTO Statement

Ordinarily, BASIC proceeds from one statement to the next, following strictly their numeric order. The GOTO statement alters this orderly march. The first type of GOTO shown below is sometimes called an *unconditional branch*. There is no question of which program statement is to be executed next. The second form, IF-GOTO, is a *conditional branch*. The transfer of execution may or may not occur, depending on the current values in memory.

Statements: GOTO *LineNumber*   (unconditional branch)
             IF *Expression* GOTO *LineNumber*   (conditional branch)
     GOTO branches execution to the statement indicated by *LineNumber,* instead of the next statement in numeric order.

Example:

```
10 PRINT "NUMBER OF DIFFERENT HANDS MADE FROM A DECK OF CARDS"
20 PRINT "CARDS", "POSSIBILITIES"
30 ANSWER = 1
40 CARDS = 1
50 IF CARDS > 52 GOTO 100
60      ANSWER = ANSWER * (53 - CARDS) / CARDS
70      PRINT CARDS, ANSWER
80      CARDS = CARDS + 1
90 GOTO 50
100 PRINT "THE END"
```

Abbreviated Computer Output:

```
NUMBER OF DIFFERENT HANDS MADE FROM A DECK OF CARDS
CARDS          POSSIBILITIES
  1            52
  2            1326
  3            22100
  4            270725
        .
        .
        .
 51            51.99998
 52            .9999996
```

The Reserved Word ELSE

The above variation on the IF statement contains the word GOTO rather than the usual THEN. IF statements may also have another reserved word, ELSE. ELSE is combined with any BASIC statement (just like the pairing of THEN with any statement) and is placed after the THEN part. The ELSE's statement is executed whenever the boolean expression is false.

Statement: IF *Expression* THEN *FirstStatement* ELSE *SecondStatement*

If *Expression* is true, only *FirstStatement* will be executed. Otherwise, *SecondStatement* will be executed.

Example:

```
10 LET RAINPERHOUR = 2.3
20 IF RAINPERHOUR > 1.5 THEN A$ = "POURING" ELSE A$ = "RAINING"
30 PRINT "IT'S "; A$; " OUTSIDE!"
```

Computer Output:

```
IT'S POURING OUTSIDE!
```

The FOR and NEXT Statements

By themselves, IF statements can be used to build powerful programs. For convenience (and sometimes additional speed when executing), BASIC has other mechanisms for altering the path of execution. The FOR statement executes a group of statements a fixed number of times. A special variable called an *index variable* is used to keep track of how many times the group has been executed. The FOR statement is sometimes called a *loop*. Note how the flowchart symbols below actually form a loop. The inner statements that make up the body of a FOR loop may contain another FOR loop, resulting in what is called a *nested FOR loop*.

Statements: FOR *Variable* = *StartValue* TO *EndValue*
              FOR *Variable* = *StartValue* TO *EndValue* STEP *StepValue*
              NEXT *Variable*

Variable is given successive values from *StartValue* until it reaches *EndValue*. The value 1 is added to *Variable* each time a NEXT statement containing the same variable name is reached.

The NEXT statement sends execution back to the statement just after its matching FOR statement.

The keyword STEP allows the programmer to specify an incrementing factor other than 1. Negative values for *StepValue* cause *Variable* to decrease in steps. In that case, the loop is broken when *Variable* goes below *EndValue*.

Example:

```
10  AMOUNT = 100
20  INTEREST = 12
30  PRINT "BANK ACCOUNT AT"; INTEREST; "PERCENT INTEREST"
40  PRINT "YEAR", "VALUE"
50  FOR YEAR = 0 TO 5
60     PRINT YEAR, AMOUNT
70     AMOUNT = AMOUNT + AMOUNT * (INTEREST/100)
80  NEXT YEAR
```

Computer Output:

```
BANK ACCOUNT AT 12 PERCENT INTEREST
YEAR          VALUE
  0            100
  1            112
  2            125.44
  3            140.4928
  4            157.3519
  5            176.2342
```

Flowchart of a FOR statement:

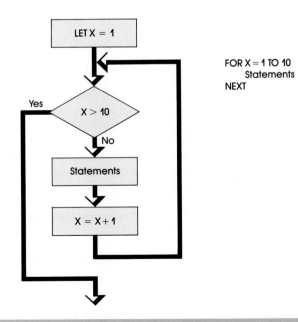

FOR X = 1 TO 10
    Statements
NEXT

The Reserved Word STEP

The amount by which an index variable is changed may be varied within the program. The reserved word STEP determines how much the variable changes on each trip through the loop. Index variables should never be changed by an assignment statement within a loop. Attempting to do so will yield unpredictable results; for example, the assignment might be ignored entirely.

This example shows both a nested FOR loop and the use of the reserved word STEP.

Example:

```
10 PRINT "FIRST FIVE POWERS OF THE FIRST FIVE EVEN INTEGERS"
20 FOR I = 2 TO 10 STEP 2
30      PRINT I; ":";
40      FOR P = 2 TO 5
50           PRINT I ^ P,
60      NEXT P
70      PRINT
80 NEXT I
```

Computer Output:

```
FIRST FIVE POWERS OF THE FIRST FIVE EVEN INTEGERS
 2 : 4          8              16           32
 4 : 16         64             256          1024
 6 : 36         216            1296         7776
 8 : 64         512            4096         32768
10 : 100        1000           10000        100000
```

The WHILE and WEND Statements

The WHILE statement provides another way to execute a group of statements repeatedly. However, unlike the FOR loop, the WHILE loop is broken when the value of a boolean expression is false rather than when a fixed number of repetitions have been done. If the WHILE statement is executed and its controlling expression is false, the interpreter scans forward to find the matching WEND (short for WHILE END) statement and executes the next statement after that. The statements that comprise the body of a WHILE loop can contain nested WHILE-WEND pairs. As long as the controlling expression is true, the WHILE statement does nothing more than serve as a place marker. Execution of the WEND always sends control back up to its matching WHILE, which evaluates the controlling expression and determines whether or not the loop is to be broken.

The summary below contains a sample program that uses Euclid's algorithm for finding the greatest common divisor of two integers. It uses the two numbers and their remainder in a repeated computation. The number of times the remaindering operation is done depends on the two input numbers.

Statements: WHILE *BooleanExpression*
                     WEND

When *BooleanExpression* is false, all the statements up to and including the matching WEND statement are bypassed.

WEND always sends execution back to its matching WHILE statement.

Example:

```
1 REM GREATEST COMMON DIVISOR OF TWO POSITIVE INTEGERS A AND B
2 REM THE VARIABLE A MUST BE GREATER THAN B
10 A = 27
11 B = 18
20 PRINT "THE GREATEST COMMON DIVISOR OF"; A; "AND"; B; "IS";
30 WHILE B > 0
40    TEMP = B
50    B = A MOD B
60    A = TEMP
70 WEND
80 PRINT A
```

Computer Output:

```
THE GREATEST COMMON DIVISOR OF 27 AND 18 IS 9
```

The ON-GOTO Statement

All the statements introduced so far make a single decision that has only two possible outcomes: a group of statements is skipped, or it is not. The ON-GOTO statement is an extension of the IF-GOTO statement, but it has several possible outcomes. Instead of working with a boolean expression, the ON-GOTO statement has a general expression as its condition. The GOTO part of the statement can have a whole list of line numbers to which control is transferred. If the controlling expression has the value 1, the first line number following GOTO is used; the value 2 selects the second line number, and so on. If the value of the expression is greater than the number of line numbers provided, the ON-GOTO statement does nothing; execution continues at the next statement in regular numerical order.

Statement: ON *Expression* GOTO *FirstLine#*, *SecondLine#*, *ThirdLine#*, . . .

Expression controls which line GOTO will cause to be executed next. Only the integer part (not rounded!) of the value of the expression is used to select the line number. That is, 1.0 and 1.99999 both select the first line number. An error is signaled if the value of the expression is less than 1 or greater than a preset maximum (MicroSoft BASIC's maximum is 255). Values greater than the number of line numbers following GOTO cause execution to continue at the next statement in regular numerical order.

Example:

```
10 FOR DAY = 1 TO 5
20    PRINT "ON THE ";
31    IF DAY = 1 THEN PRINT "FIRST";
32    IF DAY = 2 THEN PRINT "SECOND";
33    IF DAY = 3 THEN PRINT "THIRD";
34    IF DAY = 4 THEN PRINT "FOURTH";
35    IF DAY = 5 THEN PRINT "FIFTH";
50    PRINT " DAY OF CHRISTMAS MY TRUE LOVE GAVE TO ME"
51    ON DAY GOTO  70,69,68,67,66
66    PRINT "FIVE GOLDEN RINGS"
67    PRINT "FOUR CALLING BIRDS ";
```

```
68    PRINT "THREE FRENCH HENS"
69    PRINT "TWO TURTLE DOVES AND ";
70    PRINT "A PARTRIDGE IN A PEAR TREE."
80    PRINT
90 NEXT DAY
```

Abbreviated Computer Output:

```
ON THE FIRST DAY OF CHRISTMAS MY TRUE LOVE GAVE TO ME A
PARTRIDGE IN A PEAR TREE.

ON THE SECOND DAY OF CHRISTMAS MY TRUE LOVE GAVE TO ME
TWO TURTLE DOVES AND A PARTRIDGE IN A PEAR TREE.

ON THE THIRD DAY OF CHRISTMAS MY TRUE LOVE GAVE TO ME
THREE FRENCH HENS
TWO TURTLE DOVES AND A PARTRIDGE IN A PEAR TREE.
          .
          .
          .
```

This multibranching technique is often used in menu-driven systems. The programmer clears the machine's screen and writes out a list of possible actions the user can invoke. Each action is labeled with an integer, starting with 1 for the first. The peculiar behavior of the ON-GOTO statement when its condition has a value less than 1 can cause some complications in practical programs. It is seldom acceptable for a working program to abruptly stop executing because the user has entered some incorrect input. When there is any possibility that user input generate a value less than 1 for the ON part of the ON-GOTO statement, an explicit IF statement should be placed before the ON-GOTO pair, as shown below.

```
10 IF SELECTOR < 1 OR SELECTOR > 255 GOTO 30
20 ON SELECTOR GOTO Line1, Line2, Line3
30 PRINT "BAD SELECTOR VALUE"; SELECTOR
```

Summary

Certain BASIC statements cause selective execution of portions of a program.

The IF-THEN statement uses a boolean expression to determine whether or not the statement following the keyword THEN is to be executed. A GOTO causes execution to move to a particular statement in the program. That action is called branching. IF and GOTO are often combined on one line; the combination is called a conditional branch. Another variation of the IF statement uses the reserved word ELSE to separate two statements; one is executed if the controlling boolean expression is true, and the other is executed if it is false.

The FOR and NEXT statements provide a convenient way to execute a group of statements a fixed number of times. An index variable keeps track of the number of times the loop has been executed. This variable normally increases by 1 each time through the loop. The keyword STEP allows the programmer to specify a different value for the increment.

The WHILE-WEND pair are used when the statements in a loop are to be executed as long as a boolean expression is true.

The ON-GOTO statement redirects execution to one of several given line numbers.

Exercises

1. How many different values can a boolean expression have?
2. When can the THEN part of an IF statement be omitted?
3. Can the index of a FOR statement be a string variable?
4. Rewrite the following program using a FOR statement where appropriate.

```
10 X = 2
20 REM PRINT THE ELEMENTS OF THE SUM 1/2 + 1/3 + ... + 1/19
30 ANS = 0
40 ANS = ANS + 1/X
50 PRINT ANS
60 X = X + 1
70 IF X < 20 GOTO 40
```

5. Write a program that prints a diagonal line of asterisks across the computer's screen.
6. Is there anything wrong with the following program?

```
10 WHILE I < 3
20     PRINT I
30 WEND
```

*7. What is the permissible range of index values for the ON-GOTO statement on your computer? What happens when the index is a negative number or zero?
*8. What error message (if any) is given if a GOTO statement specifies a line number that doesn't exist in your program?
9. Rewrite the following program using WHILE and WEND.

```
10 REM HOW MANY PAYMENTS MUST BE MADE
20 REM BEFORE HALF OF A LOAN IS PAID OFF?
30 LET RATE = 0.02
40 LET PAYMENTS = 25
50 LET LOAN = 1000
60 LET HALF = LOAN/2
70 LET COUNT = 0

100 IF LOAN <= HALF GOTO 140
110    LOAN = LOAN * RATE
120    LOAN = LOAN - PAYMENT
130 GOTO 100
140 PRINT "AFTER"; COUNT; "PAYMENTS THERE IS"; LOAN; "LEFT"
```

INPUT TO A PROGRAM

Encoding Data Inside a Program: DATA and READ

Raw data may be entered into a program in several ways. For example, you can enter data using LET statements. This approach is rather inconvenient in that only one data item can be assigned per statement. Furthermore, the program must be modified to change any input data, and the position of those initializing statements is obviously important. Fortunately, there are other ways of entering data. The DATA statement can be used to enter data from within the program itself. As a result, the data elements can be grouped together in a convenient place for making subsequent additions.

Statements: DATA *Constant, Constant, . . .*
              READ *Variable, Variable, . . .*

DATA statements contain input data in the form of numeric and string constants. Several constants may be contained within a DATA statement; they are separated by commas. A program can have several DATA statements, occurring anywhere in the program (before or after the related READ statements).

READ statements successively pair up variables with the constants in DATA statements. Each time a READ is encountered, more of the constants are used. If all the data values have been read, an error is signaled and the program stops executing.

Example:

```
10 DATA 1, 2, "HOMETOWN, USA"
20 READ A, B
30 PRINT "A AND B = ";A;B
40 READ CITY$, QUOTELESS$, FOURDIGITS
50 PRINT "TOWN IS ";CITY$
60 PRINT QUOTELESS$
70 PRINT FOURDIGITS
80 DATA A STRING WITHOUT QUOTES BUT NO COMMAS, 9999
```

Computer Output:

```
A AND B = 1 2
TOWN IS HOMETOWN, USA
A STRING WITHOUT QUOTES BUT NO COMMAS
                9999
```

When a DATA statement is executed, nothing changes. This is just like what happens with REM statements. As you can see in the example above, DATA statements need not be placed together in a program. When READ statements acquire data items, DATA statements are used in ascending numerical order. The program in the box above shows some additional characteristics of the DATA and READ statements. Note that a single READ statement may use only part of a DATA statement. Any additional constants are available for subsequent READ statements. On the other hand, a READ that has several variables may consume as many DATA statements as are necessary to fill all its variables. For example, refer to line 40 above. The same rules apply for the variables in the READ and the data items in the DATA as for the variable and the formula in an assignment statement. The data types must match. String data items may be entered exactly as they are for an assignment statement; quotation marks surround each item. As a convenience, quotation marks around string constants are optional as long as the string contains no commas.

Since attempting to read data elements that don't exist is treated as a fatal error (the computer stops executing the program and displays a message), a programmer must have a means for telling the program where the actual end of data is. There are two principal ways of signaling the end of a collection of data. First, the person who prepared the data can count the number of items that are to be entered. That number is entered as the very first data value. After it has been read, a FOR loop will use the item count as the limiting value for its index variable. The block of statements that comprise the body of the FOR loop will read and process one data element.

Counting the number of data elements is adequate for small batches of data but is too error-prone for large collections. Using a special data value as a "flag" is another way of detecting the end of a stream of data. This data element is sometimes called a *sentinel*. Using a special value placed in the data stream is workable because legal data items are usually a subset of all the possible numbers or of all the possible strings. For example, a person's name is not likely to be the same as the string in this statement:

```
10 DATA "***END-OF-DATA***"
```

The summary below contains two programs. Both calculate the average grade given on a test where the individual student grades have been entered using DATA statements. The first program uses a count to determine when the last grade has been read; the second uses a sentinel.

Example:

```
10 REM CALCULATE THE AVERAGE SCORE ON A TEST
20 REM THE NUMBER OF TEST SCORES IS THE FIRST DATA ITEM
30 REM FOLLOWED BY THE ACTUAL TEST SCORES

100 DATA 14
110 DATA J TAYLOR,   25, C SIMON,    39, B MAC,     31, B ZUNICH, 37
120 DATA S GOODMAN, 32, L FAST,     29, S BUNCH,   40, N YOUNG,  33
130 DATA C BABBAGE, 38, A TURING,  32, B PASCAL,  36, B MCCOY,  39
140 DATA D RITCHIE, 23, S JOHNSON, 28

200 READ COUNT
210 SUM = 0
220 FOR N = 1 TO COUNT
230      READ STUDENT$, GRADE
240      SUM = SUM + GRADE
250 NEXT N
260 PRINT "THE AVERAGE OF"; COUNT; "GRADES IS"; SUM/COUNT
```

Computer Output:

```
THE AVERAGE OF 14 GRADES IS 33
```

Example:

```
10 REM CALCULATE THE AVERAGE SCORE ON A TEST
20 REM THE SENTINEL VALUE ***END OF DATA*** AS A STUDENT NAME
30 REM ENDS THE INPUT DATA

110 DATA J TAYLOR,   25, C SIMON,    39, B MAC,     31, B ZUNICH, 37
120 DATA S GOODMAN, 32, L FAST,     29, S BUNCH,   40, N YOUNG,  33
130 DATA C BABBAGE, 38, A TURING,  32, B PASCAL,  36, B MCCOY,  39
140 DATA D RITCHIE, 23, S JOHNSON, 28
150 DATA ***END OF DATA***

200 SUM = 0
210 COUNT = 0
```

```
220 READ STUDENT$
230 WHILE STUDENT$ <>   "***END OF DATA***"
240      READ GRADE
240      SUM = SUM + GRADE
250      COUNT = COUNT + 1
260      READ STUDENT$
260 WEND
260 PRINT "THE AVERAGE OF"; COUNT; "GRADES IS"; SUM/COUNT
```

Computer Output:

```
THE AVERAGE OF 14 GRADES IS 33
```

Sometimes a programmer is given a problem that requires multiple passes through a set of data. Let's expand the problem of the calculation of the average grade and print the names and scores of students who scored above the class average. But that average can't be determined until all of the grade data have been processed. The RESTORE statement indicates the line number of the next DATA statement to be read. This allows DATA statements to be reused.

Statement: RESTORE *LineNumber*

LineNumber is an optional parameter that indicates which DATA statement is to be read next. If it is absent, the first DATA statement in the program is reused.

Example:

```
10 REM PRINT THE NAMES AND SCORES THAT ARE ABOVE AVERAGE
20 REM THE NUMBER OF TEST SCORES IS THE FIRST DATA ITEM
30 REM FOLLOWED BY THE ACTUAL TEST SCORES

100 DATA 14
110 DATA J TAYLOR,   25, C SIMON,    39, B MAC,     31, B ZUNICH, 37
120 DATA S GOODMAN, 32, L FAST,     29, S BUNCH,   40, N YOUNG,   33
130 DATA C BABBAGE, 38, A TURING,   32, B PASCAL, 36, B MCCOY,   39
140 DATA D RITCHIE, 23, S JOHNSON, 28

200 READ COUNT
210 SUM = 0
220 FOR N = 1 TO COUNT
230      READ STUDENT$, GRADE
240      SUM = SUM + GRADE
250 NEXT N
260 AVERAGE = SUM/COUNT
270 PRINT "THE AVERAGE GRADE IS"; AVERAGE

300 RESTORE 110

310 FOR N = 1 TO COUNT
320      READ STUDENT$, GRADE
330      IF GRADE > AVERAGE THEN PRINT STUDENT$, GRADE
340 NEXT N
```

Computer Output:

```
THE AVERAGE GRADE IS 33
C SIMON        39
B ZUNICH       37
S BUNCH        40
C BABBAGE      38
B PASCAL       36
B MCCOY        39
```

Receiving Data from Outside a Program

The INPUT Statement

Encoding data from within the program is convenient when data change infrequently. When different data are to be used every time a program is run, the INPUT statement is used as a link to the outside. INPUT functions similarly to the READ statement except that the data come from the computer's keyboard rather than from internal DATA statements.

Statement: INPUT *"PromptString"*, *Variable, Variable, . . .*
   Data values are obtained from the keyboard and placed into variables.
   The constant *PromptString* is optional. Its value is displayed to the user to help identify what information is expected by the INPUT statement. If it is absent, a question mark is printed instead.

Example:

```
10 REM CALCULATE GAS MILEAGE
20 INPUT "INITIAL ODOMETER READING", INITIAL
30 INPUT "GALLONS USED AND MILEAGE", GALLONS, MILES
40 DISTANCE = MILES - INITIAL
50 PRINT DISTANCE/GALLONS; "MPG OVER"; DISTANCE; "MILES"
```

Computer Output (user's input in red):

```
INITIAL ODOMETER READING? 23060
GALLONS USED AND MILEAGE? 13.4, 23442
 28.2962 MPG OVER 382 MILES
```

INPUT always reads one line of data that is entered by the user at the keyboard. When the INPUT statement is executed, a message called a *prompt string* is displayed. After RETURN is pressed, the pairing of data items and variables goes on just as with a DATA statement. If there are more input variables than data elements, the interpreter prompts again, expecting more input to be forthcoming. The INPUT statement is unlike the DATA statement in that if there are more data elements than input variables, the excess data are discarded. In composing a reply to an INPUT request, the normal editing keys can be used to make corrections up to the time the RETURN key is pressed.

Defensive Programming When Using INPUT

Obviously, the programmer has no control over what the user enters in response to an INPUT statement. Therefore, an INPUT statement should always be followed with a section of code that checks the plausibility of the values that were just entered. Something that seems out of the ordinary should cause a message to be displayed, followed by an opportunity to reenter the information. The program in the example below shows two plausibility checks. The program is asking for two pieces of information, a name and an age. Names that start with nonalphabetic characters are looked upon with suspicion, but the user is given the freedom to confirm that his or her name really is 6 ⅞. Again, when age is requested, an answer indicating an infant or centenarian requires confirmation. However, a negative age, a physical impossibility, is flatly refused.

Example:

```
10 REM DEMONSTRATION OF DEFENSIVE PROGRAMMING WITH INPUT
20 REM ASK FOR A NAME AND AN AGE

100 INPUT "YOUR NAME IS: ", N$
110 IF N$ >= "A" AND N$ <= "ZZ" GOTO 40
120   PRINT "MY YOU HAVE A STRANGE NAME! IS "; N$; " RIGHT(Y/N)?";
130   INPUT YES$
140   IF YES$ <> "Y" GOTO 100

200 INPUT "AND YOUR AGE IS: ", AGE
210 IF AGE > 1 AND AGE < 99 GOTO 300
220   PRINT "THAT'S A FUNNY ANSWER! IS"; AGE; " REALLY YOUR AGE(Y/N)?"
230   INPUT YES$
240   IF YES$ <> "Y" GOTO 200
250   IF AGE > 0 GOTO 300
260       PRINT "SORRY, NOBODY CAN HAVE A NEGATIVE AGE"
270       GOTO 200

300 PRINT
310 PRINT "NAME: "; N$; " AND AGE:"; AGE
```

Computer Output (user's input in red):

```
YOUR NAME IS: 6 7/8
MY YOU HAVE A STRANGE NAME! IS 6 7/8 RIGHT(Y/N)? N
YOUR NAME IS: MR BILL
AND YOUR AGE IS: -3
THAT'S A FUNNY ANSWER! IS -3 REALLY YOUR AGE(Y/N)? Y
SORRY, NOBODY CAN HAVE A NEGATIVE AGE
AND YOUR AGE IS: 19

NAME: MR BILL AND AGE: 19
```

Receiving Keystrokes Immediately: INKEY$

The tight restrictions around the processing of input (such as having to separate all values with commas, having to enclose some strings within quotation marks, and requiring agreement between the type of the data and the variable) may make the unadorned INPUT statement tricky to use. There are other ways of reading data from a keyboard. The string variable INKEY$ is a reserved word in BASIC that returns each keystroke individually. Unlike line-oriented input, where the user can edit data before turning it over to the program, INKEY$ takes a value that changes as soon as any key is pressed. If no keys have been pressed since the last time INKEY$ was used, the value returned is that of the empty string (which is the value that is entered as" ").

Keyword: INKEY$
     Returns each keystroke in a string. If no keys have been pressed, the null string (" ") is returned.

Example:

```
10 LET COUNT = 0
20 REM PRINT UNTIL ANY KEY IS PRESSED
30 WHILE INKEY$ = ""
40       PRINT "IS ANYONE OUT THERE? (PRESS ANY KEY)"
50       COUNT = COUNT + 1
60 WEND
70 PRINT "AHHHH THANK YOU."
80 PRINT "I HAD TO PRINT THAT MESSAGE"; COUNT; "TIMES."
```

Computer Output:

```
IS ANYONE OUT THERE? (PRESS ANY KEY)
IS ANYONE OUT THERE? (PRESS ANY KEY)
IS ANYONE OUT THERE? (PRESS ANY KEY)
IS ANYONE OUT THERE? (PRESS ANY KEY)
IS ANYONE OUT THERE? (PRESS ANY KEY)
IS ANYONE OUT THERE? (PRESS ANY KEY)
IS ANYONE OUT THERE? (PRESS ANY KEY)
AHHHH THANK YOU.
I HAD TO PRINT THAT MESSAGE 7 TIMES.
```

The immediate processing of a user's input is appropriate in situations where there are a limited number of valid responses that can be made. An example of this is in a menu-oriented system, where a screenful of output is presented to the user and a single keystroke identifies which action the computer is to perform. Often the actions are labeled with the numbers from 1 to 9. Some computers have extra function keys that send unique codes to the waiting program.

Summary

Information can be contained in a program in DATA statements. The program retrieves the information via READ statements. The RESTORE statement allows the program to reread DATA statements.

Information is acquired from outside the program via an INPUT statement, which transfers data from the keyboard into a program's variables. Because the computer has no control over what is being entered, the validity of all information received should be checked.

The INPUT statement reads the keyboarded data a line at a time. Each keystroke can be sensed by using the reserved word INKEY$.

Exercises

1. Modify the program calculating the average grade to accept an additional piece of information, the maximum number of points that the exam is worth (40). Print out each student's name and score as a percentage; 100 is the grade to be given if every answer is correct.

*2. Write a program that intentionally tries to read more data than is provided in the program. What error message do you get?

3. What are the values of the variables A, B, and C at the end of the following program?

```
10 DATA 1, 2, 3
20 DATA 4, 5
30 READ A, C, B, C
40 READ B
```

*4. Write a program that uses INPUT to read several numbers and then prints their sum. What happens when an alphabetic character is typed in response to the INPUT statement?

*5. Write a program that uses INKEY$ to measure how long it takes to type a sentence. Assume that the input will be a sentence that ends with a period. Then run the program using the sentence "THE QUICK BROWN FOX JUMPED OVER THE LAZY DOG." as input.

6. Write a program that accepts the initials of some of your classmates and prints their full names in response. Let the user of the program ask for several names. Use informative prompts that guide the user through the program.

7. A small Midwestern company produces three products: flywheel gromis, muffler bearing, and widget. They cost $10, $25, and $37, respectively. Write a program to be used by a secretary who will answer the phone and take a customer's order. Try to use an ON-GOTO statement. The sales tax is 6%, except on the edible widget, which is taxed at a rate of only 1%.

8. Given the following data base of values for mileage and gallons of gasoline used, write a program that will print the average miles per gallon.

```
10 REM DATA BASE IS PAIRS OF VALUES FOR MILEAGE AND GALLONS USED
20 REM    ENDS WITH MILEAGE OF ZERO
30 DATA 12095, 12.5, 12350, 9.3
40 DATA 12795, 13.7, 13201, 14.9
50 DATA 0
```

FUNCTIONS: ANOTHER KIND OF OPERATOR

BASIC comes with a rich set of built-in functions. There are more than 60 in the IBM PC version of MicroSoft BASIC. Furthermore, we will describe a way for the programmer to add more functions of his or her own design. If each built-in function were given a special key, the computer's keyboard would need to be very large indeed. Fortunately, functional notation comes to the rescue. Functional notation is simply the name of a *function* (which will always be a reserved word) followed by a list of parameter expressions. The parameter list is encased within parentheses, as shown here:

FunctionName(FirstParameter, SecondParameter, . . .)

The parameters for a function can be formulas or variables. Each function requires a particular number of parameters. Furthermore, each parameter has a type limitation of either string or numeric.

A function performs some operation using the values of the parameters as input data.

Table A.7 Some Mathematical Functions

Function	Action
SQR (*n*)	Calculates square root of *n*
TAN (*rad*)	Finds tangent of *rad*, which is in radians
SIN (*rad*)	Finds sine of *rad*
COS (*rad*)	Finds cosine of *rad*
RND	Computes a "random" number

The output of a function is either a string or a number (depending on whether or not the function name ends with a dollar sign). The whole combination of a function name followed by parentheses enclosing the necessary parameters may be used to build up larger formulas. A function can be placed in a formula wherever a variable is allowed. In fact, the only place where a function can't take the place of a variable is on the left-hand side of an assignment statement.

Mathematical Functions

Each of the mathematical functions in Table A.7 operates on a single numeric parameter and returns another number. The parameter for the function is unchanged. The function RND is slightly different in that its parameter may be omitted in certain cases.

Square Roots

The square root of a number is computed by the function SQR. Such a calculation is required in many algorithms that deal with distance. One such algorithm you may be familiar with is the formula for determining the length of the longest side of a right triangle—the hypotenuse. Pythagoras, a Greek philosopher of the sixth century B.C., is credited with the solution shown in Figure A.3.

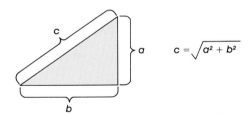

$$c = \sqrt{a^2 + b^2}$$

Figure A.3 The Pythagorean Theorem

If Pythagoras had had an IBM PC, he might have written the program shown in the box below (we've translated it from Greek for you).

Example:

```
10 REM   FROM THE SHOP OF PYTHAGORAS, PHILOSOPHER EXTRAORDINAIRE
20 REM   WRITTEN BY MY HAND, THIS 13 FEBRUARY 578 B.C.
30 REM   AN INTERESTING THEOREM ABOUT TRIANGLES FOLLOWS
40 INPUT "ENTER, O STUDENT, THE HEIGHT AND WIDTH ", A, B
50 C = SQR(A * A + B * B)
60 PRINT "MEASURE THE TRIANGLE, ";
70 PRINT "I SAY ITS HYPOTENUSE IS"; C
```

Computer Output (user's input in red):

```
ENTER, O STUDENT, THE HEIGHT AND WIDTH 4,9
MEASURE THE TRIANGLE, I SAY ITS HYPOTENUSE IS 9.848858
```

Trigonometry

BASIC also comes equipped with a small battery of trigonometric functions. The function COS computes the cosine of an angle, SIN computes the sine, and TAN computes the tangent. The angle is measured in units called *radians*. To convert from degrees to radians, multiply the degrees by π (the Greek letter pi is used to symbolize the number 3.14159) and then divide by 180.

Statement: TAN(X)

TAN computes the tangent of its parameter X, which is expressed in units of radians.

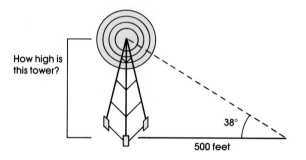

How high is this tower?

38°

500 feet

Example:

```
10 REM A SURVEYOR STEPS BACK 500 FEET FROM THE BASE OF A TOWER
20 REM HE SIGHTS THE TOP OF THE TOWER AT 38 DEGREES
30 REM HOW HIGH IS THE TOWER?
40 ANGLE = 38
50 RADIANS = ANGLE * 3.14159 / 180
60 DISTANCE = 500
70 PRINT "THE TOWER'S HEIGHT IS"; TAN(RADIANS) * DISTANCE; "FEET"
```

Computer Output:

```
THE TOWER'S HEIGHT IS 390.643 FEET
```

Random Numbers

Computers are used to simulate real-world situations. But events in the real world are rarely certain: there is a 20% chance of rain today; will I get an A on this Friday's test? The function RND allows a programmer to simulate probabilistic events. Every time RND is called, it returns a number between 0 and 1. The computer isn't guessing. It uses a special algorithm to generate what are called pseudorandom numbers. The entire sequence of numbers generated by RND is determined by a single initial number—the *seed*. The value of the seed is set by the RANDOMIZE statement.

Function: RND
Statement: RANDOMIZE *SeedValue*

RND returns a random value between 0 and 1 every time it is evaluated.

RANDOMIZE establishes a starting point for the random number sequence that is generated by RND. *SeedValue* can be any number; it is not limited to values between 0 and 1.

Example:

```
10 REM CALCULATE A SEED BASED ON THE TIME TO PRESS A KEY
20 COUNT = 0
30 PRINT "PRESS ANY KEY TO BEGIN"
40 WHILE INKEY$ = ""
50    COUNT = COUNT + 1
60 WEND

100 RANDOMIZE COUNT

200 FOR I = 1 TO 5
210    PRINT RND
220 NEXT
```

Computer Output (*note:* you won't be able to duplicate this sequence; it depends on the reaction time required to read the message and press a key):

```
PRESS ANY KEY TO BEGIN
```
User presses a key
```
        0.2354236
        0.9345738
        0.1238123
        0.0345340
        0.7234871
```

When debugging a program that uses random numbers, it is advisable to use a constant in the RANDOMIZE statement. Then any data-dependent program branches will take the same path in response to the same user input. However, if RND were used to simulate the shuffling of a deck of cards, players would probably get suspicious if every time they played the game, the jack of hearts came up as the first card. One way to get a suitable value as a seed for the random number generator is to read it from a system-provided time-of-day clock. Some computers provide a reserved variable that represents the number of milliseconds for which the machine has been on. Another technique, demonstrated in the box above, is to measure how long it takes a user to press a key in response to a message.

Functions That Deal with Strings

Cutting Strings Apart: LEFT$, RIGHT$, and MID$

There are several built-in functions that perform operations on strings. The ones that return a string as the result, such as LEFT$, have names that end with a dollar sign, just as string variable names do. There are several functions that chop a string into subparts. All functions that return strings make a copy of the information they need to perform their task. The original string is untouched by the operation.

Functions: LEFT$(*String$, Number*)
             RIGHT$(*String$, Number*)
             MID$(*String$, Position, Number*)
             LEN(*String$*)

LEFT$ returns a new string containing *Number* characters from the left part of *String$*.

RIGHT$ returns a new string containing *Number* characters from the right part of *String$*.

MID$ returns a new string consisting of the middle *Number* characters of *String$*. The first character of the new string is the one in the original string designated by *Position;* a 1 indicates the first character of the string *String$*.

LEN counts the number of characters in *String$*.

Example:

```
 5 REM PRINT A WORD DOWN THE LEFT SIDE OF THE SCREEN
10 WORD$ = "AMERICA"
30 COUNT = LEN(WORD$)

40 FOR X = 1 TO COUNT
50    PRINT LEFT$(WORD$, 1)
60    WORD$ = RIGHT$(WORD$, COUNT - X)
70 NEXT X
```

Computer Output:

```
A
M
E
R
I
C
A
```

Converting from a Number to a String

The ASCII code defines several nonprinting characters. These characters are called *control characters.* They influence how data are written on the screen or by the printer. For example, the computer's speaker beeps whenever the character with code number 7 is received. The function CHR$ converts a number to an ASCII character. The function ASC performs the reverse transformation. It returns the ASCII code number that corresponds to the first character of a string.

Functions: CHR$(*Number*)
             ASC(*String$*)

CHR$ converts *Number* into a string using the ASCII code.

ASC converts the first character of *String$* into an ASCII code number.

Example:

```
10 PRINT "THIS MESSAGE BEEPS" + CHR$(7)
20 PRINT "THE CHARACTER 7 HAS THE ASCII CODE NUMBER"; ASC("7")
```

Computer Output:

THIS MESSAGE BEEPS   (a bell will sound)
THE CHARACTER 7 HAS THE ASCII CODE NUMBER 55

User-Defined Functions

Programmers are not limited to the built-in set of functions provided by the manufacturer of a BASIC interpreter. A commonly used expression may be saved and accessed whenever it is needed by creating a user-defined function. The new function name always starts with the characters FN followed by a name that the programmer chooses. If the function's value is going to be a string, the function name must end with a dollar sign. The summary below shows how the DEF FN statement is used to create user-defined functions. These functions are a type of shorthand for programmers. They save space in the computer's memory (since the translated expression for the function needs to be stored only once) and make programs easier to read and to modify.

Statement: DEF FN*Name*(*FirstParameter, SecondParameter*, . . .) = *Expression*
        DEF FN adds a function to the list of built-in BASIC functions. The parameters that follow *Name* are used in the evaluation of the function's expression. *Expression* can be any BASIC expression whose type matches the type of the function's name. Any variables may be used in the expression. The names in the parameter list stand for the values of the first, second, and so on, parameters when the function is called from the program.

Example:

```
10 DEF FNDISTANCE(X1,Y1,X2,Y2) = SQR((X1 − X2) ^ 2 + (Y1 − Y2) ^ 2)
20 PRINT FNDISTANCE(2,4,5,8)
```

Computer Output:

5

Summary

Functions transform the value of some input formula into a result. There are two types of functions: those that return numeric results, and those that return string results. The value generated by a function can be used in other formulas.
        This section demonstrated some numeric functions: SQR for taking square roots, TAN for computing the trigonometric tangent, and RND for producing random sequences of numbers. The sequence that is returned by RND is determined by the seed value in the RANDOMIZE statement.
        The string-valued functions RIGHT$, LEFT$, and MID$ each return a segment of a string. LEN counts the number of characters in a string. CHR$ constructs a string consisting of a single ASCII character. ASC performs the reverse translation; it changes the first character of a string into a number, using the ASCII code.
        User-defined functions are created with the DEF FN statement.

Exercises

1. Can functions be the parameters for other functions? If so, what is printed as a result of the following statement?

```
10 PRINT SQR(SQR(16))
```

2. A palindrome is a sentence that reads the same forward and backward (punctuation marks and blank spaces are ignored, however). For example, the following sentence is a palindrome:

   A MAN, A PLAN, A CANAL: PANAMA!

   Write a program that will tell whether or not a sentence is a palindrome. (*Hint:* Use MID$ to access each character in the sentence.)
3. Write a puzzle-making program that uses RND to jumble the characters of a word into a new pattern. You might find LEFT$, RIGHT$, and MID$ handy for picking characters out of the original word.
4. Write a program that prints the character that follows the period in the ASCII code.
5. Define your own function for returning a random character from a string.
6. When a function is user-defined, the parameters are simply placeholders for values that will be calculated when the function is used. Ordinary variable names may also be included in the formula. Define a function that computes the price of an item. The function should have two input parameters: the basic cost of the item, and the number ordered. Allow for a changeable tax rate and a company discount when calculating the price.

SUBROUTINES: REUSING PROGRAM STATEMENTS

The GOSUB Statement

One of the indications of a good program is that it is the simplest one possible for accomplishing the task for which it was built. Simple programs avoid duplication of effort. Instead of repeating a particular set of identical instructions every time they are needed, a *subroutine* can be used to record the instructions just once and permit their repeated use. BASIC has two statements that are used to construct subroutines: GOSUB and RETURN. GOSUB acts like the GOTO statement in that it allows selection of the next statement to be executed. However, it also saves the line number of the statement that follows it. After the subroutine has performed its task, the RETURN statement uses the saved line number to determine where execution should continue.

Statements: GOSUB *LineNumber*
              RETURN
              END

GOSUB transfers control to the subroutine that begins at the designated line number. The line number of the statement following the GOSUB is saved.

The RETURN statement in a subroutine will direct execution back to the statement following the GOSUB that invoked the subroutine.

The END statement stops the execution of a program. It is often used at the end of the main routine to keep the BASIC interpreter from "falling into" any subroutines that the programmer has placed following the main routine.

Example:

```
10 GOSUB 100
20 PRINT "STATEMENT 20"
30 GOSUB 100
40 PRINT "STATEMENT 40"
50 END

100 PRINT "STATEMENT 100"
110 RETURN
```

Computer Output:

```
STATEMENT 100
STATEMENT 20
STATEMENT 100
STATEMENT 40
```

    The concept of the subroutine is extremely important. Large and complex programs simply couldn't be written without using subroutines. Programmers couldn't keep up with the interdependencies in trying to amass 10,000 statements as one tangled nest of GOTOs. The solution is to break a large, unmanageable task into smaller ones. Two benefits are immediately derived. The programmer only has to know what each smaller task is supposed to do, how it receives its input data, and where it is in order to generate its output. The programmer needn't be concerned with every detail of the overall task. The second benefit is the ability to test the subtask's proposed solution without running or reviewing the entire program.

    Subroutines do impose some burden of extra documentation on the programmer. Since the code will be shared (several GOSUBs will lead to the same subroutine), the programmer must be very careful to state which variables are going to be used for input, output, and temporary storage. Failure to adequately document subroutine interfaces can lead to bugs that are very subtle and therefore difficult to diagnose.

Example:

```
10 QUESTION$ = "HOW OLD ARE YOU?"
12 LOWLIMIT = 1
14 HIGHLIMIT = 99
16 GOSUB 1000
18 AGE = ANSWER

30 QUESTION$ = "WHAT DAY OF THE MONTH WERE YOU BORN ON?"
32 LOWLIMIT = 1
34 HIGHLIMIT = 31
36 GOSUB 1000
38 DAYOFMONTH = ANSWER

70 PRINT "AGE IS"; AGE; "BIRTHDAY ON"; DAYOFMONTH
80 END
```

```
1000 REM SUBROUTINE: ASK A QUESTION$, RETURN A NUMERIC ANSWER
1010 REM SUBJECT TO THE LIMITS OF HIGHLIMIT AND LOWLIMIT
1020 REM VARIABLE YES$ USED INTERNALLY IN THIS SUBROUTINE

1030 PRINT QUESTION$;
1040 INPUT ANSWER
1050 IF ANSWER >= LOWLIMIT AND ANSWER <= HIGHLIMIT GOTO 1090
1060 PRINT "WOULD LIKE AN ANSWER FROM"; LOWLIMIT; "TO"; HIGHLIMIT
1070 INPUT "IS YOUR ANSWER CORRECT? (Y/N) ", YES$
1080 IF Y$ <> "Y" GOTO 1030
1090 RETURN
```

Computer Output:

```
HOW OLD ARE YOU? 311
WOULD LIKE AN ANSWER FROM 1 TO 99
IS YOUR ANSWER CORRECT? (Y/N) N
HOW OLD ARE YOU? 31
WHAT DAY OF THE MONTH WERE YOU BORN ON? 25
AGE IS 31 BIRTHDAY ON 25
```

The programs that solve subtasks are often called *modules*. Modular programming is the art of designing a software solution to a problem that decomposes into nearly independent subtasks. The modules themselves may be further divided until a manageable set of specifications and programs is reached. The technique of assigning subtasks to modules is one that is probably best learned from actually writing programs. If the specifications are written with too many constraints, too many modules will be necessary. For example, the example program in the box above contains a general-purpose subroutine that asks a question and does a rudimentary first-level check on the correctness of the answer. One could have specified that there be one module to ask the first question (for a person's age) and another module to ask the second (for the birthdate). A middle ground might be to create two very small *interface* subroutines that do nothing more than establish the parameters for a more general-purpose subroutine's use. Just such an adaptation is presented below.

Example:

```
10  GOSUB 100
20  GOSUB 200
30  PRINT "AGE IS"; AGE; "BIRTHDAY ON"; DAYOFMONTH
40  END

100 QUESTION$ = "HOW OLD ARE YOU?"
110 LOWLIMIT = 1
120 HIGHLIMIT = 99
130 GOSUB 1000
140 AGE = ANSWER
150 RETURN

200 QUESTION$ = "WHAT DAY OF THE MONTH WERE YOU BORN ON?"
210 HIGHLIMIT = 31
```

```
220 LOWLIMIT = 1
230 GOSUB 1000
240 DAYOFMONTH = ANSWER
250 RETURN
```

Selecting One of Many Subroutines: The ON-GOSUB Statement

An alternative form of the GOSUB statement lets you call one subroutine out of a list. The ON-GOSUB statement is nearly identical to the ON-GOTO statement. Instead of the unconditional branch of a GOTO, a call to a subroutine is made.

Statement: ON *Expression* GOSUB *FirstLine#*, *SecondLine#*, . . .
     The expression is evaluated and the integer part of it is used to select a subroutine from the list of line numbers at the end of the statement. A value less than 1 causes an error and the program is stopped. A value greater than the number of line numbers provided causes execution to continue at the statement following the ON-GOSUB statement.

Example:

```
10 FOR I = 1 TO 3
20 ON I GOSUB 100,200,300
30 NEXT
40 END

100 PRINT "THE SUBROUTINE AT LINE 100"
110 RETURN

200 PRINT "THE SUBROUTINE AT LINE 200"
210 RETURN

300 PRINT "THE SUBROUTINE AT LINE 300"
310 RETURN
```

Computer Output:

```
THE SUBROUTINE AT LINE 100
THE SUBROUTINE AT LINE 200
THE SUBROUTINE AT LINE 300
```

Summary

Subroutines allow the reuse of valuable parts of a program. Rather than repeating a set of instructions every time they are needed, the code can be written once and then called with a GOSUB statement. Subroutines can call other subroutines. Each RETURN statement branches, in effect, to the statement following the most recent GOSUB.
     The ON-GOSUB statement selects one subroutine from a group. It is similar to the ON-GOTO statement.

Exercises

1. Write a subroutine that converts the number of seconds since midnight into hours, minutes, and seconds. (*Hint:* Use the MOD operator to compute the seconds first.)
2. Write the subroutine that converts hours, minutes, and seconds back to seconds since midnight. For consistency, set the values of hours and minutes to zero after the conversion is done.

 ARRAYS: GROUPING RELATED DATA ELEMENTS TOGETHER

Arrays gives the programmer the capability of saving several pieces of related information under one variable name. The individual pieces of information may be easily accessed in whatever order the programmer dictates. This is in contrast to the capability given by READ and DATA statements, where, to get to the fifth piece of data, the first four must be read. Also, since arrays are variables, the data elements in them may be modified during the program's execution. Individual pieces of data, which are called *elements*, are extracted using one or more subscripts. The array reference is written as a variable name followed by a list of subscripts encased in parentheses. The number of subscripts used is called the *dimension* of the array.

An array that has a single subscript can be envisioned as a line of data storage cells. As shown in Figure A.4, a two-subscript array corresponds to a rectangular table; one subscript specifies a row, the other specifies a column.

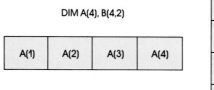

Figure A.4   How Arrays Are Arranged in Memory

Textually, an array reference is indistinguishable from a function call. But since an array is really a variable, the array reference may be placed on the left-hand side of an assignment statement. The DIM (for DIMension) statement indicates how much memory should be reserved for the elements of an array. The first use of a variable as an array variable will allocate enough memory space to work with subscripts up to 10.

Statement: DIM *Variable(MaxFirstSubscript, MaxSecondSubscript, . . .)*
Array Reference: *Variable(FirstSubscript, SecondSubscript, . . .)*

The DIM statement reserves memory space for arrays. Singly dimensioned arrays with subscripts less than 10 need not be declared. The BASIC interpreter will automatically allocate storage for them. The number of subscripts and the maximum value for each is specified for a variable. Several variables may be declared in one DIM statement by separating the individual declarations with commas.

Example:

```
10 DIM ARRAY (11)
20 ARRAY(1) = 1
30 ARRAY(2) = 1
```

```
40 FOR I = 3 TO 11
50      ARRAY(I) = ARRAY(I - 1) + ARRAY(I - 2)
60 NEXT
70 FOR I = 1 TO 11
80       PRINT I, ARRAY(I)
90 NEXT
```

Computer Output:

```
1        1
2        1
3        2
4        3
5        5
6        8
7        13
8        21
9        34
10       55
11       89
```

Arrays find many uses in programs. The program in the box below reads words into an array and alphabetizes them. The same algorithm would work with numbers if the array name were changed from a string to a numeric variable name. The program works by comparing an array element with the one directly after it. If the first element is larger than, or comes after, the next two values trade positions. At the end of one pass through the array, the largest element has made its way through the ranks and is at the end of the array. Other elements may also have traded places. Because of the way the values move, this algorithm is called a *bubble sort*.

Example:

```
10 DATA "THIS","IS","THE","BUBBLE","SORT","PROGRAM","IN","ACTION"
20 N = 8
30 FOR INDEX = 1 TO N
40     READ ARRAY$(INDEX)
50 NEXT

60 GOSUB 100
70 FOR INDEX = 1 TO N
80     PRINT ARRAY$(INDEX);
90 NEXT
91 PRINT
92 END

97 REM BUBBLE SORT SUBROUTINE IN WHICH N ELEMENTS OF ARRAY$
98 REM ARE PLACED IN ALPHABETICAL ORDER
99 REM INTERNALLY USES VARIABLES INDEX, LAST, AND TEMP$

100 FOR LAST = N - 1 TO 1 STEP - 1
110     FOR INDEX = 1 TO LAST
```

```
120      IF ARRAY$(INDEX)     <= ARRAY$(INDEX + 1) GOTO 160
130          TEMP$            = ARRAY$(INDEX)
140          ARRAY$(INDEX)    = ARRAY$(INDEX + 1)
150          ARRAY$(INDEX + 1) = TEMP$
160      NEXT INDEX
170 NEXT LAST
180 RETURN
```

Computer Output:

```
ACTION BUBBLE IN IS PROGRAM SORT THE THIS
```

Summary

Arrays are used to hold groups of related variables. The individual elements can be accessed quickly using a subscript. The number of subscripts is called the dimension of an array. A DIM statement is used to reserve space in memory for an array.

Exercises

1. Which of the following are not acceptable array references?
   SUN(3)   TAN(2)   LOTION(5)   HELPS("SKIN")
2. Rewrite the bubble sort subroutine to sort numbers instead of strings.
3. Write a subroutine that produces a horizontal bar chart when it is given an array of data points. Assume that the numbers are all positive. A negative number signifies the end of the array. Use the following function to fill the array with 24 data points:

```
10 DEF FNTEST(X) = 100 * SQR(X)
```

4. Generate 101 random numbers using RND. Their average can be computed by adding all of them together and dividing by 101. Write a program that determines how many of the values are less than the average.
5. Write a grade-calculating program. First, prompt for the maximum score on a test. Then acquire the students' names and their raw scores using INPUT statements. Save the raw data in arrays. Have program print out the grades in two blocks: first, those who scored above average, and second, those who scored below.

 ## FILES: WORKING WITH SECONDARY STORAGE

The data and information accumulated in memory when a program is running is totally erased when a new BASIC program is loaded or when the current BASIC program stops executing and returns control of the processor back to the operating system. Microcomputers can lose information stored in primary memory as a result of power interruptions. Secondary storage, usually in the form of magnetic disk or tape, retains information after the program that created it stops running.

BASIC's file-handling capabilities give programs access to secondary storage, input, and output devices. The OPEN statement identifies either a secondary storage file or a peripheral device to be operated for INPUT or PRINT statements. Any device that can communicate using the ASCII code can be operated from a BASIC program. This includes a number of nontextual output devices, such as pen plotters. OPEN converts a file name into an integer number. The file name controls which storage or peripheral device is to be manipulated.

Statements: OPEN *"Filename"* AS *#FileNumber* FOR *"Mode"*
              CLOSE *#FileNumber*

OPEN establishes a path from BASIC's INPUT and PRINT statements to a data file on a secondary storage device. The parameter *Filename* may also designate a peripheral device using the ASCII code, such as a terminal or telecommunications modem.

AS *#FileNumber* selects a file number that will be used for all subsequent operations dealing with the file.

FOR is an optional parameter that may indicate special attention should be given to a file. Possible modes are OUTPUT, INPUT, and APPEND. OUTPUT mode deletes any file that might exist when the OPEN is executed. A new file is created. With APPEND, new output is added to the end of an existing file. INPUT marks the file as being *read-only*. The file will not be modified by the program.

CLOSE *#FileNumber* breaks the path to the designated file. System resources that were allocated for the file's access are freed.

Example:

```
10 OPEN "TEMPFILE" AS #1
20 CLOSE #1
```

Several files may be opened simultaneously for processing. A file number is a value assigned by the programmer, which serves to designate a file in other program statements. Opening a file usually consumes some of the computer's memory resources. Because secondary storage devices are much slower to access than primary memory, a programming technique called *buffered I/O* is used for file access. Instead of immediately writing small pieces of information onto a disk file, a small section of memory, called a *buffer*, is used to accumulate several pieces of information. Only after enough data has been written to fill the buffer does an actual transfer to the storage device take place. The CLOSE statement informs the BASIC interpreter that no further access will be made to the indicated file. If there is any buffered data, they are written to the file at this time.

The format for a file name depends on the computer being used. There are usually restrictions on the number of characters that can be used in a file name; file names may be restricted to upper-case characters.

Information is recorded in files using the PRINT statement. Data is read using INPUT statements. A number symbol (or a sharp if you're musically inclined) and file number direct the data transfers to and from the file rather than to the screen and from the keyboard. As with normal INPUT statements, the types of variables and data must match. However, since there is no convenient mechanism for correcting data interactively, a mismatch between data type and variable type will cause an error message and will stop execution of the program.

Statements: INPUT *#FileNumber Variable, Variable, . . .*
              LINE INPUT *#FileNumber Answer$*
              PRINT *#FileNumber Formula, Formula, . . .*

INPUT reads in data records from a file and assigns values to variables.

LINE INPUT reads one line of data into a string variable.

PRINT writes formatted information into a file. Semicolons can also be used with the same effect as they normally have when using PRINT.

Examples:

```
10 OPEN "EVENFILE" AS #2
20 OPEN "ODDFILE" AS #1
30 FOR I = 1 TO 10
40      IF I MOD 2 = 0 THEN PRINT #2 I ELSE PRINT #1 I
50 NEXT
60 CLOSE #1
70 CLOSE #2
RUN
```

In a later session:

```
10 OPEN "EVENFILE" AS #1
20 INPUT #1 ANSWER
30 PRINT ANSWER
40 IF ANSWER <>  10 GOTO 20
```

Computer Output (for later session):

```
2
4
6
8
10
```

Summary

The path to a file on a secondary storage device is created by the OPEN statement. The mode in which a file is opened controls the operations that can be performed on it. Output files are created as needed. Any previous data associated with a particular file is usually removed first. The OPEN statement can also designate that output be appended to an already existing file. An input file can only be read from.

The CLOSE statement closes the path to a file. The resources that were allocated for the processing of the file are freed for other use.

The file number is an integer number. A number symbol (#) is used with the file number to cause INPUT or PRINT statements to refer to a file rather than to keyboard or screen, respectively.

Exercises
1. Write a program that copies lines of keyboard input into a file. Use an ordinary INPUT statement to read from the keyboard. Stop when a line containing only a period is entered.
2. Write a program that reads files from secondary storage and prints them on the screen. Stop when a blank line is read.

Picture Credits

Special thanks to Jeffrey Mark Dunn for his photographs taken especially for this book.

PART 1 **left** A. Woolfitt/Woodfin Camp and Assoc.; **center** Dicomed; **right** Dan McCoy/Rainbow

CHAPTER 1 **1 opener** Steven Grohe/Picture Cube **1 case** Carnegie Mellon University **1.1(a)** DAVA **1.1(b)** Bill Ballenberg **1.1(c)** NASA **1.2(a)** MSI Data Corp. **1.2(b)** Chuck O'Rear/Woodfin Camp **1.3** Ford Motor Company **1.4(a)** IBM **1.4(b)** Hewlett Packard **1.4(c)** Hewlett Packard **1.5** William Strode/General Electric **1.6** Cray Research, Inc. **1.7(a)** Chuck O'Rear/Woodfin Camp **1.7(b)** Intel **1.7(c)** Peter Menzel/Stock Boston **1.10** Hewlett Packard

CHAPTER 2 **2 opener** Pat LaCroix/Image Bank **2 case** Daniel Kottke **2.1(a)** Languepin/Rapho/Photo Researchers 6C9027 **2.2** Smithsonian Institution **2.3** Dr. E. R. Degginger **2.4** Smithsonian Institution **2.5(a)** Seth Thomas **2.5(b)** Seth Thomas **2.5(c)** Dr. E. R. Degginger **2.5(d)** Joe Demaio/Picture Cube **2.6** IBM **2.7(a)** IBM **2.7(b)** Smithsonian Institution **2.8** Smithsonian Institution **2.9** Smithsonian Institution **2.10(a)** Smithsonian Institution **2.10(b)** Smithsonian Institution **2.11** Smithsonian Institution **2.12** Sperry Corp.

APPLICATION PERSPECTIVE 1 **1** American Petroleum Institute **2** American Petroleum Institute **3** Texaco, Inc. **4** Jeffrey Mark Dunn **6** Burroughs Corp. **7** Federal Reserve Bank of Boston **8** Burroughs Corp.

PART 2 **left** Jon Goell/The Picture Cube **center** Walter Bibikow/The Image Bank **right** Dicomed

CHAPTER 3 **3 opener** Chuck O'Rear/Woodfin Camp **3 case** Data General Corp.

CHAPTER 4 **4 opener** Hewlett Packard **4 case** Hank Morgan/Rainbow **4.3(a)** 3M **4.3(b)** 3M **4.3(c)** Memorex **4.4** Mohawk Data Service **4.6(a)** Sperry Corp. **4.7** IBM **4.9(a)** Sperry Corp. **4.9(b)** Carol Lee/BASF **4.9(c)** IBM **4.12(a)** Bay Bank Boston **4.12(b)** NCR **4.13(a)** Reprinted by permission of Educational Testing Service. **4.13(b)** National Computer Systems **4.15(b)** Melchior Gigicacomo/Image Bank **4.16(a)** Apple Computer, Inc. **4.16(b)** Apple Computer, Inc. **4.16(c)** Hewlett Packard **4.16(d)** Walter Bibikow/The Image Bank **4.17(a)** Texas Instruments **4.17(b)** MSI Data Corp. **4.18(a)** Apple Computer, Inc. **4.18(b)** IBM **4.18(c)** Apple Computer, Inc. **4.18(d)** Apple Computer, Inc. **4.18(e)** WICO **4.18(f)** Apple Computer, Inc. **4.19** Hewlett Packard

CHAPTER 5 **5 opener** Sepp Seitz/Woodfin Camp **5 case** Robert Llewellyn **5.5(a)** NEC **5.5(b)** IBM **5.6(top)** Genie Technologies Corp. **5.10** IBM **5.11** AT&T **5.12** 3M

CHAPTER 6 **6 opener** Steven Grohe/Picture Cube **6 case** Apple Computer, Inc. **6.1** Enertronics Research, Inc. **6.2(right)** Burroughs Corp. **6.5(a)** Diablo **6.5(b)** Epson **6.5(c)** Apple Computer, Inc. **6.6(c)** IBM **6.7(a)** Dataproducts **6.8(a)** Dataproducts **6.9(left)** IBM **6.10** Digital Equipment Corp. **6.11** Ken Whitmore/BASF **6.12(b)** Tandy Corp. **6.13(b)** Calcomp **6.15** Apple Computer, Inc.

CHAPTER 7 **7 opener** Western Union **7 case** Ken Banks **7.1** Compuserve **7.4** Lexicon **7.9** AT&T Bell Labs **7.10(a)** D. McCoy/Rainbow **7.10(b)** NASA **7.10(c)** Peter Menzel/Stock, Boston **7.11** Howard Sochurek/Woodfin Camp & Associates

APPLICATION PERSPECTIVE 2 **1** Jeffrey Mark Dunn **2** Jeffrey Mark Dunn **3** Jeffrey Mark Dunn **4** Jeffrey Mark Dunn **5** Sperry Corp. **6** Jeffrey Mark Dunn **7** Jeffrey Mark Dunn **8** Jeffrey Mark Dunn **9** Jan Halaska/Photo Researchers

PART 3 **left** J. Freis/The Image Bank **center** Dan McCoy/Rainbow **right** A. Myerson/The Image Bank

CHAPTER 8 **8 opener** Dan McCoy/Rainbow **8 case** Ed Kasni/Time Magazine **8.8** John Terence Turner/The Image Bank

CHAPTER 9 **9 opener** Dan McCoy/Rainbow **9 case** Jeffrey Mark Dunn

CHAPTER 10 **10 opener** John Blaustein/Woodfin Camp & Assoc. **10 case** IBM **10.1** Jeffrey Mark Dunn **10.2** MicroPro International **10.3** Software Arts TM **10.4** Software Marketing Assoc. **10.6** Ashton-Tate **10.7(a)** Enertronics Research Inc. **10.7(b)** Apple Computer, Inc. **10.8** Microsoft Corp. **10.9** © 1984 Interactive Picture Systems, Inc. Published by Scholastic, Inc. **10.10** Howardsoft **10.11** Lotus **10.12** Quarterdeck Office Systems, Santa Monica, California **10.13** Jeffrey Mark Dunn **10.15** Jeffrey Mark Dunn

CHAPTER 11 **11 opener** John Blaustein/Woodfin Camp & Assoc. **11 case** Julie Houck **11.7** Apple Computer, Inc.

APPLICATION PERSPECTIVE 3 **1** Cameramann International, LTD. **2** Ed Pieratt/Stock Boston **3** Jeffrey Mark Dunn

PART 4 **left** G. Gladstone/The Image Bank **center** Frank Wing/Stock Boston **right** Digital Equipment Corp.

CHAPTER 12 **12 opener** Ellis Herwig/Picture Cube **12 case** Internal Revenue Service

CHAPTER 13 **13 opener** Ashton-Tate **13 case** Larry Williams

CHAPTER 14 **14 opener** Digital Equipment Corp. **14 case** Hewlett Packard

APPLICATION PERSPECTIVE 4 **1** Jeffrey Mark Dunn **2** Jeffrey Mark Dunn **3** Hewlett Packard **4** Jeffrey Mark Dunn

PART 5 **A** Wyle Laboratories **B** Michael Melford/The Image Bank **C** Ken Cooper/The Image Bank

CHAPTER 15 **15 opener** Dan McCoy/Rainbow **15 case** Michael Datoli **15.1** Intel Corp. **15.6** Radio Shack, a division of Tandy Corp. **15.7** Data General **15.8** Compaq Computer Corp. **15.9** IBM

SPECIAL SECTION **1** Julie Houck **2** Julie Houck **3** Cameramann International, Ltd. **4** Jeffrey Mark Dunn **5** Bill Pierce/Rainbow

CHAPTER 16 **16 opener** Chuck O'Rear/Woodfin Camp & Assoc. **16 case** Jeffrey Mark Dunn **16.1(a)** Cygnet **16.1(b)** Cygnet **16.1(c)** Cygnet **16.2(a)** Mita Copystar America, Inc. **16.2(b)** Mita Copystar America, Inc. **16.3(a)** Navopache Labs **16.3(b)** Navopache Labs **16.3(c)** Energy Optics, Inc. **16.3(d)** Navopache Labs **16.4(a)** Jeffrey Mark Dunn **16.4(b)** Jeffrey Mark Dunn

Text Credits

Glossary

access arms mechanisms that move read/write heads in and out across the surface of a magnetic disk (Ch. 5)

access log a computer-security technique for keeping track of the users who enter a system or program, when they enter, and when they exit (Ch. 22)

access time how long it takes for data to be written on or read from a given storage medium (Ch. 5)

accumulator a location in the CPU that is used to hold the results of ALU operations (Ch. 3)

acoustical enclosure units cabinets used to muffle printer noise (Ch. 22)

acoustic coupler a modem that converts digital signals into sounds that are emitted into a telephone receiver cradled in rubber cups (Ch. 7)

address a unique number identifying a memory location (Ch. 1). It is the part of a computer instruction that specifies the memory location of a data value (Ch. 3)

address space the number of binary digits required to specify a given number of memory locations. (Ch. 3)

algorithm a step-by-step method for getting from input (data) to output (results) (Ch. 8)

alphanumeric characters the letters, numbers, and punctuation marks (Ch. 3)

alphanumeric display a computer display (CRT or flat panel screen) that presents only textual material (Ch. 6)

ALU acronym for *arithmetic and logic unit* (Ch. 1)

American Standard Code for Information Interchange system see *ASCII system* (Ch. 3)

analog having a continuous range of possible values (Ch. 2)

application package a collection of related programs or subprograms designed to accomplish some specified set of tasks (Ch. 10)

architecture a specification of the construction of a CPU or computer system (Ch. 3)

arithmetic and logic unit (ALU) the part of a CPU that performs mathematical operations, compares the values of two numbers, and manipulates values in other ways based on logical comparisons (Chs. 1 & 3)

arrays ordered sets or lists of data items that are identified by a single name (Ch. 9)

artificial intelligence the branch of computer science concerned with building systems that imitate human thought processes or decision making (Ch. 23)

ASCII (American Standard Code for Information Interchange) system a 7-bit code cooperatively developed by several computer manufacturers for representing characters (Ch. 3)

assembler a special program that converts assembly-language instructions into machine language (the strings of zeros and ones that the computer can manipulate) (Chs. 2 & 9)

assembly language a low-level, machine-specific programming language that allows programmers to use mnemonics (easily remembered names) for operations and symbols for variables (Ch. 2)

asynchronous transmission the sending of one character at a time over communications channels (Ch. 7)

ATM acronym for *automated teller machine* (Ch. 7)

automated teller machine (ATM) a remote terminal programmed to perform many functions of human bank tellers, such as dispensing cash, receiving deposits and payments, and reporting account balances (Chs. 7 & 19)

automatic process control a type of regulation of any manufacturing process in which a computer program, acting through specialized peripheral equipment, assesses the state of the process and operates controls so as to maintain it, or, if it has gotten out of the desired state, to bring it back within the limits (Ch. 18)

auxiliary storage see *secondary storage* (Ch. 5)

band printers line printers having a printing mechanism consisting of a scalloped steel band with five sections of 48 characters each and an array of hammers, one for each position in the line (Ch. 6)

bandwidth the range of frequencies that can be accurately transmitted over a communications channel (Ch. 7)

bar codes a means of representing data as a series of white and black marks (Ch. 4)

batch input methods data entry techniques that involve grouping data items before submitting them to the computer (Ch. 4)

baud a unit used to measure transmission speed, equivalent to bits per second (Ch. 7)

BCD (Binary Coded Decimal) system originally a 4-bit code used to represent the decimal digits; later expanded to a 6-bit code that represents 64 different characters but is no longer widely used (Ch. 3)

Binary Coded Decimal system see *BCD system* (Ch. 3)

binary point in a binary number, the period (.) separating the digits representing positive powers of 2 from those representing negative powers of 2 (Ch. 3)

binary system a number system in which the digits of each number indicate what powers of 2 (1, 2, 4, 8, 16, etc.) it contains (Ch. 2)

biotechnology an area of scientific research concerned with the problems posed by the interactions of human beings and machines (Ch. 22)

bit one binary digit; either a 0 or a 1 (Ch. 2)

black box a symbol used to designate a piece of hardware or software that performs a certain function in an unknown or unspecified manner (Ch. 12)

blocking factor the fixed number of logical records that make up a block (Ch. 5)

blocks groups of records (Ch. 5)

bpi abbreviated form of the unit *bytes per inch* (Ch. 5)

branching a programming technique in which alternative paths are set up (Ch. 3)

broadband channels communications pathways having a bandwidth greater than 3000 hertz and a transmission rate as high as several million characters per second (Ch. 7)

buffer storage a unit inserted between two different forms of storage in order to synchronize their functioning more efficiently (Ch. 3)

bulk memory a type of supplemental memory with a size and an access speed intermediate between those of primary and secondary storage (Ch. 3)

bus a group of wires that connect all of the various internal and external components of a computer system with its CPU (Ch. 15)

byte a group of 8 bits (Ch. 3)

bytes per inch (bpi) a unit used to measure the data density on a storage medium such as magnetic tape (Ch. 5)

cache memory a type of high-speed storage that bridges the gap between primary storage and certain faster circuits in the CPU (Ch. 3)

CAD acronym for *computer-aided design* (Ch. 18)

CAE acronym for *computer-aided engineering* (Ch. 18)

CAI acronym for *computer-assisted instruction* (Ch. 20)

cathode ray tube (CRT) a device in which a rapid scanning technique produces images on a screen; the basis of the majority of computer displays now in use (Ch. 6)

C³I System abbreviated form of *Command, Control, Communications, and Intelligence System* (Ch. 21)

CDP abbreviation that stands for *certificate in data processing* (Ch. 22)

cell each usable position on an electronic spreadsheet, identified by its row and column (Ch. 10)

central processing unit (CPU) the collective name for the primary memory, the arithmetic and logic unit, and the main control unit of a computer system (Ch. 1)

certificate in data processing (CDP) document awarded in recognition of a person's experience and competence in the computer field and his or her having met the ethical standards set by the Institute for Certification of Computer Professionals (ICCP) (Ch. 22)

chain printers line printers that are similar to band printers except that the characters are embossed on small pieces of metal joined as links in a looped chain (Ch. 6)

channels special-purpose microcomputers or minicomputers that control the movement of data between a CPU and input/output devices (Ch. 11)

channels communications lines (Ch. 7)

character printers machines that print a single character at a time, one after another, across the paper from margin to margin (Ch. 6)

characters per inch (cpi) a unit used to measure the data density on a storage medium such as magnetic tape (Ch. 5)

check digit a single number that is based on an input number, calculated through the use of some predefined mathematical formula, and then appended to the input number; used for error checking (Ch. 4)

chief programmer team a collection of specialized personnel directed by a chief programmer, an individual who prepares the software requirements, designs the overall structure of the program, and oversees all of the lower-level activities of the program development process (Ch. 8)

CIM acronym for *computer-integrated manufacturing* (Ch. 18)

cipher a method of concealing the meaning of a message by making a substitution for each letter (or sometimes for a fixed number of letters) (Ch. 22)

closed-loop control a type of regulation of any manufacturing process in which feedback flows both from process to computer and from computer to process (Ch. 18)

clustered devices see *multistation units* (Ch. 4)

clustered word processors see *shared word processors* (Ch. 17)

clustering methods a class of pattern recognition techniques in which pixels in satellite images are grouped together if their values (colors) are statistically similar, as determined from some predefined criterion (Ch. 20)

CMI acronym for *computer-managed instruction* (Ch. 20)

coaxial cables communications lines consisting of a central wire or wires completely surrounded by, but insulated from, a layer of outer wires that help to reduce electromagnetic interference (Ch. 7)

coding the process of expressing a fully detailed algorithm in some standard programming language (Ch. 8)

cohesion a structured programming term used to describe the closeness of the relationships among the elements within a module (Ch. 8)

COM acronym for *computer output microfilm* (Ch. 6)

Command, Control, Communications, and Intelligence (C³I) System an integrated defense network of computers, telecommunications systems, airborne warning and control systems aircraft (or AWACS), satellites, ground radar, and flying command centers (Ch. 21)

command language a set of procedures for instructing a DBMS to perform manipulations, comparisons, and operations on its data (Ch. 13)

comments explanatory notes inserted within a program's source code to help clarify its operation; ignored by the computer during program translation and execution (Ch. 9)

common carrier a company licensed or regulated by a state or the federal government to carry the property of others at approved rates (Ch. 7)

communications channels the pathways over which data are sent (Ch. 7)

communications software the programs that enable a host computer and/or a front-end processor to establish, coordinate, monitor, and control the flow of data through data communications systems (Ch. 7)

compilers special programs that translate an entire high-level language program into a complete machine language program (Chs. 2 & 9)

computer-aided design (CAD) the application of interactive computer graphics to product design (Ch. 18)

computer-aided engineering (CAE) the application of computer programs that simulate complex electrical or mechanical systems to the design and development of products (Ch. 18)

computer-aided manufacturing (CAM) the application of shared data bases and computers to all aspects of production, including the design of special tools and dies, the programming and use of computer-controlled machines, the monitoring and control of manufacturing processes, and the overall coordination of a manufacturing facility (Ch. 18)

computer-assisted instruction (CAI) the use of computers to facilitate the process of learning (Ch. 20)

computer conferencing the use of a telecommunications link to join distant computers and terminals so that users can exchange information or messages immediately and directly (Ch. 7)

computer crime the unauthorized manipulation of computers, computer programs, or data for inappropriate or unlawful purposes (generally for personal profit) (Ch. 22)

computer-integrated manufacturing (CIM) a process in which a common data base serves the needs of all the computer programs that are involved in any part of the design/manufacturing cycle (Ch. 18)

computer-managed instruction (CMI) the application of computers to helping teachers monitor their students' progress (Ch. 20)

computer output microfilm (COM) rolls or sheets of thin plastic film on which output text is reproduced photographically at greatly reduced size (Ch. 6)

computer program a precise, ordered group of statements that specifies how a computer is to execute a well-defined task (Ch. 8)

concentrator a minicomputer or microcomputer that combines the data from a number of terminals onto a single high-speed transmission line connected to a central computer (Ch. 7)

contention a technique for maintaining smooth flow of data in a data communications system; each terminal is instructed to "listen" to see if any other terminal is transmitting and, if so, to wait (Ch. 7)

contents the value stored in a memory location (Ch. 1)

control statements high-level language statements that show how the flow of program logic proceeds (Ch. 9)

control structure a pattern for the flow of logic in a computer program; a framework that indicates the order in which the operations of a program are performed (Ch. 8)

control totals sums that are computed by hand before input, recomputed by the computer afterward, and then compared as a check for input errors (Ch. 4)

coprocessors supplemental microprocessor chips that perform specialized tasks in personal computers (Ch. 15)

coupling a measure of the strength of interconnection between two modules of a computer program (Ch. 8)

courseware software programs developed for use in specific college courses (Ch. 23)

cpi abbreviated form of the unit *characters per inch* (Ch. 5)

CPU acronym for *central processing unit* (Ch. 1)

cross-compiler a translator that allows a programmer to develop a program on one computer with the intention of using it on another computer (Ch. 11)

CRT acronym for *cathode ray tube* (Ch. 6)

cryptography the practice of transcribing messages from their original form into a secret code or cipher (Ch. 22)

cylinder method an approach to the organization of data on disks in disk packs, in which each track on the surface of one disk lines up with the corresponding track on all the other disks, creating a set of nested cylinders (Ch. 5)

DAC acronym for *digital-to-analog converter* (Ch. 20)

daisy wheel printers character printers with a printing mechanism that has raised characters on the ends of arms that are arranged like the spokes of a wheel or the petals of a daisy (Ch. 6)

data the raw materials of a problem, which are input into a computer for processing (Ch. 1)

data base one or more files of interrelated or interdependent data items stored together efficiently (Chs. 2 & 10)

data base management systems (DBMS) software used to create, maintain, and access data bases (Ch. 13)

data base record a collection of related fields; essentially the same as a file record (Ch. 13)

data base system an integrated set of computer hardware, software, and human users, that is, a working combination of data base, a data base management system, and the people who use the data base (Ch. 12)

data communications the transmission of data between geographically separated computers (Ch. 7)

data definition see *data description* (Ch. 13)

data definition language (DDL) a set of commands with a formal syntax that enables users to create logical descriptions of the contents of a data base (Ch. 13)

data density the number of bytes of data stored per given area on a storage medium (Ch. 4)

data description characterization of information for the purposes of storage and display by a computer system (Ch. 13)

data dictionary a collection of information about the data elements of a computer system; typically contains the name, description, source, format, and use of each major category of data (Ch. 12)

Data Encryption Standard (DES) a standard block cipher designed by the National Bureau of Standards for use by senders and receivers of data (Ch. 22)

data flow diagram a systems analysis tool that shows the sources, storage locations, and destinations of data as well as the directions of data flow and the processes that transform data (Ch. 12)

data manipulation language (DML) an interface between a programming language and a data base management system (Ch. 13)

data models the means by which data base systems structure, organize, and manipulate data items (Ch. 13)

data transfer time how long it takes for a data item to be transmitted from secondary storage to the CPU, or vice versa (Ch. 5)

data types the kinds of data that can be processed using a particular programming language (Ch. 9)

DBMS acronym for *data base management system* (Ch. 13)

DDL acronym for *data definition language* (Ch. 13)

debugging the process of detecting, locating, and correcting logic errors (or bugs) in a computer program (Ch. 8)

decision support system (DSS) a computer-based information system that applies statistical and mathe-matical models and simulation techniques to provide a basis for judging situations analytically, thereby giving quick answers to interactively asked "what if" questions (Ch. 14)

decision table a program design aid used for specifying complex logical conditions and the actions to be taken in response (Ch. 8)

dedicated word processors systems used solely for word processing and consisting of a microcomputer with a large CRT display screen, a full keyboard, one or two floppy disk drives, and a letter-quality printer (Ch. 17)

demodulation the conversion of analog signals into digital signals (Ch. 7)

DES acronym for *Data Encryption Standard* (Ch. 22)

desk checking the process of proofreading source code for obvious syntax errors as well as for not-so-obvious logic errors (Ch. 8)

device media control language (DMCL) a facility that may be included in a DBMS to allow users to define how data are to be stored physically (Ch. 13)

diagnostic programs special software that tests computer hardware and locates faulty parts quickly (Ch. 2)

dialects versions of a high-level programming language (Ch. 2)

digital having only a discrete set of predefined values, for example, the digits 0 through 9 (Ch. 2)

digital-to-analog converter (DAC) a device that translates a discrete data value into an electrical signal of a certain voltage (Ch. 20)

digitizer an input device having a flat surface on which the user draws with a special stylus and which senses each location where the stylus touches it, produces signals communicating the x-y coordinates of the contact points, and transmits these to the computer (Ch. 4)

direct access file a group of records stored on a direct access medium, such as a disk, according to some addressing scheme (Ch. 5)

direct access medium a storage medium that allows any particular data item to be read at any time without having to go through all the preceding items (Ch. 4)

direct-connect modems modulating/demodulating devices that plug right into standard phone jacks (Ch. 7)

direct conversion a changeover from an old computer system to a new one in which an organization simply stops using the old system and immediately starts using the new one (Ch. 12)

disaster recovery team a group composed of systems analysts, disaster recovery experts, and company or agency employees that carefully plans which programs and devices are most essential and need to be reinstalled immediately if a disaster should crash the system (Ch. 22)

diskette   see *floppy disk* (Ch. 4)

disk packs   sets of magnetic disks connected in tandem that can be removed from a disk drive and stored elsewhere or transported (Ch. 2)

distributed data-processing (DDP) networks   data communications systems consisting of several widely dispersed but interconnected computers (Ch. 7)

DMCL   acronym for *device media control language* (Ch. 13)

DML   acronym for *data manipulation language* (Ch. 13)

documentation   a detailed written description of a computer program's algorithm, design, coding method, testing, and proper usage (Ch. 8)

dot matrix printers   character printers having a printhead that constructs character images by means of a vertical column of eight or nine pins that is struck repeatedly against the ribbon and paper, forming successive columns of dots that make up the characters (Ch. 6)

double-density diskettes   floppy disks that can hold 6400 bits of data per inch (Ch. 5)

drum plotters   output devices for creating hard copy graphics, in which a continuous sheet of paper rolls over a cylinder beneath one or more pens (Ch. 6)

drum printers   line printers having a solid metal cylinder embossed across its outside surface with rows of characters, one row for each character position on a line of text (Ch. 6)

DSS   acronym for *decision support system* (Ch. 14)

dumb terminal   an on-line peripheral device, usually consisting of a keyboard and CRT display, that can only be used to send data to and receive data from a computer (Ch. 4)

EBCDIC (Extended Binary Coded Decimal Interchange Code) system   an 8-bit (4 zone bits and 4 numeric bits) BCD code that represents 256 (2^8) different bit combinations (Ch. 3)

EFT   acronym for *electronic funds transfer* (Ch. 7)

egoless programming   a model that sees the creation of programs as a social activity, open to and benefiting from the feedback of colleagues, who check each other's work for errors in a constructive rather than a negative way (Ch. 8)

ELD   acronym for *electroluminescent display* (Ch. 6)

electroluminescent display (ELD)   a flat-panel screen that consists of a thin layer of zinc sulfide and manganese sandwiched between glass panels containing an embedded network of wires and that produces an image composed of orange and yellow dots (Ch. 6)

electronic bulletin boards   data communications networks that provide a means for their users to exchange messages, programming tips, advice, comments, and software (Ch. 7)

electronic funds transfer (EFT)   the movement of money into, out of, and between bank accounts by means of computers and telecommunications technology (Chs. 7 & 19)

electronic mail   a data communications service that employs computers and telecommunications lines to send and store messages that would otherwise take the form of a phone call, memo or letter (Ch. 7)

electronic spreadsheet   software that displays a table of columns and rows that is most often used to store and manipulate financial or accounting data (Ch. 10)

electronic typewriters   electric typewriters that contain embedded microprocessors (Ch. 17)

electrophoretic display (EPD)   a type of flat-panel screen in which electrically charged particles of pigment are suspended in a fluid of a different color, which is sandwiched between two glass panels in which are embedded networks of wires (Ch. 6)

electrostatic printers   character printers that employ sparks of static electricity to burn away aluminum from special aluminum-coated, black-backed paper (Ch. 6)

embedded computers   computers that are part of larger, electromechanical systems (Ch. 9)

embedded microprocessor   a preprogrammed integrated circuit on a chip which is part of some larger device (Ch. 16)

EPD   acronym for *electrophoretic display* (Ch. 6)

ergonomics   the study of people's physical, psychological, and anatomical relationship to their working environment (Ch. 22)

executive   see *supervisor* (Ch. 11)

expansion slots   connectors that accept plug-in circuit boards containing extra components (Ch. 15)

expert systems   complex software designed to imitate the thought processes and decision-making patterns of human experts in a given field (Ch. 23)

Extended Binary Coded Decimal Interchange Code   see *EBCDIC system* (Ch. 3)

external storage   see *physical storage* (Ch. 13)

facsimile transmission   a process by which text and fixed graphic images are optically scanned, converted into electronic signals, sent over communications lines, and reproduced at a remote location (Ch. 17)

fax   abbreviated form of *facsimile transmission* (Ch. 17)

feasibility study   the first step in any system project, in which the nature and scope of the problem are examined to determine whether the project should be undertaken (Ch. 12)

fiber optic cables   communications lines consisting of very thin glass filaments that transmit light (Ch. 7)

fields   groups of characters that are somehow related (Ch. 5)

fifth generation   a new type of computer that is to be based on the principles of artificial intelligence and to excel at making inferences (Ch. 23)

file managers application packages that allow users to set up, store, retrieve, and manipulate collections of data items (Ch. 10)

files collections of data records that need to be maintained outside of a computer's primary memory (Ch. 5)

fixed bar code readers stationary peripheral devices for reading bar codes such as the UPC (Ch. 4)

fixed-point number any number whose point (decimal or binary) is always in the same place in relation to its digits (Ch. 3)

flatbed plotters graphic output devices that have a pen or pens suspended from a carriage above a horizontal surface on which paper is placed (Ch. 6)

flat-panel screen a computer display device currently used in several specialized applications and the focus of a great deal of research (Ch. 6)

floating-point number a number whose size or magnitude—position of its decimal or binary point—is given as a separate quantity: the exponent. Its digits are the mantissa (Ch. 3)

floppy disk a thin, circular sheet of flexible plastic coated on one or both sides with a magnetizable substance and enclosed in a plastic or cardboard envelope (Ch. 4)

flowchart a graphic depiction of an algorithm in which standard symbols represent the necessary operations and indicate the order in which they are to be performed (Ch. 8)

front-end processor a computer, usually located at the same site as the central computer in a data communications system, whose function is to relieve the central computer of routine transmission-oriented tasks (Ch. 7)

full-duplex channels communications pathways that allow transmission in both directions simultaneously (Ch. 7)

function a subroutine that returns a single value (for example, the square root of a number) to the main program (Ch. 9)

function keys special keys on a personal computer's keyboard that reduce certain often-used commands to single keystrokes (Ch. 15)

Gantt chart a type of bar graph that shows how long it is expected to take to complete various tasks in the context of an entire schedule (Ch. 12)

generic operating systems operating systems that can be installed in any of a number of computer models (Ch. 11)

geodemographics the statistical study of populations by geographical regions (Ch. 21)

gigabyte a unit equal to 2^{30} which is approximately 1 billion bytes; used to measure storage capacity (Ch. 3)

gigaword a unit equal to 2^{30} or approximately 1 billion words (Ch. 3)

GOTO statement a programming language instruction that causes an unconditional branch from one part of a program to another (Ch. 8)

graphic display a computer output device that can present pictorial images as well as alphanumeric characters (Ch. 6)

graphic input data that describe a pictorial image or a particular place on a display screen (Ch. 4)

graphics tablet see *digitizer* (Ch. 4)

half-duplex channels communications pathways that allow transmission in either direction, but not simultaneously (Ch. 7)

Hamming codes the most frequently used redundancy codes (Ch. 4)

hand-held wand an OCR input device; used in many large department stores (Ch. 4)

handshaking signals electrical impulses that are sent back and forth between computer and peripheral unit indicating readiness to send or receive data (Ch. 15)

hard copy any form of permanent computer output that a user can walk away with (Ch. 1)

hard disk a rigid, circular metal platter (usually made of aluminum) that is coated on one or both sides with a thin magnetizable film (Ch. 4)

hardware the physical devices that make up a computer system (Ch. 1)

hashing a transformation of a record key into an address to be used for direct access storage (Ch. 5)

head crash a collision between a disk drive's read/write head and any obstruction on the surface of a disk (Ch. 5)

help facilities software features allowing usage instructions to be presented on the user's display screen (Ch. 10)

heuristic algorithms problem-solving methods incorporating strategies that select good or adequate solutions from a large and unwieldy set of possibilities (Ch. 23)

hexadecimal system a number system for which the base is 16 (Ch. 3)

hierarchical model a data model for expressing information as a series of one-to-many relationships; each data item can have many subordinate items but only one item directly above it in the hierarchy (Ch. 13)

hierarchical network a DDP system in which computers are connected together in a pyramidlike arrangement that reflects their relative levels of importance (Ch. 7)

high-level languages machine-independent programming languages that allow users to express problem solutions in abstract terms (Ch. 2)

highlighting emphasizing particular sections of text on a display screen by means of underlining, increased intensity, blinking, or reverse video (Ch. 6)

HIPO (Hierarchy plus Input-Process-Output)

chart   a tool for designing programs that clearly displays what a program does, what data it uses, and what output it creates (Ch. 8)

Hollerith code   a coding scheme developed by Dr. Herman Hollerith for use with the 12-row, 80-column punched card (Ch. 4)

host computer   the machine that is designated as the central controlling unit of a data communications system (Ch. 7)

IBG   acronym for *interblock gap* (Ch. 5)

impact methods   printing techniques that resemble the working of a typewriter in the sense that an object is struck against an inked ribbon and a paper surface in order to produce an image of a character (Ch. 6)

index   a table of selected record keys and their addresses that is stored on the same disk as the file of records to which it refers (Ch. 5)

indexed sequential file   a group of records that is kept sorted so that transactions can be processed in batches; an index is used to speed up access when records are updated one at a time (Ch. 5)

industrial espionage   spying activities engaged in by corporations intent on stealing one another's ideas, designs, or trade secrets (Ch. 22)

information   the answer to a problem, the result of computer processing, or the human-usable output of a computer program (Ch. 1)

information services   organizations that offer interactive networking to users who have terminals or personal computers (Ch. 7)

inkjet plotters   computer-controlled output devices that produce images by spraying droplets of colored inks on paper rolled over a rotating drum (Ch. 6)

inkjet printers   character printers with a printing mechanism that shoots tiny, electrically charged droplets of ink out of a nozzle; the droplets are guided to their proper positions by electrically charged deflection plates (Ch. 6)

input   to enter data and programs into a computer (Ch. 1)

input/output (I/O) control unit   the subordinate part of the main control unit that oversees the peripheral equipment (Ch. 1)

instruction counter   a special register in the main control unit that contains the address of the next instruction to be executed (Ch. 3)

instructions   statements in a program that specify actions to be carried out by a computer; an instruction has two parts, an operation and an address (Ch. 3)

integrated circuits   small solid pieces of silicon containing all the components and all the interconnections found on a printed circuit board (Ch. 2)

integrated operating environment   see *software integrator package* (Ch. 10)

integrated software package   an application package

aiming to provide almost all of the commonly used tools that are needed in a business environment (Ch. 10)

intelligent modem   a modulator/demodulator that can simultaneously transmit both voice and data, automatically dial telephone numbers, automatically answer incoming calls, and test and select telephone transmission lines (Ch. 7)

intelligent terminal   a smart terminal that can be programmed by the user to perform simple processing tasks independently of the computer to which it is connected (Ch. 4)

Intelsat   the International Telecommunications Satellite, part of an international network linking more than 100 nations and 20,000 telephone circuits (Ch. 21)

interblock gap (IBG)   a blank space separating one block of records from the next on a magnetic tape (Ch. 5)

interface   a connection between a computer's CPU and a piece of equipment operating under its control (Ch. 15)

interpreters   special programs that translate a high-level language into machine language one statement at a time (Ch. 9)

interrecord gap (IRG)   a blank space that separates adjacent records on a magnetic tape (Ch. 5)

IRG   acronym for *interrecord gap* (Ch. 5)

iteration control structure   a loop, or pattern of program statements that causes the repeated processing of a set of operations (Ch. 8)

JCL   acronym for *job control language* (Ch. 11)

job   any program or part of a program that is to be processed as a unit by a computer (Ch. 11)

job control language (JCL)   special language used with multimode operating systems to specify how programs are to be run and what computer resources they will need (Ch. 11)

key   the data item on which the sorting of records is to be based (Ch. 5)

key-to-diskette unit   an independent data entry system consisting of a keyboard, a view screen, and a floppy disk drive (Ch. 4)

key-to-disk unit   an input device that allows direct entry of data onto hard disks (Ch. 4)

key-to-tape devices   input devices that record data entered at keyboards onto magnetic tape (Ch. 4)

kilobyte   a unit equal to 1024 bytes (Ch. 3)

kiloword   a unit equal to 1024 computer words; for an 8-bit CPU, the kiloword is equal to the kilobyte (Ch. 3)

knowledge-based systems   software that attempts to allow computers to make deductions from a stored base of facts and experience, rather than to execute precise algorithms that are mathematically guaranteed to solve problems (Ch. 23)

LAN acronym for *local area network* (Ch. 7)

laser card see *optical card* (Ch. 5)

laser disk see *optical disk* (Ch. 5)

laser printers page printers in which laser beams reflected from spinning disks onto electrically charged paper form electrostatic images that attract the oppositely charged particles of an ink solution (Ch. 6)

LCD acronym for *liquid crystal display* (Ch. 6)

leader the first 10 to 15 feet of a reel of magnetic tape, which are always blank (Ch. 4)

leased lines telecommunications links that connect computers with fixed destinations (Ch. 7)

LEGIS system a data base system that stores and displays information on the contents of all bills proposed in Congress as well as their current status (Ch. 21)

LEXIS a data base containing nearly 500,000 court decisions, administrative rulings, trade regulations, and securities and tax laws from the past 60 years (Ch. 21)

library managers utility programs that allow users to build and use their own collections of frequently needed modules (Ch. 11)

light pen a light-sensitive rod used with special graphics terminals (Ch. 4)

linear programming a computer science technique for finding the best or most favorable solutions to certain types of mathematical problems (Ch. 10)

line printers machines that print an entire line at a time (Ch. 6)

linkage editors see *linkers* (Ch. 11)

linkers utility programs that process the machine language code produced by assemblers or compilers and create executable modules (Ch. 11)

linking loaders see *linkers* (Ch. 11)

liquid crystal display (LCD) a flat-panel screen made of a thin layer of a liquid crystalline material between two polarized sheets of glass in which thin wires are embedded (Ch. 6)

local area network (LAN) a data communications system consisting of two or more microcomputers physically connected together with some type of wire or cable, which forms a pathway over which data are transmitted (Ch. 7)

local terminals terminals at the same site as the computer to which they are connected (Ch. 4)

logging on the process by which users of time-sharing systems identify themselves as being authorized to gain access (Ch. 10)

logical expressions statements constructed by connecting simpler statements with the logical connectives *and, not,* and *or* (Ch. 3)

logical records a name often given to records stored on tape or disk, reflecting the fact that there is some intrinsic relationship among the records' fields (Ch. 5)

logical storage the users' view of how stored data seem to be arranged (Ch. 13)

machine code see *object programs* (Ch. 2)

machine-independence the characteristic of a programming language that allows it to be used on any computer as long as that computer has the applicable translator program (Ch. 9)

machine language strings of binary digits providing program instructions and data to a computer (Ch. 2)

macroflowcharts flowcharts that depict the main segments of complete computer programs (Ch. 8)

maglev abbreviated form of *magnetic levitation* (Ch. 23)

magnetic bubble storage a form of computer memory that utilizes tiny spherical magnetized areas induced on chips of synthetic garnet (Ch. 5)

magnetic cores tiny doughnut shapes pressed from powdered magnetic material and strung together on wires to form the primary memory of second-generation computers (Ch. 2)

magnetic disk a secondary storage medium first utilized in second-generation computers (Ch. 2)

magnetic drums cylinders having a magnetizable outer surface; used as internal memory for many first-generation computers (Ch. 2)

magnetic ink character recognition (MICR) an input method by which characters printed with magnetizable ink are automatically entered into the computer (Ch. 4)

magnetic levitation a method of train propulsion employing a system of charged electromagnets mounted on the rails and on the train to provide a frictionless, vibrationless, high-speed ride (Ch. 23)

magnetic strips short lengths of plastic-covered, magnetizable coating that can hold data; often found on the backs of credit cards, bank cards, identification cards, and security badges (Ch. 4)

magnetic tape a recording medium used extensively for computer batch input and data storage; consists of a long thin strip of Mylar coated on one side with a film of an easily magnetizable substance, such as iron oxide (Ch. 4)

magnetic tape units see *tape drives* (Ch. 4)

mail-merge facility the capability of some word-processing software to merge a file of names from a mailing list with the text of a form letter, for example, to create a batch of ''personalized'' letters (Ch. 17)

main control unit a collection of circuits that coordinates the functioning of all of a computer system's components (Chs. 1 & 3)

mainframe computer a large-scale, high-speed computer, principally used by large organizations and government agencies (Ch. 1)

management information system (MIS) an organized means of providing managers with the information they need to do their jobs effectively (Ch. 14)

manufacturing resource planning (MRP) a computerized technique for preparing production plans by working backwards from the required completion or delivery date for assembled products (Ch. 18)

manufacturing support software a software application that gives assistance in the functions of production planning and control (Ch. 18)

mark sensing see *optical mark recognition* (Ch. 4)

mass storage a class of secondary storage devices that hold enormous quantities of data but have access times that are measured in tens of seconds (Ch. 5)

master files files of records that are updated periodically using transaction files (Ch. 5)

matching a process by which a computer is used to compare records from government or private information systems in order to find names that are common to more than one set (Ch. 22)

mathematical model a simplified representation, expressed in mathematical terms, of a real process, device, or concept (Ch. 10)

matte effect a common type of special effect used in movies (Ch. 20)

megabyte a unit equal to 2^{20} or approximately 1 million bytes; used to measure storage capacity (Ch. 3)

megaword a unit equal to 2^{20} or approximately 1 million words (Ch. 3)

memory the place in a computer system where data and programs are stored (Ch. 1)

memory location an electronic circuit in a computer's memory, composed of small groups of transistors, in which one number may be stored (Ch. 1)

message switcher a device that receives all transmissions from all terminals in a data communications system, analyzes them to determine their destinations and proper routing, and then forwards them to the appropriate locations (Ch. 7)

MICR acronym for *magnetic ink character recognition* (Ch. 4)

microcode a sequence of electrical signals that causes the ALU to execute a particular operation (Ch. 3)

microcomputers the smallest and least expensive computer systems (Ch. 1)

microfiche sheets of film holding very small photographic images (Ch. 6)

microfilm rolls of film holding very small photographic images (Ch. 6)

microfloppies small-sized floppy disks, commonly only $3\frac{1}{2}$ inches in diameter and completely enclosed in a hard plastic shell (Ch. 4)

microflowcharts very detailed flowcharts that illustrate the processing steps within program modules (Ch. 8)

microforms very small photographic images used to store both text and graphics (Ch. 17)

micrographics the area of information processing concerned with the production, handling, and use of microforms (Ch. 17)

microprocessor the CPU of a microcomputer; a chip created through very large-scale integration (Ch. 2)

microwaves radio signals with very high frequencies; used to transmit all kinds of data (Ch. 7)

MICR reader-sorter unit a device that automatically records the data from bank checks and then sorts them by means of the special characters printed on them with magnetic ink (Ch. 4)

milestone chart see *Gantt chart* (Ch. 12)

minicomputers computers in the middle range of size and power (Ch. 1)

MIS acronym for *management information system* (Ch. 14)

mnemonic symbols easy-to-remember abbreviations for computer operations (Ch. 9)

modem a modulator/demodulator, or an interface unit that enables a computer or terminal to transmit and receive data via telephone lines (Ch. 7)

modulation the conversion of digital signals into analog signals (Ch. 7)

module a relatively independent, identifiable group of related program statements that can be treated as a unit (Ch. 8)

monitor an output device consisting solely of a display screen (Ch. 6)

monitor see *supervisor* (Ch. 11)

monochrome of one color (Ch. 6)

motherboard a set of closely spaced, identical slots that incorporate the bus (Ch. 15)

mouse an input device consisting of a small plastic box having either wheels or a ball roller and producing electrical pulses when rolled on a flat surface; a part of many user-friendly microcomputer systems (Ch. 4)

MRP acronym for *manufacturing resource planning* (Ch. 18)

multidrop lines a system of wires or cables that connects several terminals to a computer via a single channel (Ch. 7)

multifunction intelligent workstation a computer terminal or locally linked personal computer, with an associated set of input, communications, and output devices, designed to serve the needs of executive, managerial, professional, secretarial, and clerical staff (Ch. 17)

multimode systems large, general-purpose operating systems that simultaneously support batch processing, time sharing, real-time processing, etc. (Ch. 11)

multiplexer a device that combines the signals from several terminals into a single transmission that can be carried by one communications channel (Ch. 7)

multiprocessing operating systems operating systems that coordinate the parallel execution of several instructions on a single computer system having several central processing units (Ch. 11)

multiprogramming operating systems operating systems that alternately carry out instructions from several jobs within a given time frame, creating the appearance that the computer is executing several jobs simultaneously (Ch. 11)

multistation units key-to-tape devices in which several keyboards and view screens are connected to a central controller (Ch. 4)

multitasking operating systems see *multiprogramming operating systems* (Ch. 11)

narrowband channels communications pathways with a bandwidth of less than 3000 hertz and a transmission rate between 5 and 30 characters per second (Ch. 7)

National Crime Information Center (NCIC) a central data repository maintained by the FBI and accessed by law enforcement agencies all over North America as well as in Europe (Ch. 21)

NCIC acronym for *National Crime Information Center* (Ch. 21)

network model a data model that specifies a set of records (also called nodes) and the links, or associations, between those records (Ch. 13)

NEXIS a computer-based text-searching system covering more than 100 legal and commercial publications (Ch. 21)

nibble one-half of a byte, or 4 bits (Ch. 3)

noise incorrect pixel values in satellite transmissions; caused by electrical disturbances in the atmosphere or by equipment malfunction (Ch. 20)

nonimpact methods printing techniques employing inkjet, thermal, or electrostatic processes to form character images on paper (Ch. 6)

nonprocedural languages recently developed programming languages that attempt to make it as easy as possible for users to tell the computer what to do (Ch. 9)

numerically controlled (NC) machine tool a power-driven mechanical device whose actions are determined by a program that describes, in detail, each step in the sequence of operations required to transform a piece of metal stock into a finished, high-precision, machined product (Ch. 18)

numerical weather prediction the computer simulation of the weather based on a mathematical model of the atmosphere's motion (Ch. 20)

object code the machine-language version of the source code (Ch. 9)

object programs machine-language code resulting from a compiler's translation of source programs; also known as machine code (Ch. 2)

OCR acronym for *optical character recognition* (Ch. 4)

OCR-A a standard typeface designed to be easily read by optical character recognition techniques (Ch. 4)

octal system a number system for which the base is 8 (Ch. 3)

office automation the application of new electronic, telecommunications, and computer technology in the white-collar workplace (Ch. 17)

off-line having no permanent physical connection to the CPU; requiring manual connection before accessing (Ch. 5)

OMR acronym for *optical mark recognition* (Ch. 4)

on-line physically connected to and controlled by the CPU (Ch. 5)

on-line input methods data entry techniques by which individual pieces of data are entered and processed as they become available (Ch. 4)

opcode abbreviated form of *operation code* (Ch. 9)

open-loop control a type of regulation of any manufacturing process in which information flows from the process to a monitoring computer, but no direct feedback returns from the computer to the process (Ch. 18)

operand the number on which an operation is to be performed (Ch. 9)

operating system (OS) software that controls, supervises, and supports a computer system's hardware, matching jobs that need to be done with the equipment that is available (Chs. 2 & 11)

operation the part of a computer instruction that specifies what is to be done with the data value stored at the memory location specified by the address (Ch. 3)

operational information information used by first-line management to control the repetitive, day-to-day activities of an organization (Ch. 14)

operational simulations computerized models that project how equipment will function in any of a number of hypothetical situations (Ch. 19)

operation code a binary code representing an elementary computer operation to be performed (Ch. 9)

operation decoder a special memory that stores all the sets of signals that can be sent to the ALU to cause operations to be executed (Ch. 3)

optical card a small, flat rectangle of plastic with a laser-encoded metallic strip (Ch. 5)

optical character recognition (OCR) an input technique that employs light beams to read alphanumeric characters (Ch. 4)

optical disk a circular platter covered with a thin metallic film beneath a layer of glass or plastic on which data are written and read by lasers (Ch. 5)

optical input the reading and direct entry into a computer of visible symbols not printed in special ink (Ch. 4)

optical mark recognition (OMR) an input technique widely used in the scoring of test forms; employs light beams to convert the pencil marks on forms into electrical signals that can be entered into a computer (Ch. 4)

optimizing compilers translators expressly designed to produce highly efficient object code (Ch. 11)

OS acronym for *operating system* (Ch. 11)

output to print or otherwise display any information processed or stored by a computer (Ch. 1)

packet-switching networks value-added networks that combine messages from several customers into a packet that is transmitted as a unit at high speed and then disassembled into the various messages at the carrier's office closest to their final destinations (Ch. 7)

page printers devices that print entire pages at a time (Ch. 6)

paging the ability to call up entire screenfuls (pages) of text to be displayed on a terminal screen (Ch. 6)

paging the process of dividing a program that is to be run into chunks of a fixed size and placing these chunks into virtual memory (Ch. 11)

parallel conversion a changeover from an old computer system to a new one in which both systems are run simultaneously for a time until users are satisfied with the operation of the new system (Ch. 12)

parallel interface a connection that transmits data from a computer to some peripheral device one byte at a time (Ch. 15)

parity bit an extra binary digit that is added to a byte for error-detecting purposes (Ch. 4)

password a specific sequence of letters and/or numbers that must be supplied by a user in order to gain access to a computer program or system (Ch. 22)

pattern recognition an application concerned with efficiently using computers to describe and/or identify objects in pictures (Ch. 20)

PCM acronym for *pulse code modulation* (Ch. 20)

PDP acronym for *plasma display panel* (Ch. 6)

pen plotters computer-controlled drawing machines that produce images by moving a pen or pens across the surface of paper (Ch. 6)

peripheral equipment components of a computer system's hardware through which data and programs are put into memory and results are communicated to the user; includes keyboards, display screens, printers, etc. (Ch. 1)

personal computer a stand-alone, general-purpose computer system, containing one or more microprocessors and peripherals, designed and priced to be used by an individual or small group of individuals (Chs. 1 & 15)

phased conversion a changeover from an old computer system to a new one in which users ease into the new system one step at a time (Ch. 12)

phototypesetting machines reprographic devices that accept text input and produce output on film or on special photographic paper (Ch. 17)

physical records see *blocks* (Ch. 5)

physical storage how the data are actually held on a secondary storage device (Ch. 13)

pilot conversion a changeover from an old computer system to a new one in which only one department, plant, or branch office switches over to the new system, in a kind of trial run, before everyone changes (Ch. 12)

pixels short for "picture elements"; the tiny dots of light

making up the images on computer display screens (Ch. 10)

plasma display panel (PDP) a flat-panel screen consisting of glass sheets criss-crossed with wires and sandwiching a neon gas mixture that glows orange at the points where current is flowing through two intersecting wires (Ch. 6)

plotters computer-controlled drawing machines used to produce paper output in the form of maps, graphs, charts, or illustrations (Ch. 6)

point-of-sale (POS) input data fed to a computer from terminals located at check-out counters in retail stores (Ch. 4)

point-to-point lines communications pathways that connect each terminal in a system directly to the central computer (Ch. 7)

polling a technique for maintaining smooth flow of data in a data communications system; each connected terminal, in turn, is "asked" if it has data to send (Ch. 7)

portability the capacity of a high-level language program to be translated by different compilers into machine-language programs appropriate for different computers (Ch. 2)

portable terminal small movable input devices ranging from ones with no display capabilities to ones that function like full-sized computer terminals (Ch. 4)

POS acronym for *point-of-sale* (Ch. 4)

precompilers translator programs that are employed to preprocess source code before a regular compiler is used (Ch. 11)

preliminary investigation see *feasibility study* (Ch. 12)

primary memory internal memory that is directly connected to the ALU and control unit and that holds the active data and program (Ch. 2)

primary storage see *primary memory* (Ch. 2)

printed circuit boards removable assembly (in second-generation computers) on which the electronic components were mounted (Ch. 2)

printer a piece of peripheral equipment that produces human-readable hard copy on paper (Chs. 1 & 6)

printer spacing chart a formatting tool that enables a user to specify the appearance of a printed report (Ch. 12)

printing terminals specialized computer terminals that produce output on paper instead of displaying it on a screen (Ch. 6)

problem-oriented language a specialized programming language designed to enable programmers to create solutions to a certain rather narrow range of predefined problems (Ch. 9)

procedure-oriented language a general-purpose programming language designed to enable programmers to express the logic of problem solutions without having to pay attention to the details of the computer's processing (Ch. 9)

process control systems   real-time systems that take input data from sensors, perform some analysis, and then initiate some actions that will change the process that is being regulated (Ch. 11)

process monitor   a computer that observes, records, and displays the state of a manufacturing system (Ch. 18)

process monitor systems   real-time operating systems that take input data from sensors and report this data without affecting the process that is being monitored (Ch. 11)

production control   the constant monitoring of labor, production standards, and performance (including quality control) (Ch. 19)

production planning   the development of long-term projections of how much a production line is able to manufacture, as well as how much it can afford to manufacture, based on forecasts of sales, orders, costs, and expenses (Ch. 19)

production scheduling   determination of the best start-up dates for production orders, the most efficient allocation of materials, and the least costly adjustment of inventories (Ch. 19)

program   the step-by-step list of instructions that tells a computer how to solve a problem or perform a task (Ch. 1)

program design aid   a tool for constructing computer programs that either outlines a program's overall organization or gives some of its specific steps (Ch. 8)

program development process   the series of activities necessary for the creation of a successful computer program (Ch. 8)

programmable automation   the use in manufacturing facilities of tools that can readily be reprogrammed, such as numerically controlled machine tools and industrial robots (Ch. 18)

program maintenance   an ongoing process of correcting any bugs in a program discovered during operation, upgrading the program to accommodate new hardware or software, and introducing minor improvements (Ch. 8)

programmer   a person who develops computer programs (Ch. 1)

programming language   a set of symbols and usage rules employed to direct the operations of a computer (Ch. 9)

protocols   sets of rules or procedures spelling out how to initiate and maintain data communications (Ch. 7)

pseudocode   an informal expression of a program's algorithm using words and mathematical symbols to represent the elements and flow (Ch. 8)

pulse code modulation (PCM)   the assigning of binary values to tonal output (Ch. 20)

punched cards   perforated rectangles of stiff paper; one of the very first ways of encoding data for input into calculating machines (Ch. 4)

query languages   nonprocedural languages that enable users to access and interrogate data bases by means of Englishlike statements (Ch. 9)

RAM   acronym for *random access memory* (Ch. 3)

random access file   see *direct access file* (Ch. 5)

random access memory (RAM)   a type of primary storage in which any randomly selected location can be accessed in the same amount of time (Ch. 3)

randomizing   see *hashing* (Ch. 5)

read-only memory (ROM)   a type of primary storage written to only once, after that it can only be read from (Ch. 3)

read/write heads   tiny, sensitive electromagnets that read data from and write data onto magnetic storage media (Ch. 4)

real number   see *floating-point number* (Ch. 3)

real-time operating systems   operating systems that control computers that interact with their environments to perform work; often used to control systems characterized by the need for immediate response, such as weapons systems or industrial plants (Ch. 11)

record layout form   a tool used to facilitate data formatting (Ch. 12)

records   groups of fields (Ch. 5)

register   special storage location directly connected to the main control unit and to the ALU (Ch. 3)

relational model   a data model that organizes data into flat (or two-way) tables, each made up of rows (representing data records) and columns (representing fields within the records) (Ch. 13)

relays   electromechanical devices consisting of an electromagnet and a switch (Ch. 2)

remote job entry systems   teleprocessing systems in which the host computer receives tasks to be processed from distant terminals and batches them (Ch. 7)

remote terminals   terminals located at some distance from a computer but connected to it by long cables or by phone lines (Ch. 4)

reprographics   the area of information processing concerned with the reproduction of documents, mainly at or near full size (Ch. 17)

reserved words   words that have set meanings in a programming language and that are not available for programmers to use as file or variable names (Ch. 9)

resident routines   the most frequently used components of the operating system supervisor, which are held on the system residence device (Ch. 11)

resolution   a measure of the density of pixels on a computer display screen's surface (Ch. 10)

retooling   the retraining of industrial workers in technologically useful skills (Ch. 22)

ring network   a DDP system in which several computers are connected directly to one another, with no central, dominant computer (Ch. 7)

ROM   acronym for *read-only memory* (Ch. 3)

ROM cartridge a plastic case containing one or more ROM chips mounted on a small printed circuit board (Ch. 5)

rotational delay the time it takes for the turning motion of a magnetic disk to bring the desired record under the read/write head once the access arm is in position (Ch. 5)

salami slice a computer-crime technique by which small amounts of money are regularly diverted to a nonauthorized account during normal processing (Ch. 22)

schema a global description of the conceptual organization of an entire data base (Ch. 13)

scrolling the ability to move lines of text up or down on a display screen (Ch. 6)

SDI acronym for *Strategic Defense Initiative* (Ch. 21)

secondary storage a type of memory with a higher capacity but longer access times than primary storage; the place where programs and data are kept when the computer is not processing them (Chs. 2 & 5)

sector method an approach to data organization in which the disk surface is divided into shapes like slices of a pie, called sectors; used on virtually all floppy disks (Ch. 5)

seek time how long it takes for an access arm to position its read/write head over the proper track or at the proper cylinder (Ch. 5)

segment see *data base record* (Ch. 13)

segmentation the process of dividing up a program that is to be run into a number of chunks of different sizes and placing these chunks in virtual memory (Ch. 11)

selection control structure a two-path pattern of computer program statements that reflects the IF-THEN or IF-THEN-ELSE logical structure of pseudocode (Ch. 8)

sequence control structure a pattern of computer program statements that specifies one step after another in a straightforward, linear fashion (Ch. 8)

sequential access medium any means for the storage of data from which the items must be accessed in the order in which they were recorded (Ch. 4)

sequential file a collection of data organized so that one record follows another in some fixed succession (Ch. 5)

serial interface a connection that transmits bytes of data from the computer to some peripheral unit one bit at a time in an asynchronous fashion (Ch. 15)

serial printers see *character printers* (Ch. 6)

service programs see *utility programs* (Ch. 11)

set a collection of records that have at least one attribute in common (Ch. 13)

shared word processors powerful word-processing systems based on a minicomputer or a mainframe and capable of serving multiple users on a time-sharing basis (Ch. 17)

signals pixel values that are a true part of the image transmitted by a satellite (Ch. 20)

signing on see *logging on* (Ch. 10)

silicon chip a small piece of the silicon wafer that is processed into an integrated circuit (Ch. 1)

simplex channels communications pathways that allow transmission in one direction only (Ch. 7)

simulation the use of some system (very often a computer) to represent selected characteristics of some other physical or abstract system (Ch. 10)

single-density diskettes floppy disks that can hold 3200 bits of data per inch (Ch. 5)

single-station unit a key-to-tape device with a keyboard, a view screen, a limited amount of memory, and a tape-recording mechanism (Ch. 4)

smart products any appliances, tools, gadgets, or knick-knacks that contain embedded microprocessors (Ch. 16)

smart terminal a terminal with an embedded microprocessor and some internal storage, enabling it to do some data editing prior to transmission (Ch. 4)

software controlling programs that drive the hardware comprising a computer system (Ch. 1)

software integration the bundling of several application programs into a single, powerful, easy-to-use package (Ch. 10)

software integrator package an application package that handles and transfers data among several other independent application packages (Ch. 10)

software licensing a method for protecting software manufacturer's intellectual property (the programming) against theft by copying; disks are sealed in plastic, with labels stating that once the seal is broken, the purchaser has entered into a legal and binding contract giving him or her the sole right of use (Ch. 22)

software requirements specifications that define what a computer program is to do, without giving any details concerning how this will be done (Ch. 8)

source code a computer program expressed in some programming language other than machine language (Ch. 8)

source data input methods techniques used to get data into the computer directly from documents or other sources by means of some type of scanning device (Ch. 4)

source program see *source code* (Ch. 2)

speaker-dependent systems the most prevalent type of voice recognition modules, which recognize only the speaker who recorded the templates (Ch. 4)

speaker-independent systems voice recognition modules that can, theoretically, recognize the words in their vocabularies no matter who says them (Ch. 4)

specialized common carriers companies that offer a limited number of data communications services in and between selected metropolitan areas (Ch. 7)

spooling an activity that enables several users to send output to the same printer while input and processing operations are also occurring (Ch. 11)

star network a DDP system consisting of several computers connected to a central computer (Ch. 7)

Strategic Defense Initiative (SDI) a still largely theoretical plan for a defense system against nuclear missiles, involving reconnaissance satellites, ground-based supercomputers, killer satellites, drones, and smart rocks; commonly referred to as the "Star Wars" program (Ch. 21)

strategic information information used by top management for long-range planning (Ch. 14)

structure chart a program design aid that helps programmers organize large, multipart programs (Ch. 8)

structured programming a set of software development techniques aimed at the standardization of programming teams' efforts (Chs. 2 & 8)

structured walkthroughs reviews by a group of peers of the design and/or coding of a computer program (Ch. 8)

subroutine a module, or a sequence of statements that performs a particular processing task and that can be called on from various locations in the main program (Ch. 9)

subschema the description of the organization of a specific portion of a data base (Ch. 13)

supercomputers the largest and most powerful mainframe computers (Ch. 1)

supermicros desktop computers that can service more than one user and that approach the speed and storage capabilities of many minicomputers at a fraction of the cost (Ch. 15)

superminis the most advanced minicomputers, which work with 32-bit words (Ch. 3)

supervisor the main control program of an operating system (Ch. 11)

supply reel the removable reel on which magnetic tape is stored (Ch. 4)

switched line communications link that can connect a computer through switching centers to any of a number of destinations (Ch. 7)

symbolic addressing the practice of using representative names in program statements instead of numeric memory addresses (Ch. 9)

synchronous transmission the rapid sending of data as blocks of characters (Ch. 7)

syntax the vocabulary, grammar, and punctuation of programming language (Ch. 8)

system "a collection of people, machines, and methods organized to accomplish a set of specific functions" (from the American National Standards Committee) (Ch. 12)

system crash a shutdown of a computer system as a result of equipment or software failure (Ch. 11)

system flowchart a flowchart that provides a broad overview of an entire operation without itemizing the specific input, processing, and output steps that will actually be performed (Ch. 8)

system residence device the permanent home of the operating system within on-line secondary storage (Ch. 11)

systems analysis the practice of evaluating an existing system to see how it works and how well it meets the users' needs (Ch. 12)

systems analysts professionals whose basic responsibility consists of evaluating existing manual and computer systems and planning new ones by translating users' needs into technical specifications (Chs. 1 & 12)

systems design the process of planning a new system based on the findings from a systems analysis (Ch. 12)

tactical information information used by middle management for relatively short-term planning (Ch. 14)

take-up reel the permanent reel on a tape drive (Ch. 4)

tape cartridges plastic cases enclosing small reels that hold 140–150 feet of ¼-inch magnetic tape; commonly used with minicomputer systems (Ch. 4)

tape cassettes plastic cases similar to regular audio cassettes and holding tape for microcomputer secondary storage (Ch. 4)

tape drives devices that write and read the data stored on magnetic tape (Ch. 4)

tape reels large spools of magnetic tape commonly used with mainframes and some minicomputers (Ch. 4)

tape transports see *tape drives* (Ch. 4)

telecommuting working at home using a computer linked to an office via telecommunications lines (Ch. 7)

teleconferencing holding audio and/or video meetings by electronically linking geographically dispersed participants (Ch. 17)

teleprocessing systems data communications systems consisting of remote terminals connected via channels to a central host computer (Ch. 7)

template matching in pattern recognition, the technique of comparing what is actually present against a predefined pattern (Ch. 21)

templates in a speaker-dependent system, the speech patterns against which the computer compares all subsequent voice commands (Ch. 4)

terabyte a unit equal to 2^{40} or approximately 1 trillion bytes; used to measure storage capacity (Ch. 3)

teraword a unit equal to 2^{40} or approximately 1 trillion computer words (Ch. 3)

TERCOM System abbreviated form of *Terrain Contour Matching System* (Ch. 21)

terminal a video screen with an attached keyboard used to enter into a computer and display data and programs; the most popular on-line input device (Chs. 1 & 4)

Terrain Contour Matching (TERCOM) System a specialized image-processing system that uses elevation maps to guide a Cruise missile on its planned flight path (Ch. 21)

text editors prewritten software packages that preceded word-processing software and have more limited capabilities; suitable for entering and editing computer programs and data files (Ch. 17)

thermal printers character printers that employ heat to produce characters resembling dot matrix ones on special heat-sensitive paper (Ch. 6)

time bomb a coded section of a program that initiates some event after certain other specified events have occurred; used by computer criminals to damage data for vindictive reasons or to destroy evidence of crimes (Ch. 22)

time sharing the parceling out by an operating system of successive connection times of a few milliseconds' duration to several users; creates the illusion for each user of having sole and immediate access to the computer (Ch. 2)

time-sharing operating systems operating systems that switch among several user programs at fixed intervals of time, creating the illusion that the computer is servicing several users simultaneously (Ch. 11)

top-down design an approach to program design that involves breaking down a large task into successively smaller subtasks, which are organized hierarchically (Ch. 8)

touch-panel screens input devices employing either a pressure-sensitive surface or crisscrossing beams of infrared light to enable users to enter data by simply touching a display screen (Ch. 4)

touch-tone devices input devices that send input data, in the form of sounds of varying pitches, over telephone lines from remote locations to a central computer (Ch. 4)

transaction the entering or updating of any piece of data (Ch. 4)

transaction files collections of additions, deletions, and changes to be made to sequential files (Ch. 5)

transient routines the less frequently used portions of the operating system supervisor (Ch. 11)

transistor an electronic device made of solid material and functioning like a vacuum tube (Ch. 2)

translation the conversion of source code into machine-language instructions (Ch. 8)

translator a computer program that converts programming language statements into the zeros and ones with which the computer deals (Ch. 2)

trapdoor a set of program instructions that allow the perpetrator of a computer crime to bypass a computer's normal internal security systems (Ch. 22)

Trojan horse a set of program instructions embedded in a legitimate operational program by a computer crim-

inal in order to access otherwise inaccessible data (Ch. 22)

Universal Product Code (UPC) a bar code identifying the manufacturer and the product; appears on most supermarket items and on books and magazines (Ch. 4)

universal workstation see *multifunction intelligent workstation* (Ch. 17)

UPC acronym for *Universal Product Code* (Ch. 4)

upward compatability a characteristic of a family of computers (a product line), in that a program written for one machine can be run on any larger one in the series (Ch. 2)

user-definable keys see *function keys* (Ch. 15)

user-friendly the characteristic of software that makes it easy to use; instructions and answers to questions are built in to guide the user in utilizing it (Ch. 2)

user interface the means by which the people using a computer program communicate with it (Ch. 8)

utility programs processing programs that provide users with common necessary functions (Ch. 11)

vacuum tube an electronic switch that operates in a matter of microseconds; employed in the first electronic computers (Ch. 2)

value-added carriers companies that lease communications channels from common carriers and add extra services beyond the basic ones provided (Ch. 7)

value-added network (VAN) a data communications system that offers some extra service to its users (Ch. 7)

VAN acronym for *value-added network* (Ch. 7)

videotex interactive information services that rely heavily on color displays and graphics (Ch. 7)

viewdata see *videotex* (Ch. 7)

viewporting a screen control feature that allows the user to have several different images displayed simultaneously (Ch. 6)

virtual machine an interface that relieves the user of any need to be concerned about most of the physical details of the computer system or network being accessed (Ch. 11)

virtual memory see *virtual storage* (Ch. 11)

virtual storage a memory management tactic that employs an area of rapidly accessible secondary storage (such as a hard disk) as an extension of primary memory (Ch. 11)

voiceband channels communications pathways with a bandwidth of about 3000 hertz and transmission rates as high as about 960 characters per second; commonly used for voice communications (Ch. 7)

voice mail an electronic message-transmitting system similar to electronic mail except that the messages are vocal ones (Ch. 17)

voice recognition modules (VRMs) input devices that can recognize from 40 to 200 isolated sounds, words, and phrases (Ch. 4)

VRMs acronym for *voice recognition modules* (Ch. 4)

WESTLAW a computerized subscription service of West Publishing Company, providing access to its law textbooks and volumes of case histories (Ch. 21)

wheel printers line printers that employ a series of print wheels, one for each position in a line of text (Ch. 6)

Winchester disk drive a device that has access arms, read/write heads, and a hard disk or disks completely enclosed in a sealed, airtight housing; originally developed by IBM (Ch. 5)

windowing a screen control feature that allows the user to select any section of the screen image and have it displayed by itself, usually on a larger scale (Ch. 6)

word a group of adjacent bits that are manipulated and stored as a unit (Ch. 3)

word-processing package a piece of software that enables a computer and a printer to do all that a typewriter does and more (Ch. 10)

workstations locations with input and output hardware set up for individual users (Ch. 17)

xerographic printers page printers in which electrically charged paper is passed over photoconductive surfaces covered with a powdery ink; the charged images on the paper attract the dry ink (Ch. 6)

Index